Humphrey Carpenter's award-winning biographies include *The Inklings* (1987), *W. H. Auden* (1981) and *A Serious Character: the Life of Ezra Pound* (1988). He and his wife, Mari Prichard, compiled *The Oxford Companion to Children's Literature* (1984) and his own children's books include the popular 'Mr Majeika' series. He is now at work on a life of Benjamin Britten, which Faber will publish in 1990.

by the same author

A Serious Character: the Life of Ezra Pound

The Brideshead Generation

EVELYN WAUGH AND HIS FRIENDS

Humphrey Carpenter

faber and faber
LONDON · BOSTON

First published in 1989
by George Weidenfeld & Nicolson Ltd
First published in this paperback edition in 1990
by Faber and Faber Limited
3 Queen Square London WC1N 3AU

Printed in England by Clays Ltd, St Ives plc

A CIP record for this book is available from the British Library.

ISBN 0-571-14414-4

Contents

Contents

Illustrations

Author's Note

This is a study of several writers and their circle, whose work has certain ideas and beliefs in common, and who, I believe, are better understood when they are considered in relation to each other. It is chiefly a work of biography, but sometimes strays into an examination of its subjects' writings, so as to identify and highlight certain strands of thought.

Evelyn Waugh is the central figure in the narrative. Indeed, as the book progresses, he comes to dominate it almost to the exclusion of the other members of his circle. This is because, in his person and his writings, increasingly as the years passed, he displayed the characteristics and conflicts of the group more intensely and dramatically, and more entertainingly, than any other member. I have not, however, tried to write an exhaustive biography of him, but have attempted instead to concentrate on and draw out what seem to me the essential features of his personality and imagination. Overall, I hope that the book will be read as a small piece of cultural history, an account of a certain strain in English life and writing during this century.

H.C.
Oxford, January 1989

PART I: 1918–1922

Eton Candle

1

'... Thought They Must Be Foreigners'

When the First World War came to an end in November 1918, Eton College still seemed firmly rooted in the Edwardian era. Reports on the Wall Game dominated the *Eton Chronicle*, and when a series of *Eton Broadsheets* was begun, to print the work of school poets, such subjects were chosen as 'Derwentwater' and 'The East Window of Eton College Chapel'. Yet Eton, secure at the top of the English social system, could afford to tolerate eccentricity in a way that lesser establishments did not dare. As George Orwell, who was a scholar there from 1917 to 1921, has written, 'Eton ... has one great virtue ... a tolerant and civilized atmosphere which gives each boy a fair chance of developing his own individuality.'

Certainly in odd corners of the school, unconventional tastes could be encountered. At Dyson's the jewellers in Eton High Street there was a wind-up gramophone in a room above the shop, and for a few pence Etonians could go up the stairs and play their own records – such machines being forbidden within the confines of the school itself. In the winter months of 1918, customers in the shop might, on certain afternoons, have had reason to glance up at the ceiling, for upstairs an entire *corps de ballet* seemed to be practising its steps.

If anyone ventured up and pushed open the door, he or she would see just a couple of young Etonians. But they were leaping around the room with the energy, if not the finesse, of Nijinsky. It was the music of the Ballets Russes to which they were dancing: *Petroushka*, and then, with a pause to wind the machine, a side or two of *Schéhérazade*.

3

Neither of them had yet seen the celebrated ballet company, but one of the boys – the one with a high domed forehead – had met Diaghilev when the impresario came to tea at the boy's family's Florentine villa. They had both avidly followed reports of the company's public appearances, cutting out pictures of Massine and other principals from the illustrated papers, and making inspired guesses about the choreography.

After a few minutes, they would pause for breath, and the other boy – tall, with jet-black wavy hair and a dead-white face – would expatiate on his latest enthusiasm, in a manner copied at fourth hand from the now dispersed followers of Oscar Wilde. It might have been absurdly precocious in a thirteen-year-old, were it not that he seemed to have been born for such a performance. His eyes, as Eton acquaintances remarked, seemed by nature to be heavily made up.

'My dear, I've just discovered a person who has something, just something, a little bit unusual, under a pimply and rather catastrophic exterior. Of course, I may be mistaken, and there is a faint risk that he may develop into a bore. But what do you think, my dear, he has a passion for *campanology*.'

'Really, Brian?' responds the other. 'And is that interesting?'

'Why, it is the art of ringing bells, my dear. He knows everything, simply everything there is to know about it. I'm trying to persuade him to write a causerie on the subject. It could be extremely suggestive. I think I shall send it with a covering letter to the *Eton Chronicle*, explaining to the editor why I think it so very important.'

He pauses and blinks his long eyelashes. He usually tells new acquaintances: 'I am said to be the image of Max Beerbohm when he was beautiful as well as brilliant,' and he does indeed bear a close resemblance to the Rothenstein drawing of the young Max.

His companion, whose vowels do not sound altogether English – a lengthened *a* here, an American twang there – asks why campanology should be so important.

'It struck me', answers the Beerbohm cherub, 'that every house' (he means every boarding house in Eton College) 'should build its own belfry. Then it could be distinguished both musically and architecturally. But I'm afraid', he adds with a sigh, 'that in my case m'tutor is bound to choose Lutyens. I suppose it can't be helped, though one hears that he has made some tolerable designs for New Delhi. You, of course, will want to erect a Florentine campanile.' The cherub pouts thoughtfully for a moment. 'Having originated the scheme, I shall insist on being Chairman of the Bell Committee. I shall choose m'tutor's bells.'

His companion laughs. 'At Cartier's, I suppose? And of platinum inlaid with cabochon rubies?'

The cherub frowns. 'Now, don't be facetious, dear, it doesn't happen to suit you. I am in earnest. Just think of the carillons, my dear! I shall commission Rimsky-Korsakov!'

'But he's with the angels, Brian.'

'Will you stop interrupting? I can see that you're getting into one of your mosquito moods. Of course Rimsky's dead, we all know that. I meant . . . Granados. It would be nice to have a Malaguena or a Seguedilla to soothe one at lock-up time. Such memories of Spain!' The cherub has never been out of England in his life. 'Memories of bullfights, and matadors with enormous shoulders and no hips – I can't think why hips were invented – and sunlit patios with Moorish fountains . . . .' He sighs again. 'I can see an endless argument about it with m'tutor, even though he is a trifle more cultivated than the average beak. He's bound to plump for Elgar or Vaughan Williams. And when the belfries are completed, there are bound to be bats, symbolically speaking. . . .'

This time it is his companion who sighs, slightly impatiently. He points out that the half-hour for which they have paid for the gramophone will soon run out, and he wants to buy something for tea before evening school begins.

The mention of food sets off an argument – the cherub and his friend are always disputing about it. Though the friend looks entirely English, he has lived in Italy for most of his life. His parents own one of the great Florentine villas, and he frequently preaches to the cherub the delights of *ravioli al sugo, sanguinaccio, panini* stuffed with white truffles (he has them sent regularly to Eton in jars), and the thousand varieties of *pizza*, as it is served in Naples, where his family has ancestral connections. After such a diet, he frequently explains, it is tantamount to torture to be ordered by one's fagmaster to fry up British sausages in malodorous lard. And he still has terrible memories of preparatory school food – 'hairy brawn . . . knobbly porridge . . . blotched oily margarine . . .'.

The cherub remains unmoved by such speeches. The only gastronomic delight which moves him is *marrons glacés*, and he and his friend now fall to arguing the virtues of their favourite varieties, Doney's in Florence versus Rumpelmeyer's in London. 'Doney's', says the friend passionately, 'are of classical proportions, neither too large nor too small, neither too brittle nor too compact. They just open their luscious chapped lips and let their somnolent juices ooze within you.

And the frosting of sugar melts gently down your throat, warming the red corpuscles so that they play gay tarantellas while you masticate – and even for some time afterwards!'

The cherub is impressed by this speech. 'Perhaps, since you are more *eloquent* on this subject than on others of greater import, there may be something in what you say.'

Descending to reality for a moment, he offers his companion a paper bag containing acid drops; for even Etonians do not have endless supplies of *marrons glacés*. Then suddenly he leaps across the room. 'My dear! I'll offer you a very special *marron*!' And, winding the handle of the apparatus, he selects another record from his box.

'What now, Brian?' asks the friend.

'Hush. Be patient and listen. Now: it's coming, it's coming.'

It is a man's voice, sinister and caressing, in some sort of foreign accent, not clearly audible, for the record is heavily scratched: '*Svengali will go to London himself, and play as nobody else can play; and hundreds of beautiful English women will see and hear and go mad with love for him. They will invite him to their palaces, and bring him tea, and gin, and* marrons glacés. . . .'

'Isn't it divine!' croons the cherub. 'Sir Herbert Beerbohm Tree as Svengali. I feel I'm eating a *marron glacé* every time he pronounces it. My dear, whenever we have a craving for them, we shall come here to Dyson's and simply *feast* off the record.'

And so, packing up their records and the acid drops, the two descend the stairs and slip out through the shop into the November gloom of Eton High Street; the cherub's companion reflecting, not for the first time, that for all his Italian upbringing, all his contacts with the rich and eccentric, all his meetings with geniuses and connoisseurs, he has never before encountered such an exotic, disarming and stimulating creature as the thirteen-year-old Brian Christian de Claiborne Howard.

The friend himself, Harold Acton, could scarcely be described as a conventional Etonian. Though English in name and descent, the Actons had adopted Italy as their homeland in the eighteenth century – an ancestor, Sir John Acton, served in the Tuscan navy and became Prime Minister of the Kingdom of Naples. Harold's mother was of wealthy American stock, and with her money the splendid villa of La Pietra was bought and restored not long before Harold's birth, which took place in 1904.

Harold's father was an amateur painter and art collector, and Harold's childhood had been spent among a swarm of connoisseurs, English, American and European, who buzzed around the villas of the rich, making pronouncements on their latest discoveries among the Italian primitives and *quattrocento* celebrities, vying as bitterly with each other as had the Guelfs and Ghibellines.

Amid the splendours of La Pietra, with its cypress avenue, its Venetian statues decorating the little open-air theatre, its orange, lemon and peach trees, and its vineyard and plantation of silvery olives, Harold had grown to dislike what little he could learn or intuit about England and the English. His nurse, a Londoner with damp eyes and projecting teeth, clicked her tongue over the garden statues and called them shameful.

'But why are they shameful, Nurse?'

'Because they're showing what they shouldn't. You don't show your little thing in public, do you? If you did, the police would soon be after you.'

'But these are only statues.'

'It doesn't matter. They're indecent, that's that they are. They ought to be removed. In England such things would never be allowed.'

The nurse would have weeping fits of homesickness, and sing hymns to herself. Harold discussed the matter of the statues with his parents, and went back to the nurse with an eloquent dissertation on the nobility of the nude; but it fell on deaf ears.

Home life for the boy meant Florentine fancy-dress parties, Harold and his brother William dressing up as Persian pages out of *Schéhérazade*, and a young *marchese* hoaxing the guests by arriving disguised as a mysterious princess from Schleswig-Holstein; D'Annunzio stirring Italy to war, during a salon in a Florentine drawing-room, with an oration against Austria and the Kaiser that was worthy of Dante; and Diaghilev and Bakst coming to tea. England, when Harold finally saw it, meant an indifferent preparatory school and a worse crammer; Kitchener's face stonily proclaiming 'Your Country Needs You'; inedible food, grey skies and visits to equally grey churches and castles which, after the *palazzi* and *chiesi* of Tuscany, had no power to stir. The only building which excited him was the Brighton Pavilion. And then the return from England, through the Alps: 'Oh, the gay rhythm of the train as we disembogued from a dark tunnel into the sudden summer of white casinos amid the palms and orange trees!'

The English had shown no more affection for the young Harold Acton than he for them. Arriving at the crammer where he was to work for the Eton entrance examination, he found that his copy of Oscar Wilde's *A House of Pomegranates* caused the drooping-moustached proprietor to turn pale and ask what other unhealthy books were in his trunk. Harold showed him Shaw's *Plays Pleasant and Unpleasant* and the poems of Ernest Dowson. 'At Lawnwood we pride ourselves on being *mens sana in corpore sano*,' the usher affirmed, 'healthy minds in healthy bodies.' He pronounced the last word *buddies*. The Dowson was taken away without explanation.

Harold had read *Dorian Grey* at twelve – he said he had devoured it like strawberries – and when homesick at prep school and crammer he wrote dozens of poems about Italy, in green and purple ink, and short stories which he illustrated in colour: '"*I am going to the ball tonight, Mario,*" *said the last rose of the Bellanozzia family, that family whose name rings in the heart of every Venetian citizen. There was a pause and then a sigh as the Contessa stepped out of the gondola. . . .*' One day somebody at school found them and destroyed them all.

At Eton, where he arrived in May 1918, Harold found himself in the ranks of the Musical Society, supposed to be singing in a choral version of the Neapolitan aria *Santa Lucia* in English. It infuriated him to hear it turned into an anthem for boy scouts, so he determinedly intoned the Italian words:

> *Sul mare luccica*
> *L'astro d'argento.*
> *Placida è l'onda,*
> *Prospero é il vento . . .*

It relieved him that he himself was not entirely English, but half American; and this was one of the things that made him gravitate, in his early terms at Eton, to Brian Howard, who was entirely American by birth.

Brian believed that he had Jewish blood on his father's side, but could discover very little about his paternal pedigree. His father, Francis Gassaway Howard (whose surname was said to have been originally plain Gassaway), an entrepreneur who had drifted from Washington DC to the fringes of the London art world, was conspicuous in the family by his frequent absences; he had allegedly been caught *in flagrante* with another female during his honeymoon. Brian's mother, a Southern belle, noted in her diary that her child's first words included 'Dada . . . all gone'.

Brian's given names suggested his mother's social ambitions. She took 'Christian' and 'Claiborne' from her mother's family, the Duvals, who had come from Rouen, and she turned it into 'de Claiborne' for good measure. But 'Howard' was rather a handicap at Eton if one happened not to be related to the Duke of Norfolk, and Brian was sneeringly referred to by at least one contemporary as '*Die geborene Gassaway*' ('the lady née Gassaway').

He had been born in Surrey in 1905, and was sent as a boarder to a preparatory school, where he had allegedly been seduced by one of the masters – 'It was there that my life was ruined,' he told a cousin melodramatically. Arriving at Eton, he protected himself from ridicule by behaving with cultivated disdain both towards his schoolfellows (he told his mother they were '*remarkably* silly') and towards the masters. One of his contemporaries, Cyril Connolly, describes a typical scene in the classroom, when the master has just caught Brian reading a book, and has asked what it is.

'*Les Chansons de Bilitis*, sir.'

'And what is this lesson?'

'You have the advantage, sir.'

'What do you mean, boy?'

'Ah, sir, fair's fair. I told you what my book was. You must tell me what's your lesson.'

'Elementary Geometry!'

'But it sounds fascinating! Then this delicious piece of celluloid nonsense is – I know, sir, don't tell me – a set square?'

'I have been teaching it for twenty years, and never met with such impertinence.'

'Twenty years, and still at Elementary! Oh sir, what a confession.'

Brian's diary entries for the autumn 'half' of 1920 show him in conflict with his tutor about his appearance: '*Rencontre* with Mr Blakiston re my hair! Do a pastel. . . . Compose *Night-Piece* (for piano). . . . Get eyeglass. Get black spats.'

The tutor, C. H. Blakiston, was in no doubt about the sort of character with whom he was dealing. He wrote to Brian's mother: 'It has seldom been my lot, in many years of work amongst boys, to come upon one so entirely self-centred and egotistical. Mentally he has some equipment – not in the ordinary school subjects . . . but he undoubtedly has some taste both literary and artistic. However . . . so far as his moral nature is concerned I cannot find what standards he has other than those of pure selfishness. . . . He disgraced himself and me by behaviour on Easter Sunday which caused disturbance to scores of boys in Chapel.' Brian's mother noted on the letter that 'he took a little toy engine to Chapel'.

He got a good review when the House Dramatic Society performed a farce – 'Of the ladies, Howard as Sybil Camberley showed real dramatic power, and made a very excellent leading lady' – but Mr Blakiston was moved to ask Brian's mother 'if you would seriously consider the advisability of removing him'. She notes that she 'had a time getting Mr Blakiston to keep him'.

One of Blakiston's complaints was that he kept breaking bounds. Harold Acton describes how, on Sunday afternoons, while other boys walked dutifully into Windsor, Brian would insist that they transgress by heading for Slough, the undistinguished railway junction for the Windsor line. Once they had reached its seedy outskirts, 'Brian was quick to detect streaks of queer cruelty and fetishism. . . . He would pause before a neo-Gothic structure with leprous walls and ask, with a startled air : "Did *you* hear anything peculiar?"' They would persuade themselves that, behind the dingily respectable façades, retired solicitors were gorging themselves on sausages of freshly minced corpse.

In the school holidays their tastes were similarly egregious. Another Etonian, Jim Knapp-Fisher, observed that

> where the average schoolboy would go to the latest Dorothy Dickson show, for instance, they would go to the latest ballet at the Alhambra. One time I happened to be with my family at the Alhambra when Brian and Harold walked into the stalls, in full evening dress, with long white gloves draped over one arm, and carrying silver-topped canes and top hats ... like a pair of Oscar Wildes. My step-mother was astonished at the sight of them, and thought they must be foreigners. I was much too nervous, at about fifteen, to say they were two of my great friends from Eton.

Knapp-Fisher visited Brian's house in Warwick Square, and found Brian making some drawings in the manner of Bakst. 'He called one of his efforts "Odalisque", to which Mrs Howard took exception. "Brian," she said, "I think that word means something horrible, and you must not call it that." "Oh – *ohh*," said Brian, in that wonderful way he had.'

Brian and Harold kept in touch when Harold went back to Florence, Brian addressing the envelopes in such manner as 'Harold Acton, who lives in discreet distinction, not unflavoured with a certain elusive gayety [*sic*], at – La Pietra, Firenze, Italia.' The letters were full of excitement at the prospect of a sparkling future: 'I saw Trefilova dancing in London – God! She is superb!... I hope that you and William [Harold's brother] are writing and painting like the very devil.... We will be reviewed all over England, and our success is certain. Oh – my friend, my friend Harold, aren't you glad!'

Come Nearer, Child

Brian Howard had been writing poetry since he arrived at Eton. At the time of the Armistice he told his mother that he had 'started writing for the Press to get some money', and he sent her some lines appropriate to the national mood, beginning:

> Quickly they gathered at the Call,
> Brave hearts that stood the test....

The press did not respond on that occasion, but during 1920 (aged fifteen) Brian manage to get an article printed in the *New Age*, a rather clumsy spoof on current intellectual fashions, entitled 'The New New':

> The New Era is coming.... There's terror abroad – who, *who* ever saw such inundations.... And Mr Huxley has written an insult to the Catholics ... dissecting our premier public school with ululant yowls.... In the swirls of derivative symbolism, there is one place to turn ... where our Ozzies and Sacheys and Ezras cannot follow with bombilatory pursuance – The LONDON MERCURY.

This, as well as its nudges at Ezra Pound and the Sitwells, refers to the presence at Eton during 1918 and 1919 as an assistant master of Aldous Huxley, who had subsequently been writing about the school.

The 'insult to the Catholics' is a joke about the title of Huxley's 1920 collection of poems, *Limbo*.*

Brian's next literary achievement was to get A.R. Orage, editor of the *New Age*, to print his poem 'Nausea', a vaguely Eliotic piece of *vers libre* which may (in view of his anti-modernist article) have been intended as parody:

> The meat is sodden (so is the bread) and unattractive;
> The greens are colding and give one the vertigo,
> Or ever the dull spoon digs at them . . .
> I am fit only for contemplation.

Certainly Orage thought it was parody; he printed it in the section of the magazine headed 'Pastiche'.

Though Brian mocked the Sitwells, he did not hesitate to try to get on their bandwagon. At the beginning of 1921 he sent some poems to Edith Sitwell for her annual anti-Georgian anthology *Wheels*, and received a not discouraging reply: 'You have quite obviously very real gifts . . . but your promise is far too real for me to risk your future by publishing these poems *in their present state.*' She said she detected 'a feeling of insincerity', and suggested he 'melt' all the best lines together into one poem and call it 'The Café by the Sea'. Brian willingly complied, and sent her more poems as well; eventually his 'Barouches Noires' appeared in the 1921 *Wheels*, Brian adopting for the occasion – presumably for fear of Mr Blakiston, his Eton tutor – the pseudonym 'Charles Orange':

> It was when I was sitting by the side of the lake . . .
> I saw a procession of old, frayed barouches filing by;
> Old, broken-down barouches that followed their
>   soundless horses soundlessly,
> And contained loads of young dead people, propped up
>   in outrageous positions . . .
> The last barouche that passed had a placard tied on with
>   string –
> 'We are the lovers that drowned themselves in this lake.'

Following this success, Brian (says Harold Acton) 'was determined to publish an illustrated magazine', with himself as editor, 'and had

* Harold Acton describes Huxley as 'one who stood out a mile' among the Eton masters. 'Walking along the Eton High like a somnambulist, or like a juvenile giraffe that had escaped from a zoo, he wore a conspicuous orange scarf which trailed behind him. One could not visualize him keeping boys in order. . . .' He couldn't; he called them 'sinister young men', and Eddie Sackville-West describes how, with his poor eyesight, Huxley had no chance of maintaining discipline: 'The general tumult was indescribable.'

asked me to collaborate. With the talent of the Eton Arts Society at our disposal, it was bound to be readable. . . .'

Brian had conceived the idea of a 'New Eton Art Club' on his fifteenth birthday, in March 1920, but did nothing about it for two years. Then in February 1922 the club suddenly became a reality, with Brian in charge and ten other boys as members, including Harold and William Acton.

The official President of the Eton Society of Arts, as constituted by Brian, was Sidney Evans, the school drawing master – occupant of what was virtually an inherited post* – who inhabited the Studio in Keate's Lane, an *atelier* that would not have disgraced the Latin Quarter of the 1850s, and who himself resembled a British painter of the *Trilby* period. A predominantly literary society would have had to invite one of the school's academic teaching staff to be its senior member, but by opting for Evans and his studio, Brian and Harold had put their group conveniently out of the way of officialdom's eye. Things could be stirred up in the drawing school that could never be debated freely in the classroom. Evans's own artistic taste was for Sickert and the Camden Town Group, but he was broadminded, and aware, rather cynically but without active disapproval, of Matisse and Picasso.

There were ten founder-members of the Society, most of them interested in painting, though none could quite make out why a quiet dark-skinned boy named Minns had been co-opted, since he hardly spoke at meetings. To Harold, Brian explained his reasons for including this young gentleman: 'Pure Hymettus *honey*, my dear. Still waters run *deep*.' Brian had evidently now confessed certain romantic entanglements to his mother, since she wrote to him on the subject of his Eton bedroom: 'And now I'm worrying for fear someone comes in tonight that you won't want to turn out. . . . Baba don't take any risks. . . .'

Henry Yorke, chosen as Secretary of the 'Arts', was the same age as Brian, the son of a wealthy Midlands industrialist, a cheerful, rather plump boy, and a commanding talker. He had made friends with Brian and Harold because he despised his games-playing schoolfellows' sneers at 'those aesthetes'; he wanted to be able to tell them that they 'were not really bad fellows'. Anthony Powell, nine months younger than

---

* Four generations of Evanses held the post of drawing master between 1796 and 1922, the first, Samuel Evans, having migrated from Flintshire to Windsor to teach drawing to the daughters of George III. The female members of the family became Dames (matrons) in various Eton houses.

Brian, had joined the 'Arts' because he was considering becoming a painter of huge 'subject' pictures, or an illustrator of historical novels. He had been at prep school with Yorke, and was the son of a regular army officer with a 'Sandhurst personality' but also a taste for Beardsley, Arthur Rackham and Bakst's ballet designs. Anthony had drawn for sheer pleasure since the earliest age.

Harold Acton says that Yorke and Powell, at meetings of the Society of Arts, 'participated discreetly without committing themselves to extremes'. Powell describes the other members of the Society as they seemed to him: 'Harold Acton's high forehead, eyes like black olives, slightly swaying carriage ... dramatic, formal, courteous, seasoned ... with a touch of impishness. ... William Acton, no less unusual, was more heavily built, in fact quite muscular, exuding energy, words pouring from him in a torrent. ... William Acton's painting at Eton tended to vary between "still lifes" severe as Cézanne's, and costume designs more exotic than Bakst's.' Robert Byron, a friend of Yorke, was the son of a civil engineer. Powell calls him 'thoroughly out of the ordinary' in appearance, with 'his complexion of yellowish wax, popping pale blue eyes, a long sharp nose'. Though he could turn out a good caricature, Byron refused to consider himself at all artistic. Indeed, the mere use of such words as 'intellectual' or 'good taste' threw him into paroxysms of rage. 'He was', says Powell, 'energetic, ambitious, violent, quarrelsome ... habitually in a state of barely controlled exasperation about everything.' Harold Acton similarly mentions Byron's 'provocative tirades', and Powell recalls that if someone tediously asked Byron what he wanted to be when he reached adulthood, Byron would snap back: 'An incredibly beautiful male prostitute with a sharp sting in my bottom.'

Powell suggests that, in these characteristics, Byron had something about him that predated his own era, 'something of the genuine nineteenth-century Englishman – a type in those days all but extinguished in unmitigated form – the eccentricity, curiosity, ill temper, determination to stop at absolutely nothing'.

Alongside Robert Byron, Brian Howard and the Acton brothers, other members of the Society of Arts seemed rather staid. Alan Clutton-Brock, the son of a professional art-critic, was preparing to pursue a similar career; he made experiments in paper-marbling which resembled early Surrealism, and wrote fantasy-stories in the manner of Lord Dunsany. Also in the group were Oliver Messel, who at this date (says Acton) was 'painting minutely in the pre-Raphaelite manner', and Hugh Lygon, son of Lord Beauchamp, leader of the Liberals in the

House of Lords (who Powell says was 'celebrated for his own brand of pomposity'). Hugh had no pretensions whatever towards the arts, but was 'fairhaired, nice mannered, a Giotto angel living in a narcissistic dream'. Powell suspected that his inclusion in the Society was due to 'a *tendresse* (probably unvoiced) felt for him by one of the more influential members, like Howard or Byron'. Of the two remaining members, Roger Spence, a quiet well-behaved son of an Indian Army officer, was self-appointed protector of the Acton brothers and Brian Howard against the hearty elements in the school, while Colin Anderson, a member of Pop – the exclusive self-electing body of senior boys who at Eton filled many of the roles of prefects at other schools – was an athlete who nevertheless drew and painted at the Studio. His inclusion was another buffer against the ridicule of the school.

The Society of Arts met on Saturday evenings. Henry Yorke describes the appearance of the Studio:

> It was a long low room with skylights and on shelves along the walls earth-red pots, unglazed jars which generations had had to draw and white casts rubbing noses. It was always dusk in there but it had charm because there was no other dirty room in the whole school. Wherever a shelf ended watercolours were hung up of the same casts and pots standing next to them and however badly these were drawn the repetition on paper and in colour of so much that was before the eye made the place amicably unreal like a living joke.

A leaflet advertising the Society records that the subjects discussed included 'Post-Impressionism; the Decoration of Rooms; Colour as applied to Decoration; Oriental Art; Spanish Painting'. Each meeting began with a paper, after which there was supposed to be a debate, though Yorke says that people did not really answer points already made – they got up and talked simply to show off. Powell cannot remember anything about the papers or debates except that Robert Byron, speaking on the Decoration of Rooms, advocated black ceilings, grey walls and white carpets.

They tried to be thoroughly modern; Yorke recalls everyone remarking over and over again, 'Art is not representation.' Powell believes that Harold Acton and Robert Byron proposed a Victorian revival, but Acton says that Byron was 'saturated in Ruskin', which meant that the two of them were automatically in opposition, as Acton, with his Florentine tastes, could not enthuse over the revival of Venetian Gothic. Victorianism was, at this time, thoroughly out of fashion. During the early 1920s some of the neo-Gothic stalls which had been placed in Eton Chapel during the 1840s were removed in order to reveal medieval frescoes which they had been hiding, and there was a widespread enthusiasm for removing and destroying such Victorian claptrap.

Occasionally, notabilities like William Rothenstein and Roger Fry came down to address the Society, and Fry agreed to judge a school painting competition. 'At first,' recalls Acton, 'there was a tendency to snigger at the gaunt bespectacled figure with the spidery gestures and the mop of grey hair, but as soon as he spoke the boys listened with rapt attention. . . . Ideas and clarity of vision [he said] were of primary importance: children of six with these gifts would succeed, and adults who lacked them would fail, whatever their technical skill.' This in itself sounded revolutionary to those who had not attended the meetings of the Society of Arts, and they were still more astonished when Fry allotted the prize for still life to a boy called Edward James (not a member of the Society), 'for the most ingenious painting in the room'.

Edward James, small, dark and pretty, was widely believed to be a bastard son of Edward VII. 'I was not,' he says in his memoirs. 'I was, in fact, his grandson.' His maternal grandmother 'had a tumble in the heather' with the then Prince of Wales in Aberdeenshire, and Edward's mother was the result. 'I once got a photograph of my mother and added a beard to it,' recalls James. 'She looked the image of George V.' He may after all have been the King's son as well as his grandson, since the Court Circular for 19 November 1906 records that His Majesty visited Mr and Mrs James that day; Edward was born almost exactly nine months later, which lends some mathematical support to the notion, as does the choice of the boy's Christian name. Edward's American father – a distant cousin of Henry James – was, however, unmoved by the widespread speculation about the paternity of his children. Edward's mother told him how one day 'Daddy received an anonymous letter telling him that your sister Audrey was not his daughter. Audrey had just been born, and he read it and said, "That's from Lady Sackfield, because we didn't invite her to the first shoot," and he paid no attention to it and threw it on the fire.'

Audrey had indeed been fathered by someone else – Sir Edward Grey, the Foreign Minister. And though Mrs James was the King's daughter, she certainly behaved like one of his mistresses:

> One day [recalls Edward James] the King arrived rather late in the afternoon with a stream of Daimler cars, and the butler came down with a very large cardboard box about the length of six flower boxes

and tied with pink ribbon. 'Mrs James is indisposed,' said the butler, 'but she sent you this instead of coming herself.' The King was handed a pair of scissors. I was watching from the oak gallery above the marble steps to the front hall, and I saw the King cut the ribbon and open the box and there was my mother inside disguised as a doll with a big key. A notice said 'Wind here', and the King turned the key, and a musical box played at the bottom of the flower box and my mother got up and performed a dance so well that she really looked like a mechanical doll. . . .

Edward also remembered the King leaning against the gallery railing, wearing a pearl-grey waistcoat and smoking a cigar. 'I said, "Mr King, why aren't you wearing your crown?" and he replied, "Oh, I'm not wearing it because it's a rainy day."'

Edward's mother took very little interest in her children (four daughters as well as Edward). She is said one day to have sent for one of them to accompany her to church, and on being asked which one, snapped: 'How should I know? Whichever one goes with my blue gown.'

Edward James says there was a great deal of insanity in his mother's family. His Uncle Charlie, who had lost a fortune at Monte Carlo and was obliged to sell all the lead off his castle roof, tried to recoup by inventing colour photography, 'but his process only showed the reds'; also, by patenting a collar-stud that went 'ping' if you dropped it on the floor, so as to help you find it in the dark (he forgot to wind it up and lost it in a taxi); and a soap for dogs that smelt of liver and bacon and so made the dogs want to be washed – 'it had the inconvenience that all the other dogs wanted to eat them afterwards'.

Edward's father died when he was five years old, in 1912, leaving him an estate in Sussex (West Dean) of twenty-two thousand acres, but (after death duties) with an income of only about six hundred pounds a year. Edward's mother had to give up the house, and she spent much of her time trying to regain the position in society that this had lost her. Edward found himself a not particularly welcome guest in an endless series of country houses. They were invited by the Harcourts to Nuneham Courtenay, 'and old Lord Harcourt asked me to go into the garden to pick gooseberries and he tried to put his hand in my pocket. . . . Later I learned that he had done the same thing to my cousin. . . . He had asked her if she would like to see the grotto, taken her there, and said, "I'll show you my stalactite."' At the end of the visit, Edward was made to go up to Lord Harcourt's bedroom and say thank you. 'He said, "Come nearer, child. Come nearer.'' So I came a little nearer. . . . And then suddenly he threw back the bedclothes revealing a large and hideous erection; he looked like an old goat with his large drooping beard and I ran out of the room.'

Edward told his mother about it, and Mrs James gossiped about it in London, with the consequence that 'the whole of London was talking about it, and not long afterwards Lord Harcourt committed suicide'. The newspapers record that Lewis ('Lulu'), Viscount Harcourt, a former Colonial Secretary, was found dead in bed at his London house on 24 February 1922. He was fifty-nine, and had taken a dose of bromide. The coroner recorded a verdict of death by misadventure.

Despite the loss of West Dean, Edward and his mother were not exactly homeless. They still had a London house, 35 Wimpole Street, and a Scottish mansion, and every year Mrs James used to rent a villa on the Riviera. She remarried, but her second husband, a colonel in the Guards, had no serious interest in women and promptly fell in love with Edward, insisting that they take baths together and writing clandestine sonnets to him. On the eve of his departure for Eton, Edward was given a terrifying warning by his mother against homosexuality. But despite all his experiences, 'I hadn't the faintest idea what she had been talking about.'

The winning of the prize for the still life was the first major event of his Eton career. 'My stepfather was rather pleased and for a long time my still-life hung on the stair. Not that he was artistic; the only things he was interested in were nude bronzes of Greek gods.' Edward left Eton when he was sixteen, 'because I had a nervous breakdown' – chiefly on account of his mother's obsessive fear of his becoming homosexual. As one of his cousins remarked, 'If Edward wasn't going to be homosexual anyway, Aunt Evie is doing everything possible to make him so.'

The 'Arts' was looked on with suspicion by most of Eton. 'The fact that we were allowed to have meetings and that the headmaster had attended one of our debates made sensibly enough no real difference to the distaste with which we were regarded,' writes Henry Yorke. 'We had hopes for several terms we might be able to interest the prefects' club [Pop] ... but this was a wild dream. . . .' And Robert Byron remarked that the attitude of the masters 'resembled that of someone discovering the first symptoms of leprosy in his mother'.

Brian Howard decided that the Arts might find an ally in Cyril

Connolly, a Colleger (that is, a Scholar) recently elected to Pop, who had covered the walls of his room with Medici prints bought with money from a history prize, and so seemed not unpromising. Connolly consequently received an invitation to tea from Brian. 'I accepted on Pop writing paper, and went round one summer afternoon to find *foie gras* sandwiches, strawberries and cream, and my postcard of acceptance proudly displayed on the mantelpiece. Seeing it up there for the world to know that Brian Howard had had a Pop to tea with him, I was miserable.... I swallowed down my tea like a lady who is offered a swig by a madman in a railway tunnel and bolted.'

Harold Acton says that, after this, Connolly 'puffed cynically on our fringe', though Connolly explains that it was not cynicism but self-protection. 'When I saw Brian alone I would talk to him; when I was with the other Pops I avoided him.... I need not have worried for he soon became the most fashionable boy in the school.' With hindsight he judged the Howard–Acton set 'the most vigorous group at Eton.... Yet my moral cowardice and academic outlook debarred me from making friends with them.'

Born in 1903, Connolly was the son of a regular army officer whose family (of distant Irish descent) had flourished in the Bath of Jane Austen's era, but had now fallen on harder times; Cyril's paternal grandmother lived in furnished rooms. His mother came from a clan of Irish landowners, and in the school holidays Cyril often visited Mitchelstown Castle in County Cork, where lived his great-aunt, widow of the Earl of Kingston. Consequently he was not altogether certain of his own social position. On his mother's side he was the great-nephew of an earl, yet his paternal grandmother was poorly off. 'I could not consider myself entirely upper class; yet I was not altogether upper middle. I had fallen between two standards of living. With the upper class I felt awkward, dowdy, introspective and a physical coward. With the middle class I felt critical, impatient, and sparkling. This class distinction, the line between Kensington and Belgravia, is a source of anguish. To consider oneself born into one and yet be slowly conditioned to the other was as uncomfortable as having one shoulder too low.'

It became a real obsession: 'Why had my father not got a title? ... Why be born, why live at all if I could not have one? ... Today [he wrote in the late 1930s] I cannot listen to any discussion of titles or open a peerage without feeling sick.... I shall never be able to breathe till they are abolished.'

Like Anthony Powell's, Connolly's father was a reserved military man. Major Matthew Connolly had a shut-in face with a heavy moustache, and Cyril's parents' marriage was not happy. 'So much was repressed', Cyril writes, 'that they found themselves without emotional resources.' Major Connolly liked to sign personal letters, even to his son, with his army rank as well as his name. The parents eventually separated, the mother to South Africa, the father to live alone in a London hotel.

Cyril was sent to a prep school he calls 'St Wulfric's', on the south coast (it was really called St Cyprian's, and was near Beachy Head). It was not a bad school, but was run on one principle: 'to attract the sons of peers and send them to Eton'. Cyril made his mark there by playing 'the gay, generous, rebellious Irishman, with a whiff of Kipling's M'Turk', but he knew he was only 'a stage rebel'. His friend Eric Blair (George Orwell) was 'a true one. Tall, pale, with his flaccid cheeks, large spatulate fingers, and supercilious voice, he was one of those boys who seem born old. . . . Alone among the boys he was an intellectual and not a parrot for he thought for himself, read Shaw and Samuel Butler and rejected not only St Wulfric's but the war, the Empire, Kipling, Sussex, and Character.' Orwell describes in his essay 'Such, Such Were the Joys' how at St Cyprian's he was beaten for wetting his bed, and how, when the headmaster's wife overheard him telling other boys that it had not hurt, the beating was repeated. St Cyprian's gave Orwell 'a sense of desolate loneliness and helplessness, of being locked up not only in a horrible world but in a world of good and evil where the rules were such that it was actually not possible for me to keep them'. Such bitter memories were common. Edward James says that at his prep school:

> there were only eight lavatories between eighty boys and only ten to fifteen minutes between breakfast and first school so constipation became our common lot. . . . I became terribly ill because only the big boys, who could knock the others down, could get into the lavatories before school, and I came home suffering violent pains. All I needed was castor oil and a rest, but my mother had me operated on and part of my intestines were removed.

Anthony Powell writes of the school he attended before Eton: 'Nothing picturesquely horrible ever happened to me there, though I should be unwilling to have five minutes of it again.'

Another contemporary of Connolly's at St Cyprian's, a boy with a 'slow, affected and creamy' voice, who 'had a charming, dreamy face, enormous blue eyes with long lashes and wore his hair in a fringe', displayed a form of independence rather different from Eric Blair. 'From Orwell I learnt about literature,' writes Connolly, 'from Cecil I learnt about art.' This was Cecil Beaton. On Saturday nights, when the boys were kept quiet with lantern slides and poetry,

> there would be a hush, and Cecil would step forward and sing, 'If you were the only girl in the world, And I was the only boy . . .' The eighty-odd Wulfricians felt there could be no other boy in the world for them, the beetling chaplain forgot hell-fire and masturbation, the Irish drill-sergeant his bayonet practice . . . and for a moment the whole structure of character and duty tottered. . . .

Beaton, the son of a London timber-merchant, was aware of Connolly's interest in him, and wrote of him a few years later in his diary: 'He is extraordinarily intellectual, but I think he has no real sense of beauty. One feels he has no fundamental basis and he always falters when talking about pictures. In a way he is charming, but he can be dreadfully nasty and deceitful.' Beaton felt that Connolly exaggerated the horrors of St Cyprian's – at least, that he over-emphasized the filth and the snobbery – but admitted that he himself had 'loathed every minute of the school regime'.

Beaton's own worst waking nightmares had been at the day-school he had attended before St Cyprian's, in Hampstead. At mid-morning break there, the leader of a gang of bullies would advance on him, 'a boy half the size of the others, wearing Barrie-esque green tweed knickerbockers'. This person fixed him with 'a menacing wild stare' and then 'stood on his toes and slowly thrust his face with a diabolical stare, closer and closer to mine, ever closer until the eyes converged into one enormous Cyclopean nightmare. It was a clever inauguration to the terrors that followed, and my introduction to Evelyn Waugh.' The school was called Heath Mount; Waugh attended it from the age of seven until he went to Lancing. Beaton passed on to St Cyprian's, then to Harrow.

While at St Cyprian's, Cyril Connolly began to be romantically attracted by other boys. 'The boy whom I loved for the last three years I was at St Wulfric's was called Tony Watson [his real name was Terry Willson]. He was small, brown, wiry, good at games. . . . He is a type that has recurred through my life and which gets me into trouble.' (Connolly was in his thirties when he wrote this.) 'By the time I was twelve all four types to which I am susceptible had appeared . . . the Faun [to which Terry Willson belonged], the Redhead, the Extreme Blonde, and the Dark Friend.' But he preserved his sexual innocence completely; a glance or possibly a touch on the arm was all he ever attempted.

Connolly himself was not conventionally handsome. At Eton he acquired the nickname 'Ugly', and one of his contemporaries referred to him as 'the tug who's been kicked in the face by a mule'. Yet his face, as Anthony Powell observes, 'was certainly one of his several means of imposing a fascination on people'. At St Cyprian's he managed to secure the affections of Terry Willson. After those days were over, he wrote to a friend describing Terry as:

> faun-like ... small and brown and wiry, with an untidy fringe and won-derful mouth and superb brown eyes.... We used to rag among the pegs in the passages at night and sometimes climb out of a window and run out on the lawn.... I told you, I think, of my fatal repression our last night in the bathroom and how I was shy and blundered when he tried to kiss me, wearing a towel round his waist, his brown skin shining, his hazel eyes very soft and his little lips parted. (I can't help 'little', they were so.) After that we've never met though we wrote a lot for two years more.... 'The Priory, Repton, Derby. My dear Tim [Connolly's nickname at St Cyprian's] ... I must end now, love and what shall I say? Terry.' Fancy getting a letter like that [at Eton] on a cold evening in the war and hugging it through tea and bread and margarine and plopping gas lights, and the smell of stale foods.

After St Cyprian's, Eton seemed 'splendid and decadent' when Connolly went there to sit the scholarship exam. 'It was summer, and ... the top hats, the strawberries and cream, the smell of wistaria ... the foppish drawl, the two boys with their hats on the back of their heads, the graceful sculler ... seemed the incarnation of elegance and maturity.' When he left St Cyprian's he was given the usual 'seedy exhortation' by chaplain and headmaster: 'We were going into a world full of temptations.... We must report any boy at once who tried to get into our bed, never go for a walk with a boy from another house, never make friends with anyone more than a year and a half older (eventually it would be younger), and above all, not "play with ourselves".' On this last topic the cautionary tale was told of the old boy of St Cyprian's who became so addicted to masturbation that when he got to Oxford he had, in a fit of remorse, put his head under a train. 'That miserable youth, I afterwards learnt,' says Connolly, 'had attended all the private schools in England.'

Eton at first seemed to offer a dignified identity: 'C.V. Connolly, Esq., ks [King's Scholar], New Buildings, Eton College, Windsor.' But in reality Connolly and the other boys who had been aristocrats of their prep schools found themselves 'pitched into the Carthaginian slave market'. The seventy scholars lived together in one house, governed by the usually ineffective Master in College, and by ten members of the Sixth Form, who had similar privileges to Pop. The youngest boys therefore found themselves to have become serfs in a feudal system: 'The masters represented the church, with the headmaster as Pope,' says Connolly; 'the boys, with their hierarchy of colours and distinctions, were the rest of the population, while the prefects and athletes, the captains of house and the members of "Pop" were the feudal overlords.' Connolly had rarely been beaten at St Cyprian's, but now 'even the little boy who was "Captain of Chamber" could beat us'. He was beaten if he had been far into Windsor to buy food for his fagmaster and had made a wrong purchase; he was beaten for speaking first to a senior boy; he was beaten for some obscure infringement of privilege. Connolly soon felt 'quite lost and friendless'. Another Etonian, Christopher Hollis, describes Harold Acton being caned by another boy at the mature age of seventeen for not knowing the football colours of the various houses. Harold told Hollis: 'Smack, smack, smack. I shifted round so that the blows might fall in a different place. "Keep still," he shouted. "It's my religion," I said. "I'm turning the other cheek."'

George Orwell reacted to all this by ignoring it contemptuously, and maintaining that it was probably even worse at inferior schools. Though Connolly was at first almost crushed by the system, he did not fight or scorn it, but threw in his lot with it. After a while he discovered that 'if I seemed unsuspecting and confident and did not smell of fear', the senior boys who had the power of beating would on the whole leave him alone. Next, he realized that he could make them laugh with his antics and wit. Eventually he reached the stage where he was able to become a bully himself: 'After two terms of being bullied, I had ... a year of bullying. ...'

By the summer of 1920, turning seventeen, he was no longer a fag, had a room of his own and belonged to the College Literary Society, for which he wrote poems, criticism and satires on the Georgians. But here, too, something was a little wrong. As at most public schools, the majority of Eton masters simply crammed boys as best they could, in the intervals of keeping order, and no real intellectual tradition was encountered until scholars reached the top forms, where there were perhaps half a dozen real teachers. These taught their own brand of learning: what Connolly calls 'the pure eighteenth-century Etonian tradition of classical humanism, which could be learnt nowhere else'.

This was the tradition of William Johnson Cory, the Eton master and poet whose *Ionica* (1858) contained his celebrated version of Callimachus' epigram on Heraclitus of Halicarnassus: 'They told me, Heraclitus, they told me you were dead ...' (Cory also wrote the words of the 'Eton Boating Song'.) Anthony Powell gives evidence that the Cory tradition was still alive in 1920; in his novel *A Question of Upbringing* the Eton housemaster Le Bas quotes the Heraclitus poem with 'reverberance'.

Actually Le Bas, in the Powell narrative, goes on to observe with some acuteness that Cory and his contemporaries suffered from 'nineteenth-century nostalgia for a classical past largely of their own imagining'; but this perception, if it was shared by the real-life Eton masters in 1920, did not stop them repeating the error. 'Homer and Virgil were the pillars of an Eton education,' writes Connolly. 'But we read them with the help of two official cribs, Butcher and Lang for Homer, Mackail for Virgil.' Mackail had given Virgil an 1880s air, so that Dido seemed a creation of Rossetti, and Andrew Lang, trying to render Homer in the language of the Norse sagas, had produced (says Connolly) 'a Wardour Street Nordic fog'.

In Powell's novel, Le Bas also quotes one of Andrew Lang's own poems which expresses a Cory-like nostalgia for the classical golden age: 'And shepherds still their songs repeat, / Where breaks the blue Sicilian sea.' He comments: 'Fine lines, you know.' In response, Charles Stringham, here representing the Howard–Acton element in the school's life, quotes from Oscar Wilde's poem on Theocritus and Sicily, and earns Le Bas's disapproval: 'Not a very distinguished versifier.'

The Eton culture, then, was romanticized classicism; Connolly calls it 'the Milton–Keats–Tennysonian culture, that profuse and blooming romanticism ... which had dominated English literature until the death of Flecker and Rupert Brooke'. Typical of those who taught this culture was the Vice-Provost, Hugh Macnaghten, an 'ogre for the purple patch' who treated English poetry as a species of Latin verse. His taste was for 'tags and useful epithets', and he encouraged Etonian poets to put their innermost thoughts into Latin rather than English verse. Consequently, says Connolly, 'no one who did his verses well could write poetry afterwards. There would be one slim Eton-blue volume with a few translations, a *Vale*, a couple of epigrams, then silence.'

Alan Pryce-Jones, also at Eton at this time, says of Macnaghten that his 'sensibility ... was so acute that, whenever the word "little" was spoken in his presence, he wiped away a tear'. The dominance of such men over the school's study of literature explains the Society of Arts establishing itself well away from the classroom. Connolly remarks that the Howard–Acton set failed to be infected by the Macnaghten virus because they were too lazy to 'gargle quotations'; also they were too hopeless at games to be given any responsibility in the school and be drawn into its culture. Ignoring most Eton conventions, they were able to stimulate each other into some sort of intellectual life.

Connolly himself, however, read widely as directed by Macnaghten : Catullus, Omar Khayyám and the *Shropshire Lad*, Tennyson and Matthew Arnold. The rest of his energy was devoted to trying to get into Pop – a particular challenge since he was a Colleger and not an athlete, not even a 'bitch' (pretty boy), which would have helped. 'At that time,' he writes, 'Pop were the rulers of Eton, fawned on by masters and the helpless Sixth Form ... an oligarchy of two dozen boys who ... were self-elected and could wear coloured waistcoats, stick-up collars, etc., and cane boys from any house. The masters could not.... Such was their prestige that some boys who failed to get in never recovered; one was rumoured to have procured his sister for the influential membership.'

Connolly managed to get in by being 'engaging and witty' to his Oppidan (non-Scholar) friends, and, having achieved this, felt that there could be 'no further social ambition'. For the remainder of his Eton career he abandoned the company of other Scholars and lived exclusively among Oppidans. On his visits to Dyson's, he became ashamed to play classical records any longer; instead he and his Pop friends would go down there to spin 'Say It With Music' on the turntable. 'The fox-trot floated away on the sunlight and we commented on the looks of the passers by.'

3

Suspended Boyhood

'Meanwhile,' says Connolly, 'a strange pink album had appeared called the *Eton Candle*. . . .' This was the 'illustrated magazine' intended by Brian Howard to reflect the glories of the Society of Arts, chiefly his own and Harold Acton's. 'Remember that the *Eton Candle* is our challenge – our first fruits – the first trumpet call of our movement – it is OURSELVES,' Brian wrote to Harold during the Christmas holiday of 1921-2.

The two of them wrote the greater part of the magazine themselves. Though there were contributions from distinguished Old Etonians, and from a few other current members of the school, all the notable pieces were by Brian and Harold. The *Eton Candle* – dubbed the 'Eton Scandal' by the school – began with an essay by Brian praising the modernist poets, specifically Ezra Pound, the Imagists and Edith Sitwell's *Wheels* group. Brian's selection from his own poems, printed later in the magazine, included a piece on the war which was close in tone to a passage in Pound's recently published *Hugh Selwyn Mauberley*:

> You were a great Young Generation –
> And then you went out and got murdered – magnificently –
> Went out and got murdered – because a parcel of damned old men
> Wanted some fun, or some power. . . .

Brian and Harold also filled up the pages of the *Eton Candle* with stories in the manner of Ronald Firbank, whose *Valmouth* had appeared in 1919. Brian's narrative was about a sexually ambiguous *grande dame* with a bass voice who lives in one of those sinister houses in the vicinity of Slough, and Harold's was a heavy piece of Nineties pastiche, with the perverse title 'Hansom Cab no. 213 *bis*', about a rich aesthete named Athelstane who lives entirely for his own sensations – he drinks milk because he finds it more stimulating than whisky, and bathes in mauve twilight to the accompaniment of organ music. It was meant to be the first chapter of a novel.

Various other Etonians did offer contributions, but Brian and Harold judged most of them too bad to print. Robert Byron wrote some *vers libre* that enchanted Brian – 'Robert has developed into a poet, my dear, an English Apollinaire,' he told Harold. But then Byron, hooting with laughter, told him it was a joke, a parody. Brian was indignant at this treachery.

There was further treachery when Alan Clutton-Brock, who had contributed some prose fables to the magazine, reviewed it anonymously in the *Eton Chronicle*, saying that overall it was rather disappointing, though 'nothing like it has ever been done before at Eton'. However, appreciative letters came from various distinguished Old Etonians, and Harold Acton was approached by Thomas Balston, a friend of Anthony Powell's father and a member of the publishing house of Duckworth. This led to their publishing Harold's first volume of poems, *Aquarium*, the following year.

The Nineties air of Brian's and Harold's stories in the *Eton Candle* was not just a personal, epicene whim on their part. Osbert Lancaster, who eventually joined up with the Eton 'Arts' set at Oxford, observes that aestheticism had been 'driven underground in the mid-nineties by the Wilde scandal'. Since then it had thrown up 'occasional gushers', such as Firbank and Norman Douglas, but had not yet managed to re-emerge in full flood. Brian and Harold were harking back to the last era when the aesthetic temperament had been given full rein in Britain.

Immediately after the publication of the *Candle*, at Easter 1922, Harold Acton left Eton. 'I was now eighteen, and in a house so pre-occupied with athletics I felt I was wasting my time.' He passed the Oxford entrance examination, Responsions, and went up to Christ Church at the beginning of the autumn term, to read Modern Languages.

Brian Howard remained at Eton, reporting his adventures by letter to Harold. He went to tea with Edith Sitwell in Bayswater, and was scathing about the refreshments: 'I got one penny bun, and three-quarters of a cup of rancid tea in a dirty cottage mug.' Hearing of the financial success of the *Eton Candle*, she appointed him business manager of *Wheels*, but he soon found that soliciting advertisements for it was far harder than keeping the *Candle* afloat in Eton waters.

Harold was continuing to write his 'Hansom Cab' novel, and Brian was unenthusiastic about the second chapter: 'I don't *very* much like it, excepting the dwarf dancers and their mistress.' He himself had begun a novel which satirized the Eton masters: '*How* it will madden them!' He remarked in one of his letters to Harold that he had decided, after reading A.J.A. Symons on Symbolism, that he and Harold were 'the new Symbolists'. He went on: 'Incidentally I think James Joyce and Proust are bad writers. . . . A welter of minute and appallingly tedious or shocking detail.' Meanwhile Alan Clutton-Brock had started his own new magazine at Eton, and had 'burlesqued you and me', Brian wrote to Harold, 'amalgamated into one person . . .'.

Brian sat his School Certificate – a usual qualification for a university place – and failed. He was removed to a crammer near Salisbury, in the hope that this would enable him to get through Responsions and straight into Christ Church, but again he failed. He was removed to a different crammer, and finally succeeded in getting a Christ Church place in time for October 1923, having participated in a certain amount of cheating – 'Like everyone else in the room . . . "x" and I . . . did our Latin and French papers largely *ensemble*.'

Cyril Connolly sat for and won a Balliol scholarship, and went up to Oxford at Michaelmas 1922, the same term as Harold Acton. Anthony Powell followed to Balliol as a commoner in October 1923. Henry Yorke went up to Magdalen a year later, also as a commoner. They were not all entirely confident of what Oxford had to offer.

Connolly had not been impressed by his first sight of Balliol, when he went there in winter-time to sit for the scholarship: 'The sheets had not been aired in my bedroom. I got rheumatism in my shoulder and could hardly hold a pen during the later papers. The dons impressed me but the undergraduates I encountered made me long to return to my suspended boyhood [at Eton], to Charles and Jackie and Nigel and Freddie, my books and Medici prints, the view from my window of wine-dark brick and the chestnut tree in Weston's Yard.' Oxford seemed a 'world of matey young men with their pipes and grey bags', which filled him with despair.

Eton, after all, had given them a particularly intense experience. 'Here,' writes Henry Yorke, recalling the Studio on Saturday evenings, 'under the yawns of the Art Master . . . we had what came as close to those talks which are supposed to be exchanged by undergraduates in which the course of life is plotted.' For Yorke, the 'Arts' had immediate, practical results: 'All I know is that it gave me confidence even if there was nothing in it so that ... I began to write a novel.' It was called *Blindness*, and much of it was completed by the time he went up to Oxford.

Writing fifteen years later, Connolly was convinced that Eton, rather than Oxford, had set the pattern for himself and his contemporaries. He posited 'the theory that the experience undergone by boys at the great public schools, their glories and disappointments, are so intense as to dominate their lives and arrest their development. From these it results that the greater part of the ruling class remains adolescent, school-minded, self-conscious, cowardly, sentimental, and in the last analysis homosexual.'

Connolly concluded his own Eton career at Corps camp, where in the privacy of his tent he lay in the embrace of another Colleger. 'It was the happiest night of my life,' he wrote to another Etonian not long afterwards. 'I did not do him or anything and I was not gone on him but in the dark one face is very much like another and it was the perfect understanding which arose out of such a close embrace that I valued so much and has lasted ever since after all.'

Certainly Connolly himself could never get away emotionally from Eton. 'For my own part,' he wrote many years after leaving,

> I was long dominated by impressions of school. The plopping of gas mantles in the class-rooms, the refrain of psalm tunes, the smell of plaster on the stairs, the walk through the fields to the bathing places or to chapel across the cobbles of School Yard, evoked a vanished Eden of grace and security; the intimate noises of College, the striking of the clock at night from Agar's Plough, the showers running after games of football, the housemaster's squeak, the rattle of tea-things, the poling of fires as I sat talking with Denis or Charles or Freddie on some evening when everybody else was away at a lecture, were recollected with anguish and College, after I left, seemed to me like one of those humming fortified paradises in an Italian primitive outside which the angry Master in College stood with his flaming sword.

Only Harold and Brian were self-confident about Oxford. Harold delightedly discovered, on his first visit to the University to sit Responsions, the joys of the Ashmolean Museum – 'Italian primitives ... a Paolo Uccello of singular beauty representing a stag-hunt ... a moving Baptism of Christ by Giovanni di Paolo'. Christ Church itself was 'love at first sight', and he found himself 'treated as an intelligent adult' by 'Mr Dundas, the Senior Censor'. The whole thing seemed 'like a holiday'.

Brian was just a shade more doubtful, when he too went to sit for Responsions. 'It is an interesting place, if the tiniest bit in the world disappointing.' But 'we will have a *violently interesting* time there'.

Et in Arcadia

1

Oxford Broom

In May 1922, visiting Oxford to take Responsions, Harold Acton was given lunch by Billy Clonmore, son of the Earl of Wicklow, who had been at prep school and Eton with him and was now up at Merton. At the lunch party he introduced Harold to what he described as an 'Oxford aesthete'. Harold thought poorly of the specimen: 'A pressed fern from the pages of the *Yellow Book*, his disjointed fragments of drawled conversation were as dull as his jaundiced eyes.' Harold tried discussing the Nineties with him, but could stimulate no response worth the name. 'What interest he could muster in life was limited to his sickly appearance.' The aesthete showed him some naughty etchings he had picked up in Venice. Harold was infuriated by their timid prurience, and told him they were just 'the messes of a miserable masturbator'.

Harold's feelings about such so-called Aesthetes were shared by a contributor to *Isis* that summer, who published a poem beginning

> I used to think they passed away
>   With rather naughty '99,
> Those gaudy insects of a day –
>   Your pardon, the mistake was mine.
> O, la, la! the Aesthete!
> I've met one in the street . . .
> I'm glad there's someone still who '*yearns*',
>   And dotes on Dowson and on Wilde. . . .

35

In an Oxford that was, as Acton says, still full of the recently demobilized who 'had not yet sloughed off their military skins', it was understandable that the few people preoccupied with the arts should wish to distinguish themselves from the beefy majority by manner and appearance. But Harold, knowing how much prejudice there already was against 'art' in Britain, feared that the Aesthete type – who was, as the *Isis* poet pointed out, merely attempting a stale revival of the Nineties manner – would damage a cause he himself cherished. Billy Clonmore told him that this particular fellow was not such a bad soul; Harold replied that he wished he *was* a bad soul – wished he had 'anything so positive as a vice'. He left the lunch party bursting with resolutions.

His own artistic inclinations were not, in fact, very different from those of the Nineties imitators. He had the advantage of a Florentine upbringing, but had formulated no plan of aesthetic campaign. He had general ideas, not yet focused on any artistic doctrine: 'We should combat ugliness; we should create clarity where there was confusion; we should overcome mass indifference; and we should exterminate false prophets.' The contempt he felt for the Aesthetes at Oxford largely sprang from the alarming proximity of their enthusiasms to what he and Brian had been attempting at Eton. The *Candle* had been a predominantly Nineties artefact, and had Harold not found such feeble mimicry of the Nineties at Oxford, he would probably have pursued that course for much longer.

He looked at other artistic currents in and around Oxford. The University's annual anthology of undergraduate verse, *Oxford Poetry*, showed the dead state of that particular art: the 1922 edition contained not a glimmer of modernism, and was stuffed with sub-Georgian pieces with titles like 'Twilight', 'Ruined Church' and 'Come, My Muse'. The most modern influence was De la Mare. Other possibilities might lie at Garsington Manor, outpost of Bloomsbury, a few miles on the London side of Oxford. Harold had met its chatelaine, Lady Ottoline Morrell, in Florence, and had also read Aldous Huxley's *roman à clef* about Garsington, *Crome Yellow*, which had been published the previous year, so when he was invited there during his May 1922 visit to Oxford he knew what to expect. He admired the house and garden, which had a certain Italianate quality, and was struck by the sight of Lytton Strachey standing beside their hostess, who was wearing, for all her considerable height, 'a Kate Greenaway costume of heliotrope silk with white stockings'. But the conversation seemed erratic rather than exciting – Lady Ottoline suddenly hissed out, for no apparent reason, 'I'm sure Mr Acton is an admirer of Belloc' – and all the other guests seemed to know each other intimately and left him 'to shift, *à l'anglaise*, to my own devices'. He wandered into the house and began to see what Bloomsbury could offer in the way of pictures.

He was just examining Augustus John's portrait of Lady Ottoline when Philip Morrell, the husband, strode in looking like a country squire, in riding-breeches, and sat down at a pianola and began to pedal away at a piano-roll of *Schéhérazade*. Acton had now seen the Diaghilev ballet, adoring it above all the company's repertoire, with its Bakst décor and the dancing of Nijinsky and Karsavina. To hear it mangled on a mechanical piano was an outrage. 'I put my hands to my ears and fled.' He walked the six miles back to Oxford in a rage.

Alongside this experience, the more traditional trappings of Oxford did not disappoint. During Harold's May visit to Christ Church, R. H. Dundas, the college's Senior Censor, invited him to dine on High Table, and he appreciated 'the excellent simple fare' – simple by the standards of La Pietra – and the 'aroma of ripe scholarship'. The dons' conversation suggested the Augustan age, and Harold was impressed that, instead of dozing over the remains of the meal, the company picked up its napkins and shifted to the Senior Common Room for the ceremony of port and madeira. (Dundas, his host, was notorious among undergraduates for his curiosity about their sex lives. 'Dr Dundas', writes Osbert Lancaster, 'extended his inexhaustible sympathy and excited interest to all those he considered to be in urgent need of sexual advice.')

Since Harold was going up to Oxford before him, Brian Howard decided to draw up plans about how, as the advance party of their *Eton Candle* team, Harold should conduct himself at the University. 'I think', he wrote to him during the summer of 1922,

> that we, at Oxford, ought to remain *exclusive*. ... *Don't* go and join any societies *please*. ... Already we have got to a stage *way beyond* the Oxford intellectuals. We are genuinely gifted people, we are comparatively mature. They are NOT. ... If you take up an attitude – not an offensive attitude – of calm, conscious superiority and aloofness – security in superior attainments and knowledge, you will get an enormous reputation as an intellectual.

Returning to Oxford in October 1922 to take up residence at Christ Church, Harold made his first bid for individuality. 'Most freshmen at "The House" [Christ Church] coveted rooms in Tom Quad, Peckwater or Canterbury, but a room with a balcony overlooking Christ

Church Meadow appealed to me more.' It was both an aesthetic and a social statement, a rejection of the classical formality of the college's principal quadrangles (Peckwater and Canterbury are fine specimens of eighteenth-century architecture, Tom Quad a grand *piazza* from the sixteenth and seventeenth centuries) for the then highly unfashionable Victorianism of Meadow Buildings, and a separation of himself from the Old Etonians who traditionally thronged Peckwater, leaving Meadow Buildings for 'dim' men from obscure schools.

Christopher Hollis, in his book *Oxford in the Twenties*, explains the social hierarchy of the colleges. Christ Church was the smartest, being crammed with Old Etonians; Wykehamists (clever men from Winchester College, the public school with the best academic tradition) generally went to New College; but in other respects intellectual superiority 'certainly rested with Balliol'. The Christ Church Etonians 'very often ... did not mix with [undergraduates] from other and despised public schools', and the smart colleges had little or nothing to do with the others. Hollis cites Michael Fane in Compton Mackenzie's *Sinister Street* (1913–14) being asked to lunch by a man at Lincoln College, and saying: 'I don't know where Lincoln is. Have you got a map or something?'

Harold Acton, then, was sitting at the top of the social tree at Christ Church. But by his choice of rooms he had turned his back on the smart set. Meadow Buildings were designed by Thomas Deane and erected in the early 1860s to replace a seventeenth-century structure. In 1922, when Harold came up to Christ Church, they could easily have won a competition for the ugliest building in Oxford. John Betjeman writes:

> They represent ... the result in stone of the mistaken doctrine that Venetian Gothic was the only genuine article, which was being preached with fatal eloquence by Ruskin. The Meadow Buildings are the memorial of Dean Liddell's reign as Dean of Christ Church. They certainly should be seen, as curiosities, as a bold Gothic block, singularly gloomy to live in, yet so vividly Ruskin's dream as to be preferable to the faint hearted attempts at Neo-Gothic-moderno-classicism practised by well-known architects in present day Oxford [Betjeman was writing in the 1930s]. Meadow Buildings are an honest expression of the gas-enlightened 'sixties. As such, they are worthy of preservation.

Harold Acton admits that 'externally, Meadow Buildings are grimly Victorian Gothic and internally they are sombre'. But it was there that he had chosen to establish himself. Given his determination not to follow the style of the Aesthetes he found at Oxford, there were really only two ways he could go: either to become pure modern (as the Auden group, also based at Christ Church, did a few years after him), or to turn antiquarian. He chose the latter, picking the period immediately before the Nineties.

He painted his rooms in Meadow Buildings 'lemon yellow' to cheer them up a little, but shrewdly realized that the best way to adorn them was in the period of the building itself. So he began to fill them with Victorian bric-à-brac, 'artificial flowers and fruit and lumps of glass, a collection of paperweights imprisoning bubbles that never broke and flowers that never faded'. By choosing Victoriana he was scorning not just the Nineties, but also Bloomsbury, which he had encountered at Garsington Manor; he says that, though Roger Fry had impressed the 'Arts' at Eton, he himself now wanted to rebel against the style of Fry's Omega Workshops, which had pioneered the use of modern art in interior decoration. The Omega approach seemed to Acton to be a visual equivalent of Rimsky-Korsakov played on a pianola.

There was – though Acton in 1922 was scarcely in a position to realize it – yet another layer of rebellion implicit in his choice of enthusiasm. Forty years later, discussing the vogue for Victoriana which had been initiated by Acton and his friends in the 1920s, Evelyn Waugh pointed out that it had an anti-parental element in it, 'the wish to scandalize parents who had themselves thrown out the wax-flowers and woolwork screens which we now ardently collected'.

The first person to take notice of what Acton was doing was Robert Byron, who came up to Merton College in January 1923, a term after Acton had arrived at Christ Church. Though the two had mostly quarrelled about the Victorians during schooldays, they now began to agree passionately on the subject. As a disciple of Ruskin, Byron found Meadow Buildings overwhelmingly splendid, and he was delighted at Acton's decision to decorate his rooms in the Victorian manner. Acton says Byron was 'a greater enthusiast [for Victoriana] than I, for he believed that never had Britain been more resplendent than between 1846 and 1865. The vision of a "large-limbed, high-coloured Victorian England, seated in honour and plenty" was constantly before him.'

Indeed, without Byron's inclination towards the Victorians, Acton would probably not have gone very far with this enthusiasm. Until now, his artistic passions had been for Bakst, the Russian Ballet and the Italian primitives and *quattrocento*; and the *Eton Candle* showed that, for all his assertions that he despised them, he tended to drift into the mannerisms of the Nineties imitators – his 'Hansom Cab' novel was pure Nineties. He was really singularly ill-equipped to cultivate the earlier Victorians. He knew almost nothing of nineteenth-century English literature, and would refer to Dickens with great contempt as 'a writer whom my nurse used to make me read'. He took no interest in English ecclesiastical architecture, really a *sine qua non* for expertise in the Victorians.

If Brian Howard had arrived at Oxford at the same time as him, Acton might well not have chosen the Victorian path. Brian, after all, believed himself to be the champion of modernism, and seemed to think he would be able to rule Oxford with the same vague artiness as he had ruled a section of Eton: 'When I go to Oxford, I am going to continue the *Eton Candle* as the *Oxford Candle*, AND I am going to have a replica of the Rhymers' Club in a Candle Club.' But without Brian there to boss him, Harold, talking to Robert Byron, began to realize the potential in a conspicuous Victorian revival.

They felt that the early Victorian era, in which Britain had made strenuous efforts to recover from the Napoleonic war, seemed closer in spirit to 1922 than did the effete Nineties: 'We wanted Dawns, not Twilights.' Also, though the previous generation had tried to sweep away the remnants of Victoriana, the period did not seem very far off, for some of Acton's and Byron's contemporaries had had first-hand contacts with it. Osbert Lancaster, who came up to Oxford in 1926, had been brought up in pure Victorian style in his parents' Bayswater villa, and lived among great-aunts and grandparents who were themselves Victorians. For example, there was his Great-Aunt Martha, born early in the reign of George IV, who 'never appeared abroad save in the prescribed Victorian uniform for old ladies', and who when animated would gesture with her arms 'in a manner that was perfectly familiar to me from the illustrations of Cruikshank'. His grandfather spoke in the style of the early days of *Punch*: ''Pon my word, ain't he a howlin' swell?' Alan Pryce-Jones, who came up to Eton just as Acton was leaving, had been brought up in similarly Victorian fashion:

My father . . . recommended special reading for Sundays, and gave me annuals of Sabbath literature from his own nursery. Cards were not allowed on Sundays, and neither horse nor car could be used. Church, in London, meant the Guards Chapel in Wellington Barracks, and for this my father put on a tail-coat, a white waistcoat under a black one, and a top-hat. In the country, church usually meant Evensong, and I still . . . hear the richly melancholy threefold sway of 'The Day Thou Gavest, Lord, is Ended' sung by a black-cassocked choir in some Butterfield chancel.

For Harold Acton to choose early Victorian objects to decorate his rooms was not, then, so very *outré* in itself. But it became quite clear that he had declared war against the Aesthetes, the 'followers of Bunthorne', when he began to dress as an early Victorian. 'I bought a grey bowler, wore a stock and let my side-whiskers flourish. Instead of the wasp-waisted suits with pagoda shoulders and tight trousers affected by the dandies, I wore jackets with broad lapels and broad pleated trousers. The latter got broader and broader. Eventually they were imitated elsewhere, and were generally referred to as "Oxford bags".'

Imitations did indeed eventually appear, and a fashion began. Tom Driberg, coming up to Christ Church two years later than Acton, in 1924, went to Hall Brothers, the smart Oxford tailors in the High, and ordered 'trousers very wide and flapping at the ankles, far wider than the Navy's bell-bottoms ... and in an unusual colour – bright green'. Henry Yorke describes the Oxford craze for Victoriana which was raging by 1925:

> We collected Victorian objects, glass paperweights with coloured posies cast in them, little eternalized baskets of flowers in which nothing could break ... and large piles of waxed fruits under high glass domes. ... A number of us bought spotted dogs in china from Staffordshire, one or two had figures of the Prince Consort in the same material. As to architecture we were for everything Gothic and Beckford was a writer much admired.

But if this suggests instant popularity for Harold Acton's tastes, it is quite misleading. The first reaction to him was sheer astonishment.

Emlyn Williams, a Christ Church contemporary, describes the apparition of Acton in Tom Quad one foggy winter evening:

> A tall plumpish young man loomed up, whom it was impossible to contemplate as an undergraduate; his umbrella was rolled cane-tight but no snugger than he was, into a long tube of a black overcoat with spilling from under it pleated trousers as wide as a skirt. As he advanced out of the swirling mist, it became clear that it was not just the weather, he was doing his own swirling. ... He swayed to a standstill; in case his kind soft-coloured features might be mistaken for the face of youth, he had flanked them with a pair of long side-whiskers and topped them with a skittishly curled grey bowler. Bowing with the courtesy of another age and clime, he spoke, an English flawlessly Italianated: 'I do most dreadfully beg your pardons this inclement night – though I have been resident a year, I find it too idio-tically diffi-cult to find my way about. I have been round Tom like a tee-toe-tum, too too maddening – where

does our dear Dean hang out?' ... 'Jesus,' said Evvers [an American undergraduate], 'what's that?'

The Christ Church 'hearties' responded to this new *poseur* in their usual fashion. Writing to Brian Howard during the summer of 1923, his third term, Harold reported that:

> no one else has had such a smash-up as I had in the House. I, tucked up in bed and contemplating the reflection of Luna on my walls, was immersed under showers of myriad particles of split glass, my head powdered with glass-dust and my possessions vitrified. A band consisting of nearly thirty big ruff [*sic*] animal louts tried to break in my 'oak' [the outer door of his rooms] – but I remained adamant and their force was wasted. Yet I had never before received a poker through my window and hope that I shall never experience it again.

Tom Driberg says that such events were commonplace, and that the festivities of the Bollinger Club in the opening chapter of Waugh's *Decline and Fall* are 'a mild account of the night of any Bullingdon Club dinner in Christ Church. Such a profusion of broken glass I never saw until ... the height of the blitz.' On such nights, any undergraduate who was believed to have 'artistic' tastes was an automatic target. Driberg himself had his Christ Church rooms raided by hearties who pulled off his green 'Oxford bags' and carried them round Tom Quad in triumph before cutting them up into strips and hanging these around the Junior Common Room. Driberg did not mind terribly – 'I had probably not paid the tailors' bill' – but he was upset by their 'Philistine destruction of some wax or glass fruit' (another imitation of Acton).

Henry Yorke, coming up to Magdalen – a college almost as full of rich public school men as was Christ Church – found it hard to believe that the authorities could encourage 'orgies' like the Bump Suppers (celebrations of rowing wins in Eights Week) for the oarsmen and their supporters, who amounted to ninety-five per cent of the college: 'It did seem to turn the rest of us into early Christians for a Roman holiday.' He found that the best remedy was to get drunk oneself, 'so that, if they did come, it would not hurt too much. ... The most that was likely to happen was that they would drop one into the Cherwell from a bridge but they were so mad drunk ... that I felt there was a chance they might do me serious injury.'

There were various ways of staving off an invasion of one's rooms. A character in John Betjeman's *Summoned by Bells*, on being told that the hearties intend to break up his fancy-dress party, responds: 'I've settled *them* all right, / I've bribed the Boat Club with a cask of beer.' A cheaper answer was to 'sport one's oak', keep the outer door locked. But Henry Yorke 'never did this because I thought if they came and could not get at me they would lie in wait to take me another day, and that the suspense I should be in of waiting would not be worth while'. He describes 'that awful screaming they affected when in motion imitating the cry when the fox is viewed'.

Yorke prepared himself for one invasion by half emptying a dozen bottles of beer and filling them up with brandy. These he passed to the rowing men 'slavering in the doorway', who 'took a pull and passed them back to the dervishes behind and soon they went away to become unconscious. They had been drinking port all night, the beer and brandy on top was too much for any stomach.'

Osbert Lancaster says that the hearties, though a threat to any 'aesthetic' gathering, did lend a certain excitement to the occasion. Moreover the toughs were not always victorious. He recalls 'one heroic evening when they fell like ninepins before a barrage of champagne bottles flung by Robert Byron from a strategic position at the head of the stairs with a force and precision that radically changed the pattern of Oxford rowing for the rest of term'. Henry Yorke achieved another form of revenge. One morning after a Bump Supper he was calling on a friend with a hangover, taking him a bottle of Eno's Fruit Salts. Hurrying through the cloisters, he came across some belatedly drunken hearties – 'two men supporting a third. His head lolled as though his throat were cut but ... he saw the bottle in my arms and it meant drink to him. He broke loose, ran forward and after a struggle he snatched it away ... and ... poured the powder down his throat. At once he fell on his back ... and began silverly frothing. We laughed until we choked.'

Harold Acton had done more to annoy the hearties than wear broad trousers and fill his rooms with Victorian paperweights. During his second term, Duckworth published *Aquarium*, his first volume of poems, 'and its red, black and yellow striped cover met me everywhere like a challenge. For a book of poems it had a prompt success.'

Reviews in the Oxford journals were slightly condescending, but definitely enthusiastic. 'Mr Harold Acton', observed *Isis* on 9 May 1923, 'has graduated with honours in the Sitwell school. ... But he is also, somehow or other, a poet. ... In a year or two he may be writing really well.' The *Oxford Magazine* said much the same, observing of the Sitwell influence: 'We should not be surprised if, with a little more sincerity and a little less straining after effect, its author went further than the leader he follows.'

The publication of *Aquarium* marked a decline in Brian Howard's influence over Harold. Brian had not been informed that the book was coming out, or sent a copy, and he heard about it only through a friend of his mother's. 'Why wasn't I told?' he grumbled to William Acton. But he wrote a congratulatory note to Harold.

Though he had forgotten to inform Brian, Harold made sure that Christ Church knew about the poems. 'Since I was free from false modesty ... and possessed a resonant voice, I never faltered when I was asked to read them, but shouted them lustily down a megaphone. Nor would I tolerate interruptions. The megaphone could also be brandished as a weapon.' In particular, 'I read them from my balcony to groups in Christ Church meadow.'

The poems in *Aquarium* have some Eliot touches – almost to the point of plagiarism – and a great deal of Edith Sitwell, but though hardly original the book was a great deal more vigorous than the average piece of undergraduate verse in 1923. The most recent Oxford stars had been Edmund Blunden, Roy Campbell and Robert Graves, who had all gone down, leaving the field to the feeble Georgian imitators. Shouted through a megaphone at the athletes returning from the rugger field and the boats, lines like these must have caused quite a sensation:

> Within, the heat is curdling into flesh,
> Vague, supple limbs to weave a night of lust
> And throats lain back to kiss at my desire
> White, soft and curving, I may nibble then
> Such mad caresses as will flay my lips.

Harold records that many copies of *Aquarium* were inscribed with 'tender dedications' to those 'witnesses of youthful passion' who had inspired such lines. He names no names, but observes that 'it is a subtle satisfaction, even in retrospect, to have kindled flames in Elgin marble breasts'.

At first, Harold ignored Brian's warning about not joining existing societies at Oxford: 'I was drawn to them like a moth. I fluttered my wings at the Italian Circle, the Spanish Society, the Ordinary, which invited me to read papers and join their discussions, and there were dining clubs as well.' But at such meetings 'poems were read in a self-deprecatory manner, amid stammerings and blushes'. This irritated him, and encouraged him to form his own clique, along the lines of the 'Arts' at Eton. Once again, the immediate outcome, even

44

before the clique was properly formed, was a magazine. At the beginning of his second term, in January 1923, Harold began to start 'sweeping away *fin-de-siècle* cobwebs' with a paper called the *Oxford Broom*. Its first issue appeared in February.

The magazine's title may have come from Harold Loeb's *Broom*, a magazine for expatriate writers in Europe, edited in Rome from November 1921. Its style was simply that of the *Eton Candle*, transplanted to Oxford. Like the *Candle*, it began with a brash statement of modernity, an editorial entitled 'A Modern Credo' which called for 'the erection of new absolute values' amid 'the exquisite chaos of modern thought'. Like the *Candle*, the remainder of the contents – indifferent poems and prose sketches by various individuals – suggested a general and rather vague interest in aestheticism rather than any deeply felt modernity. However, it was a change from the ponderous *Isis*, with its weekly 'Idol' drawn from the ranks of indistinguishable athletes, and from the grim earnestness of the *Oxford Outlook*. Together with *Aquarium*, it established Acton as a freshman to be reckoned with.

He was only nineteen, but his cosmopolitan air gave him a head start over his elders and contemporaries. 'With his tall, distinguished, vaguely Oriental looks,' writes Christopher Hollis, then at Balliol, 'with the scarf carelessly twisted round his neck, most of us did not remember, and doubtless many did not know, that he was really younger than the rest of us. We accepted him without complaint as our leader and hardly recollected that he had been still a schoolboy when we were already undergraduates.' Hollis adds that in itself the cosmopolitan manner would not have endeared him to other undergraduates. 'But he wore his culture with such an air of high spirits, kindliness and good humour, with so brave a dash that we all fell for him and even those who came to scoff were soon persuaded to remain, if not to pray, at least to laugh.'

The second issue of the *Oxford Broom* (April 1923) was no more remarkable in content than the first. But this number at least looked unconventional, for its cover bore a woodcut-style drawing of deliberate ugliness, showing an ape-like park-keeper wielding a besom. The contents page stated: 'Cover Design by Evelyn Waugh'.

2

'. . . Longed to Remain Myself and Yet Be Accepted . . .'

Evelyn Waugh was an undergraduate at Hertford College – by Christ Church standards, one of the most dim and obscure – reading Modern History. He had been up at the University since January 1922, two terms before Harold Acton, and he was older than him; he would be twenty in October. He was one of the two sons of a London publisher, and had made his mark on Cecil Beaton at their day school in Hampstead.

Beaton alleges that the torture inflicted by Waugh's gang had included bending his arms back to front. Waugh, in his own memoirs, disputes this: 'Our persecution went no further than sticking pins into him and we were soundly beaten for doing so.' He expresses no regret for his behaviour: 'I remember him as a tender and very pretty little boy. The tears on his long eyelashes used to provoke the sadism of youth and my cronies and I tormented him on the excuse that he was reputed to enjoy his music lessons and to hold in sentimental regard the lady who taught him. I am sure he was innocent of these charges.' Waugh gave the same account of the bullying when he reviewed Beaton's diaries in the *Spectator* in 1961; he observed of the book: 'He can't write for toffee.'

There was a bullying streak in the Waugh family. Evelyn's paternal grandfather, Dr Alexander Waugh, a country doctor of Scottish descent with a practice in Somerset, suffered from attacks of violent rage, was known to lay about the drawing-room ornaments with a poker, and had beaten his sons severely. 'The happiness of all', writes Evelyn, 'would depend on his temper.' He deliberately frightened his children, ostensibly to fortify their characters. Once, observing a wasp on his wife's forehead, he crushed it with his cane, thereby ensuring that she was stung. When Arthur Waugh, Evelyn's father, first heard the term 'sadist', he remarked: 'I believe that is what my father must have been.'

Arthur Waugh, mild by comparison, was nevertheless capable of bullying, at least on the printed page. In his spare time from his publishing office he wrote reviews for the London literary journals, and sometimes put on a highly irascible performance. Contributing to the *Quarterly Review* for October 1916, he poured scorn on the modernist poets, dismissing Ezra Pound's verse as 'wooden prose, cut into battens' and calling T.S. Eliot's 'The Love Song of J. Alfred Prufrock' a display of 'the banality of premature decrepitude'. He summed up the work of these 'literary "Cubists"' as 'unmetrical, incoherent banalities ... anarchy which will end in something worse even than "red ruin and the breaking up of laws"'. With them he contrasted favourably the 'humour, commonsense, and artistic judgement of the best of the new "Georgians"'.

Arthur had learned the value of a harsh pen at school at Sherborne. Despised for being a 'swot' and no athlete, he had made a name by writing lampoons of masters and other unpopular boys. Subsequently at New College, Oxford, he had contributed comic verses to an undergraduate paper and had written a humorous 'smoker' for the Oxford University Dramatic Society (the OUDS). In his memoirs, he blames the amount of time he gave to this and country-house theatricals for the fact that he left Oxford with only a Third Class in Classical Moderations and 'Greats'.

A literary cousin, the eminent Edmund Gosse, obtained him a commission to write a life of Tennyson, who was then in his eighties, and Arthur had almost finished it when Tennyson died. It was hurriedly completed and rushed through the press, and Arthur's reputation was made. This was in 1892; two years later he was invited to contribute to the first *Yellow Book*; Henry Harland, its editor, wanted him as a sop to the prim, a counter-balance to the Decadents. Arthur wrote in praise of 'Reticence in Literature', objecting to such things as descriptions of 'the sensations of childbirth'. This contrasted very oddly with the general tone of the *Yellow Book*, and Arthur's piece was picked on favourably by those reviewers who disliked most of Harland's contributors. In contrast with the Beardsley–Wilde set, Arthur Waugh was labelled 'sane and manly'.

Having taken on almost by accident the role of defender of traditional literary values, Arthur found it profitable. Literary editors from the more conventional journals, such as the *Daily Telegraph*, began to give him regular reviewing work, and he also began to write a literary gossip-column for a New York paper, thereby making a number of enemies. He explains that his chief model as critic was Samuel Johnson, whom he praises for his 'tonic, invigorating commonsense'. But he himself was not really a die-hard. In his autobiography (1930) he speaks respectfully of T.S. Eliot and Edith Sitwell, and he tended to lapse into Edwardian sentimentality of the J.M. Barrie school – he writes gushingly of 'the old nursery' in his Hampstead house, calling it 'a sort of treasure-house of our happy home life'. Anthony Powell, who was often at the Waugh house, calls this aspect of Arthur 'a bit too good to be true'.

Powell records that he was apt to begin sentences: 'Speaking as a member of the lower-middle classes ...'. In fact the Waughs were solidly upper middle class. Arthur's immediate forebears were clergymen, lawyers and the like, while his wife's family included soldiers and members of the Indian Civil Service. (One of her great-grandfathers, Henry Cockburn, an Edinburgh public servant, was created a Lord of Justiciary in 1837.) Evelyn Waugh judged his father's most obvious characteristic to be theatricality. 'The first adult visitor I introduced into the house ... said to me: "Charming, entirely charming, and acting all the time." When I consulted her, my mother confirmed this judgement.' Yet, says Evelyn's brother, Evelyn was 'very like his father'.

Arthur became managing director of the publishing house of Chapman & Hall at the early age of thirty-five, remaining there until his retirement in 1929. Early in Evelyn's childhood, he moved his family from their small North London house to a plot of land on the edge of Hampstead Heath, which he sentimentally named 'Underhill' after a lane in his native Midsomer Norton. He wrote ecstatically of the meadow he could see from his 'book-room', but other villas quickly sprang up to spoil the view, the Tube railway arrived, shops, a theatre and a cinema sprang up, and, as Evelyn says, 'our postal address was altered from Hampstead to Golders Green'. (Christopher Hollis alleges that, as a young man, Evelyn 'would walk to Hampstead to post his letters in order that they might bear a more aristocratic postmark'.)

In one of Evelyn's first pieces of prose fiction, 'The Balance' (1926), the hero, based on Evelyn himself, is described as being 'too well brought up' to remember much of his childhood. There seems to be a double meaning here: that his parents have conducted his upbringing so successfully that nothing unpleasant can be recollected of it, and that he comes from the kind of family in which it is simply 'not done' to rake over the past. Waugh certainly liked, when asked about his early life, to give both these impressions.

He was the younger of the two Waugh sons. His elder brother Alexander, named after Arthur Waugh's bellicose father, was known from birth as Alec. The younger son was given Arthur's own name: 'I was christened Arthur Evelyn St John: the first name after my father.' Until he came to write his memoirs, and looked at family papers, he believed the correct order to be 'Evelyn Arthur St John', which is how it is always given in works of reference. To avoid confusion with his father, he became known from infancy as Evelyn, but he said he had 'never liked' that name, since 'In America it is used only of girls and from time to time even in England it has caused confusion as to my sex.' He explains that the name was chosen 'from a whim of my mother's'. Does it contain a hint that Mrs Waugh, already blessed with a son, really wanted a girl? 'St John was more absurd,' he goes on. 'I had a High Church godfather who insisted that I must be given the name of a saint.'

Alec was five and a half years older than Evelyn, and found his baby brother 'too young' for companionship. He turned instead to his father, whom he calls 'a wonderful companion. . . . I confided in him all my ambitions, all my problems. I have never since been so completely myself with anyone.' Arthur Waugh reciprocated Alec's attentions. 'I must have been the youngest man of my age in London,' Arthur writes of the years in which Alec and Evelyn were children, alleging that this rejuvenated him. To which Evelyn replies: 'I never saw him as anything but old, indeed as decrepit.' Behind the joke is bitterness and a sense of exclusion from the cosy friendship that existed between father and elder son.

Alec admits that he himself was 'an indulged child, very much my father's favourite'. Nor did the mother make efforts to counterbalance this prejudice on her husband's part. Alec writes: 'Evelyn . . . once said to his mother, "Daddy loves Alec more than me. But you love me more than you love Alec." This was indeed true, but my mother felt that she should not show favouritism. "No," she said, "I love you both the same." "Then I am lacking in love," he said.' And Evelyn told Christopher Sykes, his biographer: 'I was not rejected or misprized, but Alec was their firstling and their darling lamb.'

In Evelyn's autobiographical novel *The Ordeal of Gilbert Pinfold*, it is said that Mr Pinfold loved his mother 'extravagantly' in childhood; and in his memoirs Evelyn talks of 'two adored deities, my nurse and my mother'. One notices the order in which the two women are mentioned. He goes on to write at length about his nurse, Lucy, a girl from Midsomer Norton. 'I think Lucy fully returned my love,' he says. He makes no such statement about his mother, describing her as 'small, neat, reticent'.

Catherine Waugh, the mother, had been born in India, the daughter of an official in the Bengal Civil Service, and had been sent very early to England where she and her sister were brought up in an 'elderly *ménage*' of two maiden great-aunts and a bachelor great-uncle. She had been quietly happy there – Evelyn says she looked back on it 'as the ideal of home' – and when she came to have children of her own she treated them much as she had been treated herself. She was content to let her histrionic husband dominate the household. Anthony Powell, who when Evelyn was grown up sometimes came to supper on Sunday nights, records that Mrs Waugh scarcely spoke a word at meals. Evelyn says she was happiest working in the garden, 'potting, planting, watering, weeding'. Christopher Sykes records that he 'often heard Evelyn talk of his father, but I do not remember him once mentioning his mother'.

With a less flamboyant husband, Mrs Waugh might have been able to pay more consistent attention to her younger child. But when Arthur was at home he dominated the entire family. Alec says that Evelyn's day 'ended with the click of his father's latch-key', and that Evelyn 'resented his father's intrusion' into such attention as he could get from his mother. Evelyn echoes this: 'I . . . grudged his usurpation of my mother's attention.'

Arthur Waugh made some attempt to get to know his younger son – 'I think he paid a visit to the nursery every evening and often made brief efforts to entertain,' writes Evelyn – but these few minutes at the end of the day were not sufficient to endear him to a small child, and Evelyn says he 'never particularly welcomed him' into the nursery. Until he was seven, his father was 'a figure of minor importance and interest' to him, a noisy creature who would arrive home from the office and shout 'Kay! Kay! Where's my wife?' from the hall below. 'And that', says Evelyn, 'was the end of my mother's company for the evening.'

Nevertheless in his autobiography Evelyn devotes an entire chapter to his father, whilst his mother's character is summed up in a single paragraph. This alone – quite apart from abundant evidence elsewhere in his books – suggests that his father was ultimately a figure of the greatest importance to him. 'He was restless rather than active,' he writes of him.

> In person he was small. ... I remember him as always corpulent. ... He often adverted to his imminent demise. He always referred to himself as 'incorrigibly Victorian'. ... His melancholies were brief and quickly relieved. Most of his acquaintance regarded him as exuberantly jovial. He was by nature sociable and hospitable, but he had no pleasure in large gatherings. ... Most of his acquaintances were subject to genial ridicule. ... In politics he would have described himself as a Tory but ... did not go to the polls. ... He had no itch to get to the truth of a story, frankly preferring its most picturesque form.

Each of these statements could stand, without the slightest modification, as a precise description of Evelyn himself in the later years of his life. Alec Waugh, on the other hand, never became a copy of Arthur. Auberon Waugh (Evelyn's own eldest son), writing an obituary of his uncle Alec, describes him as 'unaggressive, benign ... urbane'.

Alec himself supplies a persuasive reason for this: 'I was confident that I was going to make a considerable mark in the world,' while Evelyn 'may well have felt himself relegated to second place'. As Evelyn began to grow up, his resentment of his theatrical, self-caricaturing father was augmented by a curiosity about this florid personality, easily the strongest character in the house. But Arthur did not reciprocate his younger son's attention. He devoted such time as he spent at home to Alec, simply because the eldest son was traditionally the object of the father's special concern. Instead of getting the rewards he might expect from imitating his father's character, Evelyn was constantly rejected in favour of another.

He began to be contemptuous of his father and jealous of his brother. 'Daddy is a Publisher he goes to Chapman and Hall office it looks an offely dull plase,' he wrote at the age of seven. He expresses the same sentiment in his memoirs: 'His sedentary and cerebral occupations appeared ignominious to me in my early childhood. I should have better respected a soldier or a sailor like my uncles ... a man, even, who shaved with a cut-throat razor.' As he began to grow up, he and his father (notes Alec) began to be 'constantly in conflict', and were mostly 'irritated by each other'. By the age of seventeen, Evelyn had begun to perceive the theatrical element in his father's personality: he wrote in his diary that his father had been 'ineffably silly' throughout the school holidays, adding that he was beginning to 'see through' him.

As to his feelings towards Alec, Evelyn wrote, many years later, a bitter short story on the subject of sibling rivalry:

The two brothers developed into sturdy, unremarkable little boys. . . . They were both sandy-haired, courageous, and well-mannered on occasions. Neither was sensitive, artistic, highly strung, or conscious of being misunderstood. Both accepted the fact of Gervase's [the elder's] importance just as they accepted his superiority of knowledge and physique. . . . Tom found that his obscurity was on the whole advantageous, for it excused him from the countless minor performances of ceremony which fell on Gervase.

In this story, the elder brother gets all the prizes, including the heiress whom his younger brother had intended to marry.

In life, the Waugh brothers' achievements were eventually very different, the younger easily outstripping the elder; yet Alec constantly dogged Evelyn's steps. He became a successful author before Evelyn had been heard of, and Evelyn was not infrequently mistaken for him. In *Labels*, his 1930 travel book, Evelyn describes an encounter with 'a beautiful and splendidly dressed Englishwoman' in a Paris night club, who, on being introduced to him, praises him and his writings. Then she discovers that he is not Alec. ' "Well," she said, "how very unfortunate." ' Whether or not one believes in the incident, the fact that Evelyn chose to record or invent it shows how sensitive were his feelings on the subject. Alec, for his part, displayed not the slightest resentment of Evelyn for having swiftly overtaken him in literary reputation and earnings; he preserved the elder brother's self-confidence, nurtured long ago by paternal approval and encouragement. In *The Best Wine Last* (1978) he prints without a grumble Evelyn's scathing reference to his being 'in general not very highly regarded' as a literary figure, and cheerfully records that Evelyn's success as an author 'sent my own stock up'. On the other hand in 1957 Evelyn took a journalist to court for alleging that Alec's books had sold more copies than his own.

Alec Waugh was sent away to preparatory school as a boarder, but hated it, and when Evelyn's turn came he was allowed to remain at home until he reached his teens, attending Heath Mount as a day-boy. Though he avoided 'the bleak dormitories to which most boys of my age and kind were condemned', he had his own difficulties at Heath Mount, where his effeminate Christian name caused 'ridicule'; he says he would try to silence it by 'quoting the precedent of Field-Marshal Sir Evelyn Wood'. Further laughter was provoked by his surname, which other boys would pronounce as 'Wuff' or 'Wuffles'. Anthony Powell suggests that Waugh's fondness for mispronouncing other people's names – '*Dilwyn* Thomas' for Dylan Thomas, 'Kingsley *Ames*', and the like – was due to people's constant mishandling of his own; Powell noticed that when Waugh's second child Auberon was born in 1939 *The Times* printed the father's name as Emlyn.

'As a little boy he had been acutely sensitive to ridicule,' Waugh writes of his *alter ego* Mr Pinfold, and it may have been his schoolfellows' mockery that drove him to bullying weaker boys like Cecil Beaton. The bullying was perhaps also an attempt to compensate for being physically small, like his father; in adult life he measured about five feet seven inches, the same as Arthur Waugh, and he once observed that the Waughs had grown smaller through the generations because the bullying streak in the men made them marry small women. (However, in his diary for 1955 he makes a rejoinder to the popular notion that small men are pugnacious to compensate for lack of size: 'It is more plausible that God makes pugnacious men small because of the greater harm they could do if powerful.') A friend in his later years, Frances Donaldson, notes that when during the 1950s Evelyn began to be mocked in the press, it was as a 'prim, stuffy, cross, snobbish, *little* man', and she herself admits: 'He looked very small.' When in 1952 the aged Hilaire Belloc remarked to him that Englishmen were usually enormous, Waugh replied bluntly: 'I am short.'

Alec says that at home Evelyn was 'emotional and apt to dissolve in tears'. At school he hid his vulnerability behind a tough exterior; aged eleven, he records in his diary fighting the big brother of a boy who had picked a quarrel with him: 'We set to with a mixture of wrestling and boxing ending in my victory.'

He would have been sent from Heath Mount to Sherborne, Arthur Waugh's old school, which Alec was attending, but Alec was asked to leave because he was discovered to have engaged in homosexual practices. 'I had the bad luck to be found out,' Alec writes. 'A scandal started, a number of names were involved. . . .' This in itself might not have debarred Evelyn from going to Sherborne; minor scandals of the sort frequently disturbed the public schools and were soon forgotten. But Alec decided to get his revenge on Sherborne by writing a comparatively realistic novel of school life, which alluded delicately to the existence of homosexuality in public schools. *The Loom of Youth* found a publisher – not Arthur Waugh, though he stood by his son throughout the whole episode – and appeared in 1917, just as Evelyn was leaving Heath Mount at the age of thirteen. It became a best-seller, scandalized the older generation, and infuriated Sherborne. Arthur therefore had to find another public school for Evelyn.

He selected Lancing College, on the south coast near Brighton, a choice which Evelyn pretends to find comically eccentric; he says Arthur had 'never seen' the school and had 'no associations' with it, and that the whole decision was made and executed without proper consideration. In fact there was a perfectly good reason for the choice. Lancing had a strong Church of England tradition of the High Church variety, and Evelyn, who had been attending a church of that persuasion in Hampstead, had developed an enthusiasm for Anglo-Catholic ritual. Arthur Waugh was religious but pessimistic; during Evelyn's early years he read family prayers every morning, but when the First World War broke out had abandoned this practice on what Evelyn thought the 'very curious grounds' that it was 'no longer any good'. Arthur notes that in childhood Evelyn displayed 'a deeply religious temperament', and though he himself evidently doubted the power of the Almighty to halt the terrible bloodshed on the Western Front, he did not attempt to dissuade Evelyn from belief. Evelyn records that at the age of ten 'to the dismay of my parents [I] expressed my intention of becoming a clergyman'. His beloved nurse Lucy, a devout Nonconformist, had taught him to venerate the Bible, and had taken him on Sundays to the North End Rooms to hear sermons and sing the hymns of Moody and Sankey. Later, with his parents, he had sat in the congregation of St Jude's, Hampstead Garden Suburb, where the florid, lisping incumbent, the Rev. Basil Bourchier – whose brother had founded the OUDS at Oxford and was a popular actor–manager – delivered highly theatrical sermons. These amused but also impressed Evelyn, so that he began to take an interest in Anglo-Catholic ritual: 'The enthusiasm which my little school-fellows devoted to birds' eggs and model trains I turned on church affairs and spoke glibly of chasubles and Erastianism.' He also 'composed a long and tedious poem about Purgatory'. Lancing therefore seemed a sensible choice of public school.

After the comparatively easy life of being a day-boy at Heath Mount, within walking distance of home, it was a shock to be thrust into a community that lived in a group of flinty buildings situated in monastic isolation on the open downs. Evelyn arrived at the beginning of a summer term, when there were few other new boys, and felt completely alone. His pugnacious manner no longer served him well; he had developed the habit of making scathing remarks about other people's failings – in his Heath Mount diary he dismisses various individuals as 'repulsive', 'weird' and 'awful' – and at Lancing this began to get him into trouble. 'How often', writes Roger Fulford, another new boy that summer term of 1917, 'did I hear those ominous words "that awful little tick Waugh".'

Yet Fulford notes that he did not respond to this hostility by trying to make himself inconspicuous. In the dormitories, 'before getting into bed, we used to fall on our knees to use the chamber-pot and to address a brief word to the Almighty. Long after the pot was used, Evelyn would remain plunged in prayer by his bedside; similarly, in chapel his devotion was pronounced. Such practices . . . were not liked.' Probably he was praying for deliverance from the awfulness of boarding school. In his memoirs he notes grimly of his arrival at Lancing: 'I was not at all popular then or at any time in my first two years.' He wrote to his father asking to be taken away from school, but Arthur, in reply, 'counselled endurance'.

At Lancing, there was no escape from the barbarities of school life – no Eton High Street, no Dyson's with its gramophone, no Windsor, no comically awful Slough. Waugh describes the school as standing in 'complete isolation. . . . One might have been living on an island miles from anywhere.' And when a temporary escape was offered, it brought its own misery. On Ascension Day during his first term the school had a whole holiday, when boys were expected to go off in twos and threes into the surrounding countryside. Nobody had told Evelyn that he should pair off with someone, or, if they had, there was no one who would pair with him. When the day came, 'I had nowhere to go and no friends.' Everyone else disappeared, and he discovered that there were no meals at the school. He went to the kitchens and was given 'some ghastly galantine', and set off on foot, alone. 'Rain came on. . . . I wandered out with my damp packet of food and after a time took shelter among the trees called Chanctonbury Ring, ate a little and . . . wept. So every Ascension Day since I have felt that things can never be as bad as that.'

In 1947 he wrote in his diary: 'Ascension Day never passes without my thinking of the day now thirty years ago at Lancing which was the most miserable of my life.' These are strong words – by 1947 he had experienced many other crises – but there is no reason to doubt their accuracy, for it was now that he began to grow the hard outer shell of personality which in future would give him some protection

55

against the world and its power to humiliate. At the same time he began to make efforts to be accepted socially.

'I did not admire the other boys,' he writes of the months during which he began to adjust to Lancing. 'I did not want to be like them. But, in contradiction, I wanted to be one of them. I had no aspirations to excel, still less to lead; I simply longed to remain myself and yet be accepted as one of this distasteful mob. I cannot explain it; but I think that was what I felt.' Nearly forty years later, he wrote to his son Auberon, then having a difficult time at a public school himself: 'Don't become an anarchist. ... There is no superiority in shirking things and doing things badly. Be superior by cultivating your intellect and your taste.'

Roger Fulford soon observed the change in his behaviour. After his disastrous start, he seemed to be working strenuously to set things right. 'He moved steadily up the school in work,' Fulford writes. 'He took part in the gruelling five-mile cross-country race up the Downs [and] finished respectably. He ... began to enjoy a certain repute', the repute of a mildly successful conformist. Another Lancing contemporary, Dudley Carew, observes that Waugh would play football with considerable determination against boys older and heavier than himself, as if he were training for survival in a harsh world; Carew noticed his apparent 'indifference to kicks [and] knocks'. Fulford, who had not liked him much at first, began to think him a reasonable sort of fellow, and Carew got some amusement out of his company. Yet privately Waugh seems to have allowed himself to feel little warmth towards them or any of the other boys.

After attending a school Corps camp at the end of his third year at Lancing, he wrote in his diary that the 'increased insight into people's characters' he believed he had gained by being cooped up with them under canvas had led mainly to 'increased dislike'. And looking back on his days at Lancing in a 1953 radio interview, he tersely described his animosity towards other boys. The interviewer asked if he had been happy at school:

> *Waugh:* No. No fault of the school's. I think I shouldn't have been happy at any school.
> *Interviewer:* Why were you unhappy?
> *Waugh:* Hated the boys so.
> *Interviewer:* You didn't like them at all? I mean, they had nothing in common with you?

Waugh: I didn't discover it in the years that I was there.
Interviewer: All the boys? Did you really hate *all* the boys in the school?
Waugh: Didn't hate, but I just didn't like their company about the place.

He began to refine this scorn of the herd, to develop it in two particular directions. His diary shows that he was becoming precociously cynical about the world: 'The more I see of politics,' he wrote at the age of sixteen, 'the more dishonest and fascinating they appear.' In another entry he praises eighteenth-century court life as 'so healthily cynical', and judges 'a sense of the ludicrous' to be an essential trait for the sane individual.

At about the same time he began to show contempt towards the lower classes. 'The crowds were astounding,' he wrote in his diary after his brother Alec had taken him to a football match. 'It is extraordinary the people who can pay 10s 6d for a seat.' It was reassuring, in his insecurity, that there existed beneath his parents' social rank a whole hierarchy of persons whom he could legitimately ridicule, the middle classes' contempt for their inferiors being an acceptable emotion in British society. Evelyn evidently derived comfort from pretending to a Victorian certainty of his own position. In his diary he wrote of another boy's rudeness to the Corps bandmaster at Lancing: 'It is rather bad form to swear at one's social inferiors.' And, finding that he was beginning to like one of his schoolfellows, he described him in the diary as a 'true aristocrat', though the boy was actually of the same social class as himself. He was beginning to invent a social identity for himself that was implicitly aristocratic, and so allowed him to look down on others.

Re-reading his school diary forty years later, Waugh was shocked by the attitudes it displays. He judged its adolescent author to have been 'conceited, heartless and cautiously malevolent ... consistently caddish'. This is a slight exaggeration – there are moments of self-contempt – but at this period he was certainly cultivating cynicism and heartlessness. Insecurity at home followed by the cruel isolation of his first terms at Lancing had made him grow this shell. A little later in his school career he began to learn, not to soften it, but to make the shell more entertaining to other people.

He began to pick up a certain poise from J. F. Roxburgh, the future founding Headmaster of Stowe, who was then teaching at Lancing. Tom Driberg, another Lancing pupil of this generation, calls Roxburgh a 'magnetically brilliant' teacher with a 'polysyllabically precise delivery', and Waugh says they 'all caught' Roxburgh's elegant style of speaking. He describes Roxburgh dissecting Cowper's hymn 'God Moves in a Mysterious Way' and demonstrating the degree of self-contradictory nonsense in it: 'A mine is a hole from which you extract something or else an explosive weapon. In neither case would you "treasure up" anything in it. ... ' Such teaching inculcated in Waugh a lifelong contempt of cliché and woolly thought. It is in this mood that, in his diary while at school, he frequently castigates himself for bad writing: 'This is quite incoherent. ... A poor sentence.' Yet, for all his severe training under Roxburgh, he never mastered one aspect of the English language. 'I wish I could spell,' he remarked to Maurice Bowra in 1951. 'I often write angry letters to the headmistresses of my children's schools and after I have posted them realize they are full of mistakes.'

During schooldays he was reading Balzac and Flaubert, and probably much more, but his diary – a record of the development of his public personality – does not concern itself with such things. Towards the end of his time at Lancing he made an attempt at writing a novel, but did not consider the notion of becoming a professional author, which would have meant competing not merely with his father but with his elder brother, who after war service had entered the literary business full time (Evelyn's 1920 diary contains a sarcastic pun about 'the boom of youth'). When he and some of his Lancing schoolfellows founded a Dilettanti Society on much the same lines as the 'Arts' at Eton, Evelyn took charge of the visual arts section, and left the literary side to someone else.

He had been interested for some time in illuminated manuscripts – the shape of words appealed to him, much as the shape of sentences would do when he became a novelist – and he won a prize for illumination awarded by the school art master. This activity earned approval from Arthur Waugh, who commissioned Evelyn to design several book jackets for Chapman & Hall, paying a small fee for those which were used. But this mark of acceptance from his father had come too late to affect Evelyn's attitude to Arthur, and it was more gratifying to shock him. Evelyn says in his autobiography that for some years in adolescence he 'intermittently pretended to be a socialist' – a pose calculated to alarm the deeply conservative Arthur – and he also wrote, and managed to get published in a London art magazine, at the age of only fourteen, an essay 'In Defence of Cubism', praising those principles of modernism that his father had attacked in the *Quarterly Review*. It was a very polished piece of work, which Roxburgh would have admired, but in truth he had absorbed his father's distaste for the modern, and could not keep up the pretence for long. At the age of sixteen he visited a Matisse exhibition and wrote contemptuously in his diary of the artist's 'crude ill-drawn things'.

His taste was really for the mock-medievalism of the Pre-Raphaelites – he was proud of a family connection with Holman Hunt – and for their Arts and Crafts descendants who clustered around Eric Gill, a taste sufficiently against the mainstream to give a superficial impression of nonconformity, but not unpalatably modern, and providing an excuse for imitating traditional forms. Even here there were ways of shocking his father. His Lancing housemaster introduced him to Francis Crease, an amateur scribe and follower of the Gill group who lived in bachelor rooms near the school. Evelyn began to take lessons with him, and wrote in his diary: 'He is very effeminate and decadent and cultured and affected and nice.' He warmed to Crease as something of a fellow social outcast, and when he discovered that some of the Lancing masters doubted Crease's motives in befriending schoolboys, he decided to invite Crease to stay with his family in London, which was surely guaranteed to cause paternal alarm. However, during the visit, it was Crease who first opened Evelyn's eyes to his father's theatricality, thereby deepening Evelyn's cynicism about Arthur and his disillusion with human character.

Evelyn's conflicting feelings about his father are clearly visible in an editorial he wrote for the school magazine shortly before leaving Lancing, when he was eighteen. 'During the last few years,' the article begins, 'a new generation has grown up; between them and the young men of 1912 lies the great gulf of the war. What will they stand for and what are they going to do?' It was a pertinent question to ask at this moment, the end of 1921. The war had wiped out a huge proportion of 'the young men of 1912' who had gone to fight at the behest of their fathers' generation. The experience of 1914–18 had shown those who survived that, in the image of Wilfred Owen's parable–poem, the 'old man' would willingly slay his son 'And half the seed of Europe' through sheer stubborn paternal pride. Fathers were no longer to be trusted.

Waugh's Lancing editorial goes on to argue that those of 'Rupert Brooke's generation' who had survived the war were now 'broken . . . tired and embittered'. The way was now open for his own generation. 'What', he asked, 'will the young men of 1922 be?' One would expect the answer: they will pay no attention to their elders – the father-figures who sent Brooke and all the others to their deaths – and they will be revolutionary in their attitudes to the *mores* of the paternal generation; they will overturn everything because the war has shown them the folly of obeying their fathers. But this is not at all the line that Waugh takes. The editorial is, after all, the work of someone who, under his shell, is far too unsure of his position in his family and the world to issue a call to rebellion, and the answer he provides to his own question is thoroughly vague.

He refrains from giving any kick at his father's generation. Instead, he writes of himself and his contemporaries in stirring-sounding but quite empty terms:

> They will be, above all things, clear-sighted. . . . The youngest generation are going to be very hard and analytical and unsympathetic. . . . They are going to aim at things as they are and they will not call their aim 'Truth'. . . . They will not be revolutionaries and they will not be poets and they will not be mystics; there will be much that they will lose, but all that they have will be real.

The only clear statement here is 'They will not be revolutionaries'. If he is attacking anything, it seems to be some sort of mystical idealism, which makes him want to be 'hard and analytical' by comparison. But he is not really criticizing anything at all. He had indicated that, despite the war, his generation – or at least he himself – does not really feel rebellious.

However, in the next paragraph he does at last attack one characteristic of his father's generation – more specifically, a characteristic of Arthur Waugh himself, theatrical emotionalism: 'And they will be reticent too, the youngest generation. The young men of the nineties subsisted upon emotion and . . . poured out their souls with water and their tears with pride; middle-aged observers will find it hard to see the soul in the youngest generation.' So Evelyn is not going to be as histrionic as his father. Yet even this very limited piece of revolution is qualified in the next sentence: 'But they will have – and this is their justification – a very full sense of humour. . . . They will watch themselves with . . . a cynical smile and often with a laugh.' This sounds remarkably like Arthur Waugh's own self-aware, self-mocking theatricality.

The editorial ends on a very different note from the trumpet-call of its opening question. There is now no pretence of rebellion, merely the puzzlement of someone who confronts a chaotic scene and does not know what to do about it: 'It is a queer world which the old men have left them and they will have few ideals and illusions to console them when they "get to feeling old". They will not be a happy generation.'

By the end of his time at Lancing, Evelyn had turned against religion, informing the school chaplain that he had lost his faith. He records that he was driven to this by a young Oxford theologian named Rawlinson, later Bishop of Derby, who was temporarily teaching at Lancing, and gave his classes a taste of modern biblical scholarship, explaining that none of the books of the Bible could really be by their supposed authors and inviting them to speculate on the nature of Jesus Christ. 'This learned and devout man', writes Waugh, 'inadvertently made me an atheist.' Yet though the manner of his turning away from religion might be calculated to annoy his father – the influence of a modernist theologian – the actual rejection of Christianity recalls Arthur's own abandonment of family prayers when the war broke out, apparently because he felt that it was 'no longer any good' believing in a benevolent God.

In every other respect, Evelyn's final months at Lancing demonstrate a wish to observe the conventions and win the approval of the paternalistic school system. He was made House Captain, and played up to this part enthusiastically. In a letter to the school magazine he defends himself and his fellow prefects against the charge that boys in authority usually drop their friends: 'In the interests of discipline, it is essential that the officials shall form a caste apart.' Like Cyril Connolly at Eton, he was prepared to sacrifice friendship for advancement within the system. He wrote a satirical play about school life – just as his father had done at Sherborne – in which the hero of the final act is a rebel blackmailed into conformity; it was autobiographical, except that he himself had been the blackmailer. Leaving Lancing for Oxford, where he had won a scholarship, he was in every external respect a conventionally successful public schoolboy. J. F. Roxburgh wrote him a farewell letter in which he declared: 'If you use what the Gods have given you, you will do as much as anyone I know to shape the course of your generation.' It was the sort of praise teachers give to those who have kept the rules. Waugh notes that when he really did become famous and influential, Roxburgh 'deplored my writing and what he heard of my conduct'.

At first, Oxford seemed as daunting as Lancing had been to the new boy. Waugh had been persuaded to sit for a scholarship at Hertford, being told by his history teacher at Lancing that he stood a better chance there than at some larger and more fashionable college. He quickly found that it was 'respectable but rather dreary', with buildings that looked like a bank. He began to wish he had gone to New College, where his father had been. Moreover he had again arrived at an unfashionable time of year – January 1922 – when the previous autumn's freshmen had already settled down and made their own friendships. He found some old Lancing boys in the college, but no one he knew well. Although he was 'entirely happy in a subdued fashion' during his first two terms, doing everything that freshmen traditionally did – purchasing a cigarette box ornamented with the college arms, learning to smoke a pipe, getting drunk for the first time, exploring the villages around Oxford – he felt all the time that 'there was a quintessential Oxford which I knew and loved from afar' which had not yet become visible.

Up to this time, books had not contributed greatly to his imaginative life. 'I can remember', he wrote in 1951, answering an inquiry about writers who had 'influenced' his early years,

> that in my early youth I spent many days in attempting to construct a model town from the directions in the *Children's Encyclopaedia*. Those directions, it seems, must be the only piece of important literature I ever read [in childhood], for I cannot name any book or poem that has influenced my behaviour.

But before coming up to Oxford he had absorbed all the literature about the place that he could find, the poems of homage to University and city that Matthew Arnold, Quiller-Couch, Flecker and Belloc had written, and 'all the Oxford novels that came to hand', especially *Zuleika Dobson* and Compton Mackenzie's *Sinister Street*, in order to 'get the Oxford atmosphere'. Mackenzie provided that atmosphere in full:

> Michael . . . lay back in a deep armchair watching the candlelight flicker over the tapestries. . . . The tobacco smoke grew thicker and thicker, curling in spirals. . . . Moonbeams came slanting in and with them the freshness of the May night: more richly blue gathered the tobacco smoke: more magical became the room, and more perfectly the decorative expression of all Oxford stood for.

Cyril Connolly calls *Sinister Street* 'an important bad book . . . the first of a long line of bad books, the novels of adolescence, autobiographical, romantic'.

Hertford's version of Michael Fane's 'Chandos Society' – one of whose meetings is being described in the passage above – was less glamorous. Waugh describes how 'public-spirited men' in the college would ask freshmen to tea to enlist them in 'philanthropic and evangelistic work among hop-pickers', or persuade them to join the League of Nations Union. He guys this at the conclusion of *Decline and Fall*; yet Paul Pennyfeather 'liked the ugly, subdued little College', and so in many ways did Evelyn. Unlike most colleges there was no compulsory chapel or roll-call early in the morning, so he could lie in bed late ('I never attended chapel'). There was also an absence of extreme heartiness and anti-aestheticism: 'No one was ever debagged or had his rooms wrecked. . . . It was a tolerant, civilized place.'

Life was not exactly luxurious. In order to take a bath, he had to cross the mock-Venetian 'Bridge of Sighs' that spanned New College Lane and descend to a steamy cellar. Lavatories were remote and few, but scouts (college servants) brought shaving-water to undergraduates' rooms each morning and emptied their chamber-pots twice daily. They would also bring lunch and tea to order. Lunch was a 'commons' of bread, cheese and beer, 'delicious little fresh-baked loaves', recalls Waugh, 'wedges of well-chosen, well-kept, English cheeses, bitter ale drawn from the cask in silver tankards'. Tea was dispensed from the buttery of the Junior Common Room, over which Evelyn had his rooms, 'and my chief memory of the staircase is of the rattle of dish-covers on foggy afternoons and the smell of anchovy-toast and honey buns as the scouts filled their trays'.

Oxford in 1922 had not changed much since Arthur Waugh's undergraduate days. There was no little competition for places; certain colleges, says Evelyn, harboured 'aristocratic refugees from the examination system' who had been admitted without having to take Responsions. Apart from North Oxford, already well established, the suburbs were only beginning to spread themselves, and the town was still surrounded by streams, meadows and hamlets. Few people possessed motor-cars, and the streets – says Waugh – were chiefly filled with 'clergymen on bicycles'. Telephones were not in common use, and correspondence was written on crested cards and delivered by college messengers.

Eccentrics abounded, figures from the nineteenth century. Dr Spooner still reigned in New College, and Phelps, the Provost of Oriel, could be seen striding down the High in a black straw boater or heard beneath a window of the Provost's Lodging as he hesitated before his daily cold bath, exhorting himself to 'Be a man, Phelps, be a man!'

Even the younger generation of dons cultivated originality; for example R.M. Dawkins, Professor of Byzantine and Modern Greek, habitually clothed in thick black suits which he ordered by postcard from the general store of a small village in Northern Ireland, frequently advertised his presence with a cackling laugh that carried great distances, and when telling a funny story was known to slide beneath the table, hooting madly, completely overcome by mirth.

Evelyn had regarded Lancing as a challenge, and had won through by suppressing a large part of himself. He approached Oxford quite differently; it was time for a holiday, time to begin to lower his defences: 'From the first I regarded Oxford as a place to be inhabited and enjoyed for itself. . . . I wanted to taste everything Oxford could offer and consume as much as I could hold.' John Betjeman, arriving at Magdalen in 1925, felt exactly the same:

> Privacy after years of public school;
> Dignity after years of none at all –
> First college rooms, a kingdom of my own;
> What words of mine can tell my gratitude?
> No wonder, looking back, I never worked.

No diary survives for Waugh's Oxford years. Apparently he kept one for part of the time, but destroyed it because of what it contained. However, his letters give a clear picture of his early months. 'I am very shy and a little lonely still but gradually settling down,' he wrote to Dudley Carew at Lancing during his first term. 'I feel I am going to be immoderately happy.' And a little later in the term, also to Carew: 'I don't feel that I can tell you all about Oxford yet. Largely because I haven't got it into full perspective. All I can say is that it is immensely beautiful and immensely different from anything I have seen written about it.' And to Tom Driberg, also still at Lancing, about the middle of his first term: 'I do not work and never go to Chapel.'

Quite apart from his determination to enjoy himself to the full, the subject he was supposed to be reading, Modern History, had no essential appeal to him; he had won his Hertford scholarship 'on my English style'. Nor was he fortunate in his tutor. Charles Robert Mowbray Frazer Cruttwell had taken a double First and become a Fellow of All Souls before the war, and was an authority on the political history of the Rhineland. But this meant nothing to Evelyn, who assumed that Cruttwell was 'obsessed' with the subject solely because it concerned the territory towards which he had gazed from his wartime trench. Evelyn's generation's attitude to the Great War is evoked in

Nancy Mitford's first novel, where a young aesthete states to a returned soldier: 'We haven't exactly forgotten it, but it was never anything to do with us. It was your war and I hope you enjoyed it, that's all.'

There is no doubt that 'Crutters' was a difficult character. Prone to rheumatic fever and the painful effects of a wartime leg-wound, he would confront eighteen-year-old freshmen with bursts of barrack-room language, and await reactions. Those who responded in kind became drinking-cronies; those who reacted timidly or with resentment earned permanent bad marks. Contemporaries variously report him as 'charming', 'witty', 'erudite', 'foul-mouthed', 'ill-mannered'. His writing demonstrates a lack not merely of humour but of humanitarianism; his *History of the Great War* (1934), which became a standard work and is still consulted, displays almost no awareness of the appalling degree of suffering it chronicles. Confronted by the young Waugh, who had decided to do the minimum of work, Cruttwell snapped: 'Damn you, you're a scholar. If you can't show industry I at least have some right to expect intelligence!' (Evelyn had just translated the Latin verb *eramus* as 'Erasmus'.) J. F. Roxburgh had treated his Sixth Form as if they were undergraduates; Cruttwell behaved to Evelyn as if he were dealing with a naughty schoolboy, thereby providing Evelyn with a further motive for idleness.

By his third term, relations with Cruttwell had almost been severed. Exasperated beyond endurance, Cruttwell refused to see Evelyn at all for a while, and there was a 'blissful period' in which 'I was left without tutoring of any kind.' Then he was handed over to a young don, T. S. R. Boase, who treated him politely, 'but I did not learn very much from him'.

Indifference to academic work was common among undergraduates at this period. The syllabus had scarcely been reformed since the 1870s; the older dons seemed antediluvian, and the younger tended to be embittered veterans of the Western Front, who could not understand the deep impulse to frivolity – maybe a delayed reaction to the austerities of wartime – that moved so many of Evelyn's contemporaries. In this atmosphere, it was definitely not the done thing for one undergraduate to ask another what subject he was reading. Enthusiasm was only acceptable for sport, the OUDS, debates at the Union, and the various undergraduate magazines.

Evelyn set to work to find himself a place in this system. A second-year man at Hertford invited him to a lunch-party with the President of the Union and the editor of *Isis*, and soon Evelyn was active in both institutions. At first he met with no success in Union debates. 'Mr

Waugh appeared unaware of his audience,' reported *Isis* of one of his first speeches from the floor of the house. Evelyn told Dudley Carew he had been 'very nervous'. Then he began to discover a way of attracting attention.

The prevailing political climate at Oxford in 1922 was distinctly left of centre. Christopher Hollis, who became President of the Union during Evelyn's time, says that 'the general habit was to air liberal opinions'. In a Union debate during Evelyn's first term, a motion supporting 'The principles of Conservatism' was heavily defeated. There was a small but active Communist Party, two of whose members had been sent down for publishing seditious literature just before Evelyn arrived – a disciplinary action which aroused widespread undergraduate protest. The Labour Party flourished, and numbered many able young men among its members. Extreme Tories were very much in the minority, and were branded 'Die-Hards'.

Evelyn began to contemplate this political map. At Lancing he and his friends had sometimes posed as 'Bolshevik', but he quickly perceived that if he were to join one of the left-wing groups at Oxford he would 'find the competition too hot'. Politics did not really interest him; he 'never read' the political pages of the newspapers, but some sort of political stance, preferably outrageous, would certainly help him at the Union.

The home of such Conservatism as existed in Oxford in 1922 was the Carlton Club, which had rooms in George Street and aspired, with some success, to the atmosphere of Pall Mall. It was an elegant place to sit and write letters, and sip one's drink as the more industrious folk hurried past the window to lectures. There was also the Chatham, a Tory dining club which met in members' college rooms and drank mulled claret; before each meeting a bank messenger would bring from the vaults the Society's own silver – candlesticks, snuff box, cigar box and loving cup. Evelyn found this more appealing than the company of earnest men at Hertford who discussed the League of Nations over cups of tea. Moreover he knew the rudiments of Conservatism from his father, who, though he claimed never to vote, was a perfect specimen of an English reactionary.

Evelyn joined the Carlton Club, was invited to attend the Chatham, and by his second term at the Union was citing proofs that 'Socialism is undesirable.' By his third term he was describing himself as a Die-Hard; by his fourth he was uttering what *Cherwell*, the other principal undergraduate paper, called some of the most outrageous reactionary sentiments the Union had ever heard. They treated him (as he had intended) as a comic turn, and his speeches were reported humorously but with a distinct air of appreciation.

Comedy got him into print as well. *Isis* had plenty of reporters but few illustrators, so he decided to offer the editor caricatures. He now had a serious ambition 'to draw, decorate, design and illustrate', and he had begun to make comic drawings of other boys at Lancing. When these were widely praised, even by Roxburgh, he announced in his diary that he would 'forswear script and take to caricature'.

Punch and Max Beerbohm both offered stylistic models, but Evelyn decided instead to adopt the woodcut-style, as favoured by his hero Eric Gill and by Gill's friend Lovat Fraser. (Anthony Powell had also developed an enthusiasm for Fraser.) One of Evelyn's first caricatures published in *Isis*, on 14 June 1922, is in this style, and portrays a plump don waving an enormous pipe while he talks. His identity can be guessed from Evelyn's description of Cruttwell:

> He smoked a pipe which was usually attached to his blubber-lips by a thread of slime. As he removed the stem, waving it to emphasize his indistinct speech, this glittering connection extended until it finally broke leaving a dribble on his chin. When he spoke to me I found myself so distracted by the speculation of how far this line could be attenuated that I was often inattentive to his words.

Eighteen months later, Evelyn supplied *Cherwell* with a series of blackly comic drawings depicting a modern Seven Deadly Sins. His selection of sins was idiosyncratic. The drawings portrayed 'The Intolerable Wickedness of Him who Drinks Alone', 'The Horrid Sacrilege of those that Ill-Treat Books', 'The Wanton Ways of those that Corrupt the Very Young', 'The Hideous Habit of Marrying Negroes', 'That Dull, Old Sin Adultery', 'The Grave Discourtesy of Such a Man as will Beat his Host's Servant' and 'That Grim Act Parricide'. This last drawing showed a young man about to shoot his father.

Evelyn's first friendship at Oxford was with Terence Greenidge, the second-year Hertford man who had introduced him to the editor of *Isis* and the President of the Union. Greenidge was an Old Rugbeian with some pretence to conventionality – he was an enthusiastic classicist who ran regularly on the University track – but he was thoroughly unkempt in appearance and eccentric in habits. He objected to waste paper in the gutters, and would pick it up and put it in his pockets. He also pocketed objects which took his fancy, such as other men's hairbrushes, and these he would secrete in nests behind the books in the college library.

Evelyn was especially taken by Greenidge's habit of inventing soubriquets or epithets for individuals who caught his attention. Roger Fulford, who had come up from Lancing to Worcester College and had taken to wearing pince-nez, was christened 'Subman'. The night porter at Hertford was dubbed 'Midnight Badger'. Another Lancing contemporary of Waugh's, who refused an invitation to bread and cheese because he preferred a cooked meal at midday, became 'Hotlunch'. And most memorably – though this seems to have been a Waugh–Greenidge collaboration – a certain scholar of Balliol became 'Philbrick the Flagellant'. Christopher Hollis explains that F.A. Philbrick:

> was an able but indiscreet scholar who had confessed, or was alleged to have confessed, that at school he had derived pleasure from the beating of smaller boys. Evelyn had got hold of this story and very mischievously spread all round the University the tale that Philbrick was an unbridled sadist.

This game with nicknames was a kind of verbal caricaturing, the selection of one characteristic and its enlargement to the exclusion of everything else. It became Waugh's principal method of comic character-drawing in his novels. The use of the name Philbrick in *Decline and Fall* is an appropriate tribute to Greenidge for helping him to discover it.*

Greenidge showed, too, that it was possible to extend such joking into the realms of pure fantasy. One day in a tutorial or lecture, Cruttwell made the remark: 'Of course a dog cannot have rights.' Evelyn and Greenidge, discussing this afterwards, hazarded the notion that the man must wish to violate the creatures sexually – why else should he have said it? – and indeed was probably in the habit of doing so nightly. Evelyn, when drunk, was subsequently heard shouting across the quadrangle:

> Cruttwell dog, Cruttwell dog, where have you been?
> I've been to Hertford to lie with the Dean.

Greenidge decided that they must put it to the test, and so purchased a stuffed dog from one of the town junk shops, which, says Evelyn, 'we set in the quad as an allurement for him on his return from dining

---

* Philbrick's character in the novel, however, seems to have been based on an amiable confidence trickster who arrived in Oxford by canal barge, announced that he would take over the proprietorship of the then moribund *Cherwell*, collected advertisement fees, and then sailed away again wiht the money in his pocket.

in All Souls'. They also began the custom of barking beneath Cruttwell's window.

Greenidge had not exactly introduced Evelyn to the Oxford of *Sinister Street* but, by encouraging his taste for comic inflation of the truth, he had made life hilarious, and by March 1922, the end of his first term, Evelyn was telling Dudley Carew: 'Oxford is all that one dreams.' A term later, by which time he and Greenidge had established an informal bread-and-cheese lunch club in Evelyn's rooms, called 'The Offal', Evelyn was accumulating substantial bills, and had decided that there was 'nothing like the aesthetic pleasure of being drunk'. The term after that he met Harold Acton.

3

Hypocrites

At the beginning of his second year, Evelyn was taken by a New College acquaintance to hear G.K.Chesterton address a Catholic group, the Newman Society. At the meeting he encountered Harold Acton (himself a Catholic) who had just come up to Christ Church. 'Antithetical as we were in so many ways,' writes Evelyn, '[we] struck up ... an immediate and lasting friendship.'

Harold found Waugh strikingly attractive. 'A little faun called Evelyn Waugh,' he calls him in *Memoirs of an Aesthete*,

> a prancing faun, thinly disguised by conventional apparel. His wide-apart eyes, always ready to be startled under raised eyebrows, the curved sensual lips, the hyacinthine locks of hair, I had seen in marble and bronze at Naples, in the Vatican Museum, and on fountainheads all over Italy. The gentleness of his manner could not deceive me, nor could the neat black and white drawings, nor the taste for Eric Gill. ... So demure and yet so wild!

This Wildean fantasy seems far-fetched as a description of the distinctly cautious young man who looks out from photographs of this period, but another undergraduate of this period, Harman Grisewood, was equally struck by Waugh's vivacity: 'And there he was, very pink in the cheeks, small, witty and fierce, quite alarming. ... It was a very gloomy room ... and Evelyn Waugh was like a bright spark from the fire.' Anthony Powell, meeting Waugh at Michaelmas 1923 when he came up to Balliol, perceived – unlike Acton and Grisewood – something of what lay beneath the brittle shell:

> Small, rather pink in the face, his light brown wavy hair not far from red, Waugh nodded severely, at the same time giving utterance to a curious little high-pitched affirmative sound, a mannerism that always remained with him. He showed no disposition to chat. His air . . . was of a man disillusioned with human conduct, a man without ambition, living a life apart from the world. . . . Innate melancholy was never far away.

Acton, perceiving chiefly the good looks, began what Peter Quennell describes as 'a romantic, yet fatherly attachment' to him, presenting him (when it was published) with a copy of his own book of poems, *Aquarium*, inscribed to 'Le faune d'un après-midi ou de plusieurs'.

'Fatherly' is an odd term to use of someone several months Waugh's junior, but Waugh was dazed by Acton's experience of the world. 'I was entirely insular,' he writes. 'Indeed, at the age of nineteen I had never crossed the sea and I knew no modern language. Harold brought with him the air of the connoisseurs of Florence and the innovators of Paris.' He was also struck by Acton's physical appearance and personal style; he describes him as 'slim and slightly oriental in appearance, talking with a lilt and resonance and in a peculiar vocabulary that derived equally from Naples, Chicago and Eton'.

At first they appeared to have no tastes in common. Waugh learnt that Acton was opposed to such contemporary English manifestations of aestheticism as Eric Gill, Lovat Fraser and their disciples. But they shared one attribute. Waugh writes that Acton was 'funny and energetic', and 'loved to shock'. In Waugh's present mood of revolt against the Cruttwell generation (and his own father), this was the sort of friend he wanted. In an *Isis* article some time later, he recorded his approval of Acton's tonic effect upon the stuffiness of the University in 1922:

> When Mr Acton came up to Oxford, he found the University . . . in a very sad way. There was a grim pipe-smoking *intelligentsia* who lived in Wellington Square. . . . There were a few ornamental and rather tiresome folk who were proud of having read Mallarmé. With the *Broom* high spirits entered into this foetid atmosphere. . . . It has proved a magnificent tonic for the sullen mind of the literary undergraduate.

Learning that Waugh, too, 'loved to shock' with mock-die-hard speeches in the Union and satirical cartoons in the University papers, Acton enrolled him for his *Oxford Broom*. Waugh thereafter provided covers for the remainder of its short life – three more issues – and, to the June 1923 issue, contributed a short story, 'Anthony, Who Sought Things That Were Lost', a grim little mock-medieval tale in the manner of James Branch Cabell (whom he currently admired), about two imprisoned lovers. A skilfully written piece of pastiche, it was one of the better items the magazine had printed.

Acton began to explore Waugh's own circle of friends, and was amused to discover what he calls the 'Chestertonian' gatherings in his rooms. Accepting Evelyn's invitation to consume bread and cheese with them, he found that this unpromising set had its attractions. 'Among the "offal",' writes Evelyn, 'there was a strikingly handsome "hearty" for whom Harold conceived a romantic attachment. It was the presence of this Adonis almost daily in my rooms that drew him there. . . . While we drank beer he would sip water and gaze ardently at the inaccessible young athlete.' In return, Evelyn would receive invitations to the frequent luncheon parties in Harold's rooms in Meadow Buildings.

Writing about Harold in *Isis*, Waugh mentions 'the most incredible Early Victorian decorations' that he found there. Elsewhere, and much later, he drew this picture:

> His room was filled with a strange jumble of objects – a harmonium in a gothic case, an elephant's foot waste-paper basket, a dome of wax fruit, two disproportionately large Sèvres vases, framed drawings by Daumier – made all the more incongruous by the austere college furniture and the large luncheon table. His chimney-piece was covered in cards of invitation from London hostesses.

This is Sebastian's room in *Brideshead Revisited*, but Waugh is recalling Acton's collection of Victoriana and other curios. His *Isis* article of 1924 continues: 'He . . . purchased a megaphone through which he reads his own and the Sitwells' poetry in a way which, with all respect to the assiduity of the OUDS, is inimitable.' In the novel, after lunch, Anthony Blanche gives the performance that was earning Harold notoriety in Christ Church, though the poetry he recites is not the Sitwells' but *The Waste Land*: '*I, Tiresias, have foresuffered all*,' he sobbed to them from the Venetian arches. . . . And then, stepping lightly into the room, 'How I have surprised them! All b-boatmen are Grace Darlings to me.'

The Waste Land was published in the *Criterion* during Acton's first term at Christ Church. He notes that up to this time Eliot was regarded at Oxford only as an up-and-coming critic; his poetry was 'not taken seriously'. Throughout the 1920s, most undergraduates who took any notice of modernism in the arts thought it essentially funny. Some years after Acton's megaphonic recitals, in May 1927, John Betjeman and Tom Driberg helped to stage a hoax concert at the Holywell Music Room, a parody of modern music entitled 'Homage to Beethoven' – the title was intended to lure the unsuspecting dons' wives from North Oxford. Eric Walter White, another of the participants, describes it as consisting of a concerto for megaphone and orchestra (megaphones were widely associated with modernism since Edith Sitwell had used them in *Façade*), which 'opened with a bang from the band and an entreaty from Tom Driberg, delivered through his megaphone, that the audience would "commit no nuisance". . . . The slow movement [which featured two typewriters] was notable for the fact that it was very slow and very long.' A roll on the side drum which brought the audience to its feet, in expectation of the National Anthem, was followed by the distant flushing of a lavatory. The performance concluded with the admonition : 'Please adjust your dress before leaving.'

At Acton's luncheon parties, Waugh began to meet some of the men who had been at Eton with his host. His own initial shyness in this company is doubtless recorded in Charles Ryder's description of his fellow-guests at the luncheon party in Sebastian's rooms in *Brideshead Revisited* :

> There were three Etonian freshmen, mild, elegant, detached young men who had all been to a dance in London the night before, and spoke of it as though it had been the funeral of a near but unloved kinsman. Each as he came into the room made first for the plovers' eggs, then noticed . . . myself with a polite lack of curiosity which seemed to say : 'We should not dream of being so offensive as to suggest that you never met us before.'

However, one of Acton's frequent guests did not correspond to this description at all. Robert Byron, now installed at Merton, greatly intrigued Evelyn by his manner and appearance :

> He was short, fleshy and ugly in a painfully ignominious way. His complexion was yellow. . . . He dealt with his ill looks . . . by making them grotesque. He affected loud tweeds, a deer-stalker hat, yellow gloves, horn-rimmed pince-nez, a cockney accent. He leered and scowled, screamed and snarled, fell into rages that were sometimes real and sometimes a charade – it was not easy to distinguish. Wherever he went he created a disturbance, falling down in the street in simulated epilepsy, yelling to passers-by from the back of a motor car that he was being kidnapped. He contrasted in almost every way with the elegant and urbane Harold.

Acton says that Byron's 'vivacity and pugnacity' greatly appealed to Waugh, and Waugh himself alleges that he 'greatly relished his company' as a 'very good . . . clown'. In later years he turned against Byron, but at these luncheon parties of 1923, which drifted into the late afternoon, with Cointreau and hymns at the harmonium, he seems to have found nothing but delight in Byron's outrageous performances. Certainly the comic *persona* which he himself developed more than twenty years later would seem to owe much to Byron's noisy idiosyncracies.

The Oxford pubs were out of bounds to undergraduates. Largely in consequence of this, there flourished a number of University clubs, with their own premises, where drinking and dining could take place. Some, such as the Bullingdon and the 'Grid' (Gridiron), were socially exclusive; others, like the OUDS, would let in undergraduates from unfashionable public schools.

The clubs were not just for food and drink; they were a way of finding more congenial company than was necessarily available in the Junior Common Room of one's own college. An *Isis* correspondent wrote in May 1924:

> I penetrated into a college J.C.R. the other day. It was an amazing place, full of people whose horizon was bounded by the college lodge on one side and the college playing fields on the other, and whose only idea of self expression was to write terse remarks in the J.C.R. suggestion books about the jam roll they had in hall. I expect they will all get Blues or Firsts or something like that.

Evelyn was introduced by Terence Greenidge to one of the least smart clubs, the Hypocrites, which had rooms over a bicycle shop at 34 St Aldate's, near Christ Church. Founded by a group of Trinity and Oriel men who were fond of discussing philosophy, its members at the time that Evelyn joined were mostly (he says) 'rather sombre Rugbeians and Wykehamists with vaguely artistic and literary interests'; L. P. Hartley and Lord David Cecil were among undergraduates sometimes seen there. The club took its name from the fact that its motto, in Greek, was 'Water is best', yet it served beer.

At that time at Oxford there was, Waugh recalls, a Chestertonian–Bellocian mystique about the conviviality that results from the swilling of enormous quantities of beer, the only drink that most undergraduates could regularly afford. Moreover, he continues,

> there was at that time a real danger of Prohibition in England. It was said that a majority in the House of Commons had promised their consti-

tuents to support it, if it ever came to the vote, and that it was only the astuteness of the minority which averted the disaster. There was thus an element of a Resistance group about the drunkards of the period.

During his first year as an undergraduate, Prohibition was twice debated at the Union, and though on both occasions the vote was against it, a number of speakers gave it articulate support.

Waugh describes the premises of the Hypocrites when he first joined the club: 'One ascended narrow stairs ... into a rich smell of onions and grilling meat. Usually the constable on the beat was standing in the kitchen, helmet in one hand, a mug of beer in the other. Above and beyond the kitchen were two large rooms.' In these could be found dart and shove-ha'penny boards, while folk-songs and glees were some-times sung around the piano. Members tended to order drinks with such phrases as 'Draw a stoop of ale, prithee.'

When he first ventured up its stairs, Harold Acton was highly amused by the Hypocrites:

> A rugged set they appeared at first sight, and to me, exotic. ... But the ruggedness was an externality: it went no further than unshaven chins and beer-stained corduroys. Beneath a scowling façade most of them were sensitive and shy. Some were inclined to a Communism which expressed itself in [illicit] pub-crawls; others had hankerings after folk-dancing and the Cowley Fathers. Ale might loosen their tongues, but they preferred shove ha'penny and darts to conversation and were quite happy to shove ha'pence for hours, puffing at a clay pipe.

Though he wrinkled his nose at the frying onions, Harold found the place had gastronomic attractions: 'A figure from the music-halls of Sickert's days served drinks: nowhere in Oxford could you taste a better omelette or a juicier mixed grill.'

Anthony Powell has more to say about the staff, who consisted of a married couple called Hunt and a 'retainer' named Whitman:

> Mrs Hunt did the cooking (simple but excellent), her husband and Whit-man acting as waiters. Hunt was clean-shaven, relatively spruce: Whit-man, moustached, squat, far from spick and span. Both Hunt and Whitman were inclined to drink a good deal, but, in their different ways, were the nearest I have ever come to the ideal of the Jeevesian manservant, always willing, never out of temper, full of apt repartee and gnomic comment.

Brian Howard, who joined when he eventually came up to Oxford, observes that the club had 'entirely freed itself' from the 'jejune snobberies, various and vapid', which constricted most of the University's life. Similarly Harold Acton praises the absence of the typical Oxford languor from its members' manners. 'At all hours I could find somebody here to talk to, somebody with a congenial hobby or mania: Graham Pollard with his first editions of seventeenth-century poets, Richard Pares with his subtle theories about Edward Lear.' Waugh describes Pares as 'a Balliol Wykehamist, with ... the Lear–Carroll like fantasies of many Balliol Wykehamists.'

Greenidge brought Waugh to the club, Waugh brought Acton, and soon – presumably thanks to Acton – the Hypocrites were being taken over by what Waugh calls 'a group of wanton Etonians'. This was easily effected, since the president of the club was Lord Elmley, a solid and ultra-respectable Magdalen undergraduate who did nothing to interfere, while the nominal senior member, Professor Dawkins (he who would fall under the table while laughing at his own jokes), had never been known to set foot there. During the coup, a quorum of tipsy voters installed Waugh as secretary, but he never performed any duties: 'My appointment was a characteristic fantasy of the place.' Anthony Powell alleges that Waugh was indeed only intermittently a member, being excluded at one period 'for having smashed up a good deal of the club's furniture with the heavy stick he always carried'. Waugh did not stint himself at the bar, since drinks could be purchased on credit. Powell describes another glass being passed to him one evening just before closing time. ' "But, Whitman, I told you, when you asked, that I did *not* want another drink." "I thought you were joking, sir." '

The 'wanton Etonians' rejected the mock-Tudor speech of the former regime for a mock-Cockney: 'Just a nip of dry London, for me wind, dearie.' They were frequently found around the club piano, upon which Robert Byron would hammer, 'contorting his features' (says Powell) 'into fearful grimaces, while he sang Victorian ballads in an ear-splitting alto'. Another performer at the keyboard was an individual named Peter Ruffer, who, swathed in a long woollen muffler, would warble sadly in a high soprano. Waugh describes Ruffer as 'obese, musical, morose, often contemplating suicide in his rooms in the Turl'; Acton describes him as a 'hefty person' whose appearance gave no inkling of the complexities of his character. Built in the proportions of a rugger blue, he would sit at the piano 'mourning, at the age of twenty, the loss of his youth. He showed one photographs to prove that he had been slim. ... '. Acton adds that Ruffer liked to engage in correspondence with lonely persons who advertised in the newspapers; one of his pen-friends was an individual who claimed to experience sexual desire for hot-house plants. Eventually, thanks to a quack doctor, Ruffer slimmed himself to death.

Certain Hypocrites seemed figures of the seventeenth rather than the twentieth century. Powell was first introduced to the club by Alfred Duggan, an Old Etonian whom Waugh calls 'a full-blooded rake of the Restoration'. Besides being very rich, he was the stepson of Lord Curzon, Chancellor of the University. 'We were often drunk,' writes Waugh, 'Alfred almost always.' While Powell had some difficulty at first in getting through one pint of the dark beer served at the Hypocrites, Duggan was inclined to down a pint of burgundy from a tankard at luncheon. However, his head was not as strong as his stomach; generally in an alcoholic haze, he was often seen by Powell 'all but speechless with drink'. Duggan had come up to Oxford with his own horses, and frequently went hunting. Osbert Lancaster says that in the traffic-free Oxford streets of the 1920s it was common to see undergraduates on horseback in the town, and Tom Driberg describes a Christ Church man knocking at his tutor's door and saying, 'I thought I'd just let you know that I shan't be coming to any tutorials or lectures this term, because I've managed to get four days' hunting a week', this said 'with imperious condescension'.

Alfred Duggan – who claimed, rather improbably, to be a Communist – would spend an evening losing huge sums of money over cards in his rooms in Balliol, and then, the college gate being locked for the night, would climb out of his window, get into a waiting car hired from a local garage, and be driven to London, where he frequented the Forty-Three, the night club run by the celebrated Mrs Meyrick.* He would boast about his intimacy with one of the girls there, much as Boy Mulcaster does in *Brideshead Revisited*, where the club is portrayed as 'The Old Hundredth'.

When giving luncheon parties in his rooms in Balliol, Duggan was in the habit of laying an extra place for anyone he might have invited when drunk and subsequently forgotten; Waugh says it was often occupied. During this period there were several Etonians who would give luncheon or dinner parties for twenty or thirty guests, many of whom

---

* Kate Meyrick, daughter of an Irish doctor whose errant husband had left her with six children and no means of support, ran three or four London night clubs where illicit after-hours drinking took place, chief among them being the Forty-Three, so called from its address in Gerrard Street. She avoided prosecution by bribing the police, but at one point spent fifteen months in prison. Many night clubs did not dare evade the law, and provided no alcohol. In Nancy Mitford's first novel, *Highland Fling* (1931), there is a description of one such establishment where 'fruit drink' and disgusting coffee are the only beverages, despite a stiff entrance fee.

might scarcely know the host by sight. One such was Romney Summers, a wealthy member of the Hypocrites who had come down from Brasenose College but was unable to tear himself away from Oxford, and gave extravagant luncheons and dinners in his lodgings. Brian Howard visited him, and was received as if by some *grand seigneur* of the Bourbon court: 'With the diamond background of his exquisite collection of old English glass . . . you would find yourself listening to the seemingly rather bored recital . . . of how yesterday he had acquired a Jacobean glass for twopence-halfpenny, or to a diatribe against the inefficiency of hired aeroplanes.'

Another *revenant* or lingerer in Oxford who frequented the Hypocrites was John Davies Knatchbull Lloyd, a Montgomeryshire man who had been educated at Winchester and Trinity, taking his degree in 1922. Like Summers, he seemed unable to extricate himself from Oxford. Afterwards a Fellow of the Society of Antiquaries and Secretary to the Council for the Preservation of Rural Wales, he was known in the Hypocrites as 'the Widow', on account of a shaving lotion marketed as 'The Widow Lloyd's Euxesis', and he played up to the name. Harold Acton describes him as 'the precious "Widow" Lloyd who belonged to the world of *Cranford*', and it may be him that Henry Yorke has in mind when he describes how 'a friend would dress up as an old lady to go down to the club after dinner. He wore a Victorian costume . . . with a huge red wig and thick veil. The streets were not well lighted and with terrible obscene gestures he wavered down the road . . . . Following him we laughed and laughed . . . .'

By the spring of 1924, the new order was firmly installed at the Hypocrites, and *Isis* attempted to sum it up:

> The Hypocrites are perhaps the most entertaining people in the University. They express their souls in terms of shirts and grey flannel trousers, and find outlet for their artistic ability on the walls of their Club rooms. To talk to they are rather alarming. They have succeeded in picking up a whole series of intellectual catch-phrases with which they proceed to dazzle their friends and frighten their acquaintances; and they are the only people I have ever met who have reduced rudeness to a fine art.

To celebrate the total transformation of the club, Robert Byron and 'Widow' Lloyd organized, in March 1924, a fancy-dress party. Street musicians were engaged to provide music on barrel-organ, zither and xylophone, and Oliver Messel came down from the Slade to assist with the decorations – hence the remark in *Isis* about painting on the walls. Harold Acton describes Messel's décor:

> 'Still lifes' of lobsters, rabbits and poultry that might have been arranged by Landseer were suspended like chandeliers from the ceilings; and significant scenes of Victorian history were depicted on the walls: Queen Victoria – not amused; 'Mr Livingstone, I presume'; Alfred, Lord Tennyson nursing his whisky bottle.

As to the fancy dress, Byron attired himself as his famous namesake, and the Widow Lloyd came *en travesti*, clutching a *lorgnette*. Acton donned military uniform and a white mask, 'and I thus retained a successful incognito'. Romney Summers arrived dressed as a Regency rake, Graham Pollard the bibliophile put on a child's sailor-suit and shorts, and Anthony Powell appeared in antique military garb. There were several pirates, a courtesan out of the Mozart era, a crone with blacked-out teeth selling balloons, a nun, and an epicene figure in choirboy's surplice and cassock with vermilioned lips. Also present was an elderly gentleman in an umpire's white coat, the University lecturer in Tamil and Telugu, Sidney Roberts, always known as 'Camels and Telegraphs'. Waugh says that this individual made himself much loved in the Hypocrites 'for no other reason than that after a life spent in conventional service in India he found enchantment in our extravagances'.

Harold Acton says the party was uproarious and harmless, 'but rumour transformed it into a shocking orgy', and shortly afterwards the club was closed down by the Proctors, the University disciplinary officials. Emlyn Williams (not a member) records that lurid gossip was circulating about the Hypocrites, such as 'they're supposed to eat newborn babies cooked in wine'. Waugh explains that the members had become 'notorious not only for drunkenness but for flamboyance of dress and manner which was in some cases patently homosexual'.

Oxford was in effect still an all-male community, as it had been since the founding of the University. Colleges for women had been established in the last quarter of the nineteenth century, but were geographically and socially separated from those for men. 'Undergraduettes lived in purdah,' writes Waugh. Girls who did not belong to the University might receive invitations to attend college balls in Eights Week – in *Brideshead Revisited*, Charles Ryder reacts unenthusiastically to the 'rabble of womankind' who suddenly invade the place – but for the rest of the year they were very rarely seen there. Such girls as did attend undergraduate parties in the men's colleges (and there were a few) had to be disguised as young men. Emlyn Williams describes a certain Cara being smuggled in as 'a white wisp of a boy in Oxford bags, long scarf and green pork-pie hat; she passed among the crowd and danced from here to there, so Eton-cropped that her hair was often shorter than her partner's'. The *gamine* look was in fashion; at the OUDS ball in June 1924, which was in fancy dress, the *Oxford Chronicle* reported that 'several of the ladies, taking advantage of the fact that their hair was of the "bobbed" variety, had turned themselves into very chic page boys'; and Emlyn Williams records Brian Howard remarking: 'My dear, I've only seen one passable undergraduette and *she* looked like a vain boy scout.'*

Male undergraduates who had come from public schools had spent most of their last four or five years in a community where girls were scarcely seen, where gossip was regularly fuelled by some older boy's romantic interest in a younger, and where there had been some clandestine homosexual activity. They had had some social contact with girls in the school holidays, but the hothouse atmosphere of a boarding school was, for many, more conducive to passion than were the awkward and self-conscious encounters with the opposite sex at supper parties or dances in parents' houses. By the time they came up to Oxford, they turned almost automatically to their own sex for emotional satisfaction. Waugh writes that while most men might indulge in 'light flirtations' with young women during the University vacation, they plunged themselves more wholeheartedly into 'deep friendships' with other men in term time.

There had been at least a mild homosexual element in Oxford life in the mid-nineteenth century; the college dramatic societies had specialized in farces which required the men to dress up in women's clothes, to the extent that this became the cause of scandal and was suppressed by Jowett, the then Vice Chancellor. In the Nineties, open effeminacy had come into vogue, but the arrest of Wilde in 1895 put a sudden stop to this fashion, and only after the First World War did the Univer-

---

* By the late 1920s the purdah had been somewhat relaxed, and Osbert Lancaster says that 'members of the dimmer colleges' were known to entertain female undergraduates to morning coffee at the Super Cinema. Moreover each year one particular undergraduette was the toast of the men's colleges. 'In my first year,' writes Lancaster, 'it was Miss Margaret Lane; in my second a girl from Somerville who played Miranda in *The Tempest* . . . with whom many were in love, and to whom not a few were engaged; in my last it was Miss Elizabeth Harman, now Lady Longford, who achieved the unique distinction of being admitted into the charmed circle surrounding the Dean of Wadham [Maurice Bowra].' (Osbert Lancaster, *With an Eye to the Future*, ch. 4.)

sity again allow itself to admit the existence of 'the love that dare not speak its name'.

Homosexual practices remained illegal throughout Britain, but Christopher Hollis says that by the mid-1920s the subject was 'freely discussed' among undergraduates. To take even a detached interest in the matter was a way of separating themselves from their parents' generation, to whom the whole topic had been taboo on account of Wilde. John Betjeman recalls his father's outrage when he found that John had been corresponding, out of sheer curiosity, with the ageing and exiled Lord Alfred Douglas:

> My father took me for a walk up a lane. ... He said: 'You've been having letters from Lord Alfred Douglas.' I couldn't deny it. 'Do you know what that man is? ... He's a bugger. Do you know what buggers are? Buggers are two men who work themselves up into such a state of mutual admiration that one puts his piss-pipe up the other one's arse. What do you think of that?'

Open homosexuality was by no means universal in Oxford by 1924; Edward James, coming up to Christ Church from Eton, 'never heard an overt homosexual conversation at Oxford', though advances were once or twice made to him by other men when they were alone together. However, certain bachelor dons liked to act as panders to their male pupils' romantic interest in each other, taking them away together on vacation reading parties, or encouraging them (like Dundas at Christ Church) to unburden themselves of worries about masturbation or homosexual inclinations; and a few of them were actively homosexual themselves. While he was an undergraduate at Christ Church, Tom Driberg was picked up by a young don in the 'cottage' (underground lavatory) in Blue Boar Street, and the two engaged in *soixante-neuf* on several occasions in the don's rooms.

Alan Pryce-Jones says that, even for those who were not really homosexually inclined, 'it was *chic* to be queer, rather as it was *chic* to know something about the twelve-tone scale and about Duchamp's "Nude Descending a Staircase"'. Those who were sexually active 'had few inhibitions about their exploits', writes Christopher Hollis, 'and confessed their amours to one another'. The newspapers began to take notice of the supposed effeminacy of the University, treating it as a matter for outrage or amusement as they felt inclined. In October 1925 *Cherwell* parodied Fleet Street's reactions with the headline 'GIRL MEN AT CAMBRIDGE', beneath which was this paragraph:

> This kind of slogan in the daily papers must cease. Oxford is not easily

roused, but she cannot afford to lose her only claim to public attention. Girl men are hers, and hers alone; they have provided three dozen special reporters with their daily bread for at least six months. ... I received a cutting from a newspaper from India in which an eyewitness described how he actually saw one undergraduate produce a stick of lip-salve and paint the lips of his companion! Shall Cambridge take this away from us? Never!

The headquarters of the 'girl-men', during its brief life under Etonian rule, was the Hypocrites' Club. Lord Elmley, as president, tried to restrain behaviour by ordering: 'Gentlemen may prance but not dance.' No one paid attention. Tom Driberg, coming up from Lancing to sit the scholarship examination, was taken to the Hypocrites by Waugh, and, discovering that this was the custom of the place, danced with another young man. Meanwhile 'Evelyn and another rolled on a sofa with (as one of them said later) their "tongues licking each other's tonsils".'

Waugh is quite candid about the strength of the attachments he experienced at Oxford. 'I loved him dearly,' he says of 'the first friend to whom I gave my full devotion'. This was Richard Pares, the Balliol Wykehamist with a taste for Edward Lear and Lewis Carroll. A 1954 letter from Waugh to Nancy Mitford describes Pares as 'my first homosexual love'.

Pares was a year older than Waugh; a drawing of him by Waugh, in his Eric Gill–Lovat Fraser style, shows the outline of a small young man with an umbrella and big fists (maybe gloves). In his memoirs Waugh speaks of his 'appealing pale face and ... mop of fair hair, blank blue eyes'.

At Lancing, Waugh had fallen mildly for one or two of the younger boys. 'I was susceptible', he writes, 'to the prettiness of some fifteen-year olds.' But he refrained from pursuing them because, as he wrote in his diary, 'they can never talk intelligently.' Roger Fulford notes that Waugh 'was neither courted by older boys nor, when he grew older, did he pursue younger ones'. There were severe penalties at Lancing for any suggestion of homosexuality; Tom Driberg was reported to the Headmaster by two small boys to whom he had made nocturnal advances; the Head, the Rev. T.H. Bowlby, stripped him of his prefectship and ordered him virtually into solitary confinement for the remainder of the term (his last).* On the other hand Waugh did make some effort to bring the subject into the open. In an editorial in the school magazine he invented a conversation between a visitor to the school and a senior boy such as himself:

> A small, good-looking boy passed us, flushed with his game.
> 'And he – do you know him?'
> 'Yes – at least a little. He's a charming man. I used to like him rather a lot, but he's a good deal junior to me, you know, and it isn't encouraged by the authorities. They're quite right, of course, it wouldn't do, but it's rather bad luck when it is all right, isn't it?'

Waugh was by no means indifferent to girls. He met a number of them in the school holidays, at friends' and cousins' houses, and his diary records mild crushes on several of them. He was particularly attracted by Luned Jacobs, daughter of the writer W.W. Jacobs, 'a dark, handsome girl, slightly younger than I', whose sister Barbara married Alec Waugh while Evelyn was at Lancing. During parties at the Jacobs' house (Waugh writes),

> a children's game of undefined rules was played in the dark. The ostensible object was for one party to crawl through the ranks of the other to a goal on the further side. Here on the polished oak floor she and I would seek one another, grapple and, while the younger players squealed in the excitement of arrest and escape, would silently cling and roll together. We maintained a pretence of conflict. There was no kissing, merely rapturous minutes of close embrace. . . .

John Betjeman recalls similar moments of bliss at children's parties:

> Was it chance that paired us neatly,
> I, who loved you so completely,
> You, who pressed me closely to you, hard against your party frock?

> 'Meet me when you've finished eating!' So we met and no one found us.
> Oh that dark and furry cupboard while the rest played hide and seek! . . .
> Love that lay too deep for kissing. . . .

But it was not easy to make the transition from calf-love to a serious romantic and sexual interest in young women, when in between loomed the mountain of homosexual romance at public school.

Waugh describes Oxford homosexuality as a symptom of delayed

---

* Bowlby himself was later charged by the police with molesting little girls on a train. He stated: 'I only treated them as I treat my own grandchildren,' and was acquitted. (Driberg, *Ruling Passions*, p. 53.)

adolescence: 'We were in some respects ... sophisticated ... but in others barely adolescent.' He himself had scarcely shown any emotional signs of puberty while at Lancing, repressing the naturally rebellious and experimental inclinations of this age-group in his determination to be accepted by the school system. 'I ... never fell victim', he writes, 'to the grand [homosexual] passions which inflamed and tortured most of my friends (to whom I acted as an astringent confidant).' At Oxford he relaxed his vigilance, and let adolescence catch up with him.

It appears that he was chaste during his first two years at Oxford, confining himself to, at most, close embraces such as Driberg witnessed. 'My affections are much more romantic than carnal,' he told Christopher Hollis at this period, and Hollis believed him. In any case the relationship with Richard Pares did not last long. Pares 'did not enjoy drinking and ... this made an insurmountable barrier between us. When I felt most intimate, he felt queasy ... and as a result we drifted apart.' Hollis did not think they had been well suited:

> He and Evelyn were not a well-assorted pair. Richard Pares was the son of Sir Bernard Pares, well known as an expert on Russian affairs. He was a scholar at Balliol from Winchester and in many ways a most typical Wykehamist. His natural company was with his books. ... He was of floppy light hair and good looking and attracted, as such young men did, the attention of Sligger Urquhart, the Dean of Balliol, who christened him Wig. It would not have been at all natural for him to waste his time in dissipation, but Evelyn's personal dominance was powerful. He made strong demands on those to whom he offered affection ... and in particular the demand to join with him in the bouts of heavy drinking which he had at that time erected almost into an article of religion. Richard obeyed him for a time, but the exercise was not natural to him.

Pares withdrew not merely from Waugh but from the entire Hypocrites' circle, got a First, became a Fellow of All Souls, and was eventually appointed to a chair in History at Edinburgh. Waugh guessed that 'he would probably have been elected Master of Balliol had he not been tragically struck down by creeping paralysis' (he died in 1958).

Waugh writes in his memoirs that Pares's 'successor as the friend of my heart I will call Hamish Lennox'. This was Alastair Hugh Graham, who came up to Brasenose College from Wellington at Michaelmas 1922, two terms after Waugh arrived at Hertford. Talking to Martin Stannard, who was writing a life of Waugh, Harold Acton described Graham as 'a small man, quiet, whimsical, gentle, but, Sir Harold added, "very full of guts and invention" '. On another occasion

Acton gave a rather different account of Graham, calling him 'a pre-Raphaelite beauty' but also 'a cock-teaser'; he observed that he himself had not liked Graham, but said that Waugh was undoubtedly 'very much in love' with him.

Alastair Graham was the son of a wealthy father from a Border family, who had died, and a mother from one of the southern states of America, whom Waugh called 'high-tempered, possessive, jolly and erratic'. Mrs Graham had settled at Barford in Warwickshire, not far from Stratford-on-Avon. Immensely energetic by nature, she gardened (says Waugh) 'with all the fury of the chase', and would announce: 'I only keep this place going for Alastair.' Her son made no secret of his dislike of the house, and said he would get rid of it as soon as he possibly could.

Alastair reacted to his mother by retreating into deliberate idleness. Such few photographs of him as have survived show a small, neat, dark-haired young man, not romantically handsome as Acton's remark suggests, but good-looking, a little reserved, with a certain self-possession. Christopher Hollis, who knew Alastair well, says he was 'quite without ambition'. At Oxford, he took no interest in academic work, failed his preliminary examinations, and was sent down during his second year, Mrs Graham announcing that he would 'take a course in architecture in London'. She sent him to an architectural school, and believed that he was studying there, but later discovered that he had never attended its classes. Thereafter there was some talk of his learning printing at the Shakespeare Head Press, but this came to little, though he did acquire a printing machine. For most of the time he merely drifted, and for much of it Waugh drifted with him.

'For two or three years,' writes Waugh, 'we were inseparable or, if separated, in almost daily communication.' During the time that Alastair was supposed to be studying in London, he continued to haunt Oxford, where Christopher Hollis says he 'went about from drinking party to drinking party with Evelyn'. He was rich enough to own a car, and he and Waugh spent much of their days 'driving in his motor round the surrounding villages and our evenings in the Oxford inns frequented by townees – the Turf, the Nag's Head, the Druid's Head, the Chequers . . .'. Hollis says that Waugh's and Alastair Graham's conversation in these pubs 'mainly consisted in commenting with approval on any . . . whom [they] met who displayed any sort of eccentricity'. Unlike Richard Pares, Alastair had no objection to drink, and, says Waugh, 'we drank deep together'.

Alastair, indeed, drank far too much for his mother's peace of mind.

Irritated with his and Evelyn's idleness when they were at Barford ('Why can't you boys get out of the house and *do* something?' she would bark), she expressed a deeper concern to Alastair's friends about the life he was leading. Christopher Hollis describes a meal at Barford when Alastair refused to leave the table after it had been cleared, but sat there, refilling his glass again and again.

> Eventually Mrs Graham demanded that I should leave the table and come and talk to her. Alastair begged me to pay no attention ... but ... I felt that I had no alternative. ... She gave me a lecture. ... For his misdemeanours I was more responsible than Evelyn or any other of his undesirable friends. 'For of course you're so much older.' This was not to any significant extent true, but it was an impression she had formed.

Waugh, too, was drawn into the conflict: 'She made friends with me as a link with her wayward son and constantly appealed to me to mediate between them,' with no more effect, however, than Sebastian's mother has when she appeals to Charles in similar circumstances in *Brideshead Revisited*. Mrs Graham was, though, no Lady Marchmain in manner. Her bluff speech became a model for a much more robust character in Waugh's fiction, Lady Circumference in *Decline and Fall*. Christopher Hollis gives an example of her behaviour. Believing for some while that she was suspicious of him, he eventually discovered that 'she was convinced from the thickness of my lips that I had black blood in me. As she one day confided to Evelyn, "I've not lived in the Southern States for nothing."'

Waugh was now living the life of a true Hypocrite. In his second year he began, though he could ill afford it, to give formal luncheon parties on an Etonian scale, as well as attending countless others. 'The food was abundant and highly decorated,' he writes of these. 'In winter the staple drink was mulled claret followed by port. We drank on till dusk while the "muddied oafs" and "flannelled fools" passed under the windows to and from the river, the track and the playing-fields.'
Henry Yorke describes the preparations for such a luncheon:

> We could order lunch to be served in our rooms by going to the kitchens and talking through a hatch to the chef in his white cap. In the end, I do not know why, the main dish was always duck. Then we visited the Junior Common Room to choose wine with the head steward and this always turned out to be hock. Duck no doubt was what could most easily be cooked, and they had laid down a great store of hock.

At the luncheon, 'we fingered long stemmed glasses and sniffed the wine, holding it up to the light which came through our narrow gothic-ridden windows. We spoke knowingly of vineyards with German names but had to be told when the wine was corked.'

John Betjeman, at Magdalen with Yorke, led the same hedonistic life, and was smitten with conscience at what his parents must be thinking:

> I cut tutorials with wild excuse,
> For life was luncheons, luncheons all the way . . .
> But as the laughs grew long and loud I heard
> The more insistent inner voice of guilt:
> 'Stop!' cried my mother from her bed of pain.
> I heard my father in his factory say:
> 'Fourth generation, John, they look to you.'

Even Waugh began to feel uneasy, realising that 'I was doing no good at my books.' At the beginning of his third year 'I wrote to my father asking to be taken away and sent to Paris to enjoy the full life of *Trilby*.' Charles Ryder makes the same request in *Brideshead Revisited*, and it is granted; but Arthur Waugh told Evelyn that he must stay and get his degree. 'This reasonable verdict', writes Evelyn, 'gave me the sense that . . . I was at Oxford under protest. I perversely regarded it as the *laissez-passer* to a life of pure pleasure.'

4

Dear Private Giggles of a Private World

Cyril Connolly came up to Balliol in October 1922 and was miserable. Oxford seemed as hard a place in which to find his identity as Eton had once been. After only a few days he longed to rush back there and see his school friends. Knowing that this would be a mistake, he wept all evening. However, a visit to Alfred Duggan cheered him up; Duggan offered him 'unlimited drink'.

Duggan – who usually had to be put to bed after such occasions – was the centre of Etonian life in Balliol, and Harold Acton and others of the 'fast' set could often be found in his rooms. Yet the very luxuriance of the social life Connolly began to encounter there left him still more bewildered about how he could make his mark in such a place. 'If it was a monastery it would be all right,' he wrote to a friend still at Eton, 'a sleepy place where we could follow the advancement of learning. ... But it bristles with acquaintances, bridge, tea-parties, debts ... a round of gaiety which is rather awful.' Eton had been 'such a gorgeous setting for the jewels of my pedestal to flourish in'. Here, the competition was far more fierce.

However, he soon decided he was in love again, this time with an Etonian freshman at Trinity called Bobbie (R.P.) Longden. 'Please don't sleep with Ronnie, he is too tall for you,' he wrote to Longden. 'I always want to sleep with you more than anything but it is not very practicable at Oxford. ...' It was perfectly practicable, had they both so wished, but for all his romantic passions Connolly had passed through school without any actual sexual experience – he had never even masturbated. As for Longden, the most he would write in reply to Connolly's declarations of love was 'I think of and admire you a lot.'

Unlike Waugh at Hertford, Connolly found the Balliol dons better than his schoolmasters. In particular there was F.F. Urquhart – 'wonderfully refreshing after ushers [schoolmasters] – a Dean whom you can pinch, put your arm around his neck and call Sligger with no self-consciousness at all'.

Francis Fortescue Urquhart, son of a wealthy Scotsman with a passion for interfering in the internal affairs of Turkey, had been brought up a Catholic and educated at Jesuit schools in England, then at Balliol under Jowett, where he took a First in Modern History. During an undergraduate reading party he was nicknamed 'the sleek one' for his rather smooth features; in the Oxford parlance of the day* this soon became 'the Sligger'.

As an undergraduate, Sligger had been pretty in a rather china-shop fashion – crisp light-coloured hair and a full mouth with prominent lips. Walter Pater, then a Fellow of Brasenose, evidently took a fancy to him, since Sligger's biographer Cyril Bailey identifies him as the model for 'Emerald Uthwart' in Pater's novella of that name: 'Strangers' eyes, resting on him by chance, are deterred for a while. ... "Young Apollo!" people say ... watching the slim trim figure with the exercise books. His very dress seems touched with Hellenic fitness to the healthy youthful form.' By the 1920s Sligger was, says Peter Quennell, 'curly-headed, wrinkled and rosy-cheeked'.

Sligger had intended to become a Jesuit, but was persuaded to undertake some temporary teaching of Modern History at Balliol, and this 'temporary' contract was extended piecemeal again and again. Eventually he was elected to an official Fellowship, the first Roman Catholic to become a tutorial Fellow at Oxford in modern times. He remained unmarried, and his close interest in the private affairs of undergraduates amply qualified him for the post of College Dean, which he undertook from 1916, his forty-ninth year.

He was an undisguised snob. In a 1905 letter to an academic colleague he suggested that the best way of improving Balliol would be to 'get the best men (in several ways) from the Public Schools and let them mix up with intelligent men from Birmingham etc. ... At present we seem to have too many of the latter.' He wrote and published next to nothing – merely a few articles in the *Catholic Encyclopaedia* and an

---

* By which the Union became the 'Ugger', the Prince of Wales the 'Pragger Wagger', and the Martyrs' Memorial in St Giles the 'Maggers' Memugger'.

occasional pamphlet – and he cared comparatively little what class of degree his pupils got. He was attracted by good looks and titles.

Though power and influence appealed to him, he preferred to exercise them as an *éminence grise*. He allowed himself to be passed over for the Mastership of Balliol, commenting of the election of A.D. Lindsay, considerably his junior: 'It is rather fun to have a Master younger than oneself; one can advise him.' By 1910 he could boast that there were 'three members of the Cabinet who call me Sligger'. In the same letter he added: 'I believe that the working classes are still ready, large numbers of them at any rate, to follow the lead of the ''gentry'' if these are really prepared to understand and lead them.'

He lived on the first floor over the Balliol back gate, overlooking the Martyrs' Memorial, in a dark, dank set of rooms whose Gothic windows admitted little light. Every available inch of mantlepiece and walls was covered with photographs of previous generations of undergraduates. Here he held 'open house' late each evening. Connolly would find notes inviting him to call round, and those not resident in Balliol could get in, despite the locking of the college gates, by calling out 'Sligger!' from the street, whereupon Sligger would throw down the key to the back gate. Peter Quennell describes Evelyn Waugh taking advantage of this one night by standing beneath the window and singing, to the tune of 'Here we go gathering nuts in May',

> The Dean of Balliol sleeps with men,
> Sleeps with men, sleeps with men.

Connolly first became aware of Waugh as a noisy appendage to the Harold Acton clique. When he asked Waugh why he made such a row so often, he received the candid reply: 'Because I'm poor.' Waugh had realized that the Etonians would accept him, despite his Lancing–Hertford disadvantages, if he made them laugh.

Waugh resented Sligger because he had lured Richard Pares away from the Hypocrites; Waugh alleged that Sligger lusted after Pares himself, and a letter from Sligger to Pares rather bears this out: 'Well, Wig my dear, it is a very pleasing thought that we shall meet so soon. . . .' Uncommonly among dons at this time, Sligger called his favourites by their first name or nickname. A letter to another undergraduate includes this passage: 'If you are going through a bad time, John, this is just to hold you by the hand and wish you courage.' Peter Quennell describes Sligger's salon as very 'modest' on the intellectual plane, and consisting chiefly of 'handsome youths'.

Sligger made some attempt to win over Waugh, inviting him to lunch so that they could talk about Pares, but he never offered wine or beer to undergraduates, and on this occasion Waugh's glass was filled with lemon squash – 'an error not to be easily forgiven', says Christopher Hollis. Thereafter Waugh delighted to collect and spread stories about Sligger. Some were mild, such as the report that Sligger had gone to Cambridge to lecture, but had been unable to do so because of a severe attack of hiccups; Waugh was intensely amused by this, and caused his friends to parade around Balliol singing, to the tune of 'Pop goes the weasel', the words 'Oop! goes the Urquhart'. But the chant about Sligger sleeping with men, delivered (says Quennell) 'in a voice of thunder', was a different matter, and may have contributed to the forcible closure of the Hypocrites', a calamity which Waugh and others largely blamed on Sligger's wire-pulling.

Sligger's interest in his pupils did not cease in the vacation, for he would hold reading parties, either at some beauty spot in Italy or Sicily, or – at least once a year – at 'the Chalet', a Spartan hut erected by his father in the Alps near Mont Blanc. At the end of his first term, Connolly went on a Sicilian reading-party with Sligger; Bobbie Longden was there too, at Cyril's request. 'Longden is superb,' Cyril wrote to his father. 'Sligger in fine form.' In *Brideshead Revisited*, Charles's sour, blackly comic relationship with his father while he languishes at home, separated from Sebastian, strikingly resembles Connolly's predicament in his vacations from Oxford, much of which had to be spent at the family home, a damp mansion by a disused canal near Aldershot. His mother had long since departed, and the company of his father (who had not yet decamped to his solitary hotel room) was scarcely endurable to Cyril: 'He fusses the whole time and is irritable and ready always to think he is a martyr – from vanity and self-pity chiefly. He would read my letters if I gave him the chance. ... All that might be bearable if it wasn't for πoθoς [yearning] for Bobbie.'

In due course Connolly was invited to the Chalet, where Sligger gave him and Bobbie a room to themselves. 'This is the earthly paradise,' Cyril wrote to an Eton friend. But it was not to everyone's taste. Guests were roused by Sligger sharp at eight a.m., and were expected to pay rent – Sligger complacently referred to himself as 'M.le Patron'. Kenneth Clark, another Balliol Sliggerite who went to the Chalet, experienced hunger, boredom, constipation, cold showers and stale bread, and disgraced himself by escaping an obligatory mountain walk to consume *vitello alla Milanese* and Chianti in a village restaurant.

Connolly seems to have played some part in stealing Richard Pares from Waugh and the Hypocrites. Some time during 1923 he drew a map of friendships and enmities, in which Pares's and Waugh's names were linked with a red line that indicated love, but Waugh was listed among the 'bad-hats', who also included Harold Acton, Robert Byron and Terence Greenidge. Waugh is alleged to have said: 'I was cuckolded by Connolly.' Connolly admitted, in a letter written during his second term, that he was 'rather gone' on Pares: 'He took me round for the rest of the morning to banks and things, taking my arm outside the London County and Westminster (thrill). . . .'

Connolly's romantic letters to his Eton friends were now causing trouble: the mother of one of them implored him to cease writing, and his old tutor at Eton warned him to keep away from the school – he had broken his resolution and begun to haunt the place. However, he was settling down at Oxford. At the end of his second term he was the only candidate in History Previous (the preliminary examination) to win a Distinction and be congratulated by the examiners, and he found an alternative salon to Sligger's. His Trinity friends Kenneth Clark and Patrick Balfour (later Lord Kinross) took him to lunch with Maurice Bowra, the Dean of Wadham, who turned out to be 'very nice' and quite 'dropped his manner' when the other two had gone.

Bowra was a young don at Wadham, another of those who, in Connolly's words, 'encouraged a few undergraduates at a time, piloting them through the shoals of adolescence'. He himself had been a Sliggerite in his youth, and had modelled certain small aspects of his behaviour on Sligger – for example he liked to be addressed as 'Maurice' but signed his notes 'C.M.B.', just as Sligger signed his 'F.F.U.' but liked to be called 'Sligger'. Bowra's personal style, however, was radically different from Sligger's.

Wadham was in those days a rather dim college, so Bowra sent out his spies to find lively undergraduates from elsewhere. Though he was by no means uninterested in their private lives, he chose them not for looks but for their intelligence and capacity to amuse. Unlike Sligger, he was a real scholar – a classicist whose books demonstrated an enormous range of learning – but his prose style in print was very flat. He reserved the best of himself for conversation.

Sligger had an essentially nineteenth-century outlook; he was outraged by the publication of Lytton Strachey's *Eminent Victorians* in 1918. Bowra, exceptionally among dons, was widely read in modern poetry – he introduced Connolly to Eliot, the later Yeats, Hardy, Edith Sitwell and Proust. 'Eliot hit me very hard inside,' he wrote to Connolly, but I resisted it, because I could not quite believe that everything was so drab as he said, and I resisted the Christian part. But now I see that he was on the whole right, and that the Christian part is in fact hardly Christian at all, but really a plea for the inner life.

This was after *Ash-Wednesday* and Eliot's reception into the Church of England.

Like Sligger, Bowra (who was unmarried) delighted to bring members of his circle together in romantic bonds, and encouraged those who were already paired. He had been told about Connolly's passion for Bobbie Longden, and signalled his approval, though he warned Connolly that 'Bobbie knows too many people.' (Longden was moving among a slightly *louche* set that included a former boyfriend of Lytton Strachey.) He suggested that Connolly and Longden should find digs together in a remote part of North Oxford, where nobody would notice them; failing that, said Connolly, 'he will make us both Fellows of Wadham'. On the other hand he was aware of Connolly's lack of sexual experience, and his jokes could be cruel. 'He would introduce me to some of his older friends', writes Connolly, 'with a genial: "This is Connolly. Coming man. (*Pause.*) Hasn't come yet."'

One of his techniques with his less self-confident undergraduate friends was to help them come to terms with difficult parental figures, such as Connolly's father. Connolly describes his method of 'making a kind of therapeutic pack of cards which were then dealt out as one makes a sad child laugh – "What does Major Connolly think of the *Après-midi d'un Faune*?"' Kenneth Clark writes:

> I don't think he ever met my father, but he recreated him as a mythical personage ... and invented for him extravagant and not altogether impossible adventures. Thus he lifted from my shoulders a load of shame and resentment which had been deposited there when, as a child, I had to get my father [an exuberant gambler and drinker] out of embarrassing scrapes.

Bowra alleges in his memoirs that Connolly's father was 'a world authority on snail-shells', a complete invention which nevertheless catches the character of Connolly *père*. In the same passage he also observes that Connolly 'needed affection'. Evidently he found him fascinating, for he writes of his 'fine forehead, eager, questing eyes, a face that registered every change of feeling, and a soft hypnotizing voice'.

Anthony Powell had often heard of Bowra as a man of influence, but was quite unprepared for his striking appearance: 'Noticeably small, this lack of stature emphasized by a massive head and tiny feet

... a little like those toys which cannot be pushed over ... or perhaps Humpty-Dumpty, whose autocratic diction and quick-fire interrogations were also paralleled.' Powell records that he 'habitually wore a hat and a suit ... in different shades of brown, very neat, always tending to look a shade tight over the outline'.

Powell, who was introduced to Bowra by a Balliol friend, had never met anyone remotely like him; he found it hard to guess his origins, even his age – Bowra liked undergraduates to assume that he was their coeval, and when asked how old someone was, would often reply 'our age', a concept that covered anyone who came up to Oxford between the wars. He was in fact half a dozen years senior to Connolly and his friends, born in 1898 in China, where his father (who came from a Kentish family) was a senior official in the Customs service. Maurice had been sent back to England to be educated, and from school at Cheltenham had won a classical scholarship to New College, where he took a double First. He had fought at Ypres, and told Connolly: 'Whatever you hear about the war, remember it was far worse: inconceivably bloody – nobody who wasn't there can ever imagine what it was like.' Yet he usually avoided mention of his wartime experiences, and had nothing about him of the returned soldier, except a certain raucous army humour. 'Got a boil on your cock, old boy?' he would cry in imitation of some remembered officer. 'Then crash along to the MO, who'll soon put you right with a Number 9.'

Soon after his introduction, Powell found himself admitted into Bowra's circle – 'or rather one of them, for there were not a few'. Bowra gave select dinner parties in his Wadham rooms for six or eight men, 'always undergraduates', says Powell; 'I can never recall meeting a don.' The rooms were high up in the front quadrangle, and as guests came through the college lodge they would hear raised and cheerful voices, Bowra's loudest among them. 'His voice had the carrying power of the Last Trump,' writes Noël Annan. 'The roar so beat about your ears that you found yourself roaring too. At least one of his friends acquired his voice and manner lock, stock and barrel.'

Once reached at the top of the stairs, his rooms appeared bare compared to Sligger's: no snapshots of undergraduates, just a few carefully chosen paintings, and many rows of Greek and Latin texts. Osbert Lancaster remarks on the studied bleakness of the décor, but observes that anything more could have proved a distraction from the events of the evening.

Unlike Sligger, Bowra provided plenty to drink, almost always champagne. John Betjeman describes 'the feeling of safe elation as the glass was thrust into one's hand and the introductions made to people one knew and liked already, but given different titles in the fantastic hierarchy Maurice invented for them'. In *Summoned by Bells*, Betjeman describes Bowra's

> fusillade of phrases . . . rattled out
> In that incisive voice and chucked away
> To be re-used in envious common-rooms
> By imitation Maurices

– *bon mots* such as 'I'm a man more dined against than dining,' 'Noël feels things sin-deep; he's safe in the arms of Kleist,' or, late in the evening, when much had been drunk by his guests: 'Lead blindly tight amid the revolving room.' Second-hand versions of his witticisms did indeed pass widely around.

Much of his wit was directed against University colleagues. Contempt of other dons was undisguised: 'The Master of Balliol has been ill but unfortunately is getting better.' He judged people ruthlessly. 'Nice stupid man' was a frequent summing-up. 'Able' signified guarded approval without personal affection: 'A very able man.' 'But what's he like?' 'I've told you. He's a very able man.' An adversary to be reckoned with would be labelled 'Shit of hell'. Many were condemned from reputation alone: 'Awful shit. Never met him.' Certain people were subjected to sustained demolition: 'He is indescribably awful, positively and dynamically fourth-rate . . . infinitely pretentious and ignorant . . . physically hideous . . . embarrassing to be seen with.' (These are phrases from one of his letters.) But if he found he had said the wrong thing in influential company, he would backtrack shamelessly and lavish praise on someone he had dismembered. Similarly in college meetings, if he found that his side was losing, he would desert to the enemy, greatly to the discomfiture of his allies.

Osbert Lancaster, who joined the Bowra circle when he came up to Oxford in 1926, says that in his company 'everything seemed speeded-up, funnier and more easily explicable in personal terms. Abstract ideas . . . were, in his company, always firmly treated as extensions of personality.' He adds that Isaiah Berlin and David Cecil, Oxford's fastest talkers, owed their verbal speed to having to get everything in between Maurice's noisy outbursts. (Betjeman remarks that Lancaster himself had picked up much of the Bowra manner.)

Gerard Irvine, a member of Bowra's circle some years later, suggests that Bowra effected a significant change in the behaviour of English intellectuals. Immediately before his day, says Irvine, the prevailing accent among writers, artists and academics was the drawl, an affected languor dating from the Nineties. Bloomsbury took this over and made it its own. Then Bowra arrived with his machine-gun utterance, which immediately appealed to a generation wishing to develop its own style and not mimic the Bloomsbury manner. Certainly many of Bowra's characteristics were taken over by those who belonged to his set in Oxford in the mid-1920s – and by some, among them Evelyn Waugh, who did not. During his undergraduate days Waugh was not drawn into the Bowra circle; he writes somewhat acidly that Bowra 'became friends after I attracted some attention as a novelist'. But it is evident that Bowra's personality filtered through to him from his friends, and that he recognized its value. Isaiah Berlin writes that Bowra's style was 'a major liberating force. . . . His passionate praise and unbridled denunciation of enemies produced an intoxicating effect . . . was deeply and permanently emancipating. It blew up much that was false, pretentious, absurd; the effect was cathartic; it made for truth, human feeling, as well as great mental exhilaration.'

After the champagne, the company in Bowra's rooms would move in to dinner – 'A dozen oysters and a dryish hock,' recalls Betjeman, 'Claret and *tournedos*; a *bombe surprise*.' Anthony Powell says that during the meal there was, amid the laughter and gossip, 'always a slight sense of danger'. Bowra would stage-manage the conversation to achieve indiscretion, yet could easily take offence, announcing a day or two later that what so-and-so had said was not acceptable.

Though not insensitive himself, he took an undisguised delight in causing trouble for others. 'One continues to go out of one's way to court people's hatred,' he told Powell, and he would delightedly claim that he had 'made splendid bad blood' between others. Even his own discomforts could be the cause of malicious pleasure. 'Causes pain,' he would remark quite gleefully of somebody else's success or good luck, relishing his own envy. Isaiah Berlin observes that all the salvoes against others masked – and were really the result of – a deep lack of confidence in himself: 'He needed constant reassurance.' And Noël Annan says: 'You very soon learnt how raw his skin was.'

Annan remarks on another characteristic: 'When you were with him the large Johnsonian face was for ever mobile, responding. . . . But one feature in his face never smiled: his eyes. They were pig's eyes, fierce, unforgiving, unblinking, vigilant. They were inspecting the enemy's dispositions.' This could be a description of Waugh in his final years.

If some young man started to become a tipsy bore at the dinner table, Bowra was highly skilled at piloting him tactfully out of the room. (On a larger scale, friends might find themselves suddenly cast into outer darkness and left there for years, on the slightest of grounds – something said or done which had unexpectedly caused immense offence. Connolly later experienced this and calls it 'devastating'.) Betjeman writes that at Bowra's table 'I learned ... how not to be a bore, / And merciless was his remark that touched / The tender spot if one were showing off.' He would censure outrageousness in his guests only if it were motivated simply by a desire to shock, for he himself was quite without inhibition; Powell says he would 'proclaim the paramount claims of eating, drinking and sex (if necessary, auto-erotic)' while also accepting as absolutely natural 'open snobbishness, success worship, personal vendettas, unprovoked malice, disloyalty to friends, reading other people's letters (if not lying about, to be sought in unlocked drawers)'. Kenneth Clark found this unbelievably liberating: 'He said all the dreadful things one was longing to hear said, and said them as if they were obvious to any decent man. ... My priggish fears and inhibitions were blown to smithereens.'

For all his exhortations about the necessity of sexual indulgence, Bowra seems to have had little or no sex-life of his own. (Possibly, as with Sligger, all his manipulations and scoring off other people, and being scored off, might be interpreted as a substitute for sex.) He experienced passions for certain male undergraduates, but was apparently telling the truth when he said that for him sex was 'inescapably in the head'. He would also maintain that lust is invariably stirred by fetishism – white shorts, grey flannel trousers, plimsolls – rather than by the beauty of the person desired.

Noël Annan says that he was terrified of blackmail, which a homosexual friend of his had experienced, and would never mention homosexuality in print, even when discussing poems inspired by it. He sometimes played the hearty heterosexual; Betjeman describes him at a country house 'coming into my bedroom when we were changing for dinner and saying, "I say, old boy, shall we roger the skivvies?"' A letter to Noël Annan describing the visit of some woman friend is in this vein: 'But she brought Sebastian with her which meant no fucking and, much worse, his presence.' Annan believes that he was attracted to women, calling him 'an immensely masculine bisexual', and says that at various times he experienced passions for Elizabeth Bowen, Penelope Betjeman and Iris Murdoch. Whatever his real sexual nature, it seems to have given him little happiness. Somebody once addressed him as 'a carefree bachelor', whereupon he was suddenly discomposed: 'Never, *never*, use that term of me again.'

In conversation, he would divide the world geographically into the Drink Zone (northern hemisphere) and the Sex Zone (southern), though the division did not correspond to the equator; in France it lay north of Provence, but it ran south of Japan. This could lead to such remarks as 'America? Drink Zone pretending to be Sex.' He did not deny that sex was practised in the Drink Zone, but there it was 'cursed with guilt, darkness, despair, complexity'.

After dinner in his rooms there might be such parlour games as giving famous poets classes of Oxford degrees. Should Goethe get a First? 'No: the Higher Bogus.' 'Maurice, we've forgotten Eliot.' 'Aegrotat.'* Or the company might draw up cricket elevens of bores, or be challenged to define the quintessence of a Wykehamist. Bowra would allege that there was such a thing as a distinctive Wykehamist thigh, characterized by its massive girth; hence the opening of Betjeman's poem 'The Wykehamist': 'Broad of Church and broad of mind, / Broad before and broad behind ...'. Sometimes paper and pencils would be produced, and instructions given to write a brief biography of the President of Magdalen in heroic couplets. Or, taking a manuscript volume from a locked cupboard, Bowra would read out scabrous verses of his own composition about the sexual preferences of his friends and enemies, usually in the form of parody or pastiche:

> I will arise and go now and go to have a pee
>> Way down in Innisfree
>> That's where I wish to be
>> With a corporal on my knee.
>>> Oh, is it town or gown or tousled hair
>> A tousled boy-scout's hair
>>> Inside the wc?

The verses were rather heavy-handed after the spontaneous witticisms, but their outrageousness invariably delighted the company.

After this, if the mood had not become too hilarious, there might be real poetry. 'And as the evening mellowed into port,' writes Betjeman,

> He read us poems. There I learned to love
> That lord of landscape, Alfred Tennyson;
> There first Thomas Hardy's poetry ...

---

* An Aegrotat is awarded to a candidate who was too ill to take the examination, but has been judged worthy of a degree.

> Yeats he would chant in deep sonórous voice;
> Bring Rudyard Kipling – then so out-of-date –
> To his full stature . . . .

Bowra's taste in architecture was similarly unfashionable. He would enthuse over such Victoriana as the polychromatic Butterfield brick of Keble College and the gloomy creations of Sir Thomas Jackson, a former Fellow of Wadham who had designed the sepulchral University Examination Schools – Bowra coined the phrase 'Anglo-Jackson', afterwards taken over by Betjeman. He hated modern buildings: 'They are entirely made of some ghastly stuff called cladding.' Osbert Lancaster recalls visiting Oxford churches with him, Bowra gloating over architectural absurdities and leaping into the pulpit to give an impersonation of the lugubrious Dr Holmes-Dudden, Master of Pembroke College. Not religious by nature, he nevertheless attended the college chapel regularly as if propitiating a household god, and would cross himself in Roman Catholic churches; he had a classical and pagan attitude to the supernatural. Politically he was neutral, or rather, he had an equally passionate hatred for the extremes of both right and left.

On holiday, he operated a points system. According to the greatness of some church or work of art, so many points were earned, and when fifty was reached the party was entitled to a drink. But if the church or gallery turned out to be closed, ten points were awarded in compensation. And if they stumbled across some truly awful collection of paintings, 'Thirty points!' he would boom, striding triumphantly past.

John Betjeman judges that beneath all the foolery lay invaluable lessons for those who had been drawn into his circle. Bowra showed:

> that wisdom was
> Not memory-tests (as I had long supposed),
> Not 'first-class brains' and swotting for exams,
> But humble love for what we sought and knew.

Betjeman judges that Bowra 'taught me far more than all my tutors did'. Moreover within his rooms 'I met my friends for life.'

Certain habitués of the Bowra dinner table, Betjeman among them, also participated in another, more ridiculous salon, held after church on Sunday mornings at 38 Beaumont Street, by George Alfred Kolkhorst, University lecturer in Spanish and Portuguese, who dwelt amid Nineties clutter and a persistent smell of gas. Known variously as 'G'ug' or 'the Colonel', Kolkhorst was the cause of a whole world of childish jokes in which he participated somewhat uncertainly, being himself quite devoid of wit though a determined maker of epigrams. He is commemorated in Betjeman's *Summoned by Bells*. Osbert Lancaster, another regular at the Kolkhorst salon, wonders in retrospect 'exactly what it was which so endeared this figure of fun to so many of the brightest of my contemporaries', and Betjeman similarly observes in *Summoned by Bells*: 'How trivial and silly now they look ... / Dear private giggles of a private world!' This last phrase supplies the answer to Lancaster's question.

John Betjeman was the son of a London manufacturer of probable German descent, who claimed (by the time of the First World War) to be Dutch. The family had been in England since the late eighteenth century, and had for some while been calling themselves 'Betjemann', under which name John came up to Magdalen in 1925. The family firm made dressing-tables, household ornaments and 'Tantalus' holders for locking up the whisky-decanters against the servants. John's father, Ernest Betjemann, was proud of being in trade, and would take John, his only child, to the family works in Pentonville to remind him that he was 'fourth generation' and was expected to join the firm in due course. Alan Pryce-Jones describes Ernest Betjemann as 'a tyrant' and his wife Bess as 'a lachrymose victim', and says that, unknown to Bess, a mistress had been kept for years who bore Ernest a second family. Like Waugh, John Betjeman was trying to escape from an overpowering father.

Yet, again as with Waugh, he knew no other model. His mother, Bess, briefly ran a small millinery business during John's childhood, but she made no serious attempt to escape from, or stand firm against, her husband's tyranny. Deprived of firm maternal support, John could measure himself only against his domineering father. His poetry is full of guilt at having rejected Ernest. 'My dear deaf father, how I loved him then / Before the years of our estrangement came!' he writes of his childhood in *Summoned by Bells*, but elsewhere in the same poem he admits: 'I feared my father. . . .'

John was given the education of a gentleman, first at Highgate Junior School, where he was briefly taught by the young T.S. Eliot (whom he liked, and whose poetry he quickly came to appreciate), then at the Dragon School in Oxford, and at Marlborough College. Early in life he would sometimes overhear himself described by friends' parents as 'a common little boy' on account of his uncertain accent and not quite gentlemanly bearing. Eventually he learnt to play up to this, but when he arrived at Oxford he was still extremely sensitive to the subject, and was all agreement when another Old Marlburian claimed the right to identify with the smart set – 'Spiritually I was at Eton, John.'

Betjeman was scarcely more fortunate in his tutor than Waugh. C.S. Lewis, just appointed to a Fellowship at Magdalen, was absorbed in his own imminent religious conversion and the first stirrings of his beer-drinking, saga-reading friendship with J.R.R. Tolkien. He had no time for an undergraduate who hobnobbed with the aristocratic rakes of Magdalen, turned up for tutorials (if at all) in carpet-slippers, and would ring up from a country house to say that he could not manage his Anglo-Saxon this week as he had measles and had been forbidden to open a book. Tutor and pupil disagreed almost as violently as Cruttwell had with Waugh, and in after years, just as Waugh frequently used the name 'Cruttwell' in his novels for various unsavoury characters, so Betjeman not infrequently alluded sarcastically to Lewis. For example in his 1933 book *Ghastly Good Taste* he thanks 'Mr C.S. Lewis, of Oxford, whose jolly personality and encouragement to the author in his youth have remained an unfading memory for the author's declining years'.

At the Dragon and Marlborough, Betjeman had begun to write competent verse, and arriving in Oxford he made friends with W.H. Auden, who had just come up to Christ Church from Gresham's School in Norfolk. Indeed, the two indulged in a brief homosexual experiment together. But Betjeman's social sights were set higher than this; he admits that he aspired to move in 'the grand sets'.

He managed this despite – or perhaps because of – considerable eccentricity of manner and dress. Osbert Lancaster describes him as already presenting 'a convincing impersonation of a rather down-at-heel Tractarian hymn-writer recently unfrocked'. At the OUDS, which he frequented, he was chosen to play such comic old men as Starveling in *A Midsummer Night's Dream*; the theatrical director John Fernald, another OUDS member in those days, says that such performances demonstrated that Betjeman could 'certainly have become a professional actor had he so wished', and Emlyn Williams describes him as 'a zany wiseacre with a protruding tooth'. Harold Acton writes that 'John looked as if he had tumbled out of bed and dressed in a hurry, necktie askew and shoe-laces undone, while a school bell seemed to be tinkling in the distance. . . . We became friends at first sight.'

Betjeman made a stir at Oxford by his habit of carrying with him everywhere a well-worn teddy bear which he had preserved from childhood. Known as Archie (full name Archibald Ormsby-Gore), this object, sometimes accompanied by its friend, a bedraggled toy elephant named Jumbo, would be taken by Betjeman to country-house week-ends. Waugh was sometimes present on these occasions; hence, eventually, Sebastian's teddy bear Aloysius in *Brideshead Revisited*. This exquisite piece of foolery by Betjeman – an implicit comment on the immaturity of the English upper classes – grew from the time when his father had decided that the boy was too old for teddies:

> When nine, I hid you in a loft
>   And dared not let you share my bed;
> My father would have thought me soft,
>   Or so at least my mother said. . . .
>
> And if an analyst one day
>   Of school of Adler, Jung or Freud
> Should take this agèd bear away,
>   Then, oh my God, the dreadful void!

A friend describes Betjeman's behaviour on the Tube in London:

> We had to go on the Inner Circle, and of course he had to have Archie the teddy-bear on his lap, with everybody staring. He used to bring him out of his little brief-case and sit him up on his lap and would talk to him: 'Now, Archie, you know where we are? We're in an Underground; some people call them "tubes". See that couple over there? They're looking at you. Behave!' And he'd go on like that throughout the journey. . . . I used to be acutely embarrassed.

Betjeman knew the value of foolery as a way not merely of attracting attention but of subverting paternalistic authority. Both his father and his tutor were greatly disconcerted by what they considered to be his frivolous attitudes. Lewis grumbled to him, 'I have never heard you speak of any serious subject without a snigger,' and Ernest Betjemann frequently made the same complaint. Even friends like David Cecil were puzzled that he was always 'saying he loved a thing, and laughing at it'. Betjeman, who once described himself sadly as 'doomed for ever to be thought "a funny man"', tried to explain his behaviour in a 1929 letter to his father: 'I do not think that what is said or written matters, but what is felt. Often most "serious" feelings are expressed as a joke.' His playing of the fool was a symptom not of frivolity but of pessimism, the response of someone who knows that the world is too foolish to listen to serious things. A small girl who knew him when he was teaching at her father's prep school in the late 1920s found him anything but frivolous: 'All the time . . . he gave the impression of someone who has early looked close at life and has profoundly despaired, and from then on [is] filling in time until his death.'

At Oxford, Betjeman social-climbed with a will – 'Week after sunny week / I climbed ...' he writes in *Summoned by Bells*. He did not pose as an aristocrat himself, having found that it was far more effective to play the bourgeois, parodying his father's lifestyle. He liked to amuse his Etonian friends by pretending to be a commercial traveller, referring to his father as 'Ernie', and signing off letters with 'Tinkerty-tonk, old boy'. Beneath the comedy lay a real revulsion. A friend jotted down Betjeman's account, in conversation, of his father's behaviour: 'V. rich, gives his son nothing, forbids him to read poetry, kicks his wife, brings mistresses into the house.' Allowing for some exaggeration, Ernest Betjemann does seem to have been monstrous; Sir Horace Plunkett, for whom John worked briefly after going down from Oxford, met him and thought him 'a bounder of the worst kind'.

After a few months of social-climbing Betjeman 'reached what seemed to me the peak – / The leisured set in Canterbury Quad'. Canterbury was the neighbouring quadrangle in Christ Church to Peckwater, and contained especially grand suites of undergraduate rooms, affordable only by the very rich. Among those dwelling there was Edward James, who had come up from Eton possessed of a fortune which he had recently inherited from an uncle. He decorated his rooms (Canterbury 3:3, which included a dining room and drawing room) in silver and black, with hangings of Flemish tapestry. Tom Driberg recalls that gramophone horns concealed in busts of Roman emperors belched forth the latest French and American music. Around the drawing room was lettered ARS LONGA VITA BREVIS EST SED VITA LONGA SI SCIAS UTI, 'Art is long and life brief but you can make life long if you know how to use it.'

In this setting, James would entertain Betjeman to breakfasts of champagne and Virginia ham, while they read their own poems aloud to each other. Despite the gap in class and wealth, James encouraged Betjeman to treat him as his protégé, at least where poetry was concerned. He had discovered Betjeman's considerable facility at composing verse – he could scribble off stanzas in scarcely more time than it took to read them aloud. But though to a few intimates like James, Betjeman might confess to real ambition in this direction, he had no wish to tarnish his comic mask by appearing in public as a serious poet. When *Cherwell* published his fine piece, rather in the manner of Hardy, 'For Nineteenth Century Burials' ('This cold weather / Carries so many old people away ...'), the author was disguised behind the pseudonym 'Olivia Rembrandt'. Betjeman would sign his name only to squibs such as this impersonation of the hearties, printed in *Cherwell* a few months later:

> We'd gallons and gallons of cider, and I got *frightfully* tight,
> And then we smash'd up ev'rything, and what was the funniest part,
> We smash'd some rotten old pictures which were 'priceless works of art'.

It was the same with architecture: his contributions on this subject to *Cherwell* were invariably frivolous, and only his close friends could perceive the seriousness of his interest. This had begun at Marlborough, where participation in the Art Society – yet another group of school aesthetes opposed to the prevailing philistinism – had led him to discover volumes of aquatints portraying Georgian country houses. He began to be fascinated by the life of the landed proprietor of that period, 'with his gate lodge, park, walled garden, pinetum, icehouse, library, saloon, home farm and spreading stables'. (It was all so far from the Betjemann factory in Pentonville where he feared he would soon be imprisoned.) Near Marlborough he found a perfect specimen of the Georgian mansion, Ramsbury Manor. 'No words can express my longing to get inside this house,' he later wrote. 'I think the mystery of its winding drive gave me a respect for the system of hereditary landowning which I have never shaken off.'

In this state of mind he came up to Oxford, where he would privately disclose his obsession to certain friends – Alan Pryce-Jones was taken by him to inspect Georgian manor houses and churches in Oxfordshire villages. But the Victorian craze initiated by Harold Acton was in full spate, and Betjeman perceived its humorous possibilities. At school he had despised Victorian architecture as 'purely imitative and rather vulgar', an opinion he had not really abandoned. Yet Maurice Bowra, at whose dining table he found himself sitting, amused him with his connoisseurship of Victorian extravagances, and Betjeman began to practise a little gentle clowning in this area himself, printing in *Cherwell* a series of photographs of Victorian monstrosities, such as an Oxford shop built in the style of Blenheim Palace.

He soon found his own Alastair Graham in Lionel Perry, rich, blond and beautiful, a Magdalen undergraduate one year senior to him, who provided him with social introductions that allowed him to inspect certain great houses at close quarters. Through Perry he met Billy Clonmore, who invited him to the family home, Shelton Abbey in County Wicklow. The gloomy Irish setting and the Gothic mansion greatly appealed to Betjeman, who records his delight in 'the winding avenue and sheet of water, the fine outward show and the inward damp splendour slightly dried by burning logs . . .'. He was amused by a member of the household named Harold Newcombe, who held the post of 'social secretary' to Clonmore – in effect a combination of bodyguard and teacher of etiquette. Lord Wicklow had engaged him to keep his son on the rails of propriety and gentlemanly behaviour. From Newcombe, Betjeman learnt some of the social *faux pas* that he guys in his poem 'How to Get On in Society' (never use fish-knives, do not say 'lounge' for 'sitting-room', and so on); Clonmore's widow writes that 'Billy said that John had put in as many of Newcombe's "don'ts" as possible'. Newcombe travelled everywhere with Clonmore to keep an eye on him, not unlike Mr Samgrass in *Brideshead Revisited*.

More remarkable than Wicklow Abbey in architectural terms was the home of another of Lionel Perry's friends, John Dugdale, whose family occupied an early nineteenth-century mansion built in the Indian style at Sezincote in Gloucestershire. In *Summoned by Bells*, Betjeman describes the journey there from Oxford:

> Heavy with hawthorn scent were Cotswold lanes,
> Golden the church towers standing in the sun. . . .
> > Down the drive
> Under the early yellow leaves of oaks;
> One lodge is Tudor, one in Indian style.
> The bridge, the waterfall, the Temple Pool –
> And there they burst on us, the onion domes. . . .

In the *Architectural Review* in 1931, Betjeman writes of the surprise caused by the domes to unsuspecting passers-by: 'I have seen Americans and "hikers" goggling with amazement as they caught a glimpse of the mansion while trespassing in the park.' There may be an echo of this in Charles Ryder's experience of first seeing Brideshead when he and Sebastian motor over there from Oxford one June morning:

> . . . .suddenly a new and secret landscape opened before us. We were at the head of a valley and below us, half a mile distant, prone in the sunlight, grey and gold amid a screen of boskage, shone the dome and columns of an old house. . . .
> 'Well?' said Sebastian, stopping the car. Beyond the dome lay receding steps of water and round it, guarding and hiding it, stood the soft hills.
> 'Well?'
> 'What a place to live in!' I said.

Waugh made the journey to Sezincote one day in June 1930, with Betjeman and Frank Pakenham. 'Sezincote is quite lovely,' he wrote in his diary. 'Regency Indian style like Brighton Pavilion, only in Cotswold stone instead of plaster. Fountains all playing and ferocious swans. . . . Colonel Dugdale said, ''The twenty-fourth of May is my day for haymaking.'' . . . The most lovely view in England.'

5

He Embodied Authority

Some time during his second year at Oxford, Waugh met a Balliol undergraduate who was an old boy of Berkhamsted School – Henry Graham Greene, the son of the school's Headmaster, Charles Henry Greene.

Waugh was probably introduced to Greene by his cousin Claud Cockburn, who was then up at Keble and who had been at Berkhamsted. Cockburn describes Greene's father, the Headmaster, as:

> a man of powerful and vivid reactions. Certain events, sometimes major, sometimes quite trivial, seemed to strike his mind with the heat and force of a branding-iron. ... His history lessons were ... comments on a state of affairs in which history had taken a distinct turn for the worse. ... He treated history simply as a series of signposts ... to ruin. For Charles Greene was, in the widest as well as the party-political sense of a the word, a Liberal, and in the crack-up of Liberalism he saw the mark of doom.

Mr Greene feared the 'bolshevistic' way things were tending, which was evidenced locally by bored and frequently drunken soldiers, still in uniform months after the Armistice, who were camped outside the town; once, they rioted and broke into the school. The Headmaster and Cockburn would sit arguing politics over their lunch, Mr Greene encouraging Cockburn's Conservative inclinations so that he might become an infiltrator – he exhorted him to 'enter the Conservative Party and so stimulate its moral sense and moderate its crassness'.

Meanwhile the rest of the school would be waiting impatiently for the Latin grace that signalled the end of the meal; finally Mr Greene would cut short the discussion with: 'Well, well, Cockburn, I don't see how civilization's going to be saved, Benedictus Benedicat.'

Henry Graham Greene was the fourth of the six Greene children. Like Waugh, he was given one of his father's Christian names as his own first name, but the 'Henry' was soon dropped. Because of his position in the family he was quickly passed over in infancy, and his parents seemed to him remote figures. His mother, dignified and calm, occasionally paid what Graham calls 'state visits' to the nursery, but she played no prominent part in his childhood or the development of his imagination. His father, far more prominent than the reticent mother, was chiefly characterized by his position in the school, though this did not endear him to Graham, who writes: 'As a headmaster he was even more distant than our aloof mother.'

Never close to his father when very young, Graham became frightened and resentful of such notice as Mr Greene began to give him as he grew older: 'To be praised was agony – I would crawl immediately under the nearest table.' He felt virtually no affection for him until it was too late: 'Only when I had children of my own did I realize how his interest in my doings had been genuine, and only then I discovered a buried love and sorrow for him, which emerges from time to time in dreams.'

Elsewhere Greene has said of his father: 'I had no feelings about him. He embodied Authority too much.' Yet it was not easy to turn against him, for Charles Greene was, like Arthur Waugh, a reasonable and humane individual, despite a certain theatricality. Open rebellion did not seem justified to Graham any more than it did to Evelyn Waugh. Like Waugh, he was therefore driven to take avoiding action, to look for some way of escape from the dominance of his father.

For a long while he refused to learn to read, but this crude protest against his father's profession was abandoned when he discovered his first possible escape route – romantic adventure-fiction. By about the age of ten he was tucking greedily into boys' stories by Ballantyne, Captain Marryat, Henty and the other masters of the genre, and this species of literature eventually left a considerable mark on his own novels. Escapist fiction brought him a degree of tranquillity in childhood, but then at the age of thirteen he became a boarder in his father's school.

For any boy it would have been 'a savage country', just as it was for Connolly at Eton and Waugh at Lancing, but Greene's relationship to the Headmaster made it far worse: 'I was like the son of a quisling in a country under occupation. ... I was surrounded by the forces of resistance, and yet I couldn't join them without betraying my father.' Hence, as he says himself, the recurrent motif of divided loyalties in his books, from the smuggler's son in *The Man Within* (1929) who has betrayed his father's gang, to the MI6 officer in *The Human Factor* (1978) who is a traitor to his country.

Finding himself in this acute predicament at school, and persecuted by a sadistic boy named Carter, Greene resorted to clumsy escape-attempts – malingering, playing truant, trying to cut his leg open with a penknife, eating deadly nightshade, swallowing handfuls of aspirin. None of these did him any harm, nor was noticed by his father, so Graham tried the expedient of leaving a note to say that he had run away from school; he then took a book and went off to Berkhamsted Common, to wait for them to come and find him – which they did about two hours later. The matter would have ended there had not Graham's elder brother Raymond, who had just gone up to Oxford and regarded himself as knowledgeable in such matters, suggested that Graham must have had a nervous breakdown, and required psycho-analysis. In most families this absurd suggestion would have been ridiculed, but it touched a certain spot in the Greenes, for the Headmaster's father had suffered from manic-depression, while Mrs Greene was the daughter of an Anglican clergyman who had gone mad and taken off most of his clothes in a field. Graham was in due course packed off to an analyst in London.

This suited him splendidly, because the analyst in question, a gentle Jungian, made no greater demands than that Graham should describe his dreams. Meanwhile Graham was accommodated in great comfort in the analyst's house – a maid brought him breakfast in bed – and was allowed to spend most of his time reading under the trees in Kensington Gardens. This total escape from 'the stone steps, the ink-stained schoolroom, the numbering-off at the bogs, the smell of farts around the showers' was more than he could have hoped for. But all too quickly the so-called analysis came to an end and he was sent back to Berkhamsted.

A concession was made to his supposedly unstable nervous condition, in that he was now allowed to live in the family house while attending classes. But in a sense this made things worse. Instead of being unhappy, he became desperately bored: 'Boredom seemed to swell like a balloon inside the head.' He supposed that it must be a symptom of the family manic-depression, damped down to *ennui* by psycho-analysis. But there had been no analysis worth the name. He was bored because there was no escape. He had tried all the routes and found that they led back to his home–school captivity. He began to feel that life would always be like that.

After a while, alternating with the waves of boredom, he began to experience acute lust – for teenage girls, for soubrettes in musical comedies, for any remotely attractive female, though not for boys, for Berkhamsted, being largely a day-school, lacked the homosexuality of the all-boarding establishments. Coming up to Balliol in the autumn of 1922, he began his Oxford career by deciding that he was in love with a waitress at the George Restaurant, near his college. Next, he made advances during the vacation to a girl called Gwen Howell, the governess of his younger brother and sister, and was given some encouragement; but she was ten years his senior and already engaged to be married, so he took refuge in writing self-pitying poetry:

> Eating a Lyons' chop in nineteen thirty . . .
> I'll ponder through the scraping of a plate
> How love which should have been a blaze of wonder
> Has been a dusty and untended grate. . . .

But in another poem he admitted the real nature of his feelings:

> And when I said I loved you,
> Oh, I lied.
> The two-backed beast went trotting in my head. . . .

Those of his poems that were not about Gwen played with the notion of putting an end to the boredom by suicide:

> I slip a charge into one chamber,
> Out of six,
> Then move the chambers round.
> One cast of the dice for death,
> And five for life.

This was exactly what he had been doing: 'I can remember very clearly the afternoon I found the revolver in the brown deal corner-cupboard in a bedroom which I shared with my elder brother . . . and there was a cardboard box full of bullets.' He immediately set off for Berkhamsted Common, convinced that he had stumbled on the perfect cure for boredom. There, 'I slipped a bullet into a chamber and, holding the revolver behind my back, spun the chambers round.' He pulled the trigger, but there was only a click. In his autobiography he argues that it was not a suicide attempt but a way of discovering, through his relief when the gun failed to go off, that he really wanted to stay alive after all. Yet he would not have done it on a number of occasions, at Berkhamsted and Oxford, had he not at least half meant to kill himself.

Next, he tried drink, and went to bed in a drunken stupor every night for a term. But much of Oxford was in the same condition and no one noticed this gesture. After this, he was rather at a loss for escape-routes. Rather oddly, considering the Oxford fashion, he kept his distance from homosexuality. 'Perhaps this was just my naïvety. ... It never attracted me or interested me. ... Evelyn Waugh ... used to tease me. ... He claimed that I had lost a great deal by not going through a homosexual phase.'

6

A Dream Too Agreeable

Brian Howard eventually reached Christ Church in October 1923, a year after Harold Acton. He behaved like a guest who has arrived late at a celebration and so is doubly determined to enjoy himself. 'One lives an extraordinarily marvellous life,' he wrote to William Acton, 'a sort of passionate party all the time.' Realizing that there was little chance of wresting the leadership of their clique back from Harold, he turned instead to the rich aristocrats of the Bullingdon Club. 'I got extremely tipsy, and broke several windows in Peck,' he wrote to William after one of the club's dinners; '256 panes of glass were smashed altogether. ... After the Bullingdon dinner I had a tumultuous sleep with someone who remained extremely chilly until we actually got "between the sheets".' Waugh observes of such incidents that 'there are many placid peers today who ascribe most of their youthful fun to Brian'. Brian liked to pose as a peer himself; Waugh describes him telling some Trinity hearties who had broken up a party: 'We shall tell our fathers to raise your rents and evict you.'

Though Anthony Blanche in *Brideshead Revisited* is largely drawn from Waugh's imagination, his physical appearance is that of Brian:

> He was tall, slim, rather swarthy, with large saucy eyes. ... He had on a smooth chocolate-brown suit with loud white stripes, suède shoes, a large bow-tie and he drew off yellow, wash-leather gloves as he came into the room; part Gallic, part Yankee, part, perhaps Jew; wholly exotic.

This description was written after Brian Howard's death, and inserted into the 1960 revised edition of the novel; the first edition says nothing about Blanche's physical appearance, Waugh presumably fearing that Brian might take action against so obvious an identification.

Waugh could not help being impressed by Brian's 'gift of invective and repartee', and says approvingly that Brian's 'ferocity of elegance' belonged to 'the romantic era of a century before our own'. Yet he concludes this brief sketch, in his memoirs, with Lady Caroline Lamb's words on first meeting Byron: 'Mad, bad, and dangerous to know.' This was not so; Brian's letters reveal that beneath the flashy exterior lay a rather childish and naïve individual, incapable of posing a threat to those more mature and clever than himself. Yet evidently Waugh felt threatened. In his account of Brian he describes him as 'an incorrigible homosexual', a turn of phrase which perhaps suggests that Waugh, himself discovering the depths of feeling possible for members of his own sex, but at the same time frightened of this discovery, was disturbed by the spectacle of the guiltlessly homosexual Brian.

In *Brideshead Revisited*, Anthony Blanche takes Charles Ryder to 'the George bar', the establishment on the corner of the Cornmarket and George Street where Graham Greene had fallen in love with a waitress. The girls who worked at this establishment – a homely tea-room trying absurdly to ape the Café Royal – were a principal target of such heterosexual interest as Oxford could muster. A friend of Emlyn Williams mentioned casually one evening in the OUDS clubroom that he had had carnal knowledge of one of them, named Muriel: 'I asked her to marry me, but she was engaged either to Plunket Greene or Robert Byron, she couldn't remember which.' Such liaisons were greatly frowned on by the University authorities, who (says Anthony Powell) were 'indifferent to homosexuality'. When Powell and a Balliol friend were seen talking to another George waitress, Nelly, in the street one evening, they were sent for by the Proctors and given a warning. And when another Balliol man, Peter Quennell, actually admitted to having spent a night in term-time with a woman – even though it had happened some distance from Oxford – he was rusticated (sent down for a term), and in consequence never returned to Balliol or bothered to take his degree.

In *Brideshead Revisited* the George is visited by Anthony Blanche and Charles only for cocktails; Blanche has a more sophisticated establishment in mind for dinner. ' "We are going to Thame," he said. "There is a delightful hotel there, which luckily doesn't appeal to the

Bullingdon.'' ' John Betjeman describes how Maurice Bowra would sometimes accompany them all on expeditions to Thame, 'in hired cars driven very fast and dangerously by undergraduates. . . . We went out . . . to dine at the Spreadeagle at Thame at Fothergill's.' And Harold Acton writes: 'For a quiet dinner there was no alternative but to drive to Thame. At John Fothergill's Spreadeagle Inn one could be sure of good food and better wine in congenial surroundings with a host whose affability and erudition revived a more liberal age.'

Until 1922 the Spreadeagle was a very ordinary inn, standing on the broad principal street of the modest market town of Thame, a little over ten miles from Oxford. In that year John Fothergill arrived. 'In 1922 I found that I must do something for a living,' he writes in *An Innkeeper's Diary*, 'so I was compelled to take an Inn. Here at least I thought I might still be myself and give to others something of what I had acquired before making this clean-cut departure from an easy past.' He gives only a highly compressed and allusive account of that 'easy past'. He came from Westmorland, from a family of some means: 'Will Rothenstein once asked me what my father did, and I told him that he spent most of his time thinking out the proper thing to do and say; surely enough work for two men. Indeed many times since I took this Inn I have felt ashamed of working for a living. . . .' He had studied painting at the Slade (where he had known Rothenstein), and had also been a pupil at the London School of Architecture. Arriving in London at the age of nineteen, 'shy and tender', he had been drawn into, and become a plaything of, the Oscar Wilde circle. Wilde named him 'The Architect of the Moon', and after his own downfall presented him with an affectionately inscribed copy of *The Ballad of Reading Gaol*; he hoped that the young Fothergill would come to live with him in exile in France. Talking to Harold Acton and his friends in the 1920s, Fothergill would imitate Wilde's 'great heavy drawl', and would also recall Ruskin, whom he had known in childhood in the Lake District – he described Ruskin's 'very little bedroom in his beautiful house in Coniston, a little bed, a few sticks of furniture but about a dozen sumptuous Turner water-colours'.

After his Wilde phase, Fothergill had lived for many years in the household of E.P. Warren, an American archaeologist and antiquary who ran an all-male establishment at a country house in Sussex. 'There were six of us,' writes Fothergill,

> each with his own horse, study and dogs. No woman ever entered the
> house. . . . At breakfast Ned [Warren] would open the letters and say:

'Johnny, will you go to Athens today and see those bronzes,' and so
on. Marshall would quietly disappear and perhaps there'd be only three
left for dinner after rides on the downs.

Warren wrote a pseudonymous tract entitled *In Defence of Uranian Love*,
this being a contemporary euphemism for homosexuality. Fothergill,
however, was not content to remain in this ambience. Some time in
the early 1900s – a period when, concurrent with his work for Warren,
he was running the Carfax Gallery in St James's, where Rodin, Max
Beerbohm and Augustus John exhibited – he made a brief and disastrous first marriage, thereafter experiencing some sort of nervous breakdown; he says he had to 'retire to Church Stretton, to a sort of Farm
House in the hills where they took mainly ex-idiots'. After recovery
he married again, and while he and his second wife Kate were at Thame
she bore him two sons.

When he took over the Spreadeagle in 1922, at the age of forty-six,
it was a shabby establishment frequented chiefly by farmers coming
to market, each of them 'with his own particular time-honoured
privilege or abuse. One old farmer had to have his Market Day
dinner ... at the end of the kitchen table as he was often sick on
the floor.' Fothergill went into battle against the farmers, whom
he describes as 'medieval'. They refused to believe that the
prices, unchanged since 1914, would have to be raised, and one of
them told him: 'You're a German and a damned man.' He also had
to struggle with recalcitrant commercial travellers who, like the
farmers, all had their little ways. One of them insisted on being
provided with steak, though it was not on the menu: 'I've had a steak
five days a week for thirty years, and I want a steak now.' Fothergill
went to the butcher and asked for the toughest steak the shop could
provide.

Soon he had driven out all the old customers, and erected a magnificent signboard outside the hotel, dominating the entire street. Depicting
an eagle of heraldic magnificence, surrounded by festoons of wrought
iron, it boldly bore the name JOHN FOTHERGILL. Next, using his London connections, Fothergill began to acquire a new clientele. Several
of his Slade painter friends began to use the place, Augustus John
sent his son Romilly to learn the hotel trade, and Arnold Dolmetsch
and H. G. Wells became regular visitors. 'Brothers Sitwell dine,' Fothergill noted in his diary, 'two ordinary, stalwart, kind fellows, and so
unlike their works.' Other early guests included the writer Storm Jame-
son and her husband Guy Chapman – 'A lovable couple and a good

blend,' noted Fothergill. 'Where she is masculine he is feminine, and vice versa.' Fothergill's own wife Kate was a masculine-looking woman with a leonine jaw; Fothergill himself, a willowy young man in his Oscar Wilde days, had thickened into a powerful figure with strong black eyebrows.

The first Oxford man to discover the Spreadeagle was George Gordon, President of Magdalen, who began to hold reunions of wartime cronies there. Soon after came the Hypocrites, who during 1923 held a wake at Thame following the closure of their club by the Proctors. Fothergill did not yet know many of them personally, but recalls that the fifty people present consumed sixty bottles of champagne, besides much else, and describes Lord Elmley in a purple dress suit, Terence Greenidge looking 'quite mad', and Robert Byron 'shrouded with lace trimmings'. The principal members of the party arrived by hearse, and Harold Acton made 'a speech full of incredible precocity and rare quotation that would have surprised Aubrey Beardsley'. After dinner, writes Fothergill, 'the dancing was terrific. I have an image as of wild goats and animals leaping in the air.' In contrast with this bacchanalian behaviour, Fothergill was struck, on another occasion, by the 'shy propriety' of another undergraduate, Evelyn Waugh.

Fothergill was now determined 'to make this an Eton or Stowe of public houses'. His method was not to curry favour with those he wanted as customers, but to dissuade those he disliked. 'In an altercation I had with a scrubby undergrad, the fellow said, "I'll never come here again," to which I replied, "Yes, but will you give me another undertaking: to tell all your friends not to come?"' He reports with pride that Robert Ross once described him as the worst-mannered man in London.

If people complained about the prices or the quality of the food they were lucky to get away with mere insults; Fothergill was as likely to resort to his fists: 'An old man with a whore told Katie to tell me that 3s 6d for a four-course meal was a swindle, and when I went to him afterwards to invite a scrap he only smiled pleasantly. ... ' A diner who objected to the serving of oysters when there was no *r* in the month was told: 'Ah, but there's an *r* in Fothergill.' His pet hate was people who used the lavatories without buying food or drink; if he failed to apprehend them on the spot he would take the number-plate of their car and send abusive letters. Even reasonable requests could be treated furiously if he disliked a face or voice; he overheard a lady asking to see a room before taking it for the night, and roared out 'Don't show her the verminous room!' And when a journalist who had promised to write up the inn in his newspaper arrived at the Spreadeagle with a female companion obviously not his wife, with whom he proposed to share a bed: 'You're not married and I discourage indiscriminate coupling here.' The journalist hastily departed and the piece remained unwritten.

He made no pretence of tolerating working-class customers, objecting vociferously when he had to serve a charabanc party of 'great burly, black broad cloth-suited brutes' from the East End. In the Thame area he quickly acquired the reputation of a ruthless snob, who was alleged to bully people who turned up in little cars but was 'all over' parties in Rolls-Royces. Yet he describes the Spanish royal family, who arrived unannounced one day, as 'a pretty girl and her husband, with three gentlemen who looked like butlers discharged for taking liberties'. Certainly class mattered to him; he would refuse written applications for rooms 'simply because we don't know the people, or the writing or the address don't please', even though the hotel was barely paying its way. But appearance, behaviour and intelligence mattered more, and he summed up his policy thus: 'I've determined not only to have proper and properly cooked food but to have only either intelligent, beautiful or well-bred people to eat it.' He welcomed into the Spreadeagle only those he would have invited into his private house. It may be objected that he was playing the squire when he was really a tradesman; yet his behaviour, brought within reasonable limits, set the style for the patrician hotel proprietor or restaurateur, who until that time was almost a contradiction in terms. Fothergill himself says he was 'the first educated person to take and make an Inn after his own kind'.

The Spreadeagle was furnished like a home rather than a hotel. All the tables and chairs were Georgian or early Victorian, no two sets being identical, and meals were served on a fine collection of china; Fothergill describes the annual Fellows' Dinner of Oriel College, headed by the seventy-five-year-old Provost Phelps, being eaten off Ming and Crown Derby, with a Queen Anne coffee-pot to follow, all on a big round Regency table with a rosewood and brass inlay. (One of the Fellows, thanking Fothergill, described it as 'the pleasantest evening in our joint lives'.) Turkish Delight would be handed round on a Sunderland plate with the words 'Prepare To Meet Thy God'. Harold Acton and Robert Byron, conducting their early Victorian campaign, were promised loans of several such items from Fothergill for their planned exhibition of domestic ornaments from that period – though the display was banned without explanation by the Proctors before it could take place.

The food was not very expensive; a set dinner cost five shillings, the average charge for such a meal at this time. Fothergill himself did most of the cooking, and would adjust the bill as he saw fit. He once told the waitress to charge a party sixpence a head extra because they were all so ugly; on the other hand he marked an enormous bill run up by John Betjeman 'Less £6 for extravagance.' Tom Driberg says he would refuse to bring out his better wines if he thought the customers were incapable of appreciating them.

He constructed his menu from 'all the things I had found best wherever I'd been'. He would take delivery each day from three different bakers 'of bread made from flours that I have forced upon them'. Cheese came from East Harptree, salt from Malden, mustard from Newport Pagnell, and sausages, 'after a romantic search all over England', from the International Stores in Thame. If a guest suggested some slight change in the menu, Fothergill was liable to respond: 'Everything has been to my utmost satisfaction.'

He would be in evidence himself while the meal was served, dressed in an outfit of his own invention, a knee-length white coat such as a butcher or doctor might wear, and shoes with buckles. He would say of this: 'Every tradesman ought to wear a uniform.' He drove a four-wheeled dog-cart, in which he would deliver orders of wines and spirits to local country houses, where he was invariably treated as 'trade' and sent round to the servants' entrance.

Behind the Spreadeagle, he laid out a remarkable garden containing approximately seven hundred species of plants, over a hundred of them aromatics, so that the place was especially entrancing in the dark of a summer night. The path was tapered to give the illusion of greater distance, and at the end was painted on the wall a *trompe l'oeil*, described by Fothergill as 'cubist mountains'. There was also a row of Babylonian willows, 'which I planted in weeping memory of a barmaid for giving notice'.

Despite the enormous popularity of the Spreadeagle with the Harold Acton set, and the frequent patronage of London intellectuals, Fothergill failed to make a proper living for himself and his family, and in 1932 sold the inn for less than half what he had paid for it, moving to the Royal Hotel at Ascot, where for a while he kept elephants in the stables, using them to erect a set of full-sized dolmens in the hotel courtyard. They also provided several tons of manure for the garden. But again the venture was a financial failure, and Fothergill moved in 1934 to the Three Swans in Market Harborough, which he ran successfully until his retirement eighteen years later. He died in 1957.

While Fothergill was still at Thame, Evelyn Waugh visited the hotel frequently. Rather surprisingly he makes no mention of Fothergill in his memoirs, but there can be little doubt that the character of the gentleman inkeeper – his accomplished rudeness to those he despised, his unashamed contempt for charabanc parties and shoddy journalists, his determination to maintain the standards and style of a better age – deeply impressed him. When in 1928 he published his first novel, *Decline and Fall*, he gave a copy to Fothergill, inscribed to 'John Fothergill, Oxford's only civilizing influence'. Fothergill read the book with delight, recognizing in it his own sense of humour. Then he chained it up in the hotel lavatory, whence he had previously lost a good many treasured books, describing it as the 'best comedy in the English language'.

Dinner at Fothergill's was available nightly to those with the means and the motor-car. Another dinner took place only once a term, in curious surroundings. On 30 May 1923 *Isis* reported: 'The Aberdeen–Penzance express has been adopted as the official train of the Oxford University Railway Club. The motto is: "There is no smoke without fire." '

The founder of the Railway Club was John Sutro, a Trinity undergraduate from a well-off Jewish family living in St John's Wood. Waugh writes of his home: 'It was there – not as described in *Brideshead Revisited* – that I first tasted plovers' eggs.' It was usually Sutro's money that kept *Cherwell* afloat during the period that Waugh was contributing drawings to it, though Sutro readily let other people edit it and did not force his own writings or views on the paper. Rubber-featured, with an engaging grin, he is described by Harold Acton as 'a consummate actor, mimic, improviser, journalist, vocalist, pianist, and gastronomist'. Waugh records that, in conversation, 'he spoke in many voices. It was, indeed, rather rare for him to speak *in propria persona*.' He calls Sutro 'above all humorous; a mimic of genius. . . . He has never wearied of a friend or quarrelled with one. . . . loyal, hospitable.'

Sutro was a fervant enthusiast for the British railway system, whose plethora of independent companies had been 'grouped' in 1922 into four leviathans – the Great Western; the London Midland & Scottish; the London and North Eastern; and the Southern – but which still retained many local idiosyncracies. Waugh writes of Sutro's enthusiasm: 'John was a genuine amateur of the railway system and knew his Bradshaw as my father and brother knew their Wisden.' Sutro was probably the author of an article in *Cherwell* on 3 November 1923 (an issue largely devoted to trains) which argues that 'it is only when in the train that even the most self-sufficient man must recognize that he had not even the smallest control over his destiny'.

In the first term of the Railway Club's existence, the summer of 1923, a few members travelled informally from Oxford to Leicester and back in an evening, dining in one restaurant car on the way out and buying drinks in another on the return journey. The route was chosen not just because of the convenience of a dining car each way (on the through train from the West of England to Scotland), but because it involved running over the metals and travelling in the trains of two different companies, the Great Western providing the rolling-stock for the outward journey and the LNER that for the return. But only Sutro cared for these details; to the rest of them, as Waugh writes, 'it was merely an original way in which to spend a jovial evening'. Eccentric dinners were fashionable in Oxford. Billy Clonmore gave a supper party on the roof of the church of St Peter in the East, and there was a club in Balliol named the *Hysteron–Proteron* (Greek for 'back to front'), whose members, says Waugh, 'put themselves to great discomfort by living a day in reverse, getting up in evening dress, drinking whisky, smoking cigars and playing cards, then at ten o'clock dining backwards starting with savouries and ending with soup'.

Following the success of the first Railway Club trip, Sutro organized a more elaborate evening, on 28 November 1923, though characteristically at the same time he announced his imminent resignation as president ('M. le Chef de Gare'); Richard Pares agreed to take his place. Sutro did, however, write up this journey for *Cherwell*. A private dining car was reserved to Leicester, another for the return journey, and members were encouraged to invite guests; Sutro records that 'Mr Alastair Graham' had 'specially journeyed from London for the occasion.' Also present was 'Dr Counsell, whose green smoking jacket contrasted admirably with the dull magenta cushions in the Restaurant Car'. H. E. Counsell was an elderly Oxford doctor who lived opposite the Sheldonian Theatre in what Osbert Lancaster says 'were generally held to be the Duke of Dorset's old lodgings' (in *Zuleika Dobson*), wore a broad-brimmed hat and a flowing cape, invariably acted as prompter at performances of the OUDS, and was reputed to have 'a magic touch with the clap'. This skill was of doubtful relevance to Oxford in 1923, but 'Doggins', as he was generally known, also ran what Waugh calls 'his own welfare service' for undergraduates in emotional tangles with their own sex.

The party left Oxford soon after seven p.m., on the Penzance–Aberdeen express. 'The Great Western Railway Company', writes Sutro,

> had provided a magnificent collation for the Club, which the steward of the restaurant car served to us with splendid courtesy and efficiency. I cannot resist giving the menu, and side by side the stations at which the viands changed in their courses:
>
> 7.20 – Bletchington: Hors d'oeuvres.
> 7.33 – Fritwell and Somerton: Crème de Céléri.
> 7.45 – Aynho: Fillet de Sole, Poche Sauce Dieppoise.
> 7.51 – King's Sutton: Roast Chicken and Sausage.

Waugh points out that this was not a specially ordered meal, but 'the ordinary five shilling menu (seven courses in those days)'. Sutro's timetable continues:

> 7.58 – Banbury: Cauliflower, Brussels Sprouts, Potatoes. (Stop.)
> 8.15 – Woodford and Hinton: Cranberry Apple Tart and Cream. Mousse Framboise.
> 8.37 – Rugby: Cheese and Biscuits. (Stop.)
> 8.43 – Lutterworth: Dessert, Coffee, etc.
> 9.00 – Leicester, Central: L'Addition.

Since they all had to be back in college by midnight, it was essential that the train kept to time, and Sutro records that 'a note of peril' slightly marred the dinner because there was some delay in arriving at Banbury. 'The half-formed question was on everyone's lips: "Should we fail to catch our return express at Leicester and not arrive in Oxford till 3.48 a.m.?"' This did not stop Terence Greenidge from trying to get out of the train when it reached Rugby, where he had been to school. Sutro applauds this 'fine sentimentalism' and says that Greenidge 'was with difficulty frustrated by the Chef de Gare'. Dr Counsell generously offered to put them all up for the night should they miss the connection, after which 'we thrust it from our minds'.

They had intended to hold their first Annual General Meeting in the Refreshment Rooms at Leicester, but there was no time. A hurried farewell to engine driver, steward and chef, and the Club dashed to board the Aberdeen–Penzance express, which had already been 12 odd hours on its way. We entered the North-Eastern restaurant car this time ... [for] a rapid general meeting. M. le Chef de Gare resigned his position, and Mr Pares was unanimously elected in his stead; Mr Henderson was elected Guard, and Mr Acton Conducteur.

Toasts were drunk, to the King, to 'his late, more congenial Majesty Edward the Seventh', to the railway companies, and to the steward of the train. Dr Counsell then proposed the health of the club 'in a superb oration. ... He took the Club with rich fancy to Vienna and Rome, and sketched a glorious programme for future functions. ... But we are already at Banbury, and there is scant time for Mr Acton, the new Conducteur, to make his speech.' Waugh records: 'On the return journey Harold's speech was the chief pleasure.' Acton praised the railway as a manifestation of early Victorianism, citing Turner's celebrated 'Rain, Steam, and Speed'. Then the train steamed into Oxford. 'The Club,' writes Sutro,

> holding aloft the signals which had decorated the table, a procession of fourteen, in dinner jackets, ascended the hill from Oxford station with thankfulness in their hearts for their journey of 150 miles. They had given the answer to those who maintain that beauty and fantasy cannot be found in an industrial civilization; they had discovered the secret fascinations of the train.

The club continued its activities in the following months. Waugh drew and presented to Sutro a blackly comic tableau depicting 'The Tragical Death of Mr Will Huskisson' – the politician who was run over by a train at the opening of the Liverpool to Manchester Railway in 1830 – and this drawing was published in *Cherwell*. In the spring term of 1924, shortly before the annual Oxford–Cambridge Boat Race, *Cherwell* announced that the Railway Club would travel to Bletchley 'to compete against the Cambridge University Railway Club in the Semi-Final Round of the Huskisson Cup, which, as our readers are well aware, is offered annually for engine-racing with tender'. The report continued:

> Reviewing the prospects of the two teams, our Railway Correspondent writes: 'Cambridge are a team of fine individual players, but their diffi-culty, owing to lack of sufficient practice, is an inability to pull together. They are slow off the mark and when travelling at full steam their piston-

work is a little wild. Their fireman, however (Mr R. A. Butler)* is himself a magnificent worker and his stoking and regular shovelling does much to keep the team together. Oxford on the other hand are already stale. ... The inclusion of Acton at left buffer will probably strengthen the hands of the *Chef de Gare*.

Though this was spoof, Acton records that they did travel to Bletchley, the midway point between Oxford and Cambridge, to meet the Cambridge Railway Club. But the meeting was not a success, for the Cambridge contingent turned out to be serious students of railway engineering, who were greatly puzzled by the Oxford frivolities.

After he and his friends had left Oxford, Sutro would occasionally organize reunion dinners on other trains. 'Our journeys became longer and more adventurous,' writes Acton, and Waugh recalls how:

in later years, after we had gone down, our meetings became more elaborate and the membership widened to include friends of John's who had been at Cambridge or Sandhurst at the time of our formation. Chefs were then recruited from London restaurants and fine wines added to the fare. Silver cigarette-boxes were presented to astonished engine-drivers and reception committees met us at our destinations.

But it was hard to recapture the careless jollity of those original five-shilling dinners eaten between Oxford and Leicester. The last of these to be recorded in *Cherwell* was in June 1924, and this time the reporter was Terence Greenidge. On this occasion the LNER dining-car steward made a speech, in which 'he emphasized the rare and delightful sympathy which he and his colleagues felt' with the 'aims and aspirations' of the club. The fourteen members then adjourned to Dr Counsell's house, 'to taste Oxford's finest hospitality'. Greenidge sums up the evening as 'a dream too agreeable to last'.

Indeed, it was already dissolving. By the time this journey took place, many members of the Railway Club had reached the end of their three years at Oxford. Among those taking their Final Honours School examinations in the summer term of 1924 was Waugh.

He spent his final year living in lodgings in Merton Street with Hugh Lygon, younger brother of Lord Elmley. During this year he was sub-editor of *Isis*, and reviewed films for the magazine. The critiques were usually acid: 'Mr Barrymore looks exactly like a games master at some good public school. ... There was a drunk in *Mumming Birds* who looked exactly like Mr Arnold Bennett. ... I don't think I have ever

* The future Conservative Cabinet Minister was at this time President of the Cambridge Union.

been bored quite so much.' Another film was praised as 'intensely diverting; we have never seen anything to equal it for sheer, over-acted senseless sentiment'. In his penultimate term he also maliciously featured his tutor, Cruttwell, in an 'Isis Idol', describing him as 'a badger-like figure, clad in ancient tail coat and lop-sided white tie, which pads pensively northward across New College Lane, to go to earth near the desecrated ruins of the Octagon Bookshop'. He hinted that Cruttwell was a drunkard – 'Should we not all be the better for more malt and more hops within us ...?' And in another issue *Isis* printed a short story by him about a young man who hates his history tutor ('Curtis') so passionately that he decides to murder him. The undergraduate buys a dagger at an antique shop, attends a Union debate so as to acquire an alibi, and slips up to the tutor's rooms:

> His tutor had that habit, more fitting for a housemaster than a don, of continuing to read or write some few words after his visitors entered, in order to emphasize his superiority. It was while he was finishing his sentence that Edward killed him and the sentence was merged in a pool of blood. . . . It had been a good evening, Edward thought.

A titled and drunken undergraduate, Lord Poxe, is accused of the murder, and assumes that he did indeed commit it while inebriated, but the Warden decides to hush it up because 'my boy, you are the fifteenth Lord Poxe'. He is fined thirteen shillings and warned not to do it again. The story is slightly marred by the coda, in which it is revealed that, had the case come to trial, the Warden himself would have been a prime suspect, for his wife had been having an affair with the murdered man. Otherwise it is only a short step from *Decline and Fall*.

This gives some idea of the level to which relations with Cruttwell had descended. Also, Waugh was worried about money. He had run up enormous bills with local tradesmen, and his bank had refused to extend his overdraft; consequently during his last year he was obliged to hold a private auction of his more valuable books and pictures in order to obtain ready cash – Peter Quennell remembers 'a boisterous luncheon party where I bought his Nonesuch *Donne*'. He increased his debts further, however, by panicking about his academic work and buying large quantities of history books on credit in the hope that he could still 'master the neglected texts'.

In the spring of 1924, the term before his final examinations, he seems to have become active homosexually. He told Christopher Sykes that while at Oxford he had experienced an 'extreme homosexual phase'

(Sykes's words) which, for the short time it lasted, was 'unrestrained, emotionally and physically'. There appears to be an allusion to this in a letter to Dudley Carew from Oxford this spring:

> My life here has been extremely precarious. . . . At present I am keeping my balance but I may crash at any moment. We will then combine and run a Sadist brothel at Wigan. . . . Of course no one in our class need ever starve because he can always go as a prep school master not a pleasant job but all roads lead to Sodom.

And in another letter to Carew:

> I have been living very intensely the last three weeks. For the last fortnight I have been nearly insane. I am a little saner now. My diary for the period is destroyed. I may perhaps one day in a later time tell you some of the things that have happened. It will make strange reading in the biography.

And from a third letter to Carew this spring:

> St John [his third name] has been eating wild honey in the wilderness. I do not yet know how things are going to end. They are nearing some sort of finality. One day I will tell you things to surprise you and sell an edition of the biography if faithfully recorded.

Christopher Sykes, who either knew everything or was pretending to, writes of this in his official life of Waugh: 'Names and details need not and should not be given.' Possibly Waugh was now going to bed with Alastair Graham, but Harold Acton thinks this is unlikely – he believes that Graham's attractiveness to Waugh was increased by the chastity of their relationship. Possibly it was Hugh Lygon, handsome and fair-haired, with whom Waugh was sharing digs. Those who knew Hugh claim to perceive traces of him in the character of Sebastian in *Brideshead Revisited*. At all events this homosexual episode or phase, whatever it was and whomever it involved, passed swiftly and was not to be repeated. Waugh's letters to Carew suggest that it did not disturb his conscience. It was part of the process of relaxing his emotional guard, of lowering the defences he had carefully constructed at school, a process that had been going on steadily since he arrived at Oxford.

Possibly this sudden outburst of carnality further distracted him from his studies. He still hoped that 'comparative seclusion' in his final term might get him a Second Class degree, and even after sitting the papers in June did not give up this hope, though 'I was uneasily aware as I left the Examination Schools that the questions had been rather inconvenient.' On his last night in Oxford he attended a party in Balliol, was let out of Richard Pares's window 'by a string' some time after midnight, and travelled home to London next day in the luncheon car, 'at the next table to poor Brian Howard'. At the end of July he was back in Oxford for his *viva voce* (oral examination), but it was clearly a mere formality, and he telegraphed to his parents to warn them that he had certainly got a Third. When the expected result came, Crutwell wrote of the Third that it was 'not even a good one'.

To qualify for the Bachelor of Arts degree to which he was entitled despite his poor result, Evelyn would have had to complete a further, ninth term in residence at the University. His scholarship had been revoked as a result of his Third, so Arthur Waugh – who looked on Evelyn's result with some sympathy, having got a Third himself – decided it would be a waste of time and money for Evelyn to go back to Hertford, and instead 'entered me at an art school'.

When writing to Evelyn about his result, Cruttwell did allow that a Third was 'an inappropriate intellectual label' for him, and concluded: 'I hope you will soon settle in some sphere where you will give your intellect a better chance.'

Waugh's Third was typical of his circle. Only one member of it, Richard Pares, achieved a First; Terence Greenidge, Claud Cockburn and Graham Greene managed Seconds, but Thirds or worse were common. Robert Byron, Cyril Connolly, Christopher Hollis and Anthony Powell were among those to whom Thirds were awarded; Powell could not even console himself by saying that he had done no work. 'On the contrary, I had worked quite hard, though without the least sense of direction.' Harold Acton took a Fourth in Modern Languages, and Osbert Lancaster the same class in English. Several people did not take their degrees at all. Alan Pryce-Jones survived at Magdalen for only two terms, which he 'wasted . . . recklessly'. Henry Yorke, reading English, found that he could not learn Anglo-Saxon and that 'literature is not a subject to write essays about', so he left before his time was up. Edward James drifted away from Oxford without attempting the examinations. John Betjeman was sent down for failing persistently in 'Divvers', the compulsory examination in Holy Scripture; his tutor C.S. Lewis told him: 'You'd have only got a Third.' Maurice Bowra suggested that since Betjeman was devoted to ecclesiastical minutiae and 'Divvers' was notoriously easy, he must have unconsciously wished to fail, perhaps because he had not done enough work for finals, perhaps as some more fundamental protest against conventional intellectual achievement.

In a sense, Oxford had given them nothing, or at least they took away nothing conventional from it. But they had none of them needed the intellectual stimulus and training that Oxford claimed to offer. They had already acquired it at school. Connolly was immensely well read in classical literature by the time he came up to Balliol; Waugh had learnt the cadences of the English language from Roxburgh; Acton was immersed in European culture to a degree that few Oxford dons could rival; Betjeman had devoted himself to the study of architecture; Yorke was already writing his first novel. Oxford teaching in the early 1920s was at a very low ebb; reforms were beginning to come in – C. S. Lewis and J. R. R. Tolkien managed to recast the English syllabus in the late 1920s – but they were too late for the Waugh generation. Betjeman complained, writing to Lewis in 1939, that he had come to Oxford in search of aestheticism and found only pedantry: 'It was my ambition to become a don and read English literature to the accompaniment of lovely surroundings.' Instead he found Lewis 'reading philology in . . . that white unlived-in room of yours . . . with the tobacco jars and fixture cards'.

Waugh and his contemporaries rightly ignored the poor intellectual fare that was on Oxford's official menu, and instead used the place as a testing-ground for a new lifestyle in which writers and artists might flourish. Osbert Lancaster observes that until the 1920s English intellectuals were expected to be pillars of conventional society. On the Continent, the intelligentsia were recognized as a separate group and allowed a certain laxity of behaviour; those Englishmen who wished to follow this pattern felt obliged to exile themselves, generally to Italy, in order to do so. If they remained in England, they were expected to be 'indistinguishable in appearance and behaviour from the great army of Victorian clubmen. . . . The *haute Bohème* did not exist and the Athenaeum rather than the Closerie des Lilas shaped the social life of the literary world.' In the 1890s there had been a brief attempt to create a café society for the arts – the Café Royal life of the Wilde group – but thanks to Wilde's arrest this was very short-lived. Now, Waugh and his friends were renewing the attempt.

They were doing it at exactly the same time (1923–5) that the young American exiles of the Hemingway generation were trying the same thing in Montparnasse – again, an attempt to create a new ambience in which art and literature could flourish without social constraints. The English attempt was self-confidently self-sufficient; Harold Acton might praise Gertrude Stein, Bakst and Diaghilev – he was frequently rushing off to the Continent for first-hand contact with such people, and he brought Gertrude Stein to Oxford while he was still an under-graduate – but most of the Waugh circle were brazenly insular, choosing instead to derive stimulus and inspiration from their friends' foibles, and by cultivating that profoundly English thing, a sense of humour.

Once they had passed from Oxford, they left little trace upon the place. Brian Howard, lingering there as late as June 1927 for a second attempt at his final examinations in Law, realized that he belonged to 'the Acton period', which was now over; Oxford had 'gone dead'. This was not strictly true: there now came the Auden period, in its way as lively as the Acton, with W. H. Auden presiding over Spender, Day Lewis and MacNeice in a self-proclaimed attempt to revitalize the English arts. (Auden got a Third too.) Acton rightly describes the Auden group as his 'successors', and says they were 'organized so well that poetry at Oxford was assured of a long lease of life. They regarded me as a minor versifier since I lacked a political message. . . . I had been suspiciously enterprising and far too gay . . . a "decorative dilettante", etc.'

Osbert Lancaster, revisiting Oxford during the 1930s, found it rapidly changing culturally, thanks largely to the influence of the Auden group. In Blackwell's bookshop the 'rainbow hues' of the collected works of Ronald Firbank were soon overwhelmed by the 'yellow flood' of Gollancz's Left Book Club. 'The recorded strains of "Happy days are here again" floating across the summer quad were drowned by the melancholy cadences of "Hyfrydwl" chanted live by Welsh miners trekking southwards down the High. . . . All over Oxford the lights, if they were not yet actually going out, were starting ominously to flicker.'

Bright Young People

1

Struggle for Detachment

'I suppose I must get a job,' Cyril Connolly wrote to Maurice Bowra after hearing that he had got a Third. Bowra did not respond; he was not one of those dons like Sligger who tried to arrange careers for their undergraduates. Graham Greene describes as 'ominous' the realization that the moment had arrived to find employment – the feeling that one must now bear personal responsibility for the future. There was an Oxford Appointments Board to help graduates choose jobs, but Greene felt that it offered only a choice of different prisons, 'for how else at twenty can one regard a career ...?' Having ignored the conventional world for three years, one suddenly came face to face with it.

The most obvious job was teaching, and many of Greene's and Connolly's contemporaries passed almost without a thought through the doors of Gabbitas & Thring, scholastic agents (Auden dubbed them 'Rabbitarse and String'). It seemed slightly less grim than an office job, and might allow time for writing. This was Betjeman's experience when he went down from Oxford in the summer of 1928:

> Ah, welcome door, Gabbitas Thring & Co's
> Scholastic agency in Sackville Street!
> 'The Principal will see you.' 'No degree?
> There is, perhaps, a temporary post
> As cricket master for the coming term
> At Gerrard's Cross. Fill in this form and give
> Qualifications – testimonials

> Will help – and if you are accepted, please
> Pay our commission promptly. Well, good day!'

So Betjeman became 'A prep-school master teaching Games, / Maths, French, Divinity' at Thorpe House School, Gerrard's Cross, run by a Mr Noble. 'Harsh hand-bells hurried me from sleep / For thirty pounds a term and keep.'

He lasted there for a few months, then tried a spell as private secretary to an Irish public servant, Sir Horace Plunkett, then returned to teaching, this time at Heddon Court, Cockfosters, Hertfordshire, obtaining the job by pretending that he was good at cricket.

> 'The sort of man we want must be prepared
> To take our first eleven . . .'
> Oh where's mid-on? And what is silly point?
> Do six balls make an over. Help me, God!

In this poem, 'Cricket Master (An Incident)', two other masters take Betjeman to the nets for cricket practice, after which one of them mutters to him: 'D'you know what Winters told me, Betjeman? / *He didn't think you'd ever held a bat.*'

One day Waugh visited him at the school, and they had lunch together in a pub in Barnet, and (says Betjeman) drank 'a lot of very strong beer, and I was so drunk when I came back that I wasn't able to take the game of football, and the boys kindly took me up to my room and never said anything about it. That was the effect Evelyn had on my schoolmastering. . . .' Waugh says he told Betjeman facetiously on this or a similar occasion: 'You will remember these schooldays as the happiest time of your life.'

Connolly took a tutoring job, sailing for Jamaica, where he spent a few months coaching a thirteen-year-old boy who had been removed from Marlborough after a rugger accident. But, for Graham Greene, 'the one opening I simply couldn't face was that of teaching. . . . No doubt because of my sad experience at school . . . I was convinced that once in I'd never get out again.' So Greene applied for, and was accepted by, the British American Tobacco Company, which proposed to take him out to China. He sat for a couple of weeks in 'a large office like a classroom', then discovered that China would mean three compulsory years in the Shanghai office on a poor salary without being allowed to marry. Since he was involved in another love affair he decided to resign his post. In consequence he found himself walking through the door of Gabbitas & Thring, which he calls 'the last hope of those needing a little temporary aid. You pawned yourself instead of your watch.'

It was late in the season, and all they could offer him was a tutoring job in Derbyshire, unpaid but with accommodation in a hotel and full board. When he accepted, the interviewer 'looked at me with disappointment and suspicion – there must be something disgracefully wrong in my background'. And so Greene found himself in the Pennines, looking after the son of a widow who did not want her boy overworked. 'A little mathematics perhaps in the morning (I had forgotten all I ever knew), a quarter of an hour of Latin (equally forgotten). . . .' He decided to occupy the lad with carpentry, about which he knew as little as Betjeman about cricket. Together they attempted to build a toy theatre, which failed to take recognizable shape. 'After two days' work I decided that what we had been making without knowing was a rabbit hutch. He was quite satisfied. . . .'

In a way, the job suited Greene, 'for I had the evenings free when I could work at my novel'. He had already completed one novel while still at Balliol; he recalls that its subject,

> like so many first novels, was childhood and unhappiness. The first chapter described the hero's birth in an old country house . . . a black child born of white parents – a throwback to some remote ancestor. . . . There followed . . . a hushed-up childhood and a lonely colour-barred life at school.

It was a reworking of his own lonely childhood and school career, when he had been 'colour-barred' by being the Headmaster's son. His fictional hero ran away from home and joined a ship at Cardiff as one of the black deckhands, thereby escaping from the sense of being an outsider. Greene sent the book to the literary agent A.D. Peters, who wrote back enthusiastically, calling it eminently publishable, but as the months passed and no publisher proved willing to take it on, the enthusiasm faded from Peters's letters. Greene also had a verse collection, *Babbling April*, published by Blackwell's at Oxford during 1925. Harold Acton gave it a sneering review in *Cherwell*, castigating Greene for the banal expression of very ordinary emotions – 'the slender banjo-tunes of an adolescent hysteria'. Greene got the message 'that I wasn't a poet either'.

By the time hope had died for his first novel, a second was under way. This time the setting was Victorian and the stylistic model Joseph Conrad. The hero, another young Englishman wishing to escape from his own background, became involved in plots against the Spanish Government, and had a love affair with an exotic Spanish lady. 'I called the novel rather drably *The Episode*.' He worked at it in the intervals of making the rabbit hutch.

Cyril Connolly tried a novel too. When he came back from tutoring in Jamaica, Sligger fixed him up with a job as secretary to Logan Pearsall Smith, man of letters and aphorist; Connolly also obtained some reviewing and proof-reading from Desmond MacCarthy, literary editor of the *New Statesman*. His own first attempt at a book was a collection of *pensées* much in the Pearsall Smith style, and he offered it rather diffidently to Anthony Powell, who had taken a job at Duckworth's the London publishers, obtained through the kindness of his father's friend Thomas Balston (who had published Harold Acton's *Aquarium*). Powell and others made encouraging noises, but Connolly felt he ought to try and achieve a reputation with a novel first. He duly began work on a book reflecting the situation many of his contemporaries were in: 'a novel which would begin with the hero in a waiting-room of Gabbitas and Thring'. Connolly did not get very far with the book, which was to be called *Green Endings*, partly because it seemed too obvious an imitation of the most popular novelist of the moment, Michael Arlen.

Harold Acton set out deliberately to copy Arlen's *The Green Hat* (1924), a melodramatic romance of Mayfair life, and began work on a novel called *Humdrum*. 'The plot', he writes,

> was lively, contrasting the vicissitudes of two sisters, Linda, fast and fashionable, and Joan, conventional and 'county'. Gradually they reverse roles, Joan sliding down the primrose path and Linda landing in the country. But disgust with the style I had assumed got the better of me and the novel turned sour in the writing.

Nevertheless the book was completed and accepted for publication, and Acton began to hope he could live off literature: 'My parents gave me a liberal allowance on the understanding that I was ... to achieve some tangible evidence of literary success ... within three years. ... I felt I had to hurry.' He says it was considered *de rigueur* to begin with fiction. 'There was no escape from that first novel. ...'

Henry Yorke's novel, *Blindness*, which he had begun at Eton and finished while at Oxford, was not a Michael Arlen imitation. The Woolfs at the Hogarth Press accepted it and brought it out in 1926, with the author's name given as 'Henry Green'. Definitely 'experimental', it was written in a low-key, vaguely modernist manner that Harold Acton calls 'aloof and unpredictable', an attempt to narrate with 'scientific impartiality'. The book concerns John Haye, a sixth-former at 'Noat' (Eton) who has founded a Society of Arts with his friends Seymour (Harold Acton) and B.G. (Brian Howard). On the way home for the holidays, John is blinded when a small boy carelessly throws a stone through the train window, and the novel describes his paradoxical increase in vision and imagination as a result of this physical handicap.

The acceptance of *Blindness* by the Hogarth Press made Yorke 'the most popular man of my year' at Magdalen, 'the only undergraduate member of an exclusive London club'. Yet by choosing the authorial name 'Henry Green' he seemed to be aiming not at mere pseudonymity, but at anonymity. This was all of a piece with his decision to go and work for a while as an anonymous factory operative in his family's business in Birmingham.

'I had a complex,' he writes of this decision, 'a sense of guilt whenever I spoke to someone who did manual work . . . and in the end it drove me to go and work in a factory.' Alan Ross describes Yorke two decades later, when he was still working there, though by then on the managerial side:

> I never remember Henry in anything other than a dark grey suit and sober tie. He wore a trilby in the street and carried or wore a raincoat. He was as deeply conventional in his appearance and views, as fearful of drawing attention in person, as he was adventurous in his writing.

In his early days in the factory, Yorke lived in lodgings and worked a forty-eight-hour week, first in the stores, then as a pattern-maker, then in the iron and brass foundries, then as a coppersmith. 'I . . . wrote at night.' Waugh visited him at the factory in 1930, and was 'chiefly impressed by the manual dexterity of the workers. Nothing in the least like mass labour or mechanization – pure arts and crafts.' The firm, Pontifex, made (among other things) lavatories, and Waugh christened Henry 'Mr H. Yorke the lavatory king'.

Graham Greene soon found himself in industrial surroundings too, in Nottingham. After the tutoring had finished, he took an unpaid trainee sub-editorship on the *Nottingham Journal* in the hope of thereby qualifying himself for Fleet Street. Here, in grim lodgings, he laboured at his Spanish novel, turning out five hundred words a day, though he was already 'half aware' that it would never be published. Almost the only person not trying to write a novel was Brian Howard, now drifting about London and living off his mother, who would not give him a regular allowance but paid his debts when his cheques had proved worthless. Brian said he would wait a little before turning novelist: 'I prefer to let my juvenilia remain in my notebooks. I don't want to be handicapped, in the future, by a mass of bad early stuff.'

*

135

Evelyn Waugh resumed his diary on the day he went down from Oxford – or at least from this point on he preserved the diary. Back at Hampstead, there was nothing much to do besides potter round London with Alastair Graham and other Oxford friends, so in his spare time he too began to write a novel: 'I began "The Temple at Thatch" last night [20 July 1924] and have written a dozen pages of the first chapter.' It was about an undergraduate who inherited a property of which nothing remained but an eighteenth-century classical folly, where he set up house 'and, I think, practised black magic' (writes Waugh in his memoirs, recalling this long-vanished fragment). He worked at it intermittently during the summer, and by the beginning of September feared that it was 'becoming dull'. Evidently he had not found the prose equivalent of the wit in his drawings.

And yet in his diary he *had* found it. The immediately post-Oxford entries are full of comic distortions of real events and people, experiments in verbal caricature:

> I arrived home to find a wire from Alastair asking him to meet me for dinner. .... There we found a sweet drunk man called Wilkinson who had been at Radley. Soon we were joined by the foul Tasha Gielgud [a Russian noblewoman, sister-in-law of John Gielgud] and in her company a pert young woman dressed almost wholly as a man. ... We managed in the end to get rid of them only by leaving the restaurant ourselves and putting them to lesbianize in a taxi.

And again:

> Luckily when I arrived at Baldhead's [Alec Waugh's] dinner they were all quite drunk. .... A ghastly hullooing outside the windows announced the arrival of Tony Bushell [an actor friend of Evelyn's], indescribably drunken, waving a bowler hat in one hand and an umbrella in the other and carolling his desire to rape Lady Calthrop. He was unsuccessful in this but stripped himself naked in preparation for the act.

His letters repeat such half-invented anecdotes almost verbatim. Of one such, he writes in the diary: 'This story is not really quite true but I have recounted it in so many letters that I have begun to believe it.'

Another medium which suggested itself for humorous experiments was the cinema. During the summer term of 1924 at Oxford, the surviving Hypocrites had made a comic film. *Isis* reported on 14 May: 'Work has apparently started on the great Hypocrites' super film. ... No expense has been spared, and the early scenes of the film, taken from the top of the Radder [Radcliffe Camera], have already been perfected at the cost of several thousand wasted feet.' Neither *Isis* nor Waugh's diary record the subject of the film. It was viewed by Waugh, Greenidge and others of their circle in London in July 1924, and it pleased Waugh enough for him to decide, a few days after watching it, to 'produce a cinema film about the Pope and the Prince of Wales'.

As temporary film critic for *Isis*, though he sneered at most creations by Hollywood and the British studios, Waugh had perceived some potential in the medium. 'The real charm of the cinema', he wrote in one of his articles,

> is in the momentary pictures and situations which appear. There were two of these in *The Merry-go-Round* which made any shortcomings immeasurably worth while. One was the gorilla standing in the window before it killed the circus-master, and the other, a little before it, was the scene in which the villain pursued the heroine round the half-lighted merry-go-round. The violent struggle in the strange, unmoving jungle of monstrous animals was almost Sitwellian.
>
> It was a pity that the management did not show a comic film. . . .

Momentary images on the screen often achieved the stark impact of his Lovat Fraser-style caricatures, in a way that (as far as he could yet tell) prose did not. He began to soak himself in films; during the summer after coming down from Oxford he went endlessly to the cinema to idle away the afternoons and evenings – the diary records 'excess of cinemas'. His plan, with Terence Greenidge, to write and make a comic film was partly just an attempt to dispel *ennui*, but was also prompted by a real curiosity about what he could achieve in the medium.

He devised an absurd plot, about an attempt by the Pope to convert England to Catholicism using Sligger as his secret agent – evidently Sligger's Catholicism seemed as absurd to Waugh as did his ridiculous salon. Terence Greenidge, his brother, John Sutro and Waugh all put up five pounds each, a camera was acquired and work began. Filming mostly took place in the Waughs' garden at Hampstead, augmented by a few other locations in London and Oxford. Casting was chiefly done from the Hypocrites' ranks, with the addition of Alec Waugh and a red-headed girl called Elsa Lanchester (not yet a professional actress, but managing a night club in Charlotte Street) who was drafted in as the only actress; Waugh rewarded her with 'a dinner which cost £4 . . . a most jolly evening'.

In his memoirs, Waugh passes off the project as chiefly Greenidge's work – 'Terence produced a cinema film' – but the film's opening titles state : '*Evelyn Waugh / By arrangement with Terence Greenidge / presents /* "THE SCARLET WOMAN" / *an Ecclesiastical Melodrama. / Story by Evelyn Waugh*'. This suggests that Greenidge did little more than provide encouragement and help with what was essentially Waugh's own creation.

Most of the performances are on the level of country-house charades – for example the appearance by Evelyn's brother Alec, as 'Chiara, mother of the ambitious Cardinal Montefiasco', a bulky figure in a straw bonnet and dress, making eyes at the Pope while swigging brown ale from a bottle. The notable exception is Evelyn himself, who appears as 'the Dean of Balliol, leading Catholic layman of England'. In a crude blond wig caricaturing Sligger's hairstyle, Waugh simpers, flutters his eyelashes, strokes a soda syphon sensuously, and makes blatantly erotic advances to the Prince of Wales. This combination of predatory homosexuality with Catholic intrigue was probably derived from Ronald Firbank's *Valmouth*, where amid the sexual nuances there wander Catholic priests similarly intent upon recruitment. But the characterization is all Waugh's own, a masterpiece of mime – the film is, of course, silent – and an indication that he had fully inherited his father's histrionic powers.

The Scarlet Woman was nearly complete by the beginning of September 1924, but when he saw what had been shot and edited, Waugh was 'quite disgusted with the badness. ... I feel no enthusiasm to finish it.' Possibly he was disappointed with the crudeness of most of the acting. In fact the film is a brilliant *jeu d'esprit*, satirizing both the Church – indeed the Church of England and the evangelicals as well as Roman Catholicism – to an extent which suggests a profound contempt for religion, and mocking the genre of the melodramatic silent cinema. It shows how Waugh, in this early exercise in story-telling, has learnt the value of the short one-joke scene as a way of constructing a narrative. There also appear for the first time typical Waugh protagonists – Sligger and Montefiasco, forerunners of such characters as Grimes and Basil Seal – distortions (but not very great distortions) of recognizable types or individuals, possessors of demonic energy who are utterly unscrupulous in pursuing their ends.

Waugh never made another film, but his fiction owes much to the cinema; arguably it has more in common with it than with other works of literature. To the end of his life, he remained passionately enthusiastic for the work of the great screen comics. In 1947 he called Charlie Chaplin 'a great artist', and in the same year he remarked that the Marx Brothers' *A Night at the Opera*, which he had seen when it was first released, was still 'exquisitely funny'. His own performance as Sligger suggests that, had he not turned novelist, he could have made his name as a comic screen actor.

The Scarlet Woman was never shown in public, but received several private screenings in Oxford and London; Christopher Sykes says it 'became a legend rather than an experience' for most of Waugh's friends. Father Martindale of Campion Hall, a Catholic house in the University of Oxford, heard about it while it was being completed – he had recently instructed Alastair Graham, who was being received into the Church of Rome (an event which may have inspired the film's plot) – and asked if he could see it. Waugh was doubtful, but it was shown to him, and the Jesuit, far from taking offence, 'laughed till his tears flowed'. It was arranged that he should add an official *imprimatur* of the Church to the front of the film, and it appears after the opening titles:

NIHIL OBSTAT

PROJICIATUR

C. C. Martindale, SJ

Arthur Waugh had enjoyed seeing his garden full of film actors – 'so much like the private theatricals of his youth', writes Evelyn – but when they departed and autumn came, Evelyn found home life oppressive. His father had enrolled him at an art school, choosing Heatherley's in Newman Street, in the south of Fitzrovia, which advertised itself as 'A Paris Studio in London', but really catered for aspiring commercial draughtsmen rather than the artistically minded. Evelyn attended conscientiously for a month, and admits that he learnt quite a lot from the life classes – 'my eye grew sharpened and my hand quite responsive' – but found that he had no interest in depicting human features *per se*, and was only attracted by 'making an agreeable arrangement of line and shadow on the paper'. (Many years later he would say of his work as a novelist that words interested him more than the delineation of character.)

He began to spend weekends in Oxford, drinking riotously with old friends. 'To breakfast at the OUDS with Hugh Lygon, to Mass with Billy [Clonmore] at Pusey House, to sherry in Beaumont Street with Kolkhorst . . ..' 'At about this stage of the evening my recollections become somewhat blurred. I got a sword from somewhere and got into Balliol somehow and was let out of a window at some time having mocked Arden [Hilliard] and Tony Powell and talked very seriously to Peter Quennell. . . .' A new acquaintance made during these week-ends was 'a lean, dark, singular man named Henry Yorke'.

He might have been in danger of becoming an Oxford *revenant* like so many of them, haunting the scenes of his former triumphs, were it not that his brother Alec had introduced him to a tolerably entertaining milieu in London, 'a bohemian world among whom I found cronies'. He joined the slightly *louche* circles which gathered around various vaguely literary hostesses, and after evenings in such company would sleep on a sofa or walk home in the early hours. On one occasion he pub-crawled from central London to Golders Green and back in the company of a friend, and was arrested for being drunk and disorderly; after a night in the cells he was fined 15s 6d. To his old school-friend Dudley Carew, it seemed he was deliberately making a 'wreck' of his life, though possibly it was 'a Byronic exercise in self-disgust'. At Christmas 1924 he abandoned Heatherley's and decided to study printing instead, in the hope that he and Alastair Graham could establish a private press and 'produce books which I should decorate and sometimes write'. But a visit to a one-man press in Sussex quickly disillusioned him – the Kelmscott-style printing turned out to be done with the aid of photographically engraved plates, rather than wood-cutting – and he arrived back in London to contemplate mounting debts and the absence of a *modus vivendi*. In this predicament, 'there was only one profession open to a man of my qualifications'.

He went not to Gabbitas & Thring, but to one of their rivals, Truman & Knightley. The following days were occupied by filling in forms to say that he had been in his house-team for swimming and was amply qualified to teach games, and in sending these to 'obscure private schools'. The idea of becoming a schoolmaster seemed 'wholly absurd', but he consoled himself by remembering some of the curious figures who had passed through his own preparatory school on the way to more exciting careers. Most of the schools did not reply, but on 2 January 1925 a telegram arrived from a Mr Banks in Denbighshire telling Waugh to meet him in London in three days' time. 'I pray to God', wrote Evelyn in his diary, 'that this means a job and some money.'

Mr Banks, when they met at a hotel, proved to be 'a tall old man with stupid eyes', the headmaster and proprietor of Arnold House School, Llandulas. 'The only question he asked me was whether I possessed a dinner-jacket.' When the parents of Irish boys, who predominated in the school, came to visit their sons, such a garment helped to impress them. 'Reassured on that point he engaged me.' Three weeks later, Evelyn found himself at Euston, rounding up small boys in red caps and entraining them for a point on the Denbighshire coast between Rhyl and Colwyn Bay.

The school consisted of 'several miles of passage covered with highly polished linoleum', perched on a steep hill and surrounded by gooseberry bushes and dung heaps, and populated by 'an army of housemaids who scurry about the passages laden with urine' – or so Evelyn portrayed it in his diary, attempting to make the comic best of the situation. The diary also alleges that Mr Banks refused to run the school according to a timetable, but would summon staff from the common room to teach as the whim took him. The boys were 'quite nice', and listened patiently as Evelyn 'told them what little I knew about Henry VII and Henry VIII', and the local Welsh were so good-natured that 'when you say, "Am I going the right way to Llandulas?" they always say "yes"'. Unlike Betjeman, he was competent at organized games, and could play rugby and cricket adequately for the boys' needs. 'Yesterday I played football and scored a lot of tries. I find that I can always do that whenever I want to now.' But the pretence that it was all a pleasant joke soon wore off. After only a few weeks, he was 'too tired' to do anything with such spare time as he had, while Mr Banks 'frequently expresses himself dissatisfied with the work I am doing'.

He returned to Arnold House for a second term in a very low state – 'I think that my finances have never been so desperate or my spirits so depressed.' His only amusement now was 'making all I teach as dreary to the boys as it is to myself'. He began to contemplate suicide and, with some theatricality, opened negotiations with a new member of staff to purchase his service revolver. This man, named W.R.B. ('Dick') Young, was 'monotonously pederastic and talks only of the beauty of sleeping boys'. He described his scandalous school and undergraduate days at Wellington and Keble, and an equally stormy time in the army, and gave a lurid account of his career as a teacher (he was now thirty-one). 'He has left four schools precipitately,' wrote Waugh in his diary, 'three in the middle of term through his being taken in sodomy and one through his being drunk six nights in succession.' This provided Evelyn with a little amusement, but life continued to bring severe disappointments. In London, he had 'fallen in love with an entire family', the Plunket Greenes, one of whom had been at Oxford with him, and had 'focused the sentiment upon the only appropriate member, an eighteen-year-old daughter'. Olivia Plunket Greene gave him some encouragement, but not much, and the diary records her frequent refusal to respond to his overtures when he saw her in London or wrote to her from Denbighshire. Meanwhile he had sent the completed chapters of his novel, *The Temple at Thatch*, to Harold Acton for comment. 'His reply was courteous but chilling. "Too English for my exotic taste," he wrote. "Too much nid-nodding over port. It should be printed in a few elegant copies for the friends who love you."' Evelyn burnt the manuscript in the school boiler.

His spirits lifted when Alec managed to fix him up with a secretaryship to 'a homosexual translator' in Florence – C.K. Scott Moncrieff, who had rendered Proust into English. On the strength of this, during July 1925, Evelyn gave notice to Mr Banks, whereupon he heard that Moncrieff did not want him after all. 'It looks rather like being the end of the tether,' he wrote in the diary. He felt that, alone of his contemporaries, he had got nowhere. Christopher Hollis was travelling the world as a member of a University debating team, Robert Byron was planning an adventurous motor trip across Europe, and Harold Acton was still enjoying popularity at Oxford and seemed set for a sparkling literary career. 'I alone, it seemed, was rejected. . . .' One night he went down to the sea without a towel, having chosen a quotation from Euripides, which he left on his clothes: 'The sea washes away all the evils of men.' He swam slowly out, but met a shoal of jelly-fish and was stung into some sense. Afterwards, he could not tell 'how much real despair and act of will, how much play-acting' had prompted the suicide attempt.

He did not withdraw his resignation from Arnold House, and during the summer managed to get an appointment at a school in Aston Clinton, not very far from London and Oxford, where Olivia Plunket Greene's brother Richard was teaching. Slightly cheered by the prospect of escaping from Denbighshire and being within reach of his friends, he spent some of the summer completing a piece of prose fiction that he had begun in the spring.

On beginning 'The Balance', as this story was called, in May 1925, he noted in his diary: 'I have quite suddenly received inspiration about my book. I am making the first chapter a cinema film. . . .' This indicates that the piece was conceived as the beginning of a novel, maybe a fresh start for 'The Temple at Thatch'. Instead, it proved to be a long short story with a very unconventional structure. When it was complete, Waugh sent it to Leonard Woolf at the Hogarth Press and to a literary agent named Whitworth. Both returned it, and it was rejected by further publishers, but Alec Waugh eventually accepted it for the 1926 number of an annual Chapman & Hall anthology, *Georgian Stories*, which he was editing. In doing so, he saved from the school boiler a piece of work which is of immense autobiographical interest.

The principal character, Adam Doure, is the forerunner of all the typical Waugh heroes, a victim rather than a man of action, yet someone who survives the vicissitudes of fortune by cultivating emotional detachment from his own predicament. Faced with the collapse of a love affair – which is narrated as a silent film with captions – he attempts suicide and, when this fails, examines his life to date and realizes that it has consisted largely of a 'struggle for detachment'. The suicide attempt (a memory, of course, of Waugh's own) has been an uncharacteristic loss of equilibrium – the 'Balance' of the story's title. The narrative ends with his determination to regain that equilibrium. Alongside this piece of self-portraiture is a character recognizable as another aspect of Waugh's personality, a drunken, tousled undergraduate named Ernest Vaughan.

'The Balance' has none of the easy narrative style of Waugh's mature fiction, and its fragmented narrative form suggests an interest in modernism. A few months after writing it, Waugh noted in his diary his appreciation of T.S. Eliot's poems, and he was sympathetic to Henry Yorke's attempt to find a coolly modern voice in *Blindness*; he wrote to Yorke that the book was 'fine'.

If one regards 'The Balance' as an exercise in self-portraiture, it is perhaps a little disturbing that Waugh felt it necessary to represent the two sides of himself as separate people, Adam Doure and Ernest Vaughan. The story also indicates something of the effort he had put, since adolescence, into his 'struggle for detachment'. The pose as the detached and invulnerable observer of others' foibles – for pose it really was, as 'The Balance' acknowledges – cost him a lot. Some months after writing the story, he began to suffer from the insomnia that plagued him for the rest of his life. 'I sat up last night unable to sleep,' reads a typical diary entry from this period. And another: 'I find it hard to sleep.'

Waugh arrived at the Aston Clinton school in September 1925, and found it distinctly better than Arnold House – run by a headmaster who at least made a pretence of liberalism towards boys and staff, and within reach of a tolerable inn with a good dining room, the Bell. He bought a motor-bicycle and was able to journey to London on it, and to Oxford: 'I went to the George and ate fried oysters with Harold and Brian Howard. ... We ... became enormously drunk. It was quite like the old Hypocrite days: trying on the hats of strange men, riding strange bicycles and reciting Edith Sitwell to the chimneys of Oriel Street.'

In the diary, he began to categorize his pupils not unaffectionately as 'the mad boys' (average stupid), 'lunatics' (very stupid), 'not mad but diseased' (quite clever but with acne). By Christmas he admitted that 'some are charming. I go and talk to them in the evenings usually, and that is the nicest part of the day.' Two of them, Charles and Edmund (he does not record the surnames), were favourites who would come to tea in his room, which helped alleviate the boredom: 'On Monday afternoon I found Edmund out of bounds and beat him with mixed feelings and an ash plant. He was very sweet and brave about it all. I have given him a Sulka tie as a recompense.' There was perhaps some danger that he might go the way of the pederastic schoolmaster at Arnold House, who paid a visit to him at Aston Clinton: 'Young of Denbighshire came down and was rather a bore – drunk all the time. He seduced a garage boy in the hedge.'

The small-scale success of 'The Balance' had encouraged Waugh to contemplate authorship as an escape from schoolmastering, but Harold Acton's wholesale condemnation of 'The Temple at Thatch' made him understandably wary of attempting another novel. Instead, he turned to biography. During November 1925 he recorded that he was 'deep in the study of the Pre-Raphaelites. I want to write a book about them.' Lytton Strachey's *Eminent Victorians* (1918) had introduced a new style of biographical writing, both elegant and cynical, which appealed to Waugh (who otherwise took no interest in the Bloomsbury writers), and he had the idea of applying the Strachey technique to a group of artists who seemed comically out of date – in 1925 the Pre-Raphaelites were at the nadir of their reputation. He noted down the idea of writing 'a modish Lytton Strachey biography' of Millais. On the other hand he felt a certain family loyalty towards the Pre-Raphaelites – because a distant relative had been married to Holman Hunt – while their original Brotherhood seemed to him, the more he studied it, an admirable example of rebellious young artists going into battle against contemporary shoddiness. When in the summer of 1926 he got round to writing an essay entitled *PRB* (Pre-Raphaelite Brotherhood) for Alastair Graham to print in a pamphlet, he gave Millais and his friends credit for initiating 'a revolutionary movement . . . against technically bad painting', and obviously envied their 'first thrills of rebellion'. Yet for most of the essay he hid his admiration behind a Stracheyesque detachment; the sentence-rhythms were entirely Strachey's, as were the imagined and semi-imagined scenes he devised to tell the brief history of the original Brotherhood:

> Millais sagely nodded his 'cockatoo tuft', and began putting away his brushes, and Hunt was on the verge of departure when Millais caught his arm, and insisted on their going in for a minute 'to see the old people'.
>
> Mrs Millais sat crocheting in the parlour arm-chair under Johnnie's chalk drawing of Apollo. The needle clicked intently, and the boys' entrance was allowed to pass unnoticed. . . .

This was a kind of leg-pull, in that Strachey and the rest of Bloomsbury believed they had consigned the Pre-Raphaelites to permanent oblivion. Yet it also hid Waugh's real feelings about his subject, which he seemed ashamed to declare.

The Strachey voice is so strong in *PRB* that it almost drowns another stylistic influence. As in Strachey, vivid scenes jostle with portentous judgements and rolling Augustan pronouncements:

> Ruskin . . . was a nice judge of a painting in just the same sense that his father had been a nice judge of sherry; his faculties were keenly trained to the perception of artistic style; he could distinguish the flavours of the different schools with the utmost delicacy – and that was all. . . . He was for all his acuteness purely a superficial critic, and in him, as in so many superficial critics, all attempts at more profound thought led merely to sociology and politics.

This could certainly pass for Strachey, but the implied sneer at Ruskin's interest in the working classes also recalls Arthur Waugh in his role of defender of Victorian values. 'My father likes the PRB essay very much,' noted Evelyn in his diary. Indeed, Arthur proudly gave copies to his friends. In the middle of all his endeavours to establish a grip on his own personality and find himself some role in life, Evelyn was turning towards the cause of so much of his conflict, and the gesture did not go unnoticed.

It had proved all too easy to imitate Strachey and his father, and his next piece of literary work was in the same mode, a lengthy essay entitled 'Noah; Or the Future of Intoxication', which he offered to the publisher Kegan Paul for a series of short books entitled 'Today and Tomorrow'. He describes it as 'mannered and literary', which is probably why it was turned down; evidently he destroyed the manuscript. Another possibility lay in comic drawing, and after completing 'Noah' he drew some pictures 'for a book I intend doing to be called the Annals of Constitutional Monarchy'. This sounds like *1066 and All That*, or one of Osbert Lancaster's illustrated books, a genre that would certainly have suited Waugh's talents, but nothing came of it. Meanwhile if Arthur Waugh had taken *PRB* as an indication that his younger son was steadying down, he must have been disappointed, for in the middle of his fifth term at Aston Clinton, Evelyn and another 'usher' named Attwell – a naïve near-teetotaller whom Evelyn had set out to corrupt – were suddenly sacked, apparently for drunkenness, or for making a drunken pass at the matron. Evelyn briefly tried teaching at a school in Notting Hill, but found it awful – 'All the masters drop their aitches and spit in the fire and scratch their genitals' – and decamped to the *Daily Express*, where he persuaded the editor to take him for three weeks' trial at four pounds a week, much less than he had been paid for teaching: 'I don't know how much I shall like that but it will be worth trying.'

These restless changes of job were partly a reflection of his own uncertainties about himself, but were also symptomatic of the times. Cyril Connolly observes how difficult it was for his generation to settle down to a career in the way their fathers had. The war had killed the old expectation of security: 'They could not settle down to boring jobs and unprofitable careers with pre-war patience and their cleverness seemed a liability rather than an asset.'

Waugh did not take his *Daily Express* job seriously. When the paper sent him to cover a fire in Soho, he decided that there was no 'story' in it, and went off to the Savoy with a girl reporter, then to a cinema. After about two months of such behaviour, he was dismissed. This quite suited him, as he had obtained a commission from Anthony Powell at Duckworth. On the strength of *PRB*, Powell had invited him to write a life of Rossetti, whose centenary would fall in 1928. Powell procured him an advance of twenty pounds, which he spent in a week, but he got on speedily with writing the book, working on it at a pub near Oxford where he and Alastair Graham had stayed – the Abingdon Arms at Beckley – and in the library of the Oxford Union. 'I think it is quite amusing in parts,' he noted in his diary.

The book, *Rossetti: His Life and Works*, compiled almost entirely from published sources, certainly gets off to an entertaining start. Once again the model is Strachey, and the intention to create a 'modish' biography such as he had contemplated of Millais. The opening is both a pastiche of Strachey and a dig at him:

Biography, as books about the dead are capriciously catalogued, is still very much in the mode.

It has usurped the place held in recent years by the novel, and before that by poetry, as the regular *métier* of all those young men and women who, in every age, concern themselves with providing the light reading of their more cultured friends. Naturally enough, a new manner has resulted, and, to a great extent, a new method; and polite literature is the less polite for it.

No doubt the old-fashioned biography will return, and, with the years, we shall once more learn to assist with our fathers' decorum at the lying-in-state of great men. ... Meanwhile we must keep our tongue in our cheek, must we not, for fear it should loll out and reveal the idiot?

This is as brilliant as anything Strachey ever wrote, yet it leaves Waugh himself in something of a dilemma. From what stance is he going to examine Rossetti's life, having mocked both the sardonic and the reverential approaches? He gives no indication, and the book swiftly reveals his uncertainty on this score.

It becomes apparent that he does not want to mock Rossetti, Strachey-fashion, since he admires him too much to pass censorious judgements. On the other hand he does not immerse himself in Rossetti's personality, or manage to bring him alive. He remains rather nervously on the edge of things, trying to seem sophisticated. There are some fine phrases, several of them repeated (and improved) from *PRB* – such as 'Turner was seventy-one years old, sinking like one of his own tremendous sunsets in clouds of obscured glory' – and the rhythm of the prose is almost always fine. But the book has an oddly fusty air, as if it were the product of Rossetti's own age rather than the 1920s. So in a sense it is, for Evelyn is imitating his father's biography of Tennyson, which came at the same stage of Arthur's career as *Rossetti* did of Evelyn's. Here is Arthur musing about Tennyson:

Such specious fancies are, perhaps, a little too artificial to be insisted upon with any freedom; but much of the poet's earlier life has to be left to conjecture and imagination of one kind and another; for the actual, palpable facts that have come to hand are very meagre indeed.

And here is Evelyn on Kelmscott, William Morris's house, which was invaded by Rossetti: 'It is, of its kind, a house of unsurpassable charm, with a sweetness and repose which Gabriel appreciated but could never fully share.' When visiting the house, Evelyn had noted in his diary that it was 'rather cramped and constricted' and the rooms 'very low and dark', and that Morris's daughter May, the current occupant, was 'very awkward and disagreeable. . . . A hermaphrodite lives with her.'

The style of the Rossetti biography, then, was a pose, perhaps assumed in the hope of winning further approval from his father. Its mock-Victorianism convinced the *Times Literary Supplement* reviewer that the book was the work of a spinster with genuinely Victorian values – the reviewer referred to the author as 'Miss Waugh' and observed that 'she' approached the squalors of Rossetti's life 'like some dainty miss of the 60s bringing the Italian organ-grinder a penny'. Yet there are some patches of spectacularly good and quite un-Victorian prose, remarkable for someone just beginning his career as a writer:

> As one follows the story of his life one leaves behind the benign genius . . . and finds the baffled and very tragic figure of an artist born into an age devoid of artistic standards; a man of the South, sensual, indolent, and richly versatile, exiled in the narrow, scrambling, specialized life of a Northern city; a mystic without a creed; a Catholic without the discipline or consolation of the Church; a life between the rocks and the high road, like the scrub of a Southern hillside, sombre, aromatic, and impenetrable.

He is particularly good on Rossetti's decline into insomnia, drugs and finally paranoia, which he writes about with an insight derived, one would guess, from the sleeplessness he was already experiencing himself:

> In 1867 his melancholy and restlessness began to give place to restless insomnia. Others afflicted by this terrible disease have contrived in some measure to adapt themselves to it, to reserve their waning vitality, manage with what sleep they can get, and when not sleeping to take adequate rest. Rossetti was the last person to be able to do this. He became unable to rest and unable to work; the days dragged by in fretful melancholy. . . . More and more his thoughts and conversation tended to the subject of suicide.

There is another point of relation to Waugh's own situation, in a passage where he suggests that late nineteenth-century England could provide more economic stability for the artist than was possible in the 1920s:

> The transition from aristocracy to industrialism came very near to crushing out English art altogether; the present generation is confronted by the incalculable consequences of the transition from industrialism

to democracy. Rossetti was fortunate as far as finance is concerned in growing up with a generation between the two processes.

The incalculable consequences of the transition from industrialism to democracy: Waugh is here, first of his circle, stating a theme that would come to obsess them all.

After finishing *Rossetti* he relapsed into insomniac boredom. 'I can't sleep or work. ... How I detest this house [his father's] and how ill I feel in it. The whole place volleys and thunders with traffic.' This was on 3 September 1927. But in the same diary entry: 'I reviewed the books [for the *Bookman*] and have begun on a comic novel.'

2

A Comic Novel

Anthony Powell would sometimes come to a cold supper on Sunday nights at the Waughs' in Hampstead. 'One night Waugh asked if I would like to hear the opening chapters of a novel he was writing.' At that stage it was called 'Picaresque: or the Making of an Englishman'. Powell found himself listening to 'the first ten thousand words, scarcely at all altered later, of *Decline and Fall*. The manuscript was written with a pen on double-sheets of blue-lined foolscap, the cipher EW printed at the top of the first page of each double-sheet. There were hardly any alterations in the text.'

In the history of comic writing in English, two largely independent strains may be detected, satire and caricature. During the Augustan age, satire was brought to a fine pitch, but though satirical writing never died out during the nineteenth century (Byron, Peacock and Thackeray were masterly practitioners), the prevailing type of humour was that promulgated in *Punch* – the humour of the sporting prints that hung in parlour bars, depicting rotund country squires taking a tumble while out with the hounds (Surtees was the exact literary equivalent). Towards the end of the nineteenth century, Oscar Wilde and W.S. Gilbert appeared to be reviving satire. But Waugh was not attracted by either as a model. He perceived that Wilde was essentially a sentimentalist with a taste for epigram, the humour in his plays being (in Waugh's words) 'ornamental' rather than 'structural', while Gilbert's propensity for satirizing contemporary figures and fashions had usually been submerged by his taste for broad comic types in the pantomime tradition. Waugh described *The Mikado* as 'a detestable pantomime'.

Around the time of the First World War there arrived three English humorous writers who suggested very different literary possibilities. The first was 'Saki' (H.H. Munro), whose *Chronicles of Clovis* (1911) experimented in what Roald Dahl has called 'a wildly outrageous premise in order to make a serious point'. Waugh admired Saki hugely. 'The wit is continuous and almost unfailing,' he wrote in 1947. 'Saki has attempted and achieved a *tour de force* in limiting himself to the most commonplace material in its most commonplace aspect, in eschewing all the eccentrics which come so easily to English humorists. ...' On the other hand Saki never progressed successfully beyond short stories – his novel *The Unbearable Bassington* (1912) is a poor piece of construction – and even the stories, as Waugh admitted, often miss their mark, 'too often have the air of being fancies and passing jests unduly expanded, or of dramatic themes unduly cramped'. (Waugh's own short stories are usually in the Saki mode, and consequently have a slightly second-hand feel about them; they move too predictably towards the inevitable Sakiesque black joke at the end.)

The second English humorous writer to take his bow during this period was P.G. Wodehouse, who by contrast with Saki was a master of plot-construction. Waugh's admiration for him was unbounded, and went back to childhood. He described himself as having

> grown up in the light of his genius. By the time that I went to school his stories were established classics and in the nursery I was familiar with my elder brother's impersonations of Psmith. I have possessed a complete set of his works, now [1961] sadly depleted by theft. I still await with unappeasable appetite the publication of each addition to the *oeuvre*.

Wodehouse's stories carefully keep their distance from the real world. Whole areas of human experience – most notably sex – are deliberately eliminated, and the narratives take place, as Waugh observed, in their own hermetic compartment: 'He inhabits a world as timeless as that of *A Midsummer Night's Dream* and *Alice in Wonderland*; a world inhabited by strange transmogrifications.' Also, while (as Waugh said) Wodehouse's work is distinguished by its 'exquisite felicity of the language', his style is so distinctive as to forbid imitation. It is a style, moreover, that owes more to American comic writing than to English. The diction is that of an English aristocrat being impersonated by an American comedian; hence the frequent lapses into American slang: 'I remember

Jeeves once saying that sleep knits up the ravelled sleeve of care. . . .
Apple sauce, in my opinion. It seldom pans out that way with me.'
This impersonation of 'toffs' was also practised by 'Frank Richards'
(Charles Hamilton), creator of Billy Bunter and other comic schoolboys
in the boys' weekly comics. 'At my private school,' writes Waugh,
'these stories were contraband and I read them regularly with all the
zeal of law-breaking.'

Another figure to appear on the literary scene at the same period
offered definite hints of a possible way forward in comic writing. Ronald
Firbank's novels began to come into print in 1915, and soon gained
a small but loyal audience, Waugh among it. Firbank, imitated in
Broom and other university periodicals by Acton and Howard, was part
of the ambience of Waugh's Oxford. Betjeman says that the books
on his shelf in his rooms in Magdalen included '*Crome Yellow* [by Aldous
Huxley], *Prancing Nigger* [by Firbank], Blunden, Keats'. In an essay
written not long after the publication of *Decline and Fall*, Waugh unhesitat-
ingly identifies Firbank as a major influence on several contemporary
writers, and by implication on himself: 'In quite diverse ways Mr
Osbert Sitwell, Mr Carl Van Vechten, Mr Harold Acton, Mr William
Gerhardi and Mr Ernest Hemingway are developing the technical discoveries upon which Ronald Firbank so negligently stumbled.'

What were these discoveries? First, that it was not necessary to tell
a story according to what Waugh called 'the chain of cause and effect'.
In Firbank's fiction, events take place seemingly haphazardly, and
appear to have been selected at the author's whim. Only gradually
does their function in the story become apparent, and it is from this
gradual unveiling of the scheme that much of the humour is derived.
Firbank also discovered that it is possible to convey considerable intricacies and nuances of human relationships through dialogue cut to the
bone. As Cyril Connolly says, 'When something bored him, he left
it out (a device which might have improved the quality of innumerable
novelists).'

Waugh picked up these and other things from Firbank, not least
a habit of inventing improbable names (such as Mrs Thoroughfare
in *Valmouth* and Mrs Mouth in *Prancing Nigger*). But for all his mastery
of comic form, Firbank had one severe limitation. 'Camp' homosexual
humour was the beginning and end of his subject-matter, and Waugh
observed that Firbank's 'coy naughtiness about birches and pretty boys'
quickly becomes tedious.

Waugh's list of those writers he believed were continuing the work
pioneered by Firbank gives hints about further influences on his own

fiction. The list begins with Osbert Sitwell, whose novel *Before the Bombardment* (1926) borrowed a little from *Valmouth* in its depiction of a closed society (Scarborough before the First World War) dominated by females; but its form and narrative manner bear more resemblance to Jane Austen and Mrs Gaskell than to Firbank. Carl Van Vechten, American novelist and critic, had promoted Firbank's work in the United States, and his own fiction was decidedly eccentric, but rather in the dilettante manner, lacking Firbank's (and Waugh's) concentration of purpose. Harold Acton leant heavily on Firbank in *Cornelian* (1928), a fable along the lines of 'The Emperor's New Clothes' about a musician who conducts performances consisting largely of silence. (Acton himself denied that there was any borrowing from Firbank, but the conversations between members of the audience could have come straight from *Valmouth*.) William Gerhardi (also spelt Gerhardie), an Englishman born and educated in Russia before becoming an undergraduate at Oxford, came into prominence with his second novel, *The Polyglots* (1925), about a young officer in the First World War making the acquaintance of a branch of his family in the Far East, and becoming deeply involved with the daughter of the house. Waugh wrote to Gerhardi in 1949: 'As no doubt you recognized I learned a great deal of my trade from your own novels.'

It is hard at first glance to see the connection between Firbank, Gerhardi and Waugh (as opposed to Waugh's direct borrowings from Firbank). Gerhardi's style, exuberant and informal, bears a minimal resemblance to either of the others; his books ramble where theirs are finely wrought. The connection, in fact, is one not of style but of theme. Gerhardi specialized in narratives about the failure of hope. *Futility* (1922), his first novel, is partly a modern version of Chekhov's *Three Sisters*, and the narrator of *The Polyglots* discovers that all pleasure lies in expectation and none in consummation. Waugh's novels tread a path very close to this.

Cyril Connolly has observed that 'the idea of futility', engendered by the First World War, was a very important concept in the literature of the 1920s, dominating the poetry of Eliot, the novels of Huxley and much of the writing of D.H. Lawrence, Hemingway and Joyce, arising from 'a disbelief in action and in the putting of moral slogans into action'. Until Waugh, no writer of distinction attempted to express this sense of futility through comedy. Connolly observed in 1938 that 'This is a satirical age and among the vast reading public the power of an artist to awaken ridicule has never been so great.'

Ernest Hemingway seems an odd name to find on Waugh's list of those continuing the work begun by Firbank, but Hemingway had certainly heard of him – Gertrude Stein, his Paris mentor, praised Firbank's novels on many occasions – and there is a resemblance between Firbank's economy of dialogue and Hemingway's clipped speeches. Hemingway's first novel, *The Sun Also Rises*, was published in England during 1927 under the title *Fiesta*. Waugh read it around the time that he was beginning *Decline and Fall*. In 1961, prompted by Hemingway's suicide, he re-read it. 'It was a revelation to me when it first came out,' he wrote in his diary, 'the drunk conversations rather than the fishing and bullfighting.' And in 1950 he wrote of the novel as 'startlingly brilliant. ... How it delighted and impressed us ...!' By that time, Hemingway had fallen out of fashion, and Waugh defended him as 'one of the most original and powerful of living writers', and especially praised 'that pungent vernacular'. But it is Hemingway's economy of language – what Cyril Connolly called his 'pointillist' manner – that particularly made its mark on Waugh's early fiction.

Another contemporary writer of whom Waugh was thoroughly aware, and against whom he could scarcely help measuring himself, was Aldous Huxley. *Crome Yellow* (1921), a great popular success which was reprinted throughout the 1920s, was followed by *Antic Hay* (1923), which Waugh, writing in 1955, described as 'frivolous and sentimental and perennially delightful'. Anthony Powell was bowled over by it – 'I was prostrated by its brilliance' – and Harold Acton admired Huxley's stance in his novels as a 'detached observer, ironical and hostile'. This Olympian detachment must have appealed to Waugh, but he was not impressed by Huxley's powers as a storyteller. The novels tend towards Platonic dialogues rather than making their points through narrative, and Waugh (in his diary) was greatly disappointed by Huxley's third novel, *Point Counter Point* (1928): 'Infinitely long with all the same characters as *Antic Hay*, all the same social uncertainties, bored lovemaking ... odd pages of conversation and biology. It might have been written by an educated Alec Waugh' – a dig at the fact that his brother, since *The Loom of Youth*, had turned out entirely unremarkable fiction.

In a sense, it is misleading to look for literary precursors for *Decline and Fall*; the model for Waugh the writer was clearly Waugh the caricaturist and illustrator. His early novels are a transposition into words of the comic drawings he had done while at Oxford. The chief thing he carried from one medium to the other was economy. In both, he achieved his effects with the minimum of material on the page. (This link between the two sides of his work is particularly evident in the first edition of *Decline and Fall,* which includes several illustrations by him in the manner of his Oxford drawings.) Also, like Waugh the caricaturist and Waugh the film scenarist, Waugh the novelist preferred vignettes, short self-contained scenes constructed to make one joke at a time. This was a new notion in English comic writing.

A particular model for the transition from drawn to written caricature may have been Max Beerbohm, whose *Zuleika Dobson* (1911) and many prose parodies demonstrated that caricature could be achieved verbally as well as visually. In 1956 Waugh wrote: 'Max Beerbohm was an idol of my adolescence to whom every year . . . deepened my devotion'; and in a letter to Beerbohm in 1947 he addressed him as 'Master'. In one of his own letters Beerbohm defines the art of the caricaturist in terms which apply equally to Waugh as novelist: 'When I draw a man, I . . . see all his salient points exaggerated . . . and all his insignificant points proportionately diminished. *Insignificant*: literally, signifying nothing. The salient points do signify something.' This certainly applies to Waugh's method of character-drawing. Yet, talking to Julian Jebb in 1962, Waugh was at pains to emphasize that he did not conceive a narrative pictorially: 'Some people think in pictures, some in ideas. I think entirely in words. By the time I come to stick my pen in my inkpot these words have reached a state of order which is fairly presentable.'

In 1937, reviewing David Jones's *In Parenthesis*, the work of another visual-artist-cum-writer, Waugh discussed the relationship between the two crafts in terms that reveal much about his own work. The review starts by being dismissive of literature: 'The truth is that far higher gifts are needed to paint even a bad picture than to write a good book.' But then he distinguishes several qualities in Jones's poetry which he believes derive from his work as a painter. First, he has a 'painter's realism', an ability to depict things precisely and accurately, and without superfluous detail. Second, a 'painter's *communicativeness*', a desire to get through to an audience beyond his own studio, as opposed to the professional writer's tendency to employ a language intelligible only to himself or to other writers; consequently 'there is not a sentence which on analysis lacks a precise meaning'. Third, and most perceptively, he observes that Jones treats the craft of writing with particular respect because it is not his natural occupation: 'He knows that he is practising an unfamiliar art . . . he writes with the respect of a stranger.'

These were the qualities Waugh himself brought to writing from the visual arts: an ability to depict precisely, a desire to communicate, a precision of meaning, and an innate respect for the craft of writing itself, a respect springing from his feeling – at least in his early years – that he was on unfamiliar ground.

A few months after listening to the first chapters, Anthony Powell asked Waugh how the comic novel was going. 'I've burnt it,' Waugh replied. However, he rewrote the opening section and pressed on.

He did not usually write easily or fluently. A friend in whose house he was staying while working on a later novel describes him 'groaning loudly as he shut himself away ... for a few hours every day'. One of his travel books begins with a description of his unwillingness to begin writing; he has postponed it all morning until 'there was nothing for it but to start'. In the original version of *Work Suspended*, Waugh's unfinished novel from the late 1930s, the narrator, a professional writer, explains: 'I have the unhappy combination of being both lazy and fastidious.'

He went down to the Bell at Aston Clinton to work on *Decline and Fall* ('it is very comfortable and quiet'), and by the beginning of 1928 had completed a good deal of it, but was dissatisfied, and wrote to ask Harold Acton's opinion – which was a risk, considering Acton's wholesale condemnation of 'The Temple at Thatch', but evidently Waugh was not prepared to go on with the new book unless it pleased the severest critic he then knew. This time Acton was enthusiastic, and the novel was completed during the spring of 1928, much of the last part being written at the Barley Mow near Wimborne in Dorset, this pub being chosen because a girl in whom Waugh was interested (Evelyn Gardner) was staying nearby. Cyril Connolly describes the hotel bedroom as the writer's 'rightful place of composition, the small single unluxurious "retreat" of the twentieth century'.

Waugh wrote to Anthony Powell from the Barley Mow on 7 April 1928:

> I hope the novel will be finished in a week. I will send it to you as soon as it is typed & then want to revise it very thoroughly and enlarge it a bit. I think at present it shows signs of being too short. How do these novelists make their books so long. I'm sure one could write any novel in the world on two post cards. Do you like 'Untoward Incidents' as a title?

In another letter to Powell – whose firm, Duckworth, Waugh hoped would publish the book – he explained this title as being a quotation from the Duke of Wellington on the destruction of the Turkish fleet at Navarino in time of peace: 'It seems to set the right tone of mildly censorious detachment.'

The changes of title suggest uncertainty of purpose. A picaresque, as Waugh originally intended to label the book, is a novel depicting the career of a rogue or resourceful and resilient individual, such as *Tom Jones* or *Moll Flanders*; this and the subtitle 'The Making of an Englishman' suggest that the book was to be concerned with the effects of experience on the central character. 'Untoward Incidents' puts more emphasis on the fatalistic nature of the story. The title finally chosen, *Decline and Fall*, is misleading if taken literally as an account of the hero's fortunes, but has the right portentous ring for a story that examines modern life with the severity of a Gibbon.

At first, no such Gibbonesque stance was probably intended. Waugh had simply decided to write a story about someone in his own present situation, a young man who leaves the cocoon of Oxford for the nightmarish realities of the teaching profession and the wider social world. At the outset, he seems to have intended to portray a conventional hero, who would react with justifiable outrage to the indignities thrust upon him by Fate. Paul Pennyfeather's 'God damn and blast them to hell!' in the published novel, when he is sent down quite unjustly from Oxford, is perhaps a relic of this, as is his adeptness at coping (just as Waugh had done) with the unruliness of schoolboys when he finds himself in a teaching job:

> 'You can't keep me in,' said Clutterbuck; 'I'm going for a walk with Captain Grimes.'
> 'Then I shall very nearly kill you with this stick.'

Yet overall Paul is a strikingly passive figure, who takes his chain of misfortunes without complaint, indeed almost without comment – the first but by no means the last of Waugh's heroes to do so. He does not even meditate on his situation as Adam Doure had done in 'The Balance'. What was Waugh up to in creating such a passive central character for this and subsequent novels?

He had doubtless been familiar with the works of Lewis Carroll as a child, but it was not until he was an undergraduate that he looked closely at them. 'Between whiles I read *Alice in Wonderland*,' he wrote to Tom Driberg in the spring of 1922. 'It is an excellent book I think.' Paul Pennyfeather's detachment from the ludicrous characters who surround him bears a marked resemblance to Alice's attitude to the creatures of Wonderland. Indeed if *Alice* and *Decline and Fall* are considered in tandem, all sorts of parallels appear.

Each book begins with a fall, literal in one case and metaphorical in the other. Paul's expulsion from Oxford is as astonishing and dream-like as Alice's sudden descent down the rabbit hole; neither Paul nor Alice complains about what is happening, because the whole thing is quite beyond their control – is in any case merely a device to effect the transition from the real world to another. Hence Paul's passivity at the opening of the novel; like Alice, he is helplessly experiencing a metaphysical journey from reality into nightmare. Once he has achieved this, he can resume something of his own self again. Like Alice, he desires to get back to where he started from, but as in her adventures the way is blocked by a series of outlandish creatures, who demand that attention be paid exclusively to them:

'I expect you wonder how I come to be here?' said Philbrick.
'No,' said Paul firmly, 'nothing of the kind. I don't in the least want to know anything about you; d'you hear?'
'I'll tell you,' said Philbrick; 'it was like this –'

This is very like Alice being bombarded by the life histories of the Wonderland creatures:

'This here young lady,' said the Gryphon, 'she wants for to know your history, she does.'
'I'll tell it her,' said the Mock Turtle in a deep, hollow tone. 'Sit down, both of you, and don't speak a word till I've finished.'

Alice in Wonderland might seem an entirely obvious model for a comic novel, but Waugh may have had a particular reason for drawing on Lewis Carroll. In 1939 he reviewed Carroll's *Complete Works*; the article says little about *Alice*, concentrating mostly on *Sylvie and Bruno* (which Waugh had evidently never read before), but at the end he throws out an intriguing suggestion about the man behind the 'Lewis Carroll' pseudonym, the Rev. C.L. Dodgson:

It seems to me that Dodgson was tortured by religious scepticism; his abnormal tenderness of conscience with regard to blasphemy [expressed in many of his later works] is explicable if we think of him as treasuring a religious faith so fragile that a child's prattle endangered it. He believed that the only way he could protect his faith was by escaping more and more from contemporary life – in his scholarship into remote and fanciful abstractions, in literature into nonsense. In order to keep his mind from rational speculation he cultivated a habit of day-dreaming and peopled his consciousness with fantastic characters.

This is one of the most acute pieces of criticism of *Alice* ever written.

A careful study of the book entirely bears out Waugh's hypothesis, and indicates that it is a sustained mockery of religion, cloaked in a disguise so thick that its author evidently did not know what he was doing. The verses are parodies of religious poetry, the instructions 'Eat Me' and 'Drink Me' on the bottle and cake that change Alice's size allude to the words of consecration at Holy Communion, and the logical paradoxes constantly posed by the Wonderland creatures are explorations of the abyss caused by the non-existence of God.* Even the structure of the book is a mocking allusion to the Christian religion. If one considers what model Dodgson could have had in mind for a journey which begins with a dreamer asleep on a grassy bank, then descending via a dark opening into the depths of the earth, and meeting a series of grotesque creatures who speak of their own misfortunes, then one answer clearly appears: Dante's *Inferno*. (Dodgson claimed never to have read the *Divine Comedy*, but wrote to a child friend that he was '*not* sure whether the reading of it would *raise* one's life ... or simply be a grand poetical treat', which sounds as if he was frightened of having his faith shaken by it.)

Dodgson's comic nightmare rests on the pillars of Dante – there is no Virgil to Alice's Dante, except perhaps the Cheshire Cat, but in every other respect the copy is close – and Waugh's rests on them both. *Decline and Fall* is a modern *Alice*, and also a modern *Inferno*, an exploration of a twentieth-century hell. Paul's 'God damn and blast them to hell!' at the opening of the book is a curse that proves horribly effective, for the creatures he subsequently meets are doomed to dwell in hells of their own making. When Philbrick says of his *inamorata*, Dingy Fagan, 'That girl could bring a man up from the depths of hell,' he is acknowledging the state in which they are all languishing.

The first circle of hell in which Paul finds himself is Llanabba Castle, not hellish as schools go, for things rub along quite cheerfully, if with gross inefficiency. But among those confined there is Prendergast, a former clergyman who has abandoned Holy Orders on account of a loss of faith – or rather, a loss of belief that the universe makes any sense:

> 'You see, it wasn't the ordinary sort of Doubt about Cain's wife or the Old Testament miracles or the consecration of Archbishop Parker. ... No, it was something deeper than that. *I couldn't understand why God had made the world at all*. ... You see how fundamental that is. Once

---

* See further the chapter '*Alice* and the Mockery of God' in the present writer's *Secret Gardens: The Golden Age of Children's Literature* (1985).

granted the first step, I can see that everything else follows ... but ... *why* did it all begin?'

Beneath the comedy, the voice is Waugh's own suicidal self. (Joan in Henry Yorke's *Blindness* confronts the same question and dismisses it lightly: 'Silly to trouble about why the world was – it was, that was all.' Her father, like Prendergast, is a clergyman who has abandoned his Orders.)

Decline and Fall makes not the slightest attempt to answer this question, any more than the Mock Turtle is prepared to tell Alice what happened on the twelfth day when the lessons had lessened into less than nothingness. Both questions reveal the abyss yawning at the questioner's feet, not merely a God-less but a meaningless universe. Waugh's creatures are no more prepared to face this issue than Dodgson's, and *Decline and Fall* shows the other inhabitants of hell with their backs firmly to the chasm. It is no coincidence that Prendergast, who alone of them has been prepared to acknowledge the non-existence of the benevolent Christian universe, comes to a terrible but appropriate end: his head is sawn off by a religious maniac. Even the choice of method is not random; Waugh is carrying out the threat that hovers throughout *Alice* – 'Off with his head!' The only man who has seen the truth must be deprived of his faculties, lest his discovery makes it impossible to go on living even in hell. Off with his head indeed.

Leaving the particular circle of hell that is Llanabba, Paul comes (in Part Two) to King's Thursday, Margot Beste-Chetwynde's country house. He comes there in search of the permanent values the school cannot give him. (The boarding school and the country house are pillars of the world in which Waugh and his friends moved.) Paul understandably feels after his Llanabba experiences that he is facing 'a world that had lost its reason', and arrives at King's Thursday particularly hoping to find permanence: 'Surely, he thought, these great chestnuts in the morning sun stood for something enduring and serene. ...' But Waugh will offer no such reassurance. By 1927 there was nothing enduring and serene in the world he knew, and he makes the point brutally by revealing that Margot has destroyed the house – 'the finest piece of domestic Tudor in England' – and replaced it with a mansion of stark Bauhaus modernism. The decay and dissolution of the country house, a constant motif in Waugh's fiction, could (like all Paul's misfortunes in *Decline and Fall*) be interpreted as a symbol of the younger brother being deprived of his birthright.

In this part of the book, Waugh deserts his *Alice* model and borrows from another children's book. Kenneth Grahame's *The Wind in the Willows* was an especial favourite of his; he read it aloud to one of his pupil-friends at Aston Clinton, and in *Decline and Fall* Peter Beste-Chetwynde is said to like it even more than Havelock Ellis. The scene in the red-light quarter of Marseilles where Paul steers a nervous path between the brothels, whose occupants regard him jeeringly, recalls Mole's anxious progress through the Wild Wood before the gaze of weasels, stoats and ferrets. If this seems an unlikely parallel, it is worth noting that in his Rossetti biography Waugh describes the downfall of Benjamin Haydon as 'Poor Mr Toad, deserted by Rat, Badger, and even Mole', and Alec Waugh records Evelyn saying of himself in high spirits, 'Mr Toad on top.' Paul Pennyfeather's prison sentence of seven years' penal servitude, after he has been found guilty of white slaving, recalls Toad's harsh treatment by the judge in Grahame's story, and his escape and restoration to his old way of life are not unlike Toad's.

It is no casual detail that, at the end of the book, we see Paul not merely returning to Oxford to resume training for the Church, but giving clear indications that he will be a very strict and orthodox clergyman. Listening to a lecturer who describes a bishop in the second century who 'denied the Divinity of Christ, the immortality of the soul, the existence of good', Paul observes: 'How right they had been to condemn him!' This is reiterated in the final paragraph of the novel:

> So Peter went out, and Paul settled down again in his chair [to read]. So the ascetic Ebionites used to turn towards Jerusalem when they prayed. Paul made a note of it. Quite right to suppress them. Then he turned out the light and went into his bedroom to sleep.

With this is implicitly contrasted the case of Prendergast, who met his end because he obtained his job as prison chaplain by becoming a Modern Churchman, 'who draws the full salary of a beneficed clergyman and need not commit himself to any religious belief'. Any departure from rigid orthodoxy leads to a glimpse of the abyss of meaninglessness, and consequently self-destruction. Paul has made the decision that Waugh himself would make three years after writing *Decline and Fall*. However, the book's religious structure is effectively disguised by frequent references to the caprice of Fate; a toast to 'Fortune, a much-maligned lady' is given three times, and Otto Silenus makes an elaborate speech about the Great Wheel at Lunar Park, symbol of the Wheel of Fortune. Waugh knew he was writing for a pagan age, which required an apparently pagan story.*

'I have finished the novel,' Waugh wrote to Harold Acton from Dorset on 17 April 1928. 'I think it is quite amusing. I am at work doing illustrations for it. May I dedicate it to you.' (Acton had dedicated his own third book of poems to Waugh and Desmond Harmsworth.) *Decline and Fall* carries the dedication: 'To HAROLD ACTON in Homage and Affection', a generous acknowledgement that Acton, more than anyone else, had set the style for Waugh's generation at Oxford, and thereby created an audience for such a book.

But at first it was not easy to reach that audience. Despite Anthony Powell's enthusiasm for the book, Duckworth's would only accept it on condition that all indelicacies were removed. They would not tolerate the debagging of Paul Pennyfeather, nor the use of such words as 'lavatory', let alone anything vaguely suggesting sex. Waugh consulted Acton, who counselled him to stand firm: 'No, it must never be castrated!'

Waugh had not wanted to take advantage of his father's position as head of a publishing house, but clearly he was in an advantageous situation at Chapman & Hall, so he took the manuscript to them. Arthur Waugh was away from the office when the board of directors discussed the book – perhaps he absented himself deliberately – and it was a near thing; in the end they agreed to publish it by only one vote. They demanded almost as many bowdlerizations as Duckworth's, though the innuendoes which Waugh substituted were sometimes an improvement – Grimes's 'I like drink and sex' became 'I like drink and a bit of fun.' Waugh was also persuaded to preface the book with a note explaining that he did not intend it to be shocking, and emphasizing 'IT IS MEANT TO BE FUNNY'.

Although he had stood aside from his firm's decision on the manuscript, Arthur Waugh now did his bit for the book, bringing it to the attention of Arnold Bennett, who reviewed it glowingly in the *Evening Standard* on 11 October 1928, calling it the work of 'a genuinely new humorist ... an uncompromising and brilliantly malicious satire'. Arthur Waugh himself, though, seems not to have observed the sharpness of the satire; in his history of Chapman & Hall he calls the book

---

* The frequent references to Fortune would seem to indicate that it is the book's real subject, but the malevolent Fate which (as I shall be arguing) is the presiding deity in Waugh's later novels scarcely makes an appearance here. All the harm that is done to Paul Pennyfeather in the early chapters has been repaired by the end, and – much more than in Waugh's later, more overtly religious books – religious orthodoxy does seem to offer a safe refuge from the vicissitudes of life.

'half-cynical, half-appreciative'. Cyril Connolly, reviewing *Decline and Fall* in the *New Statesman*, was even further from the truth in his guesses about Waugh's intentions. Declaring it to be 'not a satire, but a farce', he judged that Waugh displayed 'a love of life, and consequently a real understanding of it'. Yet Connolly shrewdly perceived that the book was almost the creation of a group of people, a product of his own generation's pranks at Oxford: 'The humour throughout is of that subtly metallic kind which, more than anything else, seems a product of this generation.'

Waugh's tribute at the front of the book to Harold Acton as leader of the generation was kindly meant, but had unforeseen repercussions. Acton's own novel *Humdrum* had come out simultaneously, and several reviewers, including Connolly, contrasted it very unfavourably with Waugh's – Connolly described Acton as 'looking on at the present day from the decade of the Yellow Book'. Acton had been thought of as the likely literary star of his circle, but just as the intellectual leadership had passed to him from Brian Howard when Acton came up to Oxford and Howard was left behind at Eton, so now with the publication of *Decline and Fall* it passed from him to Waugh, never to be relinquished. Acton continued to write and be published, but Waugh now soared ahead, to the extent that Acton's name became better known as an *éminence grise* behind Waugh than as an author in his own right. Acton records this without bitterness in his memoirs: 'At a bungalow in Ceylon I was pleasantly surprised to hear: "Aha, your name is familiar to me. Now where did I see it? Of course – in *Decline and Fall*. Pretty hot stuff. What sort of chap is Evelyn Waugh? I can't quite make him out."''

3

A Sort of Cumulative Futility

Harold Acton had set himself up in London. 'He has taken rather a charming flat in John Street, Adelphi, with a Chinese servant and many paintings of himself,' Waugh wrote in his diary in February 1927. Several of the Hypocrites had settled in the Great Ormond Street area of Bloomsbury where, says Anthony Powell, they had 'reconstructed a somewhat Oxfordish mode of life'. Powell himself, reacting against everything associated with Oxford, chose another *quartier*, the little 'village' of Shepherd Market, tucked between Mayfair and the noisy thoroughfare of Piccadilly.

Though Powell did not altogether care to admit it, his choice of district was influenced by the fact that Shepherd Market is the setting of the opening chapters of Michael Arlen's *The Green Hat* (1924) – the chapters describing the arrival out of the night, and into the life of the narrator, of the beautiful and seductive Iris Storm, with her Hispano-Suiza car, her 'aura of many adventures', and her boyishly cropped hair. (She was loosely modelled on Nancy Cunard, with whom Arlen, Armenian-born and English-educated, had had an affair.) *The Green Hat* shocked the older generation with its portrayal of liberated sexual *mores* – Alan Pryce-Jones's father threw the book on the fire – but Osbert Lancaster writes that, after he had read it, London 'was suddenly transfigured', while in *Decline and Fall*, describing Berkeley Square and its environs, Waugh observes sardonically: 'All Mayfair seemed to throb with the heart of Mr Arlen.'

Powell took rooms on the ground floor of 9 Shepherd Market, and found that the district conformed pretty closely to Arlen's description – the little shops, the down-to-earth pubs, the prostitutes who would come in from their nightly beat on Piccadilly to their flats in a big block opposite Powell's digs, a segregation of housing that (says Powell) differentiated them from the 'merely raffish'. Despite these local interests, he experienced a 'rather monochromatic' twelve months before beginning to find his way around London society.

Leaving work at Duckworth's in Henrietta Street, Covent Garden, he would walk or take a Tube to Shepherd Market, and eat supper in one of the pubs there, unless he had accepted a dinner invitation from one of the senior men in the publishing house. Then it was back to his rooms, where his landlady would send in a cup of tea and a slice of cake 'last thing' before he retired to bed. After some months, the spring and early summer of 1927 brought a few invitations to débutante dances, and Powell was glad enough to accept, though this was not really the life with which he was hoping to make contact. 'I was all the time aware that a more invigorating, less staid, world existed. . . .'

Gradually, he began to make contact with more adventurous circles. Some were ostensibly fashionable – the 'smart' parties given by Lady Cunard, mother of Nancy; 'artists' parties' like small-scale versions of the Chelsea Arts Ball; and publishers' and art-dealers' parties. Yet Powell says that none of these 'was essentially a Twenties party'. The real thing was almost reached in Bloomsbury, or at Augustus John's studio in Chelsea, but not quite. The true Twenties party, says Powell, was likely to be given by a host or hostess with no personal distinction, who might not know half the guests who had strayed into his or her house – they had been invited by somebody who knew somebody who knew the person who was giving the party.

Waugh describes an evening spent largely at a party of this sort, in September 1926:

> In the evening we went to the Alhambra and then on to a party given by the lesbian girls I met the other day. It was a party [sic]. Sir Francis Laking, dressed first as a girl and then stark naked, attempted a Charleston. A Russian played a saw like a violin. Lulu Waters-Welch came. He is living in sin with [the fifth Earl of] Effingham. . . . Alastair and I both got very drunk indeed. I think I was rude to Bobbie. There was a fight between two men. Also a policewoman who scared everyone and made Joan very pugnacious.

Powell notes that for some reason hostesses 'were . . . often well-to-do lesbians'.

Fancy dress was worn more often than not, though evening dress was quite acceptable (white tie or black tie). Alan Pryce-Jones says it was useful to travel around with a *matelot* suit, 'which we had found out to be the quickest and simplest form of fancy dress', as well as a dinner jacket. 'One was always ... dressing up for a party.' Brian Howard went to one party dressed as a duchess of 1905 vintage:

> Willie Clarkson [theatrical make-up artist] took an hour to make me up. My dear, in his hands my face suddenly became that of some bastard daughter with a dozen mothers. ... A mixture, *au fin*, of Lady Tree and an Eton dame. You can imagine me, thumping, rather top-heavy, up those stairs at Grosvenor Square. Statuesque, terrific. People waiting on the landing above recoiled.

A Noël Coward song, 'I Went to a Marvellous Party', describes Cecil Beaton's equally ambitious costumes on such occasions: 'Dear Cecil arrived wearing armour / Some shells and a black feather boa. ...' Harold Acton says that Coward himself was an influence on the character of these parties: 'The talkative devised a special basic English in which to shoot wisecracks at each other in the style of Noël Coward.' This form of speech, says Acton, was favoured largely because it carried over the noise of the gramophone, which rendered ordinary conversation quite impossible:

> The invasion of Jazz had begun. ... Couples clung together forlornly, swaying to some raucous Blues. George Gershwin's 'Rhapsody in Blue' accompanied every rough-and-tumble on the sofa. It seemed to contain all the intoxication of black and chromium cocktail bars ... high-pressure vitality followed by the hangover of yesterday's newspapers blown along gusty streets soon after a sour city dawn. Gershwin himself ... I heard play it to perfection at the Savoy Hotel.

The Charleston dominated the dance-floor; Waugh records in his diary for December 1925 that 'Olivia [Plunket Greene], who is becoming literally "Charleston crazy", was miserable until in an interval after supper she found a fairly empty room to dance it in.' Certain parties had black jazz bands, or members of the Blackbirds negro revue team, who were performing in London during 1926–7. Waugh describes one such occasion:

> Alec and Harold and I dined first at the Ritz. Then ... to Oliver [Messel]'s. It was a crowded party with all the Blackbirds and the Oxford Brian Howard set and stray and squalid stragglers uninvited ... Cecil Roberts became insensible with drink and, curled in overcoat, vomited and pissed intermittently. Robert Byron made an ostentatious entry as

Queen Victoria. The Earl of Rosse and I cut each other throughout the evening. Olivia and I both felt more than a little lonely.

The more ambitious parties had themes, or were held in curious places. A 'Mozart Party' in the Burlington Galleries had a symphony orchestra playing the 'Jupiter', and everyone dressed in Mozartian costume. There was a 'Second Childhood Party' at which guests wore baby clothing and arrived in prams, a Circus Party given by the dress designer Norman Hartnell, and a Cowboy Party held by Harold and William Acton in a house they had taken together in Lancaster Gate. 'The saxophone wailed downstairs,' writes Harold, 'and a thousand feet stomped an African lullaby. Walls and floors seemed to tremble and heave. . . . Our English servants gave notice.' But the party that everyone especially remembered was the Swimming-Pool Party.

Held at the St George's Baths, Buckingham Palace Road, on Friday, 13 July 1928, beginning at eleven p.m., its hosts were Brian Howard, Eddie Gathorne-Hardy, 'Babe' Plunket Greene (sister-in-law of Olivia) and Elizabeth Ponsonby. The invitation instructed 'Please wear a Bathing Suit and bring a Bath Towel and a Bottle.' (The bottle-party was a recent invention, by which festivity might be managed on small means. Michael Arlen turned up to one of the earliest with half a dozen bottles of pink champagne.) Tom Driberg, who had recently taken a job with the *Daily Express*, reported on the evening for the paper's 'Talk of the Town' gossip column:

> Bathing costumes of the most dazzling kinds and colours were worn by the guests. Dancing took place to the strains of a negro orchestra, and the hardy leaped into the bath, of which the water had been slightly warmed. . . . A special cocktail, christened the Bathwater Cocktail, was invented for the occasion.

Driberg gave a brief portrait of one of the hosts: 'Elizabeth Ponsonby – Eternal sophistication looks out, a little wearily, from under her heavy eyelids, and her mouth, smiling as enigmatically as that of the Giaconda, can utter all knowledge and all wisdom.' The Swimming-Pool Party ended the next morning when the police were called to eject stragglers, who attempted to disrobe the constables and get them to join the party. A press photograph shows the Mozart Party concluding in the street, where puzzled night-watchmen have allowed the wigged and powdered guests to pose with a roadmender's drill. The caption reads: 'Bright Young People help to dig up Piccadilly after the Mozart Party'. The terms 'Bright Young People' or 'Bright Young Things' had been coined by Fleet Street for the set who gave these curious parties. One of Waugh's friends records that he would use it ironically of particularly serious individuals – 'Bright Young Henry Yorke'.

Anthony Powell says that, *pace* Iris Storm, the women one met at such parties were not necessarily sexually liberated; they 'expected to have passes made at them', but were well able to fend these off. 'One heard stories of debs who could be got to bed, but I should have thought such emancipation belonged, in general, to a somewhat later period, when chaperonage had diminished, and the night-club taken a firmer hold.' In his novel *Humdrum*, Harold Acton describes such sexual contacts as were achieved at or after these parties as being brittle and transitory, like the dialogue of Noël Coward: 'They were just "frightfully amusing". . . . They might bruise and press each other's flesh. . . . No hearts to break and nothing to linger afterwards behind.'

One of the regulars at the 'freak' parties, Donald Rolph, says that 'the great fun was getting ready for the occasion, making all the preparations, dressing up. The actual party was often a bit of an anticlimax.' This was certainly true of 'The Great Urban Dionysia', a Greek-mythology party devised by Brian Howard, and intended to be the biggest and best of them all. The invitation was outsize – sixteen inches high – and announced the party as taking place:

AT 1 MARYLEBONE LANE, OXFORD STREET
(BEHIND BUMPUS'S) ON THE 4th OF APRIL 1929
AT 11 p.m., CELEBRATED BY
BABE PLUNKET GREENE
IN HONOUR OF THE TWENTY-FOURTH BIRTHDAY OF
BRIAN HOWARD

Guests were instructed to be 'dressed as a *definite* character in *Greek* mythology' and to bring wine, also to carry the invitation in order to obtain admission. Gate-crashing was common; for Norman Hartnell's Circus Party, Brian Howard had several invitations forged by a printer for himself and his friends.

The Dionysia invitation was bordered by two lists of Brian's current loves and hates, headed 'J'ACCUSE' and 'J'ADORE'. The former included:

> Intellect
> Those incredibly 'Private' Dances
> The Bright Young People

The 'J'ADORE' list included 'Intuition, Jazz, Havelock Ellis'. The actual party was, by contrast, rather flat; the *Evening Standard* described it as suffering from 'lack of excitement', though some of the costumes were remarkable – 'Mr Ernest Thesiger wore menacing black robes as the Medusa.'

Not content with organizing a mere party like the rest, Brian also had the idea of staging an Oxford-style hoax on the lines of 'Homage to Beethoven', an exhibition of the works of 'Bruno Hatte', a modernist painter of German extraction. Hatte had supposedly been discovered, living obscurely in the English countryside, by Brian's friend Bryan Guinness, a member of the Anglo-Irish brewing family, married to Diana Mitford. Spoof abstract paintings were manufactured, and Evelyn Waugh wrote a catalogue for the exhibition. Bryan Guinness's brother-in-law Tom Mitford dressed up as 'Hatte' in a false moustache and dark glasses, but the disguise was penetrated after Maurice Bowra, who was among the guests at the private view, approached 'Hatte' and addressed him volubly in German, a language which Mitford did not speak. In any case the joke fell rather flat, since most of the Bright Young People knew all about the deception in advance.

The parties sometimes had unpleasant repercussions. It was not uncommon for them to end in a fight; Allanah Harper, another of the Bright Young People, describes finding herself 'in the middle of a jealous fracas ... which ... resulted in my dress being practically torn off and tufts of my hair held up as trophies'. The final party of the era, a 'White Party' at a house in Kent to which everyone had to come dressed in white, ended with a quarrel after which a young man drove off wildly with one of the girls, crashed the car and was killed (she was unhurt). Brian Howard commented of this to his mother, who was very shocked by what she had read in the paper: 'I see it as an amusing, wildish party given by the only group of young people outside the Continent who ... know genuinely how to enjoy themselves.' But Allanah Harper wonders how she and her friends could really have found it fun: 'So much has been written about the Parties in the 'twenties. ... Looking back upon them now, they appear like a Jerome Bosch hell.'

Many partygoers habitually rounded off the evening at some establishment where drinks were served after hours. Alan Pryce-Jones mentions 'an unassuming nightclub behind Piccadilly Circus, the Blue Lantern', and Anthony Powell names in this context the Cavendish Hotel in Jermyn Street, though to obtain a drink there at any time of day, let alone late at night, it was absolutely necessary to be known to and approved by the proprietor, Mrs Rosa Lewis.

Powell knew of the place from his father, who regarded it with a certain amount of awe, as a haunt of various dashing fellow-soldiers of his day. 'He would hint at orgies, but gave no clue to their nature, and I did not like to ask.' When Powell himself first entered the hotel, in the company of Richard Plunket Greene, it was on a night when Mrs Lewis happened to be absent. Consequently nothing whatever was going on: 'All Cavendish life completely depended on the proprietress.' On a later visit, Powell found her presiding over the large drawing-room on the first floor, a salon 'done up in the manner of a somewhat decayed country house'. Aldous Huxley similarly compares the Cavendish to 'a run-down country house – large comfortable rooms, but everything shabby and a bit dirty'.

The occupants of the drawing-room could not be so easily classified. Powell says that some of them usually seemed unsure why they were there. 'A couple of pink-faced Guards ensigns would not be unexpected; nor an American. ... Augustus John, sitting drinking alone in the corner, was always a possibility. Then, probably only passing through the room, would be vague individuals, or parties of people, whose presence seemed absolutely inexplicable.' Several of these would be people who came up from the country from time to time, and knew of nowhere else in the Piccadilly area so reasonable in its terms, 'remaining totally unaware of the hotel's less prim side'. Rosa Lewis herself tended to wander in and out rather than playing the formal hostess. If in good form she was unbeatable company, but she had gloomy evenings: 'Lights on all over the house! I'll go bankrupt!'

There was a piano in the corner, and someone might be playing it. Powell describes Rosa lying in an armchair and suddeningly noticing that the music had ceased. 'Go back and play "Old Man River,"' she ordered the pianist. He protested; he was an American performer of considerable skill, probably very well known, though nobody had been introduced to him. 'Do as I tell you,' snapped Mrs Lewis.

'I'm not going to be treated like a servant.'

'Don't be a bloody fool.'

'I won't be spoken to like that.'

'Don't talk so much. Let's have another bottle of wine. Go back and play "Old Man River", and do as you're told.'

The pianist gave in – 'It had been foolish to rebel,' remarks Powell – and the champagne arrived and was poured out. 'At the Cavendish "a bottle of wine" always meant champagne. It was as if champagne was the only wine anyone had heard of there. The American obliged with "Old Man River". Rosa Lewis went fast asleep in her armchair.'

The champagne was paid for by a simple system: Rosa put it on the bill of whomever she considered the most affluent person present. Consequently, says Powell, 'a sense of financial anxiety' pervaded the room. One of the comic songs of the cabaret artist Douglas Byng alludes to this:

> The bridegroom's with Rosa,
> She's saying he owes her
> For millions of magnums of Mumm.

Something like this happened to Cyril Connolly in 1934, when he was attending the wedding of his friend Lord Antrim; in his journal he records that he was 'embarrassed ... at reception by Rosa Lewis, '''ere's the man wot owes me money, Bobbie give 'im a writ'' – we had to slink out very quickly. ...' On the other hand it was by no means unknown for Rosa herself to stand guests a bottle, especially if those present were thought by her to be hard up.

Powell says that the Cavendish seemed to exist 'in a surrealist *Alice-Through-the-Looking-Glass* dimension where normal life was turned upside down'. The Lewis Carroll atmosphere was heightened by the fact that in Rosa's company people seemed to lose their identities and acquire someone else's. An acquaintance of Powell's was one day passing through the entrance hall when Rosa confronted him. 'Have you come about the drains?' 'You know me very well, Mrs Lewis, I'm staying here.' 'Then why are you wearing a brown hat?' Powell himself was once walking down Jermyn Street when he saw Rosa approaching. 'Well, *you're* a ghost from the past,' she announced. 'Come and have a drink.' In her private sitting-room at the Cavendish she introduced him to the four or five people gathered there with the words: 'This is Bimbash Stewart.' Some years later, Powell happened to discover that there really had been a Bimbash Stewart, an Edwardian man-about-town who had died in 1907.

Rosa was often known to make such confusions of present and past. Given what Powell calls 'her usual air of moving in a dream', it was understandable that her mind should slip back to the turn of the century, since that had been her heyday. Born in 1867 into a tradesman's family on the north-eastern edge of London, she had entered domestic service at the age of twelve, become a cook and been noticed by Augustus Lumley, who acted as pander for the future Edward VII's sexual requirements. To give the Prince premises for his liaisons, Lumley and another 'provider', Sir Andrew Clarke, took a house in Eaton Terrace, arranged for Rosa to be married to Sir Andrew's butler, Excelsior Lewis, and set them up as apparently respectable husband-and-wife proprietors of 'lodgings', which the Prince could use (via a back gate) whenever he wanted. It has occasionally been suggested that Rosa herself became a royal mistress, but, though she was a fine-looking young woman, love affairs played no part in her life, and she looked on sex as merely another of her business enterprises. On the other hand she was capable of the most *louche* remarks. A young Italian waiter, taking an order for drinks at the Cavendish, asked if the party would like liqueurs. 'Lick your own,' snapped Rosa.

She soon got bored with keeping a bordello for the Prince, and began to work as a freelance caterer, employing an army of young women and providing dinners for society hostesses; she was sometimes engaged at Buckingham Palace, and for a while supervised the food at White's club. It is hard to credit that she was ever a distinguished cook; one of her few surviving recipes is for snipe or quail wrapped in slices of beef and cooked in suet pudding, which produced complaints from at least one member of White's. In 1902 she bought the Cavendish. Once, in Anthony Powell's hearing, she began to explain how she had become a hotel-keeper, giving her husband as the reason: 'I took the Cavendish on because I was sorry for him. After he went bankrupt, that was.' Unfortunately in the course of the peroration the surname 'Lewis' changed almost imperceptibly into 'Lois', and she switched tracks into an anecdote about Lois Stewart, formerly wife of the second Viscount Tredegar, both of them well known in the bohemian *beau monde*. Powell 'tried to get the conversation back on to the right lines, but it was no good'.

Her views on hotels were much like John Fothergill's: 'I wanted it to be like one's own home. ... I like people, and I think if you make a place like the people you like, you get the people you like.' Her marriage had been childless, and she bullied the Cavendish guests as if they had been her offspring. Several of them have described the hotel in childlike terms, calling it 'a naughty nursery' where Nanny provided champagne and girls rather than toys. Edward VII, now King, was occasionally a discreet client for such services; Rosa earmarked one of the suites for his use (there had probably been a surreptitious royal subsidy to help her buy the hotel), and she also provided 'companionship' for a number of Edwardian aristocrats. Powell gathered that one or two of her young ladies had almost acquired titles themselves in consequence. 'Look at the way Jack Fordingbridge wanted to marry Ivy Peters,' she told him. 'He wanted to *marry* her. The Duke was almost off his head about his son and heir. I introduced Fordingbridge to Freda Brown, and he dropped Ivy Peters like a hot potato. People forget all the good I've done.' She made little use of professional tarts, but had her own methods. During the 1930s there were complaints from the shopgirls in Fortnum & Mason's, around the corner from the Cavendish, that Rosa would accost them as they left work and ask them if they would 'like a little drink' with the gentlemen in the Cavendish. Evelyn Waugh alleges:

> there was an elderly woman circa 1926 called Lady Cook who used to be a crony of Rosa's. 'Now don't you go after those street women. Why don't you have Lady Cook here?' ... Rosa often called the penis 'the WINKLE', a term I have not heard on other lips. When chaps refused to avail themselves of Lady Cook and sought pleasure outside, Rosa pounced on them and said: 'I'll get a doctor in to look at your winkle.'

This side of the hotel gave the place what Powell calls 'a touch of something a shade macabre'. Rosa sometimes mistook her visitors' intentions. When Harry Weymouth, later Lord Bath, took the wife of an American film director there one night for a late drink, without any designs on the lady, Rosa shouted out that a room had been reserved for them both. 'It was an awkward moment,' says Lord Bath. Rosa had no objection to male homosexuality; a friend of Powell's once shared a double suite with an American acquaintance, and was awakened in the middle of the night by Rosa switching on the light and regarding each of them in their single beds with obvious disappointment. 'I hoped it would be different,' she observed before snapping the light off again. On this subject she used to say: 'I don't mind the boys doing it, if they do it with their own class, but I won't have the girls doing it, because they've got nothing to do it with.'

Her activities in this field seemed all the more remarkable because of her appearance and manner; Powell emphasizes her extremely respectable exterior – 'Tall, stately, whitehaired ... formidable to a degree', resembling 'the statuesque wife of a senior civil servant'. She spoke an ancient and long-forgotten form of Cockney.

She collected around herself at the Cavendish figures of equal eccentricity, such as Sir William Eden, an irascible individual in retreat from his wife and children, who hated dogs, the sound of whistling, the colour red and the architecture of Buckingham Palace; he lived and died in a Cavendish suite, where he would sometimes entertain professional prize-fighters to dinner. There was also Scott the hall porter, who loved his pet dog Freddy so deeply that when it died he had it stuffed and presented it to another resident, Lord Ribblesdale. Scott, who hated any encounter (internal or external) with water, would meet Cavendish clients at the London railway termini, and tie a ribbon on the dog to celebrate each arrival. On a busy day Freddy might sport fifteen, including a tartan if one of them happened to be a Scot.

During the First World War, Rosa provided comforts for those on leave ('Nice clean girls'), and during the 1920s continued her life at the Cavendish much as before, though there was now a distinctly faded, melancholy air about the place. Rosa had ceased to cook and, though food of sorts could be acquired from the kitchen, most guests had meals sent in. Rosa herself barely bothered to dress in the mornings; she could be seen in a dressing-gown and bedroom slippers and, when she went out, would simply throw an ancient fur coat over this outfit. The entrance hall of the hotel was always stacked with luggage, much of it unclaimed and dating back to the war; the letter rack was bursting with *poste restante* mail, 'to be sent on' (it never was); and there was a curious clutter of furniture and other items – abandoned tennis rackets and polo sticks, plush settees and ornate armchairs bought by Rosa at country-house sales, even an entire marble staircase, acquired at a knockdown price when Dorchester House in Park Lane was demolished to make way for the Dorchester Hotel, which lay gathering moss in the back courtyard.

Waugh said he was 'never a real habitué' of the place, but was taken there occasionally by Alastair Graham, David Plunket Greene and others of his circle. Rosa would welcome them into her downstairs parlour or the upstairs drawing-room, introducing the other occupants in her usual manner: 'Here they all are. There's Snivelling Dick, knew him before he was born. Pots of money. They gave him a gold cigarette case when his trousers fell down in Piccadilly. Young Evan's upstairs having twins. Lady What's-er-name over there looks like a tart but she isn't. Edith and I stopped her brother marrying that gingerbust. Queen Mary thinks the world of her.' (Edith was Rosa's 'companion' and assistant at the Cavendish.)

Undoubtedly Rosa cultivated this ability to confuse identities. 'I won't have that tart coming in here chasing after young So-and-so,' she would observe as some highly respectable socialite from the Midland counties entered the hotel. Her biographer Daphne Fielding observes that 'she probably knew exactly who the woman was and only made the mistake on purpose'.

Cyril Connolly was an occasional habitué of the Cavendish, though not among Rosa's favourites; Waugh says that he did not look 'exactly like a cornet of the Blues', the social type that 'Rosa really accepted'.

From the autumn of 1927, for two years, Connolly was contributing a fortnightly book review to the *New Statesman*. Meanwhile, like Powell, he was finding fresh social paths to explore. At Christmas 1927 he wrote in his journal:

> *Tuesday*. Wrote my article in the morning, very cold day. Lunch at the Travellers' with Gladwyn Jebb, nice, praise of Bobbie [Longden]. Literature discussed, on to see Sligger off at Victoria but met the wrong train. ... On to the Ritz, and write to Bobbie, then go and fetch Nina Seafeld. Thrill in the drawing room at North Street, the candles, the log fire, the dull light on my top hat, the taxi waiting in the frost outside. Then Nina's footfall on the stair and delicious *roucoulement* of greeting. On to Lady Cunard's, carol singers drear, dance with Nina and talk to Patrick and Bryan Guinness who arrive. Snobbish thrill at sight of the Prince of Wales walking alone up their wide staircase and shaking hands with Maurice Baring and Diana Cooper at the top. ... Enjoyed the rich patina of the Cunard soirée, the lovely women, the vacant faces ... and the incredible stupid air of luxurious abandon on Lady Cunard's face as she danced with the Prince of Wales. We sat next to him at supper.

Connolly was in love with the seventeen-year-old Horatia ('Racy') Fisher, niece of Desmond MacCarthy, and the journal, begun that Christmas, is at first largely taken up with this, though Connolly was also still passionately attached to Bobbie Longden.

> *Monday*. ... Racy comes and we discuss our situation. ... Racy very lovely and boyish, wearing a yellow skirt that matched my cushions and altogether brown faced, green eyes, tender and jovial. ... I think she really may be in love with me and certainly would not like to let me go.

And in another entry he describes 'Racy, slim, golden, slant-eyed, in her boy's felt hat ...'.

Racy's parents called a halt to the affair, forbidding her to communicate with Connolly. In the journal he recorded 'General sense of depression and discontent with usual horror of literature and hopeless uncertainty over Racy'. He drifted off to the Continent, slept with a Moroccan girl prostitute in Paris ('young and v. lovely, but very cold, competent and costly'), visited Bernard Berenson in Florence, went to Venice and Zagreb where he 'missed Bobbie' and slept with another girl prostitute, and went on to Berlin where he accompanied Ivor Novello, a friend of a friend, in a 'dreary round of homosexual places'. Novello tried to make a pass at him in a taxi – '"How nice you are" – I thought he meant a carthorse which we were passing and said "Yes, he's grand." He seemed put out.' Another acquaintance made in Berlin was Harold Nicolson: 'He says he hates femininity. . . . He is rather protean and slippery, the adaptable diplomatic manner. . . . I think only pretending to be in love with me.' Nicolson wrote to his wife Vita Sackville-West describing Connolly as 'like the young Beethoven with spots'.

Connolly was uncertain about his own sexual nature. In Berlin he experienced 'the desire to see more of Bobbie. . . . All these weeks I have lived under his shadow.' He now believed that women found him attractive, and decided to live as an 'intolerant, indifferent, almost Bloomsbury young man', resolving to reduce sex to 'a pigeon-holed minimum', working off his desires 'by short sharp affairs with any kind of accessible women – avoid virgins, wives, boys, tarts, venereal disease, debutantes, marriage and masturbation'. Returning to England, he felt 'nothing but an intense disgust at its stupidity'; almost its only virtue was that 'Robert Longden and Racy Fisher live there.' As to literature and criticism, he determined to 'Abuse other people's novels; get on with [my] own.'

Racy fell in love with a man named Goldman. 'There it is,' wrote Cyril; 'luckily Bobbie here to break the fall.' He and Bobbie spent part of the summer on the south coast of England. 'Our chief intimacy consisted in making bad jokes. . . . We would breakfast in our dressing gowns and later in the morning walk down to the sea. . . . The heat was incredible, the haystacks and barns and trees shimmered in haze. . . . A fulfilment of one's earliest schoolboy daydreams – the summer holidays in which one had one's best friend to stay.'

Early in 1929 he went to Paris, where he met an eighteen-year-old American art student, Jean Bakewell. Back in London he felt 'miserably depressed', and returned to Paris to see her again. They set off together for Spain. 'Jean has short dark hair, green eyes and high cheekbones, olive skin and a rather oriental appearance, like a young man from Indo-China.' Elsewhere in the journal he describes her 'slightly sullen expression and short boy's hair'.

She and her friend Mara told Connolly they were lesbians, which excited him. In fact she was pregnant from a brief affair with a champagne merchant; soon, she had an abortion. She and Connolly slept together. 'Jean . . . seemed a lovely pagan from Tibullus or the Greek anthology, with her youth, her passive and natural pleasure, her lovely boy's body. . . .'

In an ebullient mood after his trip to Spain with her, Cyril wrote a mock gossip column in his journal:

ROUND THE TOWN

A sponge and barnacle party in which the guests compete to see who can stay longest is the latest amusement of the Bright Young People – 'We had to invent it,' said Miss Cetera Etcetera, 'to keep out gate-crashers, who are mostly poor people and sooner or later have to return to their work.' The winners were a young married couple – 'It solves our house-hunting,' Mrs Waugh said.

Around Christmas 1927, Anthony Powell met Waugh in an Under-ground train. He was in high spirits. 'Before a word could be said on any other subject he made a statement. "I'm going to be married." . . . "Who to?" "She's called Evelyn Gardner."'

Powell knew the name slightly: Alec Waugh had mentioned her and her flatmate Pansy Pakenham, describing them as more than usually pleasant examples of the Modern Girl, emancipated but not brassy. Dudley Carew, who claimed to have introduced the two Evelyns to each other at a party in his flat, describes Evelyn Gardner as having 'a kind of puppyish eagerness to appreciate and embrace everything and everybody'.

She and Pansy Pakenham shared a flat over a tobacconist's shop just off Sloane Square. She was the daughter of the late Lord Burghclere, and Pansy's father was the late Earl of Longford, killed at Gallipoli. Soon after his meeting with Waugh, Powell was invited for a drink at the flat. He found that Evelyn Gardner was indeed, in appearance, exactly the Modern Girl: 'Slight, boyish, an Eton crop . . .'. As Alec Waugh had said, there was nothing of Iris Storm about her; she was relaxed and easy-going. Photographs emphasize her boyishness; pic-tured alongside Evelyn Waugh, she appears almost the more masculine of the two. Nancy Mitford, who knew her well, described her in a 1967 interview in a French magazine as being smaller in stature than Waugh, adding that she resembled 'un ravissant garçon, un page'.

Waugh was undoubtedly thinking of her when he wrote his short story 'On Guard', first published in 1934. It describes Millicent Blade, who constantly breaks the hearts of young Englishmen because of the shape of her nose:

> It was not a nose to appeal to painters, for it was far too small and quite without shape . . . but . . . it was a nose that pierced the thin surface crust of the English heart to its warm and pulpy core; a nose to take the thoughts of English manhood back to its schooldays, to the doughy-faced urchins on whom it had squandered its first affection, to memories of changing room and chapel and battered straw boaters.

A portrait photograph of Evelyn Gardner displays just such a nose; the face could be that of a fifteen-year-old boy at Lancing. Harold Acton regards Waugh's attraction to her as a natural sequel to his feelings for Alastair Graham. Indeed, Waugh might never have shown an interest in her had Alastair remained in England. As it was, he had been accepted (rather improbably) for the Diplomatic Service, and was about to sail for Athens.

Evelyn Gardner's boyishness was more than an accident of appearance. She was the youngest of the four children of Lord Burghclere, all of whom were girls. For the title to have survived, Evelyn would have had to be a boy.* Her mother undoubtedly resented the fact that she was not male, and this may explain her sexually ambiguous Christian name.

She had already been engaged several times. Lady Pansy Lamb (the former Pansy Pakenham) identifies the fiancés as 'an impecunious member of the *beau monde* in the Guards', 'a frightful bounder' and an illegitimate young man who was secretary to Rupert Brooke's mother. Christopher Sykes says that Evelyn's mother sent her to Australia to get her out of one of these tangles, but during the voyage she fell in love with the purser and accepted his proposal of marriage. This engagement was in turn broken, and other alliances followed. Sykes quotes a friend describing her as having 'a very generous nature, but she was essentially light'.

Evelyn Gardner herself has said that the repeated engagements were the result of a desperate wish to get away from home. Her mother, simultaneously rejecting and domineering, had provided no affection in Evelyn's childhood, and had threatened to dismiss her daughter's beloved nanny if her own afternoon rest was disturbed by noises from the nursery. Evelyn's sisters had partly made up for this lack of love, and she was very attached to them. Still very childlike at the age of twenty-four (she was born in 1903, the same year as Waugh), she was in search of someone who, like her sisters, would make few emotional demands of her, but would take firm and kindly control of her life.

Waugh met her in April 1927, describing her in his diary as 'a nice girl called Evelyn Gardner'. Pansy Lamb says she showed no particular interest in him at first; 'the ardour was all on his side'. But Pansy herself thought him far more suitable than the previous fiancés, and did what she could to promote the match.

* The title was only a generation old; Evelyn's father, a successful politician, had been created the first Baron Burghclere. Her mother, however, came from the 'real' aristocracy – she was the daughter of the fourth Earl of Carnarvon.

Harold Acton in the costume he devised for himself as an undergraduate: 'I wore jackets with broad lapels and broad pleated trousers.' A caricature from *Isis*, 1925.

Brian Howard in Eton schooldays: 'I am said to be the image of Max Beerbohm when he was beautiful as well as brilliant.'

Evelyn Waugh at the beginning of his schooldays at Lancing: 'I did not admire the other boys.'

Harold Acton, drawn by Waugh, with the megaphone through which he recited his poetry. From *Isis*, 1923.

C.R.M.F. Cruttwell, Waugh's tutor at Hertford College, Oxford. Waugh liked to believe that he was sexually attracted to dogs.

'Sligger' Urquhart of Balliol, *bête noire* of Waugh, who would chant 'The Dean of Balliol sleeps with men'.

Richard Pares, drawn by Waugh in *Isis*, and described by him as 'my first homosexual love'.

'That grim act parricide', the fifth of Waugh's 'Seven Deadly Sins' drawings in *Cherwell*, 1926.

(Left to right) Evelyn Waugh, his father, Arthur, and his brother, Alec.

Evelyn Waugh as a young man – 'a little un', Harold Acton called him.

Evelyn Waugh's grandfather, Dr Alexander Waugh of Somerset. 'The happiness of all would depend on his temper', wrote Evelyn.

Osbert Lancaster's drawing of Maurice Bowra handing out champagne. John Betjeman describes 'the feeling of safe elation as the glass was thrust into one's hand'.

Alastair Graham, Waugh's 'friend of my heart . . . we were inseparable'.

John Fothergill, gentleman innkeeper of the Spreadeagle at Thame.

Brian Howard as he looked when Waugh first knew him: 'tall, slim, rather swarthy, with large saucy eyes'.

Two frames from *The Scarlet Woman*, showing Evelyn Waugh as 'Sligger' (in blond wig) and John Greenidge as the Prince of Wales.

Bright Young People helping to dig up Piccadilly after David Tennant's 'Mozart Party' in the Burlington Gardens.

Rosa Lewis and friends in her sitting room at the Cavendish Hotel. 'There's Mr What-d'you-call-him, and that's an American, and there's the King of Ruritania.'

Evelyn Gardner before her marriage to Evelyn Waugh. *'Un ravissant garçon, un page'*, said Nancy Mitford.

'A Bride and Bridegroom . Married Last Week: Mr Evelyn Waugh and the Hon. Mrs Evelyn Waugh, formerly the Hon. Evelyn Gardner.' A photograph from the *Sketch*.

She-Evelyn and He-Evelyn at the 'Tropical' Party on the *Friendship*, after she had confessed infidelity with John Heygate.

Evelyn Waugh photographed by Howard Coster not long after the break-up of his marriage to Evelyn Gardner. 'I did not know it was possible to be so miserable and live.'

Nancy Mitford's wedding in 1933 to Peter Rodd, one of the models for Basil Seal.

Basil Murray, who provided the first name and something of the character of Basil Seal.

Evelyn Waugh with Lady Mary and Lady Dorothy Lygon, to whom he behaved like a naughty uncle.

As Christmas 1927 approached, Evelyn Gardner began to talk of going to Canada for a while, and Waugh decided to take action. On Monday, 12 December 1927, he 'dined with Evelyn at the Ritz. Proposed marriage. Inconclusive.' The dinner was not in the main restaurant of the hotel, but in the comparatively inexpensive Grill downstairs. It has been alleged that, in his speech of proposal, Waugh suggested that they should get married and 'see how it goes', a phrase implying that he was not especially committed to marriage. Evelyn Gardner has confirmed that he used 'words to that effect'.

Although he was affecting the casual manner of the Bright Young People, it is evident from his diary that her answer mattered very much to him. After her 'inconclusive' reply, he went on to a party, then 'rang up Pansy who advised in favour of marriage. Went to Sloane Square and discussed it [with Pansy and maybe again with Evelyn Gardner herself]. Went to Bourdon Street and told Olivia [Plunket Greene]. Home late and unable to sleep.' Next morning, 'Evelyn rang up to say she had made up her mind to accept.' Evelyn Gardner has said of her decision that she thought that no one would be much hurt if the marriage did not work out.

When she learnt of her daughter's latest engagement, Lady Burghclere was at least as displeased as she had been on the previous occasions. Anthony Powell observes that Waugh was in most respects 'even less eligible' than the other fiancés, except the ship's purser; he possessed no visible means of support (this was before the publication of *Rossetti*, let alone *Decline and Fall!*), and rumours of his 'supposedly dissipated habits' began to reach Lady Burghclere's ears. Moreover he came from the middle classes. 'It never occurred to me to think I wasn't a gentleman until Lady Burghclere pointed it out,' he wrote in 1952.

He was, in fact, doing his best now to learn a trade. He had begun to study carpentry at the Central School of Arts and Crafts, giving his reason to Anthony Powell as 'Oh, Tolstoy and all that', though Powell could see more connection with the Pre-Raphaelites. In December 1927 he recorded that he had 'nearly finished making a mahogany bed table. Not very well.' This scarcely promised a distinguished career or a substantial income while, when *Decline and Fall* was completed and accepted for publication, his impending appearance as a novelist contributed nothing to his eligibility in the eyes of Lady Burghclere. Her sister happened to be married to Gerald Duckworth, whose firm had demanded the bowdlerization of the book, so she was informed in some detail about its scurrilous nature. Waugh wrote to a friend that there would 'probably be an elopement soon'.

As it happened, Pansy Pakenham had just got engaged, to the painter Henry Lamb, but since he was not yet divorced from his first wife she, too, was having trouble with her family. A double 'elopement' of sorts therefore took place. Evelyn Gardner and Pansy left Sloane Square and moved for a while to Dorset, taking rooms in a boarding house in Wimborne. Lamb had a house nearby, in Poole, and Waugh moved to the Barley Mow just outside Wimborne, where he completed the novel.

After a few weeks, in May 1928, Waugh and Evelyn Gardner returned to London. Waugh's diary describes what happened next in studiedly casual language: they set off for a cinema in Dulwich, 'but got bored waiting for the right bus so went instead to the vicar-general's office and bought a marriage licence'. In fact he was highly excited: 'Went . . . to see Harold and show him our licence. With him to Alec where we drank champagne.' Five days later – for it was a special licence, dispensing with banns –

> Evelyn and I were married at St Paul's, Portman Square [a dreary evangelical church, says Pansy Lamb] at 12 o'clock. A woman was typewriting on the altar. Harold best man. Robert Byron gave away the bride, Alec and Pansy the witnesses. Evelyn wore a new black and yellow jumper suit with scarf. Went to the 500 Club and drank champagne cocktails. . . . From there to luncheon at Boulestin. Very good luncheon. Then to Paddington and by train to Oxford and taxi to Beckley.

At the Abingdon Arms, where Waugh had stayed with Alastair Graham, everyone was 'very sweet to us', and 'the women of the village brought bouquets of flowers for our room'. They went over to Barford, Alastair's home, where Mrs Graham 'supposes Alastair [who was now in Athens] to be dying of consumption'.

Lady Burghclere had not been told about the wedding – her daughter was now twenty-five, and required no parental consent – and when Waugh wrote to her announcing it, she replied that she was 'quite inexpressibly pained'. He went to see her in hopes of reconciliation, but the diary merely records, 'Saw Lady B. in the morning.'

Her mother's violent disapproval cannot exactly have helped Evelyn Gardner, 'She-Evelyn' as she was now known to Waugh's friends, to settle down to married life. Meanwhile they had nowhere to live, and camped for a while at his parents' house in Hampstead. By September they had found a cheap flat in an unfashionable part of North London – 17a Canonbury Square – and Harold Acton witnessed a brief period of domesticity, with Waugh clearly regarding himself as a home-maker, and helping his wife to decorate the flat amusingly. Then She-Evelyn's health began to break down.

In October she developed influenza, with a temperature of 104; Lady Burghclere at last began to visit her daughter, and engaged a nurse. German measles was diagnosed, and convalescence out of London recommended; Waugh began to worry about the cost. One of She-Evelyn's sisters and her husband invited them both down to their house in Wiltshire, and the literary agent A.D. Peters, whose client Waugh now was, got them both free tickets for a cruise during the coming February of 1929, in return for a promise that Waugh would write it up in a travel book.

At this period of his life he had no interest in foreign travel; he would have agreed with John Betjeman's remark to Edward James: 'Isn't abroad *awful*?' The offer was too good to refuse, but the journey began disastrously. They travelled south from Paris in an under-heated train, and She-Evelyn once again developed a temperature of 104. Waugh engaged a couchette for her, but could not afford one for himself. Arriving in Monte Carlo, they had to walk the snow-covered streets until they could find a cheap hotel and a doctor. Then they caught their ship, bound for Port Said via Naples. 'I knew I was ill', She-Evelyn writes, 'because I spat blood.'

The ship called at Haifa, where Waugh went ashore and engaged a nurse to attend his wife. Travelling on to Egypt, she developed double pneumonia and became critically ill. At Port Said she was taken to hospital and, while her life hung in the balance, Waugh cabled bulletins to relatives. After a couple of weeks she was out of danger, but they were now stranded in Port Said in considerable financial difficulties. Alastair Graham, resident in Athens as an attaché, seemed a likely source of help, and was appealed to. He made the journey to Port Said to see what he could do, spent two days with the Waughs, and gave them fifty pounds, 'so we can just struggle along for another week or two', wrote Waugh to his father.

In his biography of Waugh, Christopher Sykes – who does not record this visit to Port Said by Alastair – says that Waugh left She-Evelyn and travelled to Cyprus to meet Alastair, who had journeyed there from Athens. Sykes says that this apparent desertion of She-Evelyn was regarded by many people as odd and callous, though he defends Waugh against the charge. The true story seems to be recorded in Waugh's letter to Harold Acton from Egypt on Easter Day 1929: 'Alastair visited us for two days at Port Said – a characteristic excursion.' On the other hand, Evelyn Gardner has said that she has a fixed memory that Waugh left her while she was recovering from pneumonia, and believes that it was to visit Alastair; she does not think that she resented it, believing that her husband was bored with sitting by the sickbed. She accepts that the memory may be entirely false.

Whether or not Waugh actually left her, it seems evident that during the time at Port Said she began to feel that she had been in some way deserted by him; that it became apparent to her that something was missing emotionally from the marriage. She may also have been bothered by the homosexual undercurrent of his friendship with Alastair.

From Port Said, the Waughs moved to a hotel outside Cairo, next to the Pyramids. It was 'hideously expensive', but seemed a good place for She-Evelyn's recuperation. When she was better they went on to Malta, where they rejoined their original ship and at last embarked on what Waugh called 'the social life of a "pleasure cruise"'; he reported that he had 'a great rival for leadership of the bright young people in a stout Belgian. Today he appeared on deck in a Royal Yacht Squadron cap so I know when I am beaten.' The ship called at Crete and Constantinople and returned via Venice. By mid-April the Waughs were back in London. In mid-July, Waugh announced to Henry Yorke: 'I have written 25,000 words of a novel in ten days. It is rather like P.G. Wodehouse all about bright young people.'

He did not yet think of himself as a professional novelist. *Decline and Fall* had done well, but not spectacularly. It sold two thousand copies in a few weeks, and a second impression quickly went to press; the *Observer* and *Evening Standard* asked Waugh to write and review for them. But the training in carpentry had been a serious enterprise – he was attracted by the life of a craftsman – and around the time of his marriage he considered jobs in advertising and typographic design. He also thought he might 'abandon writing for painting'. Setting off on the cruise, he had told a journalist friend that he intended to 'concentrate on drawing' during the voyage, and hoped to 'bring back enough sketches to hold an exhibition in June'. If it had not been for She-Evelyn's illness he might have managed this.

Yet it was evident that writing could pay. A.D. Peters had got him the free cruise on the strength of his first novel, and held out promise of other rewards. 'Please fix up anything that will earn me anything,' Waugh wrote to him, 'even cricket criticism or mothers welfare notes.'

Given the nature of *Decline and Fall*, it was inevitable that editors should expect him to be funny, but he complained to Peters: 'I find humorous articles an awful strain.' He was asked to write on such subjects as censorship in literature, good taste (for the *Daily Express* 'Home Pages'), the younger generation and its impatience with the middle-aged, and 'Careers for Our Sons' – a commission for a humorous series in a magazine called *Passing Show*. He executed all these competently, but his boredom showed through in most of the articles. If he were going to live by the pen, another novel was essential. Indeed, it seemed a less irksome way of making money than popular journalism.

Money was a pressing need on his return from the cruise. 'We found bills of over £200 waiting for us and each overdrawn at our banks,' he told Henry Yorke, 'so I must write a lot quickly.' He did not view the enterprise very seriously, explaining to Harold Acton while at work on the new novel: 'It is a welter of sex and snobbery written simply in the hope of selling some copies. Then if it is [at] all a success I want to try and write something more serious.'

On the other hand, he was intrigued by the experiments that Henry Yorke had been making in his second novel, *Living*, just published. He wrote about it to Yorke with enormous enthusiasm, in June 1929, just as he was beginning his own new novel:

> I admire so much the way you have written it – like those aluminium ribbons one stamps out in railway stations on penny in the slot machines. The absence of all that awful thing they call 'word pictures', the way in which no appearances are described. The telegraphic narrative. . . . The thing I *envied* most was the way you managed the plot which is oddly enough almost exactly the way Firbank managed his.

And in a review some months later: 'Technically, *Living* is without exception the most interesting book I have read.'

Living (1929), again published as by 'Henry Green', an astonishing advance on Yorke's *Blindness*, is set in and around a Birmingham factory like Yorke's own family business. Yorke himself becomes young Dick Dupret, son of the owner, chiefly immersed in unrequited love for a shallow débutante in London, though rousing himself at his father's death to take the factory in hand. But the narrative is overwhelmingly concerned with the shopfloor workers and their lives, which Yorke portrays with an empathy and dispassionate understanding that is remarkable considering his own social position. (The character of the proprietor-father hints at a father–son relationship in the Yorke family that in some respects resembled Waugh's or Graham Greene's. Alan Ross describes how Henry found his father's presence at the head of the firm 'evidently a burden', and says he used to mimic Mr Yorke's mannerisms in cruel fashion, mocking what he regarded as his father's geriatric incompetence in the office.)

Discussing *Living*, Waugh could find only two other novelists with whom to compare it: Ivy Compton-Burnett, whose work, he said, was 'not half as well known as it should be', and who, too, used dialogue in a manner much like Firbank's; and James Joyce, in whom he had previously shown no interest, but of whom he now spoke approvingly: 'Modern novelists taught by Mr James Joyce are at last realizing the importance of re-echoing and remodifying the same themes. Note, for example, the repeated metaphor of "pigeons" in *Living*.' (Yorke keeps referring to racing pigeons as images of restricted freedom, like the workers' lives.)

Waugh later became contemptuous of much of Joyce's work. Thirty-five years later he said of Proust: 'I thought he began well but went dotty half way through like J. Joyce in *Ulysses*.' But in 1930, soon after completing his second novel, he was sufficiently drawn to Joyce to read Stuart Gilbert's study of *Ulysses*, and it seems that at the time he began to write the novel he felt himself to belong to the group of 'modern novelists taught by Mr James Joyce', at least in such matters as structure and dialogue.

His review of *Living* ends with one other literary comparison: 'I see in *Living* very much the same technical apparatus at work as in many of T. S. Eliot's poems – particularly in the narrative passages of *The Waste Land* and the two *Fragments of an Agon* [*Sweeney Agonistes*].'

It is evident, then, that he began the new novel in a distinctly modernist frame of mind. However, the author he chose to cite in the two epigraphs to the book was neither Joyce, Eliot nor 'Henry Green', but Lewis Carroll: the passage from *Through the Looking-Glass* where the Red Queen explains to Alice that 'it takes all the running you can do, to keep in the same place', and that in which Tweedledum says to the weeping Alice: 'I hope you don't suppose those are real tears?'

Vile Bodies, like *Decline and Fall*, is a modern *Alice*, and has a hero, Adam Fenwick-Symes (whose first name, like Adam Doure in 'The Balance', suggests Everyman), who is described as utterly neutral: 'There was nothing particularly remarkable about his appearance. He looked exactly as young men like him do look. . . .' However, the book differs from its predecessor in that Adam, unlike Paul Pennyfeather, does not stand apart from the inhabitants of the dream-world and view them quizzically, but is himself caught up utterly in its madness, and cannot return to the point from which he started.

Like *Decline and Fall*, the book begins with a 'fall' into contemporary

England, but this time, to emphasize his participation in the lunacy, the hero does not fall alone. He is on board ship, returning to England (as Waugh had just done), along with a representative cross-section of its inhabitants. The various 'estates' of society are carefully represented among the passengers: Government, in the form of 'The Right Honourable Walter Outrage, MP, last week's Prime Minister'; the Church, in the person of 'Father Rothschild SJ'; the aristocracy, as 'Lady Throbbing and Mrs Blackwater'; the middle classes, portrayed by a journalist 'telling . . . smutty stories' and a group of 'commercial gents'; and finally 'all the Younger Set . . . the Bright Young People'. Only the working class is absent; perhaps Waugh felt that Henry Yorke had written the last word about them in *Living*.

Waugh had no particular wish to write about the Bright Young People *per se*, and in the typescript of *Vile Bodies* there is this angry prefatory note:

BRIGHT YOUNG PEOPLE AND OTHERS KINDLY NOTE THAT ALL CHARACTERS ARE WHOLLY IMAGINARY (AND YOU GET FAR TOO MUCH PUBLICITY ALREADY WHOEVER YOU ARE).

They interested him only as yet another helpless group of people tossed in the modern storm, their helplessness being all the more comical because of their apparent sophistication.

In this opening chapter, all the passengers are locked in their own escapist fantasies: Mr Outrage in sexual day-dreaming, stimulated by drugs; Father Rothschild (at this stage in the novel a figure out of *The Scarlet Woman* – he mentions being friendly with 'the Dean of Balliol') in dreams of power exercised through his religious office; Lady Throbbing and Mrs Blackwater in naughty speculations about their acquaintances, conducted in Firbankian style; the journalist in his smutty stories; and the Bright Young People in childish pranks: 'They had spent a jolly morning strapping each other's tummies with sticking plaster (how Miss Runcible had wriggled).' Agatha Runcible's surname is an admiring nod at Carroll's fellow-practitioner of nonsense, Edward Lear.*

The choice of a boat journey, with the passengers seasick as they approach land, as the start to the novel was possibly suggested by Norman Douglas's *South Wind* (1917), which Waugh called 'the only great satirical novel of his [Douglas's] generation', and which begins in almost identical fashion. The point of such an opening is to suggest

---

* Martin Stannard points out that Waugh undoubtedly had in mind an article by Richard Pares in *Cherwell*, 2 February 1924, in which he alleged that Lear's word 'runcible' meant 'about to crash' or 'liable to crash'.

that the characters are 'all at sea' in terms of values. Like Dr Fagan in *Decline and Fall*, they have neither vision nor absolute ideals, and are merely trying to 'do the best they can', limping along on trivial superstitions. Faced with the prospect of seasickness (a metaphor for the despair engendered by modern society),

> some had filled their ears with cotton-wool, others wore smoked glasses, while several ate dry captain's biscuits from paper bags, as Red Indians are said to eat snake's flesh to make them cunning. Mrs Hoop repeated feverishly over and over again a formula that she had learned from a yogi in New York City.

When the storm breaks, Mrs Hoop declares: 'I'm through with theosophy after this journey. Reckon I'll give the Catholics the once over.'

Into this microcosm of a pagan, superstition-ridden England, there strides the only person on board ship who takes religion seriously as a life-force: Mrs Melrose Ape, an American evangelist.* (Her nationality as well as her religion emphasizes her separation from the all-at-sea English.) Though an utterly absurd figure, even a charlatan, surrounded by a troupe of 'angels' upon whom she has lesbian designs, she none the less voices Waugh's own feelings in this opening chapter: 'You don't hear much about Hope these days, do you? . . . They've forgotten all about Hope. There's only one great evil in the world today. Despair. I know all about England. . . .' Against their inclinations, the passengers join in her gospel singing, 'and it is undoubtedly true', says the narrator, 'that they felt the better for it'. Any contact with the Absolute, however ludicrous the circumstances, is better than the chaos of arbitrary values.

When the ship disgorges its passengers at Dover, Adam mentions casually to Customs that he has 'some books' in his luggage, and he raises their suspicions – quite plausibly, for this was the period when *Ulysses* was regularly being confiscated at the Channel ports from travellers trying to smuggle it in from Paris. The officers rummage through his luggage, impound a copy of Dante (a strong hint that *Vile Bodies*, like its predecessor, is a modern *Inferno*), and discover the typescript of Adam's autobiography, which they insist on burning, despite the fact that he earns his living by the pen. Waugh makes it an autobiography, rather than a novel, so as to indicate that Adam's claim

---

* It may be objected that Father Rothschild has real faith. But he has to carry out two functions in the book, which do not altogether cohere. For much of the time he is a sinister power-figure, a machiavellian intriguer, yet at other moments Waugh presents him as a paragon of wisdom achieved through faith (for example, during the rough crossing he recites the penitential psalms). The Jesuit's surname suggests an alliance of holy and unholy interests, but his behaviour does not always correspond to this.

to individuality is being symbolically destroyed as he enters the night-mare Wonderland. This deprivation, comparable to Paul's loss of trousers at the opening of *Decline and Fall*, contains another hint of the younger brother losing his just rewards, and Adam spends the rest of the novel trying to get the two other things that are his by rights: his girlfriend, whom he loses to someone else, and his winnings at the races, which are in another man's pocket.

On the train to London, England unfolds, and Waugh indicates that his feelings about it are much the same as Connolly's on returning from the Continent: 'Rain beat on the windows; the carriage was intensely cold and smelt of stale tobacco. Inside there were advertisements of horrible picturesque ruins; outside in the rain were hoardings advertising patent medicines and dog biscuits.' Reaching London, Adam drives 'straight to Henrietta Street' to see his publishers – who must therefore be Duckworth, the only firm at that address; a dig at their attitude to *Decline and Fall*. He reports the disaster to 'Mr Sam Benfleet, the junior director with whom Adam always did his business . . . a competent young man, with a restrained elegance of appearance'. Though this description might fit Anthony Powell, Benfleet is Tom Balston, who always ran the business in Gerald Duckworth's absence. His reaction to the news is grotesque: since Adam is unable to repay the advance on the autobiography, Benfleet issues a new contract ('our standard first novel contract') with appallingly unfavourable clauses: 'No royalty on the first two thousand', and 'an option on your next twelve books on the same terms'.

Having revenged himself on Duckworth's, Waugh turns to the promising 'copy' of Rosa Lewis and the Cavendish, which he scarcely disguises at all, calling the hotel 'Shepheard's' – the famous Cairo establishment, where he had stayed during his and She-Evelyn's Middle Eastern travels – and placing it 'at the corner of Hay Hill', that is, near Shepherd Market and Michael Arlen territory. (By setting some of the book in Mayfair, Waugh seems to be mocking Arlen and his absurd romanticism.) Rosa, disguised as 'Lottie Crump', is drawn with an accuracy that is remarkable considering how little Waugh had seen of her at first hand. Nor is she brought into the book purely as a figure of fun. In a world 'parched with modernity', says the narrator, she is able, if she likes your face, to 'draw up . . . great healing draughts from the well of Edwardian certainty'. By this, he means that the hotel has the air of an Edwardian country house, suggesting a world that is certain of its own values, even if those were merely 'the sound old snobbery of pound sterling and strawberry leaves'. On the other hand Lottie/Rosa, like one of the Wonderland creatures, has a facility for confusing or blurring the identity of the individual:

> 'You all know Lord Thingummy, don't you?' said Lottie.
> 'Mr Symes,' said Adam.
> 'Yes, dear, that's what I said. Bless you, I knew you before you were born.'

Financial identity becomes equally blurred. Adam arrives at the hotel virtually penniless, suddenly wins a thousand pounds from a bet with a guest, and a few moments later has handed it over to a drunk major who promises to put it on a horse. Despite its superficial appearance of Edwardian stability, the hotel is another microcosm of the chaos of modern life.

As his financial fortunes fluctuate through the narrative, Adam is alternately engaged and not engaged to Nina Blount. A high proportion of their conversation is conducted on the telephone, an opportunity for Waugh to develop his own 'telegraphic' language, owing something to 'Henry Green' as well as to Firbank and Hemingway:

> Presently the telephone by Adam's bed began ringing.
> 'Hullo, yes.'
> 'Lady to speak to you. – Hullo, is that you, Adam?'
> 'Is that Nina?'
> 'How are you, my darling?'
> '*Oh, Nina –*'
> 'My poor sweet, I feel like that too.'

Though Adam and Nina eventually sleep together, each is conspicuously wary of emotional involvement. When Nina gets excited about the resumption of their engagement, Adam warns her: 'Don't let's get intense about it.' This is both an implicitly critical portrayal of a brittle, rootless society, and at the same time another dig at Michael Arlen, whose fiction, for all its apparent modernity of subject, portrayed people whose values were Victorian to a melodramatic degree. Iris Storm in *The Green Hat*, shortly before killing herself, declares passionately: 'Love, love, love! A glorious word, a matchless word! But isn't it? Love, love! I am in love, I glory in love, I will die in love!' Waugh knew that people in Mayfair did not behave like that.

Considering when it was written and by whom, it is remarkable how little of *Vile Bodies* is a *roman à clef*. There are passing digs at Brian Howard's enormous invitation to the Great Urban Dionysia

('Johnnie Hoop' is described as sending out a card of the same kind), and a nudge at Bryan and Diana Guinness – 'the younger members of those two or three great brewing families which rule London'. But Waugh is remarkably restrained in his portrayal of the Bright Young People. Only one 'freak party' is described, held in a tethered airship, and even the catalogue of parties which the narrator recites is a modest affair, considering that the gossip-columns had been filled with the real thing:

> Masked parties, Savage parties, Victorian parties, Greek parties, Wild West parties, Russian parties, Circus parties, parties where one had to dress as somebody else, almost naked parties in St John's Wood, parties in flats and houses and shops and hotels and night clubs, in windmills and swimming baths ... all that succession and repetition of mass humanity. – Those vile bodies.

The novel's title, despite the detached and implicitly critical stance towards its characters from the outset, seems to have been an after-thought, since it does not appear in the manuscript. It alludes to words in the Burial Service in the *Book of Common Prayer*, themselves taken from St Paul's Epistle to the Philippians: 'through Our Lord Jesus Christ; who shall change our vile body, that it may be like unto his glorious body ...'. But the novel does not offer any such promise of spiritual redemption. Its characters are permanently imprisoned in the limitations of the flesh.

The comedy is almost entirely achieved by the trick Waugh had learnt from Firbank, which he now developed into a method of overall construction: the accumulation of seemingly unimportant and discon-nected details and incidents, which are gradually brought together with explosive results. Agatha Runcible is searched by Customs officers at Dover; later she comes down to breakfast in a strange house still wearing fancy dress. These two events combine to bring about the fall of the Government. Indeed, nothing in the novel happens through anyone's design or intention. The random appearances and disappearances of the drunk major are responsible for the violent changes in Adam's situation and, as in *Decline and Fall*, everyone is spun about by a capricious Fate. Prendergast in *Decline and Fall* glimpsed the abyss, but in *Vile Bodies* all the characters are in it, being whirled about by the winds of chaos.

Adam sets out to ask Nina's father, Colonel Blount, for some money so that they can get married. The Colonel lives in 'Doubting Hall', a Bunyanesque allusion suggesting that Adam is on a spiritual pilgri-mage – as indeed he is, his quest, like Paul's in the earlier novel, being for the 'permanence' which all the characters seem to desire but none achieves. As Father Rothschild says, in a speech which ill fits his nature, but which (like Otto Silenus's Big Wheel speech in *Decline and Fall*) had to be said by someone: 'They are all possessed with an almost fatal hunger for permanence.'

The country house, like the hotel, does at first seem to offer firm values in a shifting world. At Doubting Hall, Adam finds that:

> there was a silver tea-pot, and a silver kettle with a little silver lamp underneath, and a silver cream jug and a covered silver dish full of muffins. ... Adam ... felt a thousand times better. ... When Nina and he were married, he thought, they would often come down there for the day.

However, the Colonel proves to be yet another figure from *Alice*, adept like Lottie/Rosa at confusing identities. Adam is treated as the man 'come about the vacuum cleaner' and, when the Colonel gives him a cheque for a thousand pounds, it turns out to have been signed 'Charlie Chaplin' (an illusion to the book's debt to film comedies). There is a nice irony in that the proprietors of the two 'safe houses', Lottie and the Colonel, are the craziest people in the story.

Their craziness consists of muddling people's identities, and the hotel and Doubting Hall recall the wood in *Through the Looking-Glass* where no one can remember his or her own name, or rather, as Alice says, 'where things have no name'. Lottie's and the Colonel's apparent confusion may, in fact, be clear vision, since they can perceive that, in a world where everyone is behaving in the same insane fashion, individuals' identities are perfectly interchangeable at the whim of the observer.

When Adam and Nina finally get to bed together, the experience proves – Gerhardi fashion – to be a disappointment, at least for Nina: 'I don't think this is at all divine. ... It's given me a pain.' She has 'a pain' of some kind all through the book, the ache that afflicts all inhabitants of the waste land. More personally, there is perhaps a glimpse of the Waughs' married life in Adam and Nina's conversation after their first night together:

> Adam was inclined to be egotistical and despondent; Nina was rather grown-up and disillusioned and distinctly cross. ... Nina said, 'Do be amusing, Adam. I can't bear you when you're not amusing.' ... Then

> Nina said . . . 'All this fuss about sleeping together. For physical pleasure I'd sooner go to my dentist any day.'

This seems to have been about the point that the narrative had reached by the beginning of July 1929. Waugh had been staying at Beckley for some weeks, writing the novel at the Abingdon Arms, and sending the manuscript section by section to She-Evelyn to have it typed. On 9 July she wrote to him that she had fallen in love with a man called John Heygate, and did not know what to do about it.

Her announcement came without the slightest warning. When Harold Acton learnt the news, he asked if it was 'due to quarrels and boredom'. Waugh answered: 'No. Evelyn's defection was preceded by no sort of quarrel or estrangement.'

His initial reaction was probably that which he ascribes to Tony Last in *A Handful of Dust* when Brenda tells him that she loves John Beaver: 'His first thought was that Brenda had lost her reason. "She's only seen Beaver twice to my knowledge," he said.' Waugh stopped work and hurried to London. There, he learnt from She-Evelyn that she and Heygate were not merely 'in love', but lovers.

Believing himself to be enjoying a secure and permanent relationship, he had been suddenly plunged into the very nightmare he was describing in *Vile Bodies*, a world where no one retains identity and character, or can be sure of loyalty and affection from others for more than a moment. Again, Tony's feelings in *A Handful of Dust* undoubtedly recall Waugh's own:

> It was as though the whole reasonable and decent constitution of things, the sum of all he had experienced or learned to expect, were an inconspicuous, inconsiderable object mislaid somewhere on the dressing table; no outrageous circumstance in which he found himself, no new, mad thing brought to his notice, could add a jot to the all-encompassing chaos that shrieked about his ears.

His next reaction seems to have been sheer astonishment at his wife's choice of lover. 'Certainly,' he wrote to Acton, 'the fact that she should have chosen a ramshackle oaf like Heygate adds a little to my distress.' John Heygate was an Old Etonian who had been at Balliol with Anthony Powell, and in London the two became social companions, Heygate persuading Powell to buy his first car, and the two of them went motoring in Germany during the summer of 1929, just as Waugh heard his wife's devastating news.

The nephew of a baronet (whose title he eventually inherited), and the son of an Eton housemaster, Heygate had not done well at school or at Balliol, and had failed to get into the Diplomatic Service for which he was intended. Instead, he became a news-writer at the BBC. Powell describes him as an amusing companion, a moderately heavy drinker, and 'agreeably successful with women', though 'well short of being anything like a professional womanizer'. He was handsome in a conventional, jolly, slightly messy way, a cheerful slapdash character.

She-Evelyn had seen him more than twice; Powell says he was an habitué of the Waughs' flat in Canonbury Square, where there was 'much hospitality' in the months following their marriage. Waugh had got to know Heygate through a mutual friend, and Powell says he was 'very much taken' with him. Waugh in turn introduced Heygate to She-Evelyn. Heygate had an easy, bluff manner that passed for wit, and could be 'amusing' on demand in a way that Waugh, altogether more wary by nature, could not. Heygate would tell comic stories about his father's ineffectual attempts to turn him into a country squire. He had travelled more than Waugh, spending some time studying German at Heidelberg, and his BBC job was not without glamour in some people's eyes.

Powell had seen the Waughs when they returned from the cruise in the spring of 1929. She-Evelyn 'still looked rather pale' though she seemed in good spirits, while Waugh 'seemed in the best of form, full of plans about future books'. All appeared to be well between them, though Tom Balston at Duckworth's did hint to Powell that he thought the marriage was showing signs of strain. Powell says of his own failure to observe this that, like most of his generation at that time, he was still unfamiliar with 'the whole condition of young marriage'. Waugh had been one of the first of their set to marry.

During that spring, Powell and his musician friend Constant Lambert gave a party in the basement flat at Tavistock Square, Bloomsbury, to which Powell had just moved from Shepherd Market. The party was a success – it lasted from six p.m. till three a.m. – but Powell noticed that the Waughs turned up separately, neither of them staying long, nor seeming greatly to enjoy themselves. He also observed 'Evelyn Gardner having a brisk disagreement with Heygate'. A matter of days later, Waugh set off for Beckley to begin his novel, leaving She-Evelyn at Canonbury Square in the company of her great friend Nancy Mitford, sister of Diana Guinness. The two girls began to entertain quite a lot, and both Powell and Heygate were frequently in the flat. Powell says of She-Evelyn: 'We all used to take her out when she was on her own.' Waugh generally came up from Beckley at weekends, and one weekend he and She-Evelyn went down with Powell to the Heygate family house on the Hampshire coast. It was not a happy occasion; the Heygate parents were snobbish and dogmatic – Waugh afterwards described Mrs Heygate alleging that 'dukes are mentioned in the Bible' – but Powell was not aware of any particular undercurrents between the Waughs and John Heygate.

Two weeks later, Powell and Heygate set off together for their German motoring holiday. They investigated the decadent entertainments of Berlin, then moved south, arriving in Munich to collect *poste-restante* mail. There Powell found a cable addressed to both of them: 'INSTRUCT HEYGATE RETURN IMMEDIATELY WAUGH.' Heygate, who had evidently received his own more private communications, set out the following morning, leaving Powell to finish the holiday alone. Powell notes that, because Waugh assumed him to be on She-Evelyn's and Heygate's side in the affair, 'I saw no more of Waugh for some years.'

Describing the *mores* of the period, Powell has observed that many young women who had wedded rashly, during or just after the war, 'seemed hardly to have married at all', and were 'floating on a sea of "affairs" that most of them ... showed little or no sign of wishing to make permanent'. This was the ambience that Waugh was engaged in portraying in *Vile Bodies*.

He himself had seemed to conform to it, pretending to embark on marriage with a studied detachment, implying that it did not matter if things failed to work out. Evelyn Gardner cannot be greatly blamed if she took him to mean what he had said.

There are signs that all was not well from the outset. Evelyn Gardner has stated that 'my marriage wasn't exactly warm. Evelyn was not an affectionate person. I was.' This might refer to a whole variety of things, including the fact that he had abandoned her in London and gone off to the country to write his novel. She has denied 'ever claiming (or even thinking)' that she had 'felt neglected' during this period. Yet, coming so soon after her recuperation from an almost fatal illness, his protracted absence may have been an unpleasant surprise, and she cannot have been encouraged to discover that he could apparently only pursue his profession of writing when separated from her.

It is possible that, in describing the marriage as not 'exactly warm', she was alluding to a failure of sexual relations. Waugh himself gave hints of this in an article on marriage that he wrote for the magazine *John Bull* during 1930, a few months after his wife's desertion. Under the title 'Tell the Truth About Marriage', he concentrates almost exclusively on the sexual aspect of marriage, and complains that:

> responsible people – doctors, psychologists, novelists – write in the papers and say, 'You cannot lead a happy life unless your sex life is happy.' That seems to me just about as sensible as saying, 'You cannot lead a happy life unless your golf life is happy.' It is not only nonsense, it is mischievous nonsense. It means that the moment a wife begins to detect imperfections in her husband she thinks her whole life is ruined.

It seems an odd aspect of marriage to pick on, in such an article, if something of the sort had not happened to him. Elsewhere in the article, he speaks of people who 'find that after some time of marriage sexual relations are not so absorbingly interesting as they had been led to suppose', and goes on to say that such people 'think it is because they have made a mistake in their choice of mate. Then they get into the divorce courts.'

This suggests the following scenario for the marriage: that She-Evelyn, following the popular belief of the time that sex meant everything, was disappointed when she got married to discover 'imperfections' in her husband as a lover, and also found that sex was not so 'absorbingly interesting' as she had been led to believe. She blamed both disappointments on Waugh, and went off with someone else in the hope that things would be better. Her attitude, in other words, was exactly that of Nina in *Vile Bodies* – 'I don't think that this is at all divine,' except that, unlike Nina, she believed that it *ought* to be divine, and thought it might be with another partner.

As to Waugh himself, there are grounds for guessing that he approached the marriage in some confusion and ignorance where sex was concerned. In his book on Waugh's early years, Martin Stannard suggests that Waugh may have visited a brothel during one of his visits to Marseilles, but this is speculation, and it seems likely that he had never been to bed with a member of the opposite sex until he married. In his article on marriage, he complains that 'by the present system of education the one thing that is hidden is the actual facts of sex', and asks that parents and schools should 'teach children the biology and hygiene of sex. . . . Teach them fully about birth control. . . . they will not then marry out of curiosity or inexperience.' This seems to hint that curiosity and inexperience were among the motives behind his own marriage.

In a passage which appeared in the first edition of *Vile Bodies*, but which was deleted by Waugh when he was supervising the reissue of his novels in the 1960s, the narrator observes: 'The truth is that, like so many people of their age and class, Adam and Nina were suffering from being sophisticated about sex before they were at all widely experienced.' Martin Stannard asked Waugh's surviving friends whether 'the sexual side of the marriage was inadequate', in particular, inadequately gratifying to She-Evelyn. 'Most agreed that they had long believed this to be the case.'

Quite apart from physical problems, it may be that Waugh was having difficulty conjuring up 'warmth' and 'affection' for women. At Oxford, he had experienced a strong homosexual phase, and though he stood emphatically apart from the flamboyant homosexuality of Brian Howard and other Oxford contemporaries, his feelings for Alastair Graham and perhaps other friends had been, and presumably still were, very strong. After leaving Oxford he evidently retained a certain interest in homosexuality; at Christmas 1925, in Paris with an acquaintance, he visited a homosexual brothel, and had advances made to him by 'a boy dressed as an Egyptian woman. . . . I thought him attractive but had better uses for the 300 francs which the patron . . . demanded for his enjoyment.' Waugh then 'arranged a tableau by which my boy should be enjoyed by a large negro who was there but at the last minute . . . the price proved prohibitive'.

When Waugh married Evelyn Gardner in 1928, his predicament was apparently much the same as Cyril Connolly's: 'in the last analysis homosexual', as Connolly writes of the typical public schoolboy in *Enemies of Promise*, but somewhat drawn to boyish women such as Evelyn Gardner, the difference being that Connolly had gained actual heterosexual experience with prostitutes before embarking on a love affair with a girl.

Harold Acton writes of He-Evelyn and She-Evelyn: 'They looked like a juvenile brother and sister.' Perhaps in a sense they were. Certainly Evelyn Gardner was in search of a male version of her sisters; after the marriage had ended, she told Alec Waugh she had never been as happy with He-Evelyn 'as I've been with my sisters'. And is there a fragment of autobiography in Waugh's 1953 review of an edition of Ruskin's letters, where he describes one facet of Ruskin's relationship with women as 'a lonely little boy in search of a playmate'?

Of interest, too, is the fact that his brother Alec's first marriage, to Barbara Jacobs, had never been consummated, and was dissolved for that reason. Alec himself writes of it:

195

> The marriage was never consummated. For this failure my inexperience was entirely to blame. . . . I had imagined that a few casual encounters in the red light districts of Mainz and Nancy would have been sufficient training for me. Actually I should have been better off without it. It made me think that the whole thing was simple and straightforward. . . . I had no idea of the amount of tact and skilful patience that is required to initiate an inexperienced girl into the intimacies of sex.

Though Alec gives the impression that it was simply physical clumsiness on his part that was to blame, rather than impotence or lack of interest in the opposite sex, he (like his brother Evelyn) had experienced a homosexual phase, in his case at school.

There are several hints in Waugh's later writings of sexual difficulties in his first marriage. In *Men at Arms*, Guy Crouchback's parents fail to consummate their marriage on their wedding night: 'there was a sad gap between them, made by modesty and tenderness and innocence'. And in *The Ordeal of Gilbert Pinfold*, one of the hallucinatory voices observes: 'Many a young couple spend a wretched fortnight together through not knowing how to set about what has to be done.'

Waugh's 1930 article on marriage also indicates that he did not, at this date, consider sex an important part of relationships: 'Sex instinct in most cases is a perfectly mild and controllable appetite which would never cause most of us any trouble at all if it was not being continually agitated by every sort of hint and suppression. . . . Man's sex life is only a part of his general activity.' Ironically, it seems likely that, if she had been asked, Evelyn Gardner would have said much the same. Far from resembling the wife portrayed in Waugh's article on marriage – sexually voracious and contemptuous of her husband's physical clumsiness – she seems to have been shy and naïve about sex, embarrassed by this aspect of human relations, the victim of a sheltered upbringing where sex was concerned. Probably, during the marriage, she was as confused as Waugh.

If, bearing this in mind, one returns to her statements that 'my marriage was not exactly warm', and that 'Evelyn was not an affectionate person', it begins to seem likely that there were other, more important factors in the breakdown of the marriage than sexual misunderstanding. One might guess that, through his 'struggle for detachment', Waugh had lost the capacity for conveying emotional warmth to those who attracted him, so that he indeed seemed cold and unaffectionate, leading She-Evelyn to believe that he was entirely casual about the whole relationship. Indeed, there remains the possibility that she was right: that he had drifted into the marriage, on the rebound from Alastair Graham, without any real commitment to her. Probably he was attracted by the fact that she was a peer's daughter; perhaps this was even, in his eyes, her chief quality.

There can be no doubt that the collapse of the marriage had a profound effect on him. At least one friend, Harold Acton, interpreted his behaviour in the months that followed as evidence of a broken heart. A less charitable but possibly more realistic assessment might be that he was suffering from colossally shattered pride.

Confronted with She-Evelyn's infidelity, he tried at first to maintain the mask of detachment. Christopher Sykes records that 'after a long discussion [he] said that he would forgive his wife and forget the whole business if she agreed to give up this man. She said she would do so.' Martin Stannard gives an amplified version of this, based on conversation with Evelyn Gardner:

> Waugh was ... prepared to simulate sexual liberality. He had never been able to take sexual passion altogether seriously. Their relationship was too precious to be destroyed by hurt pride over a casual affair. If she would give up Heygate, he said, he would forget the whole business and they could go on as before. Out of loyalty to him, she agreed. It was the sensible, logical thing to do.

He was playing the part of Adam in *Vile Bodies*, who takes all such misfortune monosyllabically and without fuss. However, it was not an easy part to sustain.

Sykes says that a 'happy fortnight' ensued, before Waugh left London again to get on with the novel. Evelyn Gardner, writing to Stannard, gives a different picture: 'We decided once more to try and "make a go" of our marriage. The following fortnight was a very unhappy time with E. even saying that I was trying to poison him! He had been reading the early Agatha Christies which we both enjoyed.' Alec Waugh recalls She-Evelyn saying to him: 'It's terrible. He's drinking too much. It makes him feel ill. And he thinks I'm trying to poison him.' The mask of detachment had slipped, to reveal paranoid fear and suspicion. There is even a photographic record of his misery at this time – a picture of the Waughs at a party on board a ship moored on the Thames Embankment. It was a 'Tropical' party: She-Evelyn, in straw hat and white trousers, looks strained and worn; Waugh, clutching a solar topee, stares anxiously at the camera.

In *A Handful of Dust*, Waugh describes Tony Last keeping himself awake at night trying to puzzle out what had gone wrong with his marriage: 'He could not prevent himself . . . rehearsing over and over in his mind all that had happened . . . searching for clues . . . wondering whether something he had said or done might have changed the course of events. . . . All this kept him awake.' According to She-Evelyn (as reported by Martin Stannard), at the end of the fortnight Waugh decided that they could not go on together, and it was at this point that he sent the telegram requesting Heygate to return from Germany. He intended that Heygate should come and take her away from Canonbury Square, and the marriage be abandoned forthwith. However, at this point Lady Burghclere, learning that there was trouble, insisted that her daughter go to Venice to think things over, which she did. In Italy, she heard from Heygate that he was waiting for her in London, and she returned at once and went to live with him, first in his own lodgings and then in the Canonbury Square flat, which was in her name (no doubt Lady Burghclere had been paying the rent); Waugh had cleared out his own possessions and gone.*

It was at this point – the letter is undated but must have been written some time in August 1929 – that Waugh wrote to his parents:

> I asked Alec to tell you the sad & to me radically shocking news that Evelyn has gone to live with a man called Heygate. I am accordingly filing a petition for divorce.
>
> I am afraid that this will be a blow to you but I assure you not nearly as severe a blow as it is to me. . . . So far as I knew we were both serenely happy.

His parents and Lady Burghclere tried to reconcile the couple, but both parties now wanted a divorce, and during August they, Heygate and a professional informer attended at a solicitor's office, so that a petition could be served on She-Evelyn and the 'co-respondent'. Waugh's mother wanted him to take the blame, as was conventional in such matters, but She-Evelyn insisted on being identified as the guilty party. Waugh commented of the attempts at reconciliation: 'Everyone is talking so much nonsense on all sides of me about my affairs, that my wits reel.' This letter, to Harold Acton, concludes: 'I have absolutely no plans for the future. . . . Naturally I have done no work at all for two months. I did not know it was possible to be so miserable and live. . . .'

*

* Sykes has a different and rather implausible account, probably derived from Nancy Mitford: that at the end of the fortnight Waugh went away contentedly to continue the novel, but while he was absent She-Evelyn took up with Heygate again, and when Waugh came back he found that she had flown from the flat and was living with Heygate in South Kensington.

He went off to Ireland 'for a week's motor racing', probably in the company of David Plunket Greene, an amateur racing driver, and in the following months could be found at a number of addresses – Bryan and Diana Guinness's various houses and flats in London, Sussex, Dublin and Paris (*Vile Bodies* is dedicated to them in gratitude for this hospitality), the Abingdon Arms at Beckley, and another old haunt: 'You must not think from this address that I have gone to stay with the Heygates,' he wrote to Henry Yorke on Canonbury Square paper. 'I am living at Thame at Mr Fothergill's & expect to be here off and on until Christmas.' In *A Handful of Dust* he writes of the cuckolded Tony Last: 'He was going away because it seemed to be the conduct expected of a husband in his circumstances . . . because he wanted to live for a few months away from people who would know him or Brenda, in places where there was no expectation of meeting her. . . .' Harold Acton, with whom Waugh stayed occasionally in London during this period, says that he found him 'utterly suicidal'.

By the end of the year he had, however, drawn up some sort of strategy for self-preservation, had begun to engage again in the struggle for detachment. 'I have decided that I have gone on for too long in that fog of sentimentality,' he wrote to Henry Yorke, '& I am going to stop hiding away from everyone. I was getting into a sort of Charlie Chaplinish Pagliacci attitude to myself as the man with a tragedy in his life and a tender smile for children. So all that must stop. . . .' And stop it did. Diana Mosley (formerly Diana Guinness) recalls that he soon 'showed few signs' of any emotional reaction to the disaster. 'There was no hint of painful depression . . . when Evelyn was there it was impossible to be dull for an instant.' The mask had been replaced.

He told Henry Yorke: 'One conclusion I am coming to is that I do not like Evelyn & that really Heygate is about her cup of tea.' On the surface he maintained this bullish attitude for the rest of his life. In a 1962 interview he would only say of his first marriage: 'I went through a form of marriage and travelled about Europe for some time with this consort.' Christopher Hollis records that one day during the 1930s when he and Waugh were travelling together in Greece, Waugh seemed to be taking particular trouble to buy English newspapers. 'I asked him why . . . as he was not much interested in current political affairs. "Oh," he said, "just to see if there is any good news which I might otherwise have missed – such as, for instance, the death of Mrs Heygate."' (She-Evelyn married Heygate during 1930.) He also spoke with unmitigated dislike of Heygate: 'My horror and detestation of the basement boy are unqualified.' (Heygate's presence at

Anthony Powell's party in the basement flat had led to this cognomen.) But privately his attitude was rather different. John Heygate told Michael Davie (editor of Waugh's diaries) that 'much later on EW used to ask Tony Powell about me in a friendly manner'; he also said that Waugh had defended him against an attack in an article he wrote in *Horizon* during the Second World War about the training of officers.

Heygate's involvement in the divorce led him to resign from his job at the BBC, where Sir John Reith would not employ divorcés or co-respondents. To earn a little money he wrote a novel, *Decent Fellows* (1932), set at Eton. Later he found a job with a film company in Germany, and wrote further books. He and Evelyn Gardner were divorced in 1936, and she married an estate agent, Ronald Nightingale; this marriage, too, came to an end in the early 1950s. Waugh caricatured her later history in *Men at Arms*, where she contributes much to the character of Virginia Troy: 'Tommy took her from him [Guy Crouchback], then Gussie had her for a bit, then Bert Troy picked her up when she was going spare.' To which another club gossip replies: 'She's a grand girl. Wouldn't mind having a go myself one of these days.'

Waugh was inclined to blame her defection from him on 'some odd hereditary *tic* in all those Gardner girls – I think it is an intellectual failing more than anything else'. (This is from a letter to Henry Yorke, not long after she had left him, and refers to her sisters' equally stormy marital experiences.) And he had much to say about his cuckolding in the remainder of *Vile Bodies*, written in the weeks immediately after Evelyn Gardner had deserted him.

'I was in the middle of *Vile Bodies* when she left me,' he said in a 1962 interview, but he made no comment on the effect on the book.

At the time, he said he was finding it 'infinitely difficult' to finish the novel, explaining to Henry Yorke that 'it is certainly the last time I shall try to make a book about sophisticated people. It all seems to shrivel up & rot internally. . . .' *Vile Bodies* shows none of this strain; it moves effortlessly towards the resolution of the themes already stated.

After the suicide of Simon Balcairn, the aristocratic gossip columnist (loosely based on Waugh's friend Patrick Balfour, later Lord Kinross, who at this time was 'Mr Gossip' in the *Daily Sketch*), who puts his head in the gas oven after being excluded from society, Adam gets the job of 'Mr Chatterbox' on the *Daily Excess*. Forbidden to mention most socialites, because Balcairn has libelled them and they have served writs, he invents characters to people his daily column. This is another ramification of the *Alice* game with identities that takes place throughout the novel, for Adam's readers believe utterly in these invented people, and begin to copy their styles of dress and frequent their supposed haunts. Similarly, towards the end of the book, Agatha Runcible, attending a motor race (based on what Waugh had seen of this sport in Ireland), becomes a racing driver simply because she happens to be wearing an official armband: 'I'm the spare driver. It's on my arm.' Agatha crashes the car and loses her wits; again it is her identity that is destroyed: 'In answer to some gentle questions, she replied that to the best of her knowledge she had no name. . . .'

Nina abandons her on–off relationship with Adam, and abruptly becomes engaged to the repulsive Ginger Littlejohn, a clear allusion to Waugh's own present predicament. Adam, after briefly giving way to despair at this ('I'm thinking of committing suicide, like Simon,' he tells Agatha), copes with the situation by substituting himself for Ginger, when Nina takes her supposed new husband to visit her father. He also makes Nina pregnant – 'Ginger has quite made up his mind it's his,' Nina tells him cheerfully. Nina mentions that Ginger was a childhood friend: 'I used to play with Ginger as a child. His hair was a very pretty colour then.' This alludes to *The Green Hat*, where Iris runs off with her childhood friend Napier. But the colour of the Waugh brothers' hair was ginger, and as well as being John Heygate, Ginger Littlejohn is also the elder brother depriving the younger of what is rightfully his.

Once, briefly, the mask slips, and Father Rothschild, in his out-of-character speech, gives vent to Waugh's own feelings as he tries to convince himself that some good may come out of the collapse of his marriage: '. . . young people . . . are all possessed with an almost fatal hunger for permanence. I think all these divorces show that. People aren't content just to muddle along nowadays.' Apart from this single lapse, the air of brittle futility and impermanence is maintained to the end. Colonel Blount's country house, where Adam and Nina spend their 'honeymoon', clearly stands for the old order – 'It's been just like this every year, as long as I can remember,' says the Colonel, describing the Christmas celebrations – but this glimpse of permanence is rudely shattered when the Colonel shows the ludicrous film of the life of John Wesley in which he has participated: a symbol of the inability of modern society to understand the past. Film itself is a motif in these closing chapters; Agatha Runcible's mental collapse is compared to the projection of a crazy film ('It unrolled itself like a length of cinema film'); Ginger takes Nina up in an aeroplane, and she has a cinematic vision of the contemporary English landscape, in particular of suburbia at its worst; and, in the actual film which the Colonel projects, human behaviour is distorted and speeded up almost beyond recognition, just as it has been throughout the novel. All experience, the whole of contemporary life with its impermanent relationships, seems like a badly made film.

Such a world can end in only one way, and in the last chapter the cosiness of the country house is swept away for 'the biggest battlefield in the history of the world', an imagined Second World War in which 'every visible object was burnt or broken', and 'it was growing dark'. It takes the war to provide Adam with his girl – his substitution for Ginger can be achieved because Ginger has been called up – and also his money, for at the end the drunk major appears and gives Adam his cheque. Waugh is already looking forward to the next war to resolve his own problems.

On this note of total despair, the novel ends. Waugh wondered who could possibly enjoy such a book. 'When anyone says they liked *Decline and Fall*,' he told Henry Yorke, 'I think oh how bored they will be by *Vile Bodies*. ... I am relying on a sort of cumulative futility for any effect it may have.'

In Search of a City

1

A New Order and Another Christendom

Early in 1926 Graham Greene left Nottingham for a sub-editor's job on *The Times*. There, he was put on the 'home' desk where the hours were easy and the work undemanding. After a few months, he finished writing his second novel and sent if off to Heinemann; A.D. Peters, having failed to find a publisher for its predecessor, had declined to handle it. While he waited for Heinemann's verdict he began a third novel, a detective story. He soon abandoned it, but has described the plot. A young governess is found murdered in a country house and, though the police are baffled, the local priest realizes that the killer is a girl of twelve, who has committed the crime because her beloved governess was in love with a man. At the time, Greene would have said that the story bore no relation to his personal experience. Later, he came to see that it was drawn from his own jealous passion for the Berkhamsted governess, who had married someone else. However, by this time he had found a replacement for her.

At Oxford he had written a film review which alluded to Roman Catholics' 'worship' of the Virgin Mary. A note was left for him at Balliol lodge, pointing out that this was the wrong term: it should be 'hyperdulia'. Greene was curious to discover who it was that 'took these subtle distinctions of an unbelievable theology seriously', and became acquainted with the writer of the note, Vivien Dayrell-Browning, a Catholic girl living in Oxford. Soon they were engaged.

It occurred to Greene that 'if I were to marry a Catholic I ought at least to learn the nature and limits of the beliefs she held'. One day, while still working on the *Nottingham Journal*, he went to the Catholic cathedral and left a note asking for instruction. He says he had no conscious intention of becoming a Catholic, but merely wished to satisfy an intellectual curiosity about his fiancée's religion.

He began instruction with Father Trollope, one of the cathedral staff, who at first sight 'was all I detested most in my private image of the Church. A very tall and very fat man with big smooth jowls which looked as though they had never needed a razor ...'. Himself a convert, the priest had given up a career as a West End character actor to enter the Church. The two of them often talked while riding on Nottingham trams: 'The tram clattered by the Post Office. "Now we come to the Immaculate Conception ..."'. Though Greene had embarked on instruction cynically, he says that gradually he found himself enjoying his sessions with the priest, and so beginning to consider his arguments seriously. Such details as the historical evidence for the existence of Jesus Christ and the dates of the Gospels had, however, no bearing on his state of mind: 'I disbelieved in God. If I were ever to be convinced in even the remote possibility of a supreme, omnipotent and omniscient power I realized that nothing afterwards could seem impossible.'

In his autobiography, he says he 'fought and fought hard' to defend his dogmatic atheism – 'it was like a fight for personal survival' – but that after a few weeks he gave up the struggle, and 'became convinced of the probable existence of something we call God'. He emphasizes that it was a change of mind rather than heart: 'I had not been converted to a religious faith. I had been convinced by specific arguments in the probability of its creed.' And he describes himself as 'a Catholic with an intellectual if not an emotional belief in Catholic dogma'.

There is some evidence that even his intellectual belief was not very strong. In his autobiography he states that 'my belief never came by way of those unconvincing philosophical arguments which I derided in a short story called "A Visit to Morin"'. This story, written in the early 1960s, describes an elderly Catholic author who has lost his capacity for belief, and mocks the arguments for God's existence: 'Can you find anything more inadequate than the scholastic arguments for the existence of God? ... I would prefer the thoughts of an ape. Its instincts are less corrupted. Show me a gorilla praying and I might believe again.' Yet nowhere does Greene offer any alternative to those traditional arguments, and in a 1979 interview he hints that he never really reached a state of complete belief: 'I eventually came to accept the existence of God not as an absolute truth but as a provisional one.' In the same interview, he began a sentence: 'If God exists – I'm not convinced He does . . .'.

In that interview he alleged that he had been under instruction from Father Trollope 'regularly for six months', but in fact it happened far more swiftly. He began seeing Trollope only in November 1925, and as early as January 1926 was writing to his mother: 'I expect you have guessed that I am embracing the Scarlet Woman.' This considerable haste suggests other motives than the detached intellectual curiosity which he alleges first took him to the cathedral.

The flippant tone in which he broke the news to his mother indicates a degree of embarrassment, for to become a Roman Catholic was a powerful gesture of separation from his parents and their mild Anglicanism – a real escape from the Berkhamsted household, such as he had often attempted but never yet managed. (Arguably, though, he was only exchanging one remote paternal authority for another.) More likely, though, he was spurred to become a Catholic simply because he was engaged to a Catholic girl. After losing the governess, it must have seemed prudent to reinforce this new relationship by joining his fiancée's Church.

Eight months after Greene had submitted his manuscript to Heinemann, it at last came back, with a rejection note, but a request to see his next book. Being a novice, Greene did not try another publisher, but decided to attempt one further novel, and if the third attempt failed, 'I would abandon this ambition for ever.' He began work on the new book, and finished it during the early months of his marriage. One day towards the end of 1928 he was in bed with 'flu when the telephone rang, and Charles Evans, managing director of Heinemann, told him that he wanted to publish the book, which was called *The Man Within*. 'My 'flu was gone in that moment and never returned.'

In his autobiography, Greene dismisses this first published novel as 'very young and very sentimental . . . like the book of a complete stranger, of a kind for which I have never much cared'. In fact it contains the seeds of almost all his later work. Superficially it is an adventure story, about a young smuggler who has betrayed his fellows to the law and is trying to escape their vengeance. He is sheltered in a lonely cottage by a beautiful girl with whom he falls in love, but then he clouds the purity of his relationship with her by sleeping with a harlot, and though he finally makes his peace with the smugglers' leader, it is at the cost of the girl's life. The title, *The Man Within*, refers to the fact that the hero, Andrews, is perpetually nagged by an inner voice which comments sceptically on his motives, 'an uncomfortable questioning critic'. And there is another 'man within', the memory of Andrews's dead father, the smugglers' former captain, loved by his men but feared by his family. When Andrews is asked why he has betrayed his shipmates, he answers: 'It was because I had a father whom I hated and he was always being put before me as a model.' Greene is back at Berkhamsted School.

The book is over-written, and the principal characters are stereotypes, but the narrative never flags, and the *Times Literary Supplement* reviewer (20 June 1929) commended Greene for 'a deftness astonishing in a first book'. It sold extremely well – no less than eight thousand copies – and on the strength of this Greene decided to leave *The Times*. Evans at Heinemann agreed to pay him six hundred pounds a year (more than twice what the newspaper had given him) for three years, in return for a novel each year, and at first this seemed an attractive arrangement. Then Greene began to discover that, while writing a first novel is an adventure, 'the second is a duty'.

He quickly became depressed by his next book, *The Name of Action*: 'I despaired of it often, as I plodded with my unlikely hero through the streets of Trier.' Set in an imaginary Middle European dictatorship, it again has a hero tormented by divided loyalties, a young Englishman who has promised to help the revolutionaries but is in love with the dictator's wife. The book was published in the autumn of 1930, and among the reviewers was Evelyn Waugh, who wrote in the *Graphic*:

> A second novel is always a difficult business. Mr Greene . . . has a real sense of the importance of plot and the structure of narrative. I can foresee his early elevation to the position of a respectable, romantic, best-seller. At present, however, I find many features of his style a little repugnant. It is all metaphor and simile. . . . I wish he would write more freely and directly.

Greene admits that the book was full of exaggerated similes. His wife marked many of them on the manuscript, and these had been removed, but many remained; for example: 'Somewhere from an invisible tower a clock relinquished its load of hours', 'A revolver drooped like a parched flower to the pavement.'

The Name of Action sold poorly, and its successor, *Rumour at Nightfall* (1931) even worse. It repeated what was becoming Greene's standard theme of sexual passion conflicting with idealism, this time in the setting of Spain during the Carlist rebellion, with an English journalist allowing his love for a guerrilla's mistress to overcome his political loyalties. Greene says that, like *The Name of Action*, the book was quite lifeless because 'there was nothing of myself in [it]. I had been determined not to write the typical autobiographical novels of a beginner, but I had gone too far in the opposite direction. I had removed myself altogether.' He was soon heavily in debt to Heinemann's, and faced the collapse of his career as a writer. 'If *The Man Within* had shown promise, it was the brief promise of a dud rocket on Guy Fawkes night.'

Vile Bodies was published in January 1930, and was an instant success. One or two reviewers were unsure about it (Arnold Bennett thought it less successful than *Decline and Fall*), but most praised it without reserve – V.S. Pritchett in the *Spectator* said he had 'laughed until I was driven out of the room'. Among other critics, Richard Aldington and Rebecca West remarked upon the despair in the book; West, in the *Fortnightly Review*, linked it to *The Waste Land* and called it 'a further stage in the contemporary literature of disillusionment'.

To the general public, the book appealed as a rather naughty account of the doings of the celebrated Bright Young People, and they lapped it up. Chapman & Hall reprinted it again and again during 1930; by October they had reached the eleventh impression. Sales of *Decline and Fall* were boosted, and Waugh began to be much in demand as a humorous columnist in the London papers. Suddenly he was famous, and financially very well off; the *Daily Mail*, for which he was writing throughout 1930, paid him thirty pounds per eight-hundred-word article, six times what Graham Greene had been earning each week at *The Times*.

People started to imitate the mannerisms and habits of the book's characters, wearing black suede shoes, giving parties in airships, and using expressions such as 'Too, too sick-making'. Waugh said of this: 'I popularized a fashionable language ... and the book caught on.' Rosa Lewis professed herself outraged by her appearance as 'Lottie Crump', and threw Waugh out of the Cavendish – though not on account of the novel. Waugh explains:

> The last time I set foot in the Cavendish was after dinner before Henry Yorke's wedding. We all went on to the Cavendish. Rosa was having some trouble at the time over a cheque with a man called Lulu Waters-Welch (not of our party). She fixed me with fierce eyes and said: 'Lulu Waters-Waugh take your arse out of my chair.'

Resuming his diary in May 1930 – it had lapsed during the break-up of his marriage – he recorded that at present his income was about £2,500 a year. 'I feel rather elated about it.' So he might, since it was (for example) two and a half times the salary then paid to an Oxford professor. He spent, however, as quickly as he earned, often having to borrow or beg advances from the A.D. Peters agency. This high expenditure was partly the result of having no home of his own. He used his father's house as a base, but was often travelling; during 1930 he had a holiday in France with Alec, stayed with the Guinnesses in Ireland and Sussex, and was usually on the move. But he also spent a lot of money when he was at home in London. The very first entries in the new diary record, on three successive days, drinking and eating at the Savoy, Quaglino's, the Tour Eiffel and the Ritz (virtually a second home to him at this period), mostly at his own expense, in the company of such friends as Henry Yorke and Nancy Mitford. Maurice Bowra describes him turning up with half a dozen bottles of champagne – maybe on the Michael Arlen model – and saying, 'I thought that these might prove useful before dinner.'

He plunged into a round of literary and artistic cocktail parties and publishers' lunches: 'Luncheon at the Ivy with Jonathan Cape and my American publisher. . . . Cocktail party at Cyril Connolly's. . . . Cocktail party at Cecil Beaton's. . . . Cocktail party at Francis Meynell's. . . . Tea with Edith Sitwell. . . . Dinner at Waldorf with my American publisher' – all this in six days in May 1930. Success had come at an opportune moment, to distract him from self-pity and to reassure him that, if his wife did not want him, at least the fashionable world did.

After a while, he became less concerned to avoid She-Evelyn's social circle. During the summer of 1930 he stayed for ten days at Pakenham Hall, County Westmeath, Irish seat of Pansy Lamb's brother Edward, Earl of Longford. The house party was dominated by the high jinks of John Betjeman, also a friend of the Pakenhams, to the extent that Waugh eventually noted: 'John B. rather a bore with Irish peers and revivalist hymns and his enthusiasm for every sort of architecture.'

This enthusiasm was given full rein in Betjeman's new job, on the *Architectural Review*, which he had acquired through string-pulling by Maurice Bowra. The journal was supposed to support the better kinds of modern architecture, 'what was pure and simple and Scandinavian' (as Betjeman puts it), against the vulgarities of the two prevalent commercial styles. These were 'Jazz Modern', now known as Art Deco, and what Betjeman and his friends called 'Egypto-Commercial-Renaissance', the muddled and heavyweight pastiche of traditional styles which served for most public buildings. However, the magazine was financed by glossy advertisements for the very things its contributors deplored, mock-medieval stained glass, wrought-iron work of striking hideousness, rubber floors, and bronze doors in the style of Tutankhamen's tomb.

Betjeman sometimes wrote dutifully in praise of those modern artefacts which the magazine was supposed to admire, but on the whole in the columns of the 'Archie Rev', as he and his friends called it, he could be found ignoring both this policy and the feelings of advertisers. He delighted in mocking all fake 'revivals', such as the tea-shop taste for ersatz Tudor, which he described scathingly (in the May 1930 number of the magazine) as 'Olde gonges, olde warminge pannes, hande-paintedde and verie thickke cuppes and plates'. He and his friends hated 'tea-shop Tudor' not just because it was false, but because it was a symbol of the bad taste of their parents' generation, a *kitsch* offshoot of the Arts and Crafts movement, rather than a serious expression of either art or history.

Betjeman and his cronies sometimes invented correspondents who represented bad taste, and wrote angrily to the 'Archie Rev'. One such was H. Bardsley Brushing, of Poonah Punkah, Kenilworth Avenue, Camberley' (a parody of Betjeman's idea of the typical suburban bungalow-dweller), who complained bitterly of the magazine's 'long-haired' and 'cubist' policy, and sent in his own drawing of the ideal modern building, a ludicrous engraving Betjeman had unearthed of a mock-Jacobean folly. Betjeman was the first writer to discover that bad buildings are profoundly funny. Because he wrote about them with humorous delight, it began to be assumed that he genuinely liked them – that his real enthusiasm was for, say, some grotesque piece of late Victorian church architecture. In fact, now as before, his private personal preference was for Georgian buildings, indeed for all English domestic architecture before the Victorian period. Some years after leaving the *Architectural Review*, he wrote to its editor, Hubert de Cronin Hastings, with this *cri de coeur*:

> We *must* make contemporary domestic architecture according to rules of proportion and with textures which will fit in with the buildings we have got. . . . Why do we both live in farmhouses and not at High Point [a celebrated modern block of flats in Highgate]? . . . If brick and stucco made this [a sketch of a Georgian house] which fitted in with mountains or marshes from 1800–1830, why don't we find its equivalent for the present time in England. I haven't seen it yet. . . .

However, for most of the time Betjeman did not disclose these feelings. Since he seemed to treat everything as a joke, his friends were understandably confused about what he really did or did not admire. One of them, Lady Mary Dunn, recalls having 'a lovely jokey time' with him in Reading one day in the early 1930s. 'I never knew if he was pulling my leg as he showed me the most hideous red brick church you've ever seen, and I tried to think whether there was anything beautiful about it.'

Anyone doubting that, at heart, Betjeman deplored what the Victorians had done to English architecture should study his book *An Oxford University Chest* (1938, reprinted in 1979), in which he consistently praises buildings dating from the eighteenth century and earlier for their fine proportions, and commends Victorian work such as Butterfield's Keble College and the mock-Venetian Meadow Buildings at Christ Church only because they are an 'honest expression' of the age of gaslight. Not infrequently, he uses such adjectives as 'repulsive' and 'unfortunate' of the Victorians' work. If later in his life he came genuinely to admire much Victorian architecture, it was only because in the meantime modern architecture had dropped to such a low standard that even the grotesqueries of the late nineteenth century seemed attractive beside it.

At a rare serious moment – a lecture to the Group Theatre, printed as a pamphlet by the Hogarth Press in 1939 under the title *Antiquarian Prejudice* – Betjeman revealed his real architectural *credo*. 'My preference', he told his audience, 'is for the first quarter of the nineteenth century in England, when the aesthetic outlook seems to me to have been particularly bright.' He allowed that the Greek, Norman and Gothic Revivals of the early to mid-nineteenth century were 'essentially original and vigorous . . . not dead reproduction. . . . Until the 'forties . . . architecture had full confidence in itself'. But thereafter came mere 'hothouse revivals . . . "*unimaginative* copying, and hence neither fused into harmony with itself, nor appropriate to its situation"' (a quotation from Palgrave on the Albert Memorial). Mere 'antiquarianism' took over at this time, said Betjeman, and architecture died.

For all his own enthusiasm for a Victorian Revival at Oxford, Robert Byron felt much the same when called upon to give a serious opinion about architecture. In his travel book *The Road to Oxiana* (1937), Byron praises the Palladian style as an absolute: 'You cannot analyse it – nothing could be more lucid. . . . It is a precedent, a criterion.' Byron's and Harold Acton's Victorianism had been a camp joke, taken up jokily in turn by Betjeman, a way of observing the decline of English taste during the nineteenth century rather than a serious enthusiasm. Acton, after all, had been brought up in a Palladian villa, and it was there that architecturally his real taste had been formed.

Although Betjeman's writings in the *Architectural Review* were never reprinted, his work there had considerable repercussions. He encouraged Osbert Lancaster to make humorous contributions to the magazine, with the eventual result of Lancaster's sharply funny, but ultimately serious, set of illustrated handbooks on the decline of English architecture throughout the nineteenth and twentieth centuries, beginning with *Progress at Pelvis Bay* (1936). This first volume describes a fictitious seaside resort and its architectural growth since ancient times, beginning with a Roman villa and ending with 'the Hearts Are Trumps Roadhouse (prop: Herbert Bloodworthy)', with its Olde Englishe Grille, its Pompeian Swimming Pool, and its hot jazz from Ed Sugarprong and his Twenty-Seven White-Hot Tubthumpers. At the 'Archie Rev', Betjeman also initiated what became the influential *Shell Guides* to the English counties, which in their original form had mock-Victorian title pages, and included all kinds of unpredictable information and illustrations – for example, Betjeman's own book on Cornwall (1934) includes a photograph of a blind Primitive Methodist woman preacher. Betjeman enlisted his friends to write other volumes: Robert Byron on Wiltshire (where his family lived), Peter Quennell on Somerset, Billy Clonmore on Kent. Like Waugh in *Vile Bodies*, Betjeman was attempting to identify what was individual and enduring in a world that seemed to have lost touch with permanent values.

During the early 1930s, Betjeman's friends were much more aware of these activities than they were of his poetry, but he began to have poems published in J.C. Squire's *London Mercury*, of which Alan Pryce-Jones was then assistant editor (unpaid), and during 1931 a collection of his verses appeared in book form. The book was financed and published by the wealthy Edward James, who had now left his opulent rooms in Christ Church for an equally lavish life in London, and had chosen this way of repaying his debt to Betjeman for encouragement with his own poetry. The book was described in some amazement by Alan Pryce-Jones in the *London Mercury* for December 1931:

> *Mount Zion* is printed on alternate, or roughly alternate, sheets of pink, or roughly pink, and green paper, bound up in those papers which are usually seen on indoor fireworks, and printed in blue and brown inks. On the cover is a Persian engraving of a tight-waisted lady telephoning – the sub-title is *In Touch with the Infinite* . . . and the poems are illustrated either out of bad books of 1860s ecclesiastical architecture or by the

quite brilliant line drawings of Mr de Cronin Hastings, who appears to have a unique genius for depicting Croydon.

The poems themselves often seemed to be equally spoof, with their jingly rhymes and banal metres. This was partly a joke against the modern movement, whose rules Betjeman knew perfectly well, but chose to forget. Yet he had no distaste for Eliot (who had taught him at prep school) or Auden (with whom he had been to bed), and his motive as usual was to cloak his most serious observations in comic form, so that people would at least listen to them. It was also a mockery of, and at the same time a gesture of affection towards, the poetry that his father's class and generation had written and read, a literary equivalent of the bijou trinkets and *kitsch* furnishings that the Betjemann family factory turned out in such quantities.

On the dedication page, Betjeman dismisses *Mount Zion* as merely a *jeu d'esprit*, 'this precious hyper-sophisticated book'. But behind the facetiousness lies a perfectly serious collection of poems. The theme – and it is the theme of all Betjeman's work from beginning to end – is the decay of eighteenth- and early nineteenth-century absolute values (architectural, social, spiritual) into a shallow and meaningless modern age.

The death of the old order is encapsulated in the very first poem, which was to prove Betjeman's most famous. It describes the quiet demise of an old lady in Leamington Spa, a faded Midlands town that had once been fashionable. All around her, the remains of the old 'Spa' society, and by implication the whole life of past generations, is crumbling into dust:

> Do you know that the stucco is peeling?
> Do you know that the heart will stop?
> From those yellow Italianate arches
> Do you hear the plaster drop?

In other poems in *Mount Zion*, Betjeman often laughs at eighteenth- and nineteenth-century society, as in the mocking 'Hymn' to the vanda- lizing 'restorers' of medieval churches in the late Victorian period, and the 'Eighteenth Century Calvinistic Hymn' in which the speaker blesses his mental and bodily pains, 'For without them my Faith all congeals'. But this is affectionate mockery, very different from the terrible scorn he pours on the 'Business men with awkward hips / And dirty jokes upon their lips' who typify the present-day world. He gets a certain camp amusement from the 'cosy little bungalow' of Colonel and Mrs Kittiwake, in the poem 'Camberley', but deeply regrets the passing

of the old suburban life, described in 'Croydon' ('In a house like that /
Your Uncle Dick was born ...'). There are also sneers at the pseudo-
medievalism of 'The Garden City', and at the appalling domestic inter-
iors of 'The Outer Suburbs',* where

> wifie knits through hubbie's gloom
> Safe in the Drage-way drawing room.
> Oh how expectant for the bed
> All 'Jacobethan' overhead!

Mount Zion seems superficially a casual celebration of unfashionable
British towns and suburbs – Leamington, Camberley, Croydon,
Westgate-on-Sea (which Betjeman loves for its evocation of 'Striving
chains of ordered children ... / Striving on to prunes and suet ...').
In fact each place is carefully chosen as a symbol of some aspect of
past or present society, and all through the book there is a bitter contrast
between the certainties enjoyed by former generations ('Happy bells of
eighteen-ninety') and the loss of values in post-war society: 'Young men
who wear on office stools / The ties of minor public schools, / Each
learning how to be a sinner / And tell "a good one" after dinner ...'.
Betjeman is equally scathing about those whose interest in the past
is purely antiquarian; he has written that his early interest in architecture was nearly strangled at birth by the obfuscating technical terminology of the professional antiquary, so that 'the letters F.S.A. [Fellow
of the Society of Antiquaries] after a name have always, since those
days, caused me to shudder'. In one of the *Mount Zion* poems, he mocks
a young Oxford don who nightly 'settles down to Norman fonts', studying them in some antiquarian volume.

So mere intellectual study of the past is not, in Betjeman's *credo*,
enough. What does he want? An answer may be found in *Ghastly Good
Taste* (1933), a treatise on architecture written by Betjeman at the behest
of one of the J.C. Squire circle, Eric Gillett, who worked for Chapman
& Hall, where the book was published with Arthur Waugh's warm
approval. Re-reading it many years later, Betjeman deprecatingly said
that the 'real point' of it had been the pull-out panorama at the end,
depicting the Street of Taste (the development of English architecture
through the ages) drawn by Peter Fleetwood-Hesketh. In fact *Ghastly
Good Taste* is a passionately serious piece of work, a crucial text for
understanding Betjeman and many others of the Waugh circle.

---

* Both these poems are omitted from Betjeman's *Collected Poems*, and can be found only in the
original *Mount Zion* (James Press, 1931).

It addresses, as its imaginary reader, the owner of a substantial country house upon which the twentieth century is encroaching:

> The gun-room is dusty and the stables are deserted.... Beyond the mouldering brick walls of the kitchen garden to the west ... round the park the roaring tarmac roads coil.... Outside the gates and close to the lodge is a petrol station.... Your house is too large and unmovable. You almost want to get rid of it.

He might be talking to Margot Metroland in *Decline and Fall*, or to Colonel Blount in *Vile Bodies*, whose Doubting Hall stands on the edge of a village 'in which every house seemed to be a garage and filling station'.

Betjeman declares that his purpose is to 'dissuade the average architect from continuing in his profession'. He blames that profession for the profusion of modern buildings in the worst possible pastiche, 'a colossal hideosity aping the style of Queen Anne, or neatly portraying in yellow and red terra cotta an enlarged edition of a seventeenth-century merchant's house in Delft'. And he blames the descent into such rubbish-in-the-name-of-architecture not simply on a general decline in taste, but on something more fundamental to society: the modern disunity of Christendom. 'Before the Reformation,' he writes,

> when all Europe was united in an age of faith, the Church was the dominant force in architecture. For this reason architectural style changed with the opinions of the Church; and all Europe was Christendom, with Holy Church for its expression of consciousness.

When the Reformation divided Christendom, all was still well at first, for 'individuality and doubt' were able to find legitimate architectural expression. The tune was no longer called by the Church, but by the aristocracy; hence the great houses of the seventeenth and eighteenth centuries. But 'after the Reform Bill the Middle Class, which represents industrialism, took control – or rather lost control – of the fine Regency tradition', and 'the result was chaos'. To be more specific, architects found, from the 1820s onwards, that 'money could be made out of the uneducated rich', who demanded and got ludicrous copies of aristocratic mansions, 'a farcical replica of a feudal house', even in a four-bedroom suburban villa.

Betjeman argues that 'architecture can only be made alive again by a new order and another Christendom', a return to the 'architecture of faith'. He admits that this new Christendom may not be Christian at all – it might be 'a Union of Soviet Republics' or 'a League of

Socialistic Nations' – but at all costs there has to be unity of belief before great architecture can again be created.

That this is largely nonsense can be demonstrated simply by looking elsewhere in Betjeman's own early writings. In such poems as 'The Sandemanian Meeting-House in Highbury Quadrant', and in a short story entitled 'Lord Mount Prospect' about a crazy Irish peer who is the sole member of an obscure evangelical sect,* he revels in the varieties of architecture created by schismatic religious bodies, and in the mere fact of their separateness. He has the High Church Anglican's taste for nuances of religious observance, and would obviously deplore a Christendom in which all shared the same religious practice. It was one thing to regard Georgian architecture as a Platonic ideal, another to suggest quite seriously that something like it could be achieved again by a League of Nations or Pan-Catholicism.

There is also a large element of snobbery in his account of the decline of architecture. It was absurd to suggest that the middle class was to blame. The bourgeoisie, establishing itself in England from the sixteenth century, had been responsible for creating the building which Osbert Lancaster has called 'one of the great triumphs of English architecture', the Georgian town house. The aristocracy had commissioned almost nothing of note since the early nineteenth century and, judging by the aesthetic sensibilities (or lack of them) displayed by the average English peer in 1933, was unlikely ever to do so again. Similarly, the Roman Catholic Church, which Betjeman regards as the rightful father of architecture, had by the 1930s about as bad a recent record as any institution in the Western world for creating appalling buildings with worse decorations. The voice in *Ghastly Good Taste* which denies the possibility of the middle class nurturing good architecture is that of the small boy who had overheard himself being called 'common' at children's parties in Highgate and Hampstead, and had been trying to identify with the aristocracy ever since.

Yet it is true that English public architecture in the early 1930s was almost unremittingly deplorable. Le Corbusier and his fellow-modernists had not yet broken through the mush of neo-Gothic and neo-classical, and such few seriously modern buildings as were being attempted

---

* This richly comic short story, published in the *London Mercury* for December 1929 and never reprinted, describes the formation of a society for discovering forgotten Irish peers. Eventually the members hear of Lord Mount Prospect, who belongs to an *outré* and now otherwise defunct North London congregation called the Ember Day Bryanites. His lordship is finally found, stone dead, in his remote Irish castle, having perished in the course of preaching an endless sermon to a non-existent congregation.

– like the BBC's Broadcasting House, opened the year before *Ghastly Good Taste* was published – usually emerged as ugly and ill proportioned. It was natural that someone whose architectural tastes had been formed by English churches and country houses should look back to the period before the Reform Bill as a golden age.

Also, Betjeman was not calling for religious unity for purely architectural reasons. He makes it clear that he is writing from the standpoint of faith. 'I am pleasantly awoken every morning in London by the sound of a church bell,' he writes in *Ghastly Good Taste*.

> That early morning bell is symbolic of the lost age of faith; the symbolism becomes even more pathetic when, twenty minutes after the eight o'clock bell, six strokes on the sanctus tell the people cleaning the gramophone shop and the men at the Lex Garage opposite that the Son of Man died to save the world, and has died again just across the road today.

Despite Betjeman's belief that Roman Catholicism was the father of architecture, he himself had been a fervent Anglo-Catholic (a High Church member of the Church of England) since Oxford days. Evelyn Waugh had plenty of experience of Anglo-Catholicism, gathered during his North London childhood, and despite the doubts experienced at Lancing, had never entirely abandoned churchgoing. A diary entry for 20 October 1927, the period in which he was writing *Decline and Fall*, records a visit to All Saints', Margaret Street, the celebrated Anglo-Catholic church in the West End, where Waugh was 'discomposed to observe Tom Driberg's satanic face in the congregation. . . . It is so like *Sinister Street* meeting school friends at Mass.' Driberg was pursuing an energetically homosexual life, and was also a fervent Anglo-Catholic.

On a boat to Greece in December 1926, to visit Alastair Graham, Waugh had read William James's *The Varieties of Religious Experience*, and in February 1927 he 'went to tea with a parson called Father Underhill who spoke . . . disrespectfully of my vocation to the Church'. This suggests that even before he began his first novel he was considering returning fully to religious belief and practice, perhaps as a Roman Catholic – unless, of course, he was merely being facetious.

It would have been understandable if, following the melodramatic collapse of his marriage, he had immediately abandoned the way of life of the 'crazy and sterile generation' (as he called it in a 1929 *Spectator* article) that he had chronicled so vividly in *Vile Bodies*, and had withdrawn from the fashionable world. Instead, he used his sudden financial prosperity from the novel to behave, for the first time, thoroughly like a Bright Young Person.

Probably in the interests of curing his sexual inexperience (over tea at the Ritz he discoursed to Nancy Mitford on 'sexual shyness in men'), he began to sleep with Audrey Lucas, daughter of the writer E.V. Lucas. An acquaintance of Waugh's from five years back, she was married, but was living the partygoing life to the full. Waugh's affair with her was hazardous: 'Audrey wants more money. I said no.' And on 29 May 1930: 'Audrey says she thinks she is going to have a baby. I don't much care either way really so long as it is a boy.' On 19 June: 'To dinner at Quaglino's with Audrey. She says she is not going to have a baby so all that is bogus. . . . Went to a party at Audrey's. . . . I waited for hours to sleep with Audrey but she was too tired.' In the middle of this affair he 'Went back [one night after several parties] and slept with Varda [the separated wife of an art historian], but both of us too drunk to enjoy ourselves.'

He went almost incessantly to parties, drinking a lot:

> Cocktails at Lancaster Gate. . . . Nancy Cunard and her negress [*sic*]. . . . Later the party of Olivia Wyndham and Ruth Baldwin on a Thames steamer. It was not enough of an orgy. Masses of little lesbian tarts and joyboys. Only one fight. . . . Poor old Hat [Brian Howard] looking like a tragedy queen. . . . Felt very ill [the morning after]. . . . Diana [Guinness] had a supper party. . . . I . . . became very drunk and fought Randolph [Churchill] in the servants' hall. . . . Cocktail party at Grace Ansell. All the inevitable people. John Betjeman brought Gerald Heard. . . . Dined at the Savile with Harold [Acton] and got drunk.

Meanwhile he was sleeping poorly: 'Slept very badly all the week-end. . . . Sleeping very badly. . . . Slept well for the first time for a week. . . .'

He was in the state that John Ruskin had experienced, and which he, Waugh, had described in *Rossetti*: 'all the time suffering acutely from the public humiliation of the annulment of his marriage'.* In this passage in the Rossetti biography, he quotes Ruskin's own words about his plight: ' "I believe I once had affections as warm as most people; but partly from evil chance, and partly from foolishly misplacing them, they have got tumbled down and broken into pieces. So that I have no friendship and no loves. . . ." '

It was in the middle of this wild, almost sleepless life that he turned

---

* The actual divorce proceedings took place on 17 January 1930, when a decree *nisi* was granted on the ground of She-Evelyn's adultery; costs were to be paid by the co-respondent, Heygate.

his mind once again to religion. On 2 July 1930: 'To tea at Alexander Square with Olivia. I said would she please find a Jesuit to instruct me.'

In a 1949 essay, Waugh says he returned to the Christian faith simply because the world he was then inhabiting, the world of *Decline and Fall* and *Vile Bodies*, 'was unintelligible and unendurable without God'.

Olivia Plunket Greene was a Roman Catholic (Dudley Carew writes that, like Shaw's St Joan, she was 'in love with religion', was both 'a *religieuse* and a Bright Young Person'), and so was Alastair Graham, who had been received into the Church about six years earlier. Waugh was still deeply attached to them both.

'Why Rome?' he wrote in 1949, looking back to his conversion, and answered the question on historical grounds:

> England was Catholic for nine hundred years. . . . The Catholic structure still lies lightly buried beneath every phase of English life; history, topography, law, archaeology everywhere reveal Catholic origins. . . . It was self-evident to me that no heresy or schism could be right and the Church wrong.

But it seems likely that in 1930, when he was seeking a religious solution to his own plight, he was in search not of historical continuity but of change, something that would give a clean break from his past. To return to the Anglican practices of his childhood would be undramatic. Also, he was too well aware of the comic potential of the Church of England – *vide* Mr Prendergast – and its tolerance of all shades of religious opinion from agnosticism to fundamentalism. As Graham Greene has said of Waugh's conversion, 'He needed to cling to something solid and strong and unchanging.'

A week after he had raised the subject with Olivia, he went at her recommendation to Mount Street, just off Berkeley Square, to see Father Martin D'Arcy, SJ, at the clergy house attached to the Church of the Immaculate Conception, Farm Street. Though D'Arcy happened to be in Mayfair this summer, he was really an Oxford figure. The Jesuits had sent him to the University shortly after he had joined their Order, and he had taken a First in Greats and won a University prize in philosophy. He was about to go back to Oxford, at the age of thirty-two (six years older than Waugh), to teach Aristotle and Moral Philosophy at Campion Hall, the Jesuit house there.

'Went to Father D'Arcy at 11,' records Waugh's diary for 8 July 1930. 'Blue chin and fine, slippery mind. The clergyhouse at Mount

Street superbly ill-furnished. Anglicans can never achieve this ruthless absence of "good taste".' Alan Pryce-Jones describes 'the uniquely unattractive Jesuit house in Farm Street, surrounded by a waste of brown linoleum, brown deal, leatherette, and peeling paint'.

Though Waugh was impressed with D'Arcy's 'slippery' adeptness at argument, the Jesuit was not a particularly accomplished apologist for the Catholic faith. Brought up in an English Catholic family and educated at Stonyhurst, he lacked the convert's fire and ruthless logic (such as Greene had perhaps found in Father Trollope). His little pamphlet *Catholicism*, published in 1927 in the Benn's Sixpenny Library – one of the first of his many books – is a rambling discourse on the nature of the Catholic Church rather than a finely argued tract. He was popularly supposed to prefer the company of the aristocracy and the rich. Pryce-Jones says that the Dominicans used to recite a rhyme about him:

> Are you rich and highly born?
> Is your soul with sorrow torn?
> Come, and we shall find a way:
> I'm Martin D'Arcy, sir, sj.

However, he was strikingly good at listening to other people and appreciating their viewpoint (his lack of orthodoxy in this respect eventually deprived him of the headship of the Jesuit Order in England in 1950, after he had held it for five years), and he was especially sympathetic to those who came to the Catholic Church seeking order in a world that had lost its values. In *Catholicism* he observes that:

> for a long time the civilized world has tried every kind of expedient; we have had, in turn, Liberalism, Progress, Science, Marxism, the Absolute, Eugenics, and Supermen, but one of them has proved to be that golden rod which measures all things. The craving now [1927] expresses itself particularly in the searching for an order in society, in art, and in philosophy. . . . With the memory of the war, like a writing on the wall, and books announcing the Decline of the West, anxious minds will scan any news which promises to be good.

It could be the voice of Father Rothschild amid the hubbub at Margot Metroland's party.

D'Arcy also had one essential qualification for dealing with Waugh, a sense of humour. Though not exactly prepared to call the Church the Scarlet Woman, he does describe her, in *Catholicism*, as 'a kind of spiritual Helen, saluted now as the object of the world's desire, now as the harlot of the new Troy of the Seven Hills'.

Graham Greene claimed that his own conversion took place only after a struggle in which he tried to defend his rationalism and agnosticism. It is evident that Waugh's attitude was entirely different. In 1949 he described the intellectual process that he went through during instruction. Having decided that the world was unintelligible on its own terms, 'it only remained to examine the historical and philosophic grounds for supposing the Christian revelation to be genuine'. He told D'Arcy that (in D'Arcy's words) he had 'come to learn and understand what he believed to be God's revelation'. In other words, he had virtually made up his mind about belief before he entered the clergy house; all he required was information about the Catholic Church.

Waugh only twice records in his diary the precise subjects of his conversations with D'Arcy, but in both cases these concern specific points of Catholic doctrine rather than general matters of belief: the Church's teaching on whether the Bible is literally true ('verbal inspiration and Noah's Ark'), and two of the most controversial issues relating to Catholicism, 'infallibility and indulgences'. There is no suggestion that they talked about fundamental things, such as the divinity of Christ, or the redemption of the world through the Crucifixion and Resurrection. Waugh simply wanted to know the details of the system which he had already decided to adopt as his own.

Indeed D'Arcy was struck by how 'matter of fact' was Waugh's attitude to the whole business. D'Arcy was currently instructing another writer, whom he does not name, who insisted on testing everything he was told against his own experience, and in consequence did not proceed with instruction and decided not to join the Church. 'Evelyn, on the other hand,' says D'Arcy, 'never spoke of experience or feelings.' They merely had 'an interesting discussion based primarily on reason'.

Far from offering serious arguments against the Church's teaching, Waugh (notes D'Arcy) was 'perhaps inclined to be too literal' in his acceptance of them. His attitude to doctrinal points seems to have been much as he expressed it in a 1932 article: 'It is better to be narrow-minded than to have no mind, to hold limited and rigid principles than none at all.'

At the conclusion of instruction, D'Arcy felt that Waugh had 'convinced himself . . . with only an intellectual passion' of the truth of Catholicism; it had all been done 'very unsentimentally'. The word 'only' seems to hint that D'Arcy was vaguely uneasy, but, if so, he said nothing about it, then or later. A convert was a convert, though as Waugh writes in *The Ordeal of Gilbert Pinfold*, ' "Conversion" suggests an event more sudden and emotional than his calm acceptance of the propositions of his faith. . . .'

Writing in 1949, Waugh himself expressed some amazement that D'Arcy had been prepared to accept him on these terms: 'I look back aghast at the presumption with which I thought myself suitable for reception and with wonder at the trust of the priest who saw the possibility of growth in such a dry soul.' Elsewhere he described the Catholic Church as 'a body which [I] had joined on very slight acquaintance'. And a richly comic passage in *Brideshead Revisited*, in which the would-be convert Rex Mottram accepts everything the priest tells him without a moment's hesitation, seems to be based on Waugh's uncomfortable recollection of his own instruction. 'I can't get anywhere near him,' complains the priest.

> 'He doesn't seem to have the least intellectual curiosity or natural piety. The first day I wanted to find out what sort of religious life he had till now, so I asked him what he meant by prayer. He said: "*I* don't mean anything. *You* tell me." I tried to, in a few words, and he said: "Right. So much for prayer. What's the next thing?" '

Many of Waugh's discussions with D'Arcy took place in more congenial surroundings than the clergy house: 'Lunched Savile with Frank [Pakenham, himself a Catholic] and Father D'Arcy. . . . Lunched at the St James's Club [with] Father D'Arcy and David Cecil.' While instruction was proceeding, in the late summer of 1930, Waugh continued with his round of parties and dinner parties, and with the pursuit of various women:

> Lunched at Sovrani's with Frank after a morning with D'Arcy. Excellent cold duck with *foie gras*. . . . Went to Father D'Arcy. . . . Lunched at Ritz. . . . Lunched with Beatrice Guinness. . . . I sat at a side table with Baby [Jungman] who was sweet. . . . Dined at the Savile . . . and got drunk. . . . Went to see Audrey. . . .

That Waugh's conversion required no intellectual struggle suggests that, all along, he had retained his Christian beliefs from childhood, and the only decision was whether to become a Catholic rather than revert to Anglican worship. However, *Labels*, a travel book about his disastrous Mediterranean trip with She-Evelyn, which he had just finished writing for Duckworth's, gives a very different picture. It suggests a total scepticism about everything religious.

When the book was published in September 1930, two months after he had begun instruction with D'Arcy, Waugh was obliged to add a note explaining that its opinions were 'those of ... eighteen months ago'; since then his views 'on several subjects, and particularly on Roman Catholicism, have developed and changed in many ways'. In fact *Labels* had been written much more recently than this suggests. It had only been finished in April 1930, two months before he began instruction, and he must have been reading the proofs some time around June, so that the opinions it contains could easily have been altered before publication, had he no longer held them.

The first comic incident in the book is the description of a 'stunt' flight in an aeroplane at Oxford during Waugh's undergraduate days, an experience so terrifying that (he alleges) several others who underwent it asked to be 'received into the Roman Church.... I will not say', he continues,

> that this aeronaut was directly employed by Campion House, but certainly, when a little later, he came down in flames, the Jesuits lost a good ally, and to some people it seemed as if the Protestant God had asserted supremacy in a fine Old Testament manner.

Labels continues in this vein of mockery of religion in general, and of Catholicism in particular. Waugh describes how, on the train to the South of France, 'Juliet', one half of a honeymoon couple he has invented to disguise himself and She-Evelyn, is put into a *wagon-lit* because she has a high temperature. The other occupant of the sleeping car is a young Catholic priest who, when he finds he is sharing with a young woman, decides to spend the night in the corridor instead. Waugh laughs at his predicament: 'The night air seemed to have been effective in purging him of any worldly thoughts that the encounter produced.'

Waugh also describes, in Naples, a worshipper in the cathedral detaching himself from his devotions at Mass, and offering pornographic entertainment – 'You wanna come see Pompeian dances?' – and a little girl taking him into a crypt to view some preserved corpses, presumably saints' relics, which she describes as 'the work of the priest'; she 'thrust her face' into the slit-open stomach of one of them 'and inhaled deeply and greedily'. Evidently he finds such things ludicrous, and on the final page of the book he sneers at those who 'indulge their consciences with sectarian religious beliefs'; he himself, like the characters in *Decline and Fall*, seems only to believe in what he calls 'Fortune ... the least capricious of deities ... [who] arranges things on the just and rigid system that no one shall be very happy for very long'.

On the other hand, though the author of *Labels* may seem an unlikely candidate for reception into the Catholic Church, he is thoroughly bored with the material world in all its manifestations. He judges Paris 'bogus', finds the Casino at Monte Carlo 'very shabby', decides that the Middle East in the rain resembles 'some grouse-laden corner of the Scottish highlands', and is disappointed even by the red-light district of Port Said. When he goes to sleep, he experiences only 'the most prosaic kind of dreams', and when he contemplates his profession of writer he wonders whether there is any new subject left under the sun: 'One of the acute problems of authorship today is to find any aspect of social organization about which one can get down one's seventy thousand words without obvious plagiarism.' Indeed, the title *Labels* reflects this feeling: he says he has chosen it because 'all the places I visited on this trip are already fully labelled. I was no adventurer. . . .'

Waugh had become successful almost overnight; his future seemed assured, his social life was wildly busy, and none of it offered him any enduring delight. On the surface he was terribly bored; contemplating the typical evening's amusement in London, he declared in *Labels*: 'One suffers almost every kind of boredom.' Beneath the boredom was the deep misery caused by the failure of his marriage, a misery that could not be satisfied by partygoing and womanizing.

There may also have been an element of self-protection in his conversion. He told Terence Greenidge that he was becoming a Catholic 'to prevent the foolishness of ever wanting to re-marry'. Most of his friends were inclined to take this as an act of sacrifice, perhaps undertaken in a spirit of punishing himself for the failure of the first marriage. Yet there seems no reason not to take his words as literally true. Hurt beyond measure by She-Evelyn's desertion, he may have felt that, while he might sometimes engage in casual love affairs, it would be crazy to risk another marriage and the possibility of its dissolution. Desertion and divorce were not experiences he could go through twice. By becoming a Catholic he was protecting himself against this eventuality, for Rome did not recognize divorce, and it would be laborious, perhaps impossible, to obtain permission from the Papal office should he ever wish to marry again.

Martin D'Arcy was well aware of this aspect of Waugh's conversion. 'What showed his sincerity', he writes, 'was that . . . he thought that as a Catholic he would never be able to marry again and have children. His decision to seek admission into the Church therefore meant a considerable sacrifice.' D'Arcy does not seem to have considered the possibility that it was not a sacrifice but a precaution.

Waugh made the decision to join the Church at a time when he was desperately short of sleep, not infrequently drunk, and trying to fend off acute boredom, itself a symptom of deep depression. He announced his decision in the most spectacular way imaginable, in the pages of the *Daily Express*.

CONVERTED TO ROME
Why It Has Happened To Me

So began an article by Waugh in the *Express* on 20 October 1930, some fourteen weeks after he had first called on Fr D'Arcy.

The article begins by dismissing three popular misconceptions about the typical convert: that 'the Jesuits have got hold of him', that 'he is captivated by the ritual' and that 'he wants to have his mind made up for him'. Answering this last charge, Waugh argues that someone with a lazy mind can stagnate as easily outside the Church as within it. On the other hand, for those with active minds 'the Roman system can and does form a basis for the most vigorous intellectual and artistic activity'. The real issue today, he goes on, is the choice between 'Christianity and Chaos'. By Chaos he means the 'lack of confidence in moral and social standards' which has resulted from a loss of faith, a failure to recognize that civilization really rests on a 'supernatural basis'.

Waugh had been formally received into the Catholic Church three weeks before this article was printed, on 29 September 1930, at Farm Street. The only friend to be invited to the ceremony was Tom Driberg, who decided that Waugh had chosen him because he wanted the conversion to be announced in the William Hickey gossip column of the *Daily Express*, which Driberg was then writing. Driberg duly obliged.

Waugh's parents were distressed by his becoming a Catholic, but there was no change in their behaviour towards him. Most of his friends paid little or no attention to the conversion. Almost the only person to comment on it was Edith Sitwell, whom Waugh visited at Renishaw shortly before being received into the Church. She made a remark that he recorded without comment in his diary: 'I can't see any point in being a Catholic unless one belongs to an old Catholic family.' From Waugh's later writings, one may guess that it sank in.

2

Remote People

Faced with the collapse of his hopes as a serious novelist, Graham Greene decided to write a popular best-seller. Learning that MGM were filming a novel called *Grand Hotel*, about a collection of people in a Berlin hotel whose lives intersect dramatically, he decided to begin a book of the same species set on the Orient Express. 'I had taken on a rather heavy assignment,' he remarked, since he had never been on this train, and could not remotely afford to make the full journey the novel would describe.

However, he had once spent a day in Istanbul, the train's destination, during the course of a Hellenic cruise, and he now managed to raise funds for a third-class ticket as far as the German frontier; the German authorities provided him with a writer's free pass on to Cologne. On the train, he sat scribbling furiously, recording every detail that could be seen through the window – so that the first part of *Stamboul Train* is almost overladen with scenic description. For descriptions beyond Cologne, he relied on maps, his imagination and a record of Honegger's *Pacific 231*, which he played daily as he sat writing in his Chipping Camden house, hoping that the music 'would take me far enough away from my thatched cottage, a Pekinese dog who suffered from hysteria, some barren apple trees, the muddy lane and a row of Cos lettuces'.

He wrote in a mood of deep anxiety. Not only had his second and third novels failed, but he had wasted time and effort on a biography of Lord Rochester, which Heinemann had then rejected, 'and I was too uncertain of myself to send it elsewhere'. Consequently *Stamboul*

Train became 'laden by . . . the sense of failure'. But this was the making of the book. It could have been just another *Grand Hotel*, a potboiler glamorizing the lives of those who travel on international expresses. Instead it is pervaded, like *Vile Bodies*, with a sense of the futility of all hopes. The train is an image of Greene's career as a writer, as it then seemed to him: starting off glamorously and with hope, running into danger and appalling weather, uncertain of reaching any destination. He has realized, like the travellers on the train, that he will have to be 'very flexible, very opportunist' to survive.

The novel was published during 1932 and became a best-seller. Greene's career had been saved, as he says, 'at the very last moment'.

'We are snowed up in a tunnel near Forges D'Abel. Train gone wrong. . . . Can't breathe. All over. . . . Shit! Floreat Etona. . . . Cyril Connolly, Jean Bakewell xxx Feb 17th 1929.'

Travelling around Europe with the girl he had met in Paris, Connolly was having experiences such as Greene described from imagination in *Stamboul Train*: 'Jean got out of the train thinking I had left it and it went on without her. . . . *"J'ai perdu mon mari."* She came out to Casetas in a car. We had a reunion on the platform and an omelette together.' Though he was not yet her *mari*, they became husband and wife in February 1930, and rented a house not far from Toulon. 'If you hate both diehards and bright young people,' wrote Connolly, 'you have . . . to go and live abroad.' Evelyn Waugh came to visit them. 'I did so much enjoy it,' he wrote to Jean, 'and it was exciting meeting the Huxleys. . . .' Connolly had deliberately settled near Aldous Huxley, admiring his achievement as a novelist and hoping to emulate him. But his own hedonism annoyed the Huxleys – 'liqueurs after luncheon', noted Huxley disapprovingly of the Connolly lifestyle – and, while in France, Connolly managed to write nothing other than reviews for the *New Statesman* and other periodicals. Jean had money of her own, and they could survive, but only restlessly. They took to keeping lemurs as substitute children – Connolly writes lyrically about these bewitching creatures in *The Unquiet Grave* (1944). In the future, French country life would symbolize for him an Arcadian past, never to be recaptured. At the time, he and Jean spent much of their energy looking through advertisements of houses in England, skimming the pages of *Country Life*, 'dreaming of that Priory at Wareham where we would end our days . . . of whisky, beefsteaks, expresses from Paddington, winter landscapes, old inns and Georgian houses . . .'.

*

Harold Acton was having no success as a writer, and he put it down to an excess of Europeanism. His poems did not sell, and were not read ('poetry had fallen into the hands of hot gospellers', he says of the Auden group), and Faber's demanded that he cut thirty thousand words from a biography they had commissioned, *The Last Medici*. 'I felt I was launching a cargo of Tuscan products which nobody wanted. . . . So long as I remained in Europe my writings were bound to be affected by Italy. . . . In January 1932 I left Europe not to return until 1939.'

After a trip to America, he settled in China, where 'I felt strangely at home.' He lectured in English literature at Peking National University and himself studied Chinese poetry. Friends occasionally turned up – Robert Byron and Bryan Guinness among them – and what they told him of England made him glad to stay in the Far East. 'Peter Quennell wrote to me that Europe was like a sucked orange.'

Robert Byron, unmarried and living with his family in Wiltshire, had become a travel writer and Byzantine researcher, stumbling into this *modus vivendi* while still at Oxford, where two Old Etonian friends had invited him on a car-journey to Athens. In the book that resulted from this, *Europe in the Looking-Glass* (1926), he claimed to be a citizen of Europe rather than England, but came to some Waugh-like conclusions about many of the places he visited: 'Innsbruck . . . is uninteresting and almost squalid. . . . The hotel . . . smelt strongly of rice pudding.'

Paradoxically, all Byron's travel-writing was dedicated to proving the proposition, so often voiced by his friends, that 'abroad is awful'. Waugh's contemporaries had conducted their cultural self-education as far as possible without reference to anything beyond the British coastline. It was part of their studied anti-intellectual pose, but also a reaction to the previous generation's having had to spend much of its youth overseas. 'Uncle Matthew's four years in France and Italy between 1914 and 1918', writes Nancy Mitford in *The Pursuit of Love*, 'had given him no great opinion of foreigners. "Frogs," he would say, "are slightly better than Huns or Wops, but abroad is unutterably bloody and foreigners are fiends."'

Byron's next book was about Mount Athos, and then came *The Byzantine Achievement* (1929), *An Essay on India* (1931) and *First Russia Then Tibet* (1933). Though his knowledge widened hugely, his old prejudice against received notions of 'good taste' became deeper. Christopher Sykes says he went out of his way to be anti-intellectual. For instance, he managed to write a study of the history of Western painting without even mentioning the Dutch and Flemish masters, because he considered them of no importance and would not defer to accepted authorities, while any mention of Rembrandt could move him to physical violence. Sykes says he was even puzzled by the general admiration for Shakespeare. All this gave his books a rather freakish air. Waugh described Byron's attitudes as 'insularity run amok' with 'no standards of judgement but his personal reactions'. He thought Byron's writing precariously flamboyant rather than confidently crafted. When Peter Quennell remarked to him (after the publication in 1937 of Byron's *The Road to Oxiana*), 'None of our generation has made good except you and Robert,' Waugh snapped back: 'Robert has not made good.' Byron was (discreetly) homosexual, and friends later wondered whether this had for some reason made Waugh hostile to him, though Harold Acton's explanation of Waugh's cooling feelings was that Byron had been among the very few present at the wedding to She-Evelyn in 1928; Acton, who was best man, says that he too had temporarily 'fallen from grace' with Waugh during the 1930s.

Brian Howard turned his back on England too. He drifted about Europe during the early 1930s, engaging in stormy and usually unsuccessful affairs with various young men. Eventually he settled for 'Toni', a young German he picked up in Munich. Cyril and Jean Connolly ran into them in Athens during 1933, and found them haunting the homosexual bars and cafés, Brian depending financially on funds from his mother, with whom he shared a bank account. Connolly thought him a sufferer from 'cancer of the soul', but he was still good at 'enjoying the shifting scene and enhancing it for others'.

'The more I hear of England,' Brian wrote to his mother, 'the more I ... *loathe* the idea of my clever young contemporaries ... all these Waughs and young pseudo-serious writers. . . .'

'I want very much to go to Abyssinia for the coronation of the Emperor,' Waugh wrote on a postcard to A. D. Peters early in September 1930. He asked Peters to 'get a paper to send me as a special correspondent. . . . PS. This is a serious suggestion.'

Though the suggestion was serious, the purpose of the trip was not. The idea had occurred during his visit to the Pakenhams in Ireland (the occasion on which Betjeman was a fellow-guest). Alastair Graham was there too, on leave from Athens, and conversation got round to the forthcoming coronation of Haile Selassie as the new Emperor of Abyssinia. Alastair knew something of the realities of Ethiopian politics, but the rest of the house-party delighted in contributing spurious information about the country: that the Abyssinian Church had canonized Pontius Pilate, and consecrated their bishops by spitting on their heads; that the people lived on raw meat and mead; and that the real heir to the throne had been imprisoned in a mountain fastness, fettered with chains of gold. They looked up the Abyssinian royal family in the *Almanack de Gotha*, and discovered that the emperors traced their descent from Solomon and the Queen of Sheba, and that the first ruler 'ascended the throne immediately after the Deluge'. All this was enough to persuade Waugh to visit the place. Two weeks later he had booked his passage, and a friend who worked for *The Times*, Douglas Woodruff, arranged for that paper to pay his expenses in return for reports.

Ethiopia proved, in Waugh's eyes, rewardingly comic. The book he wrote about his journey, *Remote People* (1931), describes his two weeks in Addis Ababa as a 'preposterous *Alice in Wonderland* fortnight'. The coronation itself seemed to him an absurdity, a five-hour ceremony conducted in a makeshift tent by priests who scarcely understood the archaic religious language they were chanting, watched by a bemused bunch of European visitors, some of them in evening dress, while the Ethiopian nobility were relegated to distant corners of the marquee, where they lay on the floor and dozed. Waugh evidently had difficulty in composing a serious report of the event for *The Times*, and could not help slipping in a mention of 'an American woman who wore a tweed suit and a toque decorated with a small star-spangled banner'.

He derived even more amusement from a visit to a remote monastery in the company of an American professor, who claimed to be an authority on Abyssinian Christianity but – according to Waugh – misunderstood everything he was shown. The absurdity of this expedition was summed up for Waugh when, at the monastery church, the holy of holies was opened and proved to contain 'a wicker chair, some heaps of clothes, two or three umbrellas, a suitcase of imitation leather, some newspapers, and a teapot and slop-pail of enamelled tin'.

If *Remote People* described only the Abyssinian part of the trip, the book would be no more than the comic travel narrative which Waugh's readers expected. However, he stayed on in Africa after the coronation, visiting Zanzibar, Kenya and Uganda before travelling overland to Cape Town and returning to England by boat. The second half of the book, describing these adventures, is often very different in tone.

Three chapters in this section are entitled 'Nightmares'. One of these describes the acute discomfort of the final stage of the African journey: coping with abusive steamer-captains on the great African lakes, with non-existent timetables, and with the horror of endless days spent in appallingly uncomfortable trains. This is a Nightmare the reader can share to the full, an extreme version of the horrors of travel that are experienced to a greater or lesser extent by everyone. The other two Nightmares are rather different.

The first of them describes the four days Waugh was obliged to spend in the Ethiopian town of Dirre-Dowa after missing a train. To say that they were four days of boredom, he assures us, is an understatement; they were 'four days ... as black and timeless as Damnation'. This Nightmare is in fact an essay on boredom, and on Waugh's own susceptibility to it:

> I am constitutionally a martyr to boredom ... to the stark horrors of boredom.... I sat in Mr Bollolakos' hotel.... I had nothing to read except the first volume of a pocket edition of Pope.... For an hour or two I sat in the rocking-chair reading Pope's juvenile poems. Most of the time I thought about how awful the next day would be.... It was still early in the day. I took a dose of sleeping-draught and went to bed again.

Alec Waugh, staying with Evelyn in the South of France in the early 1930s, encountered him in just such a mood:

> One morning I went into his room to find him stretched out on the bed, a leg hanging loose over the side: his hands under his head. He did not acknowledge my entrance, I went away. I returned an hour later to find that he had not moved. He was still staring at the ceiling.

The reader might suppose from his account of paralysing boredom in Dirre-Dowa that there was not another human being to talk to in the place. But in the evening he was joined by an English-speaking couple he had met in Addis Ababa, who took him back to their house and entertained him to the best of their ability. Waugh records no gratitude, but takes the opportunity to mock the wife's ornamental brooch 'commemorating the opening of Epping Forest to the public', which he had already laughed at in Addis Ababa.

Nor was he stuck in Dirre-Dowa for the entire four days. After forty-eight hours, a train arrived and took him to Djibouti on the coast. There, he had two days of uncertainty before managing to catch a boat to Aden, en route for Zanzibar. Again he had company – 'three American cinema-men' – and again he is utterly unappreciative: 'We went for an exquisitely dismal jaunt together in the native town.'

The idea begins to suggest itself that Waugh does not really like human company. He himself considers this quite candidly, and accepts it: 'I shall always be ill at ease with nine out of every ten people I meet,' he observes, comparing his own case with so-called 'men of the world', truly seasoned travellers. 'I shall always find something startling and rather abhorrent in the things most other people think worth doing.'

If this is true (wonders the reader of *Remote People*), have all the Europeans and Africans he has met in the course of his journey been quite as absurd as he has painted them? Does he find people comic simply because of his detachment from them – because a sense of the comic enables him to preserve his isolation?

One piece of evidence confirms the suspicion that Waugh's view of people and events in Ethiopia was curiously lopsided. Christopher Sykes, in his biography of Waugh, writes at some length about Professor Thomas Whittemore, the American scholar who accompanied Waugh on the expedition to the monastery. Waugh portrays Whittemore in *Remote People* as merely ludicrous, an ignoramus posing as an expert, who misunderstands everything and makes a fool of himself to the monks. Sykes describes a very different sort of man:

> A Bostonian, a friend of Henry James, an emotional enthusiast of his subject, he had delightful and unusual conversational powers. I imagine that his dramatic style of talk, and his shameless use of the ultra-poetic phrase, reflected a style of conversation once admired and now utterly out of fashion. I heard him once describe Novgorod 'as though all the golden domes of Russia were plunged into the glittering and magic seas of Venice'. I told Evelyn about this once and he was much amused. Whittemore had used precisely the same phrase to him. His theatrical manner, and his deep tremulous voice contrasting oddly with his minute neat person, often allowed him to convey a rapid description in a way that conventional talk cannot. I once asked him what was the first and immediate impression that Henry James made on those who met him, and 'O-o-o-o-h!' he moaned, almost literally cowering away, '*Heavy!*'

Whittemore as portrayed by Sykes is funny in a far more sophisticated way than the 'Professor W.' of *Remote People*, who is simply a clumsy American ignoramus – 'one of the normal manifestations of American scholarship', Waugh calls him. Maybe Sykes's description is too complimentary; certainly Harold Acton records that Bernard Berenson thought Whittemore 'a pious fraud'. Yet Graham Greene, who met Whittemore during the Second World War, gives an account of him that is as sympathetic as Sykes's: 'an elderly man with an old maid's face and feminine wrinkles and steel spectacles and an extraordinary gentleness and kindness of manner'. And Harold Acton himself encountered him after the war: 'His articulation was painfully deliberate, but there was an ironical gleam in his eye which belied his solemnity.'

Sykes adds one further testimony that Waugh's portrait of Whittemore was a caricature. He records that after the Ethiopian trip Whittemore, who had liked Waugh, 'became an enthusiastic reader of his books, would quote from them and conceived a special admiration for the picture of Ethiopia in *Remote People*'. Sykes suggests that he may have failed to spot the mockery of 'Professor W.', but himself cannot really believe this: 'He had wit and an enormous sense of humour. I believe he enjoyed the picture of himself because it was so funny.'

If this is true, the implications are rather disturbing. Waugh's comic writing is based on the assumption that only the narrator – or at most the narrator and a tiny handful of others – has a sense of humour. What the rest of the world regards as solemn, he can see in its true light as absurd. In *Decline and Fall* only Grimes shares Paul's (and Waugh's) perception of the comedy; the rest are merely creatures of Wonderland, lost souls in hell, who cannot see the humour in their plight. In *Vile Bodies* even Adam is not granted complete comic vision; for much of the book he is being swept helplessly about the whirlpool with the rest of them. Only the invisible narrator perceives the comedy from start to finish.

This detachment on the part of the narrator, and perhaps one character, who alone can see the comic side of things, is not a *sine qua non* of humorous writing. P.G.Wodehouse allows many of his characters to laugh at what is going on, and Firbank's humour largely arises from the characters' ability to share jokes among each other, by nuance – in Firbank it is the reader who tends to be excluded rather than the people in the story. Waugh had developed a different approach, which in the novels seems unquestionably successful as a way of examining humanity, yet which may have sprung from his own inability to form close friendships or even to make any sort of personal contact with most people. This only becomes apparent in the non-fiction, where he is obliged to describe real people, not mere comic cyphers in a story he has planned; and he cannot do it. The title of the Ethiopian book, *Remote People*, begins to take on a bitter meaning.

Reading the book in this light, *Remote People* ceases to be bored travelogue, and becomes instead a chilling account of Waugh's loneliness and isolation. Again and again, he finds other people intolerable. Arriving in Addis Ababa before the coronation, he is relieved to spot an acquaintance from English country-house society, Lady Irene Ravensdale, who is standing on the hotel steps in riding habit. Thereafter one might expect Waugh to treat her kindly in the narrative, or at least to use her as someone with whom he may discuss his impressions of the city and the coronation. In fact she is hardly mentioned again in *Remote People*, and Waugh's diary shows that he found her insufferable:

> Irene returned [in] greatest consternation [from a British Legation reception].... 'After all Evelyn, you may think it's nothing but I *am* Daddy's daughter. I *am* Baroness Ravensdale.'* ... Irene was put next to the Emperor [at dinner] and was translated with excitement. Coming back she said, 'That has shown all those Bartons [at the Legation]. I have come out on top. I am Baroness Ravensdale in my own right.'

Waugh comments of her behaviour, in the diary: 'I think I must be a prig, people do shock me so.' They do shock him, all through *Remote People*, where he constantly describes them as 'odious', though what moves him to amazement and alarm would, one suspects, have caused no more than mild amusement to others.

It would be interesting to have comments on Waugh himself from some of those he met on his journey; and there is one record of how he struck someone in Ethiopia. The explorer Wilfred Thesiger, who was in Addis Ababa for the coronation, met Waugh:

> He struck me as flaccid and petulant and I disliked him on sight. Later he asked, at second-hand, if he could accompany me into the Danakil country, where I planned to travel. I refused. Had he come, I suspect only one of us would have returned.

This is to take account of only one side of Waugh. Many would have chosen him for company rather than the rugged Thesiger. Maurice Bowra, who got to know Waugh well in the early 1930s, describes him as 'the best company in the world.... The better I knew him, the more I appreciated his rich character and his quite outstanding gifts.' Nevertheless he was undoubtedly beginning to drive himself towards a position of isolation, to make himself more remote from ordinary people. Even Bowra admits this: 'This spectacle of the curmudgeon which he at times presented to the public was largely an act, which it amused him to play, but it was built on something real.'

Remote People frequently portrays the native populations unfavourably. A band of Bedouin encountered in Aden seem scarcely human: 'They are of small stature and meagre muscular development; their faces

---

* She was the daughter of Lord Curzon, whose title had passed to her by special dispensation.

are hairless or covered with a slight down, their expressions degenerate and slightly dotty, an impression which is accentuated by their loping, irregular gait.' After reading this, it is not surprising to find Waugh writing in his diary of his arrival in Kenya: 'It is nice to be on English ground again.' Indeed, one of the things he took back from Africa was an increased pride in being English.

When in *Remote People* he comes to Kenya and begins to see something of expatriate British society, he admits that there has been a 'native problem', but convinces himself that the white planters' ill-treatment of blacks is a thing of the past, and that in any case it was quite natural for Englishmen to behave in that way:

> People abused their native servants in round terms and occasionally cuffed their heads, as they did their English servants up to the end of the eighteenth century. The idea of courtesy to servants, in fact, only came into being when the relationship ceased to be a human one and became purely financial.

The fact that the settlers remind him of the eighteenth-century squire-archy excuses their behaviour, indeed makes them positively charming in his eyes. 'The Kenya settlers', he writes in one of the few impassioned sections of *Remote People*, 'are not cranks ... nor criminals ... but perfectly normal, respectable Englishmen, out of sympathy with their own age, and for this reason linked to the artist in an unusual but very real way.' Waugh does not seem willing to expand the idea of the artist having a natural affinity to someone who rejects the style of the present age, and being 'out of key with his time' (Ezra Pound's words in *Hugh Selwyn Mauberley*). But it evidently fascinates him.

Waugh is quite specific, in this same section of *Remote People*, about why the Kenya settlers appeal to him. He sees them as 'Quixotic' in their attempt to create 'Barsetshire', 'the traditional life of the English squirearchy', in the middle of Africa. He admits that while the squir-earchy was 'still dominant' in English society, it 'formed the natural target for satirists', but now that it has become 'a rare and exotic survival', one can look back at it 'with unaffected esteem and regret'.

He has come to Africa to laugh; he leaves it full of enthusiasm at the possibility of recreating the life of the English squires of the eight-eenth and nineteenth centuries. And all through *Remote People* he has been writing in a prose style appropriate to those eras. *Decline and Fall* and *Vile Bodies* (especially the latter), influenced by Hemingway and Firbank, had consisted largely of dialogue faithfully reproducing the nuances and colloquialisms of daily speech, with comparatively little narration as such, effacing memories of the mock-Victorian (or mock-Arthur Waugh) tones of *Rossetti*. But in *Remote People*, where there is little dialogue and much narrative, that antique voice returns. Usually it is only mildly pitched, and Waugh's ear, finely tuned by his Hemingway–Firbank experiments, does not allow him to slip into self-parody. Occasionally, however, the twentieth century seems to dissolve:

> He was an Armenian of rare character, named Bergebedgiań; he spoke a queer kind of French with remarkable volubility, and I found great delight in all his opinions; I do not think I have ever met a more tolerant man; he had no prejudice or scruples of race, creed, or morals of any kind whatever; there were in his mind none of those opaque patches of inconsidered principles, it was a single translucent pool of placid doubt; whatever splashes of precept had disturbed its surface from time to time had left no ripple; reflections flitted to and fro and left it unchanged.

Can this be the same author who created Agatha Runcible and her Bright Young companions – 'Too, too sick-making'? Can it really be the inventor of Captain Grimes who observes of the Anglo-Saxon expatriates' belief in their superiority over all other races: 'It is just conceivable that they might be right'?

One other point in *Remote People*, and in Waugh's diary of the trip, deserves note. It may be guessed that he went to Africa largely because he was still in flight from the failure of his marriage. It was a geographical gesture comparable to the intellectual gesture of his joining the Catholic Church. The confusion of his feelings about sex is suggested by the fact that, several times in the trip, he takes the trouble to visit the red-light district of a town, but only as an observer: 'We made an excursion into the brothel quarter. . . . It is squalid and characterless. Moreover, at the sight of us the women ran into their houses or hid in their yards.' This is in Zanzibar. And in Harar: 'Went into three or four brothels. . . . Ugly women.' Occasionally he listens to accounts of others' sexual exploits: 'Raymond . . . brought a sluttish girl back to the house. He woke me up later in night to tell me had just rogered her and her mama too.' Waugh involves himself with no woman; he looks on from a distance: 'Went into three or four tedj houses. Brothels. . . . Saw exquisitely beautiful girls making basketwork. . . . Slept badly.'

Remote People ends with a third Nightmare, a short chapter in which Waugh describes his return to London and his immersion in the brittle, artificial world he had portrayed in *Vile Bodies*: a visit to an over-priced night club, portrayed as if it were a circle of hell in the *Inferno*: 'It was underground. We stepped down into the blare of noise. . . . Cigarette-smoke stung the eyes. . . . Waiters elbowed their way in and out, muttering abuse in each other's ears. . . . Familiar faces leered through the haze.' Waugh is emphasizing that his 'hell is other people' experience of touring around Africa was no worse than the hell of other people in London. He gave the same picture in a letter to Patrick Balfour, written in July 1931: 'It is very nasty in London. . . . There is a new restaurant called Malmaison so much worse than all other restaurants & that is where we spend every evening.'

He escaped from London to write *Remote People* in friends' houses and in hotels in England and France, and when it was finished, in August 1931, he began work on a novel drawn from his experiences in Africa, telling A.D. Peters that it would definitely be a best-seller. It was ready in May 1932, and he was pleased with it.

Decline and Fall and *Vile Bodies* had made conspicuously little use of his own recent experiences, but he put many details of his Abyssinian travels into the new novel, *Black Mischief*, in a fairly undigested form – such as a lorry stuck in the middle of the road and used as a home by natives, and the abbot of the monastery appearing with an umbrella and a flywhisk (which appear both in *Remote People* and in the novel). The two books are evidently meant to be complementary, which is possibly why Waugh omits any sort of 'control' character from the novel, a Paul Pennyfeather or Adam Fenwick-Symes who can view the cavortings of its inmates without being entirely drawn into their lives. By implication Waugh himself is still present in *Black Mischief* as observer and critic, as he is explicitly in *Remote People*. A more obvious reason for the omission of a Paul/Adam is that in *Black Mischief* Waugh experiments for the first time with an aggressive rather than a passive hero. Basil Seal is the exact opposite of the 'heroes' of *Decline and Fall* and *Vile Bodies*: ruthless, self-seeking, fatally attractive to women, dirty, ill-kempt and brilliant.

Though he was usually wary of identifying any of his fictional characters with real-life models, Waugh stated, in a 1962 letter, that Basil Seal was 'a mixture of Basil Murray & Peter Rodd'. The statement is both informative and misleading, for Basil is more than that.

Basil Murray's father was the celebrated Gilbert Murray, Regius Professor of Greek at Oxford and an earnest supporter of the League of Nations. His mother, daughter of the Earl of Carlisle, had been brought up a teetotaller; when her father succeeded to the title, orders were given that the entire contents of the wine cellar at Castle Howard, the family seat, should be poured into the lake. Both the Murray parents were also vegetarian, left-wing and believers in Progress; Basil's mother was heard to say: 'When we have got rid of the drink we can turn our minds to redistributing their property.' Basil reacted against all this high-mindedness by perpetually disgracing himself in his parents' eyes, doing poorly at Oxford (though a scholar of New College he took a Third in Honour Moderations and Greats), indulging conspicuously in drink, and running up enormous debts. Waugh describes him as 'satanic ... there were times when he seemed possessed by a devil of mischief'.

But Waugh did not know him well, and from other evidence Basil Murray comes across as a rebel against parental authority but also a serious-minded if weak-willed young man. Born in 1902 as Gilbert Murray's fourth child, he went to Charterhouse where (he records) he was 'almost consistently unhappy', chiefly on account of his small stature – he was only five feet three inches high at the age of eighteen – and then to New College. After Oxford he read for the Bar, worked as aide to a Japanese prince travelling about Europe, and joined the *Daily Express*, from which he was sacked for giving the wrong name to a countess who had shot her lover in the Gare du Nord. He worked in the campaign office of the Liberal Party, was himself a parliamentary candidate for that party, wrote a hasty and skimpy biography of Lloyd George, and married a girl after a week's engagement. In the early 1930s, at the time that Waugh was writing *Black Mischief*, he was drifting from job to job, frequently having to be bailed out of trouble (drunken binges and dishonoured cheques) by his father.

Waugh says he 'did not greatly like' Murray, and Christopher Hollis supplies a possible explanation. Philbrick of Balliol, the young man mocked by Waugh for his confession of sadism, was a friend of Murray's, and one night after Waugh had been inciting his cronies to further slander of Philbrick, Murray and Philbrick waylaid him in a dark corner of Balliol and beat him up, with the words 'We've had as much of you as we can stand.'

The other person identified by Waugh as a model for Basil Seal, Peter Rodd, was a close friend of Murray's – he stood as godfather to Murray's eldest daughter – and was at Balliol during Waugh's time at Oxford. Christopher Sykes notes that from the outset he 'utterly fascinated Evelyn'. In a 1951 article Waugh describes Rodd as 'a man of conspicuous versatility, an explorer, linguist, seaman, boon-companion and heaven knows what else, of startling good looks'. And there seems to be a hint of sexual attraction in Waugh's portrait of him in his autobiography as having 'the sulky, arrogant looks of the young Rimbaud'. Photographs show that Rodd was blond and very handsome. It may be that his physical glamour gave Waugh an inflated notion of his abilities, for Alan Pryce-Jones dismisses Rodd as 'a man of extreme good-looks, some literary talent, but little else'.

After being sent down from Balliol for having a woman in his rooms after hours, Rodd, whose father was a senior diplomat, was provided with various jobs around the world, from which he usually managed to be sacked, arriving home destitute, though in the process he picked up fluent Russian and Portuguese. Pryce-Jones describes him proposing to two girls at the same ball, and marrying the one who happened to have five hundred pounds in her post office savings account, though the other was an heiress (who had not yet inherited). The girl he married was Nancy Mitford, and Pryce-Jones quotes her complaining that it was no good hiding money from Peter (always known as 'Prod'), because he could always find it: 'In the lining of the curtains, under the telephone directory, at the back of the linen cupboard, he went to it ... unerringly.' This, rather than Basil Murray (who seems to have supplied little more than his first name), is recognizably Basil Seal in *Black Mischief*, who early in the novel steals his mother's emerald bracelet and sells it to pay for his journey to Azamia (Abyssinia), where he gets himself appointed Minister of Modernization and propels the country into civil war.

Basil is the book's hero, or at least the nearest Waugh offers to one. Everyone else is foolish, blinkered, lazy or bigoted. Only Basil has his eyes open, and possesses the *élan vital* of a Grimes. His appeal to women is constantly emphasized, and in Azania he achieves the seduction of Prudence, daughter of the British Envoy, acquiring her effortlessly from William Bland, a young man on her father's staff who has failed to gratify her. 'I think you're effeminate and under-sexed,' Prudence tells William when he fails to respond to her with passion, 'and I hate you.' We seem to be back with Waugh's marriage. William responds to Prudence's mockery with sophistication – 'You're too young to arouse serious passion' – but objects when she 'cuts him out' for Basil. Prudence replies: '"Cut you out" nothing. You had me all to yourself for six months and weren't you just bored blue with it?' Six months was roughly the period (subtracting She-Evelyn's ill-ness) that the Waughs had lived together.

Yet in this triangle Basil does not represent John Heygate, for whom Waugh had no admiration. Nor is he a precise portrait of Peter Rodd. Waugh indicates that women are drawn to him not because he has conventional good looks, but because of his cavalier disregard for his appearance. 'It's nice his being so dirty,' says a girl at a party, admiring him from a distance. He recalls the dishevelled Ernest Vaughan in 'The Balance', and like Ernest he seems to be an *alter ego* of Waugh himself, an exercise in wish-fulfilment. Among his many characteristics is one that certainly belongs to Waugh: Basil is described in one passage 'lying alone in his bunk for hours at a time, smoking cheroots and gazing blankly at the pipes on the ceiling'. Alec Waugh recognized the portrait: 'Paul in *Decline and Fall*, Adam in *Vile Bodies* ... that was one side of Evelyn ... but he was also Basil Seal.'*

Black Mischief is a companion piece to *Remote People* in more than just the Abyssinian setting. The travel book shows a world populated by individuals whom Waugh finds 'odious' for their surface appearance and behaviour; the novel seeks to justify this hostile reaction by demonstrating that they *are* odious. It portrays a gallery of persons who are uniformly deplorable for their loss or perversion of values. In a sense, then, the book exists to prove to its author that he has a right to dislike the rest of humanity. As reasons for writing novels go, this is not altogether attractive, and it explains why, though it is often very funny, *Black Mischief* leaves an almost consistently sour taste in the reader's mouth. It is, incidentally, Waugh's only pre-1939 novel that does not feature a country house; it lacks the positive values which the house, however decayed, stands for or implies.

Waugh's mockery of Azania's clumsy attempts at Progress – the goal of the young Emperor Seth – is central to the novel. More puzzling is his use for comic purposes of certain aspects of Catholicism. This outraged one Catholic reader, Ernest Oldmeadow, editor of the Catholic weekly the *Tablet*, who was deeply shocked to learn that the author of *Decline and Fall* and *Vile Bodies* had become his co-religionist, and devoted some space in his journal to attacking what he saw as a mockery of Catholicism in *Black Mischief*. He complained that the book was 'a disgrace to anyone professing the Catholic name', and that it was disfigured by 'outrageous lapses'.

Oldmeadow's complaints were chiefly against sexual indelicacy – Basil's affair with Prudence, implicitly condoned by the narrator – but he also pointed out that the book contained a number of jokes of a religious, or anti-religious, nature. A monastery claims to possess:

---

* What Alec could have added was '*I* am Basil Seal' – not in character, but by the mere fact of being the elder brother. Basil is what Evelyn felt he might have been had he not been deprived of the paternal attention and the paternal rewards; himself with the restraints of younger brotherhood (and recent sexual failure) removed.

David's stone prised out of the forehead of Goliath (a boulder of astonishing dimensions), a leaf from the Barren Fig Tree, the rib from which Eve had been created and a wooden cross which had fallen from heaven quite unexpectedly during Good Friday lunchtime some years back.

Oldmeadow was particularly outraged by the last of these.

All this is in the spirit of *The Scarlet Woman*, and it may be argued that what is being mocked is not the central teachings of Catholicism, but the comic trappings of religion, or the futility of trying to graft Christianity on to a pagan culture; in this context, Catholicism is simply another example of Progress. Certainly twelve distinguished Catholics, among them Father Martin D'Arcy, Father Bede Jarrett, Father C.C. Martindale and Eric Gill, were prepared to defend Waugh. They sent a terse and angry letter to the *Tablet* accusing Oldmeadow of exceeding 'the bounds of legitimate criticism' by imputing that the author of *Black Mischief* was a poor Catholic, and expressing 'our regard for Mr Waugh'. Waugh himself responded to Oldmeadow's attack in an *Open Letter* to the Archbishop of Westminster, Cardinal Bourne, who owned the *Tablet*, which he had printed as a pamphlet but then decided not to circulate. In this, he emphasized that what he was mocking was only the 'superstitious reverence for relics' practised by a 'notoriously superstitious heretical Church', and declared that he had written nothing 'irreverent towards Catholic belief' or which could 'constitute blasphemy'.*

Yet there can be little doubt that Waugh found many aspects of Catholicism, and by no means only trivial ones, extremely funny. A 1932 letter describes a Catholic priest, at a church near the West Country hotel where *Black Mischief* was largely written, telling his congregation of the sufferings of the English Martyrs, who 'had their arses cut off with red-hot scissors & things like that'. The priest went on to say that he too was a martyr; someone in his congregation was sending him anonymous letters accusing him of unchastity – and at this point (alleges Waugh) he stared Waugh himself in the face, warning the congregation that 'IT IS MORTAL SIN TO SPEAK ILL OF A PRIEST'. He then described the awful fate that had met people who did attack priests:

---

* Waugh's anger with Oldmeadow and Cardinal Bourne did not abate with the writing of the *Open Letter*. In his life of Ronald Knox (1959) he refers to Oldmeadow as 'a man of meagre attainments and deplorable manners, under whom [the *Tablet*] became petty in its interests and low in tone' (p. 243), and elsewhere in the book he describes Bourne as having 'an exceedingly lofty conception of the dignity of his position' which 'disqualified [him] from normal social intercourse' (p. 167).

Why he said I knew a man quite well who sat down to write an impertinent letter to a priest and as he stretched out his hand for the pen, it (hand not pen) fell lifeless to his side & he has never used it again. And I know another man, he said, who went to strike a priest and he (man not priest) FELL DOWN DEAD.

Pretty frightening, eh.

Waugh concludes the letter (to one of his young women friends): 'GOD BE WITH YOU TILL WE MEET AGAIN.' This flippant, mocking tone contrasts oddly with Waugh's forceful expressions of outrage to the Cardinal Archbishop that 'the sincerity of my Faith is called in question'. Oldmeadow was a fool, but he had stumbled across a very real contradiction in Waugh.

3

Very Grim

'An awful afternoon man called Keith Winter has arrived,' Waugh
wrote to Henry Yorke from a hotel in the South of France in the summer
of 1931. Winter was a young writer then making some reputation;
Waugh's epithet for him refers to Anthony Powell's first novel, *Afternoon
Men*, which had just appeared.

Powell had approached the novel methodically, considering 'in what
style' he should write. Though in his autobiography he lists a wide
variety of writers whom he studied with a view to developing his own
narrative technique – Joyce, Wyndham Lewis, Proust, Stendhal, Conrad, Lermontov – it is evident that at the outset of his career as a
novelist one author above all showed him the way. *Afternoon Men* (1931)
is an Anglicization of Hemingway's *The Sun Also Rises*.

When the Hemingway novel was published in England in 1927,
Powell initially read it 'with a fair amount of enjoyment as a picture
of American expatriate Paris life, but without noticing anything revolutionary about the method. . . . Then someone spoke of Hemingway's
style . . . and I read the book again.' Waugh had applied something
of Hemingway's method in *Vile Bodies*, but there were so many other
elements in that novel (*Alice*-like grotesques, film as a governing motif
in the latter chapters, sheer outrageous improbability of plot) that little
space could be allowed for the deadpan Hemingway-style portrayal

of London social life led by Waugh and his circle. Powell evidently decided to concentrate entirely on such a portrayal.*

In a sense, Waugh himself was an influence on *Afternoon Men*, in that the book sometimes seems like *Vile Bodies* with the camera moved to another position. Powell carefully avoids giving the impression that the world of the Bright Young People is even superficially glamorous, as it occasionally appears to be in Waugh's book, but portrays it as seedy, repetitive and dominated by *ennui*. He says that *Afternoon Men* (the title of which comes from Burton's *Anatomy of Melancholy*) 'gives a picture reasonably in focus of the kind of life I was leading at the time'.

Powell exactly picks up Hemingway's trick of conveying the futility of his characters' lives through their inert, repetitive conversations. At the end of *Vile Bodies*, Waugh at least promised that the excitement of a holocaust would one day dispel the boredom of pointless parties and bad restaurants; but Powell knows they will go on for ever:

> Harriet sat down and Atwater sat down beside her. She said: 'Do you think that one of these days everything will come right?'
> 'No.'
> 'Neither do I,' she said. She laughed again.

Afternoon Men ends just as it began – the final section is entitled 'Palindrome' – with the same characters sitting in the same bad café.

Powell's second book, *Venusberg* (1932), set in a fictitious Baltic capital, failed to match up to this brilliant start, but he equalled the achievement of *Afternoon Men* in *From a View to a Death* (1933), which in its first edition was dedicated to 'John and Evelyn', John Heygate and Evelyn Gardner. In *Afternoon Men* he had shown the city types making their statutory visit to the country – somebody's weekend cottage – but getting nothing out of it. *From a View to a Death* demonstrates that by 1933 the English countryside had become a mere extension of the city, greatly to the impoverishment of its inhabitants. The novel's theme had been exactly expressed by Robert Byron in the prelude to his 1928 book on Mount Athos, *The Station*. Having pronounced an anathema on London life, Byron goes on to curse 'those latent social aspirations and malignities which are investing English country life with an artificiality comparable to that of London, and less excusable. It seems there are only a few who comprehend the spirit of the countryside.' Byron

---

* Powell had met the heroine of Hemingway's novel, Duff Twysden, model for 'Brett Ashley', when she was passing through London. She struck him as 'boyish in appearance, emaciatedly thin, decidedly battered' (Powell, *Messengers of Day*, p. 110).

asserts that most 'country' people today never set foot in most of the landscape that surrounds their houses: 'It is the point-to-point that clamours on the morrow. Bookmakers and fish and chips ... champagne picnics; tweed skirt and plus fours; shooting-stick and glasses. ... Better take a walk up the back drive.' Powell could have taken this as an epigraph for his novel. *From a View to a Death* is a rural *Afternoon Men* whose characters drift aimlessly through the day, occasionally participating in some trivial manifestation of country life, but looking to the city for such flimsy ideals as they get. Into this marginal and crumbling society, tottering on the edge of ruin and insanity, comes a professional social-climber, Arthur Zouch, who attempts to exploit its weaknesses, but gets his come-uppance in a carefully prearranged hunting accident.

Zouch is almost unnecessary to the book, which reads like one of Betjeman's articles in the *Architectural Review* deploring the decline of the English village into a wilderness of petrol pumps. Death is not a calamity, but a merciful release from such a world.

Black Mischief was well enough received – 'To my mind it falters here and there, but we are not likely to have a more satisfactory novel of its kind during the autumn publishing season,' wrote the *Daily Telegraph* reviewer – and in the months leading up to its publication in the autumn of 1932, Waugh's private life settled into something of a pattern. He had begun a playful friendship with two sisters of his Oxford friend Hugh Lygon. Lady Dorothy and Lady Mary Lygon lived at the family home, Madresfield Court near Great Malvern, and Waugh became a regular visitor there, taking riding lessons at an establishment in the vicinity (Captain Hance's Academy), just as Zouch attempts to train himself for the hunting field in Powell's novel. He had little more luck on horseback than Zouch: 'First, on Saturday, a little horse called Tom Tit threw me on my head over a fence. ... I have also strained my back ... and it hurts like nothing on earth.'

He addressed the Lygon girls (to whom *Black Mischief* is dedicated) by private nicknames, and sent them comic letters when he was away from Madresfield. In these, he treats 'Blondy' and 'Pollen' as two little girls who know nothing about sex (they were in their early twenties), and himself behaves like a naughty uncle making oblique references to it. Of a fellow-pupil at the riding school who had asked Captain Hance to pose for a photograph with his whip raised, he writes: 'It is what is called Masochism and if you ask Elmley [their eldest brother] & he thinks you are old enough he will explain.' And in another letter:

'Last night I saw a terribly drunk man with a prostitute. WOTS A POSTA-
TUTE PLESE?' Dorothy Lygon has described how he would embroider
the diary she was keeping with 'statements of incest and immorality',
and once painted 'a large penis' on a watercolour she had made of
a carthorse. This was more than ordinarily *risqué*, considering that the
girls' father, Lord Beauchamp, had recently gone into exile in Italy
following accusations of homosexuality. Waugh's frankness about sex
may have been intended to help the sisters come to terms with what
had happened; the jokes, however, do not suggest that he was really
very interested in 'smut'.

In London he was now engaged in the pursuit of Teresa 'Baby'
Jungman, one of the Bright Young People, the daughter of a painter
whose mother had remarried to one of the Guinness family. An acquaintance describes her as a 'chocolate-box blonde . . . just the sort of girl
that every man falls in love with'. She was also a Catholic. Waugh's
pursuit of her was therefore bound to be a hazardous enterprise.

A handful of letters from her to Waugh indicate that she was disconcerted by his frequent announcement of 'evil intentions' towards her
– his desire to sleep with her without marrying her. Also as a Catholic
she knew that he was most unlikely to obtain the Church's consent
to the annulment of his marriage, a *sine qua non* of his marrying again.
In her eyes and the Church's, She-Evelyn was still his wife. She wrote
to him that 'if you weren't married' she might have considered becoming his wife; as it was, she could only offer to 'go on being your friend'.

He had, then, taken up with a girl who was unable, without flying
in the face of her religion, to respond to his advances with anything
other than a chaste friendship. Maybe there was a degree of self-punish-
ment in this, but it may have suited him to be conducting an affair
which he knew very well would lead neither to bed nor to marriage.
In his letters to the Lygon sisters he reports her coolness towards him
with something like complacency: 'Did Teresa send me a telegram
. . .? Not her. . . . Did little Miss Jungman send me a line of good
wishes . . .? Not on your life.'

Simultaneous to his pursuit of her, he was paying court to Lady
Diana Cooper, this time without any overt sexual interest. Nine years
older than him and the daughter of a duke, she was married to Duff
Cooper, then a Conservative Member of Parliament. She was currently
appearing on stage in the Max Reinhardt production of *The Miracle*,
a piece of mock-medieval *schmaltz* about a statue of the Virgin – played
by Lady Diana – which comes alive to save an erring young nun from
punishment. In her memoirs, Diana Cooper describes Waugh accom-

panying her on the play's tour around the provinces, 'to help me with my rather lonely life'. They would motor to inspect famous country houses, and he would read aloud to her from *The Wind in the Willows*.

He undoubtedly found Diana Cooper extremely attractive. 'I am ... sceptical of youth's supremacy in the very narrow field of physical attraction,' he wrote in an article during 1932, at the time that he was seeing much of her. 'Sex-appeal is made up of an infinite number of different stimuli, and in all but very few the woman of over 30 has the debutante hopelessly beaten.' Diana Cooper was forty. However, unlike her husband, she did not engage in extramarital affairs, and was uninterested in sex to the point of frigidity. This may have had advantages to Waugh; as with 'Baby' Jungman, he could be the devoted admirer without fearing that it would commit him to anything further.

He had achieved a certain equilibrium in the three years since his marriage had crashed; most of his friends were now unaware that it had left him with any permanent injury. The Lygon sisters thought him cheerful and contented, and Diana Cooper found him a consistently amusing companion. But one or two people perceived something of what lay beneath. One day Waugh asked Duff Cooper if he would introduce him to Hilaire Belloc, whom he had admired and whom the Coopers knew. A luncheon duly took place, and Waugh was on his best behaviour to the point of being deferential. Yet when he had departed, and Belloc was left alone with Duff Cooper, Belloc remarked of Waugh: 'He is possessed.'

'Dreadfully lonely.... We sailed at about 2.30. Down the river in heavy rain and twilight. Heart of lead.' When Waugh's diary resumes after another break, in December 1932, he is setting off again on an overseas journey.

That he should commit himself to the acute boredom of another voyage – this time across the Atlantic – and the *ennui* and discomfort of travel in another 'primitive' land, South America, so soon after enduring the misery of crossing Africa, was evidently a puzzle to his friends and maybe to himself. When asked why he was going, he answered that he was looking for material for another book, but admitted: 'That is an explanation which holds very little water.... People would much sooner read about Mayfair than the jungle.'

He claimed that he genuinely wanted to travel to remote places – 'I am deeply interested in the jungle and only casually interested in Mayfair.' Truly, he was interested in neither. Mayfair quickly bored him, but he had been more profoundly bored during his African travels, and there was no reason to expect that South America would have a different effect. He was temperamentally disinclined to visit hot places – 'I am a confirmed heliophobe,' he wrote after two weeks in the mild autumn sunshine of Venice in September 1932 – and he obtained no pleasure from the challenges of travel in primitive places. He claimed that he liked ambitious journeys because 'one is interested in one's fellow beings', but *Remote People* had demonstrated this to be resoundingly untrue.

A more honest answer (in the same article, written for the *Daily Mail*) was: 'The more irritable have to go away or go off their heads.' It was perhaps partly an escape from a complicated but ultimately meaningless private life in England, but also an attempted flight from his own misery and impatience. And – though he does not suggest this – he was perhaps going into a more 'primitive' society in the hope that it might display evidence of those permanent values he could not discover in his own world.

He had chosen Brazil, which he would reach via Guiana, because Peter Fleming, whom he had met, had recently been there for *The Times* to search for a missing explorer. The place therefore had some topical appeal, but was still virtually untouched by the professional travel writers. Also, Waugh knew absolutely nothing about it; it was the choice of a bored man playing Russian roulette.

Once again he kept rough notes in his diary, writing them up into a travel book after he returned. Its title, *Ninety-Two Days*, suggests a prison sentence, and this was how Waugh regarded the trip. In the book, he claims that after his initial depression when the boat sailed, 'everything ... was a holiday', but it was nothing of the sort, and his initial fears that the journey would be appallingly arduous and dull proved all too justified. The diary records many experiences of the sort he had had in Africa:

> Conversations intolerable.... Four days of degrading boredom.... Father Keary went off at 9. Glad to see last of him.... General impression of Georgetown that I don't mind how soon I leave it.... General impression of Trinidad that I don't want to see it again.... The German's conversation unbearable....

Only one episode seemed to make the journey at all worth while, a night spent at the ranch of a religious maniac named Christie, who told Waugh he had been warned in a vision of his approach. In this vision, he had seen 'a sweetly toned harmonium' which indicated the benevolence of Waugh's character. He said he was nightly shown the sight of God the Father and the elect in Heaven, and remarked, on the subject of a medal of the Virgin: 'Why should I wear an image of someone I speak to daily? Besides it is not the least like her.'

This encounter quickly inspired a short story, 'The Man Who Liked Dickens', written while Waugh was still in South America and published in *Nash's Pall Mall Magazine* in November 1933. The first version of what became the denouement of *A Handful of Dust*, its protagonists are 'Henty' (the Tony Last character, fleeing from the experience of being cuckolded) and 'Mr McMaster' (later Mr Todd, Waugh's reworking of the madman Christie). But for the time being Waugh had no plan to use the tale as part of a novel, and in literary terms the South American journey seemed, in comparison with the Ethiopian trip, to have been almost fruitless.

The exhilaration Waugh experienced on returning to England and reacquainting himself with the comfortable life quickly evaporated. He had now filed an application for the annulment of his marriage by the Catholic Church, though with little expectation that it would be granted. His grounds for requesting annulment were that he and She-Evelyn had not wished to have children, and that the marriage had been entered into frivolously, with no thought of a permanent relationship. If he believed this, he was deluding himself. Evelyn Gardner has clearly stated: 'I had not refused to have children, but we had agreed to wait until we had an income which did not depend sometimes on others.' She adds: 'My sister Mary had a letter from him, after an operation I had, saying how glad he was we could have children.' She-Evelyn was accordingly rather surprised when Waugh explained to her – at lunch in a restaurant, shortly before the ecclesiastical hearing into the marriage, which she had agreed to attend – that he was going to inform the court that they had never wanted children. She assumed that he must have 'forgotten' what had really happened. 'I didn't remind him.'

The hearing occupied five days in the autumn of 1933, and was only the first of many wearying stages through which the case would have to pass if an annulment were to be granted. Waugh, however, seemed elated that it had come to court at all, and went and 'popped question' to Teresa Jungman. She turned him down; after all, the Church had not yet made its decision. 'Got raspberry,' he wrote to Mary Lygon. 'Stiff upper lip and dropped cock.'

With *Ninety-Two Days* finished, he became determined to write another novel, as yet disclosing nothing to his friends of its subject-matter. He chose to begin work on it in Morocco, and early in January 1934 he travelled south and settled in a *pension* in Fez. To the Lygon sisters, he reported a visit to the red-light district, where on this occasion, perhaps for the first time, he engaged in a transaction: 'There were little Arab girls of fifteen & sixteen for ten francs each & a cup of mint tea. So I bought one but I didn't enjoy her very much because she had a skin like sandpaper and a huge stomach which didn't show until she took off her clothes & then it was too late.' And a few days later: 'I have written 18,500 words. It is excellent – very grim.'

It was four and a half years since his wife had left him. The wounds which his personality had suffered, and the search for some cure, had been discernible in his writing since 1929, but had not formed the primary matter of his fiction. Nina's abandonment of Adam and Prudence's of William had been shadows of his own experience, while in *Remote People* and *Ninety-Two Days* he seemed to be trying to turn from a Paul Pennyfeather into a Basil Seal – an experiment that had failed, for again and again he had fallen victim to his own loneliness and depression, in the guise of boredom; he could not pretend for long to be the ruthless adventurer.

Then came the lesser but not negligible blow to his self-esteem of rejection by Teresa Jungman. It is hard to say how serious were his feelings for her; he makes light of them in his letters to the Lygon sisters, yet when he finally remarried he named his eldest child after her, and there may be real pain in his account to the Lygons of his feelings in 1933 when she turned him down – 'oh dear oh dear I wish I was dead,' he wrote to Mary Lygon, and perhaps he meant it. Even if, as seems not unlikely, he had never seriously wanted to marry her, it was another slap in the face. Escape from his sterile way of life seemed permanently blocked.

It was in the weeks following her rejection of him that he must have begun to contemplate, and maybe plan, the novel that would, at last, put his own experience at the centre of the stage, and try to create some sort of order out of the chaos he was still experiencing. After four and a half years he had decided to come face to face with his own unhappiness, perhaps in the hope that to portray it in a novel might alleviate it. Shortly after beginning work, he observed: 'for the first time I am trying to deal with normal people instead of eccentrics.'

The break-up of his marriage was not, however, the starting point of the new book. Its germ was 'The Man Who Liked Dickens', with its description of an Englishman imprisoned in the jungle by a

Christielike jailer; once he had written and published it, Waugh 'wanted to discover how the prisoner got there, and eventually the thing grew into a study of other sorts of savage at home and the civilized man's helpless plight among them'.

He generally had difficulty with the titles of his novels. (Even *Black Mischief* went through several changes before the final choice was made.) Though Eliot's *The Waste Land* seemed an utterly appropriate text in which to search for title and epigraph for a novel about savagery in modern civilization, the lines which Waugh chose, concluding 'I will show you fear in a handful of dust', appear less pertinent than other passages in the poem. Waugh himself originally fixed on 'A Handful of Ashes', and when his American publisher objected he suggested 'Fourth Decade', a reference to the fact that Tony Last's experiences take place in his early thirties. He chose the final title only after a long discussion with A. D. Peters. Even the loyal Christopher Sykes says he feels *A Handful of Dust* was 'not apposite' to the themes of the book. Yet the chosen title does suggest the total desolation conveyed by the novel, while at the same time hinting, by its reference to *The Waste Land*, at the possibility of a religious solution to the dilemma of modern existence.

The Proustian title of the opening section of the novel, 'Du Côté de Chez Beaver', is meant to underline the shallow socialite's life led by dilapidated man-about-town John Beaver, who lives off his mother, herself a parasite on society (an entrepreneur in the interior-decorating business). The Beavers' surname, however, suggests a certain animal energy, and Mrs Beaver is, in Waugh's own analysis of the novel (in a letter to Henry Yorke), the first of a whole string of 'savages' which it portrays.

Waugh's *alter ego* in the drama is this time neither a Paul Pennyfeather nor a Basil Seal. Instead, he creates a character whose beliefs and attitudes are almost entirely his own, and who differs from him only in his more exalted place in society. Tony Last, as his surname clearly states, is one of the last of the landowning English country gentlemen, or at least one of the last to preserve their traditional values, a fair-minded, modest individual who devotes all his resources to the maintenance of his family's mansion and estate. Tony has frequently been regarded as a prig and a bore, but this is a misreading of the novel. Certainly Tony's wife's London friends see him in this light, but from the beginning to the end of the novel his actions and thoughts are beyond reproach. He takes sober delight in the pleasures of playing squire, but Waugh admires rather than satirizes this. Tony's only weaknesses are his excessive innocence – he continues to believe the best of Brenda long after she has betrayed him – and his failure to take the Christian faith with complete seriousness. He regularly attends Matins in the village church, but when tragedy strikes the family he observes that 'the last thing one wants to talk about at a time like this is religion'. Waugh is here, however, attacking the failure of the Church of England to offer the consolation of faith, rather than blaming Tony's individual inadequacy. (There is much fun in the novel at the expense of the Vicar of Tony's parish church, a decrepit ex-colonial who delivers sermons written fifty years ago for an expatriate congregation.)

Waugh is, in a sense, granting Tony Last the lands and pedigree he himself would wish to have, but this is justifiable in the scheme of the book; Tony needs to be a landowner rather than, say, a novelist because Waugh wants him to represent the old order on which the modern world is now impinging with such disastrous consequences. And Hetton, Tony's house, is no Brideshead. All through, Waugh emphasizes that it is in need of repair, that the beds badly require new mattresses, and that in no respect does the possession of such a heritage guarantee personal comfort. Tony's life is ascetic, not luxurious; he goes about his squirearchical duties with almost monastic dedication. (His situation is that of the younger brother who has been allowed to inherit, but the inheritance has been sadly depleted by the time he gets it.)

Waugh also resists the temptation of making Hetton an architectural jewel. The house, we are told, 'was entirely rebuilt in 1864 in the Gothic style' and is architecturally deplorable, though 'already it was referred to as "amusing", and a very civil young man had asked permission to photograph it for an architectural review'. Approval by Betjeman was not, in 1934, regarded as a real mark of distinction, and we are meant to assume that Hetton is a burden to Tony rather than an enviable asset. He is doing his duty to his family and its history by keeping it up.

On the other hand the 'English Gothic' in which it is built (and which gives the title to the novel's second chapter) has certain moral and narrative overtones, for the rooms have been 'each named from Malory', so that Tony's wife's bedroom is 'Guinevere' – a hint that she will commit adultery later in the novel. By 1934 the Victorian passion for Arthuriana was universally regarded as absurd, but Waugh intends to remind us that chivalry, even in mock-medieval form, is still a reaching-out for permanent and altruistic values.

When he discovers his wife's infidelity with John Beaver, Tony at first behaves like a passive Paul Pennyfeather, but then abruptly sets off for Guiana and Brazil in the company of an eccentric explorer, who is searching for a fabulous City supposedly built by the Incas. This quest parallels Tony's search for some evidence of permanence and certainty now that his English Gothic ideals have been smashed: 'A whole Gothic world had come to grief. There was now no armour glittering through the forest glades, no embroidered feet on the green sward; the cream and dappled unicorns had fled. . . .' *Ninety-Two Days* had anticipated this search for the City. In the passage in which Waugh describes his expectations of Boa Vista, the southernmost point on his journey, where he had expected to find rest and refreshment and to be able to take a boat back to civilization, he writes: 'I had come to regard it as Middle Western Americans look on Paris, as Chekhov peasants on St Petersburg.' And when he actually saw it: 'the Boa Vista of my imagination had come to grief. Tall Troy was down.'

Henry Yorke wrote to Waugh that he felt Tony's fate at the end of *A Handful of Dust* – grotesque imprisonment by a madman – to be a piece of fantasy which did not fit the rest of the book. Waugh's own uncertainty about the conclusion of the novel is suggested by his provision of an alternative ending for the pre-publication serialization in *Harper's Bazaar*. In this version, Tony goes away for some months, pottering about the West Indies and thinking 'less and less about Brenda'. On his return they resume married life, except that Tony, asked by Brenda to dispose of the London flat, secretly arranges with Mrs Beaver to keep it on for his own infidelities. (By an ironic coincidence, the issue of *Harper's Bazaar* for June 1933 which contained the first instalment of the novel also carried an article by John Heygate, on holidays out of season.)

When he had read Yorke's objections to the conclusion, Waugh said he was inclined to agree that it was too 'fantastic' for the scheme of the book. Yet Tony's fate, endlessly to repeat the same action like a lost soul in Hades, entirely suits the book's exploration of yet another modern hell. It also reflects Waugh's grim view of his own condition at the time he wrote the novel.

The last scene reverts to 'English Gothic', with the poor-relation branch of the Last family in possession of Hetton. Waugh indicates in his letter to Yorke that these are meant to be the final tribe of 'savages' to whom civilization has fallen prey. Tony's English Gothic idyll has become a fur-farm, and the owners of the house are called Teddy and Molly and speak like characters from a Betjeman poem. The greater part of the house, including the state apartments and library, is kept locked and shuttered. This is very near the nightmare envisaged earlier in the book, when Brenda's horrible brother tells Tony: 'There's a lot in what these Labour fellows say, you know. Big houses are a thing of the past in England.'

Yet the new owners of Hetton are not on quite the same level as Hooper in *Brideshead*, spokesman for the clumsy bad taste of the middle classes. Teddy Last does at least appreciate what he has inherited. In the final sentence of the novel we are told that, by means of the fur-farm and its earnings, he hopes 'one day to restore Hetton to the glory that it had enjoyed in the days of his Cousin Tony'. Hetton is the one thing in the novel that has proved permanent and indestructible. Tony, on his way to his fate with Mr Todd, had imagined that the City would look exactly like it:

> He had a clear picture of it in his mind. It was Gothic in character, all vanes and pinnacles, gargoyles, battlements . . . a transfigured Hetton. . . . Carpet and canopy, tapestry and velvet, portcullis and bastion, waterfowl on the moat and kingcups along its margin, peacocks trailing their finery across the lawns. . . .

For all Tony's – and Waugh's – searches for it, the City, always there to be rediscovered by the true in heart, is none other than the English country house.

PART V: 1934–1939

The Gentleman's House

1

Berners Betjeman Country

Nancy Mitford had now published two novels. Waugh describes these early books of hers as 'full of private evanescent jokes', and says they 'never enjoyed much success outside the circle of her own friends'.

Highland Fling, which appeared in 1931 when she was twenty-seven, is the story of a couple of penniless Bright Young People obliged to host a dreary house-party in Scotland. Modelled on the country-house satires of Thomas Love Peacock, it is less a novel than a series of conversation-pieces emphasizing the generation gap between the veterans of the Great War and the young partygoers. The slight plot concerns the romance between Jane Dacre (resembling Nancy Mitford herself) and Albert Gates, a Harold Acton-style aesthete who collects Victoriana. The character is actually a compound of Robert Byron and Hamish Erskine, a young man (second son of the Earl of Rosslyn) whom Nancy hoped to marry, and to whom *Highland Fling* is dedicated. (She married Peter Rodd instead, in 1933.) 'General Murgatroyd' in the novel is closely modelled on Lord Redesdale, Nancy's father – a portrait she later perfected as 'Uncle Matthew' in *The Pursuit of Love*. 'Yesterday,' says Albert of the General, 'I heard him say that before the War the things he hated most were Roman Catholics and Negroes, but now, he said, banging on the table, now it's Germans.' Nancy's sister Jessica Mitford records that their father took quite kindly to this portrait, and indeed began to play up to the part, 'to take on some of the qualities of raw material for fiction'.

Nancy's second book, *Christmas Pudding* (1932), set in a Cotswold manor house, similarly contrasts the ferocious Lady Bobbin, virago of the hunting field, with a young novelist, Paul Fotheringay. He is obsessed Betjeman-fashion with a mid-Victorian lady poet, ancestor of the Bobbins, whose works he can quote by heart and whose biography he hopes to write. Nancy modelled young Bobby Bobbin on Hamish Erskine as a schoolboy, and said specifically: 'Betjeman is co-hero.'

The real-life Betjeman had been courting Nancy's sister Pam, or at least pretending to; nobody could tell whether he was serious. Pamela Mitford lived on her sister Diana Guinness's estate at Biddesden near Andover, and ran the home farm for Diana and Bryan. She was a beefy girl whom Betjeman, imitating the cowhands, addressed as 'Miss Pam'. (Jessica Mitford observes that in childhood her sister had hopes 'of becoming a horse'.) A Betjeman poem published a few years later, 'Pot Pourri from a Surrey Garden', enshrines his supposed love for this type of girl: 'Pam, I adore you, you great big mountainous sports girl....' In his 1947 novella *Scott-King's Modern Europe*, Waugh guys Betjeman's obsession with this type of female. Whitemaid, an elderly academic, becomes obsessed with an enormous female Swede. 'You must remember how she looked in shorts?' he muses.

> 'A Valkyrie. Something from the heroic age. Like some god-like, some unimaginably strict school prefect, *a dormitory monitor*,' he said in a kind of ecstasy. 'Think of her striding between the beds, a pigtail, bare feet, in her hand a threatening hairbrush. Oh, Scott-King, do you think she rides a bicycle?'
> 'I'm sure of it.'
> 'In shorts?'
> 'Certainly in shorts.'
> 'I can imagine a whole life lived riding tandem behind her, through endless forests of conifers, and at midday sitting down among the pine-needles to eat hard-boiled eggs. Think of those strong fingers peeling an egg, Scott-King, the brown of it, the white of it, the shine. Think of her *biting* it.'

Waugh wonder whether he had gone too far in this exploration of Betjeman's erotic tastes. 'I hope John did not resent the parody,' he wrote in a letter.

Betjeman played around with the Mitford girls rather as Waugh did with the Lygons. He wrote to Nancy Mitford: 'If Pamela Mitford refuses me finally *you* might marry me – I'm rich, handsome and aristocratic.' Maurice Bowra, who shared something of Betjeman's camp taste for beefy girls, alleges that Betjeman had been cultivating their company even in Oxford days; there was one, a clergyman's daughter, who bicycled over to see him in 'a strangely unbecoming raincoat'.

It may, then, have been partly in jest that Robert Byron sent to see Betjeman at the *Architectural Review* a young woman recognizably of the sports-girl type. Penelope Chetwode was no beauty in the conventional sense; Betjeman afterwards drew caricatures of her with absurdly prominent cheekbones and a sulky schoolboy mouth. But she had an intellectual vitality that was rare among the Bright Young People – her first visit to Betjeman was to offer an article on Indian temples – and she behaved with refreshing originality.

Edward James first glimpsed Penelope's 'stubby face' at a London ball. He was struck by her *retroussé* nose, her 'ugly muslin dress that must have been made for her on her mother's order by a dressmaker in Wiltshire', and her conversation – she talked about India and the *quattrocento*. 'I thought to myself, "I have got to find out who this is," because all the girls that I had talked to were saying, "Have you seen any plays lately?" "Oh! Have you seen *Bitter Sweet*?"'

She was the daughter of Field-Marshal Sir Philip (later Lord) Chetwode, Commander-in-Chief in India, a formidable soldier of ferocious appearance who is described in the *Dictionary of National Biography* as 'not intellectual' and speaking with 'a racy "Newmarket twang"'. No less daunting was Penelope's mother, Lady Hester ('Star') Chetwode, a colonel's daughter who resembled Queen Mary.

The Chetwodes were not exactly delighted when they realized that John Betjeman was paying court to their daughter. Quite apart from his penury and lack of social position, his appearance was not in his favour; Edward James describes him at this period as prematurely bald, 'with very green teeth that stuck out'. Alan Pryce-Jones observes: 'John's appearance was slovenly. . . . He did not trouble to brush his teeth or change his shirt.' But class was the Chetwodes' chief cause of anxiety; Pryce-Jones describes Lady Chetwode wondering why Penelope had 'thrown herself away on a little middle-class Dutchman'.

Betjeman's surname at least allowed the pretence among Lady Chetwode and her kind that he was not simply a member of the English middle class, which would have been worse; Edward James says his aunt would refer to Betjeman as 'that Dutch friend of yours'. But Betjeman himself took every opportunity to play the *déclassé* Englishman. Edward James writes that Lady Chetwode

had always told Penelope that one must not say 'Town' for London, or call an umbrella a 'brolly' or a 'gamp', and one mustn't talk about a 'mac', one must always say mackintosh. So John, on being introduced, said: '. . . I have got to get my mac and my brolly and pop up to Town.' Lady Chetwode was very upset . . . .

James adds that Betjeman would address Lady Chetwode as 'Auntie Star', and Osbert Lancaster says that he turned up to dine with the Chetwodes at the Savoy in an elasticated bow tie, such as was worn only by waiters. 'Throughout dinner he plucked the bow forward six or seven inches and let it snap back – purely to annoy his future mother-in-law.' Another ploy, when asked how he earned his living, was to answer: 'I'm in lino.'

For all his fooling, Betjeman was desperately sensitive about his social position. When Edward James's aunt observed of the Betjeman–Chetwode courtship, 'One can know people like that, but one doesn't marry them,' James repeated this remark to Betjeman, with striking results. 'It was the sort of joke he would make about himself,' says James, 'but he was deeply offended.'

The Betjeman–Chetwode affair took some time to mature and, though Penelope's parents never tried to prevent the marriage, they made their opposition vociferous. For a while, Penelope contemplated becoming a professional Indologist and remaining unmarried; she went to an aunt's house in the South of France to think things over, and on Nancy Mitford's advice Betjeman followed her there – one of his rare trips to hated 'abroad' – to plead his case. Shortly afterwards (during 1933) they were married half-clandestinely at a North London registry office. Betjeman's parents were there, but Penelope had not told hers. (Earlier in the engagement there had been some Jane Austen-ish negotiations between the Field-Marshal and 'Ernie' Betjemann about marriage settlements.) The reception was held at the Great Eastern Hotel, Liverpool Street Station, Betjeman's favourite railway hotel, and there was a service of blessing at an obscure Edwardian church. When Penelope finally told her parents, many weeks later, they were greatly distressed.

Long after the marriage, Penelope explained her choice of husband to Edward James: 'I wasn't pretty enough to marry one of the aristocracy, so I thought I'd marry one of the intelligentsia, an intellectual . . . and look what I got!'

At first, the Chetwodes continued to treat their son-in-law with disdain and suspicion, as a frivolous writer of 'burlesque poems', and in the early days of their marriage the couple were poorly off, making do in a series of squalid flats in North London. However, Betjeman's income increased when, early in 1934, he was appointed film critic of the *Evening Standard*. His cinematic taste was predictably anti-high-brow – he preferred Walt Disney and gangster pictures to more intellectual efforts – and in any case he was more interested in the cinema buildings and their architectural absurdities. He sampled the delights of the Regal, Edmonton, with 'its crystal organ and disappearing footlights', and of the Gaumont British Palace, Hammersmith, where with 'the biggest proscenium in Europe' there was sung 'a serious song in a perfect dream heaven of purple light on shimmering silver paper accompanied by notes on the organ of an organ-like quality'.

His trips round the cinemas made him increasingly aware of the nuances of suburbia. 'On no account', he told his readers, 'confuse Meeda Veel with Kilburn. Both banks of the valley will resent it.' In another article he suggested that:

> the possibilities of London [for the film camera] have never yet been explored. There are the corrugated lanes of Finsbury Park, the clatter round the Peckham High-road, the quiet squares of Clerkenwell and Islington, the rutty roads of some half-finished bit of Metroland, all waiting to be photographed as René Clair has immortalized Paris.

Yet when he and Penelope set up permanent home, they chose the countryside, moving during 1934 to a farmhouse at Uffington in the Vale of the White Horse, described by Osbert Lancaster as 'one of the least spoiled villages in Berkshire'.

Betjeman became a churchwarden at the local parish church – a fine example of Early English – while Penelope kept a goat which provided the household with milk, and lavished much attention on her Arab mare, Moti, a present from her father. Maurice Bowra notes that the Field-Marshal seemed more concerned about the horse's health than his daughter's, and would write copiously about its diet and care. The mare was well trained, and would often be allowed into the house; Bowra says there were generally marks of lipstick on its neck. Penelope rode it to hounds, and would harness it to a phaeton, conscripting visitors for journeys across the downs. The Betjeman visitors' book records that those who went on such trips in the mid-1930s included Cyril Connolly, Peter Quennell and Evelyn Waugh, who behaved to Penelope much as he did to the Lygon girls – a mixture of avuncularity and schoolboy smut. 'Be a good girl about this,' he wrote to her when asking her to run an errand while he was abroad, 'and I will reward you with a fine fuck when I get back.' Penelope was irritated by this, but she knew how to cope with the childish games of her husband's circle. Once when she and Betjeman were quarrelling, she threatened to throw his teddy bear Archie down a well.

The somewhat exotic Betjeman household at Uffington soon began to attract other decorative figures, such as Frank Bishop, a flamboyantly Wildean Anglo-Irish friend of Maurice Bowra, who took a house near the Betjemans while recovering from an attack of sleeping-sickness. He had briefly taught at Haileybury, alongside the painter and art historian Wilfrid Blunt, who describes Bishop issuing an invitation to tea to meet 'the six most *beautiful* boys in the school'; Blunt arrived to find a carefully chosen selection of the six ugliest. Bishop was acquainted with Lord Alfred Douglas, and he introduced Betjeman to this ageing survivor of the Wilde scandal, with whom the youthful Betjeman had once corresponded. Douglas was invited to Uffington, and there is a photograph of him and Wilfrid Blunt scrubbing down Moti, who had been rolling in a dung-heap. Even more improbably, Lord Alfred was enrolled by Penelope to help her, Blunt and Bishop judge the local baby show.

Among the Betjemans' other neighbours was the owner of Faringdon House, a Georgian mansion on the Oxford side of Uffington. Waugh referred to him delightedly, in a letter, as 'the wicked Lord Berners'. Gerald Tyrwhitt-Wilson, fourteenth Baron Berners, had inherited his uncle's title just after the First World War, when he was in his thirties and had served for a decade as a diplomat. Thereafter he settled at Faringdon to pursue the life of a dilettante in the arts. He had already studied music with Stravinksy, and had begun to acquire some reputation as a composer; he was also a painter – generally in the manner of Corot – and a writer of fiction and memoirs. All his prodigious output showed some accomplishment, but everything he composed, painted or wrote tended towards parody. Nancy Mitford observes of him, in the guise of 'Lord Merlin' in *The Pursuit of Love*, 'As [he] was a famous practical joker, it was sometimes difficult to know where jokes ended and culture began. I think he was not always perfectly certain himself.'

The practical joking was not on a very sophisticated level. Berners liked to play the piano with his bottom, draw moustaches on photographs of royalty, and hang comic notices about his house. His fiction included a privately printed spoof girls'-school story, full of giggling allusions to lesbianism, and entitled *The Girls of Radcliff Hall*. Berners himself lived with a young protégé, Robert Heber-Percy, known among the Berners circle as 'The Mad Boy'. Slim and good-looking ('He resembled an attractive ape,' writes one of the bitchier members of the Berners crowd), Heber-Percy usually dressed in loud colours – a scarlet shirt, a blue jumper, green trousers and a yellow belt made up one ensemble – and was prone both to bouts of rage and to suicide attempts. Once, for a joke, Berners announced his engagement to the lesbian Violet Trefusis. When persuaded to issue a denial he said he would put in *The Times*: 'Lord Berners has left Lesbos for the Isle of Man.'

Diana Mosley (formerly Diana Guinness) describes Faringdon House as 'a mecca of beauty and fun . . . [with] Gerald's pigeons dyed saffron yellow, shocking pink and turquoise blue'. Her sister Nancy Mitford observes that the local county families were surprisingly tolerant of Berners's flamboyance, and even of the folly that he had built on the top of a nearby hill:

> Though they were puzzled beyond words by the aestheticism and the teases, they accepted him without question as one of themselves. Their families had always known his family . . . . He was no upstart . . . simply a sport of all that was most normal in English country life. Indeed, the very folly itself, while considered absolutely hideous, was welcomed as a landmark by those lost on their way home from hunting.

John Betjeman wrote an ode on the folly in the manner of the early nineteenth-century poet Thomas Moore:

> Oh fair be the tower that Lord Berners is rearing
> And fair be the light that illumines its walls
> But fairer to me are the trees in the clearing
> And the firs on the hill top are fairest of all.

A line in a later stanza describes the folly 'Surveying the seats of the baron and serf', probably a *double entendre* referring to its somewhat phallic protuberance from its clump of trees on the top of Faringdon Hill.

Berners took a great liking to the Betjemans, and to the exquisitely behaved Moti, and one day asked Penelope to bring the horse into the drawing-room at Faringdon House, so that he could paint its portrait with her standing alongside. This was afterwards repeated as a party piece, and a later photograph shows Evelyn Waugh sitting beside the horse, which stands on Berners's carpet while Robert Heber-Percy and Penelope Betjeman look on.

In the village of Uffington and the surrounding neighbourhood, Penelope Betjeman became known as an organizer of every kind of cultural and educational event. Osbert Lancaster describes how she:

combined a missionary zeal for widening the cultural horizons of her
rural neighbours with an energy and force of character inherited from
her mother.... Under her direction the Uffington Women's Institute
... were tirelessly lectured on Nepalese architecture and Indian religions,
instructed in the preparation of mayonnaise (which, as none of them
ever ate salad, they were rather puzzled to know what to do with), and
firmly encouraged to keep and milk goats – animals they quite rightly
detested and which regularly chewed up all their chrysanthemums. For
their industry and perseverance they were from time to time rewarded
by musical evenings in which all her guests, even if tone-deaf, were
expected to take part.

Lancaster recalls that at the most memorable of these musical *soirées*,
held in Uffington Village Hall at the conclusion of the prize-giving
for the best home-made wine,

> the principal item on the programme was a performance of 'Sumer is
> icumen in' sung by Adrian Bishop, Maurice Bowra, my wife and the
> poet himself, accompanied on the piano by Lord Berners, and by Pene-
> lope on a strange instrument resembling a zither. My own contribution
> to the ensemble took the form of a flute *obbligato*. So powerful was the
> effect that all present remained rooted to their seats even when, as hap-
> pened from time to time, a home-made wine bottle exploded.

For a while, Penelope was enlisted by a neighbouring parish priest
to play the harmonium, when his wife, the regular organist, was ill.
This she did in her own fashion, choosing strikingly secular works
for voluntaries – Maurice Bowra mentions 'German folk-songs or
Offenbach's *Goddesses Three to Ida Went.*' Bowra says that for a time
all was well, but one morning she received a letter:

Baulking Vicarage

My dear Penelope,
  I have been thinking over the question of the playing of the harmonium
on Sunday evenings here and have reached the conclusion that I must
now take it over myself.
  I am very grateful to you for doing it for so long and hate to have
to ask you to give it up, but, to put it plainly, your playing has got
worse and worse and the disaccord between the harmonium and the congregation is becoming destructive of devotion. People are not very sensitive
here, but even some of them have begun to complain, and they are not
usually given to doing that.... Thank you ever so much for stepping so
generously into the breach when Sibyl was ill; it was the greatest possible
help to me and your results were noticeably better then than now.
                    Yours ever,
                    F.P. Harton

*

Evelyn Waugh contemplated joining the Uffington community. 'When i get home i shall buy a cottage,' he wrote during one of his overseas trips. 'I wouldn't mind the Berners Betjeman country. . . . Sanitation light etc no consideration. Find me a house like that theres a poppet preferably thatch but not beams.' This letter was addressed to a girl thirteen years younger than him, to whom he became attracted around the time he was finishing *A Handful of Dust*. Laura Herbert, then aged eighteen, was the daughter of a Conservative MP who had died when she was small. Waugh met her and her family while he was on a Hellenic cruise in the summer of 1933.

He was accompanied by Alfred Duggan, the wealthy Old Etonian who at Oxford had lived in an alcoholic haze, and whose habits had not changed since the days of the Hypocrites. On the cruise, Waugh and Duggan got to know one of the Herbert girls, Gabriel, who invited them to stay at her family's Portofino villa at the end of the voyage. While there, Waugh infuriated Mrs Herbert, a Catholic convert who had been brought up an Irish Protestant, by making derogatory jokes about Ireland, and Duggan would roam the house at night searching for strong drink. However, Father Ronald Knox, who was staying at the villa too, spoke well to Mrs Herbert of Waugh, and in due course – some time in 1934 – Waugh was invited to Pixton Park near Dulverton in Somerset, the Herbert country house.

At Portofino, Waugh had thought Laura, the youngest of three daughters, merely a 'white mouse', and was more attracted by her sister Bridget – 'fat girl full of sex appeal'. (He added that the only son, Auberon, was an 'astute urchin with neurotic tendencies', and said that Mrs Herbert 'barks' but was a 'very decent hostess'.) At Pixton, he changed his mind about Laura. 'I have taken a *great* fancy to a young lady named Laura,' he wrote to Mary Lygon.

> What is she like? Well, fair, very pretty, plays peggoty beautifully. . . .
> She has rather a long thin nose and skin as thin as bromo and she
> is very thin and might be dying of consumption to look at her and
> she has her hair in a little bun at the back of her neck but it is not
> very tidy and she is only 18 years old, virgin, Catholic, quiet & astute.
> So it is difficult.

Looking at photographs of Laura Herbert in those days, one would not quarrel with any of this description except 'very pretty'. Her thin, striking face is in no respect conventionally beautiful; she looks like a sad head girl at a convent boarding school who is herself destined to become a nun.

It must indeed have been 'difficult' to make an impression on her if, like Waugh, one was old enough to be her uncle, with a reputation for writing rather *risqué* novels, and somewhat inclined to shock young ladies with 'smut'. In a typical letter to the Lygon girls around this time, he reported that he had been reading *The Perfumed Garden*: 'It says that in rogering the cock should never be withdrawn so much as a millimetre and this gives the maximum pleasure to the lady on account of pressing her bladder.' The most he could manage at this first house-party at Pixton, he told Mary Lygon, was to 'pinch [Laura] twice in a charade and lean against her thigh in pretending to help her at peggoty'.

There was also the problem that, while Laura's mother was the daughter of a viscount, and her father had been the younger son of the Earl of Carnarvon, Waugh, like Betjeman, was a member of the middle class. Moreover the Herberts were related to She-Evelyn; Lady Burghclere, Waugh's former mother-in-law, was the half-sister of Laura's father. His reported interest in Laura provoked the observation from her: 'I thought we'd seen the last of that young man.'

Indeed Waugh, in the eyes of his and Mrs Herbert's Church, was still married to She-Evelyn. Though the ecclesiastical court in London had given judgement in favour of annulment, the matter was now being considered by Rome, and there was no knowing how long this would take nor what decision would eventually be reached. Where any Catholic girl was concerned, he was still in matrimonial limbo.

In the period immediately following She-Evelyn's desertion and his joining the Catholic Church, he may well have welcomed the protection that his Catholicism gave him against a rash second marriage. By 1933, four years after the break with She-Evelyn, he probably wanted to be free of this restraint. In becoming a Catholic, he had caged himself away from marriage in an impetuous gesture much like his sudden journeys to Abyssinia and the South American jungle. Reaching both those geographical destinations, he had almost immediately wanted to come back, and it may have been the same in the matter of marriage and his religion.

Laura Herbert was, as Waugh pointed out, 'only 18 years old', but this seems to have been an attraction to him. In his unfinished novel *Work Suspended*, and again in *The Ordeal of Gilbert Pinfold*, a middle-aged writer is strongly attracted to a very young girl, who is portrayed as doting utterly on him. The teenage Julia in *Work Suspended* is described as having 'that particular kind of succulent charm – bright, dotty, soft, eager, acquiescent, flattering, impudent – that is specially, it seems, produced for the delight of Anglo-Saxon manhood'. She has had a 'crush' on the novelist John Plant from a distance, at school, and Plant responds to her puppyish devotion by judging her a 'delicious girl'. Gilbert Pinfold in the later book responds with equal enthusiasm to the romantic advances of the very young 'Margaret' (one of the hallucinatory voices which disturbs him on board ship). Though both these passages are, as Agatha Runcible might say, blush-making, they seem to reflect a definite predisposition in Waugh towards girls in their teens.

Even so, Laura Herbert may seem an odd choice as the potential second Mrs Waugh. Julia in *Work Suspended* and Margaret in *Pinfold* are strong self-assertive characters, but Laura was indeed a 'white mouse' by comparison. Christopher Sykes describes her as reserved to the point of silence, and a friend of later years, Frances Donaldson, calls her 'neurotically shy'. Sykes remarks that, at least on the surface, she and Waugh seemed 'an ill-assorted couple', though her silence and reticence appeared to give her a certain insulation from Waugh's variable moods and frequently outrageous performances.

It is understandable if, after the disaster of his first marriage, Waugh did not want to risk himself with anyone of independent spirit. Similarly Laura's extreme youth and lack of sexual experience may have seemed less of a threat than a mature woman might offer. Yet he was also conforming to family pattern, copying – as in so much else – his own father. Arthur Waugh, exuberant and melodramatic, had made just such a choice of a reticent, reserved spouse. Laura Herbert's thin face, peering rather sadly from photographs, is not so very different from that of Catherine Charlotte Raban, Evelyn's mother.

Mrs Herbert was understandably uncertain about Waugh as a suitor. 'I think I may be able to see you,' Laura wrote to him some months after he had begun to pay serious attention to her, 'because Mother agreed to it before she left for Ireland but when she got back today she was in a filthy temper and very tired and seemed to want to take it all back.' Waugh's own behaviour was always liable to let him down. 'The young lady of whom I spoke to you named Laura', he wrote to Mary Lygon in February 1935, 'came to London with me yesterday but it was not a success for I had a hangover & could only eat 3 oysters and some soda water and I was sick a good deal on the table so perhaps that romance is shattered.'

Nevertheless the arrival of Laura Herbert in his life led to certain adjustments. The collapse of his self-esteem with the break-up of his marriage had prompted him to engage in restless and sometimes dangerous travelling, and the last of these virtually pointless journeys took place in the summer of 1934, before he had got to know Laura properly, when at literally two days' notice he joined an expedition to Spitzbergen in the Arctic Circle. (Hugh Lygon was another member of this trip, a reconnoitre for a full Oxford University Arctic Expedition the following year.) The Spitzbergen journey proved even more dangerous and uncomfortable than Waugh's Guiana–Brazil travels, and he did not write it up into a book, perhaps feeling that his public would not stand for yet another tale of penitential travel. Instead, on his return, he set himself a punitive task of a different kind, the writing of a biography of Edmund Campion.

He chose this subject because Campion Hall, the Jesuit house in Oxford of which Father Martin D'Arcy had become Master, was moving from St Giles to a site near Christ Church, and need to raise money for the new building; Waugh offered the profits from the book. He also stated, in the Author's Note to the finished biography, that 'I wished to do something to mark . . . my gratitude to the . . . Master, to whom, under God, I owe my faith.' There may have been a third motive. Oldmeadow's attack on his novels in the *Tablet* may have been ludicrous, but they were doing nothing to give him a good reputation in Catholic circles at a time when his divorce was still under consideration in Rome. Whether or not this was directly in his mind, it would certainly do him no harm to write a serious book on a Catholic subject. If Rome took little notice, Laura Herbert and her mother could not help being aware of it.

Much of his work on the book was done at Mells in Somerset, which was a centre of Catholic intellectual life much as Uffington was a hotbed of Betjemanic Anglicanism.* A Catholic friend of Waugh's from Oxford days, Christopher Hollis, lived there, and the manor was occupied by Lady Horner, née Katharine Asquith, who had become a Catholic after the death of her husband in the First World War. Father Ronald Knox frequently stayed there.

Until now, Catholicism had brought Waugh no companionship. 'Even in his religion he felt no brotherhood,' he was to write of Guy Crouchback in *Men at Arms*: 'He never went to communion on Sundays,

---

* Uffington had its serious religious side. Penelope Betjeman introduced Frank Bishop to Father Harton, the parish priest for whom she played the harmonium, and under his guidance Bishop eventually became a novice at the Anglican monastery of Nashdom.

slipping into the church, instead, very early on weekdays when few others were about.... Often he wished that he lived in ... a solitary outpost of the Faith, surrounded by aliens.' Mells probably gave Waugh his first experience of the Catholic Church as a community. He seems to be writing about it when, in his *Edmund Campion*, he describes Campion's arrival at Douai:

> For the first time he found himself living in a completely Catholic community, and, perhaps for the first time, began to have some sense of the size and power of the world he had entered, of the distance and glory of the aim he had set himself. The faith of the people among whom he was now placed was no fad or sentiment ... no dry, logical necessity ... it gave them their daily life, their entire love and hope....

'Dry, logical necessity' probably sums up the nature of Waugh's Catholicism at the time of his reception into the Church, and maybe later too, but at Mells he at least discovered that not all Catholics regarded it that way, and that there was a strong intellectual element among English Catholics, a highly intelligent audience for whom he could write, if he so chose.

Edmund Campion pretends not to be a work of original research. In his prefatory note, Waugh implies that he has chiefly worked from secondary sources, and from material assembled by one of the Farm Street fathers who had planned to write a biography, but died before completing it. However, Waugh did his own researches in the Public Record Office, and read widely in Tudor history, labouring seriously at his task. In October 1934 he turned down a lucrative contract for a series of short stories for the *Strand Magazine*, on the ground that he was committed to a 'pious book'. The project fully occupied his attention for nine months, a long time by his standards.

The argument of the book is that Catholicism, to which Campion, a leading young intellectual and writer of Elizabethan England, became a convert at the age of thirty-one (Waugh's own age at the time that he began to write *Edmund Campion*), is not merely the former national religion of England, but 'something historically and continuously English' which had been 'taken ... by theft' from the English people. In contrast, the Elizabethan Protestants are represented as men of worldly ambition, place-servers without moral scruple.

While this is not altogether a distortion of the truth, Waugh goes to considerable trouble to weight the argument on the Catholic side. The book naturally deals in some gory detail with the martyrdom of the English Catholics, and Waugh sidesteps the fact that this persecution was largely brought on by Pope Pius v's ill-judged excommunication of Queen Elizabeth. He suggests that Pius was ultimately wise, that he had 'seen through and beyond the present and the immediate future; understood that there was to be no easy way of reconciliation, but that it was only through blood and hatred and derision that the faith was one day to return to England'. Besides being historically implausible, this – as Christopher Sykes, a fellow-Catholic, has pointed out – evades the blunt fact that Pius himself was a persecutor who, in Sykes's words, 'never seems to have scrupled to support his principles by the use of atrocity'. Waugh's handling of his evidence was, then, not altogether honest, but to judge from one reader of *Edmund Campion* it was effective. Frank Pakenham (Lord Longford) writes in his autobiography of his wife's reaction to the book: 'The first time Elizabeth felt a really strong emotional feel from Catholicism was actually after she had been received [into the Catholic Church] when she read Evelyn Waugh's *Edmund Campion*. Now at last she thought of the Catholics as "we" and of their opponents as "they".'

While the content of the book tells us much about Waugh's feelings towards his Church, the style is a revelation of a different sort. Like his *Rossetti*, the book is written in language of striking and unrelieved formality. Though, in his Author's Note, Waugh claims to have used a novelist's rather than a scholar's criteria – 'I have merely attempted to put into a single, readable narrative the most significant of the facts' – the story plods its way heavily, giving no internal evidence that it is the work of an accomplished writer of fiction. Many of the most exciting and revealing episodes in Campion's life are severely compressed, or referred to so obliquely as to be virtually incomprehensible. There is remarkably little quotation from contemporary sources (which would have given the book some life), and the authorial voice is that of a portentous academic historian.

Possibly Waugh's evident fondness, in certain contexts, for formal style had something to do with the depressive side of his personality. Cyril Connolly writes, in *Enemies of Promise*, that he finds 'Augustan Latin and Augustan English' the 'best correctives' to his own 'addiction to melancholy'. Formality has a strong appeal to a mind sensitive to chaos in the world and in itself. Also, it provided Waugh with another *persona* for expressing his own feelings, an alternative to the deliberately farcical description of them that he provided for the Lygon sisters. One might say of his use of formal prose, as he himself said of Rossetti's medievalism, that it was 'the language in which he most easily recorded his emotions'. Formal prose is also heavily authoritarian and paternalistic, and it suited Waugh's increasing tendency from the middle years of his life to play the *paterfamilias* and imitate his own father – Arthur Waugh himself had written in much the same manner.

Waugh's technique as a writer of fiction is to impose a classical formality of narrative upon a world that is chaotic to the point of incoherence. The dialogue may be recorded colloquially, on the model of Hemingway, but the narrator's own voice is consistently formal, imposing the verbal equivalent of Georgian architecture upon the messiness of experience.*

But while Waugh's novels gain their vitality from the tension between the chaos that they portray and the formality with which they portray it, his biographies of Rossetti and Campion (and later of Ronald Knox) are acts of piety, which lack the electrifying tension between form and subject-matter. While it was comic and effective to write about the doings of the Bright Young People in classical prose, little was achieved by applying the same style to incidents in Elizabethan England or among the Pre-Raphaelites. Waugh was also severely hampered as a biographer by his evident feeling that the close investigation of motives in the lives of real people was an impertinence, an attitude no doubt formed by his wariness of revealing too much about himself.

* In his novella *Love Among the Ruins* (1953), Waugh uses this technique visually, illustrating his Orwellian parable about the horrors of a future society with formal line-drawings, in the manner of classical friezes, adapted from a book of engravings of the works of the eighteenth-century neo-classical sculptor Antonio Canova.

2

A Fascist Tract

'Get there if you can and see the land you once were proud to own,'
W.H. Auden wrote in the spring of 1930, as the Depression began
to grip Britain. 'Smokeless chimneys, damaged bridges, rotting
wharves and choked canals, / Tramlines buckled, smashed trucks lying
on their side across the rails.' By October 1932, unemployment had
reached two and three-quarter millions, and thousands of workers converged on London in a vast 'hunger march'. In Parliament, the Labour
Party was reduced to an impotent fifty-six members, when Ramsay
MacDonald set up a coalition government to tackle the economic crisis,
and many young intellectuals, disaffected by the collapse of parliamentary socialism, began to be drawn to the Communist Party. Oswald
Mosley's New Party, formed in 1931 with vaguely socialist aims, was
reconstituted the following year as the British Union of Fascists.

In May 1933, returning to England from the Brazilian jungle, Waugh
was mildly scandalized to learn that Diana Guinness had deserted her
husband to have an affair with Mosley, but the political implications
did not interest him. He seems to have found Mosley mildly comic
– there are faintly sardonic references to 'Sir Oswald Mosley' here
and there in his letters – and the activities of the BUF never attracted
his serious attention.

Most of his circle lived on private means, or had lucrative jobs which
were not affected by the slump. Their attitude to the Depression and
its possible social consequences is summed up by Diana Guinness's
sister, Nancy Mitford, in her *Highland Fling* (1931). Walter Monteath,

a Bright Young Person, speculates about a possible revolution, and how the mob would know who were the nobles: 'Personally I've always been terrified that I should be left behind when all my friends were being hurried off to the tumbrils. . . . As for all those old peers, they'll have to parade up and down Piccadilly in their coronets if they want to be taken in the smart tumbrils, and even then I expect people would think they were an advertisement for something.' Later in *Highland Fling*, at a shooting party on the Scottish moors, the heroine espies 'a rabble of half-clothed and villainous-looking peasants' – the local people, acting as beaters – and 'supposed that they were the local unemployed, soliciting arms', evidence of the joke that the Depression was to the upper classes.

Nancy Mitford's third novel, *Wigs on the Green* (1934), concerns an heiress, Eugenia Malmains, who has joined the 'Union Jackshirts', led by one Captain Jack. She stands on an upturned washtub on the village green, spouting a parody of Mosley:

> 'Oh! British lion, shake off the nets that bind you. . . . Respect for parents, love of the home, veneration of the marriage tie, are all at a discount in England today. . . . The rich have betrayed their trust, preferring the fetid atmosphere of cocktail-bars and night-clubs to the sanity of a useful country life. . . . How if a real Captain, a man, and not a tortoise, shall appear suddenly at their adulterous bedsides, a cup of castor oil in the one hand, a goblet of hemlock in the other, and offer them the choice between ignominy and a Roman death? . . .'
>
> At this point a very old lady came up to the crowd, pushed her way through it and began twitching at Eugenia's skirt. . . . 'Go away, Nanny,' said Eugenia. . . . 'Get out you filthy Pacifist, get out I say, and take your yellow razor gang with you. I will have free speech at my meetings.'

This is a caricature of Nancy's sister Unity, who had become passionately pro-Hitler during a visit to Germany with her sister Diana and Oswald Mosley in 1933. Nancy herself, and her husband Peter Rodd, briefly joined the BUF – 'Prod looked very pretty in a black shirt,' she told Waugh – but behind Diana and Unity's backs she would refer to Mosley as 'TPOL', The Poor Old Leader. The Rodds soon abandoned Fascism, and Nancy wrote *Wigs on the Green* to tease her sisters, who were not amused.

The only writer in Waugh's orbit to give even a superficial impression of taking the English political situation seriously at this period was Graham Greene. His next novel after *Stamboul Train, It's a Battlefield* (1934), concerns the family of Jim Drover, a bus driver sentenced to death for stabbing a policeman at a Communist rally in Hyde Park.

Drover is a Party member; he attacked the constable because he thought he was about to hit his wife. The Party itself fails to stand up for him, and he is saved from the rope only by the machinations of his family, who virtually destroy themselves in the process. Though some of the descriptive writing in *It's a Battlefield* is excellent, Greene is quite unable to make convincing the characters of Drover's wife Milly, his brother Conrad and his sister-in-law Kay, around whose lives the story revolves. It is abundantly clear that he has had no real contact with working-class London life, and though he tries hard not to sentimentalize the portrait, it comes out as insufferably condescending.

The atmosphere of the Depression is more effectively conveyed by Greene's next novel, *England Made Me* (1935). Though set mostly in Sweden, it portrays the effect of the slump on members of the British lower-middle class, a social echelon in which Greene is much more at home. The book's unheroic hero, Anthony Farrant, has drifted from one form of mean employment to another, as can be seen from his physical appearance: 'The grit of London lay under his eyes, he was at home ... in the one-night hotels, in the basement offices, among the small crooked flotations of transient business, jovial among the share pushers.' The Eliotic allusions should not blind us to another literary model. With his posing as an Old Harrovian, and his seedy dependence upon the public-school caste to save him from utter disaster, Anthony could be Captain Grimes.

'Seediness has a very deep appeal,' Greene wrote in his next book. 'It seems to satisfy, temporarily, the sense of nostalgia for something lost; it seems to represent a stage further back.' This observation appeared not in a novel but in *Journey Without Maps* (1936), a travel book. Neither *It's a Battlefield* nor *England Made Me* was a commercial success, and Greene was financially still 'very poor'. The current popularity of travel books encouraged him to try his hand in this genre. He picked on Africa, and chose Liberia in particular, chiefly because there were no up-to-date and detailed maps, except for American military charts which 'showed whole areas left blank except for the word "cannibals"'. At his brother Hugh's wedding, he asked his twenty-three-year-old cousin Barbara to accompany him, chiefly because 'I had drunk too much champagne.' He did not expect her to accept, but she did, and Greene 'panicked' at his choice of companion. Indeed, to take any companion seemed excessive in what, though he does not admit it, was almost a carbon copy of Waugh's expedition to South America.

Greene's account of the expedition, in *Journey Without Maps*, says so little about how the two cousins got on as travelling-companions that one is inclined to suspect either that they were not on speaking terms or that they had a love affair. However, Barbara Greene wrote her own book about the trip, *Land Benighted* (1938), in which she shows how her cousin Graham deliberately avoided getting to know her well during the trip, but seemed to want to remain remote and detached. When it was all over they were, she says, 'still not more than friendly acquaintances', and during the journey they 'never once walked together'; Graham usually went some distance ahead, like Waugh avoiding his native servants in South America. Barbara says she found his mind 'sharp and clear and cruel', the professional novelist on the look-out for good copy: 'If you are in a sticky place he will be so interested in noting your reactions that he will probably forget to rescue you.' Reading her account, one begins to feel that the absence of any clearly defined narrator in Greene's books is not an authorial trick, but a reflection of the man's character. As Waugh said of his writing, 'The reader has not had a conversation with a third party such as he enjoys with Sterne or Thackeray. . . . It is the camera's eye.'

The cousins walked for hundreds of miles, from the Sierra Leone border across the interior of Liberia, accompanied by a band of native carriers whose welfare and health caused them as much concern as their own. Greene calls the employer–servant relationship on this trip 'almost as intimate as a love-affair', and stresses the carriers' expertise: 'One didn't have to condescend; one knew more about some things, but they knew more about others. And on the whole the things they knew were more important.'

The discomforts that Greene and his cousin endured were as great as those experienced by Waugh, and so was the boredom. Greene, too, found himself detained for days in unfriendly villages and towns, unable to sleep for illness and discomfort, and like Waugh he fretted at the monotony of hour upon hour of travelling through featureless under-growth. Yet, unlike Waugh, at the most unlikely moments he experienced a soaring of the spirit – 'the happy sense of being free; one had only to follow a path far enough and one could cross a continent'. In the latter part of the journey he fell ill, and began to fear he would never make it back to the coast ('Graham would die,' writes Barbara Greene; 'I never doubted it for a minute'). This produced a curious effect in him, the experience of something that he had believed, since the imprison-ment of his Berkhamsted schooldays, was not in his nature, 'a passionate interest in living'. Also, in matters of race and class, while he began his journey with the feeling that the African blacks had about them a touch *of Firbank's Prancing Nigger* – the 'painful attempt at playing the white man' which resulted in 'the chimpanzee's tea-party' (remarks one would expect of Waugh) – he ended it by feeling that the joke was the other way round. Returning to white society many weeks later, on the coast at Grand Bassa, he found it impossible not to laugh at the expatriates who drank endless *crème de menthe* and tuned in promptly at six o'clock to the Empire Programme from Daventry. Not for him Waugh's admiring identification of the white settlers with the English squires of a utopian past; he saw, all too clearly, that the so-called 'civilization' which the whites claimed to have imported into Africa was just a euphemism for exploitation: 'We had hardly, it seemed to me, improved the natives' lot at all.... We had introduced new diseases and weakened their resistance to the old.... Civilization ... was ... the sixpenny wage. It was not civilization as we think of it.' Barbara Greene, trying to describe London to a black schoolmaster she met in the interior, experienced a similar revulsion against her own culture: 'I almost felt that I did not want to go back – till, of course, I remembered Elizabeth Arden, my flat, and the Savoy Grill.'

Greene concludes *Journey Without Maps* not merely with a despairing view of the settlers' influence on the natives, but with doubts about the prospects for European society itself; he says that his Liberian journey had given him 'a distrust of any future based on what we are'. Evelyn Waugh's next book set out to argue exactly the opposite: that Africa was in its natural state barbarous and benighted, and that one should applaud every effort to import European civilization. In writing it, Waugh at last began to take sides in the contemporary British political conflict.

On 5 December 1934, an Italian expeditionary force crossed the border from Italian Somaliland into Ethiopia, and clashed with Ethiopian troops at an oasis fifty miles into their territory, with heavy losses on both sides. The matter came before the League of Nations, which refused to intervene, and early in 1935 it became clear that Mussolini had plans to establish an East African Italian Empire.

Popular opinion in Britain was not with Mussolini. When he first came to power in 1922, British intellectuals had taken a sympathetic interest in his improvements of Italian agriculture, roads and railways, and some of them found his strong-man methods preferable to the alternative of Communism. But Hitler's seizing of power in Germany in 1933, the reports of anti-Semitic atrocities there, and the violent reputation of Mosley's blackshirts in Britain, alerted everyone to the real nature of Fascism. By 1935 virtually its only supporters among British writers were Wyndham Lewis and Henry Williamson.

Most of the younger British *literati* were explicitly left-wing, massing behind W. H. Auden's banner to denounce, specifically or by implication, the Fascist menace which they believed to lie beneath the surface of British middle-class life as well as in Germany and Italy. As Alan Pryce-Jones writes,

> a new quarrelsomeness entered social life. . . . I remember an elaborate dinner at Londonderry House when a daughter of the house threw a silver cigarette box across the dining-room table because she held the opposite [political] view to her vis-à-vis. This violence was new. The English do not normally become rabid in discussion. . . .

Given this contentious atmosphere, and his own first-hand knowledge of Ethiopia, Waugh was not inclined to keep silent.

On 13 February 1935, a few days after fighting had broken out again on the Ethiopian border, an article by him appeared in the *Evening Standard* on the subject of Italian ambitions in Ethiopia. Headed 'We Can Applaud Italy', it dismissed as mere 'sentimentalists' those of the liberal or left-wing persuasion who assumed that Ethiopia was a charming medieval backwater full of picturesque and immemorial folk-customs. In reality it was 'capriciously and violently governed', a nation which practised barbarities towards its neighbours, exploited its own peasantry, and owed its existence as an independent country not to ancient tradition but to recent force of arms, the Emperor Menelik's seizing of power and defeat of the Italian colonists in 1896. Its culture, alleged Waugh, could not be taken seriously: the table manners of the native noblemen were 'entertaining', and Addis Ababa was simply 'a great village of tin huts'.

Italian conquest of such a land, continued Waugh, seemed positively 'desirable'. It was 'one of the facts of history' that barbarous and civilized nations could not live peaceably side by side: the victor would not necessarily be the possessor of the higher culture, but 'the more virile' of the two. In the case of Italy, Ethiopia's neighbour in East Africa by virtue of its colony in Eritrea as well as Somalia, its triumph over the barbarians could by no means be predicted. Had Mussolini's programme of military training really produced an effective army, the first that Italy had had since the fall of the Roman Empire? If so, continued Waugh,

> no greater triumph has been achieved by a single man, and no more severe test could have been chosen than the conquest of Abyssinia. It

is an object which any patriotic European can applaud. Its accomplishment will be of service to the world.... It will be the supreme trial of Mussolini's regime. We can, with clear conscience, fold our hands and await the news on the wireless.

It was the sort of thing he had said when posing as a die-hard at the Oxford Union. He may have felt, as a Catholic, that a strong Rome had its attractions: at this time, Catholic conservatives regarded Mussolini as Hitler's rival for power in Europe, rather than his natural ally. But the degree to which Waugh was parting company even from the British right wing is indicated by a leader in *The Times* the day before his article appeared. This expressed 'sympathy' with Emperor Haile Selassie of Ethiopia for his 'foreign and internal troubles', and said that the build-up of Italian troops seemed clearly an act of aggression, and was 'certainly to be regretted'.

The whole subject did not really interest Waugh very much, and he would probably have paid it little further attention had any major project been occupying his mind. In fact he was casting around for a new book to write, with *Edmund Campion* nearing completion and no new novel as yet in view. Various things were in the air: he thought of writing a life of Mary Stuart for Chapman & Hall, and a film company seemed about to ask him to go to Hollywood. But neither of these projects came to anything, and a short story, written four months after the article on Ethiopia, suggests that he was in need of new subject-matter. This is the narrative about the younger brother who always gets a poor deal in the family, both in childhood and as an adult, and it is obviously drawn from Waugh's feelings about his own elder brother. Entitled 'Winner Takes All', it reads rather like the synopsis of a novel, and has sufficient in it to form the bones of one. Yet there is a slightly bored air about the whole proceeding. It gives the impression that English social black-comedy no longer interests Waugh very much.

By the summer of 1935, it was clear that the Italians would soon invade Ethiopia. In July, Waugh asked A.D. Peters to get him a commission for four articles on the Ethiopian question; a month later he wanted to write a book on it, preferably for a Catholic publisher (Tom Burns of Longman's), but said he would accept the highest bid. Another firm put in an offer, and Burns had to pay £950 – an outsize advance for those days – before he could sign up Waugh. On top of this, Waugh got himself appointed war correspondent in Ethiopia for the *Daily Mail*, which was sympathetic to Italian ambitions in East Africa.

He sailed for Djibouti in August, and found himself travelling with the correspondent of the liberal *News Chronicle*, which strongly opposed Mussolini. Waugh missed no opportunity to make the journalist nervous about Ethiopia. 'He is a married man and does not want much to be killed,' he wrote to Laura Herbert, 'and has a gas mask and a helmet and a medicine chest twice the size of all my luggage and I have told him so often that he is going to certain death that I have begun to believe it myself.' He was entertained by the conscientiousness with which the man carried out his job – 'he was continually jotting things down in a little notebook' – and the degree to which he shared the opinions of his paper: 'The [political] situation, obscure to most of us, was crystal clear to him – the Emperor was an oppressed anti-fascist.'

Arriving in Addis Ababa exhausted from the journey and with a mild attack of dysentery, Waugh showed no inclination to embark on his new profession until 'a series of peremptory cables from Fleet Street' roused him to the papers's expectations: 'REQUIRE COMPREHENSIVE CABLE GOOD COLOURFUL STUFF ALSO NEWS.... PLEASE INDICATE WHEN CAN EXPECT COMPREHENSIVE CABLE.... PRESUME YOU ARE MAKING ARRANGEMENTS GETTING STUFF AWAY.... WHAT ALTERNA-TIVE MEANS COMMUNICATION IN EVENT BREAKDOWN?' Waugh grumbled to Laura about these missives from 'my idiot editor', but he roused himself enough to send off a 'colour' piece, which the *Daily Mail* printed on 24 August 1935, under the headline 'Evelyn Waugh's Vivid Addis Ababa Cable'. It describes the rainswept desolation of the capital, with the native inhabitants unable to perceive that their country is under serious threat: 'They are like children with noses pressed at the nursery window-pane longing for the rain to clear.' During the following week he sent two more cables, reporting on the pathetic Ethiopian attempts at military training, and the end of the rainy season.

Meeting up with Patrick Balfour, who was representing the *Evening Standard*, Waugh decided that they should go east to Harar, the direction from which the Italian offensive was expected to come. En route, they were joined by another acquaintance, Charles Milnes-Gaskell, a wealthy individual who 'had come out primarily in search of amuse-ment'. Balfour engaged the services of a tip-off man, whom Waugh labelled 'Patrick's spy', and nicknamed 'Mata Hari'. At Jijiga, a settle-ment beyond Harar, while Waugh's party breakfasted off Chianti and tinned partridge, this individual informed them that the French consul was about to be shot, while twelve Roman Catholics who had also been arrested would be sewn into animal skins and burned alive. There were, he said, also 'four Maltese Popes' in the town who would probably be shot too. These proved to be Franciscans, surviving in squalor – 'They lived on boiled beads out of their rosaries,' Waugh told Katharine Asquith. The Frenchman (an obscure Count) had indeed been arrested, on suspicion of spying for the Italians, and Waugh and Balfour sent off cables to their papers, fondly imagining that they had scooped their rivals. The *Daily Mail* ran the story, but on their return to the capital Waugh and Balfour found reproofs from their papers for missing the real news.

A mysterious individual named Rickett, who had joined Waugh's ship at Port Said, had been receiving incomprehensible cables during the voyage; he had told Waugh that he was Master of a Berkshire hunt, and that the messages were from his huntsman. Deeply suspicious, Waugh wrote to Penelope Betjeman to see what she could discover; he guessed that Rickett was an arms dealer. Later, Waugh shared lodgings with Rickett in Addis Ababa, found him thoroughly genial, and so lost interest in him. While Waugh was away from the capital, Rickett, who was in fact the agent of a group of American financiers, got Haile Selassie to sign a concession giving his employers mineral rights in much of the territory bordering on Italian possessions. As Rickett was himself British, this prompted the suspicion that Britain intended to involve itself in the conflict, in opposition to Italy. In Waugh's absence, the story had been broken by the *News Chronicle* man whom he so much despised, and by a doyen of war correspondents, Sir Percival Phillips of the *Daily Telegraph*. As Phillips had only recently left the *Daily Mail* after quarrelling with its proprietor Lord Rothermere, Waugh's paper was particularly furious to have been scooped by him.

'BADLY LEFT OIL CONCESSION', the *Mail* cabled to Waugh, and Waugh reported glumly to Laura that he and his editor were now accustomed to 'telegraph abuse' at each other, while at the British Legation his name was 'mud' on account of *Black Mischief* and his portrayal of the household there. He continued to send frequent cables to the *Mail*, and they printed a story under his name almost daily (usually a mangling of what he had sent them), but he now found the other journalists far more interesting than the events he was supposed to be reporting:

> They showed almost every diversity which the human species produces. There was a simian Soudanese ... a monocled Latvian colonel, who was said ... to have worked as a ring-master in a German circus; there was a German who travelled under the name of Haroun al Raschid. ... his head was completely hairless; his wife shaved it for him, emphasizing the frequent slips of her razor with tufts of cotton-wool. ... These formed

an exotic background that was very welcome, for the majority of the regular pressmen were an anxious, restless, mutually suspicious crowd, all weighed down with the consciousness that they were not getting the news.

Meanwhile the war obstinately refused to start. Fleet Street kept cabling the impatient inquiry 'WHAT TRUTH GENERAL MOBILIZA-TION?' But the Ethiopian troops remained mostly invisible, and the journalists now found it impossible to get official permission (from the head of the Press Bureau, Dr Lorenzo Taesas, who was also head of the secret police and Haile Selassie's personal adviser) to leave Addis Ababa and investigate. They were obliged to rely on the reports of their own paid informers, most of whom were also being bribed by the Italians, and sold lies to both sides. The situation began more and more to resemble the opening chapters of *Black Mischief*, with the Emperor, like Seth in the novel, at the mercy of those of his polyglot advisers who had not already gone into hiding. For some reason official notices began to be posted in three languages forbidding cruelty to animals, recalling the efforts of Dame Mildred Porch and Miss Tin in the novel (had somebody in authority been reading it?). And there was an echo of *Vile Bodies* in the official banquet for the press at which Haile Selassie wished to give a cinema show, but was frustrated by the failure of the electric light.

At last, on 2 October 1935, came the long-awaited announcement that the Italians had violated Ethiopian territory in the south-east, and that Haile Selassie's army was mobilizing. For a few hours the journalists' mood was almost festive, but Addis Ababa soon settled back into its usual lethargy; the hostilities were hundreds of miles away, where no one from the capital had ever been, and the calm was punctured only by 'the contending loudspeakers of the two cinemas, the hyaenas howling in the cemetery'. Reports came that the Italians had bombed a hospital in Adowa, and blown up a nurse, but careful investigation suggested that neither nurse nor hospital had ever existed. 'NURSE UNUPBLOWN', cabled Waugh.

The journalists continued to provide him with entertainment. A Foreign Press Association was formed among them, to protest against government censorship of outgoing cables, but at its second meeting 'two Americans challenged one another to fight and a third was sick'. Besides the newspapermen, a number of newsreel cameramen had arrived in Addis Ababa, and these managed to stage 'some fairly effective charades' which passed for footage of the fighting, 'with iodine for blood and fireworks for a bombardment'. Indeed, 'one prominent photographer had brought out with him a set of small bombs which he was able to discharge from his position at the camera by means of an electric cable.'

Eventually, permission was granted for the pressmen to leave Addis Ababa and journey to Dessye, to the north of the capital, where it was believed that the Emperor would establish new headquarters. Waugh and some of his colleagues suspected that this was merely a ruse to get them out of the way, but he joined the expedition, which at its outset was on a magnificent scale – a New York newsreel company had hired a lorry, and blazoned it with the words 'Expedition to the Front with HM the Emperor of Ethiopia'.

The convoy set off with an air of good humour, but was soon brought to a halt by a chief who pointed out that, while they undoubtedly had permission to visit Dessye, they had neglected to get permits to leave Addis Ababa. They were detained in his village, then sent back ignominiously. 'On the whole,' writes Waugh sardonically, 'it had been an enjoyable excursion.'

He perceived the value of what he was witnessing. 'All this will make a funny novel so it isn't wasted,' he wrote to Laura. 'You will have received a copy of *Campion* by now dont try and read it put it on the shelf and wait for the novel about journalists.' It was the first time that he had identified 'copy' for fiction while it was actually taking place.

He eventually got to Dessye, where the Emperor duly arrived, but by now the war seemed likely to drag on indefinitely, and end inconclusively, and (as he told Laura) he was 'sick to death of this country and these lousy blackamoors'. The *Daily Mail* finally decided it had had enough of him, and cabled in polite terms that he was sacked. Waugh travelled back to England via Jerusalem, where he spent Christmas 1935, and Rome, where in January 1936 he applied for an interview with Mussolini, and was granted one, on condition that no report of it be published.

He had expected to find Il Duce a somewhat ridiculous figure, and was amused by the theatrical throne room in the Palazzo Venezia. But Mussolini himself turned out to be 'very impressive'; he asked Waugh how conditions in Ethiopia seemed from behind the lines, and Waugh gave 'a very gloomy account' of the difficulties the Italian army would face, though he guessed that Mussolini dismissed this as 'British propaganda'.

Soon after his return to England, he began work on the commissioned book about the Ethiopian war. When at Dessye, shortly before Christmas, he had written to his parents: 'I believe the Italians are beaten.' While actually in Ethiopia it had been impossible to sustain his attitude, expressed in the *Daily Mail* the previous spring, that an Italian conquest was 'an object which any patriotic European can applaud'. For all its failings, the country had many endearing qualities and, even if most of its inhabitants were 'lousy blackamoors', Italy seemed no better – he described it to Katharine Asquith as 'Mussolini's bughouse'. But a meeting with Mussolini, geographical separation from Haile Selassie and his entourage, and the need to fulfil his commission for the book were enough to make him change his attitude, and revert to the die-hard position.

The opening chapters of the book, written in April and May 1936, are in the severely formal style of *Edmund Campion*. While admitting that the original colonization of Africa by the European nations had been a demonstration of 'avarice, treachery, hypocrisy and brutality', he declared – taking exactly the opposite view to Graham Greene in his book on Liberia – that the settlers had nevertheless introduced to the African continent 'many of the high qualities of European civilization'. He now had nothing to say in favour of the Ethiopian people. Haile Selassie's mind was 'pathetically compounded of primitive simplicity and primitive suspicion', and the country merely possessed 'a low ... culture ... marked down for destruction'. All Waugh's amused, detached observation of the absurdities of Addis Ababa life, which had enriched his letters home and had even crept now and then, when the sub-editors were not looking, into his *Daily Mail* reports, vanished to be replaced by the pose of high Tory historian – a pose which Waugh himself found dreary. 'If this book bores its readers half as much as it is boring me to write it, it will create a record in low sales,' he wrote to a friend shortly after beginning it.

He did his best to portray Haile Selassie's government as despicable, contrasting it with the many admirable qualities of white imperialism:

> However sordid the motives and however gross the means by which the white races established – and are still establishing – themselves in Africa, the result has been, in the main, beneficial, for there are more good men than bad in Europe and there is a predisposition towards justice and charity in European culture; a bias, so that it cannot for long run free without inclining to good; things which began wickedly have turned out well.... Even in the terms of nineteenth-century liberalism there has been more gain than loss to the African natives.... The Abyssinians had nothing to give their subject peoples, nothing to teach

285

them. . . . They squatted in the villages in the thatched huts of the conquered people, dirty, idle and domineering.

What prompted him to these facile assertions, based on a superficial
knowledge of Ethiopia, and in such stark contrast to his novels? Had
he been seduced by Mussolini's personal magnetism which, in a similarly brief audience three years earlier, had been enough to make Ezra
Pound, previously without political convictions, into a passionate supporter of the Italian dictator? Or was it that, with the annulment of
his marriage still under consideration by his Church, Waugh hoped
to convince the English Catholics – among them the Herbert family –
of his rectitude and seriousness?

Graham Greene had undertaken his journey to Liberia largely in
order to discover himself, but Waugh repudiates the personal in his
Ethiopia book. At one point he fumes against the tendency of journalists
to search for 'impertinent personal details'. His move to the right politically was the adding of another layer to his hard protective shell.

Having adopted his pro-Italian political stance, he realized, as the Ethiopia book neared completion, that he lacked information to support
that attitude. He had left Ethiopia long before the Italian conquest
really began; in May, Haile Selassie had fled before the advancing
Italians, and his regime had collapsed. 'What was really happening?'
Waugh wonders aloud in the book. He decided to pay another visit
to Ethiopia.

He tried to get another Fleet Street commission to pay for the trip,
but the *Daily Mail*'s experiences with him had become well known,
and virtually all the other papers were anti-Italian in their sympathies.
Waugh could have afforded to make the trip at his own expense –
Longman's had paid substantially for the book, and Chapman & Hall
had promised him a large advance for his next novel – but he had
other plans. Arriving in Rome, he negotiated with Fascist government
officials, and persuaded them to give him a free passage on one of
their ships to Djibouti.

Arriving there, he was told that the Italians had only 'conquered'
certain key towns; the remainder of Ethiopia was in its usual state
of semi-anarchy, with heavily armed guerrillas roaming throughout
the country. His summary in his diary was: 'Truth appears to be
Wops in a jam.'

He was driven about by the Italians, and was impressed by the new
roads they had built. But, otherwise, conditions did not delight him.

In one town his hosts put him up in an 'absolutely disgusting' bungalow, and when he complained about the filth, they replied 'We are in Africa.'

There had been many reports in the British press of atrocities by the invaders, and at Harar he asked about the Italians' alleged use of poison gas. 'Gas used four or five times on Southern front,' he wrote in his diary. 'Some blind brought back to hospital.' He made no comment.

On 26 August 1936, in Addis Ababa, he attended 'Fascist meeting in honour of German consul', where he listened to 'speeches in praise of Hitler and the unforgettable friendliness of Germany [to Italy] during the outrageous pro-barbarian sanctionist campaign' – that is, the sanctions against Italy in protest against the invasion of Ethiopia. Again, he made no comment in his diary.

After three weeks, he was flown out of Ethiopia, to Tripoli, and was back in England in the second week of September, where he resumed work on the Ethiopia book. He added two more chapters, some twenty-five pages in all. The first chapter opens with a description of conditions in Djibouti and Harar, and Waugh's argument is that the Italian bombardment of Harar had not really mattered: 'There had always been a large proportion of ruinous houses in Harar. . . . The town was nearly empty at the time of the attack. When the inhabitants returned they . . . settled down to their normal life. . . . It was a revelation to me to see how little damage a bomb does.' Turning briefly to the matter of poison gas and its use by the advancing Italians, he asserts that it 'was used but accounted for only eighteen lives', though he admits that 'it is difficult to get reliable figures'. He makes no mention of the reports of gas-blindness he had heard at Harar. (In a 1937 article he says of the Italians' use of gas that they sometimes 'allowed themselves to behave as outlaws' because they had been 'condemned to outlawry by the world', though he agreed that 'it was an action which all friends of Italy must deplore'.)

He reports his meeting with the Italian Viceroy, Marshal Graziani: 'I have seldom enjoyed an official audience more. . . . He was like the traditional conception of an English admiral, frank, humorous and practical.' Waugh briefly mentions the meeting at Fascist headquarters to honour the German consul, and is disparaging about the behaviour of the 'blackshirt political boss', who he says addressed his audience of six as if he were Mussolini speaking from a balcony, but he makes no mention of the speeches in praise of Hitler. (In *Men at Arms*, though Guy Crouchback remains neutral about Italian Fascism – 'He disliked the men who were edging themselves into power [in Italy] . . . but

English denunciations sounded fatuous' – he is certain that 'the German Nazis' are 'mad and bad'. In 1936, Waugh himself made no such distinction in print.)

Waugh faithfully reports the depressing situation in Addis Ababa, the 'general sense of insecurity' and 'illusion of being besieged', and says it would be 'easy to write ironically about the Pax Romana', but prophesied that a 'second decisive campaign' was about to open in Ethiopia, the reconstruction of the country under Italian rule. And he declared: 'The new regime is going to succeed.'

Waugh in Abyssinia (the punning title annoyed Waugh) was published a few weeks after he had finished the extra chapters, in October 1936. The English Catholic press liked it, the *Catholic Herald* suggesting that the forty-odd nations who had imposed sanctions against Italy 'could after all be largely wrong', but David Garnett in the *New Statesman* was bitter about Waugh's praise of the Italian Viceroy: 'He does not tell us how many [natives] that "most amiable and sensible man", Graziani, is hanging and shooting every day.' The *Times Literary Supplement* observed that Waugh was a 'cynic turned idealist', and said it hoped he was right in his prophetic conclusion, though some might think that the foundations of his mighty road had been 'laid in arrogance and dishonour'. Writing in *Horizon* ten years after its publication, Rose Macaulay bluntly judged *Waugh in Abyssinia* 'a Fascist tract'. This in itself (she said) was regrettable enough, yet she regretted even more Waugh's failure as an artist in the book, and in its immediate predecessor, *Edmund Campion*: 'What has gone from his view is detachment. . . . He is no longer objective: he has come down on a side. In art so naturally ironic and detached as his, this is a serious loss; it undermines his best gifts.'

3

Setting Myself Up as a Squire

Cyril Connolly observed Waugh's changing political position even before the Ethiopia book was published. In January 1936 he wrote of him, in an article on contemporary novelists:

> I regard him as the most naturally gifted novelist of his generation . . . but his development has taken him steadily from the Left towards the Right, and Right Wing Satire is always weak – and he is a satirist. The anarchist charm of his books . . . was altered in *A Handful of Dust* to a savage attack on Mayfair from a Tory angle. And though there on safe ground, it is going to be difficult for him to continue, since Tory satire, directed at people on a moving staircase from a stationary one, is doomed to ultimate peevishness. . . . *A Handful of Dust* is a very fine novel, but it is the first of Evelyn Waugh's novels to have a bore for a hero.

Waugh himself, in Connolly's eyes, was anything but a bore. Connolly records of a meeting in April 1934, their first for two years: 'Evelyn very crusty and charming . . . so mature and pithy, and religion apart, so frivolous. Made most of the people we see seem dowdy.' The Connollys had returned to England and taken a flat in the King's Road, where Cyril gave dinner parties that were carefully orchestrated socially but unpredictably gastronomically; Anthony Powell describes how:

> the succession of cooks went up and down in quality, sometimes sharply. Whether or not the proprietor of a mobile coffee-stall got wind of this,

289

one of these was certainly parked every night in a strategic position just opposite the house. There Connolly dinner-guests would sometimes end the evening with a sausage-roll or two.

One evening in the mid-1930s, Powell and his wife – Lady Violet, née Pakenham, sister of Pansy Pakenham, whom he married during 1934 – came to dinner with Connolly. Powell asked Connolly what was his opinion of himself and Waugh as novelists. 'I said', writes Connolly, 'I thought Tony had more talent and Evelyn more vocation. Tony is likely to dry up and Evelyn to make mistakes, but you can learn from mistakes, you can't learn from drying up.' Powell was possibly drying up already. He admits that his fourth novel, *Agents and Patients* (1936), 'did not entirely satisfy my standards in breaking fresh ground'. The novel is a re-run of *Afternoon Men*, with the additional motif that people are either manipulators or victims. It precisely exemplifies Connolly's description of Powell's fiction, written early in 1936, before this novel was published: 'The novels of Anthony Powell are unaffected monochromes of realism. Anything which might heighten the colouring is scrupulously omitted. They deal in nuances of boredom, seediness, and squalor [and] contain much of the purest comedy that is now being written.' Powell says he was not finding it easy to develop, to move his novels away from their perhaps rather dated preoccupation with futility. He writes that *Agents and Patients*, though it was supposed to be set contemporarily in the mid-1930s, 'showed little or no departure from the mood of the Twenties'.

Shortly after the book appeared, Powell resigned from his job in publishing, and worked for a while in the script department of a film company. A little later, in the spring of 1937, he went to Hollywood with the hope – or his agent's hope – of participating in the writing of *A Yank at Oxford*. While there, he 'found myself unable to write a line of a new novel' and, after a few months, returned to London 'without even the germ of a book in my head'.

Henry Yorke had published nothing since *Living* (1929). He was working as managing director of the family business. Graham Greene's output had been substantial – six novels by 1935 – but only *Stamboul Train* had broken through what he calls 'public indifference'.

Cyril Connolly had long nurtured the intention to write a novel, but complained that his regular work as a reviewer of fiction for the *New Statesman* and other journals had made it virtually impossible to turn novelist himself. 'Reviewing', he wrote gloomily, 'is a whole-time job with a half-time salary ... in which our best work is always submerged in the criticism of someone else's.' He felt it was a despised job too: 'Who would not rather than the best of reviewers be the worst of novelists ...?' He believed that his years of reading indifferent modern fiction had blunted his ability, had silted up his mind 'with every trick and cliché, every still-born phrase and facile and second-hand expression that one has deplored in others'.

In fact the very opposite was true. Far from being, as he called it, 'the white man's grave of journalism', the reviewing of bad and indifferent novels had often inspired Connolly to exquisitely funny parodies, which demonstrate an adeptness at social nuance and comedy that easily equals Powell's and Waugh's. For example, there is his review of a typically bad light novel of the period, Eric Linklater's *Ripeness Is All* (1935), which takes the form of a lesson to schoolboys in how to write 'middlebrow satire', a parody of Aldous Huxley entitled 'Told in Gath',* and (though it is not based on a real book) 'Where Engels Fears to Tread', a masterly spoof-autobiography of Brian Howard.

This supposed memoir, '*From Oscar to Stalin: A Progress*, by Christian de Clavering', opens with the dedication 'To the Bald Young People'. It describes Brian's childhood and Eton education ('While the battle of Waterloo was being fought all around me, I just sat still and watched my eyelashes grow'), his notoriety as a young man ('At seventeen it was rather odd to figure fairly recognizably in five novels in three languages'), and his delight at this sort of fame: '"Dear Evelyn, *of course*, put me into it!"' (here Connolly is anticipating Waugh's use of Howard in *Put Out More Flags* and *Brideshead Revisited*). The 'autobiography' then follows Brian on his travels about Europe – 'My slim figure lingered, winterbound, in dim cathedrals, and there were beaches where summer licked me with its great rough tongue. Ah, summer! There's a crypto-fascist for you!' – and describes his recent flirtation with the Auden group (Brian had been fraternizing with Auden, and was talking about collaborating with him on a book). Connolly's 'de Clavering' remarks: 'From that moment I've never looked back. It's been pylons all the way. . . . See you at the Mass Observatory.'

Brian was 'mortified' when Connolly's piece first appeared in 1937, but he had the good grace to review it appreciatively when it was reprinted in *The Condemned Playground* in 1945, saying that it 'still makes me laugh almost aloud'.

Besides producing these brilliant ephemera, Connolly did manage

---

* These are collected in Connolly's *The Condemned Playground* (1945, reprinted 1985).

291

to complete a short novel. He had intended it to form the middle section of a trilogy dealing with English snobbery at home and abroad, but the other two books were never finished, and he felt it was a 'personal triumph' to have achieved even a single volume. He had written it by 1935, but it failed to find a publisher in London, because it was considered too *risqué*. Jack Kahane, who published Henry Miller and much erotica at his Obelisk Press in Paris, took it on, though Connolly said he 'found my book so little salacious that he used to tell me it was "a disgrace to his list"'. It appeared in 1936.

The Rock Pool is based on Connolly's experiences while living in the South of France in the early days of his marriage to Jean. Though he claimed that the hero, Naylor, was based on two of his acquaintances, Naylor's agonizing romantic passions and his sexual orientation – he is always falling in love with boyish girls in shorts – are closely drawn from Connolly's own. More than this, *The Rock Pool* charts the sort of progressive failure, romantic, sexual and intellectual, which Connolly believed would be his own fate. Naylor arrives in Trou-sur-Mer (the town's Firbankian name indicates its sexual appetites) determined to view the expatriate community with the detached curiosity of a botanist examining the contents of a pool left stranded by the tide. But in a matter of days he has become a helpless victim of the community's sexual and financial intrigues. He is sponged off, beaten up, occasionally bedded, and by the end of the book has been reduced to a solitary alcoholic, lingering in the now deserted end-of-season resort like the helpless Aschenbach in Thomas Mann's Venice.

The story bears a resemblance to Powell's *Agents and Patients*; Connolly has observed that Naylor (like Blore-Smith in that novel) 'represents a certain set of English qualities, the last gasp, perhaps, of *rentier* exhaustion', and his capacity for being duped and used recalls Blore-Smith making his innocent way through Montmartre. The narrative is crudely constructed, a series of all too similar incidents jumbled together in great haste, with dreamlike transitions, so that the book is at the same time very short and very repetitive. These failings are made up for by innumerable passages of brilliant impressionist writing, in the manner of Connolly's journal entries, and by *pensées* and epigrams in the best Connolly manner.

Like Connolly himself, Naylor has spent years contemplating the writing of a novel, and has such an acute sense of its flavour that it seems scarcely necessary to get it down on paper. He has not written it, partly because he has been brought up on a 'dead literary English' which stifles impressionism, but also because the feeling that he is promising' is itself enough to satisfy – themes that Connolly would develop in his next book. He consoles himself that at least he has not churned out the typical young Englishman's first novel, 'a slop-pail for sex, quotations and insincerity'. He wants instead to devote his novel to 'the central concept of the nineteen-twenties – futility', and for all its imperfection as a narrative *The Rock Pool* precisely catches that theme, conveying the amorality and aimless hedonism of that period more realistically than Waugh or Powell, whose comic plots inevitably get in the way of sheer accuracy of reporting. At the end of the novel, Naylor is a more genuinely pathetic figure than Tony Last, because he is trapped in a jungle of his own making, a tangle of false hopes, conceit and foolish romanticism. As he subsides over his Pernod bottle in the hotel bedroom, he reassures himself that 'so far his life had only been ... false starts. ... Now it was going to break into a symphony. ...'

On 7 July 1936, Evelyn Waugh received a telegram from Rome that the annulment of his marriage had been allowed. 'I have got engaged to be married to Miss L. Herbert,' he wrote shortly afterwards to Mary Lygon. 'When I say engaged Miss H. and the Pope and I and Gabriel [Laura's sister] have made up our minds but it is not to be announced until after Xmas. ...'

By the time the annulment came through, Laura's mother had begun to regard Waugh as an acceptable son-in-law. For two years he had abstained from writing novels, and both *Edmund Campion* and *Waugh in Abyssinia* had raised his stock in the English Catholic community. Oldmeadow had not been roused again. When the Campion biography won the prestigious Hawthornden Prize in the spring of 1936, Waugh wrote to Mary Lygon that this recognition of the book's 'bon gout' had done him 'beaucoup de bon avec Mme Herbert'.

He proposed to Laura in the spring of 1936, before the annulment was granted, in a letter:

> You might think about me & whether, if those wop priests ever come to a decision, you could bear the idea of marrying me. ... I think it would be beastly for you, but think how nice it would be for me.

He was highly conscious of the difference in their ages – she was now twenty, he thirty-two – and tried to make light of it. Douglas Woodruff describes him, when Laura had been given a present, telling her to 'say thank you to the kind gentleman'. He told Laura: 'I dont look on you as very young even in your beauty.' (In photographs she does

293

not look much younger than him, thanks to her withdrawn, often sad expression.) His letters to her before their marriage are sometimes in playfully mock-childish language, with punctuation omitted, as if he wished to seem a fraction of his real age.

In his letter of proposal, he tried to emphasize his defects: 'I am restless & moody & misanthropic & lazy & have no money except what I earn and if I got ill you would starve.' But he told her he thought he might be able to:

> reform & become quite strict about not getting drunk and I am pretty sure I should be faithful. Also there is always a fair chance that there will be another bigger economic crash in which case if you had married a nobleman with a great house you might find yourself starving, while I am very clever and could probably earn a living of a sort somewhere.

Only at the end of the letter did he explicitly reveal the depth of his feeling: 'Eight days from now I shall be with you again, darling heart. I don't think of much else.'

Though in this letter he pictured himself as a nomad – 'we could do what we liked & go where we liked' – he determined, as the wedding approached, to buy himself a country house. 'Busy looking at houses which I find very pleasant indeed,' he wrote to his brother Alec. 'Have found a lovely one but dont know if I can get hold of it.' And in a later letter to Alec:

> Now that I am marrying procreating & purchasing property there is a thing which excites my curiosity . . . the validity of our coat of arms & crest. I may want to use it at my house. . . . I have always had some doubts as to whether we are entitled to it. We have certainly used it since the 18th century. I have some bookplates of our great-great-grand-father with it engraved. But stationers at that time had a way of inventing arms without reference to the College of Heralds. Do you think it worth asking them, and, if it proves spurious, having grant [a granting of arms] made? . . . It seems to me the kind of thing which isn't important now but which our children might well be grateful for if there were a change of fashion & heraldry came into general use again.

His evident desire to turn country gentleman was partly a protection of his and Laura's independence. During their engagement, it was proposed that they share Mrs Herbert's London house. Waugh, who had already 'worked myself into rage' with Mrs Herbert, would not contemplate the idea: 'Mind boggled at it.' To settle in the country in some style would also allay the fears that Laura's mother still sometimes felt about Waugh's suitability – it would be evidence that he wished to give up his nomadic ways, and by implication many other traits too.

He also had his own independent impulse towards the life that went with a country house. Indeed, he seems to have half-suspected that he wanted to get married largely so that he could experience that life. 'So often when people fall in love & want to be married,' he wrote to Laura, 'it is because they foresee a particular kind of life to which the other is necessary.' He reassured her that 'I don't feel that,' and said that in many ways it would be 'lovely' if they continued in the nomadic style to which he was accustomed – 'no possessions, no home, sometimes extravagant & luxurious, sometimes lying low & working hard'. Yet 'at other times I picture a settled patriarchal life with a large household, rather ceremonious & rather frugal . . .'.

Once embarked upon, the search for a country house began to take him over, to give this dream alarming scope. 'Am I getting folie de grandeur?' he wrote to Laura from Mells, where he was looking at several pieces of property. 'I originally thought of a £2,000 vicarage. Now I seem to be setting myself up as a squire.'

Financially, it did seem like folly. His income was as mercurial as he had suggested to Laura. During the autumn of 1936, he began work on a new novel in order to raise money for his marriage, and his letters to A.D. Peters show that he was as concerned about finance as ever. He was risking a lot even to contemplate a '£2,000 vicarage'.

Yet it was no random inclination. For years now, his life had revolved around great country houses and the families who inhabited them, Madresfield, Pixton Park, Mells Manor, Pakenham Hall and many others which he had visited. In his writing, the houses might themselves be superficially ludicrous – the ultra-modern King's Thursday, the farcical Doubting Hall, the monstrous mock-Arthurian Hetton Abbey – but they and the way of life for which they stood represented stability.

In his unfinished novel *Work Suspended*, written in 1939, Waugh suggests that his generation's enthusiasm for the architecture of the country house was a substitute for more common kinds of aesthetic emotion: 'We none of us wrote or read poetry, or, if we did, it was of a kind that left unsatisfied those wistful, half-romantic, half-aesthetic, peculiarly British longings which, in the past, used to find expression in so many slim lambskin volumes.' But there was more to it than that. Waugh's life from the beginning of his second marriage shows an almost anguished determination to identify with the landed aristocracy. In this, he was not alone among his generation.

*

Cyril Connolly expresses the feeling sharply in *Enemies of Promise*, when he speaks of the 'anguish' caused him by his uncertain position in the social system – the passage where he writes: 'Why had not my father got a title? ... Why be born, why live at all if I could not have one?' (In *The Rock Pool*, Connolly's hero has a nasty moment when, in conversation with a girl, he 'suddenly realized that she was middle-class and, worse, was assuming that he was'.) In his later years, Waugh admitted openly, if self-mockingly, to such sentiments. In 1951 Christopher Sykes happened to mention that his father had employed an Italian valet, whereupon Waugh was:

> overcome by self-pity. 'My father never had an Italian valet,' he whimpered.
> 'Well, my father never published any books, so we're quits,' I replied.
> 'Anyone can publish books,' he moaned, 'but only the great ones of the earth can have Italian valets.'

Waugh never made any pretence – which he could easily have done – that his forbears had been landed gentry. When Cyril Connolly implied, in the draft of a 1952 'profile' he was writing of Waugh, that they had been persons of means, Waugh wrote to him:

> The Waughs ... populated Berwickshire centuries ago & never knew the English distinction of squire and tenant.... [The] Rabans [his mother's family] were of Staffordshire yeoman stock who went to India at the end of the eighteenth century, made a modest fortune there & bought a modest Somerset property.

On another occasion, when reminded that he was descended from a peer, his great-great-grandfather being Lord Cockburn, a distinguished Scottish judge, he replied: 'Lord Cockburn was ennobled for practical reasons. I would like to be descended from a useless Lord.'

This was partly spoof. In 1933 he wrote: 'The larger one's humour and sensitiveness, the more readily does one's life slip into a habit of parody.' But it was only an exaggerated version of the aspirations of so many of his contemporaries, who moved among the aristocracy, married into it (Betjeman, Powell and even the egalitarian Henry Yorke, whose wife was the daughter of a peer), and identified with it as closely as they could.

These social aspirations sometimes caused amusement to those who had been born into the upper classes. Cyril Connolly, who, despite his anxieties, felt a cut above many of his friends, wrote in his journal in 1934: 'It amused me to hear Peter [Quennell] laughing at Evelyn's "provincial little Arnold Bennett *arriviste* appearance".' Quennell might laugh, but Waugh and others of his set were aping the aristocracy for reasons that ran deep into English cultural life.

Since the rise of the professional man of letters in Britain, writing had been regarded as a middle-class occupation. Hence Quennell's jibe. Even ultra-successful pre-1918 authors like Arnold Bennett and H.G. Wells had never managed to shake off their social origins, while by the 1920s and 1930s the notion of 'author' summoned in most people's minds the image of some thoroughly bourgeois figure such as J.B. Priestley. When Anthony Powell passed through Passport Control on his way back from Hollywood in 1937, the official glanced at his statement of 'Profession', and then at Powell's own appearance, remarking: 'Author? Where's your pipe?'

He might have added: 'And where's your country cottage?' First the Georgians and then the popular novelists had taken over the belief, derived from Wordsworth's circle, that literature should be written beneath a thatched roof with roses round the door. By 1935, the cottage was the symbol of success for the middlebrow author. Anthony Powell mentions that when John Heygate briefly became a popular novelist he took to living in one with She-Evelyn, and even writers who were making a fortune, such as Enid Blyton, disguised their substantial residences as country cottages. Higher up the intellectual scale, Hilaire Belloc's Kingsland and G.K. Chesterton's villa at Beaconsfield ('Top Meadow') were manifestations of a taste for simple rural pleasures, rather than statements of any aristocratic inclinations.

In *Enemies of Promise*, Cyril Connolly argues that the English writer's identification with the bourgeoisie had generally been his downfall, that while nineteenth-century France had produced Flaubert and Baudelaire, England had created Matthew Arnold and Tennyson, artists who, 'hamstrung by respectability', had been prevented from reaching their full dimensions by the 'snobbery and moral cowardice' of the class with whom they identified. Arguably, to have spawned even these two poets was no negligible achievement, and Connolly is (of course) omitting a host of other Victorians whose work shows little or no such limitation. Yet if the intellectual climate of nineteenth-century England was not nearly as poor as Connolly suggests, it is undeniable that soon after the First World War 'middle class' in England began to mean 'middlebrow'. Betjeman, guying the ghastly bad taste of suburbia, was recording the descent of the British bourgeoisie into a popular culture derived from the wireless, the illustrated magazines and the department stores, the process which Waugh refers to in *Rossetti* as 'the transition from industrialism to democracy'.

Betjeman's second collection of verse, *Continual Dew* (1937), is a tract against this general lowering of taste. It opens with a poem which records the moment in English cultural history when, Betjeman believes, the rot really began – the day on which the bourgeoisie made it clear to the artist that he must conform to middle-class behaviour, or suffer for it. This is 'The Arrest of Oscar Wilde at the Cadogan Hotel'. Surrounded by bourgeois architecture and decoration ('the Nottingham lace of the curtains ... Pont Street ... in her new built red'), and by the commercialization of what the Nineties had stood for ('So you've brought me the latest *Yellow Book*: / And Buchan has got in it now'),* Wilde, the symbol of the artist who lives for beauty and truth, is taken into custody by two policemen, whose distorted and pretentious vowels emphasize that they belong to the petty-bourgeoisie:

> 'Mr Woilde, we 've come for tew take yew
>   Where felons and criminals dwell:
> We must ask yew tew leave with us quoietly
>   For this *is* the Cadogan Hotel.'

Cyril Connolly, too, identifies Wilde's arrest and trial as a tragic turning point in English cultural life. 'The trial of Oscar Wilde', he writes in *Enemies of Promise*,

> was responsible for a flight from aestheticism which ... lasted twenty years.... From that moment the Philistine triumphed and ... romanticism was forced to be hearty. Hence the cult of beer and Sussex.... Hence the leanest years in the history of English verse.

Betjeman's *Continual Dew*, which was published by John Murray in the same mock-Victorian style as *Mount Zion*, quickly became notorious for the third poem in it, which states more passionately than anything else written by a member of the Waugh circle a hatred of the values of mid-twentieth-century bourgeois life. It therefore deserves to be quoted in full:

> Come, friendly bombs, and fall on Slough
> It isn't fit for humans now,
> There isn't grass to graze a cow
>   Swarm over, Death!

* In *Here, of All Places* (1959), Osbert Lancaster classifies 'Pont Street Dutch' as a perfect specimen of bourgeois degradation of fine architecture. Similarly *The Yellow Book*, the series of anthologies often thought of as enshrining the pure spirit of the Nineties, was a bourgeois commercial venture launched by John Lane with the intention of profiting from the Wilde group; Wilde himself was excluded from it as too extreme, whereas Arthur Waugh was invited to contribute.

Come, bombs, and blow to smithereens
Those air-conditioned, bright canteens,
Tinned fruit, tinned meat, tinned milk, tinned beans
   Tinned minds, tinned breath.

Mess up the mess they call a town –
A house for ninety-seven down
And once a week a half-a-crown
   For twenty years.

And get that man with double chin
Who'll always cheat and always win,
Who washes his repulsive skin
   In women's tears.

And smash his desk of polished oak
And smash his hands so used to stroke
And stop his boring dirty joke
   And make him yell.

But spare the bald young clerks who add
The profits of the stinking cad;
It's not their fault that they are mad,
   They've tasted Hell.

It's not their fault they do not know
The birdsong from the radio,
It's not their fault they often go
   To Maidenhead

And talk of sports and makes of cars
In various bogus Tudor bars
And daren't look up and see the stars
   But belch instead.

In labour-saving homes, with care
Their wives frizz out peroxide hair
And dry it in synthetic air
   And paint their nails.

Come, friendly bombs, and fall on Slough
To get it ready for the plough.
The cabbages are coming now;
   The earth exhales.

For Betjeman, as for Waugh in his first two novels, the modern waste land is not merely awful; it is quite literally Hell. And, as at the conclusion of *Vile Bodies*, a hypothetical Second World War is summoned up to destroy it.

The sentiments in Betjeman's 'Slough' can be found reflected and repeated in the writings of Waugh and every other member of his circle. In a 1938 article, Waugh fulminates against 'the style of the arterial highroads, the cinema studios, the face-cream factories, the tube stations of the farthest suburbs, the radio-ridden villas of the Sussex coast', while in *Vile Bodies* Nina's vision from the aeroplane of the awfulness of suburbia makes her vomit:

> Nina looked down and saw inclined at an odd angle a horizon of straggling red suburb; arterial roads dotted with little cars; factories, some of them working, others empty and decaying; a disused canal; some distant hills sown with bungalows; wireless masts and overhead power cables; men and women were indiscernible except as tiny spots; they were marrying and shopping and making money and having children.... 'I think I'm going to be sick,' said Nina.*

It is not merely a case of suburbia being awful; even the countryside suffers from the same blight. Anthony Powell's novels constantly imply this, with their emphasis on the aimlessness of country life. 'This waste land', Powell writes in his 1939 novel *What's Become of Waring*, describing a tract of Surrey heathland, 'might have been some walled-in space in the suburbs where business men practised golf-strokes; or the corner of a cinema studio used for shooting wilderness scenes. It had neither memories of the past nor hope for the future.' In such a setting there is, of course, no worthwhile occupation. 'I say, I hope you won't be bored,' remarks a character in the same novel, having invited the narrator down for the weekend. 'There is nothing whatever to do. Especially as you don't play golf.'

But it is suburbia that comes in for most of the assaults from the Waugh group. In *A Gun for Sale* (1936), Graham Greene describes a typical recently built suburban housing estate, with an implied distaste almost as strong as Betjeman's in 'Slough':

> She read the name of the new street: Shakespeare Avenue. Bright-red bricks and Tudor gables and half timbering, doors with stained glass, names like Restholme.... A big placard said: 'Come in and Inspect A Cozyhome. Ten Pounds Down and a House Is Yours.'

---

* Waugh does not seem to have observed that he and Betjeman were motivated by the same feelings. In a review of *Continual Dew* (in *Night and Day*, 25 November 1937), he describes Betjeman as 'an enthusiast' who, inspired by such oddities as Victorian Gothic, is definitely not a satirist. He makes no mention of their shared attitude to suburbia, and remarks on the 'haphazardness' of Betjeman's craftsmanship: 'No poem ... comes within measurable distance of artistic finish.'

And in *Brighton Rock* (1938), when Pinky and Rose tentatively venture out from the urban sprawl into the countryside:

> 'It's lovely,' Rose said, 'being out here – in the country with you.' Little tarred bungalows with tin roofs paraded backwards, gardens scratched in the chalk, dry flower-beds like Saxon emblems carved on the downs. Notices said 'Pull in Here', 'Mazawattee Tea', 'Genuine Antiques'.

Elsewhere in this novel, the gangsters drive out to the Queen of Hearts roadhouse, a Tudor barn converted into a restaurant and bar. 'This is *real* country,' observes one of them. 'I saw a hen just now. They use their own eggs in the gin slings.' In the opening passage of *The Lawless Roads* (1939), Greene describes his native Berkhamsted – a nondescript town within commuting distance of London – in the same terms:

> Smoke waved in the sky behind the Tudor Café and showed the 8.52 was in. You couldn't live in a place like this – it was somewhere to which you returned for sleep and rissoles.... Yellowing faces peered out of the photographer's window, through the diamonded Elizabethan pane – a genuine pane, but you couldn't believe it because of the Tudor Café across the street.... Boards marking desirable building lots dripped on short grass, and the skeletons of harrows lay unburied on the wet stubble.... Metroland loneliness....

In a 1944 satirical article, Cyril Connolly seems to be distancing himself from the anti-suburban passions of his friends, as he imagines how Betjeman's proposals for Slough might be put into action, so that 'bombs fell day and night on Bournemouth and Brighton, Southampton and Slough', until 'the landscape of England was revealed ... as if it were an eighteenth-century nobleman's deer park'. Yet in *The Unquiet Grave* (1944), he himself judges suburbia to be worse than the slums: 'Slums may well be breeding-grounds of crime, but middle-class suburbs are incubators of apathy and delirium. No city should be too large for a man to walk out of in a morning.'

No one living in England between 1918 and the present day would be likely to quarrel with Waugh and his friends for regretting the relentless growth of suburbia, the sprawl of the industrial cities, on purely architectural and environmental grounds. Yet Waugh and the others are objecting not just to suburban buildings, but to the people who live in them: Betjeman wants to destroy not merely Slough itself, but the businessman who has created it – 'Smash his hands ... make him yell.' A whole section of British society is being written off in much the same way as the Nazis were currently writing off the Jews.

Graham Greene, in *The Lawless Roads*, hints at a religious justification for this attitude; he calls the lifestyle of suburbia 'a sinless empty graceless chromium world'. A more plausible explanation for the passionate hatred he and the others directed towards suburban life is that the culture of Slough seemed to offer a serious threat to their very existence as artists. In *Enemies of Promise*, Connolly lists the manifestations of suburban taste in contemporary prose, fulminating against what he calls 'the new vernacular'; to be specific,

> the familiarities of the advertisements in the morning paper, the matey leaders in the *Daily Express*, the blather of the film critics, the wisecracks of newsreel commentators, the know-all autobiographies of political reporters, the thrillers and 'teccies, the personal confessions ... the gossip-writers who play Jesus at twenty-five pounds a week, the straight-from-the-shoulder men, the middlebrow novelists. . . .

The last figure in this list was the one Connolly and his friends feared and hated the most because, by making concessions to popular taste, he was undermining literature itself. In 1943 Waugh met J.B. Priestley, whom he considered to be the epitome of this breed of writer, and noted contemptuously in his diary: 'He sees himself as a man of great responsibility, as the epitome of the Common Man.' Another specimen of the middlebrow writer was Waugh's own brother Alec. In the summary of his own life that Evelyn Waugh wrote for the Penguin editions of his books, he states that he is 'brother of Alec Waugh the popular novelist', a statement that looks odd if 'popular' is taken to mean successful, since Evelyn's books always had immeasurably greater popularity. But he is defining terms. 'Popular' means middlebrow.

He and his friends admired the Nineties and the Wilde set (and began their own careers by imitating them) because Wilde and his associates had attempted to create a milieu for art that was remote from the common herd – and in consequence had been stamped out. Since then the scene had been barren. About fifteen years after Wilde's arrest, around 1910, the Bloomsbury Group had offered a new model of behaviour for the serious artist, but it was both too earnest and too exclusive for Waugh's generation. Harold Acton records Robert Byron praising the Paddington district of London as 'the symbol of all that Bloomsbury is not', and in *Enemies of Promise* Connolly complains that Virginia Woolf's early novels had spun 'cocoons of language out of nothing' (though he allowed that *The Waves* was a masterpiece).

Elsewhere, Connolly praises the Sitwells (another starting point for Acton and his friends) for combining 'art with dandyism', and so offering 'the only valid alternative to Bloomsbury'.

Modernism had scarcely scratched the surface of English cultural life. The so-called Georgians cornered the market in poetry until 1922, and Waugh's father's response to T.S. Eliot, in his blimpish review, was typical of the middle class of his generation. *The Waste Land* made its first appeal to those who were undergraduates when it appeared, not to the established literary set. *Ulysses* was only trickling into the country via smuggled copies until the end of the 1920s; a British edition was not published until 1936. Britain had produced few modernist painters of any importance, while its composers seemed not to have heard of Stravinsky. On this barren English soil was planted, during the 1920s, the culture of Slough. Small wonder that writers and artists who came to maturity during these years turned away from bourgeois values and sought other ideals.*

They were reacting not just against 'the new vernacular' in general, but specifically against their own fathers' taste. Ernest Betjemann's factory made such things as a 'Reynard the Fox' coffee set, with the handle of the pot in the shape of a hunting crop and the tray handles as horse-shoes. Betjemann *père* had no sense of history, not even of the immediate past, and accepted the notion of progress quite uncritically. He wrote to his son: 'The Victorians were unpleasant as a rule.... But let's not bother our heads about them, there is so much in the present world pulsating with thrills.' Arthur Waugh's taste had been uncompromisingly middlebrow. He regarded J.C. Squire as a bolder innovator in verse than 'the younger poets' (that is, the modernists and the war poets), praised *kitsch* historical novels like *Ben-Hur* and *The Cloister and the Hearth* for their 'opulent imagination', and called R.H. Benson's sentimental religious fiction 'almost blameless artistically'. He admired Galsworthy for his 'self-evident and open-hearted sincerity', and spoke of popular novelists such as Gilbert Cannan and Hugh Walpole in the same blandly enthusiastic tones as he judged Conrad and Henry James – 'Mr Conrad has the spirit of the sea in his veins....'

Immediately after Waugh's generation at Oxford came what Connolly called the 'pylon boys', W.H. Auden and his associates, who attempted to come to terms with contemporary English life by

---

* Ernest Hemingway and other young American writers had done much the same in Montparnasse between 1921 and 1928, beginning the search for a new lifestyle for the artist just as Waugh and his friends were making similar experiments at Oxford and in Mayfair.

embracing its most apparently unattractive elements – pylons, factories, the externals of industrialization – and by identifying with the common people, rather than trying to separate themselves from them. Waugh (writing in 1942) described their outlook as 'the new, complicated and stark crazy philosophy that only the poor are real and important and that the only live art is the art of the People'. Looking back at the 1930s (in his review of Stephen Spender's autobiography), he complained that they had 'ganged up and captured the decade', and alleged that they had really been sustained not by politics but by mutual admiration. (He did, however, admire Christopher Isherwood's novels.) Another link between many members of the Auden group, though Waugh did not mention this, was homosexuality. If Waugh and his associates tended to react against, and also imitate, their fathers, Auden's circle tended to be mother-dominated; Auden ascribed his homosexuality to his close childhood relationship with his mother, and later in life took to referring to himself as 'mother', just as Waugh turned himself into a caricature of a Victorian father.

Waugh's set took the other path from the 'Auden generation', attempting to revert to that period in English cultural history when, as Waugh states in his *Rossetti*, the controlling factor in the careers of artists had been the aristocracy. This choice offered obvious physical attractions – the life of country houses, Mayfair and St James's – and also seemed natural in a post-war world where hedonism was an automatic response to the prevailing sense of futility. In *The Pursuit of Love*, Nancy Mitford shrewdly points out that conservatism is partly a consequence of frivolity, of refusing to be 'committed' politically : 'You know, being a Conservative is much more restful ... whereas Communism seems to eat up all one's life and energy.'

One member of Waugh's circle did throw out lines into the Auden group. In *Living*, Henry Yorke had shown himself immensely skilled at describing the lives of working people with what seemed an insider's understanding; this earned him high praise from Auden, who once called him the finest living English novelist. A later 'Henry Green' novel, *Party Going* (1939) is unusual in portraying the potential class warfare in English society of the Thirties. It presents a group of idle rich shut up in a hotel at a fogbound railway terminus, while outside the crowds shout and roar in their thousands. *Party Going* is an unfunny version of Powell's *Afternoon Men*. Imprisoned by the steel doors which the hotel staff have shut against the impatient crowd, Yorke's characters flirt and fuss, deceive each other in a bored fashion, and revert again and again to speculating pointlessly about the comic antics of a legendary socialite, 'Embassy Richard'. Waugh had suggested that in Yorke's *Living* it was difficult to tell one factory worker from another, but in *Party Going* the not-so-bright young people remain virtually indistinguishable from start to finish. Outside in the station, the common people are having a good time – laughing, chanting, kissing – but, inside, the rich begin to fear that Armageddon has indeed arrived. 'Oh Moddom,' says one of their maids, 'do you think it's the revolution, Madam, and I have your bath-salts unpacked and your bath is ready for you now.'

Waugh made no pretence of tackling the class struggle.* In a 1937 *New Statesman* article, Connolly examined Waugh's motives for his perceptible drift to the right, and suggested that it was simply due to his taste for good living – that he had realized 'how entirely the kind of life [he] liked depended on close co-operation with the governing classes'. (Connolly liked it too, as his increasing physical bulk testified during the 1930s.) Nancy Mitford gives much the same explanation in *The Pursuit of Love*, defending high society as a desirable setting for lively minds because:

> whatever one may be in politics, right, left, Fascist, Communist, *les gens du monde* are the only possible ones for friends. You see, they have made a fine art of personal relationships and of all that pertains to them – manners, clothes, beautiful houses, good food, everything that makes life agreeable. It would be silly not to take advantage of that . . .

Waugh himself, in a 1943 *Tablet* review, examined his own motives less caustically, in the guise of discussing a past age when art was kept alive solely by the patronage of aristocrats:

> Aristocracy saved the artist in many ways. By its patronage it offered him rewards more coveted than the mere cash value of its purchases; in its security it invited him to share its own personal freedom of thought and movement; it provided the leisured reader whom alone it is worth addressing; it curbed the vanity of the publicist and drew a sharp line between fame and notoriety; by its caprices it encouraged experiment; its scepticism exposed the humbug.

In plainer English, this seems to mean that it is good for a writer to write for, and dwell among, the upper classes because it gives him social position and freedom to say what he likes about the rest of society; also, he acquires readers who have time to read his books, and are

---

* He did not, of course, see it in Marxist terms, as capitalism versus the working class, but as the English upper classes versus the rest, lumping bourgeoisie and proletariat together as the common herd.

used to all kinds of eccentricity, so that they tolerate literary experiment and are (through the excellence of their education) more discriminating than a mass audience.

In fact Waugh's audience has always been chiefly among the middle classes, who who have enjoyed his books not least because they give a vicarious experience of aristocratic life. If he had been more honest, he would have admitted that the standard of literacy among the titled and rich was considerably lower than that among the traditional (bourgeois) 'intelligentsia', while, as to the social position supposedly conferred upon an author who hobnobs with the titled, many of the titled felt that Waugh had conferred such a position upon himself, and unconvincingly at that.

Elsewhere, in a 1946 article in *Life*, Waugh argues that the English language requires the protection of an aristocratic society if it is not to become eroded through careless usage:

> It is the most lavish and delicate [language] which mankind has ever known. It is in perpetual danger of extinction and has survived so far by the combination of a high civilized society, where it was spoken and given its authority and sanctity, with a thin line of devotees who made its refinement and adornment their life's work.

Again, the argument that the English aristocrats (who, if they have any special linguistic character, tend to be monosyllabic and slangy) have made any contribution to the preservation of the language is hard to sustain, while the notion that language is a hothouse plant that requires delicate attention seems equally debatable.

What the society of the rich and titled indubitably gave Waugh was 'copy'. This, and his desire to resist the middlebrow populism which threatened to swallow the artist, might seem to provide sufficient reasons to identify with the aristocracy. Yet in *Enemies of Promise*, Connolly suggests a third, more purely artistic motive.

According to Connolly, there is a species of writer who may be labelled a dandy. Just as a dandy in fashionable society aspires to the greatest possible elegance, desiring to distinguish himself utterly from the herd, so the literary dandy separates himself from the bourgeoisie, whom he despises for their stupidity and hypocrisy, taking pains to avoid any 'vulgarity of writing'. He idealizes the aristocracy because they can indulge in style for its own sake, and the only non-aristocratic figures he admires entirely lack bourgeois ambitions and *mores* – they are unaware of evil, and display 'a muddled goodness'.

Connolly picks as his principal example of a literary dandy Ronald

Firbank, whose novels he examines at some length in this light. His list of other dandy-writers includes such diverse figures as Congreve, Beckford and T.S. Eliot, and excludes Waugh. Nevertheless, everything he picks out as characteristic in Firbank of the dandy-writer – the social attitudes, the love of language for its own sake, the characters who ignore bourgeois *mores* – is typical also of Waugh's fiction.

Connolly's definition of the literary dandy does not so much explain Waugh's desire to identify with the aristocracy as place him in a group which *per se* experiences such feelings. Like all labels, it has its limitations and dangers.* Nevertheless Connolly's passage usefully warns of the equal danger of treating Waugh merely as the puppet of cultural and social forces. While it is possible to argue that he wrote as he did in reaction to middlebrow culture, and that he identified with the aristocracy because he was dissatisfied with what had become the conventionally bourgeois image of the artist, Connolly reminds us that he may simply have been acting according to his own nature as a writer.

Malcolm Muggeridge has compared Waugh's posing as a country squire with George Orwell's adoption of the dress and style of the working class. Waugh perhaps perceived this, since he always wrote respectfully of Orwell, both in public and in private, though he felt that Orwell had 'not achieved neutrality' in the class war. Anthony Powell believes that, at the deepest level, Waugh did not really identify with the rich, that even when he was playing the prosperous country gentleman with right-wing views, 'something always remained beneath the surface of a kind of social resentment'. Christopher Sykes points out that Waugh's snobbery took the form less of looking up at the rich and titled than of looking down at the common herd, despising the culture that he wished to escape from: 'His belief in the existence of the "right" kind of people was very much weaker than his belief that there are "wrong" kinds.' Perhaps the most uncharitable and prosaic analysis of Waugh's motives in playing the squire was provided by Diana Cooper. She told him she thought his preference for 'marble halls' was 'hopelessly middle class', and added that he was 'like Arnold Bennett' – in other words, for all his desire to distinguish himself from the Bennett–Wells–Priestley species of literary man, he was simply behaving like the typical successful author.

*

* In his book *Children of the Sun* (1977), Martin Green treats Waugh and his circle exclusively as dandies, scarcely considering other aspects of their character and work. Though the book contains some sensible observations, it is overall a *reductio ad absurdum* of Connolly's definition of the literary dandy, pressing home its thesis so ruthlessly as to distort the real character of many people whom Green discusses.

His first plan was that he and Laura should make a home in the vicinity of Mells, but there was nothing in that district available on the right terms, and by the end of 1936, after he had been staying there for most of the autumn, he found the place 'oppressive'. For all his desire to impress the English Catholics, he did not want to live in a ghetto. He and Laura looked at a couple of houses in 'Berners Betjeman country', but this, too, was a clique with which he did not want to identify exclusively, so with a 'sense of guilt' at deserting his friends, he went to the area around Stroud, on the edge of the Severn Estuary, just below the Cotswolds. Here, he quickly found a house named Piers Court in the village of Stinchcombe. 'Absolutely first-rate, delighted,' he wrote in his diary. The village (and thus the house) were soon nick-named by him 'Stinkers'.

Piers Court in 1936 was exactly the sort of house Waugh described in an article on architectural style two years later:

> the gentleman's house, 'standing,' as the house-agents say, 'in twenty acres of park-like grounds; three acres well matured gardens; entrance lodge, carriage drive, stabling for twelve and other outbuildings . . . farmland at present let to long-established tenants; four recep., ten bed, usual offices, water by gravitation. Electric light available in near future. A feature of the property is the wealth of period decoration.' A lovely house where an aged colonel plays wireless music to an obese retriever.

Architecturally, Piers Court was an expression of Waugh's own personality at the time that he bought it. A severe Georgian frontage had been imposed on an essentially untidy house, mostly of Elizabethan date, that rambled on many unpredictable levels once the formal dining-room and library had been passed through. From the garden, the Severn Estuary could just be glimpsed, but the house resolutely turned its back on this and stared formidably at the visitor as he came up the drive.

In the mid-seventeenth century the house had been occupied by the Pynffold or Pinfold family, whose coat of arms was set in the Georgian façade; Waugh removed it and replaced it with his family's own, duly verified by the College of Heralds. He bought the house for £3,350, initially out of his own pocket – it was far more than he could easily afford – but then Laura's grandmother sent a cheque for the entire amount as a wedding present.

The wedding was arranged for mid-April 1937. In the preceding weeks, Laura paid two visits to Paris to buy her trousseau, and Waugh 'bought a chimney-piece and mirror, both Adam, and two very fine carved pedestals which I am having converted at enormous expense into bookcase ends'. The ceremony, on 17 April, at the Church of the Assumption, Warwick Street, was attended by Henry Yorke, John Sutro, Billy Clonmore, Hubert Duggan and a few others of Waugh's more respectable friends. Afterwards there was a reception; it was all a far more resplendent affair than his 1928 marriage. Waugh had written to Tom Driberg asking him not to mention in his *Daily Express* column that he had been married before – 'I think that by now most people have forgotten. . . .' The Waughs flew to Paris, dined at the Tour d'Argent on Laura's favourite dish (pressed duck), and spent 'some delicious days at Portofino'; the honeymoon was paid for by a wealthy lady whom Alec Waugh had recently married.

By mid-November, Evelyn and Laura had settled at Piers Court. Evelyn would wake in the morning to the sound of the tenant-farmer calling his cows in the field below the bedroom windows. A married couple had been engaged to serve them; there were also staff in the garden, where Waugh threw himself energetically into clearing and planting. A carpenter was engaged on a weekly wage, to build cupboards in the room that had been designated the night nursery. The first child, Maria Teresa, was born in March 1938. Waugh's public reaction was studiedly cool; in a note to A. D. Peters he refers merely to 'Laura's baby'.

He furnished the house chiefly in the Victorian style, with paintings by such nineteenth-century academicians as Augustus Egg, and was soon writing in *Harper's Bazaar* on how to keep a wine cellar, in the manner of someone who had been doing it for years: 'For the civilized Englishman port will always be a major interest. . . .' He said he found an 1860s hunting port 'a fine eleven-o'clock drink'. He dressed for dinner, whether or not there were guests. 'Yes, I normally wear a dinner jacket in the evenings,' he wrote to an acquaintance who was planning a visit.

It was all very far from the modest Waugh family home in North London. Yet Evelyn's affection for Georgian architecture and the aristocratic life suggests a fondness for symbols of firm paternal authority, a search for a sense of order that childhood had not given him. The opening chapter of his unfinished 1939 novel *Work Suspended* was originally entitled 'My Father's House', an image which might be applied to so much of his life and work.

4

Ourselves Against the World

In the intervals of establishing himself as a country gentleman, Waugh worked on his new novel, the book about journalists that he had intended to write since his experiences as a war correspondent. The opening chapter of *Scoop*, the only one of his pre-war novels to have an obviously appropriate title, concerns the efforts of the society beauty Julia Stitch to obtain for novelist John Boot the job of war reporter in Ishmaelia for the *Daily Beast*. In his diary, Waugh described this chapter as 'Diana's early morning'. Visiting Diana Cooper in 1972, Michael Davie found her behaving exactly like Mrs Stitch:

> She was in bed, wearing a pink peignoir; white face, brilliant red lips, arm in plaster, the counterpane smothered in catalogues, books, morning papers and Christmas cards. . . . When the telephone was not ringing, and Lady Diana was not searching for her spectacles or explaining the rudiments of flower arrangement to a Chinese servant, or talking to Randolph Churchill's second wife, she elucidated obscurities in [Waugh's] diaries. . . .

The account of Mrs Stitch driving her tiny car along the pavement was suggested by Lady Diana's antics in a baby Fiat, which she and Duff Cooper had spotted in a shop window in Venice, and driven back across Europe. The model for John Boot, who has punctuated his elegant fiction with 'unprofitable but modish works on history and travel', is Waugh himself.

From the London scene, *Scoop* shifts to Boot Magna, country home of William Boot, who is sent to Ishmaelia in mistake for his namesake. Like 'Last' in *A Handful of Dust*, the name 'Boot' suggests the final and in this case absurd extremity of the English landed gentry, though there is also a hint of the French *butte* (which Waugh informs us was the Norman version of the family's name) meaning 'butt' and often 'butt of a joke', which fits William's Paul Pennyfeatherish role in the novel. The Boot household, with its decaying parkland, its half-insane family, its attic full of superannuated nannies, and its ten servants whose time is chiefly occupied in consuming 'the five meat meals which daily tradition allowed them', may be even more of a caricature than Doubting Hall or Hetton Abbey, but it seems to have been drawn from life. Waugh's close involvement with Laura's family had plunged him into the eccentric realities of upper-class life; his diary records such details of the Herberts as that Laura's grandmother had 'taken a dislike to toast, believing the holes to be made by worms'. *Scoop* locates Boot Magna in the West Country near Taunton, exactly where Laura's home, Pixton Park, was to be found.

However comic Boot Magna may be, it represents, like all Waugh's country houses, permanence and self-certainty, and it is because he comes from such a home that William remains untainted by the tawdry world of the *Daily Beast* and its proprietor Lord Copper, who inhabits a fake Byzantine horror of an office such as Betjeman frequently mocked in the *Architectural Review*. The *Beast* as depicted by Waugh is a satirical portrait not so much of Fleet Street as of the notions of civilization held in contemporary suburban society. Mr Salter, Lord Copper's stooge, is Slough Man: 'Normal life, as he saw it,' writes Waugh, 'consisted in regular journeys by electric train, monthly cheques, communal amusements and a cosy horizon of slates and chimneys.' The novel reaches its comic climax when Salter with his suburban ways is pitted against the half-dotty but infinitely more resourceful family of Boots.

Though *Scoop* is chiefly a comedy of mistaken identities, it also, like most of Waugh's fiction, involves deprivation. William is plucked away from his secure country life and whisked off to Ishmaelia, where he falls in love but then loses the girl to someone else; moreover the knighthood intended for him goes by mistake to John. As usual, an elder brother figure has triumphed, though it is a member of the paternal generation – William's Uncle Theodore – who alone gets any material rewards from the whole business. However, the book is altogether sunnier than any of Waugh's fiction since *Decline and Fall*, reflecting the optimism with which he was embarking on his new marriage. It seems to have been intended partly as a tribute to P.G. Wodehouse, since Boot Magna bears more than a faint resemblance to Blandings Castle, and the elaborately layered misunderstandings recall the fine construction of a Wodehouse plot. Indeed, Waugh acknowledges Wodehouse in the final scene, where at Lord Copper's banquet Uncle Theodore and his neighbour discover a mutual acquaintance with one 'Bertie Wodehouse-Bonner'. As Waugh several times pointed out in print, Wodehouse's method was to create comedy out of a world which 'has never existed'. The triumph of *Scoop* was to achieve the same effect with real people and recent events.

Perhaps because *Waugh in Abyssinia* had been criticized for its pro-Italian sentiments, Waugh made obvious efforts to avoid political bias in *Scoop*. Though the Jackson family who control Ishmaelia are ludicrously given the names of prominent British liberals and left-wingers – Pankhurst Jackson, Huxley Jackson, General Gollancz Jackson, Mrs Earl Russell Jackson – Waugh balances this with a caricature of Fascism. The White Shirt movement, which is rebelling against the Jacksons, holds a comic version of the Fascist theory about an international Jewish conspiracy – the White Shirts fear the influence of 'international Negro finance and secret subversive Negro Bolshevism'. The book's villain, the black Communist would-be dictator, is named Mr Benito. In her 1946 *Horizon* article mapping out Waugh's changes of political attitude, Rose Macaulay noted approvingly that, compared to its immediate predecessors, *Scoop* was 'entirely good-tempered'.

Yet the novel is not quite neutral politically. By depicting Ishmaelia as a country where a Soviet-backed dictatorship is attempting to take power from the established rulers, Waugh was making an oblique comment on a conflict that was at its height while he was working on the novel, the Spanish Civil War.

At first he was inclined to treat that war as a joke: 'Well you only have to read the paper and see what is happening in Spain where the lower classes have the upper hand' (this was in the summer of 1936). Later, when asked for a public comment in Nancy Cunard's questionnaire *Authors Take Sides on the Spanish War*, published by the *Left Review* in November 1937, he sent a reply that was printed in the pro-Franco section. Since out of the 148 replies only four others had been so classified by Nancy Cunard, this effectively identified Waugh as against the views of the vast majority of his fellow-writers, and suggested that he was pro-Fascist.

The question sent out to the authors ran: 'Are you for, or against, the legal government and the people of Republican Spain?' – a loaded way of putting it, clearly hinting at the answer Nancy Cunard hoped for. In reply, Waugh declared himself dissatisfied with the wording:

> I know Spain only as a tourist and a reader of the newspapers. I am no more impressed by the 'legality' of the Valencia government than are English Communists by the legality of the Crown, Lords and Commons. I believe it was a bad government, rapidly deteriorating. If I were a Spaniard I should be fighting for General Franco. As an Englishman I am not in the predicament of choosing between two evils. I am not a Fascist nor shall I become one unless it were the only alternative to Marxism. It is mischievous to suggest that such a choice is imminent.

It was a clever answer, and by putting it in the pro-Franco section Nancy Cunard was ignoring its ambiguities.

In her defence, it should be noted that in his 1939 book *Robbery Under Law*, Waugh described himself as 'a partisan of Franco'. Yet even if he had come out unambiguously on the Fascist side of the conflict in 1937, his position would not have been so isolated as the Cunard questionnaire implied. Four British national newspapers supported Franco (the *Daily Mail, Morning Post, Daily Sketch* and *Observer*) and several others preserved neutrality. Nor had Nancy Cunard presented a complete and fair consensus of literary opinion; a number of writers – among them Hilaire Belloc, Roy Campbell and W. B. Yeats – would undoubtedly have taken the side of Franco if they had been asked (which they were not). She and her fellow-organizers wished to make the right wing appear as underpopulated as possible.

Moreover, several writers who visited Spain with a left-wing attitude to the conflict had come back with their ideology more than a little dented. Among these was Cyril Connolly. He made his first trip to the civil war in the summer of 1936, when idealism and hope were high on the Republican side, and he wrote about what he had seen in the *New Statesman*, in terms so eulogistic that they almost amounted to a parody of that journal's political viewpoint. He said he had found an 'absolutely new and all-pervading sense of moral elevation' among the various factions of Republicans, a marvellous 'flowering of humanity ... something which it would be an unimaginable piece of human malignity to destroy'. After a second and third visit (the latter in January 1937), his perceptions had changed, and he had to admit that 'it would be hard to find an atmosphere more full of envy, intrigue, rumour, and muddle than that which exists at the moment in the capitals of Republican Spain'. The idealism had collapsed into 'mutual accusations and reproaches'.

This report, again in the *New Statesman*, made Connolly very unpopular with the left wing; he says he was called 'a coward, a Fascist, a stabber-in-the-back, etc.' He did not attempt to respond, having no serious pretensions to political journalism; he noted in his journal that the first of his Spanish war journeys had been part of a 'Food Trip' that also took in a good deal of France. The January 1937 Spanish visit was in the company of Lord ('Ran') Antrim, who seems to have given the expedition rather a Pall Mall air: 'We motored to Valencia,' writes Connolly, 'and there things began to go wrong. Ran was given a terrible grilling by the communists – what did he want in Spain, what did he do etc? It shook him very much as he had never been treated except as a peer before. . . .'

Anthony Powell's closest contact with the Spanish war was while he was in Hollywood, where he attended a charity performance of Hemingway's film *Spanish Earth*. Hemingway himself made an appearance: 'He wore a dark-blue suit and leant against the lectern. . . . What he read had no very personal touch, except perhaps when he referred to a shell's direct hit on a train: 'Two persons were taken to hospital, the rest removed with shovels.' This report by Powell appeared under the heading 'A Reporter in Los Angeles' in a new London magazine, *Night and Day*. One of the founders of this journal was Graham Greene; contributors included Waugh, Connolly, Betjeman and Osbert Lancaster. Powell explains that the Waugh 'set was making an attempt 'to dislodge *Punch*'.

Night and Day – the Cole Porter title was intended to suggest metropolitan sophistication – was launched at a cocktail party for eight hundred guests at the Dorchester Hotel. The publishers were Chatto & Windus, Graham Greene was one of the three editors, and the first issue, dated 1 July 1937, promised well. In appearance the magazine closely resembled the *New Yorker*, with sophisticated cartoons, a film column by Greene, and the first of a weekly series of book reviews by Waugh. He had originally been offered the theatre column, but declined it because 'I can't bind myself to be in London every week. . . . I remember', continued this letter to Graham Greene, 'being approached in 1929 by a London *New Yorker* that never materialized. Is yours soundly backed?'

It was – the Chatto partners and other shareholders had raised £19,000 capital – and at first *Punch* was scared. It soon appeared that the editorial policy was to invite well-known people to write on unlikely subjects. Herbert Read undertook to review detective fiction, while Pamela Hansford Johnson reported on croquet, William Plomer on all-in wrestling, A.J.A. Symons on restaurants, and Louis MacNeice on the Kennel Club. More conventional allocations of author and subject were Hugh Casson on architecture and Osbert Lancaster on stately homes, while Alastair Cooke contributed an occasional letter from America.

Though there was no overt political stance, the prevailing tone was affluent, upper class and implicitly anti-left. Advertisements were directed at a Mayfair (or would-be Mayfair) readership. The weekly profile 'In the Lions' Den' turned its attention on 14 October 1937 to Ribbentrop, at that time German Ambassador in London, whom it praised as a 'charming amateur diplomat'. An article on wine expressed relief that the civil war had not interrupted the Spanish sherry trade, and though the literary left was allowed to put in an occasional appearance – besides MacNeice there was a contribution from Christopher Isherwood (an excerpt from his forthcoming *Lions and Shadows*) – the magazine's detachment from the Auden gang was summed up in an unsigned cartoon which has been attributed to Cyril Connolly. It depicts a young man, with features resembling Auden's, informing a portly dame stretched before him on a chaise longue: 'I'm sorry, my dear Countess, but I still feel pretty Left Wing.'

This attitude often became explicit in Waugh's weekly book reviews. On 8 July 1937 he laid into *The Mind in Chains*, a symposium on the benefits to be obtained from the Marxist state, edited by C. Day Lewis. 'Marxians', declared Waugh contemptuously, 'believe, more firmly than any Rotarian, that prosperity is round the corner.' Though MacNeice was an occasional contributor to *Night and Day*, Waugh savaged his and Auden's *Letters from Iceland*: 'The book, if book it can be called, is flabby, pretentious, and humourless.' Reviewing *May the Twelfth*, an account by Mass Observation (an offshoot of the Auden group) of the British public's behaviour on the day of the coronation of George VI, Waugh said he found much of it 'highly amusing', but he took issue with the Mass Observation philosophy. Claiming that most Mass Observers were members of 'the middle forms of the Gollancz extension school' (Victor Gollancz was the publisher of the Left Book Club), he pointed out that 'Mass Observation is based on the rudest of classifications – upper class, middle class, lower class; old, middle-aged, young', whereas 'it is the basic assumption of all traditional Christian art and philosophy that every human being is possessed of free will, reason and personal desires'. It became his habit, when matters of class-distinction were raised in print, to assert that Christianity teaches that we are all individuals in the sight of God, and therefore class distinctions must be meaningless.

John Betjeman had a regular column in *Night and Day*. For its readers, he invented a character called Percy Progress, an embodiment of all that seemed deplorable in modern urban, and especially suburban, life. Like Captain Grimes, Percy is proud of his public school education. He went to (the fictitious) Carshalton, and refers to other old boys as 'Old Cag Bags', but 'I wear the Old Harrovian tie for business purposes, of course'. Percy has made his pile from Back Numbers Ltd, a firm which hires out old magazines, bought at waste-paper rates, to dentists' waiting rooms, though later he expands into the manufacture of (dangerously inflammable) cigarette holders, and engages in such ventures as Hoots Waha! Synthetic Whisky, Chemical Fruits Ltd, the Beautisite Billposting Co., and property development – he is managing director of Tudor Bungalettes Ltd ('for a trifling extra payment stained glass may be set in the upper lights of the windows').

Percy lives in the heart of suburbia, at Olde Chimneys, 142 Maconochie Way, Iver, Bucks (on the edge of Slough), and gives his recreation as 'platinum blondes'. He possesses 'a honking little sports car that'll rev up to fifty', in which 'little bus' he spends much of his spare time. 'I must say there's nothing like spinning down a by-pass when you've got a drop of drink in you and a couple of cuties to while away the irksome.' One afternoon, he and 'some really good sports' have a 'paper chase' all over a peer's country estate, which means scattering waste-paper out of the car as they drive. Another country outing involves experiments with a mammoth loudspeaker, which broadcasts to the surrounding population from the top of the Wiltshire Downs: 'We called ourselves "The Noise Gang". I took some records – Bing Crosby crooning, and some experimental ones of gear-changing on a cheap car, realizing that these are the two chief noises you hear nowadays.' Percy buys the loudspeaker from his friend who has invented it for ten pounds, and sells the patent for half a million. 'That's the way to do business, boys. Cheer-bye.'

In his weekly film column in *Night and Day*, Graham Greene was moved to anger as white-hot as Betjeman's, in his case by the dubious motives of the film industry. He was particularly sensitive to the nuances of screen sexuality, describing how Jean Harlow in *Saratoga* 'toted a breast like a man totes a gun'. He extended this sexual scrutiny to the reigning child star Shirley Temple, then aged nine, with serious consequences for himself and *Night and Day*. Earlier, while reviewing films for the *Spectator* in 1936, Greene had commented of her performance in *Captain January* that she had 'an oddly precocious body' and was 'as voluptuous in grey flannel trousers as Miss Dietrich'. On 28 October 1937, in *Night and Day*, he turned his attention to the Twentieth Century Fox screen version (or travesty) of Kipling's *Wee Willie Winkie*, in which Miss Temple starred. Reminding himself of her 'neat and well-developed rump' in *Captain January*, he declared that her resemblance to a child was only skin deep. 'Middle-aged men and clergymen' found her sexually alluring, he alleged, and were protected from conscious awareness of this only because of the 'safety curtain' of her juvenile mannerisms.

Readers of *Night and Day* might have surmised from this that Greene himself was powerfully attracted to her, but Twentieth Century Fox chose to read it as a slur on their own good name, and they served writs on magazine and reviewer. Greene, who was abroad, told a friend that he had received a cable 'asking me to apologize to that little bitch Shirley Temple'. An apology was not enough, and the case came to court, resulting in the payment of £3,500 damages, the film company insisting that Greene contribute £500 of this himself. There was even a threat that he might be prosecuted by the Crown for criminal libel. *

The libel settlement would probably have closed *Night and Day* had not the magazine already ceased publication by the time the case came to court. Sales had not been high, the circulation of *Punch* was never seriously threatened, and no more issues appeared after Christmas 1937. Waugh had already been commissioned by Greene to write his next book review when the news of closure reached him. 'I received your telegram this morning,' he replied to Greene, 'after the enclosed article had been written. As it had been definitely commissioned, and as it is unsaleable elsewhere, I am afraid that I must hold you to your offer, whether you print it or not.'

The failure of *Night and Day* was partly due to its lack of professional humorists, experts in the short comic piece that was the chief ingredient of *Punch*. An exception was Cyril Connolly, whose contributions are among the few really funny things in it.

* It was Greene's third libel suit. J. B. Priestley had sued because he believed himself to be portrayed unsympathetically in *Stamboul Train*, and a government doctor in Sierra Leone had insisted upon the withdrawal of *Journey Without Maps* because Greene had inadvertently taken his name for a character in the book.

Like Betjeman's, they take the form of a diary supposedly written by a representative of a facet of contemporary society which Waugh and his friends regarded with particular horror, in this case the middle-class middlebrow. The Arquebus family lives in Hampstead. 'Dads is the head,' explains Felicity Arquebus, daughter of the house and author of the diary. 'He is Philip Arquebus and I expect not unknown to you.' A man of letters by profession, he bears a strong resemblance to Arthur Waugh. Felicity describes him as an 'author, essayist, talker, quoter, no mean cricketer and philosopher, an earl's great great nephew through Granny, and literary adviser to some publishers, and "the famous critic" too, of course. And he wields no mean skittle either.' Felicity's own bookshelves are crowded with middlebrow fiction: 'Phyllis Bentley, Phillis Bottome, Helen Waddell, Helen Simpson, G.B. Storm . . . new writers who left one rather breathless, and whose books had lovely cold names like *Open the Sky* and *Armed October*.' Her room is decorated with 'plaster gargoyles from the little shop near Notre Dame'.

The family, 'The House of Arquebus' as Felicity calls it, exists in an atmosphere of cosy jollity, with much use of nicknames and family jokes. The only cause of strife is Felicity's brother's political inclinations: 'Chris who's at Cambridge and terribly Left. All his friends are communist and one is CP!' When Chris comes into dinner, 'Dads' observes: 'Well, Chris, not gone to Madrid yet?' By the end of the evening, Chris is seen sloping out with a suitcase:

> Uncle Pat makes one of his Eyeless in Gaza noises. Chris goes out and is tiresomely careful *not* to slam the door. 'Supposing he does go?' says the B[oy] F[riend].
> 'How's the exchequer, Mrs Arquebus?' says Dads.
> 'He had nine and elevenpence when Nurse turned out his suit this morning.'
> 'And I've locked his passport up – he won't get farther than Cook's. I think somehow before the night is out we shall be a united family again.' Dads *can* be sweet.

If Connolly had collected his Arquebus pieces and written some more, the result could have been one of the funniest books of the decade. Instead, during the few months in which *Night and Day* was appearing, he completed *Enemies of Promise*, which was published at the end of 1938. Waugh reviewed it in the *Tablet*, and described Connolly as 'the only man under 40 who shows any sign of reaching . . . the Art of

Criticism', but he judged the book to be 'structurally jerry-built', alleging that it consisted of 'the secondary stages of three separate books'.

There are indeed three separate treatises in *Enemies of Promise*, an autobiography (which comes last in the volume), an examination of the contemporary predicament of English prose, and an analysis of the various snares that lie in wait for the 'promising' writer. The three parts do not really cohere into one argument – it scarcely matters in which order they are read – but the random and unpredictable form of the book entirely suits Connolly's aphoristic talents.

Waugh, however, felt the lack of structure to be a serious fault, and this goaded him into one of his rare statements of artistic principle. He said he did not like the term 'creative' as a term for writers:

> A better word, except that it would always involve explanation, would be 'architectural'. I believe that what makes a writer, as distinct from a clever and cultured man who can write, is an added energy and breadth of vision which enables him to conceive and complete a structure.

It was lack of this 'architectural' faculty that seemed to him the cause of Connolly's literary failure – if failure there had really been. He faulted Connolly for allowing the book to become 'jumbled up with the flattest clichés', and called the autobiographical section of *Enemies of Promise* 'highly embarrassing to the reader', but described Connolly's literary career to date as one 'which some of us might envy and all of us honour'. He did, however, conclude the review by taking issue strongly with Connolly's observations about writers and politics.

Though, in *Enemies of Promise*, Connolly lists politics among the various 'weeds' that have tangled the growth of writers, he comes down firmly on the left-wing side, in terminology that again seems almost a parody: 'Today the forces of life and progress are ranging on one side, those of reaction and death on the other. We are having to choose between democracy and fascism, and fascism is the enemy of art.' Another thrust seems to be aimed even more closely at Waugh himself:

> there is a seediness, an ebb of life, a philosophy of taking rather than giving, a bitterness and brutality about right-wing writers now which was absent in those of other days, in seventeenth-century Churchmen or eighteenth-century Tories. There is no longer . . . a Doctor Johnson . . . on the reactionary side.

From this, Connolly goes on rather lamely to admit that he himself is only a fellow-traveller with the left: 'There is a general left-wing position which has never been defined but which . . . is well suited to a writer.' He declares that such a writer is convinced 'that his future is bound up with the working classes', which in practical terms means 'a disinclination to wear a hat or a stiff collar, an inability to be rude to waiters or taxi-drivers or to be polite to young men of his own age with rolled umbrellas, bowler hats and "Mayfair men" moustaches'. Connolly also conveniently forgets his own disillusionment with the Spanish Civil War: 'Spain has done an immense amount for writers. . . . many . . . have come back with their fear changed to love, isolation to union, and indifference to action.' Waugh's response to all this was predictable: 'Mr Connolly finally surrenders himself [to] the cold, dark pit of politics into which all his young friends have gone tobogganing; the fear of Fascism, that is the new fear of Hell to the new Quakers. It is indeed a sorry end to so much talent.' He hoped, in conclusion, that Connolly would one day 'think out for himself what Fascism means'.

Precisely what Fascism did mean was not explained by him in this review, but in the *Spectator* a few weeks later, reviewing a new book by H.G. Wells, he gave his own definition of it. He said that Wells had perceived that 'the preposterous distinction between Left and Right' was sheer nonsense as an analysis of contemporary politics. England was not torn between Communism and Fascism. What had arisen was 'a single proletarian movement aimed at the destruction of traditional culture'. The apparent split between left and right was only a distinction made by those too puerile and ignorant to observe the 'basic agreement' between these two proletarian movements. Both movements, he might have added, could find their way of life portrayed in Betjeman's 'Slough'.

Although it was more than a decade since he had joined the Catholic Church, Greene had so far left religious questions outside his novels. Now, he says, the Spanish Civil War had 'inextricably involved religion in contemporary life', and he felt he must begin 'to examine more closely the effect of faith on action'. (He himself had tried, but failed, to get to Bilbao to observe the strongly Catholic Basque separatists' resistance to Franco.) However, a sceptical observer of Greene's career might suspect a more mundane motive for the introduction of Catholicism into his fiction. Although he had now published seven novels, he had experienced little critical or commercial success, and it was clearly time to try something different. Spain had made Catholicism a fashionable subject.

The assassin Raven in Greene's 1936 thriller *A Gun for Sale* knows all about religion but despises it – 'You believe in this? This junk?'

Pinkie, the teenage gangleader of the racecourse mobsters in *Brighton Rock* (1938), does believe. He and Rose, the waitress he is obliged to marry to stop her 'grassing' on the gang's murder of the seedy journalist Hale, are both Catholics, and Pinkie is conscious and proud of his own evil, like Milton's Satan. 'I don't take any stock of religion,' he tells Rose. 'Hell – it's just there. You don't need to think of it – not before you die.' He vaguely trusts in the possibility of a merciful God who will save his soul at the last moment. The book appears to be built around this religious crux; yet there is something not altogether serious about it.

Greene says that after its publication 'I was discovered to be – detestable term! – a Catholic writer.' Catholics began to treat him with special kindness, as a member of the clan who should not be disowned in any circumstances, while non-Catholic critics tended to blame his faults on his religion. He emphasizes that this seemed strange to him, since 'the ideas of my Catholic characters, even their Catholic ideas, were not necessarily mine' – a key to *Brighton Rock*.

Greene's own childhood had not been coloured by the fear of Hell and hope of salvation which is at the centre of Pinkie's and Rose's lives. As an adult convert, a man of intellect who by his own account had joined the Catholic Church without emotion, he inevitably felt some detachment from these attitudes. In *Brighton Rock* he is portraying the sort of people he knew to belong to his Church, but the authorial camera is as far above them as it was above the working-class characters in *It's a Battlefield*. The social snobbery has disappeared to be replaced by a kind of religious snobbery. *Brighton Rock* is not really a Catholic novel in the way that, say, Chesterton's Father Brown stories are Catholic fictions, exercises designed to prove that Catholicism is paradoxical yet true, but a novel about a certain kind of Catholic. The absence of any real religious feeling at the heart of the book is demonstrated by Pinkie's abrupt death, which Greene narrates in a manner that entirely ignores the supposedly central question of his salvation or damnation, but satisfies a very secular lust for justice. Greene was being honest with himself when, in a reissue of *Brighton Rock* a few years later, he subtitled the book 'An Entertainment'.

Though *Brighton Rock* is a melodrama rather than a genuinely serious study of 'the appalling strangeness of the mercy of God' (words used by a priest in the final chapter), Greene alleges that the writing of it increased his desire to investigate what he calls 'the effect of faith on action', and he obtained a commission to write a book on the condition of Catholicism in Mexico, where it had been persecuted by the nominally socialist dictatorship since the mid-1920s. The persecution had mostly abated by 1938, though the majority of churches were still ruined or in secular use, and memories were fresh of such incidents as the execution by firing squad of a young Jesuit, Father Miguel Pro; Greene was given a picture postcard depicting his last minutes and the administration of the *coup de grâce*.

Greene's account of what he saw in Mexico, *The Lawless Roads* (1939), describes the country as riddled with corruption and violence, and shows that the so-called socialist reforms had amounted to little more than religious persecution and the building of showy roads which were already collapsing. He refrained from comment on the wider political implications of this, confining himself for the most part to an investigation of the effects of persecution on the faith of the population. In the early part of the book, he speaks of Catholicism with a fervour not previously found in his writings. In Monterrey, he went to Mass in the Cathedral and, finding a congregation of old women and giggling girls, wondered if the government's prophecy that the churches would soon empty themselves might not come true. But:

> what did it matter in the long run, anyway? God didn't cease to exist when men lost their faith in Him.... During the ... persecution ... He had been carried in a small boy's pocket into prisons; He had been consumed in drawing-rooms and in garages. He had Eternity on His side.

On occasions like this, Greene felt a deep affinity with his co-religionists. 'It was home,' he writes of Benediction in a luridly decorated church. At last there was a strong emotional element to his faith: 'Even if it were all untrue and there was no God, surely life was happier with the enormous supernatural promise than with the petty social fulfilment, the tiny pension and the machine-made furniture.' Catholicism seemed the only acceptable alternative to Slough.

However, as he penetrated deeper into Mexico, this feeling of elation gave way to more mixed emotions. He had chosen to travel to regions of the interior where Catholicism was still suppressed, and he found his journey – by river-steamer, light aeroplane, motor-car and mule – almost as arduous as Waugh's trip in South America had been some years earlier. Like Waugh, he experienced the horrors of acute boredom, waiting endlessly in small settlements for unpredictable transport, having exhausted his reading-matter, and like Waugh he finally succumbed to misanthropy. After a few weeks Mexico began to seem a 'hating and hateful country'. Ill with dysentery, disillusioned with the way many Catholics degraded their religion – a supposedly miraculous shrine which Greene had travelled to see proved to be a cheap picture of a saint kept, for motives of profit, in a tea-caddy – he wrote bitterly in his diary: 'If Spain is like this, I can understand the temptation to massacre.'

Yet, returning to London, he wondered why he had particularly disliked Mexico. England seemed just as bad: 'Victorian houses falling into decay . . . a coal merchant's window with some fuel arranged in an iron basket, a gas showroom . . .'. He was at one with the conclusion of *Vile Bodies* and with Betjeman's hopes for Slough: 'How could a world like this end in anything but war?'

Reviewing Greene's book on Mexico, Evelyn Waugh said he had awaited it eagerly, since he himself had set out for Mexico shortly after Greene had returned. He felt Greene's *The Lawless Roads* to be 'a formidable rival' to his own book on conditions there, shortly to be published.

In the spring of 1938 he had been offered a journey to Mexico at the expense of the wealthy Pearson family, on condition that he would write a book exposing the injustice of the Mexican government's recent appropriation of international oil companies, in which the Pearsons had a financial interest. Waugh accepted the large cash payment that was offered, plus an expense account of £800, and Laura accompanied him. The trip occupied three months, from August to October 1938, and his book appeared the next year. Though it duly fulminates against Mexico for confiscating the oil companies' assets – its title is *Robbery Under Law* – nowhere does Waugh mention that his trip was paid for by the Pearsons.

Unlike Greene, he lived in comfort – his and Laura's base was the Ritz in Mexico City – and travelled comparatively little. Besides being drawn from only a very limited knowledge of Mexico, the book is not crafted to his usual standard; its tone alternates between heavy didacticism and peevish bickering. Whereas Greene had made the persecution of the Church into gripping, horrific reading, Waugh spends much of his chapter on this subject quarrelling with one Ernest Gruening, who had written in defence of Mexican socialism.

Waugh mocks socialists who come to Mexico to observe the benefits of the revolution: 'These credulous pilgrims pursue their quest for the promised land; constantly disappointed, never disillusioned.' And he defines socialism as a creed which teaches man that 'his real duty in life ... is to get through the largest possible amount of consumable goods and to produce these goods in the largest possible quantities so that he may consume them'. The book ends, not so very differently from Greene's, by taking Mexico as a cautionary tale for the rest of civilization: 'Barbarism is never finally defeated.... There is nothing, except ourselves, to stop our own countries becoming like Mexico.' Indeed, the whole book is a laboured attack on the socialist outlook, ignoring the fact (made clear by Greene) that the Mexican government was not really socialist at all.

For all its blimpishness on the subject of socialism, *Robbery Under Law* does not mark a further stage in Waugh's journey into the right wing. He concludes his introduction with a declaration of apparently reactionary political opinions, beginning with the statement 'I was a conservative when I went to Mexico and ... everything I saw there strengthened my opinions. ... I believe', he continues,

> that man is, by nature, an exile and will never be self-sufficient or complete on this earth.... I believe in government ... but [this] should be kept to the bare minimum of safety; that there is no form of government ordained from God as being better than any other.... I believe that inequalities of wealth and position are inevitable and that it is therefore meaningless to discuss their elimination; that men naturally arrange themselves in a system of classes; that such a system is necessary for any form of co-operative work, more particularly the work of keeping a nation together. I believe in nationality; not in terms of race or divine commissions for world conquest, but simply [that] mankind inevitably organizes itself into communities. ... I do not think that British prosperity must necessarily be inimical to anyone else, but if ... it is, I want Britain to prosper.... Most of the greatest art has appeared under systems of political tyranny, but I do not think it has a connection with any particular system, least of all with representative government.... Artists have always spent some of their spare time in flattering the governments under whom they live, so it is natural that, at the moment, English, American and French artists, should be volubly democratic.

Under the apparently conservative surface this is a mild, pragmatic view of humanity, short on sympathy for the underdog, but in no respect extremist or Fascist, and amounting to little more than *sauve qui peut*. Taken alongside the rest of *Robbery Under Law*, it may sound like a blustering English squire, but on its own it can be read as an attack on all forms of totalitarianism, and on the infiltration of politics into art. Elsewhere in the Introduction, he attacks the Nazi attitude towards race: 'Education was a monopoly of the Church [in Mexico];

which is the sounder, the catechism, or the race-mythology taught in half the schools of Europe today?'

Graham Greene had not intended to write a further book on Mexico, but was greatly struck by a story told him during his travels there. Staying with a doctor of Scottish extraction in Villahermosa, capital of the state where the persecution had been worst, he asked about a certain priest who had fled: '"Oh," [Dr Fitzpatrick] said, "he was just what we call a whisky priest." He had taken one of his sons to be baptized, but the priest was drunk and would insist on naming him Brigitta.' From this there grew, during the months following Greene's return to England, the novel that gave him 'more satisfaction' than any he had yet written, which was also 'the only novel I have written to a thesis'.

The Power and the Glory (1940) does indeed seem to be a simple exposition of a clear idea, that a man does not necessarily save his soul by keeping the rules. The unnamed 'whisky priest' who is the book's hero is an alcoholic and a fornicator, weak and fearful, yet twice in the story he turns his back on an easy escape from his persecutors because a priest is needed by someone sick or dying, and when he finally goes to execution it is not with the proud certainty of some copybook martyr, but with fear, humility and a conviction of his own worthlessness.

The novel appears to be a radical departure from Greene's authorial detachment and impersonal cinematic manner. Virtually everything is seen through the eyes of the priest, and Greene totally rejects the secular socialism represented by the police lieutenant who is pursuing him, accepting the priest's argument that it is better to leave the poor in poverty if their souls are thereby saved: 'It's better to let [the poor man] die in dirt and wake in heaven – so long as we don't push his face in the dirt.' Such a reaction might seem natural after Greene had witnessed the results of the Mexican persecutions, and seen the shoddiness of the country's attempts at socialism.

Yet the dissimilarity to his earlier novels is not as great as might at first appear. Once again, the narrative concerns a man on the run who is saved from complete moral failure by the opposite sex – except that this time it is not an adult woman who helps him, but two children, Coral, daughter of a British plantation owner, who shelters him and is converted by him from the shallow rationalism in which she has been brought up, and the priest's own daughter by a village woman, a child whom he loves and prays for in spite of her brutal scorn for him.

Though the novel is superficially set in Mexico, Greene makes strikingly little effort to evoke a specifically Mexican atmosphere. The terrain of small villages and shoddy towns is the usual anonymous setting of his novels, a place where life is lived in a seedy, dangerous way. Certainly Greene took the surface details of most of the subsidiary characters from people he had met in Mexico, a shabby dyspeptic dentist, an ingratiating half-caste, a priggish Lutheran and his sister, originals of whom may easily be found in *The Lawless Roads* ('I was handing out alternative destinies to real people whom I had encountered on my journey,' Greene writes). Yet the central character of the whisky priest himself bears no resemblance to the dissolute figure Dr Fitzgerald had described to him. Instead of an amiable Mexican scoundrel, holy in spite of himself, Greene portrays somebody very different.

The very title 'whisky priest' is misleading. The priest's preferred drink is brandy, and his craving for it is very mild; he uses it only as an analgesic to drive away fear and misery, and nowhere in the book does he get drunk. When he spends his few remaining *pesos* on drink, it is in the hope of obtaining wine with which he can say Mass. Certainly he has begotten a daughter on a village Indian woman, but only in a moment of tipsy exuberance long before the beginning of the novel, and this single indiscretion is contrasted with the pathetic and ludicrous Father José, who has obeyed the decree that, to escape the firing squad, all priests must marry; he has saddled himself with his former housekeeper, who keeps crying 'Come to bed, José!'

The whisky priest, then, does not altogether behave according to Greene's thesis. Far from being a degraded wretch who is saved in spite of his failings, he is the only man in the story with integrity. His lapses do not amount to much when set against his capacity for fidelity, love and self-sacrifice, which the novel constantly emphasizes. In fact the lapses enhance him, for they keep him on the fleshly level and prevent him from becoming inaccessibly good. He is the kind of man whom reader and author would like to be; indeed, Greene seems to be hinting that he himself is the priest. This is how he first introduces the man: 'He had protuberant eyes; he gave an impression of unstable hilarity, as if perhaps he had been celebrating a birthday, alone.' This recalls descriptions of Greene himself. 'Most of all,' writes A. L. Rowse, who knew him at Oxford, 'one was struck by those staring, china-blue eyes. . . .' And Peter Quennell writes of Greene at school: 'His contemplation of the horrors of human life appeared to cause him unaffected hilarity.' Even the fact that the priest drinks brandy rather than whisky is another detail hinting at self-portrait. In *The Lawless Roads*, Greene describes how he frequently had to resort to 'the brandy I had bought in Veracruz (poisonous stuff)' to ward off boredom and discomfort.

The whisky priest, then, is Greene himself, confronted on one hand by the Catholic Church with its pieties and self-certainties, and on the other by the equally pious and self-certain socialist ideals of so many 1930s intellectuals. He feels drawn to both, and at the same time can see the limitations of each. As he has said of his 'divided loyalties' in schooldays – son of the Headmaster and victim of the school – 'I belonged to neither side.'

Waugh did not contemplate writing a Mexican novel. After his trip was over and *Robbery Under Law* written, he subsided into what had already become the bore of country life. 'In the twenty-five mile radius of my house there are three great houses,' he wrote in *Harper's Bazaar* in July 1939; 'each is in the possession of the family which has held it for generations.' What this meant in practice is recorded in his diary: 'Dined with Lady Featherstone Godley. Bad dinner, bad wine, middle-aged military men boasting about their ancestry.'

When he did began a new novel, it had nothing to do with his recent travels. It was started during July 1939, while he was staying with Laura's family at Pixton. The book was going well by the end of August, though he was becoming distracted by the obvious imminence of war.

The new novel contains two self-portraits. For the first time, Waugh tells the story in the first person, as John Plant, a bachelor and an established writer of thrillers, who goes to Fez in Morocco to compose his books, as Waugh himself had done when writing *A Handful of Dust*. There is also much of Waugh in Plant's painter father, whose death takes place at the beginning of the novel, and who is described as having behaved in Waugh's own manner – or, rather, in the manner Waugh would adopt some ten years later.

Mr Plant senior, whose canvases are ludicrously old-fashioned (mid-Victorian in style and subject-matter), is chiefly concerned to cultivate aloofness from the attitudes of his contemporaries: 'It was enough for him to learn that an opinion of his had popular support for him to question and abandon it.' He dresses in outrageous checks and other loud items of clothing: 'He thought it fitting for a man to proclaim un-equivocally his station in life, and despised those of his colleagues who seemed to be passing themselves off as guardsmen and stock-brokers.'

Although he seems 'a man of indestructible sanity', his son observes that 'there had always seemed an element of persecution-mania about his foibles which might, at a time of great strain, go beyond his control'.

Work Suspended, as Waugh called the novel after abandoning it, indicates more clearly than any other work of fiction by him the importance of his father to his own character and imagination. It indicates, but it does not explain. The story presents father and son as living in amicable accord, and gives no hint of the complexity of the real Arthur–Evelyn relationship. It is wish-fulfilment; this is how Evelyn would like it to have been.

Nevertheless the father's death produces a kind of emotional release, a sudden sense of freedom in the son. He abandons his latest novel and goes to his publisher to explain:

> 'I have been writing for over eight years . . . and am nearing a climacteric . . . a turning point in my career. . . . I feel in danger of turning into a stock best-seller . . . becoming purely a technical expert . . . turning out year after year the kind of book I know I can write well. . . . I need new worlds to conquer.'

This may well have been Waugh's own feeling by 1939.

With the money from the sale of his father's London house, Plant decides to buy a mansion in the country, admitting that this is not merely for domestic convenience. He has lived among a set of friends nearly all of whom:

> professed a specialized enthusiasm for domestic architecture. It was one of the peculiarities of my generation, and there is no accounting for that. . . . When the poetic mood was on us, we turned to buildings, particularly those in the classical tradition, and, more particularly, in its decay. It was a kind of nostalgia for the style of living which we emphatically rejected in practical affairs. The nobilities of Whig society became, for us, what the Arthurian paladins were in the time of Tennyson.

Plant goes house-hunting with Lucy, the wife of his old friend Roger Simmonds, with whom he has fallen in love. She is heavily pregnant, which makes the relationship safe for the time being. In any case, he is not a man to let his emotions show. 'For the civilized man,' he declares, 'there are none of those swift transitions of joy and pain which possess the savage; words form slowly like pus about his hurts; there are no clean wounds for him; first a numbness, then a long festering, then a scar ever ready to re-open.' This is surely a recollection of Waugh's response to the collapse of his first marriage. 'Not until they have assumed the livery of the defence', continues Plant, 'can his emotions pass through the lines. . . .'

This honest statement of Waugh's own reserve is also a critique of his current limitations as a novelist. *Work Suspended* was his first attempt at self-portraiture since 'The Balance', and he left it unfinished because he was not yet capable of it. He had not yet learnt to select and highlight aspects of his own personality in the manner he had perfected with other people. Later, that skill would come, with the creation of Charles Ryder and Guy Crouchback, but for now all he could produce was a very thin sketch of a highly reserved individual.

He could not even write eloquently of Plant's love for Lucy – a composite portrait of many women Waugh had been attracted to, including Diana Guinness (now Diana Mosley) and Waugh's own wife Laura, who was expecting their second child while *Work Suspended* was being written. 'To write of someone loved,' says Plant, 'of oneself loving, above all of oneself being loved – how can these things be done with propriety? How can they be done at all?' The narrative comes to an abrupt end with the birth of Lucy's child. Waugh's own son Auberon was born on 18 November 1939, shortly before the novel was abandoned.

Waugh professed himself pleased with what he had written – 'It would have been OK,' he told John Betjeman – and the outbreak of war provided a convenient excuse to stop. Indeed, it seemed a veritable godsend, offering boundless possibilities of change and new experience. 'The war seems to be developing into ourselves against the world,' he remarked jauntily in this letter to Betjeman, looking back on their anti-Slough crusade of the 1930s, 'so we shall all have some fighting to do between our 40th and 80th birthdays. . . .'

It was more than just an enthusiasm for change. The point of *Work Suspended* is that, despite their idyllic relationship, John Plant cannot begin to be himself until his father has died. Arthur Waugh was still alive in 1939, and Evelyn could not yet expect such a change to take place in his own life. On the other hand the army, which he was already making efforts to join, offered the possibility of a new form of paternal authority, to which he could relate without complications. As a soldier, everything would become simple for him. He could go back to the beginning again.

PART VI: 1939–1945

Arcadia Revisited

1

Buggered About

Cyril Connolly wanted a war job, and a good one: 'If we're all back at school one must be a prefect.' But it proved surprisingly difficult to get called up, even for those like Anthony Powell who had been in the Territorials and had placed their names on the officers' Emergency Reserve. Powell sent his pregnant wife off to an aunt's castellated mansion in Wales, and delivered their Siamese cats to a boarding establishment run by a Mrs Perkins, then found himself in a 'state of suspended animation', waiting restlessly for his call-up, trying to write a life of John Aubrey, and envying those few friends who appeared in uniform.

Eventually Powell's telephone rang: 'This is Captain Perkins. We haven't met, but my wife is looking after your Siamese cats. I thought you would like to know they are well.'

'That's very kind of you.'

'I'm at the War Office,' continued Captain Perkins. 'I've just seen your name there. . . . Do you want to be called up?'

'Very much indeed.'

'What regiment would you like to join?'

So three weeks later, thanks to his cats, Powell was on his way to a battalion of the Welch Regiment in Pembrokeshire.

Graham Greene had to wait until the authorities calling up the Emergency Reserve had reached the letter G. He went before a board consisting of a major-general and two colonels. 'How do you *visualize* yourself?' the General asked. 'How do you *see* yourself?' Greene knew that they expected him to apply for Intelligence. He decided to be helpful, and answered: 'I suppose . . . the Infantry.' One of the colonels gave a sigh of relief.

He asked if his call-up could be postponed for a few months, while he finished writing *The Power and the Glory*. Permission was readily granted: 'Shall we say until June? Try and keep fit, though, Mr Greene, in the meanwhile. What I mean is . . . sometimes when you want to take a bus, walk instead.'

John Betjeman volunteered for the Royal Air Force, but was turned down because he told the examining psychologist that he was terrified of spiders. Alan Pryce-Jones was posted, with the rank of captain, to Tidworth camp in Wiltshire, where he was to serve as an interpreter for prisoners of war. He found that his military duties 'were confined to giving or acknowledging salutes', and he was able to stay with friends on the downs near Marlborough in a ravishing eighteenth-century house. Betjeman gave him a copy of Hardy's collected poems, in anticipation of a long war abroad, and there was a picnic with Robert Byron near his family's house in Savernake Forest, 'he looking, as always, like Queen Victoria *en travesti*'. Life was 'as serene as September on the Downs could make it'.

Just before the outbreak of war, families evacuated from London began to arrive in Waugh's village of Stinchcombe. 'Some of the evacuees', Waugh wrote in his diary, 'are under the impression that they are taking refuge from the IRA.' He sent long letters to the Ministry of Information 'pressing my qualifications as liaison with foreign war correspondents', and put the house into the hands of several agents, with instructions to let it. But there were no favourable responses from either quarter. 'A tedious time,' he recorded in the diary. 'Had I no garden to dig in I should be in despair with lack of occupation.'

Eventually a community of Dominican nuns arranged to take Piers Court from the beginning of October 1939, to use it as a convent school. Waugh and Laura moved down to her family house, Pixton, where Waugh received an invitation to call at Naval Intelligence in London. He hurried up by train, was told simply that his name was 'on the list', and went to the War Office, where he found total confusion and no possibility of a job. He left for the St James's Club, 'where I had half a dozen oysters, half grouse, a whole partridge, and a peach, half bottle of white wine and half Pontet Canet 1924. From then my day began to improve.'

He called on the Welsh Guards and was told that there might be something for him in six months, but two days later they wrote 'unaccountably telling me that their list had been revised and that they had no room for me. My first feeling was that there must be someone at the War Office occupied in blocking my chances. . . . I was thrown into despair. I now had no irons in the fire. That night I tried new sleeping draft [*sic*].'

He went off to his favourite writing refuge, Easton Court Hotel at Chagford in Devon, where he did some final work on *Work Suspended*. While there, he learnt that the War Office had at least allocated him a number; also, after a great deal of string-pulling, the Marines sent him a form to fill up. 'Perhaps I shall be able to join the war yet.'

The form asked, among many other personal things, 'if I am a chronic bedwetter'. He went to London to be interviewed by them. The doctor diagnosed 'middle-aged spread', and gave him a sealed envelope to take to the Admiralty. Waugh opened it in the taxi 'and found a chit to say that I had been examined and found unfit for active service'. However, the officer who saw him ignored the medical report, observing of Waugh's poor eyesight, 'Anyway most of your work will be in the dark.' He allowed Waugh to put himself down for Marine Infantry, 'a force being raised for raiding parties'. Waugh left in excellent humour, a mood reinforced by a meeting at the Savoy with 'a lugubrious kind of baboon', the editor of the American magazine *Life*, who commissioned two articles at the startling price of a thousand dollars each. Elated by all this, Waugh drank champagne at his club, and at dinner at Patrick Balfour's, and again at Mrs Meyrick's latest night club, topping it up with rum. 'I was sick at about 5.'

Military life seemed at first like an extension of clubland. Anthony Powell, who at thirty-five was considerably older than most of his fellow-officers, was given a welcome of great cordiality at the Mess in Haverfordwest, where he found that the command of his battalion was virtually a hereditary post, both the father and grandfather of the present C.O. having held it before him. Waugh, reporting to the Marines at Chatham early in December 1939, was led to the supper table with profuse apologies for the meal being cold – the officers were about to attend a play – and found 'lobster, fresh salmon, cold birds, hams, brawn exactly like the cold table at the St James's. Afterwards several rounds of excellent vintage port.'

Like Powell, he was, at thirty-six, considerably older than his brother officers, but the rule in the Mess was to defer to age rather than rank. Physical comforts ceased abruptly when he was sent to Deal for infantry training; on the other hand the Brigade Commander, St Clair Morford, was an eccentric of the highest calibre who provided a great deal of 'copy' for Waugh's diary and letters: 'Teeth like a stoat, ears like a faun, eyes alight like a child playing pirates. "We then have to biff them, gentlemen."' The Brigadier carried Waugh off to his house, 'which was the lowest type of stockbroker's Tudor. . . . The Brigadier's madam is kept very much in her place and ordered about with great shouts: "Woman, go up to my cabin and get my boots."'

Training seemed – indeed was – endless. It was still continuing when France fell to the Germans in June 1940, though Waugh could relieve the boredom by spending weekends in hotels with Laura. 'I have been to London every weekend,' he wrote in his diary during the spring, 'dining and lunching at the Ritz and spending a very great deal of money. We are now about £500 overdrawn. I owe £200 in income tax and see no possibility of getting my finances square except by prodigious national inflation.'

After assault training at Scapa Flow, Waugh, now a captain, sailed in September 1940 for French West Africa, as part of a joint expedition with the Free French to retake Dakar from Vichy France. It was a fiasco, and Waugh (acting as Battalion Intelligence Officer) was among those who never even landed. However, he derived some amusement from defending one of the men on a charge of buggery: 'He got eight months. His companion in pleasure got eleven. I did quite well for him.'

Life as a Marine was mostly unrewarding. 'I do wish sometimes I could meet an adult,' Waugh wrote to Laura while returning from Dakar. 'They are all little boys. Some of them naughty little boys like the Brigadier, most of them delicious & just what I want Bron [his son Auberon] to be at the age of ten, but not one of them a mature man.' He swiftly did something about it. 'I have transferred to something more unusual,' he wrote to Henry Yorke in November 1940, 'under Bob Laycock whom you may remember. . . . It is a corps of Buck's toughs doomed no doubt to ignominy like the marines, but at the moment promising. Anyway a change.'

Lieutenant-Colonel Robert Laycock, an acquaintance of Waugh's from London life before the war, was in charge of five hundred men known as 8 Commando. Waugh had first heard of the Commandos from Brendan Bracken, Winston Churchill's Parliamentary Private Secretary, whom he had known casually since the 1920s. Waugh went to see him at 10 Downing Street, and 'Brendan said: "You ought to be with Bob Laycock's tough boys."' Waugh wrote to Laycock and the transfer was arranged.

The Commandos were still regarded very much as 'irregulars'. Originally raised to supply raiding parties against the occupied coast of France, they operated much like independent bands of mercenaries. While in training, they were allowed to find their own accommodation – which particularly appealed to Waugh, who had by now had enough of unspeakable billets and camps – and there was an abnormally high proportion of officers to men. To join them would be a tough assignment for a man in his late thirties who had 'middle-aged spread' and liked soft living, but they seemed likely to offer more stimulus than the Marines, and the physical stamina required was the sort of challenge Waugh wanted. He was treating the war as a kind of pilgrimage or penance, much as he had treated his travels abroad in the 1930s, though his decision to join the 'tough boys' also recalls his determined participation in tough sports at Lancing.

He caught up with 8 Commando at Largs in Scotland, and found it very far from tough. 'All the officers have very long hair & lap dogs & cigars,' he wrote to Laura from the Marine Hotel, where they were all staying. 'I have done nothing so far except take a cuckoo clock to pieces & play a lot of ludo.' The lap dog (a pekinese) was owned by Randolph Churchill, son of Winston, whom Waugh had known since they both stood godfather to Bryan and Diana Guinness's son Jonathan. Now Waugh found him quarrelling over his hotel bill, refusing to serve under people he disliked, and being expelled from a training course for heckling the instructors. The other officers, who included several peers, were 'divided more or less equally into dandies and highly efficient professional soldiers'. The dandies ate expensive dinners in Glasgow most nights, and there was a great deal of heavy drinking. 'Setting out drunk for one of the night operations,' Waugh recorded, 'I fell down and cut my lip but no one thought the worse of me for this accident. ... The whole thing was a delightful holiday from the Royal Marines.'

After some weeks of time-wasting and muddle, 8 Commando sailed for Egypt, at the beginning of February 1941. On board, there was much gambling for high stakes: 'Randolph lost £850 in two evenings.' They were promised 'a bellyful of fighting', but found themselves doing general defence duties in the Alexandria area. To placate a now very restless 8 Commando, a series of minor operations was planned against the enemy's lines of communication, each with the name (appropriately enough) of a Ben Travers Aldwych farce – 'Rookery Nook' and so on. On each occasion they set out and were promptly turned back. These events were summed up by 8 Commando in a parody of Randolph

Churchill's father's famous *dictum*: 'Never in the history of human endeavour have so few been buggered about by so many.'

Meanwhile, in the middle of all the frustrations and amusements of Commando life, Waugh wrote to Laura: 'I think I shall start writing a book, for my own pleasure, probably not for publication – a kind of modern Arcadia.'

From Haverfordwest, Anthony Powell's Division was ordered to Newry in Northern Ireland, where local feeling was openly anti-British and pro-German; youths lounging in the streets would sing 'We're going to hang out the washing on the Maginot Line.' From there, Powell found himself sent to a tactical training establishment in a mock-Norman castle in County Armagh, staffed by a 'crew of seedy bad-mannered middle-aged officers'. He was learning that second lieutenants like himself were 'the army rank most buggered about'. He was moved to Belfast, where his duties included the disposal of ash and swill. His only expectation was of automatic promotion to lieutenant (the rank to which Waugh had returned when joining the Commandos), which was due soon. 'The prospect was not inspiring.'

John Betjeman reached Ireland during 1941, as Press Attaché to the British Representative in Dublin. Penelope and their son Paul, born the year before war had broken out, accompanied him, and they were given a damp Georgian mansion near the airport to live in. Betjeman's duties included entertaining distinguished visitors, among them Laurence Olivier, who had come over to film the battle of Agincourt for his *Henry V*, since Ireland was still plentifully supplied with young men and horses. Consequently, unlike Waugh and Powell, Betjeman actually saw some fighting, if only in front of the camera.

Henry Yorke had chosen to work as a London fireman during the Blitz. When he and Waugh met, he told Waugh 'things about the fire brigade which' (wrote Waugh) 'made it clear that they are much braver fellows & have seen more real action than the army'. Graham Greene similarly experienced bloodshed simply by remaining in London while waiting for his call-up and doing duty as an air-raid warden. 'One really thought that this was the end,' he wrote in his journal describing a bad evening rescuing bomb casualties while the raid was continuing around him, 'but it wasn't exactly frightening – one had ceased to believe in the possibility of surviving the night.'

Like so many people, Greene finally got what seemed a worthwhile war-job by private wire-pulling: his sister Elizabeth recruited him for

Penelope Betjeman, Moti the Arab mare, Robert Heber–Percy, and Evelyn Waugh in one of Lord Berners' drawing rooms at Faringdon House.

Waugh photographed by Yevonde Middleton during the 1930s. 'I am deeply interested in the jungle and only casually interested in Mayfair.'

Osbert Lancaster's drawing of the Uffington House village concert. Lord Berners is at the keyboard; Lancaster himself plays the flute and Penelope Betjeman, 'a strange instrument resembling a zither'; the singers are Adrian Bishop and Cara Lancaster (in the back row) and Maurice Bowra and John Betjeman. They are performing 'Sumer is icumen in'.

Laura Herbert leaves her family's London house for her wedding to Evelyn Waugh in April 1937. She is twenty-one; accompanying her is her sixteen-year-old brother, Auberon, who is to give her away,

Laura Herbert and Evelyn Waugh on their wedding day. 'You might think ... whether ... you could bear the idea of marrying me.'

Piers Court, Waugh's home from 1937. 'I seem to be setting myself up as a squire.'

Evelyn Waugh and his brother Alec, in the South of France.

'I'm sorry, my dear Countess, but I still feel pretty Left Wing.' A cartoon defining the boundary between the Auden group and the Waugh set, attributed to Cyril Connolly and published in *Night and Day* on 7 October 1937.

Cyril Connolly photographed by Howard Coster in 1942, at the height of his *Horizon* period.

Waugh in Marines uniform soon after the outbreak of war. 'We shall all have some fighting to do...'

Waugh, with moustache, rather later in the war. 'I'm so unpopular as to be unemployable.'

Graham Greene (right) on duty as a 'Catholic novelist', with the Papal Nuncio to Belgium and François Mauriac.

Anthony Powell in 1953, as *A Dance to the Music of Time* was getting into its stride.

The Burges washstand, subject of one of Waugh's delusions just before his 'Pinfold' hallucinations. Note the heavily Victorian surroundings of Waugh's house in which it stands.

John Betjeman in Betjemanic mood in 1955.

Waugh caught by the camera in Gilbert Pinfold mood.

...augh and family photographed at Combe Florey in 1959. Auberon Waugh stands next to his ...her; seated (left to right) are Harriet, Teresa, Laura, Margaret (turning to look at her father), ...d James. Septimus is on the floor.

Waugh in the study at Combe Florey. 'I get up late. I try to read my letters. I try to read the paper. I have some gin. I try to read the paper again. I have some more gin. . . . That's my life.'

MI6, and in the winter of 1941 he sailed by cargo-ship for West Africa. In the trunkload of books he took to alleviate the tedium of the voyage was a Michael Innes detective story, which entertained him so much that 'I developed the ambition to write a funny and fantastic thriller myself.' He wrote *The Ministry of Fear* during the following year, while living a lonely but contented existence in Freetown, in the intervals of decoding messages, writing reports, drinking whisky, and listening to the rats swinging on his bedroom curtains.*

Waugh, similarly suffering a tedious voyage during 1941, wrote a new novel to dispel the boredom. From the Middle East – where he had finally taken part in a little fighting, a night raid on the coast of Libya – he and 'Layforce' (the Commando units organized by Laycock) were moved in mid-May to Crete, where British troops were under severe bombardment. Layforce was supposed to march inland and provide reinforcements for the defenders. In the chaos which followed, Waugh 'learned that the most valuable piece of equipment one can have in action is a pillow', since for much of the time all he could do was lie low. The ineffectiveness of Layforce was partly due to the cowardice and incompetence of the officer afterwards portrayed in *Officers and Gentlemen* as 'Major Hound', but morale was altogether low. Waugh records a Presbyterian chaplain announcing 'It's *sauve qui peut* now,' taking himself away from Crete as quickly as possible, and afterwards sending in a large bill for kit lost in enemy action. After embarking from Crete, Waugh wrote to Laura: 'It was tedious & futile & fatiguing. I found I was not at all frightened; only very bored & very weary. . . .'

In July 1941 he started a twenty-thousand-mile sea journey home, via Cape Town, Trinidad, the American coast and Iceland. On board ship he began the new novel. It was finished during September, while he was still at sea – the fastest he had ever written. It was not the Arcadian narrative he had spoken of to Laura, but (he told his father) 'a minor work dashed off to occupy a tedious voyage'; by comparison the abandoned *Work Suspended* would have been 'major'. To Randolph Churchill he admitted that the new book was 'quite funny', but said that thanks to the paper shortage it would probably not appear in print 'until it has lost all point'. He was unduly pessimistic, for the novel came out early in 1942, when memories were still fresh of the first

---

* Greene's *The Confidential Agent* (1939) is an escapist romantic thriller in much the same mode as *The Ministry of Fear*. Undertaken purely to earn money, it was written in six weeks, at the same time as *The Power and the Glory*, Greene fortifying himself with the drug Benzedrine while he worked on it.

months of the war, in which it is set. Not since *Vile Bodies* had Waugh so swiftly turned the contemporary scene into fiction.

Put Out More Flags – the title, from a Chinese sage, is, as usual with Waugh, slightly obtuse – resembles *Vile Bodies* in that it deals with the interlocking fortunes of a set of characters rather than with a single hero. There is not even a particular point of focus, as with Adam in the earlier novel. The narration shifts between five principal figures, Ambrose Silk, Basil Seal, Alastair Trumpington, and Angela and Cedric Lyne. Waugh's intention was evidently to portray the spirit of the months known as the 'phoney war' or, as he put it in his Dedicatory Letter to Randolph Churchill, 'that odd, dead period before the Churchillian renaissance' (the ascent of Randolph's father to the premiership) 'which people called at the time the Great Bore War'.

The novel's theme is clearly stated by Peter Pastmaster (Margot Metroland's son, one of many characters who reappear from Waugh's earlier novels), towards the end of the story: 'Most of war seems to consist of hanging about.' When they are not hanging about, the characters are frequently being 'buggered about' by officialdom, or by each other. Waugh's and Powell's use of that phrase is echoed by the troops whose embarkation is being supervised by Cedric Lyne: 'I'm —ing —ed with being —ed about,' mutters a military voice in the darkness.

The point of the novel is that all this hanging around, and being buggered about, offers boundless potential for hostilities of a non-military kind. Basil Seal fails to get any kind of war job, but consoles himself by conducting his own war against the middle class who have overrun the villages surrounding his sister's country house. Having accidentally encountered the awful Connollys (the use of Cyril Connolly's surname no doubt amused Waugh), he extorts large bribes from the bourgeoisie in return for not billeting these outrageously behaved evacuee children on them. Waugh has the wisdom, however, not to make the Connollys simply a caricature of slum children. They are junior versions of Basil, who use their terrible social handicaps to get the maximum return from life.

Basil's nefarious operations with the Connollys are described in military language. Informing his first victims that the children are about to be billeted on their perfect Arts and Crafts household, Basil imagines himself throwing a grenade into their midst:

'We pay eight shillings and sixpence a week,' he said. That was the safety pin; the lever flew up, the spring struck home. ... Five, six, *seven*. Here it comes. Bang! 'Perhaps I should have told you at once.

I am the billeting officer. I've three children for you in the car outside.'
It was magnificent. It was war.

It is, of course, war against the class that Waugh most despised, the one from which he himself was trying to raise himself by setting up as a squire.

At the other end of the seesaw from Basil – for the book deals in balanced opposites – is Ambrose Silk, in most respects a portrait of Brian Howard as he had become by the 1940s, 'a cosmopolitan, Jewish pansy', who has been forced to abandon his German boyfriend to the Nazis and is back in London looking for war-work – almost precisely Brian's situation in 1940. (Though usually unwilling to make such identifications, Waugh admitted in a 1951 letter to Nancy Mitford that *Put Out More Flags* was 'a book about . . . B. Howard'). The real Brian's German boyfriend Toni had been interned in France at the outbreak of war, and Brian himself, returning to London from his European wanderings, had taken only a few weeks to inveigle himself into (of all things) a job in MI5. He managed to look at the 'screening' report on him, which said 'Has compelling eyes.' He was supposed to report on possible Nazi sympathizers, but when he informed his superior officer that a certain prominent person had displayed strong Fascist sympathies before the war, he was told: 'Don't be ridiculous – he went to Eton with me!'

In the summer of 1942 Brian was sacked from MI5, probably for too many tipsy indiscretions in night clubs ('If you aren't careful, my man, I'll have you put *inside* . . .'), and to everyone's surprise he volunteered for, and was accepted by, the Royal Air Force. Aircraftman Howard reported to his mother: 'I like *all* the NCOs – they're so like nannies at heart.' He was frequently in trouble for minor infringements, such as 'the day I lost my uniform. Seems no one'd ever done that before. People are really *too* extraordinary. I just left the silly thing in a public lavvy.'

He remained an Aircraftman almost until the end of the war, and was finally discharged honourably, despite many scrapes. The most celebrated of these took place at the Ritz, where he was heard discoursing noisily on the incompetence of those in charge of the war, from Churchill downwards. As he was wearing his uniform, a high-ranking RAF officer came over and angrily demanded Brian's name, number and station. Brian replied: 'Mrs Smith.'

Given the circulation of these and many other comic tales about Brian's recent activities, Waugh could have made Ambrose Silk purely a figure of fun. Instead, he is portrayed with cruel candour but complete understanding, as an ageing juvenile from the Twenties who has pitched his camp uncomfortably with the Auden–Isherwood supporters (the two writers, who remain offstage, are thinly disguised as Parsnip and Pimpernell, both of whom have 'fled' to the United States), and who is trapped inside his own dandyism and camp manner.

In a letter to his Toni, Brian described the character of Ambrose Silk as 'an absolutely vicious attack on me'. Waugh may have meant it to be, but, far from mocking Ambrose, the novel emphasizes that he is a 'sane individual' among lunatics, and credits him with a more sensible attitude to the war than is displayed by most of the characters in the book:

> If, thought Ambrose ... I were not all that the Nazis mean when they talk about 'degenerates' ... I wouldn't sit around discussing what kind of war it was going to be. I'd set about killing and stampeding the other herd as fast and as hard as I could. Lord love a duck, thought Ambrose, there wouldn't be any animals nosing about for suitable jobs in *my* herd.

After the successful conclusion of his rural campaign with the Connollys, Basil Seal transfers his private military operations to London, getting himself a job as a Fascist-hunter at MI5 (much like Brian Howard's position there), and persuading his superior that a literary magazine which Ambrose Silk is publishing from his own desk at the Ministry of Information contains Fifth Column pro-Hitler propaganda. This strand in the narrative is pure farce, but Alastair Trumpington's activities in the book seriously reflect Waugh's view of himself in 1940. Alastair abandons soft living (jugs of Black Velvet at midday while still in pyjamas) to enlist as a private in the army, explaining to Sonia his wife: 'We've had a pretty easy life up to now. It's probably quite good for one to have a change sometimes.' Sonia comments: 'He went into the ranks as a kind of penance or whatever it's called that religious people are always supposed to do.' Though Waugh did not go into the ranks, he had thrown himself into military training as just another officer, in something of the spirit that he credits to Alastair.

While Basil's activities rise to a farcical pitch, Alastair experiences the comparative satisfaction of the steady routine of army life, and (like Waugh) spends as much of his spare time as possible with his wife, in hotels or rented houses. Meanwhile the novel also deals with the decline into lonely alcoholism of Basil's mistress, Angela Lyne, whom Waugh uses as a symbol of pre-war Mayfair life. Peter Pastmaster and his fiancée find her collapsed in drunken confusion at a cinema, and take her home to the care of her maid. Waugh plays the scene entirely straight; indeed Angela, her estranged husband Cedric, and their uncomprehending prep-schoolboy son Nigel, are handled with a simple seriousness not attempted in Waugh's previous books, even *A Handful of Dust*. At the end of *Put Out More Flags*, Cedric is killed in action – heroically but pointlessly – in circumstances recalling the evacuation of Crete.

Put Out More Flags is a transitional book, deliberately avoiding for much of the time the farcical element that up to now had played a large part in Waugh's fiction, but not yet completely devoted to the handling of serious themes in a manner that consistently subordinates comedy to a larger purpose. The passages describing Cedric's feelings when he encounters Angela after a gap of three years look forward to Guy Crouchback's reunion with his estranged wife. Basil Seal, on the other hand, belongs firmly to the pre-1939 Waugh, and remains, despite Waugh's evident enjoyment of his outrageousness, a little too monstrous to be believable. The book does not altogether amount to a novel, but is more a set of experiments in voices, some old, several new, another cautious step forward, like *Work Suspended*, but not yet a confident change of manner.

Its only unattractive feature is its exclusively aristocratic outlook. Up to now, Waugh's novels had always distanced themselves a little from the rich and titled, or had allowed them some redeemingly unglamorous feature, such as poverty or the decay of their houses. *Put Out More Flags* does not stand back from them in this way. Everyone in it, except Basil, has an abundant income and lives in a luxurious London flat or a splendid country house. There is a slightly unpleasant air about this, observed (among the book's reviewers) by Alan Pryce-Jones, writing in the *New Statesman*:

> Aren't the great, ramshackle houses now too finely observed? Don't the casual details [of aristocratic life] ring too carefully true? One cannot imagine any of these young men, shameless as they are in the conduct of life, doing up the bottom button of their waistcoat; and is not each overtone of adultery – in not somewhere obvious like Berkeley Square but a knowing by-street, say Montpelier Walk – recorded with rather too modish an air?

2

A Total Misfit

Ivory Tower, the literary magazine that Ambrose Silk edits in *Put Out More Flags*, is a dig at Cyril Connolly's war-work. At the outbreak of hostilities in the autumn of 1939, Waugh himself had thought of founding a new magazine to keep culture alive: 'I have opened negotiations with Chapman & Hall's, Osbert Sitwell and David Cecil with the idea of starting a monthly magazine under the title of *Duration*.' Nothing came of it, because Waugh discovered that Connolly was already putting a similar plan into action.

Like many of his literary friends, Connolly had often dreamt of starting his own magazine, and now suddenly found he had a backer, an Old Etonian named Victor Watson, always known as 'Peter', wealthy son of the inventor of margarine, an art collector and one of the great loves (but not lovers) of Cecil Beaton. Connolly had known this rather *louche*, faunlike individual for several years, and in October 1939 Watson undertook to subsidize *Horizon*, as the new magazine was to be called. The first issue appeared in January 1940.

It announced itself as a definite departure from the Thirties. 'The war', wrote Connolly in his opening editorial,

is separating culture from life and driving it back on itself, the impetus given by Left Wing politics is for the time exhausted, and however much we should like to have a paper that was revolutionary in opinions or original in technique, it is impossible to do so when there is a certain suspension of judgement and creative activity. The aim of *Horizon* is to give writers a place to express themselves, and to readers the best

344

writing we can obtain. Our standards are aesthetic, and our politics are in abeyance.

The first issue demonstrated the breadth of contributors who were willing to come together under this manifesto, or non-manifesto. There were poems by Auden, Betjeman, Walter de la Mare and Louis MacNeice, articles on the war and the future by J. B. Priestley and Herbert Read, prose by Connolly and H. E. Bates, and reviews by Stephen Spender and Geoffrey Grigson. Connolly was trying to bring together the Auden camp (of which the house magazine had been Grigson's *New Verse*) and his own set, seasoned with some popular middlebrows. Despite the claim of 'no politics', the prevailing tone was mildly left. Waugh noted in his diary that *Horizon* was being run by 'the rump of the left wing'. To Connolly in 1953, he wrote: 'I always enjoyed the magazine & was grateful to you for printing my work in it, but there was an ugly accent – RAF pansy – which kept breaking in. . . . That spoiled the enterprise for me.' Spender was co-editor with Connolly until 1941, and Connolly admits that the presence of Spender's friends tended to give it the air of 'a Left-wing "school magazine"'. Connolly himself contributed trenchant editorials defending Auden and Isherwood for settling in America, which he called 'a land richer in incident and opportunity' than Britain.

Early issues provoked complaints not of political bias but of 'sameness and tameness', and the magazine certainly seemed bland after the hot tempers of the Thirties. But the quality of individual contributions made it required reading for anyone seriously interested in the survival of the arts during wartime. There were drawings by Henry Moore, John Piper (who had designed the cover) and Osbert Lancaster, fiction by Elizabeth Bowen, V. S. Pritchett, and J. Maclaren-Ross, and photographs of wartime Britain by Cecil Beaton. 'My Father's House', the first section of Waugh's *Work Suspended*, was published in the issue for November 1941. The political viewpoint became more detectably left when Connolly published an attack on army life by an anonymous conscript, and when news came of the death of Robert Byron, torpedoed on his way to Egypt as a war correspondent, 'Ran' Antrim contributed an obituary which concluded:

> We must be determined that no lack of vigour will spoil our intention that it is to be impossible for the Roberts of the next generation to be drowned in a barbarous war initiated by the folly of weak-kneed and incompetent politicians.

This, though, was not an exclusively left-wing viewpoint; Ezra

Pound, supporting the Axis, was saying much the same on Rome Radio.

In the October 1941 issue, Connolly published a manifesto asking 'Why Not War Writers?', signed by himself, George Orwell (a frequent contributor), Arthur Koestler, Arthur Calder-Marshall and others of known left-wing sympathy, proposing 'the formation of an official group of war writers' who would be exempted from military service and 'used to interpret the war world', writing 'novels about ... the planning of wartime services, the operation of ... an evacuation scheme ... satires on hoarders ... novels of army life'. Their aim would be to see 'that cultural unity is re-established and war effort emotionally co-ordinated'. This drew an anonymous riposte in the issue for December 1941, signed 'Combatant', and in fact written by Waugh, who added: 'I may not sign my name to a letter dealing with military matters, but if anyone has any curiosity about my identity, please inform him.'

Waugh described the manifesto as a 'preposterous document'. He sneered at 'the book-reviewers and mass-observers and poets (of a kind) and Left-Book-Club-sub-group-assistant-organizing-secretaries' who he said had been holding back from military life, and announced:

> If they want to write about the war, the way is clear for them. ... They must be, or have been, part of it. ... The atmosphere [in the armed forces] is uncongenial to writing, but that is all to the good. It has been too easy to write in recent years. Genius overcomes privation and inferiority. If these young men *must* write, they will do it the better for suffering some inconveniences. If they are under no immediate compulsion, let them sit tight and store their minds with material for future use.
>
> But what do your chums propose doing? ... They would 'co-ordinate war effort emotionally'. Cor, chase my Aunt Nancy round the prickly pear! The General Staff love initials; they would, I am sure, rejoice to put an armlet, D.A.E.C.W.E., on someone's arm and call him Deputy Assistant Emotional Co-ordinator of War Effort.

Connolly made no direct reply, but in a later editorial (May 1942) he observed caustically: 'All writers who feel that they are in the war and responsible for winning it should be excused literary activity, and even forbidden it.' In the same issue he printed a sharp review of *Put Out More Flags* by Peter Quennell, who described Waugh as 'some sort of romantic Tory', and said that passages in the book were 'faintly reminiscent of Mr Michael Arlen'.

*

For all his protests that writers were better off serving in the armed forces, Waugh was no longer even intermittently happy with military life. On his return from Crete he took a company commanders' course, then went back to the Commandos with the firm hope of being given his own company. But this did not happen. 'I was told by my NCOs that Tim Porter was taking over D Company,' he wrote in his diary on Friday, 13 March 1942, in camp in Scotland.

> I asked the Commanding Officer if this was true and he said it was. I asked to see the Brigadier and saw him next day. I stated my case that I was qualified to command a company. ... The Brigadier ... said I was only suitable to command one in battle.

The Brigadier was sugaring the pill. Christopher Sykes, who saw much of Waugh during this period, says that Laycock and other senior officers had come to realize that Waugh was utterly unsuited to commanding other ranks in any circumstances whatever, simply because of his 'total incapacity for establishing any sort of human relations with his men'.

Sykes regards it as a plain manifestation of class-prejudice. The men, he says, 'were working-class people and Evelyn had (I regret to say) an instinctive dislike for the working classes'. This seems to have been less the case earlier in Waugh's army career; he had obtained some amusement from defending the man court-martialled for homosexuality, and he records that a half-mad NCO who kept a scurrilous diary during the fighting on Crete was viciously critical of almost all the officers, but 'seemed to have some liking for me'. However, boredom with hanging about in a series of nondescript camps, waiting for something to happen, had increased Waugh's irritability, and he took it out on the other ranks. 'The men mean-spirited, lazy, untruthful,' he wrote in his diary early in 1942.

Another officer, the Hon. 'Jakie' Astor, who was in camp in Dorset with Waugh, told Sykes that he hated to see Waugh drilling the men, or assuming any kind of command over them, however trivial: 'He never hesitated to take advantage of the fact that while he was a highly educated man, most of them were barely literate. He bullied them in a way they were unused to. He bewildered them, purposely. I found it embarrassing.'

Sykes himself, always eager to defend Waugh whenever it was reasonable to do so, makes no attempt in his biography to justify Waugh's tendency to be rude to his social inferiors, or to those he considered inferior:

> To the naturally weak [writes Sykes] he was as merciless as he had

been in his bullying school days. I witnessed the spectacle many times and it always utterly disgusted me. It was useless to remonstrate as I sometimes did because he was always ready with a witty and plausibly logical defence.

Sykes suggests that this form of bullying 'was a perversion . . . of his aggressive spirit which rejoiced in conflict'.

There is a hint of explanation in a 1953 letter from Waugh to Nancy Mitford, in which he remarks of the servility of Indians (he had just been to Goa): 'I can only bear intimacy really & after that formality or servility. The horrible thing is familiarity.' This seems to hint at a deep-seated shyness, a horror of normal social contact with anyone who was not a carefully chosen intimate.

Nancy Mitford tackles the subject herself in *The Pursuit of Love*, in a passage which suggests that the middle classes automatically fear those immediately beneath them, whereas the upper classes, being at a greater social distance, do not feel similarly under threat; moreover they have usually been brought up by members of the working classes – nannies and other servants – and so regard them as part of the family. 'I love them, anyway I was brought up with them,' says Linda in the novel. 'The trouble with you', she adds to her bourgeois husband, 'is that you don't know the lower classes and you don't belong to the upper classes. . . .'

Waugh had been 'brought up with them', in the sense that as a small child he had had a working-class nurse, Lucy. But a girl from rural Somerset in the early 1900s was scarcely a preparation for dealing with the men from industrial and urban backgrounds who made up the majority of conscripts in 1943. In any case, by now Waugh simply did not like people of any kind in the mass, and his aggression towards his men in the Commandos was not just snobbery, but a manifestation of this wider disaffection with humanity.

During the fighting in Crete, a Commando officer named Pedder was shot in suspicious circumstances. 'We shall never know who killed him', records Waugh. 'Many of his men had sworn to do so and he was shot in the back by a sniper.' Christopher Sykes says Laycock feared the same fate for Waugh, and 'set a guard on Evelyn's sleeping quarters'. Another officer, Colonel Brian Franks, described to Sykes his conversation with Laycock, when Laycock proposed taking Waugh into action again: 'You will regret it,' said Franks. 'Apart from anything else, Evelyn will probably get shot.' Laycock answered: 'That's a chance we all have to take.' 'Oh,' said Franks, 'I don't mean by the enemy.'

Consequently Waugh spent the whole of 1942 in the United Kingdom, much of it hanging about London waiting for orders, and the rest of the time doing what seemed to him pointless office work. He deliberately made this even more pointless: 'I mainly open the letters and send them on to DAQMG. One or two I address to myself, post them in the OUT tray; they disappear for about three hours into the "Central Registry" and return to the IN tray. ...' It brought out the worst in him, whereas Anthony Powell, now pushing paper as a major in Military Intelligence (Liaison), derived some quiet enjoyment from the regular rhythm:

> My own normal War Office routine was to arrive at half-past nine, knock off as a rule at seven or soon after in the evening. ... After dinner I would return to my one-room flat, get into bed right away with some book likely to be useful in writing the Aubrey biography. ...

And John Betjeman, who had come back from Dublin to a desk in the Ministry of Information, seemed in his element in an office, gazing at 'sports girls' in the canteen and fantasizing about their home life. One of these reveries inspired a poem, 'A Subaltern's Love-song', in which Betjeman imagines himself in romantic pursuit of an ornament of the Surrey stockbroker belt, a fellow Ministry worker named Joan Hunter Dunn. (The poem guesses that she comes from Camberley; the real Miss Hunter Dunn's home was in Aldershot, so he was out by only a few miles.)

Waugh's sole distraction from the boredom of office work was drinking with friends. After one binge he 'saw myself in a mirror ... like a red lacquer Chinese dragon, and saw how I shall look when I die'. On his thirty-ninth birthday, in the middle of this boredom and boozing, he wrote in his diary, trying to persuade himself that all was well: 'A good year. I have begotten a fine daughter [Margaret, born in June 1942], published a successful book, drunk 300 bottles of wine and smoked 300 or more Havana cigars ... health excellent except when impaired by wine; a wife I love. ...' In fact relations with his family were rather distant at present. He saw Laura now and then at weekends, but from her scarcity of letters he began to suspect that she was not terribly interested in him. 'It has been a great sorrow to me to hear nothing of you,' he wrote to her from London. 'I should like to feel that once or twice a week you felt enough interest in me to write & say so.' He suggested ironically: 'If by chance my children should die, do come to London. I miss you every hour.'

This seems a particularly black joke considering that one of his children *had* died, a daughter, born in November 1940, who survived for only one day. 'Poor little girl, she was not wanted,' Waugh wrote in his diary at the time, for Laura's unexpected pregnancy had come in the early days of the war when she was already finding it a struggle to manage her children. Although Margaret's birth and survival a year and a half later were entirely welcome, on his visits to Laura and the family (at Pixton) Waugh usually found his children 'uninterested' in him, and he reciprocated this attitude. In his memoirs, he writes:

> My eldest child's [Teresa's] first memory of me is of the head and shoulders of a strange, angry man in military uniform, who had arrived on leave the night before at her grandmother's house [Pixton] and now appeared at a window under which she was playing with her cousins, shouting: 'For God's sake, someone take those children to the other lawn.'

By the spring of 1943, Waugh had sunk into miserable *ennui*. At night he suffered 'dreams of unendurable boredom – of reading page after page of dullness, of being told endless, pointless jokes, of sitting through cinema films devoid of interest'. He had still hoped to go into active service again, but was now told the blunt truth by Laycock: 'Bob explained to me that I am so unpopular as to be unemployable.' Waugh's only comment in the diary was: 'My future very uncertain.'

In July 1943 it became known that Laycock and his Commandos were about to depart for 'Operation Husky', the long-awaited expedition against the Axis via the toe of Italy. Despite knowing that he was not really wanted, Waugh hoped to accompany Laycock and brigade headquarters, but then without warning, on 24 July, his father died. The same day Laycock set out, leaving Waugh behind. 'It was an unfortunate coincidence,' Waugh wrote in his diary, 'as I was distracted from one by the other. I was angry with Bob for leaving me behind. My father died with disconcerting suddenness.' It did indeed seem unfortunate. By dying just as Evelyn hoped to be in the thick of things at last, Arthur Waugh had dealt a severe blow. Far from his demise liberating Evelyn, in the way that John Plant is liberated in *Work Suspended*, he had timed it so as, yet again, to deprive his son of what seemed rightfully his.

Though Waugh believed that Laycock was using the bereavement as an excuse to leave him behind, Laycock had in fact left clear instructions that Waugh was to follow with the first reinforcements; friendship had evidently overridden powerful doubts about the advisability of taking him into action. However, this was overruled by the man who became Waugh's commanding officer with Laycock's departure, Lord Lovat, who regarded Waugh as 'a source of constant trouble', and could not believe that Laycock really wanted him on his staff. Questioned about Waugh more than forty years later, Lovat described him as, from the army's point of view, 'a total misfit'.

A series of angry confrontations followed between Waugh and Lovat, and Waugh took his case as high as possible, to the Chief of Combined Operations, Lord Louis Mountbatten, with whom he had lunched earlier in the year. But this did him further harm. The case was passed to Mountbatten's deputy, Brigadier Charles Haydon, who bluntly advised him 'to leave the Special Services Brigade [Commandos] for the Brigade's good'. Waugh, immeasurably hurt, applied for posting to the Royal Horse Guards.

He tried to persuade himself that it did not matter. 'I dislike the Army,' he wrote in his diary in August 1943, the month after the crisis.

> I want to get to work again. I do not want any more experiences in life. I have quite enough bottled and carefully laid in the cellar, some still ripening, most ready for drinking, a little beginning to lose its body. I wrote to Frank [Pakenham] very early in the war to say that its chief use would be to cure artists of the illusion that they were men of action. It has worked its cure with me. I have succeeded, too, in dissociating myself very largely with the rest of the world. I am not impatient of its manifest follies and don't want to influence opinions or events, or expose humbug or anything of that kind. I don't want to be of service to anyone or anything. I simply want to do my work as an artist.

In truth, the army's rejection of him was a blow comparable to his first wife's unfaithfulness. Like that earlier calamity, it was to have a profound effect on his life and character, deepening his misanthropy, making him hereafter regard himself as inexorably *contra mundum*, against the world, committing him more than ever to his Church, and causing him to take refuge from all forms of public action by regarding himself – as he had never really done before the war – as a writer by vocation, whose task was to nourish and protect the English language.* It was no coincidence that as soon as the army had rejected him he began to plan a novel.

*

* I owe this last point to an excellent essay by Donat Gallagher on Waugh's changes of attitude at this period, in his edition of Waugh's *Essays, Articles and Reviews* (1986), pp. 289–300.

By the end of January 1944, he was able to announce to the commanding officer of the Household Cavalry Training Regiment at Windsor, to whom he had been attached (instead of the Horse Guards), that 'I have formed the plan of a new novel which will take approximately three months to write. ... If, in fact, the book is not written now it never will be written.'

He had begun to 'meditate starting a novel' as early as October 1942, possibly beginning with the concept of the 'modern Arcadia' which had been his mind early in 1941. Seeds of the new book can also be found in his increasingly pessimistic expectations of life after the war. 'Everyone I meet is despondent of the future,' he wrote in his diary in April 1943. The London crowds suggested the sort of world victory would bring: 'Horrible groups of soldiers in shabby battledress with their necks open, their caps off or at extravagant angles, hands in pockets, cigarettes in the sides of their mouths, lounging about with girls in trousers and high heels and filmstar coiffures.'

There are no further references in his diary or letters to the projected novel until he began work on it, but in October 1943, four months after the crisis caused by his father's death and Laycock's departure for the Mediterranean, he was involved in a drama which added another element. His Oxford contemporary Hubert Duggan was dying at the age of thirty-nine, a lapsed Catholic who had begun to talk of returning to the Church. Waugh decided that 'he has no strength for reasoned argument and needs the presence of someone holy'. Duggan was apparently hesitating because he felt that to return to Catholicism would be a betrayal of his mistress, who had herself died earlier in the year; it would seem, noted Waugh, like 'repentance of his life with her'. Duggan's sister was trying to persuade him to have nothing to do with a priest; Waugh records her as saying: 'You are getting well, you have nothing on your conscience.' On his own initiative, Waugh himself fetched a priest, who gave Duggan absolution and then anointed him. 'Father Devas very quiet and simple and humble,' Waugh recorded,

> trying to make sense of all the confusion, knowing just what he wanted. ... 'Look all I shall do is just to put oil on his forehead and say a prayer. ...' And so by knowing what he wanted and sticking to that ... he got what he wanted. ... We spent the day watching for a spark of gratitude for the love of God and saw the spark. ... Hubert crossed himself and later called me up and said, 'When I became a Catholic it was not from fear', so he knows what happened and accepted it.

He died a few days later. Quite apart from the buttress for Waugh's religion which the incident must have provided, it had come as a substitute for Arthur Waugh's death, which had been 'disconcerting' in its suddenness, offering no chance for reconciliation. In the novel, Waugh was to give the holy death-bed to an elderly father.

Having applied to his Household Cavalry commanding officer for 'leave of absence from duty without pay for three months' to write the novel, Waugh decided not to wait for the reply, and set off for his favourite work-place, the hotel at Chagford in Devon, arriving there on 31 January 1944 'with the intention of starting on an ambitious novel tomorrow morning', he wrote in his diary. 'I still have a cold and am low in spirits but I feel full of literary power which only this evening gives place to qualms of impotence.'

3

Mag Op

The new novel, narrated like *Work Suspended* in the first person, began with the very thing that had just happened to Waugh, the moment at which, as the narrator says, 'love . . . died between me and the army'.

The voice of the narrator, Charles Ryder, was almost identical to that of John Plant in the abandoned novel. But Plant – as his name suggests – had been a rather cold-blooded individual with little indication of emotional depth. Waugh organized the new story so that Charles is examining its events across a gap of years, recollecting with the conflicting feelings of middle age looking back on youth. 'When I reached "c" Company lines, which were at the top of the hill,' begins the first sentence of the book, 'I paused and looked back . . .' The entire novel is an act of pausing and looking back. Begun a few months after Waugh's fortieth birthday (Charles Ryder is 'at the age of thirty-nine'), in a mood of profound distaste for what life could offer him at present, it is a revisiting of the most heightened and vivid feelings of his early years, undertaken with the conscious motive of uncorking and tasting a fine vintage, but arising also from a loss of direction. The army, on which he had staked so much, did not want him, and his wife and family seemed to have little use for him either. It was time to reconsider the past, in the hope of rediscovering who and what he was. 'My theme is memory,' says Charles at the beginning of Book Three. 'These memories, which are my life . . .'

Hence the second word in the title, *Brideshead Revisited*, which otherwise (like so many of Waugh's titles) seems misleading, for Charles only literally revisits the great house near the beginning and end of the story. And the book opens at the precise opposite of Brideshead, in the type of place so often used by Waugh and his friends as a symbol of the desolation of the contemporary scene. 'Here the tram lines ended,' Charles tells us of the Scottish army camp which his battalion is leaving at the beginning of the Prologue. 'This was the extreme limit of the city. . . . Here the close, homogeneous territory of housing and cinemas ended and the hinterland began. . . . Another year of peace would have made the place part of the neighbouring suburb.'

In the first chapter of Book One, Waugh manages in a few thousand words to re-create a whole series of heady things from his own youth – his first visit to a great country house, the delights of Oxford in Eights Week, his first luncheon party of Christ Church Etonians, and falling in love. The 'dissolve' from each of these scenes to the next is almost unnoticeable, but Waugh says in his diary that this section had to be rewritten several times, 'before I got the time sequence and the transitions satisfactory'.

He wrote to Graham Greene that the 'only excuse' he could offer for the self-indulgence of these passages was wartime deprivation, 'spam, blackouts and Nissen huts'. This does not quite convince, for a great deal of his war had been spent in comfortable hotels and London clubs. Alec Waugh suggests a more private motive for the sense of luxury and self-indulgence that pervades the early chapters of the novel. In his view, it was their father's death six months earlier that made Evelyn desire to write in this manner. Until now, he says, Evelyn had always been wary of copying Arthur's emotionalism, but 'the warning example was now removed'.

After examining the modern hell in his early novels, and portraying the limbo of wartime life in *Put Out More Flags*, Waugh is in *Brideshead Revisited* at last letting himself into the earthly paradise; and once again, as in his first two novels, there are strong hints of *Alice in Wonderland*. 'I was in search of love in those days,' says Charles, describing his emotions on the brink of the Christ Church luncheon party, 'and I went full of curiosity and the faint, unrecognized apprehension that here, at last, I should find that low door in the wall, which . . . opened on an enclosed and enchanted garden. . . .' *Alice* itself, one remembers, was written in Christ Church.

Sebastian Flyte, the younger son of Lord Marchmain (owner of Brideshead) and the host at the luncheon, who becomes the object of Charles's love in the first half of the novel, has often been identified with Alastair Graham, to whom Waugh was greatly attached at Oxford. There can be no doubt that Charles's idyllic days with Sebastian owe much to Waugh's recollections of his happy abandon with Alastair. But Sebastian's 'epicene beauty which in extreme youth sings aloud for love' does not sound altogether like Alastair, while his playful dependence on his teddy bear, Aloysius, is taken from John Betjeman and 'Archie'. Sebastian is not, in fact, drawn from life at all, nor is any of the principal characters. 'None except one or two negligible minor figures is a portrait,' wrote Waugh (in *Life* magazine in 1946). The Lygons and the Plunket Greenes may have contributed to the concept of the Flyte family, but there is no casual copying of real-life detail; everything has a function. And in the early part of the book, Sebastian represents childhood.

He meets Charles by vomiting through his open window in college – the sort of thing a child might do – and writes a note of apology in crayon all over a sheet of Charles's best drawing paper. Then, after the luncheon party (at which he eats more than his share of plovers' eggs, like a greedy child), he decides impetuously to take Charles to Brideshead, not to see the house, but to meet his nanny. Arriving there, the two climb 'uncarpeted, scrubbed elm stairs, followed more passages . . . covered with linoleum . . . up a final staircase, gated at the head. . . . Here were the nurseries.' It is a purely symbolic journey back to childhood, led by an irresponsible, innocent child.

Two other characters in the novel underline Sebastian's role in the story as a symbol of childhood. Cara, Lord Marchmain's mistress, remarks that Sebastian is 'in love with his own childhood', and Anthony Blanche, the feline Old Etonian whom Charles meets at Sebastian's luncheon party, observes the element of the child in Sebastian, and hints that it may be fake. 'You know, when I hear him talk,' he says, 'I am reminded of that in some ways nauseating picture of "*Bubbles*". . . . When dear Sebastian speaks it is like a little sphere of soapsud. . . .'

Blanche conducts this conversation with Charles over dinner at 'a delightful hotel' at Thame (the Spreadeagle, though Waugh avoids introducing Fothergill, knowing that such things would reduce the book to a mere *roman à clef*). Like Ambrose Silk, he is superficially modelled on Brian Howard – 'part Gallic, part Yankee, part, perhaps, Jew' – while his recitation of *The Waste Land* through the megaphone from the Christ Church balcony recalls Harold Acton. But his chief characteristic is taken from neither Howard nor Acton; it emanates from Waugh himself.

In a passage deleted when Waugh revised the novel in 1960, Blanche is described as 'shedding a vivid, false light of eccentricity upon everyone so that the three prosaic Etonians [at the luncheon] seemed suddenly to become creatures of his fantasy'. This is a description of Waugh's own technique in his diary and letters: to highlight and exaggerate eccentricities to the extent that real people become fictional characters – a technique he had learnt among the exquisitely comic members of the Hypocrites' Club. In *Brideshead Revisited*, Anthony Blanche is representative of the entire Hypocrites' set; he stands for the implicitly homosexual and precociously sophisticated group of people who had brought Waugh out of his shell and turned the serious youth from Lancing into a rake, a dandy, and an artist. But he is also an aspect of Waugh himself, his capacity to imagine life in more lurid colours than it really displays. Just as Blanche suggests that Sebastian may be fake, so Sebastian casts doubt on Blanche's lubricious tales of seduction and intrigue. 'I just wanted to find out how much truth there was in what Anthony said last night,' Charles asks Sebastian after his dinner with Blanche, and gets the answer: 'I shouldn't think a word. That's his great charm.'

Each of them is, in Blanche's own word, an 'exquisite', a Firbankian confection designed to tease, amuse, and excite; an aspect of Waugh himself, raised in his imagination, rather than a real remembered person. If the idea of Sebastian as Waugh seems far-fetched, one should remember Harold Acton's description of the young Evelyn: '. . . a prancing faun . . . wide-apart eyes . . . the curved sensual lips, the hyacinthine locks of hair . . .'

Sebastian's first name is that of the saint who, in medieval iconography, was the symbol of male homosexual beauty. 'My dear, I should like to stick you full of arrows like a p-p-pin cushion,' says Anthony Blanche to him. Yet though Waugh implies (and only implies, never states) that a sexual relationship develops between Sebastian and Charles, he speaks of it entirely in terms of childhood innocence:

> It seems to me that I grew younger daily with each adult habit that I acquired. . . . That summer term with Sebastian, it seemed as though I was being given a brief spell of what I had never known, a happy childhood, and though its toys were silk shirts and liqueurs and cigars and its naughtiness high in the catalogue of grave sins, there was something of nursery freshness about us that fell little short of the joy of innocence.

The only judgement he will pass on the homosexuality of his generation at Oxford, 'the wickedness of that time', is that it was 'like the spirit they mix with the pure grape of the Douro, heady stuff full of dark ingredients; it at once enriched and retarded the whole process of adolescence as the spirit checks the fermentation ... so that it must lie in the dark ... until it is brought up at last fit for the table'.

Brideshead itself, the great house, has no more basis in reality than do Sebastian or Anthony Blanche. In setting and architecture, with its dome distantly visible across the fields, it suggests Castle Howard in Yorkshire, which Waugh had visited several times (the actual address, given in a letter from Sebastian to Charles, is 'Brideshead Castle'). The *art nouveau* decorations of the chapel are taken from Madresfield, the Lygons' house, where the chapel had been refitted in this style as a wedding present from Lord Beauchamp to his wife. Waugh locates Brideshead, however, neither in Yorkshire nor Worcestershire, but somewhere near Swindon, in the area of England which includes both Mells (the railway station for Brideshead is 'Melstead') and Lord Berners's Faringdon House. Indeed, the westward journey which Charles and Sebastian take from Oxford could also lead to Waugh's own home, Piers Court. If Waugh himself can be found in Sebastian and in Anthony Blanche – symbols of what one might call the child and the wild imagination in him – then surely Brideshead is an aspect of him too, his vision of the English country house as the city, the possibility of earthly perfection.

Having established these three facets of himself, he creates, in the third chapter, another self-identity. Charles's father, with whom Charles is cooped up in their stuffy Bayswater house during the long vacation, has a certain resemblance to the self-dramatizing Arthur Waugh. Like Arthur, Mr Ryder is characterized by a determination to seem much older than he is ('He was then in his late fifties, but ... to see him one might have put him at seventy, to hear him speak at nearly eighty'), though when by himself he reverts almost to childhood; Charles observes him feeding on 'meagre nursery snacks – rusks, glasses of milk, bananas, and so forth', an indication of the extent to which he is posing. On the other hand, far from sentimentalizing over his son as Arthur had done with his boys, he behaves to Charles 'in a spirit of careful mockery', arranging a dinner party of the most boring individuals he can find, and deliberately misunderstanding Charles's hints that he needs money. Though Waugh is certainly caricaturing the father–son strife which had marked most of his friends' lives, he is doing so not by portraying a real father but by endowing Mr Ryder with his own wicked sense of humour. Charles's father is the sort of parent Waugh was no doubt already hoping to be, and which in time he certainly became.

Similarly, the other father in the book, Lord Marchmain, contains an element of self-portraiture in that he is a grown-up Basil Seal, with Byronic good looks, an encyclopaedic understanding of the world, and a fondness for mocking others. 'Even now they come back again and again to be snubbed and laughed at,' says Cara of his friends.

Waugh finished writing the third chapter on 26 February 1944, having completed 33,000 words in less than four weeks, despite spending much of that time in 'spinsterish' rewriting with an eye to style. For him, it was an astonishing speed. He says in the Preface to the 1960 edition: 'I wrote with a zest that was quite strange to me.' He told A.D. Peters that he expected to be finished by mid-May, though he was not sanguine about the novel's prospects: 'It would have a small public at any time. I should not think six Americans would understand it.'

No sooner was Chapter Three done than Waugh heard that 'the War Office had turned down my application for leave'. He was to be ADC to some General nobody had heard of. 'So that ends my hopes of another two months' serious work.' He went off to the General's HQ for a week's trial, got drunk in the mess on the first evening, and was 'returned unaccepted'. Another General was immediately produced for him, 'like a rabbit from a hat', but Waugh persuaded this one to give him six weeks' leave, and returned to Chagford to get on with the book, 'in a state of intense nervous excitement which must be calm before I start work'. No sooner had he 'planned the work of the next five weeks' than a letter arrived from the General cancelling his whole arrangement with Waugh. Consequently Waugh resumed work with the expectation that he would be summoned away at any moment. Nevertheless, in just over a week he had written another 13,000 words.

The fourth chapter deals with Brideshead itself, describing the house in considerable architectural detail. Its style is predominantly baroque ('that high and insolent dome ... those coffered ceilings'), as is frequently Waugh's own prose, most notably in a florid paragraph which opens the chapter: 'The languor of Youth – how unique and quintessential it is! How quickly, how irrecoverably, lost! The zest, the generous affections, the illusions, the despair, all the traditional attributes of Youth – all save this – come and go with us through life. ...' Yet baroque is the ornamentation of classical formality rather than a free indulgence in romantic licence, and Waugh's chapter is built upon a strict plan. It is concerned with two issues, the right to identify oneself with (claim ownership of) a great house, and Catholicism.

When Charles shows curiosity about the dates of various parts of the house ('Is the dome by Inigo Jones too?'), Sebastian reproves him: 'Oh, Charles, don't be such a tourist.' Charles has been relegated to those who pay their half-crowns and troop dutifully through with guidebooks. He tries to brush the insult aside: 'It's the sort of thing I like to know.' But throughout the chapter Waugh reminds us that Charles still belongs to the tourists and not yet to the family.

When (later in the chapter) Charles and Sebastian travel to Venice – a city, as it were, of still greater Bridesheads, the *palazzi* – Charles notes how Lord Marchmain disdains tourism. 'Alex has not once let me inside San Marco,' complains Cara. But then, like Sebastian at Brideshead, he has no need to be a tourist, since he occupies a *palazzo* as fine as any, 'a narrow Palladian façade . . . the *piano nobile* . . . ablaze with frescoes of the school of Tintoretto. . . .' When he wants to, Lord Marchmain can beat the tourists at their own game. Sebastian mentions that Charles is 'very keen on painting', whereupon Lord Marchmain, giving a hint of 'deep boredom', asks Charles:

> 'Yes? Any particular Venetian painting?'
> 'Bellini,' I answered rather wildly.
> 'Yes? Which?'
> 'I'm afraid I didn't know there were two of them.'
> 'Three, to be precise.'

Snubbed by both father and son, branded as an ignorant tourist, Charles has recourse to the one thing that can confer some status upon him with the family. He identifies himself as an artist.

At Sebastian's instigation, he draws the fountain at Brideshead, producing 'a very passable echo of Piranesi'. Next, he moves on to decorating a little half-abandoned room with mural panels. It is a small thing, but significant enough for one of the army officers to notice it at the end of the book – 'modern work but, if you ask me, the prettiest in the place'. In any case, to have left his mark on the actual structure of Brideshead is enough. He is joining the ranks of the artists, architects and landscapers who in past generations had a defined role in the great families.

The painting of the garden room at Brideshead eventually inspires Charles to become, by profession, a painter of great houses – a metaphor for Waugh's particular specialization as a novelist, probably derived from the work of John Piper, who had come to prominence in the late Thirties as an artist specializing in drawings of Georgian and Victorian architecture. Waugh first met him at Renishaw, the Sitwells' home, in 1942: 'There is an extremely charming artist called Piper staying here making a series of drawings of the house.' At one point it was proposed that Piper should illustrate a private edition of *Brideshead Revisited*. 'I don't much admire Piper's work, but know no one else,' Waugh wrote to John Betjeman.

Charles is also separated from the Flyte family by their Catholicism. At first, he regards the fact that Sebastian is a Catholic as merely 'a foible, like his teddy bear'. When he suggests to Sebastian that religion is 'an awful lot of nonsense', Sebastian replies: 'Is it nonsense? I wish it were. It sometimes sounds terribly sensible to me.' Charles swiftly realizes that this, too, is excluding him from the family and the house.

Sebastian's attitude to his religion is as deliberately childish as everything else about him. He says he believes in things like the Christmas story because they are 'a lovely idea' (Charles is scornful, but to no effect), and describes how he prayed to St Anthony of Padua when his teddy bear went missing, whereupon the bear was returned by a cab driver. On the other hand, he makes it clear that Catholicism, like the aristocracy, is a clique to which Charles does not belong. Sebastian describes his fellow-Catholics in terms such as he might use of fellow-aristocrats. 'They seem just like other people,' says Charles hopefully, but receives the withering reply:

'My dear Charles, that's exactly what they're not – particularly in this country, where they're so few. It's not just that they're a clique – as a matter of fact, they're at least four cliques all blackguarding each other half the time – but they've got an entirely different outlook on life; everything they think is important is different from other people. They try and hide it as much as they can, but it comes out all the time. It's quite natural, really, that they should.'

However, unlike the aristocracy, Catholicism opens its doors to anyone, and Charles makes it clear to the reader that, since the events of the book have taken place, he himself has become a Catholic. 'I have come,' he tells the reader even before Sebastian makes this speech, 'to accept claims which then, in 1923, I never troubled to examine, and to accept the supernatural as the real.' This revelation rather defuses the end of the book, but Waugh wants it to be absolutely clear in the reader's mind, as early as possible in the novel, that the story is being narrated by someone who is no longer a tourist, but an insider.

*

Sebastian's family may seem to be secure at the top of English society, but there are hints that they are on the edge of decay, like the Lasts and the Boots. Neither Lord Marchmain nor his elder son has been laying down wine, and the butler shakes his head over this: 'There's enough here for ten years at the rate it's going, but how shall we be then?' Chapter Five takes up this motif and gives further hints of erosion – this time the erosion of the aristocracy by the middle class.

This chapter, which concludes the Arcadian Book One, introduces two non-aristocratic figures who are worming their way to the core of Brideshead via the family's weakest point of defence, Sebastian. 'Mr Samgrass of All Souls' becomes keeper to Sebastian when he takes to drink, and Rex Mottram, a politician of Canadian birth, gets into a position of influence with the family by rescuing Sebastian from the police after a drink-driving charge.

Waugh emphasizes that neither of these figures belongs to the same caste as Sebastian's family. Samgrass's interest in genealogy is described as that of 'the Victorian tourist', and Mottram's origins are left deliberately obscure: 'His life, so far as he made it known, began in the war. . . .' Each is dismissed by Sebastian as a nobody: '"Who is this Samgrass? . . ."' "Just someone of mummy's".' And Rex is '"just someone of Julia's"' (he is a friend of Sebastian's sister). But by the end of the chapter Rex has established himself as 'the embodiment . . . of power and prosperity', and Charles has lost Sebastian to Samgrass, who takes him on a trip to the Levant.

Waugh admitted to Christopher Sykes that Rex Mottram, unlike the other characters, was drawn from life – a portrait of Brendan Bracken – while Samgrass has been identified with Maurice Bowra. Certainly his physical appearance is Bowra's ('a short, plump man . . . with sparse hair brushed flat on an over-large head'), and though there is not the slightest resemblance in character, Bowra himself delighted in the identification. 'I hope you spotted *me*,' Christopher Sykes reports him as saying: 'what a piece of artistry that is – best thing in the whole book.' (On the other hand Waugh records Bowra maliciously describing the novel as 'Cecil Beaton's favourite book', and adding: 'Connolly does a funny imitation of Marchmain's deathbed.')

By the end of the fifth chapter, Brideshead almost seems to be owned by Samgrass and all he represents. Charles observes this when he encounters Samgrass one evening in the Tapestry Hall: '"You find me in solitary possession,"' he said, and indeed he seemed to possess the hall and the sombre scenes of venery that hung round it, to possess the caryatids on either side of the fireplace. . . .' This is part of a larger process, as again Charles perceives. Looking through the memoir of Lady Marchmain's brother, killed in the 1914–18 war (edited for publication by Mr Samgrass), he observes that 'the Catholic squires of England' are now doomed: 'These men must die . . . so that things might be safe for the travelling salesman, with his polygonal pince-nez, his fat wet handshake, his grinning dentures.'

What, then, distinguishes Charles himself from Mr Samgrass, Rex Mottram, and the other non-aristocrats who are making inroads into the fortress of the upper class? In the earlier chapters he has escaped any taint of social climbing through his love for Sebastian; he declares that 'to know and love one other human being is the root of all wisdom'. But by the end of Book One the unselfishness of that love is being tempered by a rather bourgeois feeling, prompted by Sebastian's mother, Lady Marchmain, that he should try to save Sebastian from alcoholism. His motives in this are distinctly mixed.

He knows perfectly well that Sebastian only drinks heavily when he feels oppressed by his mother, yet he himself increases Sebastian's sense of oppression by cooperating intermittently with Lady Marchmain in her attempts to restrain him, rather than refusing to have anything to do with her. 'Have you gone over to her side?' Sebastian asks. Charles's excuse is good manners; he refuses to leave Brideshead with Sebastian in the early morning without saying goodbye to his hostess because 'I don't happen to like running away'. Sebastian is contemptuous of this display of bourgeois manners; a true aristocrat never bothers with such things – just as, in the previous chapter, he is scornful when Charles says he will present his painting of the fountain to Lady Marchmain. 'Why? You don't know her,' he says to Charles. 'It seems polite,' answers Charles. 'I'm staying in her house.' 'Give it to nanny,' answers Sebastian.

Love for Sebastian is not enough. Charles wants to curry favour with Lady Marchmain, just as he also takes care not to offend 'Bridey' (Lord Brideshead), the emotionally stunted elder son and heir. In making this choice, he has both found a way into the family and stumbled upon the thing that will destroy it, for it is Lady Marchmain and her elder son who are throwing down the defences and letting in the bourgeoisie. Samgrass owes his place in the family to Sebastian's mother, and later in the book Bridey marries a Mrs Muspratt, a caricature of the middle classes. Indeed, there is some suggestion that Lady Marchmain herself is not quite 'top drawer'.

Much attention is devoted by Waugh to the description of her small upstairs sitting room at Brideshead. She has put in a false ceiling, decorated the room with 'innumerable little watercolours', and filled a small rosewood bookcase with 'works of poetry and piety' bound in lambskin. The result is 'intimate, feminine, modern', and Charles deplores it. Indeed, Lady Marchmain's femininity may be the cause of that oppressiveness which so overwhelms Sebastian and Charles but cannot be explained by them. When speaking to Charles of Sebastian's decline, she takes hold of her subject (says Charles scathingly) 'in a feminine, flirtatious way'. Sebastian's sister Julia is acceptable in the homoerotic world of Sebastian and Charles because she looks like her brother – when introduced in the third chapter of Book One she is described as having identical features and hair 'scarcely longer' than his – and behaves with boyish carelessness. Cordelia, the youngest member of the family, is only a child and therefore sexless. Lady Marchmain, however, exudes a sinisterly feminine odour.

Early readers of the novel puzzled over the fact that Lady Marchmain has many objectionable characteristics, yet represents the Catholic viewpoint which the story is clearly intended to uphold. Waugh admitted to A.D. Peters that 'Lady Marchmain is an enigma', and wrote to Nancy Mitford, who had raised the same point: 'No, I am not on her side; but God is, who suffers fools gladly; and the book is about God. Does that answer it?' It may in theological terms, but not in narrative, and Lady Marchmain remains contradictory. She has two conflicting functions in the book. She causes Sebastian to go to the bad – a role that, if he had been true to the experiences of his generation, Waugh would have given to the father rather than the mother; indeed Lady Marchmain's self-dramatizing sentimentality has a hint of Arthur Waugh and Ernest Betjemann. On the other hand it is she who has introduced Catholicism to Brideshead; Lord Marchmain's own family were not Catholic, and he converted when he married her. It is hard to know what to conclude of this; Waugh could so easily have made the Flytes 'typical of the Catholic squires of England' – a phrase used of Lady Marchmain's brothers. Nothing seems to be gained by making Lord Marchmain a convert, unless one accepts that everything in the novel, including the great house itself and its occupants, is an idealization of the personality of Waugh, who was a convert himself.

As March 1944 drew to a close, Waugh, still at Chagford, pressed on with the book as fast as ever, expecting a summons from the army any day. His only problem was that he found himself rushing the narrative. 'It is always my temptation in writing to make everything happen in one day,' he noted in his diary on 22 March – indeed, 'in one hour on one page and so lose its drama and suspense. So all today I have been rewriting and stretching until I am cramped.' Despite these hold-ups, by 29 March he had completed more than 60,000 words of what, writing to Laura, he called his 'Mag Op' – *magnum opus*. Meanwhile Mrs Cobb, the proprietor of the Chagford Hotel, attended to his special need for peace and quiet. 'An Air Force honeymoon couple over my head made work impossible all day,' he noted in his diary. 'Today I had the couple moved.'

He realized that the first draft would require extensive rewriting, particularly expansion. But he preferred to hurry on rather than go back; his mind was rushing ahead with the story at such speed that he found it difficult to sleep: 'Wrote 2,700 words today. ... Weary, but I don't sleep and have taken drugs every night this week.' There is a reference within the novel itself to the speed and certainty with which it was written. Describing his painting of the drawing room of Marchmain House in London, just before it is destroyed to make way for a block of flats, Charles says:

> I was normally a slow and deliberate painter; that afternoon and all next day, and the day after, I worked fast. I could do nothing wrong. At the end of each passage I paused, tense, afraid to start the next, fearing, like a gambler, that luck must turn and the pile be lost. Bit by bit, minute by minute, the thing came into being. There were no difficulties; the intricate multiplicity of light and colour became a whole; the right colour was where I wanted it on the palette; each brush stroke, as soon as it was complete, seemed to have been there always.

The imminent destruction of Marchmain House is a metaphor for the annihilation of the old aristocratic society which Waugh believed was inevitable with the arrival of peace. Like Charles, he was trying to get it all down on canvas before it was too late.

The first chapter of Book Two charts the decline of Sebastian into a drunkard, the predicament Waugh probably now feared for himself. Drink had contributed to the ruin of his army career, and writing to Lady Dorothy Lygon he admitted that he was getting worried about its physical effects:

> ... in London it is not unfair to say I never drew a sober breath. I was beginning to lose my memory which for a man who lives entirely in the past, is to lose life itself. In fact I got a little anxious about it but I found all I needed was congenial work. I have been here [at

Chagford] six weeks, the nut has cleared and I am writing better than ever I did.

However, on several occasions before the novel was finished he went back to London to try to sort out his position vis à vis the army, and while there drank himself into what he admitted in his diary was 'an alcoholic stupor'. Soon after the book was finished he made a resolution 'never to be drunk again', and for a while managed to keep this pledge.

Sebastian is now dismissed from the story with ruthless speed – it is the only point at which the temptation to rush, of which Waugh speaks in his diary, becomes evident – and Julia, and Charles's interest in her, takes over the stage completely. This has led some readers to take *Brideshead Revisited* as two novels, a homosexual love story followed by a heterosexual one. If the book were really about the two love affairs, this would be true. A more cynical interpreter might feel that Charles, having failed to become 'one of the family' at Brideshead by attaching himself to Sebastian, is now trying again via his sister. Also Waugh, revisiting his own past, has moved on from the romantic friendships of Oxford to the heterosexual experiences which followed them. But most of all, Sebastian can be dismissed because in one respect he and Charles are the same character. Sebastian is a real younger brother, kept out of his inheritance by the ridiculous Bridey, resorting for consolation to drink and homosexual flirtation. In the second part of the book, Charles himself takes over the younger brother role, and is the landless young man who pines to inherit Brideshead and all its riches. Sebastian is no longer needed.

When Charles first meets Julia she is 'just eighteen . . . flat-chested, leggy', terms which fit Laura Herbert at the time Waugh got to know her. If Waugh were writing true autobiography, Julia would be She-Evelyn. But the book is an exercise in reorganizing the past as well as revisiting it.

Like Laura, Julia has been brought up by a mother who has imported Catholicism into the family – Mrs Herbert was a convert, and her husband's family were not Catholic by tradition. Like Laura, Julia's father is absent from the scene (Laura's was dead). And when Julia allows herself to drift into the companionship of Rex Mottram, many years her senior, a man with a matrimonial past, not of noble birth and financially self-made, this, surely, is Laura being courted by Waugh himself.

Rex is, in other words, Waugh as he must have feared that he seemed in the eyes of Laura's family. He was, of course, a Catholic, but only a convert of very recent date, and in the novel he makes Rex try to join the Church virtually overnight, so as to ingratiate himself with Julia's family. This produces a very comic passage, with Rex readily agreeing to believe anything he is told by the instructing priest – and by Cordelia, who deliberately misleads him – but one recalls Father D'Arcy's account of Waugh's disarming readiness to accept all Catholic doctrine unquestioningly.

Lady Marchmain and her family respond to Julia's engagement to Rex with pain and a sense of outrage, such as Waugh must have suspected he had aroused in the Herberts, and when it is discovered that Rex is in fact a *divorcé* and cannot be married in a Catholic church, Waugh seems to be imagining the worst that could have happened to him with Laura and her family.

Up to this point in the novel, one might suppose that Waugh has chosen to omit any reference to his disastrous first marriage. Then, in the first chapter of the final Book, we are introduced to Charles's wife Celia, née Mulcaster, high-born, wealthy, with a 'curiously hygienic quality' to her prettiness, a brittle, ambitious woman of whom Charles has quickly tired, and who has caused him to spend two years painting in South America because he has discovered her in adultery. This seems to be an imagining by Waugh of what might have happened had he not left She-Evelyn as soon as she became unfaithful. Charles's first reaction to the discovery of adultery is to go abroad, then to try to pick up the threads of the marriage, then to have an affair with Julia, then to be divorced from Celia. It is like a rewriting of *A Handful of Dust* without the melodramatic ending.

There is also a little stab at Laura. Celia has two children by Charles, who feels utterly remote from them – he calls them 'her children'. There is something here of Waugh's own feeling of exclusion from the nursery. On 13 May 1944, while he was working on the novel at Chagford, he wrote in his diary: 'Telephone message that Laura has had a daughter and is well. A dull day's work.' Although Pixton was not far from Chagford, he did not visit Laura or see the baby (christened Harriet) until two and a half weeks had passed, when he wrote in the diary: 'My children were much in evidence and boring.'

That this was a pose, and that his real feelings were more complicated, is suggested by his diary entry on his forty-first birthday the following October, when he listed the achievements of the year as 'a daughter born, a book written', apparently rating Harriet's birth higher than the composition of *Brideshead Revisited*. Nor was he unfeeling about the birth; to Laura he wrote, shortly before the baby was delivered: 'My heart is with you in this time of waiting. I pray God that by the time you get this you will be happily delivered. I will come as soon after the birth as you think fit.' There is also a suggestion in the novel that he is reproaching himself for his lack of feeling at the death of Laura's baby in 1940; Julia says bitterly of her stillborn child: 'She was a daughter, so Rex didn't so much mind her being dead.'

Nevertheless, he now felt so completely excluded from family life that, late in 1944, he suggested to Laura that after the war she should settle on a farm (Laura liked farming) while he should 'retain my aunts' house at Midsomer Norton . . . for my work and collecting mania [he had begun to collect Victorian bric-à-brac] and your frequent visits. . . . It is not an attempt to set up a separate household, but . . . I could not work near my children.' A factor in this sense of separation was Laura's youth. A letter from him in January 1945 shows that in many ways he still regarded her as a child:

> Darling Laura, sweet whiskers, do try to write me better letters. Your last . . . so eagerly expected, was a bitter disappointment. . . . I know you lead a dull life, my heart bleeds for it, though I believe you could make it more interesting if you had the will. But that is no reason to make your letters as dull as your life. I simply am not interested in Bridget's children. Do grasp that. A letter should be a form of conversation; write as though you were talking to me.

Laura was now in her late twenties; this is the sort of letter a father might write to an adolescent at school. When her next letter arrived he gave her an equally condescending pat on the head: 'A much better one.'

So, though Julia rather than Celia is the character in the novel who most approximates to Laura Waugh, Charles's sour relationship with his wife does seem to reflect something of Waugh's discomfort in his second marriage.

Charles begins his affair with Julia on board a transatlantic liner, amid 'Jazz Modern' (Art Deco) surroundings which, in contrast to Brideshead, are meant to symbolize the brutal world of Slough and the *Daily Beast*. There are a number of references in this last part of the novel – recalling *A Handful of Dust* – to modern civilization as 'just another jungle closing in'. The great bronze doors of the ship's dining room break loose during a storm and clash so dangerously that almost all except Charles and Julia stay below in their cabins – an image of modern life destroying its own inhabitants.

Julia doubts the stability of Charles's feelings, and reproaches him for disloyalty to her brother. Charles answers: 'He was the forerunner', but Julia is not altogether content with this explanation and says: 'Perhaps I am only a forerunner too.' As the book moves towards its conclusion, it becomes clear that she is right.

When she and Charles first become lovers, Waugh describes the sexual act as if Charles were acquiring a piece of property: 'It was as though a deed of conveyance of her narrow loins had been drawn and sealed. I was making my first entry as a freeholder of a property I would enjoy and develop at leisure.' This tasteless image becomes explicable if one considers the practical consequences of the love affair. If Julia divorces Rex and marries Charles, then Charles will be able to regard Brideshead as to all intents his own.

Rather than countenance this wish-fulfilling ending to the novel, Waugh makes Julia's Catholic conscience, dormant for many years, rear up in a histrionic speech ('They know all about it ... they bought it for a penny at the church door. ... *Living in sin.* ...') which seems out of character and is untypical of Waugh's naturalistic dialogue; Graham Greene has described it as 'a little over-written ... a bit gamey', and in a memorandum to MGM, when they wanted to film the book in 1946, Waugh himself, evidently uneasy about the speech, alleged that it 'was not intended to be a verbal transcription of anything she actually said, but a half-poetic epitome of what was in her mind'.

Once again, when Lord Marchmain comes home to die, it seems possible that Charles may acquire the house. 'It opened a prospect,' says Charles drily of this, 'the prospect once gained at the turn of the avenue, as I had first seen it with Sebastian, of the secluded valley, the lakes falling away one below the other, the old house in the foreground, the rest of the world abandoned and forgotten; a world of its own of peace and love and beauty. ...' It is of this prospect, of Brideshead becoming his and his children's, that Sebastian and Julia have been the forerunners. He is now face to face with his true love, the house.

Again, it is the Catholic Church that intervenes, for Lord Marchmain's return to the faith on his deathbed – a scene copied directly from the Duggans – moves Julia to tell Charles they must part. The function of Catholicism in the novel, then, is to deprive Charles of his prize. The father, though allowed a holy death, is made the instrument of that deprivation. If Lord Marchmain had not died, Julia and

Charles would have been left in possession of Brideshead. (If Arthur Waugh had not died, Evelyn might have led his men heroically in battle.)

Lord Marchmain's conversion leads Charles himself to join the Church, and when in the Epilogue he returns to Brideshead with the army, it is as a Catholic. Kneeling before the altar in the chapel, he tells himself that the burning of the sanctuary lamp means that Brideshead has been put to a far greater use than its builders had ever intended, for amid 'the age of Hooper' (the sloppy young subaltern who represents what England will be like after the war) the flame of faith is still alight.

It is an ingenious ending, but not quite true to the novel. The great prize has slipped from Charles's grasp, and however much he may claim that his heart has been lightened by prayer before the altar, the truth, as he has told Hooper a few lines earlier, is: 'I'm homeless, childless, middle-aged, loveless, Hooper.' The real *genius loci* of Brideshead is not to be found in the chapel, but in the high garret where the aged Nanny Hawkins still presides. 'Mrs Hawkins is up in her old room,' Charles is told by an elderly housemaid, and he duly begins the ascent 'up the uncarpeted stairs, to the nursery'.

In his 1960 preface, Waugh claimed that *Brideshead Revisited* was a novel about 'the operation of divine grace'. But until the last chapters the novel is very little concerned with God. Its theme is thoroughly mundane: the erosion of the Flytes by the middle class – Mr Samgrass, Rex, Mrs Muspratt, and most of all Charles himself, who plays the chief role in the destruction of the family.

It is he who, by currying favour with Lady Marchmain, drives Sebastian into alcoholic exile, who hastens her decline by failing to remain loyal to her, who breaks up Julia's marriage, who connives at a plan which will exclude Bridey from his inheritance, and who tries at first to dissuade the family from bringing a priest to Lord Marchmain on his deathbed. Such behaviour is not very unusual for a Waugh hero – Basil Seal would have done as much – but it does not fit Charles's sudden acquisition of holiness at the end of the book. If his part in the story is analysed, Charles begins to bear an unpleasant resemblance to Zouch in Anthony Powell's *From a View to a Death*, another novel about a landed family nearly dispossessed by a middle-class intruder. On Waugh's own territory, his conduct is much closer to that of John Beaver than Tony Last.

Far from demonstrating 'the operation of divine grace', the book shows the same malicious fate at work that can be found in all Waugh's novels. The presiding spirit of *Brideshead Revisited* is not divine grace, but the power Waugh refers to at the conclusion of *Labels* as 'Fortune ... the least capricious of deities ... [who] arranges things on the just and rigid system that no one shall be very happy for very long'.

Among the earliest readers of the novel was Lady Pansy Lamb, née Pakenham, who had moved freely in those circles which *Brideshead Revisited* might be supposed to portray. She wrote to Waugh, however, that it could not 'make me nostalgic' for the aristocratic society of the Twenties, for the simple reason that this world had not resembled the novel at all:

> Nobody was brilliant, beautiful, rich & owner of a wonderful home though some were one or the other. Most were respectable, narrow-minded with ideals in no way differing from Hooper's except that their basic ration was larger. Hooperism is only the transcription in cheaper terms of the upper class outlook of 1920. . . .
>
> You see English Society of the Twenties as something baroque and magnificent on its last legs . . . I fled from it because it seemed prosperous, bourgeois and practical and I believe it still is.

Similarly Harold Acton, when he received an early copy of the book from Waugh, did not recognize it as in any way an accurate portrait of their young days. Such lack of recognition is understandable, for Waugh was not recalling a historical golden age but inventing one.

Like all his writing, the novel was a conscious exercise in language, in this case an experiment in baroque. And here, as with the use of Catholicism in the story, Waugh was not being altogether true to his own nature. 'Charles,' asks Cordelia in Book Two, Chapter One, 'Modern Art is all bosh, isn't it?' Charles answers: 'Great bosh.' His reply is not lightly given. In *Brideshead Revisited*, Waugh abandons his stance as scrutineer of the chaotic contemporary world through rigorous classical language. No longer is there an invigorating tension between subject and style. The language attempts to mimic the subject, to copy the baroque of Brideshead itself, reflecting Charles's attempts to get inside the family and take them over.

Charles's baroque reveries, generally at the opening of a chapter or after a pause, are usually overdone. On a far higher level are the more casual, small-scale images which seem to have come from a late awakening in Waugh of the possibility of 'fine writing': Rex courting Julia 'with a passion that disclosed the corner of something like it in her', or (better still) the description of Charles putting a lighted cigarette between her lips when he and Julia first meet, and catching 'a thin bat's squeak of sexuality, inaudible to any but me'. Some weeks after starting the novel, Waugh wrote in his diary: 'English writers, at forty, either set about prophesying or acquiring a style. Thank God I think I am beginning to acquire a style.' It was the sort of style he had despised in his early days as a novelist.

Also, Charles is too lightweight a character to justify his big speeches. There is little to distinguish him from Paul Pennyfeather or William Boot – Waugh's passive Alices in Wonderland – other than his ambitions to acquire Brideshead. After reading the novel, Nancy Mitford wrote to Waugh that she found Charles 'a tiny bit dim', and wished he had 'a little more glamour'. She could perceive that he was only the narrator, but this did not eradicate the shortcoming: 'I can quite see how the person who tells is dim but then would Julia *and* her brother . . . be in love with him if he was?' Waugh replied: 'Yes I know what you mean; he *is* dim, but then he is telling the story and it is not his story. . . . I think the crucial question is: does Julia's love for him seem real or is he so dim that it falls flat; if the latter the book fails plainly.'

It may be objected that Sebastian and Julia are themselves 'dim' if examined closely. Sebastian's charm lies in his great physical beauty, which the book can scarcely be expected to convey, and many readers would agree with Christopher Sykes that Julia 'remains dead as mutton . . . a carefully modelled wax mannequin'. The old Waugh skill, however, is undimmed in the comic and semi-comic characters, especially Samgrass and Bridey, while in Cordelia he manages for the first time to create an entirely plausible and lifelike individual without any sort of exaggeration or caricature. (She is portrayed so sympathetically that Nancy Mitford asserted that Charles was really in love with her and not with her elder sister.)

Waugh's 1960 trimmings pruned a little of the book's lushness, but in his preface to the new edition he admitted that the baroque passages of the narrative were 'an essential part', and he left them mostly untouched. They are essential because the whole novel is a kind of linguistic delayed adolescence, a sudden surrender to romanticism by a writer who had reached the middle of life and wanted to open doors he had previously held shut; also an attempt at self-reassurance by a man who, at his worst moments, could say with Charles Ryder: 'I'm homeless, childless, middle-aged, loveless.'

4

Up in the Best-seller List

The passage describing Lord Marchmain's death was written on the morning of 6 June 1944, D-Day ('This morning at breakfast,' noted Waugh, 'the waiter told me the Second Front had opened'), and the Epilogue ('which is easy meat') followed. During the last stretch, Waugh was 'in alternate despondency and exultation about the book. . . . I think perhaps it is the first of my novels rather than the last.'

He was now willing to return to army life, but the army was not enthusiastic. He wrote to Colonel Brian Franks, who was nominally in command of him at present, and Christopher Sykes was there when the letter arrived. 'What on earth shall I do with him?' Franks groaned. 'I can't very well tell him to take another three months' leave and write another book, which is what I would like to do.'

Waugh spent a couple of weeks with the Special Air Service regiment commanded by Franks, but knew he was not wanted. It was possibly at this juncture that he wrote to Randolph Churchill offering to command his father Winston's personal bodyguard (who were Royal Marines). Instead, he received an invitation from Randolph to join a mission to Yugoslavia, whose Partisans were thought to require encouragement in their efforts against Hitler; Waugh might be able to deal with the Catholic Croatians (the Serbs were Orthodox), and in any case Randolph wanted 'someone to talk to'.

Waugh's first contribution when they arrived, in the summer of 1944, was to suggest that the Communist leader Tito, whom the British supported, was really a woman in disguise. 'Tito like Lesbian', he wrote in his diary, and he went about saying this until advised to shut up. When Waugh was formally introduced to Tito a day or so later, the leader was heard to say: 'Ask Captain Waugh why he thinks I am a woman.' Discreet political missions were not really in Waugh's line, and he might have got into serious trouble had not Randolph Churchill exceeded him in drunken blusterings. In contrast, Waugh lived soberly, slept well, contemplated starting another novel, and corrected the proofs of *Brideshead Revisited*, which were being sent to him via 10 Downing Street.

His chief daytime occupation was baiting Randolph Churchill, accusing him of cowardice because he had ordered everyone to shelter during an air-raid (Waugh had refused). When Churchill, in his cups, pleaded with Waugh not to be so beastly to him, Waugh redoubled the taunts. In his diary, he described Churchill as 'a flabby bully who rejoices in blustering and shouting down anyone weaker than himself and starts squealing as soon as he meets anyone as strong'. It was back to prep school again, and the same Waugh *persona* was in evidence when Nancy Mitford, working for the London bookseller Heywood Hill, sent him a parcel which included Cyril Connolly's latest volume, *The Unquiet Grave*, recently published from the *Horizon* office under the pseudonym 'Palinurus'. Waugh set to work, and in the margins of his copy was soon baiting Connolly in the school-playground manner he had applied to Churchill.

The book was a more formal version of the journal-with-aphorisms that Connolly had been keeping for nearly twenty years. Taking its title from a poem in *The Oxford Book of Ballads* ('O who sits weeping on my grave, / And will not let me sleep?'), and its authorial pseudonym from the pilot of Aeneas' ship in Virgil's narrative who falls into the sea, comes to land and is murdered, *The Unquiet Grave* continued the self-reproaches of *Enemies of Promise* but ranged over wider topics than literary non-fulfilment.

When Waugh first opened the book, he was delighted, calling it (without malice) 'an authentic breath of Bloomsbury air'. (Bloomsbury itself was not particularly well disposed towards Connolly; Virginia Woolf had christened him 'Smartyboots', abbreviated to 'Boots' by the Waugh circle.) But soon Waugh began to be annoyed by Connolly's jibes against Christianity and the character of Christ himself, whom he called 'a prig . . . a petulant man'. Waugh protested against this, and was puzzled that Connolly had concerned himself with religious matters at all, and could not write unashamedly as an ageing epicurean looking back on past pleasures. Certainly the best parts of the book are those which deal, in a mood of *où sont les neiges*, with vanished days of pre-war good living in France with his wife Jean, from whom he had now parted following multiple infidelities on his side.

Waugh made no comment on the complexities of Connolly's private life (Connolly was at present involved with one of the *Horizon* secretaries, Lys Lubbock), but he was moved to wrath by those passages of *The Unquiet Grave* which anatomize broken romances and marriages. Remarks such as 'The person who has been abandoned is always psychologically groggy; the ego is wounded in its most tender part and is forced back on the separation and rejection phobias of infancy' infuriated him with what he called their 'clichés from Freud' and, reviewing the book in the *Tablet* some time later, he dismissed them as the work of a 'flushed and impetuous woman novelist'. Admittedly Connolly is not at his best in this context, but Waugh's snorts of rage are more ferocious than is deserved, and suggest that the mere attempt to probe the feelings of an abandoned partner (such as he himself had been not many years earlier), or indeed to undertake any sort of psychological map-making, would inevitably meet with a profound resistance. 'The secret of happiness', writes Connolly, 'lies in the avoidance of Angst ... the condition of all unhappiness. ...' As a generalized comment on the human predicament this is not unreasonable, but Waugh only snorted, in a letter to Nancy Mitford: 'I have no Angst and I don't believe you have.'

By no means all his comments on *The Unquiet Grave* were scathing. In his copy he noted approval of many passages, and when reviewing the book particularly commended Connolly's lament for the pet lemurs he and Jean had once kept – 'as beautiful as any passage of modern English prose that I know'. It may have occurred to him that the book shared many characteristics with his new novel, an evocation of lushness in wartime austerity, a lament for lost loves, and a fear of what was to come in peacetime. Like the novel, Connolly's aphorisms frequently turn with gloom to the prospect of a socialist society. Writing as what he calls a 'Liberal die-hard', Connolly prophesies that 'sooner or later the population of England will turn Communist, and then take over'. He feared the tyranny of the 'insect society', and asked if he was exceptional, 'a herd-outcast', in wishing to separate himself from the crowd and engage in solitary contemplation.

Passages like this cannot have been inimical to Waugh, but there was one respect in which *The Unquiet Grave* was radically different from anything he had written, or would wish to write. Connolly had identified himself with Palinurus because the Homeric ghost seemed to him to stand for 'the core of melancholy and guilt that works destruction on us from within'. Throughout the book, Connolly's chief lament is not for the loss of Jean and pre-war life but, as in *Enemies of Promise*, for his own failure as a writer and a man. The book is a kind of penitential psalm, an attempt by Connolly to escape from his own nature, occasionally with a wry joke ('Imprisoned in every fat man is a thin one wildly signalling to be let out'),* but usually in a mood of despair: 'Sometimes at night I get a feeling of claustrophobia, of being smothered by my own personality. . . .' Marriages and love affairs (it is asserted) are undertaken only as escapes from oneself, from 'the dread of loneliness'. And there is no escape for long. 'Angst descends,' intones Connolly the psalmist. 'I wake up in anxiety; like a fog it overlays all my actions, and my days are muffled with anguish.'

Not since 'The Balance' had Waugh gone anywhere near this abyss. If he knew it was there, he kept it out of his books, his diary and his letters. Hell was other people, boredom was a lack of good companionship or stimulating work, misery was not his fault. Drink and sleeping-draughts were the easiest escape (marriage had not provided any serious diversion). Connolly was a flabby ass to moan like this. He could sort himself out by returning to religious faith. 'Almost all Cyril's problems', Waugh wrote in the margin,

> are fully and simply explained in the catechism. . . . It is a strong buttress of faith in times when one's problems appear insoluble to study the problems of one's friends and to reflect how they would all be happily resolved by acceptance of the truths of the catechism.

Connolly had his chance to be revenged for Waugh's *Tablet* review of *The Unquiet Grave* when, during 1950, he was commissioned to write a 'profile' of him for *Time*. When Waugh heard about it, he wrote to Graham Greene that he might have to 'horsewhip' Connolly on the steps of White's, to which club they all belonged. But the article was never published, and the surviving drafts are very flat – with the exception of the opening paragraph:

> There are two of them: Evelyn Waugh the writer and 'Evelyn' (to his friends) the man. The names are not pronounced in quite the same way. 'I saw Evelyn' is uttered with a meaning pause, for the speaker will have a story to tell. His audience will conjure up the familiar vision of a short, stout, militant, brick-faced figure with a neat moustache,†

---

* In *Officers and Gentlemen* Waugh turns this into: 'Enclosing every thin man, there's a fat man demanding elbow-room.'
† Waugh grew a moustache when he joined the army, and was sometimes seen smoking a pipe.

smiling at the fatal thrust he is about to deliver, his sharp eyes fixed on an opponent whose retreat he has pincered off by a glass of port in one hand and (except in Lent) a Havana cigar which he brandishes in the other. Yet on such an occasion he may equally well have proved courteous, sympathetic and warmly aglow with a faint melancholic all his own, his batteries masked, his inquisitorial curiosity benevolently muted, even though he will be tearing the departing victim to pieces a few minutes later; for certainly there lurks in Evelyn a demon of destruction. How came he by it?

Connolly could not answer this question, which was perhaps why he abandoned the 'profile'. He observed, in the concluding paragraphs, that Waugh's Catholicism was a force that saved him from the worst effects of this 'demon of destruction' – it had 'ripened and mellowed his talent and set within bounds the demon which might have destroyed him'. On the other hand his religion 'does not seem any better fitted than his devotion to wine or architecture to dispel his strange melancholies'.

At Christmas 1944, Waugh's friends received copies of *Brideshead Revisited* as a gift from him. Chapman & Hall had issued this advance private edition at his request; publication proper took place at the end of May 1945. Waugh himself was certain that it was his 'best book' to date – he mentioned that his 'favourite hitherto' had been *A Handful of Dust*.

Its reception by friends was generally, but not universally, enthusiastic. Henry Yorke greatly disliked the Catholicism, and told Waugh that all through Lord Marchmain's deathbed scene he had been 'hoping against hope that the old man wouldn't give way', though he added, 'I don't know when you have written more powerfully.' Father Ronald Knox was not attracted by the Flytes – he said that for most of the book he had wished Waugh would 'write about characters whom one would like to meet in real life' – but by the end felt that the 'twitch of the thread' (the power of Catholicism to reclaim its lapsed adherents) had been 'inconceivably effective'. Nancy Mitford, writing to Waugh who was still in Yugoslavia, summed up friends' reactions as:

Cyril: Brilliant where the narrative is straightforward. Doesn't care for the 'purple passages' i.e. deathbed of Lord M. Thinks you go too much to White's [apparently an imputation that the over-writing was due to alcohol, or possibly that clubland had affected Waugh's attitude to the aristocracy]. But found it impossible to put down (no wonder). . . .

Maurice [Bowra]: showing off to Cyril about how you don't always hit the right word or some nonsense but obviously much impressed & thinks the Oxford part perfect. . . .

Lady Chetwode: Terribly dangerous propaganda [for Catholicism]. Brilliant.

General view: It is the Lygon family. Too much Catholic stuff.

When the trade edition appeared, the dust jacket carried a lengthy note by Waugh himself, recalling his preface to *Decline and Fall* sixteen years earlier, which had warned readers that the book was meant to be funny. This time he wished to emphasize that the story 'is *not* meant to be funny. . . . It is ambitious, perhaps intolerably presumptuous; nothing less than an attempt to trace the workings of the divine purpose in a pagan world.' The *Tablet* reviewer took no issue with this, proclaiming the novel to be 'a great apologetic work in the larger and more humane sense'; another Catholic critic remarked that all non-Catholic reviewers were missing the point of the novel; and most of Waugh's co-religionists seemed to accept the author's own analysis of his story. However, the Irish politician and author Conor Cruise O'Brien, writing from a Catholic standpoint in the journal *Bell* under the pseudonym 'Donat O'Donnell', questioned Waugh's religious orthodoxy in the novel.

In his view, 'the main emotional constituent of Mr Waugh's religion – using the term in a wide sense – is a deep English romanticism'. Other elements in the Waugh *credo* were 'nostalgia for the period of extreme youth' (O'Brien cited Sebastian and Charles's reliving of childhood), a 'schoolboy delight in cruelty', and 'snobbery', though Waugh's 'veneration for the upper classes' had become 'more marked than his contempt for the social inferiors'. O'Brien felt that:

> this whole complex of longings, fears and prejudices . . . must be taken into account in approaching the question of Mr Waugh's Catholicism. In Catholic countries Catholicism is not romantic nor invariably associated with big houses, or the fate of an aristocracy. . . . But the Catholicism of Mr Waugh . . . is hardly separable from a personal romanticism and a class loyalty. Is Lord Marchmain's soul more valuable than Hooper's? . . . *Brideshead Revisited* almost seems to imply that the wretched Hooper has no soul at all.

O'Brien also observed that in the novel Catholicism is a force of destruction. He cited an American reader who had written to Waugh: 'Your *Brideshead Revisited* is a strange way to show that Catholicism is an answer to anything. Seems more like the kiss of death to me.' Waugh had quoted this in an article in *Life*, responding with the sneer:

'I am not quite clear what you mean by the "kiss of death". . . . Is it something to do with halitosis?' O'Brien thought the reader was on to something: 'It is much more to the point than are the *Tablet*'s eulogies.' He himself judged that in the novel Catholicism had become 'dark and defeatist', a force that prised lovers apart, scattered a family and left a great house deserted. True, at the end Charles had been converted, and had prayed before the altar in the chapel at Brideshead, but (said O'Brien) 'when he leaves the chapel, he leaves it empty of worshippers'. O'Brien concluded that Catholicism had been super-imposed on 'Mr Waugh's private religion', just as 'newly-converted pagans are said to superimpose a Christian nomenclature on their ancient cults of trees and thunder'.

If these remarks had appeared in a non-Catholic journal, Waugh would probably have ignored them. Since the *Bell* was widely read by Irish Catholics, he sent a reply. 'I think perhaps', he wrote,

> your reviewer is right in calling me a snob; that is to say I am happiest in the company of the European upper-classes; but I do not think this preference is necessarily an offence against Charity, still less against Faith. I can assure you it had no influence on my conversion. In England Catholicism is predominantly a religion of the poor. There is a handful of Catholic aristocratic families, but I knew none of them in 1930 when I was received into the Church. . . . Nor, I think, does this preference unduly influence my writing. Besides Hooper there are two characters in *Brideshead Revisited* whom I represent as worldly – Rex Mottram, a millionaire, and Lady Celia Ryder, a lady of high birth. Why did my reverence for money and rank not sanctify those two?

Many other reviewers' comments on the novel included, in varying degrees of subtlety, accusations of snobbery. In the *New Statesman* it was analysed by the poet and satirical radio playwright Henry Reed, who judged it 'deeply moving in its theme and design. . . . it haunts one for days after one has read it', but felt that it was shot through with 'an overpowering snobbishness'. Rose Macaulay in *Horizon* judged that it suffered not so much from snobbery as 'self-indulgence in the pleasures of adolescent surrender to glamour, whether to the glamour of beauty, food, rank, love, church, society, or fine writings'. Edmund Wilson in the *New Yorker* made no such qualification. Judging the book as a whole to show a disastrous decline in Waugh's powers as a stylist and portrayer of character, he ascribed this calamity simply to 'Waugh's snobbery'. Hitherto held in check by 'his satirical point of view', it had now 'emerged shameless and rampant'.

Wilson felt that the aristocrats portrayed by Waugh were 'terribly trashy', the upstarts 'rather crudely overdone', and he was doubtful whether the Catholicism in the novel conveyed 'any genuine religious experience'. However, he predicted that the book would be an enormous commercial success, 'soon ... up in the best-seller list'.*So it was. Book clubs on both sides of the Atlantic selected it for their subscribers, and sales soon exceeded those of anything Waugh had previously written.

He left Yugoslavia rather abruptly in the early spring of 1945, having aroused local suspicion and resentment by undertaking, without any official brief, an investigation of Communist intolerance of Catholics. His report on this issue, to the British Foreign Office, failed to stop Whitehall from supporting Tito; doubt was cast on the veracity of information he had gathered from sources in Yugoslavia, and there was even talk of charging him under the Official Secrets Act because, as a member of the British armed forces, he had discussed his findings with the Pope, at a private audience in Rome on his way back to London. The Pope seems to have paid little attention; Waugh records in his diary 'his English parrot-talk', asking Waugh how many children he had.

Waugh was back in England by the second half of March. He noted that there was 'no exhilaration anywhere' at the prospect of peace, and that he himself had 'gloomy apprehensions of V Day. I hope to escape it.' The nuns were still in residence at Piers Court, and Waugh lived extravagantly at the Hyde Park Hotel, occasionally visiting his wife and children at Pixton. At the end of July, the General Election brought a landslide victory for Labour under Clement Attlee – the first time the party had achieved an overall majority in the Commons. 'My congratulations on retaining your seat,' Waugh wrote to Tom Driberg, who was already an MP and had now joined the Labour ranks. 'I ... face the Hooper–Attlee terror with fortitude.'

---

* Wilson's animadversions on the book included some harsh words on the passages of lush narrative, which he described as full of 'dispiriting clichés'. Waugh, who a short time before had been hunting clichés in *The Unquiet Grave* (where his marginal comments frequently mock Connolly's more hackneyed expressions), must have been especially stung. Replying to some of the comments on his novel in *Life* (8 April 1946), he wrote, with obvious reference to Wilson's review: 'I am not the least worried about the charge of using clichés. I think to be oversensitive about clichés is like being oversensitive about table manners. It comes from keeping second-rate company. Professional reviewers read so many bad books ... that they get an unhealthy craving for arresting phrases.'

Contra Mundum

1

Down with the Horrible Counter-Honnish Labour Party

Tom Driberg had entered Parliament in 1942 as an Independent member for his home constituency in Essex, hoping to stir into life the stuffy figures who made up Churchill's wartime government. It was not easy for party-less members to achieve anything, and as the war came to an end Driberg decided to throw in his lot with Labour's energetic promises of social reform. His sympathies had always been with the left; he had joined the Communist Party in schooldays, as a protest against the stuffy *ennui* of his upper-middle-class home. On the other hand he lived in a Georgian-fronted manor house not unlike Waugh's Piers Court. Richard Crossman, a fellow Labour backbencher, went down there and found it 'a Tudor house with magnificent Robert Adam additions, including a little room on the roof where Gainsborough painted. Tom has done it all up exquisitely. . . .'

During the two years preceding the 1945 General Election, Cyril Connolly could be seen, in the pages of *Horizon* and other magazines, arguing with himself about how he would vote when the war was over. In one article he admitted that he found the prospect of socialism governing Britain quite frightening – it seemed to threaten 'propaganda, bureaucracy and a secret police with every man his own informer'. Nevertheless, as the July 1945 election approached, Connolly announced to readers of *Horizon* that he was going to use his vote for Labour, since it was high time for 'a levelling up which socialism alone can provide; we cannot continue to maintain two utterly different standards of living'. Waugh, meanwhile, had decided not to vote at all; apparently he never had, and from now on he never did. At different times he gave different reasons: 'I have never found a Tory stern enough to command my respect', 'a man's chief civic duty consists in fighting for his king', and 'I would consider it an impertinence to advise my sovereign on whom she should select for the government of her country' (this was after the accession of Elizabeth II). In his memoirs, he mentions that his father had never voted – though this was because Arthur Waugh always lived in safe Tory constituencies, and considered it unnecessary to go to the polls.

Connolly hailed the Labour electoral victory as 'one of the few good things to have come out of the war', though in the same *Horizon* editorial he grumbled about the current shortage of domestic servants, which seemed ridiculous considering that there were 'millions of displaced persons who would be only too glad to find places'. By the next summer, returning from the Continent, he was telling his readers that he felt a 'patriotic glow' at Labour's nationalization and Welfare State achievements, though he admitted that this glow was enhanced by travelling from Dover to London in 'the new cocktail bar on the Golden Arrow', just the sort of thing that a utopian post-war society ought to institute. In this editorial, he set out a ten-point plan which he urged the Labour government to implement in order to round off its egalitarian policies: the abolition of the death penalty; the establishment of model prisons; the elimination of slums; the free supply of light and heat; vocational training for all; the abolition of censorship and passports; the repealing of laws against homosexuality, divorce, bigamy and abortion; a limit on the acquisition of property; encouragement of the arts; and no discrimination against colour, race, class or creed. This sparked off a facetious reply from Waugh in the *Tablet* (27 July 1946), in which he painted a picture of Britain after Connolly's proposals had been implemented – a country in which half the population had been consigned to model prisons for 'rehabilitation' – and pointed out that Connolly himself was guilty of virulent discrimination against 'the nobility, gentry, yeomanry, burgesses and vagabonds', all of whom he wished to suppress in order to create 'the modern two-class State of officials and proletariat'. Some time later he noted that Connolly had, on a visit to Piers Court, 'recanted his socialist opinions, saying that his father's death had liberated him from guilt in this matter'. Precisely what this means is not clear, but evidently Connolly's shifting political views were bound up with his awkward relationship with his father.

The facetious tone of Waugh's *Tablet* piece might be taken to indicate light-heartedness at the prospect of socialist Britain, but if he did not respond with total seriousness it was only because he had long expected the calamity of a Labour government as part of the inexorable destruction of England by Slough Man. Also Labour was not, in his opinion, the only contemptible political party at Westminster, for he believed that the Churchill government had callously betrayed millions of Eastern European Catholics into Communist hands when post-war settlements were negotiated. By 1947 he was of the opinion that the war had been merely 'a sweaty tug-of-war between teams of indistinguishable louts'. The Welfare State seemed merely a trivial distraction, a piece of absurd idealism based on the fallacy that the classless society could be achieved by gentle English methods. If such a society eventually arrived, it would (he wrote in a 1946 article) be 'through foreign intervention and by the use of "social engineering" of the sort that is prevalent in half of what was once Europe' – another reference to the persecution of Catholics in Yugoslavia and other Communist-controlled countries.

The war, then, had been a grave disappointment to him, and its aftermath was utterly deplorable, but he could still conduct his own war. His mood after the Labour victory was that which he ascribes to Guy Crouchback in *Men at Arms*: 'now, splendidly, everything had become clear. The enemy at last was plain in view, huge and hateful, all disguise cast off. It was the Modern Age in arms. Whatever the outcome there was a place for him in that battle.'

His first military engagement in this conflict was against his own children. Reunited with his family on their return to Piers Court, he found himself surrounded by infants. A fifth child, James, was born in 1946 and a sixth, named Septimus as a reminder that one had died, in 1950. Waugh constantly maintained that their company gave him little pleasure. 'My children weary me,' he wrote in his diary. 'I can only see them as defective adults; feckless, destructive, frivolous, sensual, humourless.' He had abandoned his plans to live apart from them, but firm rules were made to ensure that they did not interfere with him. Margaret, the third surviving child, writes that:

> our nursery life was deliberately old-fashioned. As small children we lived behind a green baize door, with a nanny and nursery maid. We came down to the drawing-room for half an hour in the evening. Our parents came up to kiss us goodnight in bed. The worst punishment our nannies would threaten us with was to be sent down to the library to see our father. In fact they were so frightened of him themselves that they never dared send us.

It was not only the nannies who were frightened. Margaret admits that to the younger children their father was 'a nursery ogre'.

As usual, it was a performance modelled on his own father. In his autobiography, he writes that while Arthur Waugh was out at work 'I lunched in the dining-room,' but 'had my other meals upstairs in the nursery so as to be out of my father's way'. This lay behind his impersonation of a Victorian *paterfamilias*. In 1946 he wrote: 'I have numerous children whom I see once a day for ten, I hope, awe-inspiring minutes.'

When the children reached an age for them to be admitted into his company at greater length, his strategy was to treat them as adults. By the time they were about eight, they were allowed to take their meals in the dining-room, and were (writes Margaret) 'treated as a grown-up and expected to make conversation and attend to the conversation of others'. On the other hand if they ate too slowly they might be banished to the cellar to finish their meal.

In a 1953 BBC radio interview, Waugh maintained that he did not join in his children's amusements: 'When they get to the age of clear speech, and an appearance of reason, I associate with them. I wouldn't say "play" with them; I don't bounce balls with them, or stand on my head, or carry them about on my shoulders.' On the other hand, in *The Ordeal of Gilbert Pinfold* there is a glimpse of Waugh's *alter ego* 'joining his family in charades or Up Jenkins, playing the fool to the loud delight of the youngest and the tolerant amusement of the eldest of his children, until in degrees of age they went happily to their rooms'. Certainly there were charades at Piers Court, but they were charades of Waugh's own choosing. The children might be instructed to mime the deathbed scene of some crony of his, or to portray grotesque incidents from his own past life. When guests were present, he encouraged them (in Margaret's words) 'to taunt his friends or discomfort his acquaintances'. Cyril Connolly, staying for a few days, found it impossible to walk undisturbed in the garden because the children would keep popping up from the undergrowth, strangely attired, with the words: 'Mr Connolly, I presume?' Similarly, when the family was being driven about the countryside (either by Laura or Mr Prothero from the village garage, whom Waugh was always hoping to clothe in chauffeur's uniform), the children were instructed to recite benedictions or maledictions to the neighbours as they passed their houses, dependent on their father's likes and dislikes.

Frances Donaldson, who became a friend of the Waughs in the late 1940s, says that life at Piers Court 'revolved around jokes; very, very funny jokes'. The jokes were entirely of Waugh's making; the children could participate in his world, but only when he chose, and on his own terms. He sent them away to boarding school, the girls as well as the boys, as early as was practicable, at the age of about seven, and Auberon, the eldest son, recalls the 'tremendous festivities' at the end of each holiday, on the eve of their return to school, their father 'not disguising his joy' that he would soon be rid of them; Auberon admits that they 'did rather resent' this. Harriet (Hatty), the third in the family, sums up her father by saying: 'He gave glamour to things.' But Margaret's short memoir of him, at the end of Sykes's biography, gives reminders of the black side: 'My mother's main role [she writes] was protecting us from my father's anger, which could be truly terrible. She was always stepping in and deflecting his rage on to her own head and away from some child who had committed a misdemeanour.' These misdemeanours ranged from the breaking of a plate to some social solecism. Auberon says that their father particularly resented the children's 'vulgarity', and would frequently take against one of them 'for snobbish reasons'.

All this made their father, in Auberon's words, 'a figure to dodge'. Quite apart from the rigid code which they must not break, there were also his unpredictable shifts of mood. 'Much centred on meal times,' writes Margaret. 'There were terrible rages, chilling depressions, jolly jokes and tipsy revelry. One never knew what was in store.'

A letter from Waugh to Nancy Mitford in January 1946 contains some typical grumbles about the family – 'My two eldest children are here and a great bore' – and also drops twice into Mitford language: 'Picasso is the head of the counter-hons. I went to his disgusting exhibition to make sure. . . . Counter Hon Quennell behaved well about *Love* in his *Daily Mail*, I was glad to see. I look for other reviews but don't see them.' These are references to Nancy Mitford's *The Pursuit of Love*, recently published, in which Waugh had had a considerable hand.

The book's portrait of the highly irascible, ludicrously prejudiced, but fundamentally kind-hearted 'Uncle Matthew', father of the Radlett girls, is a masterly depiction of Lord Redesdale, Nancy's father, whom Waugh once described as 'a retiring but violent nobleman'. Uncle Matthew is, of course, the father-figure *par excellence*, the ultimate expression of paternalism in the writings of the Waugh 'set'. Nancy Mitford could have made him into a creature of pure horror, but she defuses him by surrounding him entirely with women, so that, since his daughters have no chance of inheriting, and do not need a male role-model, 'Farve's' monstrosity is little more than a decorative detail;

he cannot deprive them of anything, since he has nothing to give them. It is up to them to forage for themselves, as they do.

'Did I begin it before reading B[rides]head or after I can't remember,' Nancy wrote to Waugh of *The Pursuit of Love*. She was in no doubt that her readers would spot the point of resemblance between the two books, the first-person narrator describing the life of an aristocratic family in the country. 'Everybody will say what a copy cat,' she told him before he had a sight of the manuscript. 'It's about my family, a very different cup of tea, not grand & far madder.' It does indeed seem like a deliberate response to Waugh's novel. It, too, portrays its family being gradually dismembered, as the children leave home for marriages or liaisons that cause grave disappointment to the parents. And, as in Waugh's book, the narrator is a semi-outsider, the patient and loyal Fanny.

There is one specific nudge at *Brideshead Revisited*. When Linda Radlett becomes the mistress of Fabrice, she expresses surprise that he goes to church; does this mean he is a Roman Catholic?

'Of course I am. . . . Do you think I look like a Calvinist?'
  'But then aren't you living in mortal sin? . . .'
  'These little sins of the body are quite unimportant. . . .'
  'In England,' she said, 'people are always renouncing each other on account of being Roman Catholics. It's sometimes very sad for them. A lot of English books are about this, you know.'

The book also has some fun with the absurd linguistic etiquette practised by the upper classes – Uncle Matthew raging against Fanny for using such expressions as 'notepaper' instead of 'writing-paper'. After he had read Nancy Mitford's manuscript, Waugh began to play this game too. He noted in his diary that his eldest child Teresa, arriving home from her convent school at the age of seven, was 'neurotically voluble with the vocabulary of the lower-middle-class – "serviette", "spare room"'. (To say 'spare room' implies that you have only the one available for visitors; an aristocrat has a whole castle-full.)*

Later, Waugh applied the same close attention to the sequel to *The Pursuit of Love*, Nancy Mitford's *Love in a Cold Climate* (1949), sending her a severe critique of the manuscript. She continued to show him

---

* The game became public in 1956, with the publication of *Noblesse Oblige*, a volume containing essays by Professor Alan Ross and Nancy Mitford on 'u' and 'Non-u' (vocabulary acceptable, or otherwise, to the upper class), together with contributions by Betjeman (his poem 'How To Get On In Society'), Waugh and others of their circle. Waugh remarked to Nancy Mitford that he regarded the expression 'Non-u' as itself 'vulgar in the extreme' (*Letters*, ed. Amory, p. 444).

her work in progress, and he pronounced *The Blessing* (1951) 'admirable, deliciously funny, consistent & complete', making virtually no disparaging remarks – 'I am immensely proud of it & you.' However, he did not regard her as in any way his professional equal. In a 1955 article he argues that, because most women have not received a classical education, they write 'as though they were babbling down the telephone – often very prettily, like Miss Nancy Mitford'.

Meanwhile *The Pursuit of Love* seems to have made a mark on Waugh himself – as a person rather than a writer. His own behaviour, especially to his children, in the years that followed its appearance, bore more than a passing resemblance to Uncle Matthew's.

By June 1946, after nine months of country life, Waugh was 'stale and bored'. He had been briefly to Germany, to observe the Nuremberg war trials, but these yielded little of interest ('Ribbentrop was like a seedy schoolmaster being ragged,' he wrote to Randolph Churchill). There had also been bouts of high life in London, with the usual consequences: 'On the last evening I dimly remember a dinner party of cosmopolitan ladies where I think I must have been conspicuous,' he told Nancy Mitford. 'I awoke with blood on my hands but found to my intense relief that it was my own. I sometimes think I am getting too old for this kind of thing.' As to literary work, he occupied himself for a while attempting to write a narrative about the schooldays of Charles Ryder, based on his own Lancing diaries, but it came out like a pale imitation of *The Loom of Youth*, and he abandoned it after a few thousand words. (It is only of interest as an indication that he was now considering his own schooldays as material for a novel. The subject would require far more subtle reworking before it could rise above banality.)

In the summer of 1946, bored and at a loose end, he gladly accepted an invitation to Spain, the only European country that was still Fascist. The invitation was to attend a 'congress with junketings' in celebration of the life and work of a sixteenth-century Spanish Dominican, Francisco de Vittoria. 'I doubt if Evelyn had heard of him before,' writes Christopher Sykes. De Vittoria was one of the fathers of international law, but owing to Spain's political position most of the distinguished jurists who had been invited declined to attend, and Waugh was added at the last minute as a make-weight. He travelled with Douglas Woodruff, editor of the *Tablet*, who felt doubtful about the venture. Waugh disliked the 'suave lawyers' and 'young shits' who conducted them around Madrid and other cities, and found the congress 'ineffably tedious and pointless'. At its conclusion, he and Woodruff discovered that no air tickets had been booked for their return. They got places on a plane only by appealing to the Spanish Foreign Ministry.

Waugh wrote no direct report of the trip, nor did he mention it in letters to friends. But the following year Chapman & Hall published his novella *Scott-King's Modern Europe* (1947), which records at length his feelings about Spain under Franco. 'I am writing a dreary short story about Spain,' he told Nancy Mitford while at work on it.

Spain is disguised as 'Neutralia' (because it had nominally kept out of the Second World War), and Waugh himself becomes Scott-King, an ageing classics master from a minor public school, whose speciality is the obscure sixteenth-century Neutralian poet Bellorius (a pun on 'war/Waugh'), and who is invited to a Neutralian congress celebrating this figure. The discomforts and irritations of Waugh's trip, which he had recorded briefly in his diary, are expanded to make a mildly comic narrative, and there is also a good deal of implied distaste for Spain under Franco – the shoddy individuals who hold public office, the dreary official banquets, the ludicrous renaming of institutions (the Ritz in the Neutralian capital has become The Hotel 22nd March, to commemorate 'some forgotten event in the Marshal's rise to power'), and the universal atmosphere of uneasiness, arising from all-too-fresh memories of 'police rounds-ups and firing squads'. Before he sets off for Neutralia, Scott-King's left-wing colleagues at school project a picture of chaos in Neutralia/Spain: 'They've got teams of German physicists making atomic bombs.... Civil war raging.... Half the population in concentration camps.' The reality for Scott-King is even worse. Once he has served his hosts' purpose, they abandon him to pay his own hotel bill and find his way back to England, which he attempts to do with the aid of an underground escape organization. He leaves Neutralia disguised as a nun, and fetches up stark naked in a camp for illicit immigrants in Palestine.

Scott-King does not, however, emerge from this experience as a convert to the left wing. He admits that contemporary Neutralia has nothing whatever to contribute to Western culture, and abandons any further interest in Bellorius (possibly a hint that Waugh now repudiated his support, in print during the Thirties, for Mussolini and Franco), but his only firm resolve after his Neutralian misadventures is that 'it would very wicked indeed to do anything to fit a boy for the modern world'. In other words, the dreadfulness of modern Spain seemed to

Waugh only another manifestation of that 'huge and hateful' enemy, the Modern Age.

Understandably, *Scott-King's Modern Europe* was not publicly received as any sort of recantation of sympathy with Fascism. Waugh had refrained from specifying that the Neutralian regime was right wing (though Scott-King is branded a 'Fascist beast' by his fellow delegates when they believe him to be supporting it), and few even of Waugh's friends knew he had been to Spain. The Franco figure in the novella is referred to as 'the Marshal', and this, together with knowledge of Waugh's involvement with the Tito partisans in 1944–5, led many readers and reviewers, including George Orwell, to suppose he was writing about Yugoslavia. However, Orwell, in the *New York Times Book Review*, was perfectly correct in deducing Waugh's message to be 'There is nothing to choose between Communism and Fascism.' Orwell concluded his review by suggesting that Waugh 'could fight the modern world more effectively' if he troubled to 'read a sixpenny pamphlet on Marxism'.

After the Spanish trip, Waugh was once again 'bored bored bored', as he wrote in a letter to Nancy Mitford. Resuming life at Piers Court, he complained, in another letter to her:

> If only country neighbours would talk like Jane Austen's characters about gossip & hobbies. Instead they all want to know about Molotov & de Gaulle. . . . I am anxious to emigrate, Laura to remain & face the century of the common man.* She is younger, braver & less imaginative than I. If only they would start blowing the place up with their atoms.

He had alienated most of the neighbours by his behaviour. When John and Frances Donaldson moved into the district in the autumn of 1947, Waugh was described to them by other inhabitants as 'frightening' and 'ruthless'. The general verdict of the hunting and stockbroking set was 'he goes a bit far'.

Visitors were disconcerted by his blend of extreme formality with complete unpredictability. He expected his guests, like himself, to dress for dinner, but when they arrived they might find him suffering from what Frances Donaldson calls 'a melancholia of Johnsonian proportions', slumped in a chair and muttering: 'My wife will entertain you.' Five minutes later, if the visitor happened to make some remark to

---

* He had picked up the phrase 'the Century of the Common Man' from some politician, and had taken to using it mockingly.

Laura which caught his attention, he might spring up, take command of the conversation and race off into fun and jokes. Frances Donaldson describes his mimicry and command of language, when he was on form, as 'in no way inferior to the best of his writing', but she says it was necessary to understand his own milieu to get the best out of him: 'So often his jokes fell by the way [with strangers], were not recognized as jokes. . . . They were so stylized that one needed some previous knowledge of him or his world to catch them as they passed.' He could crush instantly if he chose to: 'He had the faculty of pulverizing other people, reducing them to silence. . . . I have seen intelligent and worldly men simply unable to answer Evelyn when he asked them some ordinary question.' Also, guests who did not share his extreme Toryism – and in the late 1940s there were few who did – might be dismayed to learn that he regarded Britain as 'an occupied country' under the socialists, and believed that it was right for his children to cheat the nationalized railways by travelling without tickets.

It was no good trying to talk to him about his books; he could not bear to have them praised as an opening gambit in conversation. He would allow friends to make some particular and pointed comment about a character or incident, but attempts at flattery were brushed aside (says Frances Donaldson) 'sternly and coldly'. The only subject of conversation he really liked was the foibles and peculiarities of others, and in this he preferred the absurd and scandalous to any serious discussion of character – an 'extremely narrow vision of the human race', writes Frances Donaldson, and one which contributed to making so many social occasions at which he was present 'a flop'. He delighted to exaggerate or misrepresent the misfortunes of others. 'I should like very much to know more of Quennell,' he wrote to Nancy Mitford after a visit to Paris and the British Embassy. 'At five a.m. on my last morning he had a seizure brought on by sexual excess. Did he die of it?' (Peter Quennell had been suffering from a hangover.) A very ordinary encounter could be turned, in the diary or in letters, into material for farce:

> Mass at 12 at Farm Street where I met the shambling, unshaven and as it happened quite penniless figure of Graham Greene. Took him to the Ritz for a cocktail and gave him 6d for his hat. He had suddenly been moved by love of Africa and emptied his pockets into the box for African missions.

Of Cyril Connolly, who had been to a health farm, Waugh wrote to Nancy Mitford:

Did I tell you of Boots' stroke? Not I think paralysis ... but a definite seizure. His doctor sent him to Tring where he was strapped to his bed for three weeks & treated with enemas and synthetic orange juice. He lost 21 lbs. Well that is a lot for a shortish man. I think it will be the end of him.

And to John Betjeman, who had complained that he was short of money: 'I say it is good news about your bankruptcy. You will be sold up and I shall get your books.' It was a performance which owed something to Belloc, whose stocky bulldog appearance Waugh was now acquiring, and whose humour, particularly in *Cautionary Tales for Children* (1907), similarly delights in gruesome misfortunes.

Even friends were wary of this aspect of him. When he asked Connolly to send some 'social gossip' from London, Connolly replied: 'I have none of the qualifications. . . . I don't find other people's misfortunes uproariously funny.' Waugh affected to find this incomprehensible: 'I was moved by your verdict that the misfortunes of your friends are not the proper subject for humour. I do not know how you can bear to go so much into society if you feel this.' Frances Donaldson points out, however, that he never used gossip maliciously, repeating it to someone else to create bad blood, as Bowra had done. He liked it for its own sake, as an enlargement of his understanding of human frailty.

All this isolated him from his neighbours; yet, as Frances Donaldson discovered, he pined for human company, and if he really liked people would swallow all prejudice. 'Is it true,' he asked the Donaldsons with great curiosity when they first dined at Piers Court, 'is it true what Laura and I have been told? Are you Socialists?' Jack Donaldson replied that they were both 'fully paid-up members of the Labour Party'. A few seconds later, Waugh dropped the subject and turned to other things, and at the end of the evening he implored them to come again soon. Thereafter he would send them postcards adorned with a hammer and sickle, and written in red ink in childish capitals, in the pretence that they were the work of Anthony Crosland, Labour MP for the local constituency, signing them 'COMRAD TONI CROSLAND'.

The Donaldsons were the only real friends he acquired in the locality. A notice in Gothic script on the gateway of Piers Court, 'No Admittance on Business', was taken by most of the neighbours as a general interdict of all human company. In his 1960 television interview with John Freeman, Waugh observed: 'It's not really accurate to say I lead a squire-archic life. A squirearchic life means sitting on the bench of magistrates, and going round cattle shows, and that kind of thing. I lead a life of absolute solitude.' But solitude was not really what he wanted, when he was not writing, and at Piers Court he devised various methods of combating the boredom it induced, none of them very successful. Sometimes he went for long walks, keeping entirely to the road (presumably because he did not wish to trespass), but Stinchcombe was being encroached upon by the nondescript town of Dursley, which had been designated a 'London overspill', and Waugh had taken a strong dislike to the area – several times he went house-hunting in Ireland. On other days he might occupy himself with various projects in the garden, such as The Edifice, a semi-circular ornamental stone wall which he himself erected to one side of the house, surrounding it with a paved area. When this was finished he advertised for human skulls to adorn it, and received a large number; Frances Donaldson says that the whole effect was generally judged 'hideous'. Twice a week after lunch he would visit the cinema in Dursley (the programme changed on Mondays and Thursdays), irrespective of what was showing. 'I . . . find it the best way to get through the early afternoon,' he told an interviewer. Graham Greene recalls that Waugh said he used to put the same amount in the church collection plate as he was paying for his cinema ticket, 'and when the cinema ticket goes up my contribution goes up'.

Reaching his forty-third birthday in October 1946, he told Nancy Mitford that already 'I strain forward to senility.' He consoled himself with the thought that 'I have two shots in my locker left. My war novel and my autobiography. I suppose they will see me out.'

He began to turn his attention to the religious position of the Betjemans, who were now living in a Georgian rectory near Wantage. Waugh found it 'lightless, stuffy, cold, poky', and described Candida Betjeman, born four years earlier, as 'a daughter of grossly proletarian appearance and manner' (she was a child of striking, patrician beauty). 'A horse sleeps in the kitchen,' Waugh told Nancy Mitford. 'Harness literally everywhere.'

Betjeman's most recent verses, in *Old Lights for New Chancels* (1940) and *New Bats in Old Belfries* (1945), had mostly abandoned the harshness of 'Slough' for a more subtle mockery of suburbia, and he was becoming especially popular for his 'sports girl' pieces – such as his two 'Myfanwy' poems, inspired by Myfanwy Piper, wife of John Piper, Betjeman's collaborator in many projects. He was also beginning to make a name as a broadcasting 'personality', and Waugh neither enjoyed nor approved of these performances. He said he had 'attempted to listen on several occasions and each time turned off the machine in embarrassment', dismayed by 'the jauntiness, the intrusive, false intimacy, the sentimentality . . . which seem inseparable from this medium'.

During a visit, Waugh discovered that Penelope Betjeman wished to become a Roman Catholic, but was postponing instruction because the idea upset John so much. He began to bombard Betjeman with polemic against the 'handful of homosexual curates' whom he declared constituted the Anglo-Catholic wing of the Church of England, to which Betjeman adhered, with the consequence that Betjeman – or so Penelope reported to Waugh – 'thinks you are the devil and wakes up in the middle of the night and raves and says he will leave me at once if I go over'. Part of the trouble, Penelope explained, was that John was terribly conscious of the existence of the 'smart catholic set', consisting of Waugh himself, together with:

> Laura's relatives and Asquiths, the Pakenhams, D. Woodruff, C. Hollis and in fact any English RC he knows. He thinks if I go C[atholic] and he doesn't you will all persecute him and there will be plots and counter-plots and the only thing for him to do is to get right away from it all and go and settle on his own in Swindon.

Waugh responded that Betjeman's horror of Catholicism was 'a very good sign . . . far more promising than the tolerant ''each-worshipping-in-his-own-way'' attitude'. He told her that she was 'in formal heresy' as long as she remained in the Anglican Church. By August 1947, when he visited the Betjemans again, she had resolved to go over to Rome. She duly did so a few months later, and Waugh wrote: 'It is a particular joy for me to be able to welcome you home. . . .'

During all this, Waugh had continued his attempt to convert John Betjeman, playing particularly on the idea of hell and damnation for non-Catholics: 'Awful about your obduracy in schism and heresy. Hell hell hell. Eternal damnation.' This was Betjeman's vulnerable point, as he admits in his poem 'Before the Anaesthetic, or, A Real Fright', written during 1945 before a minor operation for the removal of a cyst, in which he describes himself as 'dull with death and hell', and fearful of 'those echoing hells / Half-threaten'd in the pealing bells'. He also allows the possibility that, for all his obsession with Victorian churches and Anglo-Catholic ritual, '*I never knew the Lord at all.*' In view of this terrible insecurity, his refusal to give way to Waugh is impressive.

 He and Waugh remained on friendly enough terms – Waugh put Betjeman up for the Beefsteak Club around the time of Penelope's instruction – but in 1950 Waugh observed to Penelope, not altogether unseriously, 'I don't think John likes me.' Though Betjeman's threat of leaving Penelope should she convert did not materialize immediately, they began to spend more and more time apart, eventually setting up separate establishments. Waugh had perhaps played some part in bringing this about.

For all his avowed horror at the vulgarity of Betjeman's radio broadcasts, Waugh seemed ready enough to involve himself in another massmedium, the film industry. When an invitation came to visit Hollywood and discuss the 'film treatment' of *Brideshead Revisited*, for a fee of several thousand dollars, he accepted.

He and Laura sailed to New York in January 1947, and travelled from coast to coast by train. At Metro Goldwyn Mayer's Culver City, he met the writer assigned to the adaptation of his novel, who proved to be the 'awful afternoon man' Keith Winter, whom he had met briefly in the early Thirties. 'He has been in Hollywood for years and sees *Brideshead* purely as a love story,' Waugh noted. As the weeks passed, it began to seem unlikely that the film would be made. The religious element, emphasized by Waugh in discussions, held no interest for MGM, and also 'the censor made some difficulties'. However, the film company was 'constantly munificent', and Waugh was able to meet Charlie Chaplin and to visit the Walt Disney studios – 'to pay my homage', as he put it, 'to the two artists of the place'.

But what really excited him was a visit to another Californian establishment. 'I found a deep mine of literary gold in the cemetery of Forest Lawn and the work of the morticians and intend to get to work immediately on a novelette staged there,' he wrote in his diary. And to A.D. Peters: 'I am entirely obsessed by Forest Lawns [*sic*]. . . . I go there two or three times a week, am on easy terms with the chief embalmer. . . . It is an entirely unique place – the *only* thing in California that is not a copy of something else.'

The literary model for this 'novelette' set in California, *The Loved One*, which first appeared as a special issue of *Horizon* in February 1948, was, rather oddly, Henry James, whom Waugh had been reading for the first time just before he left for America. 'What an enormous blessing', he wrote in his diary in November 1946, 'to have kept Henry James for middle age and to turn . . . to a first reading of *Portrait of a Lady*.' When he sent *The Loved One* to Cyril Connolly at *Horizon*,* he provided him with a note about the story's origin which strongly

---

* Generously, he gave Connolly the use of it free of charge.

suggests James: 'The ideas I had in mind were . . . the Anglo-American impasse – "never the twain shall meet" . . . [and] the European raiders who come for the spoils and if they are lucky make for home with them.' Dennis Barlow, expatriate English poet turned animal mortuary attendant, is so contemptuous of the American way of life that he takes the most ludicrous of jobs – providing lavish death-rites for household pets – and dallies heartlessly with the young mortician Aimée Thanata-genos (her Greek surname is an allusion to her profession), driving her to suicide; he then returns to England with the intention of using it all as raw material for his art.

More than any other of Waugh's books, *The Loved One* has been regarded as a satire – on the American desire to sugar the fact of death, and more generally on the horrors of life in the USA. Yet true satire requires a moral premise, and, as R.D. Smith pointed out when he reviewed it in the *New Statesman*, this is conspicuously lacking from *The Loved One*. Dennis, with whom the reader is encouraged to identify, is (in Smith's words) 'unstable, immoral, dishonest and, in the literary sense, phoney' – he presents Aimée with items from *The Oxford Book of English Verse* as if they were his own poems, to impress her.

If he is really writing a satire, Waugh throws away a lot of opportuni-ties. He says almost nothing about the lunacies of the film industry nor the luxury homes of Beverly Hills; instead, he opens the novella with a rather laboured portrait of the English exiles in Hollywood. As to the American way of life, Waugh did not find it strikingly more horrific than the British. He liked the USA enough to return there two years later, to write an article for *Life* on the state of Catholicism in America, and told Nancy Mitford that New York was 'the most wonderful health resort in the world. I look to it to revivify me.' Even his treatment of Forest Lawn (which in the novella becomes Whispering Glades) is documentary rather than satirical. On 18 October 1947 the *Tablet* carried an article by him describing the real Forest Lawn in much detail – the names of the various divisions ('Eventide, Babyland, Graceland, Inspiration Slope, Slumberland, Sweet Memories'), the loudspeakers carrying sentimental music and artificial birdsong, and the exposure of embalmed corpses on sofas in the Slumber Room – which indicates that there is very little exaggeration in *The Loved One*.

In the midst of the almost universally enthusiastic critical reception of the novella (which went down as well in the USA as in Britain), Cyril Connolly raised the question of whether 'Mr Waugh has or has not returned to his earlier manner', that is, to the manner of his pre-*Brideshead Revisited* novels. Connolly did not answer this, but there was a general feeling that the old Waugh had reappeared. A close consideration of *The Loved One* confirms this, for the story is simply *Black Mischief* in a new setting.

Waugh found America comic for the same reasons that he had laughed at Ethiopia, the ridiculous and incompetent aping by the natives of European customs, and the equally ridiculous self-absorption of the European expatriates. The pseudo-religious trappings of Whispering Glades play the same part in *The Loved One* that the ludicrous heresies of the Nestorian monks do in the earlier book; they are both examples of savages getting hold of the Faith, and turning it into mumbo-jumbo. The English expatriates may seem to loom tediously large in Waugh's account of Hollywood but, as in *Black Mischief*, they are there to remind us that savagery is not confined to the native population of distant lands.

As in the former novel, there is no hope in this society of savages for those who are merely guilelessly good. Aimée's ignorant innocence leads her to her death, and earlier in the story a harmless elderly littérateur turned scriptwriter hangs himself because he cannot cope with the savagery of studio life. As in *Black Mischief*, the one figure that emerges triumphant from the jungle is that of an Englishman without remorse, filled with cunning and quite devoid of scruples. Dennis Barlow is even more possessed of a devil of mischief than Basil Seal. At the end of *The Loved One*, Waugh even allows him to pose as a clergyman – 'All non-sectarian services expeditiously conducted at competitive prices.' It is no worse than the savages deserve.

Just as *Black Mischief* ends with the diabolical Basil eating the innocent Prudence, so *The Loved One* concludes with Dennis cremating Aimée without a shred of regret: 'The fire roared in the brick oven. Dennis must wait until all was consumed. He must rake out the glowing ashes, pound up the skull and pelvis. . . .' Unlike Basil, Dennis is a writer, and at the end we are told that he will return to Europe carrying 'the artist's load, a great, shapeless chunk of experience'. All through the story, Waugh has emphasized that Dennis is in a superior position by being an artist, and has suggested that this licenses his ruthlessness and dishonesty, and even permits him to destroy Aimée. The image of his smashing her burnt bones brings home violently what the novella has been telling us all along, that the writer has the right to manipulate, deceive and finally destroy those around him if they can provide fuel for his art.

Graham Greene had been working productively in the cinema – *The Fallen Idol*, scripted by him from one of his own short stories, was released during 1948 – and he too visited Hollywood, to discuss a new project with David O. Selznick. When Greene explained that the film would be called *The Third Man*, Selznick shook his head reproachfully: 'You can do better than that, Graham.'

At one point in the progress of the *Brideshead Revisited* film project, Waugh heard that Greene had agreed to write the script. He sent him a postcard: 'If true, thanks most awfully. It is more than I ever thought possible.' Reviewing Greene's first post-war novel, *The Heart of the Matter* (1948), Waugh observed that Greene's narrative style was essentially cinematic: 'The writer has become director and producer. It is the camera's eye.'

Looking back at this novel in his autobiography, Greene compared its origins to those of *Brideshead Revisited*:

> Evelyn Waugh once wrote to me that the only excuse he could offer for *Brideshead Revisited* was 'spam, blackouts and Nissen huts'. I feel much the same towards *The Heart of the Matter*, though my excuse might be different – 'swamps, rain, and a mad cook' – for our two wars were very different.

Scobie, the middle-aged police official who is Greene's hero, becomes adulterously involved with a young widow, and is tormented less by his infidelity to his wife than by his religious scruples, for he is a Catholic. Helen, his mistress, taunts him much as Charles taunted Julia in Waugh's novel:

> 'It's a wonderful excuse being a Catholic,' [Helen] said. 'It doesn't stop you from sleeping with me – it only stops you marrying me.'
> 'Yes,' he said.

In a sense the novel explores what might have happened had Julia not rejected Charles but gone on living with him 'in sin', or married him without the sanction of the Church. Scobie becomes increasingly tormented by his disloyalty to God; he makes his Communion without having received absolution from the priest for his confession of adultery, and believes that he has thereby committed a mortal sin; eventually this drives him to suicide.

Scobie's conviction of his own damnation, which drives the novel on towards this melodramatic conclusion, is a reworking – as Waugh pointed out in his review of the book – of Pinkie's predicament in *Brighton Rock*. The new Greene novel seemed to Waugh to tackle this subject in a 'vastly more subtle' way than the earlier one. He judged that Greene had surpassed any of his Thirties achievements in his evocation of the West African port in wartime: 'The characters are real people. . . . It is so well done that one forgets the doer.' Certainly for the first two-thirds the characters, unlike most of those in Greene's earlier books, do seem entirely plausible, victims of their environment and way of life. Yet as the story reaches its climax, Scobie's belief that he is damned makes Greene revert to the hysterical tone of the religious passages of *Brighton Rock*, and one is also uncomfortably reminded of Julia's bombastic speech in *Brideshead Revisited* about living in sin:

> [Scobie] drove down towards the police station and stopped his car outside the church. . . . He had no inclination to pray – what was the good? If one was a Catholic, one had all the answers: no prayer was effective in a state of mortal sin. . . . Human love . . . had robbed him of love of eternity. . . .

Waugh took such passages with complete seriousness. 'It is a book which only a Catholic could write and only a Catholic can understand,' he asserted in his review. But Greene himself felt, or came to feel, rather differently.

'The scales to me seem too heavily weighted,' he writes of *The Heart of the Matter* in his autobiography, 'the plot overloaded, the religious scruples of Scobie too extreme.' He explains that he had intended to write about 'the disastrous effect on human beings of pity' (it is pity for his wife which causes Scobie to pretend that he still loves her, and pity for the widowed Helen which leads him into the affair with her). Greene also felt, looking back, that he could have written a more subtle novel around the character of a young Catholic priest he had met in Sierra Leone, about whom he made notes at the time: 'Poor little red-headed north country boy neglected by his fellows. . . . Apparently no interests. 6 year tour – 3½ done. The old raincoat over a dirty white shirt.' He felt this man might have engendered 'a better book than *The Heart of the Matter*'.

The decision to concentrate on Scobie seems to have arisen from Greene's own predicament when he came home from West Africa. An extremely private person, he gives virtually no information in the two volumes of his autobiography about his own marriage, scarcely even mentioning that he and his wife had children (a son and a daughter). One of the few hints he drops about his domestic situation is the almost passing mention that his brief taking of Benzedrine shortly before the war, to increase his literary output, was 'more responsible than the separation of war and my own infidelities for breaking our marriage'. However, when discussing *The Heart of the Matter* (in *Ways of Escape*, the second volume of his memoirs) he does hint that Scobie's predicament in the novel – caught between two women – grew out of his own. 'The booby-traps I had heedlessly planted in my private life were blowing up in turn,' he says of the months during 1946 when he was writing the novel.

> I had always thought that war would bring death as a solution in one form or another ... but here I was alive, the carrier of unhappiness to people I loved.... So perhaps what I really dislike in the book is the memory of personal anguish.... I was even contemplating one night the first move to suicide when I was interrupted in that game by the arrival at ten in the evening of a telegram ... from someone whom I had made suffer and who now felt anxious for my safety.

With which he turns back abruptly to a discussion of the novel, revealing nothing else about his own life at the time it was written.

Waugh was unaware of all this when he reviewed *The Heart of the Matter* – he did not yet know Greene very well – and he treated the novel more as a work of theology than of fiction. 'The reader', he wrote, 'is haunted by the question: Is Scobie damned?' He devoted several hundred words to considering this. He was particularly concerned with the book's epigraph, taken from the French theological writer Péguy: 'Le pécheur est au coeur même de chrétienté.' Waugh, too, had read Péguy, and in his review (in the journal *Commonweal*) he expounds the French writer's belief that sinners may be truer Christians than good men. He concludes that Greene accepts this view and uses it to mould the character of Scobie: 'I believe that Mr Greene thinks him a saint.'

Greene immediately wrote to Waugh that this was not so: 'I did not regard Scobie as a saint, and his offering his damnation up was intended to show how muddled a man full of goodwill could become once "off the rails".' Waugh replied: 'It was your putting that quotation from Péguy at the beginning which led me astray. I think it will lead others astray.' Greene raises the issue again in his autobiography, saying he has become:

> wearied ... by reiterated arguments in Catholic journals on Scobie's salvation or damnation. I was not so stupid as to believe that this could ever be an issue in a novel. Besides I have small belief in the doctrine of eternal punishment (it was Scobie's belief not mine).

Realizing that he had misrepresented Greene, Waugh instructed that a reprint of the review should have the sentence 'I believe that Mr

Greene thinks him a saint' changed to 'Several critics have taken Scobie to be a saint.' But he said he would 'very much like' the review to appear elsewhere, without further changes; it was evidently a subject which greatly interested him.

It seems hard to reconcile the creator of *The Loved One* with the theologically minded reviewer, mulling over Péguy. Waugh the Catholic reviewer might consider Scobie's predicament soberly but, theologically speaking, Dennis Barlow in his novella is damned on every possible ground, and evidently the Waugh who wrote it did not care.

Since the mid-Thirties and the writing of *Edmund Campion*, two authorial Waughs had been separating themselves from each other, the creator of the godless, amoral novels – or of novels in which God, if He exists, is simply a malevolent Fate – and the Catholic apologist concerned to stamp out heresy. Cyril Connolly noticed that Waugh's ideas no longer cohered in one intellectual scheme, or rather that they were held loosely together only by his own forcible personality. 'Under its spell,' wrote Connolly, 'the separate components are united as by the patter in a conjuring trick.'

Yet if there were two Waughs by the late Forties, they shared a belief in, and were motivated by, one thing. Waugh could never have said with Graham Greene that he found the doctrine of eternal punishment scarcely credible. Certainty of the existence of Hell, in a variety of manifestations, had always been at the heart of all his writings, and one of his objections to the Century of the Common Man was that it eliminated such a belief. In his *Tablet* article on Forest Lawn, he explained that his real objection to the Californian cemetery was that it pretended there was no such thing as the Last Judgement: 'We are very far here from the traditional conception of an adult soul naked at the judgement seat and a body turning to corruption. . . . In Forest Lawn . . . the body does not decay [and] the soul goes straight on from the Slumber Room to Paradise.' As to the extent of the literalness of his belief in Hell, Christopher Sykes, himself a Catholic of more modernist inclinations, describes Waugh as having become by this time 'a fundamentalist' who liked many articles of faith simply because they 'defied rationalism'. The more literally the Church demanded that he believe something irrational, says Sykes, the more 'delighted' he was.

Another way to mock the Century of the Common Man, with its Welfare State of free health care, teeth and glasses, was to grow old prematurely and grotesquely. 'I am a very much older man than this time last year,' Waugh wrote in his diary on his forty-fourth birthday in

October 1947, 'physically infirm and lethargic.' He seemed pleased that his hand had begun to shake. 'It is a great thing to be old and I am sorry you are not older,' he wrote to Douglas Woodruff, who had just turned fifty. 'Still you have definitely passed the watershed & that is everything. Downhill now all the way into deep pasture & long evening shadows.'

Another Waugh *persona*, which had always been present in the pack, was beginning to become prominent: the comic actor with a whole range of self-mocking performances. Often, as in the letter to Woodruff, the role resembled Charles Ryder's father. At other times he might play the spoilt child. Christopher Sykes, who was then the literary editor of the *New English Review*, met him for lunch one day at Wilton's restaurant in London and offered him a book for review. At first Waugh said no, then, when he heard what it was (a catty memoir of Logan Pearsall Smith), changed his mind and demanded the book at once. Sykes said he would send it tomorrow; he wanted to read it himself. 'At this Evelyn began to cry. When I say he cried, I mean that he began to yell in the manner of a two-year-old child, gurgling between ear-splitting ululations "I-WANT-THE-BOOK-NOW". In the confined space of the little restaurant the noise caused much sensation. I hastily gave him the book and his howls of agony stopped.'

On the same occasion Laura, who was with them, asked Evelyn to look after a watch she had just bought; she thought it would be safer in his waistcoat pocket. He would not. Laura appealed in vain: 'All your pockets are empty.' 'By no means *all*,' responded Waugh with a glare. Laura then turned to Sykes, who:

> adopted a conciliatory tone. 'Why don't you put the watch in your pocket?' I pleaded. Evelyn put on a judicial air. With glaring eyes, and in a serious manner, he explained the situation. 'Because,' he said in a voice of thunder, 'if I were to put the watch in my pocket, and if later someone were to pick me up by the heels and shake me, then *two* watches would fall out of my pockets and I would thus be made to look ridiculous.'

He had, says Sykes, 'the great comedian's ability to follow up one *coup* with another', for when Sykes asked him if being held upside down and shaken by the heels was something that often happened to him, '"Not much outside the St James's Club," he said with the same gravity, "but it is sinful to expect that God has made any man capable of predicting what may or may not happen to him, or immune from possible calamities."' Writing in *The Ordeal of Gilbert Pinfold*, Waugh describes the character he was playing here as 'a combination of eccentric don and testy colonel'.

Mr Ryder senior was in evidence again when Waugh made attempts to get Sykes to introduce him to T.S. Eliot, whom Sykes knew slightly through John Hayward. Waugh spoke of him as 'This close companion of yours, Eliot, a poet almost as famous as Stephen Spender I believe.' Sykes adds: 'He always pronounced the name Spender in Germanic style, though he always pronounced the names of German nationals in English style: Goering became Gorring and Hegel, Heegle.'

In an article in the *Strand Magazine*, John Betjeman described Waugh as he now appeared on visits to London: 'Those angry eyes looking out on to St James's, the neat clothes, cigar and carefully rolled umbrella. . . . Never did man look less like an author.' These remarks, prefacing the publication of one of Waugh's short stories ('Tactical Exercise'), were accompanied by a drawing of Waugh by Osbert Lancaster – red-faced, glaring from the steps of his club, just as described by Betjeman. Waugh's comment was: 'O. Lancaster's sketch good in conception but poor in execution.' He himself described this pose in *The Ordeal of Gilbert Pinfold*: 'He offered the world a front of pomposity mitigated by indiscretion, that was as hard, bright, and antiquated as a cuirass.'

Chiefly, of course, it was yet another way of protesting against the Century of the Common Man. But it is notable that these comic performances began in earnest only after his father's death. With the melodramatic Arthur Waugh out of the way, Evelyn could for the first time enjoy being an actor himself.

2

Back to Prep School Again

Waugh suggested to Connolly that the number of *Horizon* which was to contain *The Loved One* might also include a serious essay on Monsignor Ronald Knox, which he had just written: 'I think it would be what the Mitfords used to call "a good tease".' And he observed to Nancy Mitford: '*Loved One* is being well received in intellectual circles. They think my heart is in the right place after all. I'll show them.' In another letter to Nancy Mitford, written in November 1949: 'My *Helena* is a great masterpiece. How it will flop.'

Helena, Waugh's most uncharacteristic work of fiction, is a historical novel about the mother of the Emperor Constantine, who journeyed to Jerusalem and discovered the True Cross. Published in 1950, it had been begun five years earlier, while Waugh was in Yugoslavia. It is only a short book, but he worked at it intermittently and with little evidence of enthusiasm ('I write a sentence a week on the Empress Helena'). Though not unrelieved by humour, and with witty colloquial dialogue, it nevertheless totally lacks the ironical method of character-portrayal that he practised in all his other narratives.

In a sense there is nothing puzzling about *Helena*. Once again, Waugh is writing about civilization and savagery. Rome is presented very much in terms of the City that Tony Last sought in *A Handful of Dust*. 'I'm not a sentimental man,' says Constantius, Helena's husband, as he contemplates the boundary of the Roman Empire, 'but I love the wall. Think of it, mile upon mile, from snow to desert, a single great girdle round the civilized world; inside, peace, decency, the law ... outside, wild beasts and savages. . . . Doesn't it make you see what The City means?' Helena's discovery of the Cross is a civilizing act. By reminding her fellow-Christians that their faith has a historical and factual basis, she is bringing daylight into the mental darkness caused by heresy, gnosticism and the leftovers of the pagan world. Waugh's personal interest in her is understandable too. As he makes clear towards the end of the book, he regards her as the patron saint of latecomers to the Faith (like himself), and also of intellectuals. In a finely written passage – the more purple language does not embarrass, as it did in *Brideshead Revisited* – Helena prays for those 'who stand in danger by reason of their talents . . . the learned, the oblique. . . . Let them not be quite forgotten at the Throne of God when the simple come into their kingdom.'

With her brusque enthusiasm and obsession with horses, Helena is also a portrait of Penelope Betjeman. 'As I told you I am writing her [Penelope's] life under the disguise of St Helena's,' Waugh wrote to John Betjeman in May 1945. 'She is 16, sexy, full of horse fantasies.' His own encouragement of Penelope's wish to convert to Rome, during the period that he was writing *Helena*, is reflected in the novel. Helena is no hasty convert to the Church, and finally takes the step because she has been persuaded of the historicity of Christianity by a scholar named Lactantius, who is a portrait of Waugh himself: 'He delighted in writing, in the joinery and embellishment of his sentences, in the consciousness of high rare virtue when every word had been used in its purest and most precise sense. . . .' Besides these personal details, the book has certain characteristic Waugh touches. Roman soldiers and civil servants are made to resemble their 1939–45 equivalents. 'I've applied a dozen times to rejoin the army,' complains Constantine's son Crispus. 'No reply. Some eunuch just goes off with the papers and that's the last one hears of it.' The murderous machinations of the Imperial family receive the same light touch that sketches blackly comic disasters in Waugh's early novels. Nor does *Helena* descend to the tushery that mars so much historical fiction.

But it is not really Waugh, not a proper use of the talents that were distinctively his. Robert Graves or Rosemary Sutcliff could have done the historical portraiture better, and at the end the book declines into a religious tract: 'Above all the babble of her age and ours, [Helena] makes one blunt assertion. And there alone lies Hope.' For all its avowed seriousness, *Helena* does not really seem as serious as *Brideshead Revisited* or *A Handful of Dust*. In the scene where Helena converses with Pope Sylvester 'in a small loggia overlooking what had once been the park, now almost filled by Constantine's new church', one cannot help recalling another conversation between a Pope and a supposedly holy woman – 'Chiara, mother of the ambitious cardinal Montefiasco', alias Alec Waugh, swigging brown ale in the Waughs' back garden.

Helena was partly an act of self-sacrifice by a man who wished more than ever to identify himself as a Catholic, *contra mundum*, and was prepared to leave his real talents unused while engaging in a fairly humble task for the sake of his Church. It was also, like so much of what Waugh said and did nowadays, a good tease, an elaborate and lengthy way of frustrating his readers' expectations and refusing to dance to their music. Hereafter, he always named *Helena* as his favourite book, knowing that this would astonish and dismay his admirers. 'It's just much the best, you know,' he told John Freeman on television in 1960, 'the best written, most interesting theme.'

Towards the end of *Helena*, Waugh introduces the character of the Wandering Jew, who tells Helena in a dream where the True Cross is to be found. Though Waugh portrays him in modern fashion, as an East End entrepreneur ('I'm in incense, see. . . . All the leading shrines are on my books'), he wrote to Nancy Mitford that the Jew was 'B. Howard again'.

Though the Jew in *Helena* resembles neither Brian Howard nor Waugh's caricature of him as Ambrose Silk, it may be that Brian's own wanderings through Europe suggested a resemblance – his post-war meanderings with another boyfriend, a beefy Irishman named Sam, were as aimless as his Thirties travels with Toni. 'The fact remains that I am OLD now,' Brian wrote to his mother, 'and I've done NOTHING.' During the 1950s his health broke down, he became dependent on sedative drugs, and when (in January 1958) Sam died accidentally by asphyxiation from a faulty gas heater, Brian killed himself with an overdose. Waugh wrote a brief epitaph in a letter to a friend: 'I used to know Brian Howard well – a dazzling young man to my innocent eyes. In later years . . . I kept clear of him. . . . There is an aesthetic bugger who sometimes turns up in my novels under various names – that was ⅔ Brian ⅓ Harold Acton. People think it was all Harold, who is a much sweeter & saner man.'

Waugh still occasionally saw Acton. In the spring of 1950, visiting Italy, he stayed in a *pensione* near the Acton villa, La Pietra, where Harold's parents were still living. 'Harold lives a life of great severity,'

Waugh reported to Nancy Mitford.

> His parents will not permit his going out when they have guests or
> his staying at home when they are alone, so half his time is spent being
> polite to aged American marquesas and half eating in poky restaurants.
> He is not allowed in his fathers car and lives three miles out of town. . . .
> But he knows everything about ART. . . . La Pietra really is very fine.
> Much more than I expected.

Acton's parents had fled Italy when it declared war on the Allies, and
Harold had served as an RAF intelligence officer and a press censor.
After the war he wanted to return to China but, as Waugh records,
he was under his parents' thumb – especially since the death, during
the war, of his brother William – and he lingered in Italy, publishing
his *Memoirs of an Aesthete* (1948) and becoming a much loved figure
in the art world. Waugh renewed their friendship, and expressed gratitude for Acton's leadership in the Twenties – 'My sympathies still
stand where you grounded them,' he wrote to him in 1948.

He also kept up his friendship with Henry Yorke, while criticizing
his books behind his back. 'I think nothing of *Nothing*,' he wrote to
Nancy Mitford of the 1950 'Henry Green' novel, complaining that
there was no proper delineation of the characters' social position (the
novel is about a widower and his daughter). And in 1952: '*Doting*
is pitiable but I dont at all rejoice. There are not enough writers for
one not to mind one going to seed and there are too many contemporaries in decay.' In Yorke's case, the decay was physical as well as (in
Waugh's opinion) literary. After a visit from Yorke and his wife to
Piers Court, Waugh recorded that Henry 'looked GHASTLY. Very long
black dirty hair, one brown tooth, pallid puffy face, trembling hands,
stone deaf . . . drinking a lot of raw spirits . . .'. And in another letter
to Nancy Mitford: 'The habits of G. Greene's characters are *precisely*
and in *every detail identical* to those of the Bright Young Yorkes.'

Alan Ross, editor of the *London Magazine*, explains that Henry Yorke
had for years imitated his aged father's feebleness, 'shuffling across
his room, transferring a paper from one desk to another and then
a few minutes later taking it back again.' Then the father died and
'Henry breathed more freely. But . . . it was not long before he himself
withdrew, falling into a rapid physical decline which was accelerated
by gin.' What had formerly been mockery became Yorke's own mannerisms – 'a tottering, unshaven recluse, hard of hearing, short of
breath and teeth, who nevertheless lingered on for another twenty
years'. He died in 1973, having published nothing since 1952.

Graham Greene was almost the only friend of Waugh's who continued to please him as a writer. Waugh wrote of Greene's next novel, *The End of the Affair* (1951), in the Catholic journal *Month*, that the book 'shows that in middle life his mind is suppler and his interests wider than in youth; that . . . he has triumphantly passed the dangerous climacteric where so many talents fail'.

Begun in 1948, *The End of the Affair* was startlingly different from anything Greene had previously written. Narrated in the first person by an author, Maurice Bendrix, whose published work sounds much like Greene's own novels, it describes the complexities of his affair with Sarah, wife of a stiff-upper-lip civil servant, Henry Miles. During an air raid when they have been making love, Bendrix is buried beneath rubble, and Sarah, believing him dead, makes a promise to the god in whom she scarcely believes that if he can be brought back to life, she will renounce him. Bendrix, who has only been slightly injured, walks into the room, and Sarah keeps her promise without explaining to her lover why she is rejecting him. Eventually he discovers the truth, but Sarah, who has begun instruction as a Catholic, dies before they can be reconciled.

Thematically, the novel seems like another meditation on the dilemma of Charles and Julia in *Brideshead Revisited*, though, as Waugh pointed out in his review, the story stops before its implied conclusion, the conversion of Bendrix to the Catholic Faith. Like *Helena*, it comes perilously near to being a religious tract – after her death, Sarah apparently performs two miraculous healings. But unlike *Helena* it is entirely characteristic of its author – there are the usual shabby 'Greeneland' characters on the periphery – while the story achieves a passionate intensity never before found in Greene's fiction.

In the autumn of 1948, just as he was starting to plan *The End of the Affair*, Greene invited Waugh to lunch at his flat at 5 St James's Street. Waugh had suggested they eat at his club, but Greene insisted on being the host. When Waugh arrived, he discovered that this was because Greene wanted to introduce him to a neighbour, a young lady named Catherine Walston, who lived in the next-door flat in the same house. 'Luncheon plainly had been brought from her flat,' noted Waugh with the skill of one of Greene's sleuths, 'for there was no salt. She sat on the floor and buttered my bread for me and made simple offers of friendship.' She insisted that Waugh come and see her house in the country, near Cambridge, the very next day. Rather uncharacteristically, he agreed, and set off 'with a pleasant sense of having an interesting time ahead'.

When he arrived, Greene was already there: 'She and Graham had been reading a treatise on prayer together that afternoon.' There is no mention in Waugh's diary of Catherine Walston's husband, who had the same first name as Sarah's husband in the novel – Henry Walston, later Lord Walston, a Cambridge scientist who in those days was working for the Foreign Office. Waugh was captivated by Mrs Walston, who poured champagne into silver goblets and talked to him 'barefooted and mostly squatting on the floor. Fine eyes and mouth, unaffected to the point of insanity, unvain, no ostentation – simple friendliness and generosity and childish curiosity.' And to Nancy Mitford, Waugh wrote that he had found the Walston household:

> extraordinary.... A side of life I never saw before – very rich, Cambridge, Jewish, socialist, high brow, scientific, farming. There were Picassos on sliding panels & when you pushed them back plate glass & a stable with a stallion looking at one. No servants. Lovely Carolean silver unpolished.... The house a series of wood bungalows, more bathrooms than bedrooms. The hostess at six saying 'I say shall we have dinner tonight as Evelyn's here. Usually we only have Shredded Wheat.' ... It made quite a change from Stinkers [Piers Court].

Waugh continued to see something of Mrs Walston in Greene's company, and in August 1951 he wrote to her: 'I met you first as a friend of Graham's but I hope I can now look on you as a friend in my own right.' The idea had been mooted that she and Greene should come and stay at Piers Court, and she had wondered what Waugh felt about this. 'Please believe me', he replied,

> that I am far too depressed by my own odious, if unromantic, sins to have any concern for other people's. For me, it would be a delight to welcome you here. But when you say Graham is sometimes happier without you, that is another matter. You know & I don't. I did detect in his letters a hint that he looked forward to a spell of solitude. Only you can decide whether that mood is likely to persist. If you think it a bad time, come later....

Greene and Mrs Walston came down to 'Stinkers', and Waugh reported to Nancy Mitford:

> G. Greene behaved well & dressed for dinner every night. Mrs Walston had never seen him in a dinner jacket before and was enchanted and will make him wear one always. G. Greene spent his days patrolling the built up areas round Dursley noting the numbers of motor-cars. He takes omens from them.

This jest refers to a remark by Bendrix in *The End of the Affair*:

> 'During the last year, Henry, I've been so bored I've even collected car numbers. That teaches you about coincidences. Ten thousand possible numbers and God knows how many combinations, and yet over and over again I've seen two cars with the same figures side by side in a traffic block.'

Greene himself refers, in his autobiography, to his need for solitude even during a happy love affair: 'the chief difficulty was my own manic–depressive temperament ...'. Two years after the visit to Piers Court, another friend of Waugh's (Ann Fleming) described Greene at a party held for him by Catherine Walston: 'Is he living in sin? Is he tortured? He remained remote from all, totally polite and holding the cocktail shaker as a kind of defensive weapon.' Waugh replied: 'Graham Greene's life is as mysterious to me as to you.'

By now, Greene's own Church had begun to be aware that Greene was not simply a 'Catholic novelist' propagating the Faith. Pope Pius XII read *The End of the Affair* ('Strange reading for a pope,' comments Greene) and told Bishop (later Cardinal) Heenan: 'I think this man is in trouble. If he ever comes to you, you must help him.' In 1954 *The Power and the Glory* was officially condemned by Cardinal Pizzardo of the Holy Office, on the grounds that it was 'paradoxical' and 'dealt with extraordinary circumstances', and Waugh noted in his diary that by now 'a lot of Catholics were suspicious of [Greene's] good faith'. Their suspicions were not unfounded; Waugh recorded of a 1953 visit to Piers Court by Greene:

> Graham ... is ... it seems, in an unhappy state. He told the Italian ambassador, as an excuse for not visiting [a] conference at Florence, that he was 'no longer a practising Catholic'. [At Piers Court] he asked for a biscuit before Mass as though to provide (like his hero in *The Heart of the Matter*) a reason for not taking communion, but went off to early train fasting on Monday.

However, Waugh chose to ignore these signs, and on a number of occasions accepted invitations from Catholic groups to address them on Greene's and his own fiction, treated under the umbrella of 'Catholic novelists', reassuring his audiences of Greene's orthodoxy. To Nancy Mitford, he described 'an excruciating week-end in a convent in Surrey conducting a "Catholic Booklovers Week-End". The nuns were very attentive with little packets of chocolate and glasses of milk.... Can you wonder that the mere breath of White's intoxicates?'

*

411

Cyril Connolly's private life was only slightly less mysterious than Greene's, and just as fascinating to Waugh. 'G. Orwell is dead and Mrs Orwell presumably a rich widow,' Waugh wrote to Nancy Mitford in January 1950. 'Will Cyril marry her? He is said to be consorting with Miss Skelton.' Sonia Brownell, one of the assistants on *Horizon*, had married George Orwell shortly before his death. Barbara Skelton was another member of the *Horizon* set. Waugh continued to take an interest in her relations with Connolly. 'There is I believe', he wrote to Nancy Mitford nearly a year later, 'no doubt that Boots has married. . . .'

The daughter of a Gaiety Girl, Barbara Skelton had a long history of mildly scandalous *amours*. She had become a rich man's mistress while still in her teens, had caused a court-martial in India, and was asked to leave Egypt because of her involvement with King Farouk ('I am deadly tired,' she wrote in her diary after one dinner with him, 'and ache all over from a flogging of last night on the steps of the Royal Palace. I would have preferred a splayed cane, but instead had to suffer a dressing-gown cord . . .'). Once, she allowed two men to toss a coin for her favours on board ship, and when in the later days of the Second World War she agreed to share a Highgate house with Peter Quennell, with whom she had already had an affair, and also George Weidenfeld (whom much later she married), it seemed likely that a similar situation would develop. Instead, she took up with Connolly, having been told that 'Cyril was bored with Lys [Lubbock] and was seeking someone new.'

Though past her first beauty, Barbara Skelton was strikingly good-looking, with high cheekbones and what a French friend called 'panther's eyes'. However, Nancy Mitford claimed that what attracted Connolly was her car, a red convertible Sunbeam Talbot. They drove in it through France and Switzerland, where Barbara, a heavy smoker, suffered the first of Connolly's deflating quips. 'I was lighting up during the cheese course, when he said acidly, ''I suppose you think the hollows in the gruyère are there for you to stub out your cigarette.''' By the spring of 1950 Connolly had abandoned Lys, who had taken another lover, and was showing a considerable interest in Barbara. Peter Quennell asked her sarcastically: 'Has Baby read her Palinurus yet?' and got the reply: 'Why should I read it, when I live it every day?'

Certainly the self-pity of *The Unquiet Grave* was fully displayed in Connolly's daily life. 'Cyril rang up in a terribly self-pitying state,' Barbara wrote in her diary.

412

How could I have been so beastly as to send him back to his cold empty house? ... That I was a selfish bitch.... That he had no money.... So, I packed my basket and trekked off to Sussex Place, expecting to find him in a terrible state of gloom, but he was prancing about the bedroom barefoot, very pleased with himself.... Said he was pleased to see me, whipped off his dressing-gown, sprang into bed and was asleep in no time.

Connolly still loved making lists and catalogues, just as he had in his journal twenty years earlier. One day he told Barbara that:

he had spent the greater part of the night allotting marks to all the women of his circus, according to their suitability as wives. I, of course, got fewer than any of them for spirituality, but top score for sex appeal, followed by Sonia Orwell, who had tremendous appeal in a blowsy way when blotto.

Waugh, hearing about the affair, did not give her high marks for anything. 'Oh dear I do hope he doesnt settle down with that drab,' he wrote to Nancy Mitford. 'Why cant ones friends marry *nice* girls?'

At first, Connolly thought that marriage was out of the question, observing to Barbara that 'we don't get on at all well when things go wrong and you couldn't bear being poor'. But in October 1950 they went to the registry office, taking as their witness the village policeman who looked after Barbara's country cottage when she was away – the improbably named PC William Boot. 'Darling Nancy,' announced Waugh a couple of months later,

There is I believe no doubt that Boots has married.... The evidence is conclusive tho it is not known whether he gave her a ring. A Mrs Hulton [a friend of Connolly's] gave him a wedding breakfast. After the first course Boots had a seizure, fell off his chair frothing & gasping, was carried straight to a waiting van & whisked off to Tring where he spent the first fortnight of married life in a padded cell being starved and hosed and worse.

The truth was more exotic than Waugh's fantasy. There was no wedding breakfast, and with William Boot still in tow they ate a cold lunch in a pub 'in sullen silence'. Five days later, Barbara found Connolly in the bedroom:

standing naked in an attitude of despair staring into space. Take my bath, return to bedroom and find C still gazing into space. Go into the sitting room, to write a letter, return to bedroom, C still with his back to the room propped against the window ledge. I ask, 'What's the matter?' 'It's marriage,' he says. 'I feel trapped.'

Barbara soon realized that she had saddled herself with 'a slothful whale of a husband' who 'spends his time soaking in the bath and then plods despondently to White's where he studies the racing form'. They spent their first Christmas at Faringdon House, which Robert Heber-Percy had just inherited from Lord Berners, who had died earlier in the year. 'Garth ... acted as hostess,' noted Barbara. 'A strong smell of incense. ... There were two other queens. ... We had dinner with Sir Oswald and Lady Mosley. ... The following day we dined with the Betjemans. ... I suddenly turned to Hubby ... and screamed, "My God, you are a bore." ... Everyone stopped talking and looked very shocked.'

For a while they pigged it in Barbara's London flat. Conditions were scarcely tolerable with a narrow bed and 'Hubby heaving about like a giant seal' or 'sitting brooding like a furious fallen emperor'. Word went around that the telephone had been cut off; Waugh commented that from Connolly's appearance it looked as if the water had been cut off too. Later they moved to Barbara's cottage. *Horizon* had come to an end, thanks to Connolly's boredom and disillusionment, and he was writing reviews for the *Sunday Times*. He had nothing to do for most of the day except quarrel with Barbara. Guests who visited this *ménage* were accommodated in an outside shed; Angus Wilson 'slept in it once' (writes Barbara) 'and seemed none the worse for wear', but when Rosamund Lehmann saw it she 'suddenly recollected she had a breakfast appointment and insisted on taking the last train back to London'. The house was called Oak Cottage; Cyril dubbed it Oak Coffin. Summonses for unpaid bills arrived by almost every post. 'Cyril remains in his bed, sucking the sheet.'

Though they had no money, Connolly was always fretfully looking through agents' advertisements for Georgian manor houses, just as he and Jean had done in the Thirties. In London, at yet another party among familiar faces, 'Cyril said all those people make one feel we are all part of a dead civilization.' The quarrels got worse. 'Seeing some red wine all over his face, I say, "What have you got all over your face?" "Hate," says Cyril.'

Waugh continued to gloat over Connolly's marital misfortunes. One day Connolly told him: 'I am going to become a waiter at a fashionable restaurant so as to humiliate and reproach my friends for their ingratitude.' Waugh looked worried. 'Ah,' said Connolly, 'I see now I have touched even your cold heart.' Waugh replied: 'Well, no, Cyril, it isn't quite that. I was thinking of your finger-nails in the soup.'

Another contemporary, who had been silent as a novelist for twelve years, was now resurfacing as a literary success. Anthony Powell's last novel, *What's Become of Waring* (1939), an intricate little farce about a non-existent travel writer, had rounded off his pre-war exercises in the ironic portrayal of futility. Now in 1951 he brought out *A Question of Upbringing*, the first in a projected series of novels following the same set of characters from the Twenties to the present day.

A Question of Upbringing is set at Eton and Oxford in the Twenties, but these places as portrayed by Powell bear not the slightest resemblance to the Eton of Brian Howard and Harold Acton, nor the Oxford of *Brideshead Revisited*. Eton is reduced to a series of nondescript school buildings, swathed in river-mist and surrounded by suburban wasteland, and Oxford is painted as almost intolerably lugubrious. Powell was by now a master at reducing character to subtle shades of grey, and the book contains four triumphantly funny portraits in this manner, Le Bas the Eton housemaster, the narrator's down-at-heel Uncle Giles, Sillery the manipulating Oxford don (a blend of Sligger and Bowra), and most of all Widermerpool, the supremely graceless misfit who nevertheless has the secret of worldly success.

Waugh described typical Powell characters in terms not of greyness, but of dimensions: 'They can be observed from one position only. We cannot walk round them as statues. They present, rather, a continuous frieze in high relief, deep cut and detailed.' He observed a certain similarity in this respect to the characters in the 'Henry Green' novels, and wondered whether Yorke and Powell shared a dislike of human beings as individuals: 'I think Tony Powell suffers frightfully from all human contact,' he wrote to Nancy Mitford. 'There is an affinity between him & Henry Yorke which, no doubt, the Cambridge School of Literature will eventually investigate.'

Powell's previous novels had each presented a set of self-contained characters leading lives of almost total futility, who are gradually brought into juxtaposition with each other. No change takes place in any of them, and the process is then reversed, so that the book generally ends much as it began. This scheme was not appropriate to a longer venture, so for a method of manipulating his characters, and an image to govern the sequence, Powell turned to Poussin's picture 'A Dance to the Music of Time', which he had looked at in the Wallace Collection. In practical terms, 'the music of time' in Powell's novel-sequence means coincidence, a device of which he makes extensive use, reintroducing characters whenever he chooses without much regard for plausibility. Waugh's equivalent device in *Brideshead Revisited* was the 'twitch upon the thread', the working of divine purpose, but religion plays no part in Powell's imagination ('I suspect [him] of agnosticism,' Waugh wrote to Nancy Mitford), and usually appears in his narratives in the form of séances and other lunatic-fringe cults, supplying further evidence of human futility.

In his memoirs, Powell says he decided to begin the long sequence because he felt he would repeat himself if he continued to write single novels, and also because it seemed a waste to dismiss a set of characters once a book was finished. Yet 'A Dance to the Music of Time' is peopled with such superb characters – and such an enormous number of them – that clearly there was no danger of Powell's imagination running dry. This richness of characterization was soon winning enthusiasts for the series, among them Waugh, who did not review the early books, but wrote to Powell: 'I feel each volume of this series is like a great sustaining slice of Melton Pie. I can go on eating it with the recurring seasons until I drop.' When he finally published a review, of *Casanova's Chinese Restaurant* (1960), the fifth book in the sequence, he wrote: 'I have few reasons to desire longevity. One of them is the hope that I ... may be spared to see the completion of [this] fine sequence.'

Nevertheless, Waugh does seem to have felt certain private doubts about aspects of Powell's series. In a 1952 letter to his friend Ann Fleming, after the first two Powell volumes had appeared, he remarked that there was 'No competition here [i.e. among British novelists] except Angus Wilson whose *Hemlock and After* I have read three times and think *awfully* clever. ... ' Christopher Sykes says that, while he would not allow anyone to criticize Powell's writing, Waugh did 'allow ... that the sequence of novels ... was in danger of becoming self-defeatingly long. Evelyn would have liked the sequence brought to a conclusion after three or four volumes. ...' A 1961 letter to Nancy Mitford, describing his literary contemporaries in terms of steeplechasing, says that Powell 'is sitting unsteady with his arms round the horse's neck'. Possibly he was among those readers who, while enormously admiring Powell's pre-war work and many qualities in 'A Dance to the Music of Time', nevertheless found the long novel-sequence over-stretched and even pretentious, not least because of the weighty style of the first-person narrative.

Powell has claimed that a first-person narrator was a necessity in a long sequence, because it would avoid 'the artificiality of the invented "hero", who speaks for the author'. Yet there seems no reason why a first-person narrator should be more, or less, artificial than any other character. The suspicion arises that Powell chose to narrate in the first person, in an expansive and reflective manner, because Waugh had done so in *Brideshead Revisited* with considerable popular success.

If Waugh had a little influence on Powell's sequence, it is possible that 'A Dance to the Music of Time' helped to shape his own next work of fiction. Though he had mentioned his project of writing a novel about his war experiences as early as October 1946, it may be that *A Question of Upbringing*, which was published just as he started to write *Men at Arms*, encouraged him to plan not one volume but several. 'I am writing an interminable novel about army life,' he told Graham Greene in August 1951, a few weeks after he had begun work. And to Nancy Mitford: 'My novel is unreadable & endless.' He seems to have contemplated a sequence comparable in length to Powell's; he told Winston Churchill's niece Clarissa in January 1952 that *Men at Arms* was 'the first volume of four or five, which won't show any shape until the end', and to Ann Fleming he spoke of 'the succession of volumes that I plan'. To Cyril Connolly he explained that 'all the subsidiary characters, like ''Trimmer'' & ''Chatty Corner'' & ''de Souza'' will each have a book to himself'. Powell had been similarly uncertain at the outset just how many volumes his sequence would require.

Men at Arms lays two ghosts who had troubled Waugh's life, his father and his first wife. To do this, Waugh creates the character of Guy Crouchback, last male member of a great English Catholic land-owning family, who can beget no heir because his wife, the ironically named Virginia, has deserted him for a whole series of other men. Her desertion, eight years before the outbreak of war (the period which had elapsed between She-Evelyn's infidelity and Waugh's second marriage), has given Guy a 'deep wound' which has gravely impeded his life. The striking thing is that Virginia/She-Evelyn is presented sympathetically in the novel. Though she has a reputation as a loose woman, when Guy meets her for the first time for years he finds her charming and sensible, in no way a grotesque 'Bolter' like Fanny's mother in *The Pursuit of Love* (who cannot shake off the mannerisms of the Twenties and is pursuing men half her age), but a mature and witty woman of the world.

The portrait of old Mr Crouchback, Guy's father, is equally benevolent, conveying a real feeling of sanctity and modesty while also endowing him with enormous social self-certainty:

> Only God and Guy knew the massive and singular quality of Mr Crouch-back's family pride. . . . He was quite without class consciousness because he saw the whole intricate social structure of his country divided neatly into two unequal and unmistakable parts. On one side stood the Crouch-backs and certain inconspicuous, anciently allied families; on the other side stood the rest of mankind . . . all of a piece together. Mr Crouchback acknowledged no monarch since James II.

This is more than just Waugh as he would like to have been; it is a symbol of total paternalism. Mr Crouchback's lineage, his religion, his politics, all cohere into an unchallengeable – and to Waugh lovable – figure of authority.

The details of this are not new. The novelty lies in Mr Crouchback's lovableness. Waugh had tried to come to terms with fathers in *Work Suspended*, but had produced only an unfinished caricature. In *Brideshead Revisited* he had split the father-figure into two, creating the admirable but absent Lord Marchmain, fine enough in himself but abdicating all responsibility, and the all-too-present and positively malevolent Mr Ryder. Only now, eight years after Arthur Waugh's death, was Evelyn able to portray a loving father in harmony with his son. It is a portrait conceived in the same spirit as that of Virginia/She-Evelyn, an act of reconciliation with someone whom Waugh believed had done him wrong.

There are other scores to be settled, the terrible loneliness of Waugh's first months at Lancing, and his rejection by the army. Deftly, he combines these two private crises into one, and organizes his account of army life so that it is in effect a revisiting of his schooldays; at one point Guy observes of the petty disciplines of army life: 'It was back to prep school again.'

Like the young Waugh at school, and the mature man whom Bob Laycock did not want to take into action, Guy knows he is not liked by the people who see him daily. Waugh makes this clear even before Guy enters the army; his servants in Italy do not find him *simpatico*, but regard him as aloof and unlovable. Waugh indicates that this remoteness is the result of Guy's 'wound'; and certainly Waugh's own estrangement from humanity during the Thirties, his sense of being among 'remote people', was largely caused by She-Evelyn's desertion. Yet *Men at Arms* gives the strong impression that Guy has been like this all his life.

In a passage which touches on what Waugh's military colleagues regarded as his most unacceptable quality as a solider, Guy admits to himself that he cannot make any kind of human contact with his men, the other ranks:

> Guy knew every name. The difficulty was to identify them.... Most
> English gentlemen at this time believed that they had a particular aptitude
> for endearing themselves to the lower classes. Guy was not troubled
> by this illusion, but he believed he was rather liked by these particular
> thirty men. He did not greatly care. He liked them. He wished them
> well. ... But he did not distinguish between them as human beings.

Guy does not meditate on this, but simply accepts it as a fact about
himself. At moments like this, the reader is led to suspect that the
'wound' was there before Virginia left him, and that she walked out
because of his remote, aloof nature. Indeed, after the failure of Guy's
attempt to seduce her at their reconciliation, she hurls abuse at him
which virtually confirms this – she calls him 'wet, smug ... pompous,
sexless', and throws in a taunt at his lack of sexual prowess: 'If I
remember our honeymoon correctly, you weren't so experienced. ...
Not a particularly expert performance as I remember it.'

This is ultra-sensitive ground for Waugh, and not surprisingly the
scene soon comes to an abrupt end, thanks to drunken telephone interruptions by Guy's brother officer Apthorpe. Waugh evidently does
not want to explore the black depths of the Guy–Virginia relationship,
or to answer the charges of smugness, pomposity and lack of passion.
In general, *Men at Arms* avoids prying into Guy's character, and wherever possible puts the blame for his failures on other people. However,
the real nature of the handicap from which Guy suffers is ultimately
made clear in the novel.

Guy and Apthorpe are both addressed by the younger officers as
'Uncle', on account of their greater age. Waugh does not record in
his wartime diaries that he was ever so addressed, and his use of the
term in the novel suggests another layer of meaning in *Men at Arms*
– that he is writing about family life. Since Guy and Apthorpe are
both 'Uncles' one might assume that they are, in a sense, brothers
to each other. So they are: they represent the elder and the younger
brother, with the Brigadier, Ben Ritchie-Hook, as the histrionic, unpredictable father, judging the merits of each and making a ludicrously
wrong evaluation of both. (Waugh partly models Ritchie-Hook on
Nancy Mitford's grotesque father-figure in *The Pursuit of Love*; like
Uncle Matthew in that novel, he goes into battle with an entrenching
tool or machete, and 'once came back from a raid across no-man's-land
with the dripping head of a German sentry in either hand'.) Apthorpe
is patently ludicrous, yet it is he, the incompetent elder brother, who

is given command of a company while Guy remains two ranks lower. Guy is promised that his turn will come, but the promise is not kept. Apthorpe becomes a captain and pulls rank on Guy, while Ritchie-Hook manages to get Guy into serious trouble, encouraging him to lead an illicit night raid and then joining it himself in disguise, disobeying Guy's orders, and exposing the raid to angry official notice. Guy has been doubly let down by the father-figure. The other 'brother' has been rewarded (though he does not in the least deserve it), and Guy is on the scrap-heap. It is a vivid parable of how Waugh saw his childhood.

Alec Waugh had long ceased to be a literary success – nothing he had written since *The Loom of Youth* had made any lasting impression – but Evelyn's resentment of him was evidently still present beneath the surface. When Cyril Connolly made some reference, in the draft of his *Time* 'profile' of Waugh, to Alec's supposed heroism in the First World War, Evelyn wrote to him: 'My brother was no hero. He was a regular officer who passed through Sandhurst to a line regiment. Without any discredit he was taken prisoner in 1918. If I needed relations to emulate I have many others.' These still-smouldering feelings explain why Waugh concludes *Men at Arms* by killing off Apthorpe, wastefully in terms of the novel-sequence (the 'Sword of Honour' trilogy would have been greatly improved by the retention of Apthorpe for the remaining books), but understandably from the purely personal point of view. The elder brother is dead, and at Guy's own hands, for the death is caused by Guy clandestinely bringing a bottle of whisky to the fever-ridden Apthorpe as he lies in hospital, forbidden alcohol. The rival has at last been eliminated.

3

Acute P.M.

Writing in his *Sunday Times* column, Cyril Connolly judged *Men at Arms* to be 'a chronicle rather than a novel', beer rather than champagne, and wondered whether 'Atwater' (*sic*) was meant to be a reappearance of the character of that name from *Work Suspended*. Waugh was not offended by the review – ' "Beery" is exactly right,' he told Connolly – though he reproved him for the error in Apthorpe's name: 'It will make your readers think you did not give full attention to the book.'

A few weeks after writing this, he went with Diana and Duff Cooper to visit Connolly and his new wife. Barbara Skelton (Connolly) was greatly struck by his appearance:

> Waugh dressed in a black and white check suit. He has a check waistcoat and cap to match, and a ginger tweed overcoat, a flabby bulging stomach and a small aggressive gingerbread moustache. . . . He tries to be pleasant to me, looking down at my shabby grey checks and saying, 'You have trousers like mine.'

The clothes that Waugh was now wearing had begun to cause considerable surprise and amusement. Christopher Sykes was in at the birth of such an outfit as Barbara Skelton described:

> There is a cloth exclusively woven for officers of the Household Cavalry, used in the making of travelling and sporting overcoats and now usually for country caps. Never in history had this cloth been used for the making of a suit. On a light reddish-brown background it has a bright

red check about three inches square. Evelyn made tailoring history by ordering a suit in this cloth.

Not only was the material outrageous, but Waugh had it cut (adds Sykes) so that 'a bright red line ... ran down the fly buttons'. To the suit, he added a grey bowler hat from a shop in St James's. 'The result', says Sykes, 'surpassed the wildest extravagances of an old-fashioned music-hall comedian.'

Sykes assumed he was witnessing the ludicrous failure of an attempt to dress as 'the Old English Squire', since in this outfit Waugh, far from looking the gentleman, 'could easily be mistaken for a book-maker'. Similarly Anthony Powell, who describes the outfit as 'a sort of sponge-bag suit which made him simply look like a bookmaker', believes that Waugh really thought these were the right clothes for a country squire. Yet Waugh, always an acute observer of social nice-ties, must surely have been the first person to appreciate the comedy of the outfit. As with his impersonation of a Victorian father, he deliber-ately went over the top, and chose clothes in which no real squire would be seen dead.

Another eccentricity made its appearance around this time. 'I am quite deaf now. Such a comfort,' Waugh wrote to Nancy Mitford in March 1953, at the age of forty-nine, and in another letter he explained that he was 'stone deaf in one ear'. John Betjeman's father, another sufferer from deafness (though far more acutely than Waugh) had used an ear-trumpet: 'If he didn't want to hear you,' Betjeman would tell his friends, 'he would roll it up and put it in his pocket.' This probably gave Waugh the notion of acquiring such an instrument. He soon got hold of what Harold Acton calls a 'formidable' specimen 'which he must have disinterred from some country junk-shop', and began to use it, in Sykes's words, as 'an infallible way to make a shy person yet more ill at ease or make the most self-confident shy'. He only abandoned it after his friend Ann Fleming lost her temper and banged it with a spoon. 'The noise, Evelyn told me later,' writes Sykes, 'was that of a gun being fired an inch away.'

While the clothes and the ear-trumpet were funny, a third eccentricity was decidedly not. His pose as an irascible Victorian *paterfamilias*, an Uncle Matthew, tended to make him rude to strangers and social in-feriors, and by the time he reached his fiftieth birthday in October 1953 this habit had begun to annoy and embarrass his friends.

Much of his rudeness was in answer to fan-mail from American readers who wrote in praise of *Brideshead Revisited*. When the letter was from a married woman, he liked to reply to her husband, with the request to 'use whatever disciplinary means are customary in your country to restrain your wife from writing impertinent letters to men she does not know'. In the same vein was his response to a fan-letter from an American schoolgirl – he wrote to the child's headmistress, suggesting that she should 'mete out condign punishment to this unhappy child' for pestering him, and wondering from her peculiar name if the pupil 'is a Red Indian'. In an even less attractive category was his behaviour to the wife of an American theatrical producer, who praised *Brideshead Revisited* to his face; according to Lady Mary Lygon, who was present, Waugh replied: 'I thought it was good myself, but now that I know that a vulgar, common American woman like yourself admires it, I am not so sure.' He said much the same in letters to friends – that it was 'upsetting' that the novel had become popular in the United States: 'I thought it in good taste before and now I know it can't be.'

It was neither one of his best jokes, nor a pose that he maintained consistently. He was fond enough of America to accept a third invitation there in October 1950, to lecture to Catholic groups. He liked many American artefacts – Christopher Sykes records that he was entranced by *Kiss Me Kate*, which he saw in New York and went to again 'at least half a dozen times' when it opened in London, and he told Nancy Mitford that he always answered correspondence from 'very rich' Americans, politely, since 'they are capable of buying 100 copies for Christmas presents'. He was only too willing to accept highly paid commissions from the American-owned *Life* magazine to travel abroad and write for them; in January 1951 he and Sykes went to the Middle East at the magazine's expense, living well.

Sykes was nervous of how he would behave on this trip, but found him tolerant of the discomforts and snags of the journey. However, a trip Waugh made to Sicily with Harold Acton in the spring of 1952 was disastrous, at least for Acton, who says that he behaved like a caricature of the Englishman abroad – refusing to look at the sights, talking pigeon Italian to the natives ('No speaka da English?'), sending food back untasted in restaurants, and 'even going so far as to kick the waiters'. Back in London, at the Beefsteak Club, he picked a quarrel with the hall porter, and would have been expelled from membership had the porter not behaved as badly himself, following Waugh into the street and shouting abuse. As it was, says Sykes, 'Evelyn never went to the Beefsteak again.'

Sykes regarded this incident as more serious than the usual irascible performances designed for comic effect. 'I had noticed a change coming over Evelyn lately, and not a change for the better. He was becoming more arrogant, more quarrelsome. . . .' Others began to feel the same disquiet. After the Sicily trip, Harold Acton wrote to John Sutro quite seriously suggesting, says Sykes, 'that Evelyn was becoming mentally unbalanced'.

Waugh was, of course, only behaving as a caricature of the upper-class Englishman, an exaggerated version of the figure so many of his friends had chosen to become. Yet he seems to have been aware that one day this performance might have unpleasant consequences. Even before the Second World War he had experienced odd, disturbing little losses of memory, though he had usually put these down to drink. During 1949 he had noted, in a letter to Nancy Mitford, that when he came back to Piers Court after one of his drinking sessions in London, it was no longer merely a question of a hangover 'but of complete collapse, with some clear indications of incipient lunacy. I think I am jolly near being mad & need very careful treatment if I am to survive another decade without the strait straight? jacket.' He did not specify what form the 'lunacy' took, but in view of what was to come it may have been mild delusions of persecution. Back in 1928 in his life of Rossetti he had written at length of Rossetti's paranoia – 'Malevolence stared at him in the eyes of strangers in the street; every tiny mishap in his everyday life . . . had become in his mind the work of his enemies' – and had added a comment that suggests he may already occasionally have experienced such feelings himself; he spoke of Rossetti's condition as 'that distressing and not uncommon delusion that the whole world was banded against him in a conspiracy of infinite ramifications'.

Any disposition Waugh may have had towards this would have been exacerbated by the behaviour of the Beaverbrook press during the summer of 1953. The three national Beaverbrook papers – the *Daily Express, Sunday Express* and *Evening Standard* – all printed violently unfavourable reviews of his recently published novella *Love Among the Ruins*, a Huxleyan–Orwellian narrative set in an imagined near future in which socialism rules triumphant.* (Elsewhere the book had been received unenthusiastically, but by no means abusively.) The article in the

* *Love Among the Ruins* (1953), which reads like a delayed response to Cyril Connolly's 1946 utopian socialist plan in *Horizon*, describes Britain under an imaginary Labour–Conservative coalition of the near future, in which the State has replaced all prisons by luxurious rehabilitation centres, and euthanasia (supplied free of charge, in the manner of the National Health Service) is much in demand among the populace.

Evening Standard, by one George Malcolm Thomson, went beyond the bounds of mere reviewing, heaping personal abuse on Waugh, who was described as holding contemptible opinions and looking like 'an indignant White Leghorn'. Waugh responded with quite a mild protest in the *Spectator*, suggesting that the Beaverbrook hostility might have arisen from his recently having declined, in a rather curt manner, two journalistic commissions from that group of newspapers. In *The Ordeal of Gilbert Pinfold*, Waugh maintains that he was not seriously disturbed by such mud-slinging in the newspapers: 'It was part of the price he paid for privacy.' Yet he probably achieved such calm detachment only by repressing his fury.

Shortly after the episode with the Beaverbrook reviewers, the BBC wrote asking Waugh to take part in a radio series entitled *Frankly Speaking*. Three interviewers would come to Piers Court and record half an hour of informal conversation, soliciting his opinions on matters of general interest. Rather surprisingly, he agreed, 'provided the fee is adequate', though he said he would not wish to give 'the impression that I am taking part in a three-cornered intimate chat with personal friends, with the bandying about of Christian names and so forth, of the kind which deeply shocks me in some of the performances I have sometimes begun to hear'. The three interviewers duly arrived at Stinchcombe on 11 November 1953, two weeks after Waugh's fiftieth birthday.

In *The Ordeal of Gilbert Pinfold* the men – whose real names were Charles Wilmot, Jack Davies and Stephen Black – are described as 'youngish ... thin of hair, with horn-rimmed eliptical glasses, cord trousers, and tweed coats; exactly what Mr Pinfold was expecting. Their leader was named Angel [Stephen Black]. He emphasized his primacy by means of a neat, thick beard.' Christopher Sykes, who at this time was working in the Features Department of the BBC, spoke to Black, Wilmot and Davies after their return from Piers Court, and asked what impression Waugh had made on them:

> Evelyn did not give them a very friendly reception. Before they started the recording Evelyn said to them: 'Please understand that you address me as *Mr* Waugh. My surname is pronounced that way,' 'Of course,' said one of the interviewers, 'we know that.' 'Do you?' said Evelyn. 'I distinctly heard one of you say Wuff.' They laughed till they saw to their amazement that Evelyn was serious.

Waugh was convinced, even before the recording began, that their purpose was to get him to make a fool of himself. 'They were attempting', he writes in *The Ordeal of Gilbert Pinfold*, 'to emulate a series that had been cleverly done in Paris with various French celebrities, in which informal, spontaneous discussion had seduced the objects of inquiry into self-revelation'. He describes how, as the questions were put to him, he began to sense the hostility – specifically the class hostility – felt towards him by the interviewers:

> The commonplace face [of 'Angel', i.e. Black] above the beard became slightly sinister, the accentless, but insidiously plebeian voice, menacing. The questions were civil enough in form but Mr Pinfold thought he could detect an underlying malice.... There was a hint of the under-dog's snarl which Mr Pinfold recognized from his press-cuttings.

Although himself a BBC man, Sykes accepts Waugh's analysis of the programme: 'The interviewers ... presumed ... that this crusted conservative would be easy game, easily flustered and put on the defensive.' When the interview was broadcast a week later, an anonymous columnist in the *Spectator* was struck by the tone of the questions: 'I never heard an interview conducted in public on such ill-natured terms.' The recording itself, which survives in the BBC Sound Archives, shows Waugh's feelings about the programme to have been fully justified. The interviewers, whose contemporary middle-class accents contrast markedly with Waugh's clipped Victorian vowels and formal diction, put their questions more in the manner of a police interrogation than a radio conversation. Waugh, however, scores runs off every ball from the start.

The programme begins as follows:

> *First Interviewer (probably Black; the three are not identified, contributing to the impression of a police inquiry)*: 'Good evening, Mr Waugh. May I say to begin with that I, personally, find reading your books that you are to me perhaps the most interesting, amusing, and at the same time *depressing* person now writing. Can you tell me, do you really feel that there's any future for mankind at all?'
>
> *Waugh (beginning on the high-pitched note he sometimes used for effect)*: 'That a little smacks of the "Have you stopped beating your wife?" question. If you mean "future" in the sense you say, "There's a future for that boy," in the sense of a prosperous and happy time to come, I'm afraid I don't.'
>
> *Second Interviewer (making the question sound sinister and threatening)*: 'Where were you born, Mr Waugh?'
>
> *Waugh*: 'In London, Hampstead.'
>
> *Third Interviewer (snapping out the question)*: 'And when?'

> *Waugh*: 'Nineteen hundred and three, on the Feast of St Simon and St Jude. . . .'
> *Second Interviewer*: 'I'm not very good at arithmetic, Mr Waugh. How old does that make you now?'
> *Waugh*: 'I'm just at the dangerous age of fifty.'

After questioning Waugh about his schooldays and army career, and his methods as a writer, Black and his colleagues begin to probe for his opinions on contemporary matters. Waugh mentions that he enjoys collecting paintings, and answers the question 'What painters do you admire most?' with the reply: 'Augustus Egg I'd put one of the highest.' This leads him into a denunciation of modernism, Waugh specifically attacking Picasso (whose name he pronounces 'Pee-cass-o') and Gertrude Stein who, he declares, wrote 'gibberish' (this word pronounced with a hard *g*).

Does Waugh like the human race *en masse*? 'I loathe crowds.' Does he find it easy to get on with the man in the street? 'I have never met such a person.' Does he prefer women to have more humility than men? 'Oh, it's their nature.' Then comes the bait of capital punishment: does he believe in it?

> *Waugh*: 'I think it's one of the kindest things you can do to the very wicked, to give them time to repent.'
> *Interviewer*: 'You are in favour of capital punishment?'
> *Waugh*: 'For an *enormous* number of offences.'
> *Interviewer*: 'And you yourself would be prepared to carry it out?'
> *Waugh*: 'Do you mean, actually do the hangman's job?'
> *Interviewer*: 'Yes.'
> *Waugh*: 'I should think it very odd for them to choose a novelist for such a task.'
> *Interviewer*: 'Suppose they were prepared to train you for the job, would you take it on?'
> *Waugh*: 'Oh, certainly.'
> *Interviewer (unbelievingly)*: 'You would?'
> *Waugh (high note)*: 'Certainly!'
> *Interviewer*: 'Would you like the job, Mr Waugh?'
> *Waugh*: 'Not in the least!'

Sykes says that, listening to the broadcast, 'I almost began to feel sorry for them. It was like watching inexperienced toreadors taking on a bull who knew all the tricks of the ring.'

They questioned him about the Welfare State, of which he was predictably contemptuous, calling it a fraud to catch votes. Finally, they asked if he were conscious of any particular failing in himself.

> *Waugh*: 'Are you asking me to confess to some moral lapse? Or to inadequacies in talent?'
>
> *Interviewer*: 'Well, I should *like* to ask you to confess to some particular moral lapse! But what I really mean is, in what respect do you, as a human being, feel that you have primarily failed?'
>
> *Waugh*: 'I've never learned French well, and I never learned any other language at all – I've forgotten most of my Classics. I can't often remember people's faces in the streets, and I don't like music. Those are very grave failings.'
>
> *Interviewer*: 'But no others you are conscious of?'
>
> *Waugh*: 'Those are the ones that worry me most.'
>
> *Interviewer*: 'Well now, finally, may I ask you this, Mr Waugh? How, when you die, would you like to be remembered?'
>
> *Waugh*: 'I should like people of their charity to pray for my soul as a sinner.'

When he listened to the programme, Waugh found his own voice 'strangely old and fruity', but felt he had acquitted himself adequately. 'They tried to make an ass of me,' Mr Pinfold says of the broadcast in the novel, adding: 'I don't believe they succeeded.' Waugh used almost identical words in a letter to Nancy Mitford a few weeks later: 'They tried to make a fool of me & I don't believe they entirely succeeded.' Yet Sykes notes that the experience had shaken him: 'He looked on the occasion as an ugly humiliation.'

In the past, Waugh had relieved the tedium and sluggishness of country life by working hard in the garden, but now he had slipped into sloth. 'Physically,' he writes of Mr Pinfold, 'he had become lazy. . . . Now he spent most of the day in an armchair. He ate less, drank more, and grew corpulent.'

During the spring of 1953 he had begun work on a sequel to *Men at Arms* – 'very good too', he wrote in his diary – but in the early summer he had put it on one side. The current tax laws made it disadvantageous to complete it too quickly, and in any case he had lost interest. 'I am stuck in my book from sheer boredom,' he told Nancy Mitford. 'I know what to write but just cant make the effort to write it.' He had admitted to the BBC interviewers that boredom was at present his principal emotion: 'At fifty one's got bored with the pleasures of youth, and one hasn't yet quite acquired the pleasures of age; so at the moment you find me rather bored.' In his diary, not long after

Christmas, he described his present debilitating routine:

> By the time I have written my letters* the papers come and when I have read them it is nearly noon so I do a little work before luncheon and then don't get out after luncheon and then have tired eyes by 8 o'clock and don't want to sit up reading and not sleepy so take drugs at 11.

Insomnia may be caused by a wide variety of things. Discussing it in *The Ordeal of Gilbert Pinfold*, Waugh refutes the notion that his own sleeplessness was symptomatic of any deep-seated uneasiness: 'On most nights he was neither fretful nor apprehensive. He was merely bored. . . . He would find the sentences he had written during the day running in his head, the words shifting and changing colour kaleidoscopically. . . .' Yet in a 1952 review of Ronald Knox's *The Hidden Stream*, he does hint that his wakefulness in the early hours was not only due to boredom and lack of exercise. He speaks of 'the fidgeting doubts that disturb the early hours of the light sleeper', and describes how 'in what Mgr Knox calls "the 4 a.m. mood" a sense of futility creeps in, a suspicion that the Christian system does not really hang together, that there are flaws in the logic . . . that there are too many unresolved contradictions'. Did he remember that Charles Dodgson – Lewis Carroll – who Waugh believed was tortured by religious doubts, was another chronic insomniac?

When he could not get back to sleep, Waugh would take a second dose of his sleeping-draught. The one he was using at present was extremely powerful. 'For twenty-five years,' he writes of Mr Pinfold, 'he had used various sedatives, for the last ten years a single specific, chloral and bromide which, unknown to [his local doctor], he bought on an old prescription in London'. Chloral had been used as a sedative since about 1870, but by the 1950s was scarcely ever prescribed for insomnia. It is especially powerful when mixed with alcohol, thereby creating the celebrated 'Mickey Finn' knockout drops. Waugh was supposed to take his chloral and bromide with water, but it tasted bitter, and he chose instead to dilute it with crème de menthe.

Chloral has no marked toxic or hallucinatory effects if taken in modest doses, but bromide – another Victorian sedative which had virtually gone out of use by this date – accumulates in the body tissues, and in a few weeks may cause unpleasant side-effects. According to W.C. Bowman and M.J. Rand's *Textbook of Pharmacology* (1980), the symptoms of chronic bromide poisoning include:

---

* Frances Donaldson says he had an enormous correspondence largely because he refused to use the telephone. He claimed not to know his own telephone number.

impaired thought and memory, drowsiness, dizziness, irritability, emotional disturbances, loss of sensitivity to touch and pain, slurred speech, anorexia, gastric distress and constipation. With continued use there is insomnia, restlessness ... disturbance of vision, hallucinations, delirium and coma. ... Recovery from symptoms often takes 1–3 weeks.

It was therefore crucial that Waugh should not overdose himself. In fact he paid little attention to dosage and frequently exceeded the prescribed amount. 'He was not scrupulous in measuring the dose,' he writes of Mr Pinfold. 'He splashed into the glass as much as his mood suggested and if he took too little and woke in the small hours he would get out of bed and make unsteadily for the bottles and a second swig.'

At the beginning of Lent in 1953, evidently aware that these drugs were doing him no good, he had made a 'resolution to give up narcotics' – but then changed his mind and gave up wine instead. By November 1953, the month of the *Frankly Speaking* broadcast, he was showing signs that all was not well physically. He found himself becoming 'disagreeably flushed', especially after drinking his 'normal, not illiberal' quantities of alcohol, when 'crimson blotches appeared on the backs of his hands'. He consulted the local doctor, who, unaware that he was taking chloral and bromide in substantial quantities mixed with alcohol, pronounced it to be an allergy and recommended a temporary change of scene – in other words, a foreign trip. (Frances Donaldson says that Waugh's Gloucestershire doctor, a 'nervous man' known to the Waughs as 'the Medical Attendant', was 'terrified of Evelyn'.)

The bromide may also have been the cause of the 'agonizing rheumatism' Waugh reported that he was suffering soon after Christmas 1953, but this only led to more drugs. When he mentioned it to the doctor, the response was to prescribe him 'some pills which he said were "something new and pretty powerful"', together with 'a new sleeping-draught'. Waugh added both these prescriptions to his bromide and chloral and crème de menthe.

He was now suffering from alarming tricks of memory. His diary entry for 2 January 1954 records a 'curious illusion'. John Betjeman had made a present to him of a fine Victorian wash-handstand, designed in 1865 by William Burges. Waugh was first shown it at the London house of Patrick Balfour, now Lord Kinross, and when it was delivered to Piers Court shortly before Christmas he believed it to be lacking a piece he had not merely seen but handled – 'an ornamental serpentine bronze pipe which led from the dragon's head in the tank to the bowl below'. He protested to the removal company, and wrote to Kinross to ask if it had been left behind. A parcel duly arrived from Kinross, but contained something quite different – 'a kind of zinc funnel' which Waugh suspected Kinross had 'kindly torn out' from some Victorian possession of his own. Waugh wrote to Betjeman: 'The missing organ is something quite other – either a hallucination of mine or an act of theft on the part of one of his [Kinross's] bohemian friends.' He drew a picture of it and asked: 'Did I dream this or did it exist.' Betjeman replied that there had been no such piece; Waugh had imagined it.

He had apparently been experiencing such hallucinations for some time, for he had written to Betjeman several months before this incident: 'My memory is not at all hazy – just sharp, detailed & dead wrong. This affliction leads me into countless humiliations.' The striking thing is that, though he now knew his memory had fooled him over the washstand, he was unwilling to abandon his conviction that such a pipe had once existed. 'Either I have suffered a complete delusion,' he wrote in his diary, 'or I saw the pipe as originally designed by Burges. The latter seems more probable....' He was the more inclined to believe this because of 'Maurice Bowra's recent vision in Ashmolean'. Sitting next to Waugh at dinner, Bowra had claimed that Arthur Hughes's Pre-Raphaelite painting 'Return from the Sea', which hangs in the Ashmolean Museum in Oxford, depicts only one child, a boy, looking out to sea. Waugh answered (quite correctly) that there were two, a boy and a girl, but later investigated the history of the picture, and discovered that when first exhibited it contained only the boy, just as Bowra had described it: 'It failed to sell so Hughes painted in sister to add pathos. No living eye ... has seen original version.' It does not seem to have occurred to him that Bowra might once have read the history of the painting himself, or merely made a mistake.

The washstand and Bowra episodes were the sort of comic grotesqueries he and his friends might have used for farcical purposes in their novels. That he should take them seriously indicates the degree to which he had driven himself into a corner of his own making. To them should be added his interest in 'The Box', a device to which he had been introduced by a neighbour at Stinchcombe, Diana Oldridge, known to the Waughs as 'Tanker'. Supposedly scientific (Christopher Sykes connects it vaguely with radar), it adapted an old witchcraft belief that sufferers from various ailments could give some physical part of themselves – hairs, a little blood, nail-clippings – to a possessor of the Box, into which these would be put, supposedly effecting a cure by 'sympathetic life-waves'. Several of Waugh's acquaintances claimed to have been cured by it, or to know of cures. Waugh himself did not disbelieve, but (says Sykes) regarded it as 'probably diabolical'. In *The Ordeal of Gilbert Pinfold*, Waugh represents himself as judging the Box sceptically – 'It's just a lot of harmless nonsense' – but also fearing that it might be 'an extremely dangerous device in the wrong hands'.

Shortly after the washstand episode, Waugh found himself under attack again in the press. He had written to the *New Statesman* protesting about inaccuracies in an article on the English Catholic martyrs by the Oxford historian Hugh Trevor-Roper. An acrimonious correspondence developed, Trevor-Roper accusing Waugh of appointing himself leader of the modern English Catholics, and pointing out that Waugh's conversion to Rome was 'still rather crude and green', whereas Trevor-Roper (though not himself a Catholic) came from a family who had been 'recusants for two hundred years'. Waugh replied that the taunt of self-appointed leadership was 'preposterous', and concluded his letter: 'I cannot accept that because Mr Roper's family apostasized more recently than mine, he has inherited a superior insight into the proper use of language.' He may now have begun to feel not merely that he was *contra mundum*, against the world in a philosophical sense, but that a great deal of humanity had got it in for him personally.

Early in January 1954 he decided to follow his doctor's advice and seek a change of scene – to book a passage (he told his daughter Margaret) on 'the first available ship', which happened to be a small passenger vessel heading for Ceylon. On board, he would resume work on the war novel: 'I shant come back until I have finished my book but I hope I shall do that on the voyage.' As the date of departure approached, and he found himself daily becoming more clumsy and erratic, he allowed that the sleeping-draught (or draughts) might be responsible, and assured Laura that he would give them up as soon as he was at sea, where he always slept better. He packed only enough sedatives to last him for a few nights.

Gwendoline Sparkes, another passenger on the voyage, has described his appearance when he came on board: 'He looked awful . . . desperately ill.' A friend of hers thought he must be drunk. They were several days out to sea when, on 31 January, he finished the sleeping-draughts. Three days later he wrote to Laura:

> My rheumatism is much better – quite tolerable. It is Feb 3rd and we are not yet in the Mediterranean. My nut is clearing but feeble. It is plain that I had been accumulatively poisoning myself with chloral in

the last six months and might easily have had a much longer spell of idleness than my present little †rouble will cause. I will come home and lead a luny bin life for a bit. It was at 50 [Waugh's present age] that Rossettis chloral taking involved him in attempted suicide, part blindness & part paralysis. We will avoid all that.

Like Waugh, Rossetti had taken chloral with large quantities of alcohol. These opening sentences of Waugh's letter must have been a relief to Laura. However, the letter then changed course somewhat:

I find it hard to keep sentences connected even in a letter like this. It is 3 nights now since I had the last dose of sleepers & have had little continuous sleep as a result. That is why it is fortunate that I am absolutely alone I mean alone from everyone & thing except you. When I wake up which I do 20 or 30 times a night I always turn to the other bed and am wretched you aren't there & puzzled that you are not – odd since we usually have different rooms.

Now came a passage which may have indicated to Laura, if she considered it closely, that, far from Evelyn's symptoms clearing up, he was embarking on fresh trouble:

The ship is not luxurious & the diet would be meagre if one were hungrier. Pretty empty and the passengers pleasant. The chief trouble is the noise of my cabin. All the pipes and air shafts in the ship seem to run through them. To add to my balminess there are intermittent bits of 3rd Programme talks played in private cabin and two mentioned me very faintly and my p.m. took it for other passengers whispering about me. If a regular rural life out of doors doesn't work the trick I'll see an alienist. But I want to be back with you now.

Evelyn

'P.m.' was his abbreviation for 'persecution mania', and the fact that Evelyn knew Laura would understand these initials suggests that they had joked, in the past, about his tendency to believe himself persecuted.

The BBC Third Programme carried serious drama and talks as well as classical music, and it was quite reasonable that Waugh, hearing (or believing himself to be hearing) a disembodied voice mentioning his name, should assume he was listening to a broadcast on it discussing his work. (His own recent experience with the BBC made him associate hostile comments with their programmes.) In *The Ordeal of Gilbert Pinfold* he describes this 'broadcast' at some length, as supposedly a talk by 'Clutton-Cornforth ... the editor of a literary weekly, an ambitious, obsequious fellow' – a clear reference to Alan Pryce-Jones, who had become editor of the *Times Literary Supplement* (though the name is taken from Alan Clutton-Brock, another Old Etonian active in the arts). In the 'broadcast', Clutton-Cornforth accuses Pinfold of writing 'gross and hackneyed farce alternating with grosser and more hackneyed melodrama', and indulging in 'cloying religiosity' – the sort of comment that *Brideshead Revisited* had attracted from some reviewers.

As well as believing that he was listening to broadcasts, Waugh thought he was overhearing conversations from other parts of the ship. In the novel, Mr Pinfold begins to experience a whole variety of sounds, some of them initially not unpleasant – such as a prayer-meeting with evangelical hymns – but after a while the scenes on which he believes himself to be eavesdropping become consistently nasty. He listens with horror to a gory accident on deck, to the Captain and his sinister female accomplice torturing a young sailor to death, and to an elderly father urging his nubile daughter to seduce Pinfold himself. Waugh undoubtedly invented much of this for the novel, but Sykes says he certainly claimed to have 'heard' the burial of a murdered man at sea.

According to Sykes, Waugh was at this stage inclined to take the whole business quite lightly, and his letter to Laura of 3 February does not seem very concerned about the voices. However, a day or so later he spotted an attractive young woman passenger whom he believed to be a Mrs Wilson, whose acquaintance he and Sykes had made during their Middle East trip. 'He rose and greeted her,' writes Sykes.

> She looked bewildered. . . . 'I'm sorry,' she said at length. 'I'm afraid you've made a mistake. I am not called Mrs Wilson. I've never been to Tel Aviv or Jerusalem. I know no one called Christopher Sykes, and I don't remember ever having met you, Mr Waugh.'

As with the washstand, Waugh refused to admit to himself that he had simply been deluded, and decided that 'Mrs Wilson's' refusal to recognize him was proof that his fellow-passengers were involved in some sort of conspiracy to make a fool of him – that there was 'a well-organized plot'. He also became convinced that the ship's wireless operator was showing the other passengers copies of the telegrams he had sent Laura on departure, and he complained to the Captain about this (as Pinfold does in the novel). Meanwhile, Gwendoline Sparkes, among the passengers, noticed Waugh 'talking to the toast rack' at breakfast, and also addressing the electric lamps on the tables as if they contained microphones.

In the novel, the voices heard by Mr Pinfold gradually sort themselves out into identifiable characters. Initially, Pinfold can only make out a group of latter-day Bright Young People, who perform primitive music to wear down his nerves. Later, he becomes convinced that their leader is none other than 'Angel' (Stephen Black), the principal BBC interviewer who had visited his house. The other conspirators are a malevolent woman whom Pinfold nicknames 'Goneril' – the Captain's partner in crime – and a girl called 'Margaret', described by Pinfold as 'a sort of Cordelia', who alone among the voices speaks kindly of him. Indeed, her voice claims that she is in love with him, and it is she whom the voice of the elderly father – a retired general – urges to sleep with Pinfold.

The character of 'Margaret' in the novel may have been based on the supposed Mrs Wilson, but her name is that of Waugh's second daughter, who was eleven years old at the time of Waugh's voyage to Ceylon. He had become markedly more attached to her than to his other children. 'My sexual passion for my ten year old daughter is obsessive,' he wrote to Ann Fleming in 1952. 'I can't keep my hands off her.' A letter to Margaret when she was unhappy at her convent school tries to maintain a stance of severity – 'Your last letter was a disgrace' – but at the end gives way to open affection, such as his children rarely received from him : 'I really am very worried you should be unhappy, darling little girl. All my love, Papa.' In a letter written just before the cruise, he addresses her as 'Sweet Meg'.

In *The Ordeal of Gilbert Pinfold*, it is the elderly father of 'Margaret' who urges her to go to bed with Waugh's *alter ego*, Mr Pinfold :

'I want to talk to my daughter. Come here, Meg, Peg o' my heart, my little Mimi.... You're a woman now and you've set your heart on a man as a woman should.... And an old man can show you better than a young one. He'll be gentler and kinder and cleaner; and then, when the right time comes you in your turn can teach a younger man – and that's how the art of love is learned and the breed survives. I'd like dearly to be the one myself to teach you, but you've made your own choice and who's to grudge it you?'

Mr Pinfold (who does not seem to notice the incestuous implications of the last sentence) has been sexually aroused by what he believes he has overheard, and decides he will make love to Margaret when she arrives :

Somehow he must dispose her, supine, on the bunk. But how to get her there silently and gracefully. How to shift her? Was she portable? He wished that he knew her dimensions.

He took off his pyjamas and hung them in his cupboard, put on his dressing gown, and sat in the chair facing the door, waiting. . . .

In the American edition of the novel, three sentences are added after 'supine, on the bunk':

For the opening phase her upper parts should be in the open space, her lower enclosed. He moved the pillows from the head to the foot of the bunk. He would be able to kneel beside her and so begin the conventional preliminary caresses.

'Margaret', of course, does not materialize, and Pinfold dozes off to the sound of 'Goneril' accusing him of impotence.

For an account of the remainder of Waugh's voyage it is necessary to rely on *The Ordeal of Gilbert Pinfold*, since no other detailed record exists. Waugh himself stated in a letter that the book was essentially a true narrative:

Mr Pinfold's experiences were almost exactly my own. In turning them into a novel I had to summarize them. I heard 'voices' such as I describe almost continuously night and day for three weeks. They were tediously repetitive and sometimes obscene and blasphemous. I have given the gist of them.

By the time of the 'Margaret' episode in the novel, Pinfold is suffering under a rain of accusations supposedly made by other passengers. Some are clearly absurd – that he is a recent immigrant, a 'filthy Jew' whose real name is 'Peinfeld', and that he has driven a farmer near his home to suicide. Others are less easy to refute.

He is taunted with being a false Catholic: 'He doesn't really *believe* in his religion, you know. He just pretends to it because he thinks it aristocratic. It goes with being Lord of the Manor.' The most frequent accusations are sexual. Mr Pinfold, allege the voices, 'was a sodomite . . . he was Jewish and homosexual. . . . "Queer, aren't you, Gilbert?"' . . . He's attractive to women – homosexuals always are.' He is also accused of being a Fascist – 'I've got a photograph of him in a black shirt,' says one of the voices, 'he was up to his eyes in it' – and of suicidal tendencies: 'He longs to kill himself, don't you, Gilbert. . . . You wish you were dead, don't you, Gilbert?' But it is the sexual remarks which predominate: 'There are different types of homosexual, you know. What are called "poufs" and "nancies" – that is the dressy kind. Then there are the others they call "butch". I read a book about it. Pinfold is a "butch".'

Throughout these accusations, Mr Pinfold behaves stoically, telling himself that he is 'entirely indifferent to their good or bad opinion; that he regarded their friendship and their enmity as equally impertinent'. He loses his nerve only when, for a moment, he believes that the voices have been a delusion and he is becoming insane: 'He was possessed from outside himself with atavistic panic. "O let me not be mad, not mad, sweet heaven," he cried.' But then the voices start again, and he is reassured that there really is a plot. By the time the ship reaches Port Said, he has had enough, and decides to complete his journey to Ceylon by air.

On 8 February 1954, five days after his last letter and just over a week after he had finished the chloral and bromide, Waugh wrote to Laura from the Continental-Savoy Hotel in Cairo, not explaining why he had left the ship, but simply stating: 'I am here waiting an aeroplane to Colombo.' The remainder of the letter alarmed Laura greatly:

> I must have been more poisoned than I knew. Then when I was beginning to rally I found myself the victim of an experiment in telepathy which made me think I really was going crazy. I will tell you about it when I get home. It has made me more credulous about Tanker's box.

Margaret Waugh, too, had a letter from her father at this juncture, and 'was fairly sure that something was badly wrong', though her sisters (who were at the same boarding school) tried to convince her it was just one of his jokes. He reported to Laura that he was now 'sleeping better & quite naturally', and that his appetite had somewhat returned. He went on: 'Hand is steady today and the malevolent telepathy broken for the first time – perhaps not permanently.'

In the novel, Pinfold assumes that the voices will stop as soon as he leaves the ship with its air-shafts, pipes and wires. Sure enough, as he walks down the gangplank they fall silent. But when he reaches Cairo and goes to a dinner party, sees a photograph of a peer whom he knows on the mantelpiece, and tells his hosts that the man is a friend of his, a voice breaks into his calm: ' "No you don't, Gilbert," said Goneril. "Liar. Snob. You only pretend to know him because he's a lord." ' Thereafter Pinfold has no further peace; the voices follow him wherever he goes. He has found out that he can 'speak' to them merely by thinking the words to himself, and assumes that it is all the work of 'psycho-analysts and their infernal Box', also somehow related to 'existentialism', though he adds, in a letter to his wife: 'Sometimes I wonder whether it is not literally the Devil who is molesting me.'

Waugh says much the same in his letter to Laura written from Cairo, which continues:

> Please don't be alarmed about the references to telepathy. I know it sounds like acute p.m. but it is real & true. A trick the existentialists invented – half mesmerism – which is most alarming when applied without warning or explanation to a sick man.

It is evidence of his steely control of himself that he did not now abandon his trip and fly back to England, but continued with his planned tour. Laura had reported the discomforts of cold weather at Stinchcombe, and he announced, at the end of this letter of 8 February: 'I shall fly back as soon as conditions sound better at home.' He stayed on in Cairo for another day or two, writing on 9 February a perfectly lucid, sensible letter to John Lehmann, who wanted to print a section of the forthcoming sequel to *Men at Arms* in the *London Magazine*, which he was then editing:

> Dear Mr Lehmann,
> Please forgive my delay in answering. . . . If you like to use the opening, you are welcome to it. . . . I have not been well but hope to complete it in the summer. . . .

From Cairo, he flew to Colombo, where he wrote to Laura on 12 February:

> My Darling,
> It is rather difficult to write to you because everything I say or think or read is read aloud by the group of psychologists whom I met in the ship. I hoped that they would lose this art after I went ashore but the artful creatures can communicate from many hundreds of miles away. Please don't think this is balmy. I should certainly have thought so three weeks ago, but it is a fact & therefore doesn't worry me particularly. All it means is that this trip has been a complete failure as far as settling down to work as we hoped. Also a failure as far as getting any pleasure from it. But it is a huge relief to realize that I am merely the victim of the malice of others, not mad myself as I really feared for a few days.
> I must stay on at this island for a week or so & then will come back & no doubt I shall be able to find some rival telepathist who will teach me how to ward these people off.
> It is really a very rum predicament. Dont worry darling & tell Tanker I now believe in her box.
> > All love
> > E

It was now almost two weeks since he had given up the chloral and bromide mixture, and the hallucinations showed no signs of retreating. Four days later, Waugh sent another letter from Ceylon, announcing that he had had 'great fun sightseeing' with an American acquaintance, that the British Council had been 'most helpful' in finding accommodation, and that he intended to return home shortly. The letter seemed perfectly normal until the last paragraph:

> As I write this I hear the odious voices of the psychologists repeating every word in my ear. As they are in Aden & I am here it is a more remarkable feat than Tanker's box. You must realize that this is the reason for the rather cold tone of this letter.

Laura was now in a panic about him. She came over to the Donaldsons, swore them both to secrecy, and implored their help, reading out passages from Evelyn's letters. She said that someone clearly had to fly out and bring him back, and she felt it must be a man. She asked Jack if he would go, and he immediately agreed; Laura of course promised to pay his fare. But before arrangements could be completed – there was a delay for inoculation – Waugh wrote that he was about to come home:

> Darling Laura,
>   I have just got your cable urging me to return. I need no urging & will start for home as soon as I can make arrangements. . . . I am still grossly afflicted by the psychologists. I think they can be better dealt with from England.

This was written from Ceylon on 18 February.

Laura discussed with the Donaldsons how she should behave when she met him. She said she would treat him just the same as usual, which alarmed Frances Donaldson, who felt that he was 'quite clearly insane'. Laura warned them that, when he had recovered his mind, he might be angry with her for confiding in them, to the extent that the friendship might come to an end. With this, she set off for London.

Afterwards, she told the Donaldsons what had happened there. She was summoned to meet Evelyn at the Hyde Park Hotel, and when she arrived she heard a voice ask 'in a high, unrecognizable squeak' whether she had yet turned up. She concluded that Evelyn's voice 'was distorted by disuse, because for weeks he had spoken to no one'. In fact his letters indicate that he had had plenty of company in Ceylon. The high pitch was perhaps due to extreme tension.

'As soon as they reached their bedroom,' continues Frances Donaldson, 'Evelyn began to tell Laura what had happened.' He put the whole thing down to 'the man who had interrogated him in a broadcast interview', who had been on board ship with his wife, son and daughter, 'and the whole family used the infernal powers he had told her about to persecute him. Only the daughter ['Margaret' in the novel] showed any mercy.' He told Laura that they knew this girl: 'She was engaged to a young man – he mentioned the name – who lived in Wotton-under-Edge and who had brought her to luncheon at Piers Court.' Laura pointed out that the girl in question had quite a different name from the BBC man (Black), and could not have been his daughter.

Laura told Frances Donaldson that when she pointed this out, 'Evelyn saw almost at once it was true,' reacting 'in the manner of the sane'. They discussed the matter for some time, and Laura tried to persuade him that he had been ill and must see a doctor. 'Very well, he replied, but before doing so they would test other links in his story. He took command of the situation, devised a plan and told Laura how to carry it out.'

He instructed her to telephone the BBC and ask for Stephen Black. 'To her horror,' continues Frances Donaldson, 'the answering voice said that Mr Black was away.' She was told, however, that he was not on holiday, but in hospital. He had been ill for some weeks, and it was not yet known when he would return.

Waugh now accepted that neither Black nor his family was involved. 'Yet Evelyn could still hear their voices. They decided at this point to ask Father Caraman to come round and advise them.' Father Philip Caraman was a Jesuit, editor of the *Month*, and a man entirely trusted by Waugh. He describes how the telephone rang at Farm Street, and he received a sudden summons from Laura to dine at the Hyde Park Hotel. She gave no hint of what was going on. 'When I arrived at the Hyde Park,' writes Father Caraman,

I was surprised to be hustled straight into the dining-room without any preliminary conversation or drink. Almost immediately after sitting down, Evelyn, who was opposite me at a square table, leaned across and asked me abruptly to exorcize him: this (he explained) was the reason why I had been invited to dinner. He said he was being tormented by devils; then he repeated aloud to me what his voices had just told him about myself: nothing insulting (as far as I recollect), simply that I was a priest who had power to put his tormentors to flight. My first reaction was to suppose that Evelyn was acting the madman. Only when he persisted and began pressing in his demand for an exorcism did I begin to fear he might be in earnest.

Elsewhere, Father Caraman has described Waugh that evening as 'as mad as a coot. He asked me to exorcize him.'

Still pressing for exorcism, Waugh briefly went out to the lavatory, and in his absence Father Caraman asked Laura what was going on – whether Evelyn was serious. 'In retrospect it was the most foolish question I have asked anyone in my life. Laura was white with anxiety. She told me hurriedly about the letters Evelyn had been sending. . . .'

When Waugh came back to the table, Father Caraman told him that 'there could be no exorcism until he had seen a doctor. Then I excused myself, went to the telephone and called up my friend Dr Eric Strauss, the head of the psychiatric department at St Bartholomew's.' Strauss (a Catholic) was at home in Wimpole Street; Caraman told him that 'the case was urgent and asked him to come round instantly. By the time we had moved into the lounge for coffee Eric had arrived.'

After a few polite exchanges, Strauss began to question Waugh, who (says Caraman) 'was just like a child in his hands'. He asked what medicines he had been taking – particularly what sleeping-draught, and how much alcohol. Waugh answered in detail, though Caraman thought he was 'exaggerating the alcohol'. Strauss then said: 'The first thing you must have is a good night's sleep.' He wrote out a prescription for a new sleeping-draught, paraldehyde, and gave it to Laura, who took it to the all-night chemist in Piccadilly Circus.

Paraldehyde is a strong sedative, sometimes used to calm epileptics or unusually violent psychotics. It is prescribed for insomnia only if a patient suffers intractably from this condition, and can no longer be sedated by barbiturates. Strauss presumably prescribed it because he felt it was essential to calm Waugh down before tackling the delusions – though in fact Waugh, after his initial bout of insomnia when the chloral and bromide mixture ran out, had apparently been sleeping naturally and well in recent weeks.

Laura came back with the paraldehyde, and she and Evelyn went up to bed. Caraman says that Strauss now explained that the hallucinations might have been caused by the combination of chloral, bromide and alcohol. 'Wouldn't it be wonderful,' he said, 'if the voices stopped tonight.' And Caraman reports: 'The voices did stop that night.'

This account does not altogether tally with other versions of Waugh's recovery. According to Frances Donaldson, a few days later Waugh admitted that he was 'still . . . occasionally and faintly hearing the voices'. In *The Ordeal of Gilbert Pinfold*, the voices stop not because Mr Pinfold has been prescribed a new sleeping-draught (no such drug is given to him in the novel), but because he has been reassured by his wife, by 'Father Westmacott' (Father Caraman) and by the evidence of the telephone call to the BBC that the whole thing has been a work of his imagination. Once he is convinced of this, the voices simply fade away: 'Mr Pinfold sat in the silence. . . . He was alone with his wife. "They've gone," he said at length.'

In the novel, no figure appears who corresponds to Dr Strauss. The suggestion that the delusions have been caused by the bromide and chloral is made by 'Dr Drake', Pinfold's local doctor in the West Country, when he discovers that Pinfold has been taking the mixture secretly: 'It sounds like a perfectly simple case of poisoning to me.'

It was not perfectly simple. While Waugh's mental disorder was undoubtedly triggered by withdrawal from drugs (just as *delirium tremens* occurs after the sufferer has given up alcohol, not while he is still drinking), the form that it took was not some random psychosis, but an exaggeration of the role in which he had been casting himself for many years – the stoic English upper-class male standing alone against a deplorable world. It was a role that had attracted many of his friends, but none of them had played it so relentlessly as he, and it was therefore he who suffered the full consequences.

Philip Toynbee, reviewing *The Ordeal of Gilbert Pinfold*, made the point that the persecutors are not the kind of adversaries one would expect Waugh to imagine – 'parlour pinks, pacifists, non-believers with the wrong accents'. They are 'colonels, public school men, upper-class thugs, anti-Semites, Fascists and bullies', the sort of people towards whom Waugh (said Toynbee) had been 'a little over-indulgent'. In other words, Toynbee seemed to be hinting, the hallucinations were aspects of his own personality, and the real persecutor was none other than himself.*

In the novel, after his recovery, Mr Pinfold dismisses the voices' accusations as 'a lot of rot', and wonders why, if they really emanated from his own mind, they did not make out 'a far blacker and more plausible case than they did'. This is a smoke-screen. Though they are camouflaged with some genuine nonsense, the accusations include all the major charges that had been made publicly against Waugh in recent years – sentimental over-writing, Fascism, snobbery and insincere Catholicism – plus one that had not been openly voiced, but must have been in the minds of many readers of *Brideshead Revisited*, the charge of homosexuality. Recalling this particular taunt by the voices,

---

* This is the point which Freud emphasizes constantly in his writings on paranoid schizophrenia, the condition into which Waugh was precipitated during his Pinfold experience.

one remembers Cyril Connolly's analysis, in *Enemies of Promise*, of the typical English upper-class male as 'adolescent, school-minded, self-conscious, cowardly, sentimental, and in the last analysis homosexual'. *The Ordeal of Gilbert Pinfold* suggests that, at the deepest level, Waugh was of the same opinion.

4

The Death Wish

After Waugh's recovery, one of his doctors suggested that he give up all narcotics; but he did not follow this recommendation. He managed to get repeat prescriptions for paraldehyde, the drug which Dr Strauss had prescribed, and was soon swigging it in the quantity in which he had absorbed chloral and bromide. For a while, he also took a strong barbiturate, sodium amytal, but he was still inclined to wake in the small hours.

He took to announcing loudly to his friends that he had been mad, as if to prove how sane he now was. 'I've been absolutely mad,' he shouted to Christopher Hollis during a service at Downside Abbey. 'Clean off my onion.' And to Lady Mary Lygon: 'I am terribly afraid that the coming eclipse of the sun may drive me mad again.'

In the autumn of 1954, eight months after the hallucinations had stopped, he managed to finish the next volume of the war novel. When *Officers and Gentlemen* appeared the next summer, it carried a note by Waugh explaining that, while he had originally intended *Men at Arms* to be the beginning of a long sequence, he had brought the story to a close with the new volume. 'The two books constitute a whole.' In his 1962 *Paris Review* interview, he explained that 'originally I had intended ... *Officers and Gentlemen* to be two volumes. Then I decided to lump them together and finish it off.'

Had he changed his mind because of the Pinfold experience, or was he merely bored with the war sequence, and sinking further into torpor? Cyril Connolly, reviewing the new book in his *Sunday Times* column, inclined to the latter judgement. 'I am disappointed', Connolly wrote bluntly. He had looked to *Officers and Gentlemen* to 'make amends' for the shortcomings of *Men at Arms*, and here instead was a narrative which 'suffers from a benign lethargy which renders it very slow reading, and which affects both treatment and subject'. Other reviewers took much the same line.

However, if there seemed to be a failure of inventive powers in the first part of the novel, the book (as most reviewers pointed out) suddenly comes alive when the story reaches Crete, and Waugh proves himself the equal of Tolstoy as a narrator of the intricacies of military disorganization. Connolly called these pages 'a magnificent description of modern warfare ... equal to the best Mr Waugh has done'. There is a glimpse here of Waugh's hallucinations, when a sapper in the open boat in which Guy and others are escaping from Crete goes mad and hears voices. And in the closing pages of the novel, when Guy experiences a profound disappointment that idealism and heroism have come to nothing, there may be an echo of Waugh's own feelings when he came round from the hallucinations to find that the world was the same as it had always been – that there were no 'psychologists' to vanquish, no telepathists with their Box. Guy speaks of military idealism as 'a Holy Land of illusion', an 'hallucination' from which he has awoken, to find himself back 'in the old ambiguous world'.

During 1955, the Beaverbrook press renewed its attack on Waugh. In the summer of that year, an uninvited visit to Piers Court was paid by the chief book reviewer of the *Daily Express*, Nancy Spain, who was writing a series of 'reappraisals' of British celebrities and had suddenly decided to call on Waugh, accompanied by an acquaintance, Lord Noel-Buxton. They arrived one evening without warning, and Laura tried to send them packing, whereupon Lord Noel-Buxton, mindful of the notice at the gate ('No Admittance on Business'), is said to have uttered the words: 'I'm not on business, I'm a member of the House of Lords.'

Waugh stormed out of his library, and slammed the front door in their faces. A few days later (23 June 1955) Nancy Spain published an account of the visit in the *Daily Express*, whereupon Waugh rejoined in the *Spectator* with his own maliciously funny version – he described Lord Noel-Buxton as 'the second generation of one of Ramsay Mac-Donald's creations', and said that he 'clearly cannot have met many other lords'.

A farcical correspondence ensued in the *Spectator*, and the following spring Waugh opened the attack again, alleging in the same magazine that the Beaverbrook press was no longer an arbiter of literary taste, or had any influence over the sale of books. Miss Spain took this as the personal slight Waugh doubtless intended it to be, and responded with the assertion that, by giving it an enthusiastic review, she had been single-handedly responsible for the enormous success of Alec Waugh's latest novel, *Island in the Sun*, which had sold sixty thousand copies. This figure – she added, rashly – dwarfed 'the total first edition sales' of his brother Evelyn's titles.

Certainly *Island in the Sun* had been a huge success, Alec's first since *The Loom of Youth* forty years earlier. Evelyn had written to him to say how 'elated' he was by this, and commented of the book, 'how well you deserve it'. (But he was more honest in a letter to Ann Fleming: 'Well its rather good if you think of it as being by an American which he is really.' Alec was now living in the United States.) He was not, however, going to sit by and let Nancy Spain allege that his elder brother was now the more successful – she had no idea on how delicate a spot she had trodden. Waugh initiated legal action, and the case came to court in February 1957. Lord Beaverbrook himself took a close interest, perhaps still smarting from the implied insults in *Scoop*. 'You know as well as I do', he told Ann Fleming, 'that Alec has made more money with his books than Evelyn, and Evelyn is most horribly jealous.' But Alec himself came to court, loyally and generously, to testify that this was not the truth, and the jury awarded Evelyn two thousand pounds with costs. Moreover, Nancy Spain had by this time published yet another hostile article about Waugh in the *Daily Express*, and this resulted in an out-of-court settlement for another three thousand pounds in Waugh's favour.

Waugh did not allow these goings-on to stir up a fresh bout of 'p.m.' Though publicly litigious about Nancy Spain, in private he treated the business fairly placidly. Auberon Waugh has written that those who saw much of his father after 1955 will know that this was a comparatively 'mellow and tranquil' period of his life, certainly much more so than the preceding ten years. Yet this seems to have emanated from boredom rather than any inner calm. 'A sultry day of unrelieved boredom,' Waugh wrote in his diary during July 1955. 'My life is really too empty for a diarist. The morning post, the newspaper, the crossword, gin.'

His mother died in December 1954, aged eighty-four, causing no disruption to his life (as his father's death had), but arousing remorse. 'It fills me with regret', he told Nancy Mitford, 'for a lifetime of failure in affection & attention.' It was one of his rare moments of self-reproach.

In the spring of 1956, Anthony Powell was awarded a CBE. Waugh wrote to congratulate him: 'Delighted to read of your decoration. I should rather like something of the sort myself. How does one set about it? I hope it doesn't block you from a knighthood. That's what one really needs.' Three years later, Waugh received an offer of the CBE, but declined it, because (says Christopher Sykes) he considered that he was worth something better. Later, Maurice Bowra interceded in vain for a knighthood or an equal honour, but was told that, once an honour is refused, no further offer is made. Anthony Powell believes that the failure to gain honours peeved Waugh greatly: 'I think he wanted a knighthood very much to the end of his life.'*

Disappointments added to his boredom. 'You see nothing that happens to one after the age of 40 makes any impression,' he wrote to Nancy Mitford. 'My life ceased with the war.' Graham Greene, however, was still in search of experience. 'I am interested in life,' observes a character in Greene's *Our Man in Havana* (1956). 'If you are interested in life it never lets you down.' Greene was now travelling restlessly, much as Waugh had done in the Thirties, journeying to dangerous places throughout the Fifties, propelled by his own swings of mood – 'The fifties were for me a period of great happiness and great torment,' he writes. 'Manic depression reached its height in that decade.' Waugh's diary, no doubt with much exaggeration, gives a glimpse of Greene in manic mood, on an expedition to Rheims some time in the Fifties to visit the champagne vineyards:

> Graham ... had a bottle of whisky with him and swigged for comfort. He swigged throughout the *vin d'honneur* and the banquet. At 11 o'clock the dinner party broke up. Graham wanted to find a brothel and would not believe that they had all been closed.†

Greene visited Malaya in 1951 as a war correspondent for *Life*, covered the French war in Indo-China on four visits between 1951 and 1955 for the *Sunday Times* and *Figaro*, reported on the Mau-Mau outbreak in Kenya during 1953, and in 1956 went to Stalinist Poland. Waugh found him more mysterious than ever. 'Mystified by your

---

* The CBE was offered not in recognition of Waugh's distinction as a novelist, but on account of his biography of Ronald Knox (1959) (see below), in the course of which he had consulted Harold Macmillan, the then Prime Minister, who had known Knox well in his teens. (The offer of the CBE came from the Prime Minister's office.)

† Greene's rather strained comic novel *Travels With My Aunt* (1969) seems to present a portrait of the manic side of Greene, in the guise of the narrator's irrepressible Aunt Augusta.

predilection for son-in-law,' he wrote on a postcard in reply to a cryptic communication from Greene. 'If it is really a CAMEL OWNER you seek, you should – surely? – try further East. If CANAL OWNER, I think John Betjeman can fix you up in England.' Betjeman was writing a weekly column for the *Spectator*, defending Victorian forms of transport against modern vandalism – during 1955 he complained about the British Transport Commission's peremptory closure of the Kennet & Avon Canal. He became a national celebrity when his *Collected Poems* were published in 1958. Waugh rather regretted the popular 'Betjemanian' fad for 'Surrey villas and dripping evergreens', which had once been an agreeably cliquish joke, but now seemed overblown.

Cyril Connolly's marriage to Barbara Skelton reached breaking point by the end of 1955. One evening in December, Waugh and Greene had dinner with Connolly in White's (Greene says that Waugh 'drove me to become a member of White's. I'm not a clubbable man'). Waugh noted in his diary: 'Cyril obsessed by his cuckolding and very bad company.' To Greene he wrote: 'I wish we had not had Cyril. He is a man of moods. We met next day & he was bright and funny.' Waugh was pleased that the obviously disastrous marriage was ending, but told Greene he found it 'indecent' of Connolly to discuss the intimate details with everyone. 'But I am a prig. He said you comforted and strengthened him greatly.'

Waugh regularly did his best to comfort and strengthen the obviously vulnerable Greene. In April 1953 Greene's first play, *The Living Room*, was produced in London, and though Waugh wrote in his diary that – after being lavishly provided with champagne – he had found it difficult to concentrate on the action, he wrote encouragingly to Greene: 'The play held me breathless.' *The Living Room* reads like yet another version of the last part of *Brideshead Revisited*, an examination of what happens when a Catholic decides to 'live in sin' (a young girl's adultery with a family friend finally drives her to suicide). It is dedicated to Catherine Walston.

Greene's novel *The Quiet American* (1955), based on his experiences in Saigon, elicited another flattering letter from Waugh – 'I have . . . read it with deep admiration' – though again in his diary he was critical: 'A masterly but base work.' He disliked the character of the narrator, an English foreign correspondent who smokes opium, sleeps with one of the local girls, and is an atheist.

Waugh was evidently displeased to find the writer he had trumpeted as a Catholic novelist turning to secular, cynical stories about politics. That he believed, or affected to believe, in the concept of the 'Catholic novel' is indicated by his 1950 review of *The Last Traveller* by Antonia White, in the *Tablet*:

> Discussion groups all over the country are debating: 'What is the Catholic novel?' Many have begun to doubt whether there is such a thing. Well, here they can find it in a complete and very beautiful form. ... Miss White's characters are all infused with the Catholic faith. God is the supreme influence to whom everything returns in their lives. ... When disaster threatens they all turn to prayer. Their religion is their life although superficially they are occupied with other things. There is no question of 'dragging religion in'. It is there all the time at the centre of the story.

In the bar of White's one day in 1953, Greene told Waugh and Christopher Sykes that he was going to turn political after being refused a visa for the United States because he had admitted to having once belonged briefly to the Communist Party. 'It will be fun to write about politics for a change,' he said, 'and not always about God.' Waugh rejoined sharply: 'I wouldn't give up writing about God at this stage if I were you. It would be like P.G. Wodehouse dropping Jeeves halfway through the Wooster series.'

By August 1955, Waugh's utter boredom was prompting him to move house. 'I am sick of the district,' he wrote to a house agent. 'If you happen to meet a lunatic who wants to live in this ghastly area, please tell him.' Stinchcombe was now on the edge of the dreariest sort of suburbia.

He and Laura looked at various houses, including a Jacobean mansion not very far from Stinchcombe, with a pre-Reformation Catholic chapel where Mass was still said twice a year, but it was sold before they could buy it. Then there were various other houses – 'appalling ... no use ... quite hopeless and inhabited by a poor mad German chemist'. Before they had found anywhere, Piers Court was sold to a Mrs Gadsden for £9,500. They were now looking at houses in Devon and Cornwall, and in July 1956 came to Combe Florey, near Taunton, where the manor house was for sale – 'cosy, sequestered, with great possibilities'. The price was £7,500; the Waughs bought it, and moved there in October. 'Laura has moped a little at seeing her house [Piers Court] dismantled. I am exhilarated,' wrote Evelyn.

Combe Florey, where Sidney Smith had been rector in the early nineteenth century, was chosen largely because Waugh's daughter Margaret liked it. 'Oh please do get Combe Florey,' she wrote to him. 'I liked it so much & its so nicely situated and I like it so much and

I know I'd be happy there and perhaps we could keep a horse. . . .'

Christopher Sykes found the plain, solid eighteenth-century house disappointing after Piers Court: 'There was a grace and elegance about "Stinkers" which I found absent from the Somerset house, handsome though it is.' Life at Combe Florey was much less formal than it had been in the heyday of Piers Court. It soon became impossible to get living-in staff, and Laura had to manage with the aid of daily helps.

During the period of house-hunting and moving, Waugh worked the story of his 1954 hallucinations into *The Ordeal of Gilbert Pinfold*, taking his hero's surname from the family who had owned Piers Court in the seventeenth century. The novel appeared in the summer of 1957. Frances Donaldson, who was well versed in the true history of Waugh's 'voices', found it far less moving than the real story she had heard from his lips. Waugh himself was evidently not very satisfied with it – at least, not after reading Muriel Spark's *The Comforters*, published the same year, which also deals with hallucinations. 'I was struck', he wrote, reviewing this novel, 'by how much more ambitious was Miss Spark's essay [on delusions] and how much better she had accomplished it.' Most reviewers admired Waugh's self-portrait in the opening chapter, but there was a general feeling that the hallucinations themselves were treated too farcically.

One reviewer, J.B. Priestley in the *New Statesman*, went beyond a consideration of the novel to examine the whole question of the writer who adopts the *modus vivendi* of a country gentleman. Priestley's theme was that Pinfold (that is, Waugh) should not have dismissed the voices as 'a lot of rubbish' just because some of their accusations were nonsensical:

> He is ignoring the underlying truth uniting them all, the idea that he is not what he thinks he is, that he is busy deceiving himself and other people. Consciously he has rejected this idea for some time; he has drowned it in alcohol, bromide and chloral; and now it can only batter its way through to him by staging a crude drama of lunatic voices. . . . It is of course Pinfold remonstrating with Pinfold; the fundamental self telling the ego not to be a mountebank. What is on trial here is the Pinfold *persona*. This *persona* is inadequate; the drink hinted at it; the dope more than suggested it; the voices proved it.

Priestley went on to assert that there was a basic incompatibility between being an author and being a Catholic landed gentleman, and that what the voices were really trying to say was: 'Pinfold, you are a professional writer, a novelist, an artist, so stop pretending you represent some obscure but arrogant landed family that never had an idea in its head.' The boredom that Pinfold (Waugh) suffered from when not working was, said Priestley, 'very revealing', because it indicated that 'the role he has condemned himself to play is too sketchy and too empty'.

Priestley was himself the very type of the middlebrow, middle-class, 'professional' author against whom Waugh had reacted so strongly in the Thirties, eventually creating the Pinfold *persona* largely in consequence. Yet Waugh's choice of this role did not seem very shocking or surprising to Priestley, or even very original. He pointed out that 'Pinfolding' was an 'old trick' among English writers and artists, 'thanks to our aristocratic tradition and our public suspicion of intellect and the arts', and cited Congreve pretending to be a gentleman of leisure rather than a playwright, and Elgar acting like 'a retired colonel with a passion for horse-racing'. Such poses certainly saved British artists 'from the solemn posturing we have observed among our foreign colleagues, who are more portentous about a short review than we could be about an epic creation. We avoid the *Cher Maître* touch.' But for all its dangers of pretension, the Continental attitude (said Priestley) seemed 'saner, healthier, better for both the arts and the nation' than the British. To act the Pinfoldian philistine was to 'go over to the enemy', to hide among the brainless landed gentry. Priestley concluded with a dire prophecy:

> Let Pinfold take warning. He will break down again, and next time may never find a way back to his study. The central self he is trying to deny ... will crack if it is walled up again within a false style of life. ... If he cannot discover an accepted role as English man of letters – and I admit this is not easy – he must create one, hoping it will be recognizable. He must be at all times the man of ideas, the intellectual, the artist, even if he is asked to resign from Bellamy's Club.* If not ... then not poppy, nor mandragora, nor all the drowsy syrups of the world, shall ever medicine him.

Priestley had gone to the heart of the matter – avoiding only the sexual implications of the hallucinations – but Waugh, in public, refused to take him seriously. He responded in the *Spectator*, two weeks later, under the heading 'Anything Wrong With Priestley?' Citing Priestley's warning about the dangers of combining the roles of artist and Catholic country gentleman, he asked which particular snare Priestley thought the more deadly:

> Not living in the country, surely? Unless I am misinformed Mr Priestley

---

* Waugh's fictional version of White's, in the Guy Crouchback novels.

was at my age a landed proprietor on a scale by which my own modest holding is a peasant's patch. Catholicism? It is true that my Church imposes certain restrictions which Mr Priestley might find irksome, but he must have observed that a very large number of his fellow-writers profess a creed and attempt to follow a moral law which are either Roman Catholic or ... almost identical. Mr T.S. Eliot, Dame Edith Sitwell [a recent Catholic convert], Mr Betjeman, Mr Graham Greene, Miss Rose Macaulay – the list is illustrious and long. Are they all heading for the bin?

He asserted that 'what gets Mr Priestley's goat ... is my attempt to behave like a gentleman', and suggested that Priestley might prefer it if he were to 'hire a Teddyboy suit and lark about the dance halls with a bicycle chain' – though would not Priestley 'be quick to detect and denounce this new *persona*'?

Waugh entirely ignored Priestley's central point, that the British author refuses to take his profession seriously, and instead picked on Priestley's phrase about going over to the enemy:

> I say, Priestley old man, are you sure you are feeling all right? Any Voices? I mean to say! No narcotics or brandy in your case, I know, but when a chap starts talking about 'the enemy' and believing, for one, that he is singled out for unjust treatment, isn't it time he consulted his Jungian about his *anima*?

In conclusion, he branded Priestley as one of those authors who, before the war, 'went to great lengths to suck up to the lower classes', foreseeing the present 'social revolution', and knowing 'who would emerge top dog'. Was it surprising, in view of the failure of the Welfare State to reward him for these sycophantic attentions, that Priestley was becoming inflamed with 'persecution mania'?

As if in lengthier answer to Priestley, Waugh now began work on a book that would put his role as a loyal Catholic to a rather unusual test, a biography of Ronald Knox.

Knox represented everything Waugh persuaded himself that he admired, a brilliant intellectual who had subordinated his literary powers to the Catholic Church, and who in its service had won fame and become the darling of the English Catholic aristocracy. In 1950, Knox had asked Waugh to be his literary executor, and seven years later, when he was dying of cancer, he agreed to Waugh's suggestion of writing his biography. The book took eighteen months. 'It will be a magnum opus,' Waugh told A.D. Peters.

He had not written a biography since his life of Campion (1935), and it was the first time he had tackled a contemporary subject. His study of Knox, which came out in the autumn of 1959, is composed in his most formal prose, and the narrator's voice is that of Mr Pinfold, writing in his eighteenth-century library. Not surprisingly, this individual does not choose to examine his subject in the manner of a modern biographer.

Judging by the opening chapters, the book seems intended to be read only by Old Etonians. Waugh describes Knox's schooldays at Eton in terminology apparently designed to befuddle outsiders:

> In his first half Ronald was 'up to' Ford in the lower division of V Form. ... At Christmas 1903 he scored a record of 1,290 marks out of a possible 1,450 in Trials. This should have put him into First Hundred and established his order so as to make him, when his time came, Captain of the School.

Waugh had had to learn all this Eton lore for the biography, since it bore no resemblance to anything he had experienced at Lancing. While he was at work on the book, he reported gleefully to Ann Fleming: 'Mr Peters, my man of business, says he can't understand a word of my life of Knox.'

Following Knox from Eton to Balliol, Waugh devotes some space to portraying the set of Etonians who arrived there with him. This, he tells us, was a particularly arrogant group, whose behaviour frustrated Balliol's efforts to integrate grammar school and public school boys. These Etonians bear a strong resemblance to the Bollinger Club in *Decline and Fall*, for Waugh describes them sending 'waterfalls' of crockery down their college staircase and 'chasing nonentities out of the quad'. But the Waugh who is writing *Ronald Knox* approves of them: 'They had standards of behaviour. ... They paid for the damage they did. They talked well. All of them loved poetry, and many of them wrote it. Several had outstanding good looks.' The last sentence seems very odd as a justification of their behaviour.

Waugh also records that, before becoming a Roman Catholic, Knox experienced profound religious doubts. Like Prendergast in *Decline and Fall*, 'such temptations against the Faith as he suffered were total. Either the whole deposit of Faith was divinely inspired ... or it was false.' But Waugh does not give the reader more than this passing glimpse of these doubts.

Like Waugh, Knox left Oxford to become (in Waugh's words) 'a temporary schoolmaster', and began his literary career as a humorist, writing parodies. Again, Waugh passes briskly over this, quoting nothing from Knox's comic writing, as if it would mean digging up his own past. More remarkably, when he deals with Knox's priesthood, he cites scarcely anything from his celebrated addresses to under-graduates while he was Catholic Chaplain at Oxford, and instead emphasizes the monotony, frustration and boredom of the job, and Knox's proneness to depression and insomnia. Angus Wilson, reviewing the biography in *Encounter*, observed of passages like this that:

> Mr Waugh seems determined to give us a downward curve whichever way we look. ... It's a dismal story wherever you pick it up; but can it really have been felt so dismally by Knox? ... The portrait [Waugh] gives ... is ... uncomfortably in tune with the mood of *Men at Arms* and *Officers and Gentlemen*.

The chief lacuna in the biography is that Waugh totally avoids discussing, and scarcely quotes from, Knox's translation of the Bible, the work for which he was best known. Sykes explains this omission:

> The fact was that, although he admired the clarity of the Knox version, Evelyn did not admire it as literature. He was as shocked as the most hostile critic at the philistine way Ronald had removed all poetry from the translation. ... This was Evelyn's *secret du roi*, never directly mentioned even to close friends, though he allowed such friends to draw the conclusion.

Waugh does pass a brief comment on Knox's translation in his 1948 *Horizon* article on him, where he calls it 'grimly functional'.

As a biography, *Ronald Knox* is neurotically impersonal. So many aspects of Knox's life and character resemble Waugh's own, yet Waugh constantly shies away from discussing them, as if to do so would reveal too much of himself. The most moving thing in the book is not in the main narrative, but in an Appendix, in which Waugh, quite gratuitously and without explanation, prints a letter from G. K. Chesterton to Knox, written at a time when Chesterton was hesitating on the brink of becoming a Catholic. Two passages in it seem to reflect Waugh's own situation at the time that he was writing the Knox biography:

> I am in a state now when I feel a monstrous charlatan, as if I wore a mask and were stuffed with cushions, whenever I see anything about the public G.K.C.; it hurts me, for though the views I express are real, the image is horribly unreal compared with the real person who needs help just now ....
>
> I am not troubled about a great fat man who appears on platforms and in caricatures, even when he enjoys controversies on what I believe

to be the right side. I am concerned about what has become of a little boy whose father showed him a toy theatre, and a schoolboy whom nobody ever heard of, with his brooding on doubt and dirt and daydreams of crude conscientiousness so inconsistent as to be near hypocrisy; and all the morbid life of the lonely mind of a living person with whom I have lived. It is that story, that so often came near to ending badly, that I want to end well. Forgive this scrawl; I think you will understand me.

If Waugh had not refused to let his own mask slip, he could surely have written this letter himself.

The mask was in position more firmly than ever when John Freeman interviewed Waugh for his *Face to Face* series of interviews on BBC Television, in the summer of 1960. As usual, Waugh deflected any attempt to investigate his personality. For example, when Freeman asked him if his life in the country was 'a kind of charade . . . whether . . . you've decided to assume the attitude of country life, which doesn't seem as if it's entirely natural', Waugh replied: 'It's quite true that I haven't the smallest interest in country life, in the agricultural sense, or the local government sense. The country to me is a place where I can be silent.' Freeman (rather feebly) left it at that. As in *Frankly Speaking*, Waugh took the chance to score off his opponent. Having got Waugh to say that he was contemptuous of all public attention, whether flattering or hostile, Freeman asked why he had agreed to appear on the programme. 'Poverty,' rejoined Waugh in a flash. 'We've both been hired to talk in this deliriously happy way.'

By the rules of the programme, Freeman's face was not seen, so that viewers were treated to a long series of memorable close-ups of a beady-eyed Waugh, puffing at a Churchillian cigar. Seeming to ignore the camera, and never letting his performance slip for an instant, he proved himself a consummate television performer. Indeed, Anthony Burgess, reviewing Waugh's autobiography in 1964, even hinted that his public *persona* was a typical product of the television age – he called it 'that charming television act'.

In the spring of 1960, Waugh began work on a third volume of the war novel. It took almost a year to write, was published in the autumn of 1962, and was dedicated to his daughter Margaret, of whom he wrote to Diana Cooper in 1960: 'Margaret is my darling still – much prettier again after a time of looking like a toad.'

It was six years since *Officers and Gentlemen* had appeared, nine since the publication of *Men at Arms*. Waugh prefaced this final volume, *Unconditional Surrender*, with a 'Synopsis of Preceding Volumes' which, as several reviewers noticed, omitted all mention of Apthorpe, an indication of how Waugh's conception of the novel-sequence had changed since the outset, when he had said that each volume would have its own main character, of which Apthorpe was the first. The sequence had also been thrown off-course by Waugh's changes of mind about how many volumes there would be. *Officers and Gentlemen* had proclaimed itself to be the last, but *Unconditional Surrender* carried a note that 'This was not quite candid. I knew that a third volume was needed.'

If *Unconditional Surrender* had dealt fully with the concluding phase of Waugh's wartime experiences, its subject-matter would have been the army's increasing hostility towards him, and the death of his father preventing his going on active service again. Waugh, however, had no wish to reopen these sores. Guy Crouchback's father dies, but thereby causes his son no inconvenience, and though Guy grows disillusioned with the army it does not rebuff him, but merely lets him drift through the remainder of the war without useful employment. It is mild stuff compared to the real events.

The main character in this volume besides Guy is Ludovic, the sinister Jeeves figure from *Officers and Gentlemen*, who now becomes an amalgam of contradictory characteristics – a Palinurus (he writes a book of aphorisms which is intended as a spoof of Connolly), an Ambrose Silk (he has a homosexual past), a Gilbert Pinfold (he believes that Guy is persecuting him for two murders he has committed), and even a Waugh, for Ludovic turns novelist and produces a book, *The Death Wish*, which is a parody of certain aspects of *Brideshead Revisited* :

> It was a very gorgeous, almost gaudy, tale of romance and high drama. ... The characters and their equipment were seen as Ludovic in his own ambiguous position had seen them, more brilliant than reality. The plot was Shakespearean in its elaborate improbability. The dialogue could never have issued from human lips. ... But it was not an old-fashioned book. Had he known it, half a dozen other English writers, averting themselves sickly from privations of war and apprehensions of the social consequences of the peace, were ... composing ... books which would turn from the drab alleys of the thirties into the odorous gardens of a recent past transformed and illuminated by disordered memory and imagination.

This indicates the degree of detachment Waugh now felt from *Brideshead*

Revisited. He had recently pruned the text for a new edition (1960), explaining in the preface that its 'more glaring defects' now embarrassed him – he said he had 'modified the grosser passages'. The alterations consisted merely of certain cuts in Charles Ryder's narration; David Pryce-Jones (son of Alan), in *Time & Tide*, judged them 'few and unimportant'.

Reviewers of *Unconditional Surrender* were less concerned with the book's success or failure as the concluding part of the trilogy than with Waugh's social attitudes as displayed in it. Philip Toynbee in the *Observer*, describing himself as of 'a conventionally liberal turn of mind', said that the book displayed a 'vulgar . . . deep snobbery', and Cyril Connolly, while judging the sequence as a whole to be 'unquestionably the finest novel to have come out of the war' (had he forgotten his criticism of *Men at Arms* as beer rather than wine?), alluded to 'the essential biliousness of Mr Waugh's gaze', which he felt made too many minor characters 'too dreary to hold the reader's attention'. Kingsley Amis in the *Spectator*, who alone among reviewers pointed out how the last volume 'disappoints hopes of final coherence', commented acidly on the 'souped-up traditionalism' of old Mr Crouchback's funeral, and complained that the 'baronial wrought-iron' of Brideshead was 'back in full profusion'. Reviewers were, however, generally respectful and often positively admiring, Toynbee alone dissenting from the mood of appreciation, and wondering whether Waugh's popularity as a novelist was 'a very happy portent of our times'. Toynbee observed: 'In a very sophisticated form he appeals to us in the same way as the *Queen* magazine.' Auberon Waugh was now working for this publication. 'Poor Bron has become involved in a very common paper called *Queen*,' Waugh wrote to Ann Fleming. 'Not, as you'd think, about buggery. A sort of whining *Tatler*.'

Oddly, no reviewer pointed out one apparent inconsistency in the novel. Guy is portrayed at the end as having settled happily with his second wife Domenica, and starting a new family. Such a fate would have been inconceivable for him only a little earlier in the same volume, where Waugh consistently emphasizes that his hero is suffering from a death wish – Book Three of *Unconditional Surrender* is entitled 'The Death Wish'. This, besides being the title of Ludovic's novel, is Guy's state of mind, as we see when he makes his confession to an Italian priest. 'Father,' says Guy, 'I wish to die. . . . Almost all the time.' The finest moment in the novel – indeed in the whole trilogy – comes when Ritchie-Hook, briefly reappearing in the closing chapters, goes voluntarily and dramatically to his death, with an American press-photographer in attendance:

Ritchie-Hook ... was signalling fiercely, summoning to the advance
the men behind him, who were already slinking away; he went forward
at a slow and clumsy trot. ... He did not look back to see if he was
being followed. He did not know that he was followed, by one man,
Sneiffel, who like a terrier, like the pet dwarf privileged to tumble about
the heels of a prince of the Renaissance, was gambolling round him
with his camera, crouching and skipping, so small and agile as to elude
the snipers on the walls. A first bullet hit Ritchie-Hook when he was
some 20 yards from the wall ....

Ritchie-Hook's batman comments that it was what the old man would
have wanted: 'More than once he's said to me right out: "Dawkins,
I wish those bastards would shoot better. I don't want to go home." '

Waugh himself had not wanted to die in 1945, the year in which
Guy Crouchback's final adventures are set, but the Waugh who wrote
Unconditional Surrender was suffering from the effects of five years of
profound boredom – the boredom that had set in after the retreat of
the Pinfold hallucinations – and there is every reason to suppose that
the death-wish on which the novel dwells was his own. Indeed, the
end of Ritchie-Hook reads like a kind of idealized suicide by Waugh
himself, going without hope into battle against the modern world, letting
himself be destroyed by its snipers in a blaze of publicity.

As to the supposed happy ending, when friends wrote to him about
this, Waugh argued that the novel did *not* end happily. In a letter
to Anthony Powell, he explained that the real point of Guy's final
situation was not his contented marriage to Domenica (a character
who strongly resembles Laura), but that he was bringing up Virginia's
bastard son by Trimmer, as if the child were his own legitimate heir,
so that 'real heirs' were being 'dispossessed by Trimmer'. This final
act of dispossession brings *Unconditional Surrender* into line with the rest
of Waugh's novels.[*]

During 1960, John Betjeman published his verse autobiography, *Summoned by Bells*, much of which was an expression of guilt at not having
followed his father's wishes and joined the family firm. Waugh commented: 'John ... raises the question: *why* did he not go into his
father's workshop? It would be far more honourable and useful to
make expensive ashtrays than to appear on television and just as lucra-

---

[*] Waugh admitted that he had failed to make this clear, so in the one-volume edition of the
trilogy, *Sword of Honour* (1965), he removed Guy and Domenica's children, leaving the couple
with just Trimmer's bastard to bring up.

tive.' Betjeman was inclined to agree. In a *Horizon* symposium in the late Forties he had written:

> If I had my life over again, I think I would take up some handicraft
> – making stained glass or weaving or french polishing or woodcarving
> – and with this to fall back on ... I would be refreshed and confident
> when I wrote.... Journalism ... is a ... way out for weak characters.

In January 1961, Waugh wrote in his diary: 'It has been a bad year for the old steeplechasers ... John Betjeman ... down and out of the race; Nancy Mitford and Tony Powell just clinging in the saddle.' But any private sense of disappointment he may have felt with Mitford and Powell (who had, respectively, just published *Don't Tell Alfred* and *Casanova's Chinese Restaurant*) was nothing to the shock with which he read Graham Greene's *A Burnt-Out Case*, when an advance copy came in the post at Christmas 1960, from the *Daily Mail*, asking for a review. 'I have had to refuse,' wrote Waugh in his diary. 'There is nothing I could write about it without shame one way or the other.'

The novel concerns a Catholic architect, Querry, who has lost his faith, and is exasperated by having all his works specifically labelled 'Catholic'. Waugh wrote in his diary:

> Coming so soon after his Christmas story it emphasizes a theme which
> it would be affected not to regard as personal – the vexation of a Catholic
> artist exposed against his wishes to acclamations as a 'Catholic' artist
> who at the same time cuts himself off from divine grace by sexual sin.
> The hero of *A Burnt-Out Case* is a bored, loveless voluptuary. ... It
> is the first time Graham has come out as specifically faithless – pray
> God it is a mood, but it strikes deeper and colder. What is more –
> no, less – Graham's skill is fading. ... I am not guiltless as one of
> those who put him in the odious position of 'Catholic artist'. He com-
> plained of the heat of his sexual passions, now at their coldness. A book
> I can't review.

The 'Christmas story' to which Waugh refers was 'A Visit to Morin', published that Christmas in a magazine, and collected in Greene's *A Sense of Reality* (1963), in which an elderly Catholic author speaks sardonically about his loss of faith, and is bitter about the effects of his books on readers:

> They used to come here in their dozens to see me. I used to get long
> letters saying how I had converted them by this book or that. Long
> after I ceased to believe myself I was a carrier of belief. ... Women
> especially ... I only had to sleep with a woman to make a convert.
> ... What sort of Rasputin life was that?

Greene echoes Morin's attitudes in the first volume of his autobiography, *A Sort of Life* (1971), in which he says he has 'forgotten' the arguments for the existence of God, and in any case has come to 'dislike' the word God, 'with all its anthropomorphic associations. ... I ... prefer Chardin's Omega Point.' As to faith, 'With the approach of death I care less and less about religious truth. One hasn't long to wait for revelation or darkness.' In the short story, Morin's loss of faith and abandonment of religious observance, like Querry's in *A Burnt-Out Case*, is explained as largely the consequence of having led an irregular sexual life:

'For twenty years,' Morin said, 'I excommunicated myself voluntarily. I never went to Confession. I loved a woman too much to pretend to myself that I would ever leave her. You know the condition of absolution? A firm purpose of amendment. I had no such purpose. ... I ... cut myself off for twenty years from grace and my belief withered as the priests said it would. I don't believe in God ... but I know the reason why I don't believe and the reason is – the Church is true and what she taught me is true. For twenty years I have been without the sacraments and I can see the effect.'

In a 1979 interview, Greene covered much the same ground when talking openly about his own case. Asked whether he still went to Communion, he answered:

No, I've broken the rules. They are rules I respect, so I haven't been to Communion now for nearly thirty years. ... In my private life, my situation is not regular. If I went to Communion, I would have to confess and make promises. I prefer to excommunicate myself.

Yet he would not describe himself as having lost his faith, and called himself 'semi-lapsed', explaining:

There's a difference between belief and faith. ... Faith is above belief. One can say that it's a gift of God, which belief is not. Belief is founded on reason. On the whole I keep my faith while enduring long periods of disbelief. At such moments I shrug my shoulders and tell myself I'm wrong – as though a brilliant mathematician had come and told me that the solution of an equation was wrong. My faith remains in the background, but it remains.

In 'A Visit to Morin', Morin's questioner begins: 'Because you've lost your faith —' whereupon Morin interrupts him ferociously: 'I never told you that. ... I told you I had lost my belief. That's quite a different thing. But how are you to understand?'

In 1961, Waugh was not aware of such subtleties in Greene's mind.

After reading 'A Visit to Morin' and *A Burnt-Out Case* he wrote to Greene that it was:

> plain that you are exasperated by the reputation which has come to you unsought of a 'Catholic' writer. I realise that I have some guilt in this matter. ... I am deeply sorry for the annoyance I helped to cause & pray that it is only annoyance, and that the desperate conclusions of Morin & Querry are purely fictional.

Greene replied that in the novel he had wanted 'to give expression to various states or moods of belief or unbelief', and assured Waugh that he was in no way to blame for anything. He did not give Waugh any account of his own state of belief, or faith, or make any observation about whether the novel and the short story were autobiographical. Waugh wrote back bluntly:

> I don't think you can blame people who read the book [*A Burnt-Out Case*] as a recantation of faith. ... I cannot wish your book success. ... God forbid I should pry into the secrets of your soul. It is simply your public performance which grieves me.

'I don't think I shall write another novel for five or six years,' Waugh told A.D.Peters after finishing *Unconditional Surrender*. He said he was 'open to offers & still more, to suggestions for non-fiction work. ... I might write a 3 volume autobiography over ten years.' In July 1961, he was 'clearing up papers, preparing to start on my autobiography (with some misgivings about what Alec is going to say in his)'. He need not have worried: Alec's *The Early Years of Alec Waugh* was mild and bland.

Evelyn was at work on *A Little Learning*, the first volume of his memoirs, by June 1962. 'What a dull life I seem to have had,' he wrote to Nancy Mitford, but after the book was finished he said it had been 'quite easy' to write, because 'I'd never written about my own youth.' The book does have a surface dullness; it is written in the same formal prose style as *Ronald Knox* and the other biographies, and one reviewer (Malcolm Bradbury) called it 'reticent, low-keyed'. But beneath the surface a good deal is going on.

Only the opening chapter, 'Heredity', seriously drags, with its slow-paced examination of Waugh's gallery of ancestors ('It is the only part Tony Powell enjoyed,' Waugh told Maurice Bowra), and even this section contains a highly revealing portrait of his paternal grandfather – revealing because Evelyn could be writing about himself:

> The happiness of all [his children] depended on his temper. Would he

461

be jocose? Would he be loving in his demonstrative hectoring way? Would he be cross? ... I never knew him, nor my grandmother, who was by all accounts a fond, timid woman ... entirely subject to his will and moods.

A Little Learning also contains a sustained account of Waugh's father, which again reads like a self-portrait. For example:

The illusion of old age was much enhanced by his utterances. ... he often adverted to his imminent demise. ... As he gew older and deafer he was happiest with a single companion. ... He had no itch to get to the truth of a story, frankly preferring its most picturesque form.

Although the book begins with the jaundiced statement 'Only when one has lost all curiosity about the future has one reached the age to write an autobiography,' Waugh usually refrains from snarling at the Century of the Common Man. An exception is a brilliant passage comparing present-day literary life with that in his father's time:

Today ... there are the reporters of the popular papers who interview authors rather than review their work; there are the charmers of Television; there are the State-trained professional critics with their harsh jargon and narrow tastes; and there are the impostors who cannot write at all, but travel from one international congress to another discussing the predicament of the writer in the modern world.

Though the narrative style is almost consistently eighteenth century this mask here fits Waugh snugly. He writes like Samuel Johnson in *Lives of the Poets*, alive with curiosity for *outré* detail – like the 'bearded and monoglot Italian' who occupied a 'windowless glory-hole' in the offices of Chapman & Hall: 'He had originally been introduced to make plaster busts of Charles Dickens and could not be dislodged. He did a good deal of spicy cooking there on a little stove.'

The Oxford chapter of *A Little Learning*, though full of entertaining vignettes, is a little less fresh than what has gone before. Waugh is now reaching territory he has already explored in his novels. The final chapter deals with the real events and people behind *Decline and Fall*, and is inevitably far less entertaining than that book. Understandably, Waugh was worried about the next volume of the autobiography; around the time that *A Little Learning* was published he told an interviewer: 'After twenty-one I've used all my most interesting experiences, in one form or another, in novels.' There was also the question of his first marriage and its collapse. 'A second volume', he admitted to Diana Mosley, 'presents graver problems because I must mention several living people.' Evelyn Gardner and John Heygate were still alive.

In August 1962, a few weeks after he had begun to write *A Little Learning*, Waugh sent a rather stunned letter to Diana Cooper:

> You are in Venice & I don't know where. I hope someone will forward this letter for it is the announcement of Meg's engagement. She has fallen head over heels for an Irishman, 27 years old [Margaret was twenty], short, rather oriental in face, raffish, penniless, stock-broker's clerk of ten days' experience, but a gentleman and a Catholic – name Giles FitzHerbert. I have not the heart to keep them apart. . . . Meg is bird happy about her affair. Let her enjoy it quick before the Light of Common Day.

The previous November, he had taken Margaret on a journey revisiting British Guiana, where he had not been since *Ninety-Two Days*. They had travelled together for four months.

Diana Cooper wrote back, and Waugh replied:

> Your letter full of understanding. It is, to me, a bitter pill and ungilded. I would forbid the marriage if I had any other cause than jealousy & snobbery. As it is, I pretend to be complaisant. Little Meg is ripe for the kind of love I can't give her. So I am surrendering with the honours of war – without war indeed. The wedding will be at the end of October. . . . I suddenly yesterday began a story about Basil Seal at 60.

This letter itself is extraordinary enough, with its admission of 'jealousy' of Margaret's fiancé, and its echo of the hallucinatory father in *The Ordeal of Gilbert Pinfold*, urging his daughter towards Mr Pinfold's cabin: 'Little Meg is ripe for the kind of love I can't give her.' But it is nothing compared to the feelings that were unleashed in the 'story about Basil Seal at 60' alluded to so casually here. *Basil Seal Rides Again*, which was finished in a few weeks and published in the *Sunday Telegraph* the following February (and later as a small book), is an alternative autobiography, sparked off by Waugh's grief and jealousy at Margaret's engagement, and containing, under the thinnest of disguises, a portrait of himself far more honest and revealing than anything in *A Little Learning*.

From the beginning of *Basil Seal Rides Again*, it is evident that this is going to be something very different from Waugh's recent fiction. He brings back a handful of his pre-war characters – Basil Seal, Peter Pastmaster, Ambrose Silk, Margot Metroland, Alastair Trumpington – and, as in the pre-war novels, tells most of the story in dialogue.

(The dedicatory letter to Ann Fleming describes the story as 'a senile attempt to recapture the manner of my youth'.) At a dinner in the Ritz, where deplorable people (Parsnip, Pimpernell and other literary parasites) are celebrating what he considers to be a deplorable event – the conferring of the Order of Merit on Ambrose Silk – Basil Seal opts out of the proceedings, in the company of Peter Pastmaster, and reviews his own life. 'Slowly and stiffly they left the hotel dining-room ... two stout, rubicund, richly dressed old buffers.' Always implicitly an *alter ego* of Waugh, Basil is now clearly identified as him, at least to readers of Waugh's posthumously published diaries:

> *December 1960*. ... I must have given my hat many times to the old porter at the Ritz (London). The other day when I came to leave after luncheon he was not on duty, so I went behind his counter and collected my belongings. In my hat he had put a label with the one word 'Florid'.

So of Basil in the story:

> A week or two ago he had had a disconcerting experience in this very hotel. ... Basil ... assumed he was known by name. Then a day came when ... in the ribbon of [his] hat he found a label. ... It bore the single pencilled word 'Florid'.

Even without this detail, Basil's career is self-evidently Waugh's own. Before the war, Basil experienced a 'decade of adventure', of foreign travel and love affairs, which now seems to him to have happened to an individual immeasurably distant from the *persona* he has developed for himself. We are told that the major change in Basil's character came when he had to leave the army abruptly (after laming himself accidentally with explosives – a metaphor, perhaps for the damage Waugh's explosive character had inflicted on his soldiering). Returning to civilian life, he married, and metamorphosed almost overnight into 'a creature of habit and set opinions', who joined a sombre London club and began to dress with antiquarian formality.

On the evening when the story begins, Basil and Peter, having walked out of the dinner in honour of Ambrose Silk, take the lift to an upper floor of the Ritz, where Peter's mother, Margot Metroland, now lives. The old lady is watching television, and dismisses them irritably: 'I'm busy ... don't disturb me.' Peter comments: 'She's always looking at that thing nowadays.' In this little episode, Waugh sums up the disintegration of pre-war society into the television age.

Depressed by the encounter, Basil says goodnight to Peter and goes home, where he is welcomed affectionately by his daughter Barbara, his one delight – she calls him 'Pobble' because his toes were blown

off in the war: ' "Oh, Pobble, you toeless wonder. ..." Two arms
embraced his neck and drew him down, an agile figure inclined over
the protuberance of his starched shirt, a cheek was pressed to his and
teeth tenderly nibbled the lobe of his ear.' But Barbara is dressed for
a party, 1962 style ('very tight very short trousers, slippers and a thin
jersey'), and has brought a young man back to the house, who has
broken into Basil's cellar to look for whisky. Basil, confronting him
apoplectically, fails to recognize someone very like himself when young:
'a slender youth . . . who had a mop of dishevelled black hair . . . formidable, contemptuous eyes . . . a proud, rather childish mouth'.

Realizing that he has a rival for his daughter's love, Basil goes off
to a health farm, in the hope that he can get rid of the 'florid' appearance, but refuses to take the regime there seriously, and bribes one
of the staff to provide him with alcohol. To his astonishment, the resident doctor diagnoses his rage with young men like Barbara's boyfriend
as 'repressed and unsuspected inclinations' towards 'a preference for
your own sex'. Basil comments unbelievingly: 'That booby thought
I was a pansy.'

Though he gets hold of drink, Basil is obliged to endure the starvation
diet of the health farm, and, when feeling light-headed from lack of
food, he examines his conscience, in the hope of discovering how his
'florid' personality grew out of his pre-war self:

> he ruefully contemplated the change he had wrought in himself. He
> had first assumed it as a conscious imposture; it had become habitual
> to him; the antiquated, worldly-wise moralities which, using that voice,
> he had found himself obliged to utter, had become his settled opinions.
> It had begun as nursery clowning for the diversion of Barbara; a parody
> . . . darling, crusty old Pobble performing the part expected of him;
> and now the parody had become the *persona*.

Is this the real explanation for the construction of Waugh's Pinfold
persona, 'hard, bright, and antiquated as a cuirass'?

Certainly the dates fit. Margaret, born in 1942, began to attract
Waugh's serious attention (even infatuation) in 1952, when she was
ten years old. This was roughly when his Pinfold personality established
itself. There were other motives – in particular, mimicry of his own
father – but *Basil Seal Rides Again* indicates that it was Margaret, laughing at the imposture, who had made the Pinfold performance go on
and on until Waugh could not shake it off.

Basil comes home from the health farm much improved in appearance, and Barbara rewards him by flirting with him: 'Basil sat and

Barbara wriggled round until her chin rested on his knees. "Famine baby," she said. Star-sapphire eyes in the child-like face under black tousled hair gazed deep . . . .' Then she breaks it to him that she has become engaged to the young man, Charles Allbright. Basil takes the news very badly:

> 'Have you been to bed with this man?'
> 'Not to *bed*.'
> 'Have you slept with him?'
> 'Oh, no *sleep*.'
> 'You know what I mean. Have you had sexual intercourse with him?'
> 'Well, perhaps; not in bed, on the floor and wide awake. . . .'

He throws her out of the house, intending to have a violent confrontation with the fiancé. Then a more subtle plan occurs to him.

He has at last begun to realize that Charles resembles himself when young: 'The eyes, the whole face, seemed remotely familiar; the reflection of a reflection seen long ago in shaving-mirrors.' Now he decides to capitalize on this resemblance, and on his own past reputation as a rake. He tells Barbara that long ago he had an affair with Charles's mother, and implies that Charles is his own illegitimate son. Barbara reacted to the news very badly, departing with 'a face of tragedy', but Basil gleefully contemplates his destruction of her engagement.

Treated purely as Waugh's last piece of fiction, *Basil Seal Rides Again* is a disappointingly nasty little story, a resurgence of the Saki element in his humour (never his strongest point). Viewed as Waugh's private reaction to his daughter's engagement, it is infinitely sad. No such trick could be played on Margaret in real life, and the writing and publication of the story seems a strange way to come to terms with his feelings. The portrait of the father–daughter relationship in the story is alarming rather than endearing, while Basil's imposture at the end only adds another layer to the incestuous theme.

Margaret was married in the autumn of 1962; Waugh noted that she 'looked very pretty', though the reception was a 'ghastly expense'. His sixtieth birthday the following year brought letters from old friends, among them Nancy Mitford, who had just read *Basil Seal Rides Again*, and thought it too long. 'A sharp reminder that my powers are fading and that I am a bore,' Waugh wrote back bitterly. 'The story is too short, not too long. It would have made a novel.'

Changes in the Roman Catholic liturgy now began to distress him greatly. 'The Mass is written of as a "social meal",' he noted sourly in his diary, 'in which the "people of God" perform the consecration.' It was another manifestation of the Century of the Common Man. 'Pray God I will never apostatize but I can only now go to church as an act of duty and obedience.'

His consumption of drink and drugs was as great as ever. 'When I saw the doctor,' he told Ann Fleming in March 1964,

> he asked about my habits. I said 'I have practically given up drinking – only about 7 bottles of wine & 3 of spirits a week.' 'A week? Surely you mean a month?' 'No, and I smoke 30 cigars a week & take 40 grains of sodium amytal.' He looked graver & graver. 'Oh, yes, a bottle of paraldehyde a week.' He brightened greatly & said: 'Now *that* is an excellent thing. Far too few people use it.'

He was bored almost all the time. 'I read my letters & work at *The Times* cross-word & never set foot out of doors,' he reported to Nancy Mitford in August 1964. The next month, he wrote to Margaret:

> Darling Pig,
>   Don't worry about me. I am low spirited old and very easily fatigued. I find all human company increasingly distasteful. . . .

Margaret has written that by now he 'longed for death'.

He made some slight attempt to start the next volume of autobiography, choosing the title *A Little Hope*, and writing (and rewriting) the opening sentences, describing his return to London from teaching in North Wales. But he could get no further. One day, Christopher Sykes joked with him about this next volume, saying he was afraid what Waugh would write in it about him. Waugh:

> sighed and with a sudden change from the joking manner of our conversation he said: 'You've no reason to fear. No one has. I wish they had. My life is roughly speaking over. I sleep badly except occasionally in the morning. I get up late. I try to read my letters. I try to read the paper. I have some gin. I try to read the paper again. I have some more gin. I try to think about my autobiography. Then I have some more gin and it's lunch time. That's my life. It's ghastly.' About the same time he told my brother-in-law, Ran Antrim, that he spent his morning breathing on his library window and then playing noughts and crosses against himself, drinking gin in the intervals between play.

During 1965, he had many of his teeth removed – and delayed in having false ones fitted: 'I have a deep horror of them.' In this toothless interim he ate very little, and when dentures were finally fitted (after about six months) he found that 'the false snappers ruin my appetite for solid food'. Lack of food, combined with the vast intake of alcohol and sedatives, began to have a serious effect. 'Diana [Cooper] says I am dying of drugs,' he wrote to Nancy Mitford in September 1965. He did not, however, contemplate giving up the sleeping-draughts. 'It is true that all last year [1965] I was idle and low spirited,' he wrote to his brother Alec, 'but I was free from hallucinations.' By December 1965, he was swallowing very little apart from the drugs. When Christopher Sykes saw him at a luncheon in London that month, 'he ate nothing. He drank nothing.' Shortly before Christmas he wrote to Margaret:

> The awful prospect is that I may have more than 20 years ahead. Pray that I 'make my soul' in this period. I shall just become more and more boring I fear. Don't let me in my dotage oppress you. ... All love darling Pig,
>
> E.W.

On Sunday, 10 April 1966, Easter Day, after attending Mass said in the traditional rite by Father Caraman in a Catholic chapel not far from Combe Florey, Waugh pottered in his library, then went to the lavatory, where he suffered a thrombosis, and was found dead some time later by Laura.

Waugh was buried at Combe Florey, and a few days later a Requiem Mass was sung in Westminster Cathedral – according to the Latin rite, despite initial objections by the authorities. In their obituaries, many newspapers and magazines concentrated on Waugh's personal outrageousness, rather than his achievement as a writer; *Time* magazine summed him up as 'a flabby old Blimp with brandy jowls and a menacing pewter complexion'. Other journalists took the opportunity to revive old grudges, such as Alan Brien, who in the *Spectator* described how Waugh had once behaved badly to him in White's. As spokesman for the family and Waugh's literary executor, Auberon Waugh replied to Brien with an article attempting to redress the balance. 'The main point about my father', he wrote, 'is simply that he was the funniest man of his generation.' Graham Greene gave Waugh a higher accolade, in *The Times*:

> Evelyn Waugh was the greatest novelist of my generation. ... We were deeply divided politically, we were divided even in our concept of the same church ... but [he] had an unshakeable loyalty to his friends, even if he may have detested their opinions and sometimes their attitudes.

Elsewhere, Greene summed up Waugh as 'incomparably the best of my generation. One felt as if one's commanding officer were dead.'

Certainly *The Comedians*, Greene's 1966 novel, demonstrated a debt to Waugh once again; the character of the seedy 'Major' Jones is little more than a reworking of Captain Grimes. Waugh had read the novel shortly before he died, and wrote to Greene: 'I greatly admire *The Comedians*. What staying power you have. It might have been written 30 years ago and could be by no one but you.' Greene was indeed reworking his old formula – a rootless hero in flight from an evil conspiracy, consoled sexually by a good woman. He had now settled into a 'political period' (*The Comedians* takes place in Haiti, during the brutal regime of Papa Doc), which conformed to contemporary taste, just as Greene's left-wing novels of the Thirties and his Catholic books of the Forties had fitted the fashions of those decades. By 1978, John le Carré had created a new literary vogue, for novels about 'leaks' and 'moles' in the Secret Service, and that year Greene produced *The Human Factor*, a novel in this genre which became a best-seller. By the mid-1980s, Greene's paperback publishers, Penguin, were billing him as 'The greatest English writer of our time', a judgement which, devoted as he was to Greene, might have surprised Waugh. He might have had much to say, too, about the knighting of John Betjeman and the choice of him, in 1972, as Poet Laureate.

Cyril Connolly survived Waugh by eight years, marrying for a third time. Towards the end of his own life, Waugh noted: 'Boots is up to something rather fishy in collecting letters, I think for sale in America. ... There is a nice nest egg for us all in our senility. ... ' Connolly's papers eventually fetched up in Tulsa, Oklahoma; meanwhile Waugh's manuscripts and the books from his library, sold after his death, arrived at the Humanities Research Center in Austin, Texas. Not long before he died, Connolly visited Austin and examined the Waugh collection. He was deeply upset to discover Waugh's annotations to *The Unquiet Grave*, and on his return to England sold many of his inscribed Waugh first editions at Christie's.

The publication of Waugh's work did not by any means end with his death. Following Christopher Sykes's biography (1975) came an edition of Waugh's diaries (1976), and a selection of his letters (1980). The appearance of each of these books led to a renewal, in the review pages, of the old controversies about Waugh. Frederic Raphael called the diaries 'a portrait of the artist as a bad man', and Philip Larkin felt that the letters evoked a world that was 'curt, cheap, brutal'. Even the sympathetic Geoffrey Wheatcroft, in the *Spectator*, allowed that

Waugh's correspondence gave plenty of evidence 'of what made and still makes people loathe Waugh'. Then, in the autumn of 1981, came Granada Television's serial of *Brideshead Revisited*.

The review of the first two episodes in *The Times* (by Michael Ratcliffe) was headed ' "Brideshead": A Brilliant and Sensual Impact', and judged the dramatization 'a triumph of beauty, fidelity and relevant embellishment'. Many reviewers agreed with this, but there were dissenters, among them Kingsley Amis in the *Times Literary Supplement*, in an article headed 'How I Lived in a Very Big House and Found God'. Judging the book to be Waugh's worst, on account of its undisguised snobbery, Amis felt that the screenplay (by John Mortimer) highlighted 'the vacancy of the novel'. As to the use of Catholicism to break off the Julia–Charles affair, Amis called it 'no worse than something out of Graham Greene'. William Boyd, in the *New Statesman*, likewise wrote of the novel as 'in many respects' Waugh's worst, and emphasized the homosexual element in it:

> Waugh clouds the issue but the homosexual references are so numerous that only a wilful stubbornness could ignore their implications. . . . Waugh fudges the issue on the first theme [homosexuality] and takes up the second [Catholicism] half-way through the book. . . . The faults of the book are carried over to the film [though] the acting is of a uniformly high standard.

In an article in the *Spectator*, Auberon Waugh commented on the homosexual element in the story, made slightly more explicit on the screen. He felt that Charles came over in the television version as an 'oafish pooftah' who kept 'showing us his bum' to an unnecessary degree.

This article, 'Bums in Brideshead', was part of a jokey exchange between Auberon Waugh and Richard Ingrams, television critic of the *Spectator*, and also editor of the satirical magazine *Private Eye*. In 1962 the *Observer* had asked Evelyn Waugh to review an early number of *Private Eye*, but he declined because 'Not one of the objects of its jokes was known to me & the drawings seemed incompetent scrawl. . . . Try my son A.A. Waugh. . . . He is in touch with modern London.' Auberon eventually became closely involved with *Private Eye*. From 1970 to 1986 he contributed to the magazine a humorous diary which somewhat resembled the more fantastic inventions in his father's diaries and letters.

During the 1960s, *Private Eye*, if not explicitly left-wing, certainly contained the same kind of 'anti-establishment' satire that could be seen in television programmes like *That Was The Week That Was*, in which mockery of Harold Macmillan's Conservative government predominated. By the mid-1970s the magazine's political orientation had changed. Laughs were now largely at the expense of the 'Loony Left', with its militant support for 'gay rights', and feminism. At the same period the *Spectator*, for some while an unpolitical and unfashionable paper, began to be known as the voice of right-wing opinion, often expressed comically, and many *Private Eye* contributors began to appear in its pages – 'Pretty well the same people write for both publications,' noted Auberon Waugh in the *Spectator* on 7 November 1981.

These developments among a small journalistic clique in London were reflections of a major shift in political opinion throughout Britain. By the mid-1970s, a series of Labour governments, weakened by struggles against the trade unions who were supposed to be their principal supporters, was about to give way to a new style of Conservative administration, under Margaret Thatcher. It was no longer *de rigueur*, as it had been throughout the Sixties, for British intellectuals to espouse socialism and favour proletarian, rather than patrician, styles of life. The ideal of a classless society began to give way to a new spirit of individual self-advancement. Public school accents again became fashionable, and the gossip-columns once again concerned themselves with the scandalous behaviour of junior royalty and the aristocracy, just as they had in the days of the Bright Young People.

Even the craze for Victorianism, invented in 1922 by Harold Acton, began to come into fashion again. While members of the Thatcher government were calling for a return to 'Victorian values', Victorian paintings and *objets d'art* began to sell for enormous sums – by 1983 works by Millais and other Victorians were changing hands at half a million pounds, and Auberon Waugh was able to sell his father's Burges washstand for £45,000. The 'style editor' of *Harper's and Queen*, Peter York, noted that the revival was largely due to '[Evelyn] Waugh, Betjeman and Osbert Lancaster'. In a 1984 book, York described the growth of this 'Reactionary Chic':

> Forward into the past, backward into the future. . . . People who lived for the look of the thing were recognizing that straight-ahead modernism was just too drab. . . . After the rhetoric of the high sixties . . . all the intellectual energy . . . seemed to lie with the New Reactionaries, and they made the most of it. . . . Mrs Thatcher had said 'rich men have rights too' and a new visible group of Young Fogeys seemed to be endorsing her. . . . Charles Moore [editor of the *Spectator*] and A.N. Wilson [novelist and columnist] and all their little friends seemed to be endorsing a favourite Thatcher position, that *then* was better than *now*.

By 1982, the right-wing journalist Peregrine Worsthorne,* writing in the *Spectator*, was able to announce the death of the socialist-egalitarian movement, which had dominated British political and intellectual life from 1945 until the early 1970s. Reviewing a new edition of Anthony Sampson's *The Anatomy of Britain*, first published in 1962, Worsthorne blasted Sampson for failing to revise his book properly, in view of the changed political climate. 'Back in 1962,' he wrote, 'Mr Sampson purported to demonstrate that Britain was still governed by a lot of *ancien régime* institutions populated by fuddy-duddy aristocrats.' Sampson's recipe for the survival of Britain had been to sweep all this away – to 'get rid of the class system' and govern by meritocracy rather than aristocracy. Sampson was still saying much the same thing in 1982, but Worsthorne pointed out that in the interim the meritocrats had had their chance, and had messed it up. The governments of Harold Wilson and Edward Heath had been filled with just the sort of classless intellectuals whom Sampson admired, and where (asked Worsthorne) had it got Britain? If there was an economic crisis at the end of it, then no one could blame the class system and the aristocracy. 'It is not', wrote Worsthorne, 'the Cavendishes and the Cecils who should take the blame, but the Wilsons, Heaths, Jenkinses, Jays, and Anthony Sampsons.'

As to those élite institutions that Sampson had so roundly condemned and despised in 1962 – the public schools, the House of Lords, the Brigade of Guards, Eton and Christ Church, the City and the Inns of Court – far from weakening, as Britain went through the 1960s and 1970s, they seemed (in Worsthorne's view) to have grown in strength and influence:

> The most remarkable and fascinating aspect of Britain during the last twenty years has been the way these ancient institutions seem to have outlived the egalitarian *zeitgeist*. In a profound sense, it is *their* values which are now returning into fashion, to the point where it is not them but Mr Sampson who begins to look like the proverbial dodo or dinosaur.

Evelyn Waugh had projected some such revival of the right in a 1959 article in the *Daily Mail*, in which he prophesied the eventual death of the Labour Party as a parliamentary force – and, incidentally, also guessed that Britain would soon consist of 'speedways' (that is, motorways) and car parks, though 'there will be no inducement to

---

* Whom Evelyn Waugh had once met and dubbed 'a civil young man', though he noted that the Worsthornes were Belgian immigrants who had adopted an English-sounding surname (*Letters*, ed. Amory, pp. 552f.).

go anywhere because all buildings will look the same'. His political forecast was that 'the Labour Party will continue its useful function of posing annoying questions to Ministers but I do not think the electorate will ever again vote them into authority'.

Whether a resurgence of political Conservatism on a popular scale, accompanied by a return to traditional values in the arts and British social life, would seriously have pleased him must, however, be gravely open to doubt. All his professional life, he refused to go along with the majority, adopting right-wing views and mannerisms in protest against the decline of English culture into middlebrow trash, and playing Gilbert Pinfold, the barricaded artist *contra mundum*, as a response to the trivial values of modern society. It is hard to imagine him willingly accepting homage from the mass of people who turned Tory in the 1970s and 1980s, or delighting in the fact that the Century of the Common Man had evolved into the Century of Get Rich Quick. 'An artist must be reactionary,' he told an interviewer four years before his death, using that word not in the sense of 'conservative', but (as he always used words) with its precise and literal meaning. 'He has to stand out against the tenor of the age and not go flopping along.'

Appendices

Appendix A

DRAMATIS PERSONAE

This is merely a list of people who recur frequently in the story, and is intended simply as an aid to the reader in identifying them within this book. It makes no pretence of providing comprehensive information about them.

Acton, Harold (b. 1904). Born in Florence, educated at Eton and Christ Church, Oxford, where he led the eccentrically aesthetic group to which Waugh soon attached himself. After Oxford, Waugh's meteoric literary success at first submerged Acton's own career as a writer, and he moved to China, where he lived from 1933 to 1939. After war service, he returned to his parents' home, La Pietra in Florence, and re-emerged publicly as an author and art connoisseur. He was knighted in 1974. His books include *Aquarium* (1923), *Humdrum* (1928), *The Last Medici* (1932), *Modern Chinese Poetry* (1936), *Memoirs of an Aesthete* (1948), *The Bourbons of Naples* (1956), *More Memoirs of an Aesthete* (1970), *Nancy Mitford, A Memoir* (1975) and *Florence, a Traveller's Companion* (1986).

Balfour, Patrick (1904–77). Educated at Winchester and Balliol College, Oxford. Gossip-column writer and journalist in Fleet Street during the 1930s. Succeeded as third Baron Kinross in 1939.

Betjeman, John (1906–84). Son of a London manufacturer; educated at Marlborough and Magdalen College, Oxford. Began to publish poetry during the 1930s (see Appendix B: Bibliography), and worked on the *Architectural Review* from 1931. Married Penelope Chetwode in 1933; they had one son and one daughter. The publication of his *Collected Poems* in 1958 brought him widespread popularity, and he also became very well known for his television programmes on Victorian architecture and kindred topics. Knighted in 1969; appointed Poet Laureate in 1972.

Bowra, Maurice (1898–1971). Fellow, Dean and later Warden of Wadham College, Oxford. A classical scholar, who also translated Russian verse and wrote on modern literature, he was renowned not for his books but for his conversation and his stimulus to the young, who in their time included Cyril Connolly and John Betjeman. Set the style of behaviour for a generation of English intellectuals. Believed himself to be the model for 'Mr Samgrass' in *Brideshead Revisited*. Knighted in 1951.

Byron, Robert (1905–41). A member of the Brian Howard–Harold Acton Society of Arts at Eton, and a pioneer with Acton, there and at Oxford (he was at Merton College), of the Victorian revival. Became a travel-writer with *Europe in the Looking-Glass* (1927). His subsequent books included *The Byzantine Achievement* (1929), *First Russia, Then Tibet* (1933), and *The Road to Oxiana* (1937). He was killed when the ship on which he was travelling was torpedoed. Waugh had been initially delighted by his exuberance, then became contemptuous of his writing, and was possibly disturbed by Byron's (discreet) homosexuality.

Clonmore, Billy (Viscount) (1902–78). Educated at Eton and Merton College, Oxford. Trained to be an Anglican priest, but converted to Roman Catholicism. Became eighth Earl of Wicklow.

Connolly, Cyril (1903–74). At preparatory school with George Orwell and Cecil Beaton; at Eton with Harold Acton and Brian Howard; at Balliol College, Oxford while Waugh was an undergraduate. Became a literary journalist in London, married Jean Bakewell in 1930, and went to live with her in France. Returned to England during the Thirties, and during the Second World War founded and edited *Horizon* (1939–50). Apart from collections of his reviews and articles, his principal books are his novel *The Rock Pool* (1936), *Enemies of Promise* (1938) and *The Unquiet Grave* (1944), published under the pseudonym 'Palinurus'. Married Barbara Skelton in 1950, and after being divorced from her married Deirdre Craig in 1959, by whom he had a son and a daughter. In his later years, reviewed regularly for the *Sunday Times*.

Cooper, Lady Diana (1892–1986). Daughter of the Duke of Rutland, and wife of Sir Alfred Duff Cooper, who was created Viscount Norwich in 1952. Society beauty and the original of 'Mrs Stitch' in Waugh's fiction.

Cruttwell, C. R. M. F. (1887–1941). Waugh's hated tutor at Hertford College, Oxford. Waugh afterwards used his name for a variety of unsavoury minor characters in his novels. Cruttwell was elected Principal of Hertford in 1930.

Driberg, Tom (1905–76). At Lancing with Waugh, then at Christ Church, Oxford. Worked as a journalist on the *Daily Express*, 1928–43, part of that time writing the 'William Hickey' gossip-column. Entered Parliament as an Independent MP in 1942, and joined the Labour Party in 1945. He became a prominent Labour MP, but was never given a Cabinet post, probably on account of his flagrant homosexuality, about which he writes in his autobiography, *Ruling Passions* (1951). Also a fervent High Church Anglican. Was married in 1951 to a Mrs Ena Binfield, but makes no mention of this in his memoirs. Created a life peer (Lord Bradwell) the year before his death.

Duggan, Alfred (1903–64). Stepson of Lord Curzon. Educated at Eton and Balliol College, Oxford, where he lived the life of a rake. In middle age he gave up the bottle and took to writing historical novels.

Fothergill, John (1876–1957). Gentleman innkeeper. Bought the Spreadeagle at Thame in 1922, made it famous, but nearly went bankrupt. Subsequently kept the Three Swans at Market Harborough.

Gardner, the Hon. Evelyn (b. 1903). Youngest child of the first (and only) Baron Burghclere. Married Evelyn Waugh in 1928; left him for John Heygate the next year. She married Heygate in 1930, and this marriage was dissolved in 1936. The following year she married Ronald Nightingale.

Graham, Alastair (1904–85). Educated at Wellington and Brasenose College, Oxford. Inseparable companion of Waugh at Oxford; their friendship inspired much of *Brideshead Revisited*. In Diplomatic Service 1928–33; thereafter lived a reclusive life in Wales.

Green, Henry, see Yorke.

Greene, Graham (b. 1904). Son of the Headmaster of Berkhamsted School, where he was educated before going up to Balliol College, Oxford. On the staff of *The Times* 1926–30. In 1927 married Vivien Dayrell-Browning, by whom he had a son and a daughter. His first published novel was *The Man Within* (1929); for his subsequent literary career, see Appendix B: Bibliography. Made a Companion of Honour in 1966 and awarded the Order of Merit in 1986.

Greenidge, Terence. Educated at Rugby and Hertford College, Oxford. Eccentric friend of Waugh's in undergraduate days. Was involved with the making of the film *The Scarlet Woman* in 1924. Little is known of his later life.

Herbert, Laura (1916–73). Daughter of the Hon. Aubrey Herbert. She married Evelyn Waugh in 1937.

Heygate, John (1903–76). Son of an Eton master; educated at Eton and Balliol College, Oxford. Worked for the BBC from 1926 till 1929, when he was obliged to resign because he was co-respondent in the Waugh divorce case. Subsequently wrote novels, inherited a baronetcy, and had two further marriages after Evelyn Gardner had left him.

Hollis, Christopher (1902–77). Son of the Bishop of Taunton; educated at Eton and Balliol College, Oxford. Because a Roman Catholic in his third year as an undergraduate, and 'Sligger' provided him with a teaching post at Stonyhurst. Subsequently an author, publisher and Conservative MP.

Howard, Brian (1905–58). At Eton with Harold Acton, where he organized the Society of Arts, whose members included Anthony Powell and Henry

Yorke. Edited the *Eton Candle* (1922) and seemed set for a sparkling literary career. Failed to get into Oxford until a year after Acton, thereby losing leadership of their 'aesthetic' movement to him. When he came up to Christ Church, became known for flamboyant homosexuality, which made Waugh wary of him. Never fulfilled his early literary promise, and wandered Europe with a series of boyfriends. Often portrayed cattily in Waugh's novels (as 'Ambrose Silk' and 'Anthony Blanche'), but in reality a sadder and more naive character.

James, Edward (b. 1907). Reputedly the grandson, and possibly also the son, of King Edward VII. At Eton with Brian Howard and co. At Oxford, his Christ Church rooms were the grandest in the University. Published John Betjeman's first book of poems in 1931, and the same year was married to the actress Tilly Losch, who appeared in *The Miracle* opposite Lady Diana Cooper; the marriage lasted about three years. A notable collector of the Surrealists. In the 1970s was living in Mexico.

Jungman, Teresa ('Baby'). Bright Young Person, and *inamorata* of Evelyn Waugh between his two marriages.

Kinross, Baron, see Balfour.

Kolkhorst, George Alfred ('Colonel') (1898–1958). Lecturer in Spanish at Exeter College, Oxford; subsequently University Reader in Spanish (1931). Held a Sunday morning salon in his Beaumont Street rooms, which was the cause of almost uncontrollable mirth in those who attended it.

Lancaster, Osbert (1908–86). Educated at Charterhouse and Lincoln College, Oxford. Became known as a cartoonist while an undergraduate. During the Thirties (thanks to Betjeman) wrote and drew for the *Architectural Review*. Later became known for his scathingly funny books charting the decline of English architecture, culminating in *Here, of All Places* (1959). From 1939 contributed a 'Pocket Cartoon' to the *Daily Express*. After the death of his first wife, married Anne Scott-James. He was knighted in 1975.

Lygon family, children of the seventh Earl Beauchamp. **Viscount Elmley** (1903–79), later Lord Beauchamp, was President of the Hypocrites' Club at Oxford. His younger brother **Hugh Lygon** (1904–36), a friend of Waugh's in undergraduate days and perhaps part-model for 'Sebastian' in *Brideshead Revisited*, died suddenly while on a motoring tour of Germany. **Lady Mary Lygon** (b. 1910) and **Lady Dorothy Lygon** (b. 1912) had a playful friendship with Waugh which began in the early Thirties.

Mitford, the Hon. Nancy (1904–73). Daughter of the second Baron Redesdale. Educated at home. Published her first novel, *Highland Fling*, in 1931, and continued to write light fiction during the Thirties. In 1933 she married Peter Rodd (q.v.), whom she divorced in 1958. Made her literary name with *The Pursuit of Love* (1945). Subsequently published other novels about the Radletts, and also wrote biography and history, notably *Voltaire in Love* (1957) and *The Sun King* (1966). Edited *Noblesse Oblige* (1956), which popularized the concept of 'U' and 'Non-U'.

Murray, Basil (1903–37). Son of Professor Gilbert Murray. Educated at Charterhouse and New College, Oxford. Contributed something to the character of 'Basil Seal' in Waugh's fiction. After leaving Oxford, worked in politics and journalism, and died of pneumonia while covering the Spanish Civil War (he was strongly sympathetic to the Republican side) for a Fleet Street newspaper.

Powell, Anthony (b. 1905). The son of a professional soldier. Educated at Eton, where he joined the Society of Arts and had aspirations to be a painter and illustrator. Went up to Balliol College, Oxford, then joined (in 1927) the publishing house of Duckworth, and wrote a brilliantly funny first novel, *Afternoon Men* (1931). See Appendix B: Bibliography, for his later work. In 1934 married Lady Violet Pakenham.

Pryce-Jones, Alan (b. 1908). Educated at Eton and at Magdalen College, Oxford, which he left during his second term. Worked for J.C. Squire on the *London Mercury*, where he published some of John Betjeman's earliest poems. Lived in Vienna during the Thirties, and after the war joined the *Times Literary Supplement*, which he edited from 1948 to 1959. His son David has written and edited several books relating to members of the Waugh circle.

Quennell, Peter (b. 1905). At Berkhamsted School with Graham Greene, then at Balliol College, Oxford. Published first book of poems at the age of twenty-five, and a very successful life of Byron in 1934. Thereafter active as an author and critic.

Rodd, Peter (1904–68). Son of a titled diplomat. Educated at Wellington and Balliol College, Oxford, where he became known to Waugh. Later, along with Basil Murray (q.v.), provided part of the model for 'Basil Seal' in Waugh's fiction. Was married to Nancy Mitford in 1933; they were divorced twenty-five years later.

'Sligger', see Urquhart.

Sutro, John (1904–85). Oxford contemporary of Waugh's. Founder of the Railway Club, and participant in the 1924 film *The Scarlet Woman*. Subsequently worked professionally in the film industry.

Sykes, Christopher (1907–87). Second son of Sir Mark Sykes, the sixth Baronet. Educated at Downside and Christ Church, Oxford. Worked in the Foreign Office (1928–31) and the BBC (1949–68). Married in 1936 Camilla, daughter of Sir Thomas Russell ('Russell Pasha'), head of the Cairo police. Knew Waugh well from the 1940s, and (among other books) wrote the first biography of him (1975).

Urquhart, Francis Fortescue ('Sligger') (1868–1934). Fellow of Balliol College, Oxford, from 1897, and Dean from 1917. A Roman Catholic, who held a salon for undergraduates, preferring those who were titled and handsome. Much mocked by Waugh in the Twenties.

Waugh, Alec (1898–1981). Elder brother of Evelyn Waugh. Educated at Sherborne, and wrote his first novel, *The Loom of Youth* (1917), after being expelled for homosexuality. Worked for a while in his father's publishing firm, Chapman & Hall, married three times, and wrote about fifty books, though he had no great success between his first novel and *Island in the Sun* (1956). Frequently the cause of jealousy in his younger brother, he was himself a man of sunny temperament; his nephew Auberon Waugh has described him as 'unaggressive, benign'.

Waugh, Arthur (1866–1943). Father of Alec and Evelyn Waugh. Educated at Sherborne and New College, Oxford. Began his literary career with a life of Tennyson (1892), contributed to the first *Yellow Book* (1894), and became known as a middlebrow critic of conservative tastes. Managing director of the publishers Chapman & Hll from 1902 until 1930.

Waugh, Evelyn (1903–66). Second son of Arthur Waugh. Educated at Lancing and Hertford College, Oxford, then worked as a schoolmaster before beginning his literary career with a life of Rossetti and the novel *Decline and Fall* (both 1928). He became famous with *Vile Bodies* (1930), and his literary career (see Appendix B: Bibliography) was thereafter consistently successful, but his private life was disfigured in 1929 by the collapse of his marriage to Evelyn Gardner. In 1930 he became a Roman Catholic, and in 1937 he married Laura Herbert, by whom he had six children: Teresa (b. 1938), Auberon (b. 1939), Margaret (1942–86), Harriet (b. 1944), James (b. 1946) and Septimus (b. 1950). During the Second World War, Waugh served in the Royal Marines and the Commandos, but was never given a position of much responsibility because of his attitude to his men. When attempting to give up sleeping-draughts in 1954, he experienced severe hallucinations. From the age of about fifty he began to adopt the mannerisms of an old man; his dependence on sedatives hastened his early death, at the age of sixty-two.

Waugh, Laura, see Herbert.

Wicklow, Earl of, see Clonmore.

Woodruff, Douglas (1897–1978). Educated at Downside and New College, Oxford. Editor of the *Tablet*, 1936–67, and chairman of the Catholic publishers Burns & Oates, 1948–62.

Yorke, Henry (1905–73). Son of a Birmingham businessman, and related to the earls of Hardwicke. Educated at Eton, where he belonged to Brian Howard's Society of Arts, and at Magdalen College, Oxford, where, like John Betjeman, he failed to get on with C.S. Lewis, his tutor. Published his first novel, *Blindness* (1926), while still an undergraduate, using then and thereafter the pseudonym 'Henry Green'. Married the Hon. Adelaide Mary ('Dig') Biddulph, daughter of the second Baron Biddulph. Joined the family firm, H. Pontifex & Co., eventually succeeding his father as head of the business. Went downhill after his father's death, drinking himself into premature old age. His writing is much admired by critics and other novelists, though his books have never yet found a large audience. His other novels are *Living* (1929), *Party Going* (1939), *Caught* (1943), *Loving (1945)*, *Back* (1946), *Concluding* (1948), *Nothing* (1950) and *Doting* (1952). He also wrote an autobiography, *Pack My Bag* (1940).

Appendix B

BIBLIOGRAPHY

This is intended to serve two purposes. First, to provide a handlist of the principal published writings of four of the authors whose works are frequently cited in the text. (I have omitted from this selection the writings of other prolific authors referred to in the book – Harold Acton, Robert Byron, Cyril Connolly, Tom Driberg, Osbert Lancaster, Nancy Mitford, Peter Quennell, and Henry Yorke ('Henry Green') – because only certain works by them have been cited at any length.) Second, it provides bibliographical details of books by other authors which are cited.

The abbreviations in **bold type** are those used in Appendix c, Notes on Sources.

JOHN BETJEMAN

PRINCIPAL WORKS

Mount Zion, or, In Touch with the Infinite, James Press, 1931; St Martin's Press, 1975.

Ghastly Good Taste, Chapman & Hall, 1933; St Martin's Press, 1971.

Continual Dew, a Little Book of Bourgeois Verse, John Murray, 1937.

An Oxford University Chest, John Miles, 1938.

Old Lights for New Chancels, John Murray, 1940.

New Bats in Old Belfries, John Murray, 1945.

First and Last Loves, John Murray, 1952; Soccer Associates, 1961.

A Few Late Chrysanthemums, John Murray, 1954; Transatlantic Arts, 1954.

Collected Poems, John Murray, 1958; Houghton Mifflin, 1959. References are to the enlarged edition, John Murray, 1987 [**Betjeman, *CP***].

Summoned by Bells, John Murray, 1960; Houghton Mifflin, 1960 [**Betjeman, SBB**].
Uncollected Poems, John Murray, 1982.

BOOKS ABOUT BETJEMAN

Bevis Hillier, *John Betjeman: a Life in Pictures*, John Murray, 1984 [**Hillier, LP**].
Bevis Hillier, *Young Betjeman*, John Murray, 1988 [**Hillier, YB**].

GRAHAM GREENE

PRINCIPAL WORKS

All books were published in Britain by Heinemann unless otherwise stated.

Babbling April (poems), Blackwell, 1925.
The Man Within, 1929; Doubleday, Doran, 1929.
The Name of Action, 1930; Doubleday, Doran, 1932.
Rumour at Nightfall, 1931; Doubleday, Doran, 1932.
Stamboul Train, 1932; American ed. published as *Orient Express*, Doubleday, Doran, 1933.
It's a Battlefield, 1934; Doubleday, Doran 1934.
England Made Me, 1935; Doubleday, Doran, 1935.
Journey Without Maps, Bodley Head, 1936; Doubleday, Doran, 1936. References are to the 1971 Penguin edition [*JWM*].
A Gun for Sale, 1936; American ed. published as *This Gun for Hire*, Doubleday, Doran, 1936.
Brighton Rock, 1938; Viking, 1948.
The Confidential Agent, 1939; Viking, 1943.
The Lawless Roads, Longman's, Green and Co. 1939.
The Power and the Glory, 1940; Time, Inc., 1946.
The Ministry of Fear, 1943; Viking, 1943.
The Heart of the Matter, 1948; Viking, 1948.
The End of the Affair, 1951; Viking, 1951.
The Quiet American, 1955; Viking, 1956.
Our Man in Havana, 1958; Viking, 1958.
A Burnt-Out Case, 1961; Viking, 1961.
The Comedians, Bodley Head, 1966; Viking, 1966.
Travels with my Aunt, Bodley Head, 1969; Viking, 1969.
A Sort of Life, Bodley Head, 1971; Simon and Schuster, 1971. References are to the 1972 Penguin edition [*ASOL*].
The Honarary Consul, Bodley Head, 1973; Simon and Schuster, 1973.
The Human Factor, Bodley Head, 1978; Simon and Schuster, 1978.
Doctor Fischer of Geneva, or, The Bomb Party, Bodley Head, 1980; Simon and Schuster, 1980.

Ways of Escape, Bodley Head, 1980; Simon and Schuster, 1980; references are to the 1981 Penguin edition [*WOE*].
Monsignor Quixote, Bodley Head, 1982; Simon and Schuster, 1982.
Getting to Know the General, Bodley Head, 1984; Simon and Schuster, 1984.
The Tenth Man, Bodley Head/Anthony Blond, 1985; Simon and Schuster, 1985.
The Captain and the Enemy, Reinhardt, 1988; Viking, 1988.

BOOKS ABOUT GREENE

Marie-Françoise Allain, *The Other Man: Conversations with Graham Greene*, Bodley Head, 1983 [**Allain**].
Norman Sherry, *The Life of Graham Greene, Volume One, 1904–1939*; Jonathan Cape, 1989.

ANTHONY POWELL

Afternoon Men, Duckworth, 1931; H. Holt, 1932.
Venusberg, Duckworth, 1932; American ed. published as *Two Novels: Venusberg and Agents and Patients*, Little, Brown, 1952.
From a View to a Death, Duckworth, 1933; Vanguard, 1934.
Agents and Patients, Duckworth, 1936; American ed. published as *Two Novels: Venusberg and Agents and Patients*, Little, Brown, 1952.
What's Become of Waring, Cassell, 1939; Little, Brown, 1963.
John Aubrey and his Friends (biography), Eyre & Spottiswoode, 1948; Charles Scribner's Sons, 1948.
'A Dance to the Music of Time' (sequence of novels), all published in Britain by Heinemann:
  A Question of Upbringing, 1951; Little, Brown, 1955.
  A Buyer's Market, 1952; Charles Scribner's Sons, 1953.
  The Acceptance World, 1955; Farrar, Straus & Cudahy, 1956.
  At Lady Molly's, 1957; Little, Brown, 1957.
  Casanova's Chinese Restaurant, 1960; Little, Brown, 1960.
  The Kindly Ones, 1962; Little, Brown, 1962.
  The Valley of Bones, 1964; Little, Brown, 1964.
  The Soldier's Art, 1966; Little, Brown, 1966.
  The Military Philosophers, 1968; Little, Brown, 1969.
  Books Do Furnish a Room, 1971; Little, Brown, 1971.
  Temporary Kings, 1973; Little, Brown, 1973.
  Hearing Secret Harmonies, 1975; Little, Brown, 1975.
'To Keep the Ball Rolling' (four volumes of autobiography), all published in Britain by Heinemann:
  Infants of the Spring, 1976; Holt, Rinehart & Winston, 1977 [Powell, *Infants*].
  Messengers of Day, 1978; Holt, Rinehart & Winston, 1978 [Powell, *Messengers*].
  Faces in my Time, 1980; Holt, Rinehart & Winston, 1981 [**Powell, *Faces***].

The Strangers Are All Gone, 1982; Holt, Rinehart & Winston, 1983.

O, How the Wheel Becomes It!, Heinemann, 1983; Holt, Rinehart & Winston, 1983.

The Fisher King, Heinemann, 1986; Norton, 1986.

EVELYN WAUGH

PRINCIPAL WORKS

All books were published in Britain by Chapman & Hall unless otherwise stated.

'The Balance', in *Georgian Stories, 1926*, 1926; American ed. published as *Georgian Stories, 1927*, Putnam's Sons, 1928.

P.R.B.: an Essay on the Pre-Raphaelite Brotherhood, 1847-1854, privately printed, 1926.

Rossetti: his Life and Works, Duckworth, 1928; Dodd, Mead and Co., 1928.

Decline and Fall: an Illustrated Novelette, 1928; Farrar & Rinehart, 1929.

Vile Bodies, 1930; Farrar & Rinehart, 1930.

Labels: a Mediterranean Journey, Duckworth, 1930; American ed. published as *A Bachelor Abroad*, Farrar & Rinehart, 1930. References are to the 1974 Duckworth edition [***Labels***].

Remote People, Duckworth, 1931; American ed. published as *They Were Still Dancing*, Farrar & Rinehart, 1932. References are to the 1985 Penguin edition [***Remote People***].

Black Mischief, 1932; Farrar & Rinehart, 1932.

Ninety-Two Days, Duckworth, 1934; Farrar & Rinehart, 1943. References are to the 1985 Penguin edition [***Ninety-Two Days***].

A Handful of Dust, 1934; Farrar & Rinehart, 1934.

Edmund Campion: a Biography, Longman's, Green & Co., 1935; Little, Brown, 1946.

Waugh in Abyssinia, Longman's, Green & Co. 1936. References are to the 1985 Penguin edition [***WIA***].

Scoop: a Novel about Journalists, 1938; Little, Brown, 1938.

Robbery Under Law: the Mexican Object Lesson, 1939; American ed. published as *Mexico: an Object Lesson*, Little, Brown, 1939.

Put Out More Flags, 1942; Little, Brown, 1942.

Brideshead Revisited: the Sacred and Profane Memories of Captain Charles Ryder, 1945; Little, Brown, 1945; references are to the revised edition, 1960 [***BR***].

Scott-King's Modern Europe, 1947; Little, Brown, 1949.

The Loved One: an Anglo-American Tragedy, 1948; Little, Brown, 1948.

Helena, 1950; Little, Brown, 1950.

Men at Arms, 1952; Little, Brown, 1952.

Love Among the Ruins: a Romance of the Near Future, 1953.

Officers and Gentlemen, 1955; Little, Brown, 1955.

The Ordeal of Gilbert Pinfold: a Conversation Piece, 1957; Little, Brown, 1957 [**Pinfold**].

The Life of the Right Reverend Ronald Knox, 1959; American ed. published as *Monsignor Ronald Knox*, Little, Brown, 1960.

A Tourist in Africa, 1960; Little, Brown, 1960.

Unconditional Surrender, 1961; Little, Brown, 1961.

Basil Seal Rides Again or The Rake's Regress, 1963; Little, Brown, 1963.

A Little Learning: the First Volume of an Autobiography, 1964; Little, Brown, 1964 [**ALL**]

Work Suspended and Other Stories, Penguin, 1967 [**WS**].

The Diaries of Evelyn Waugh, edited by Michael Davie, Weidenfeld and Nicolson, 1976; Little, Brown, 1976 [**Davie**].

The Letters of Evelyn Waugh, edited by Mark Amory, Weidenfeld and Nicolson, 1980; Ticknor & Fields, 1980 [**Amory**].

The Essays, Articles and Reviews of Evelyn Waugh, edited by Donat Gallagher, Methuen, 1983; Little, Brown, 1984. References are to the second (corrected) ed., Penguin, 1986 [**EAR**].

BOOKS ABOUT WAUGH

Donaldson, Frances, *Evelyn Waugh: Portrait of a Country Neighbour*, Weidenfeld and Nicolson, revised edition 1985 [**Donaldson**]

Pryce-Jones, David (ed.), *Evelyn Waugh and his World*, Weidenfeld and Nicolson, 1973 [**EWAHW**].

Sykes, Christopher, *Evelyn Waugh: a Biography*, Collins, 1975 [**Sykes**].

Stannard, Martin (ed.), *Evelyn Waugh: the Critical Heritage*, Routledge and Kegan Paul, 1984 [**CH**].

Stannard, Martin, *Evelyn Waugh: the Early Years, 1903–1939*, J.M.Dent, 1986 [**Stannard**].

INTERVIEWS WITH, AND ABOUT, WAUGH

'Frankly Speaking' (BBC Home Service, 16 November 1953); recording in BBC Sound Archives [**Frankly Speaking**].

'Face to Face' (Waugh interviewed by John Freeman, BBC Television, 26 June 1960; soundtrack recording in BBC Sound Archives [**Face to Face**].

'Evelyn Waugh talks to Elizabeth Jane Howard. Edited extracts from "Monitor", BBC tv, 16 February 1964.' Recording in BBC Sound Archives [**Monitor**].

Waugh interviewed by Julian Jebb, in April 1962, in *Writers at Work: the Paris Review Interviews*, Third Series, Secker and Warburg, 1968.

'The Waugh Trilogy': three documentary programmes on Waugh made for BBC Television's 'Arena' (interviewer: Nicholas Shakespeare) and first screened during 1987 [**Waugh Trilogy**].

OTHER MATERIAL FREQUENTLY CITED IN THIS BOOK

Acton, Harold, *Memoirs of an Aesthete*, Methuen, 1948 [**Acton**].

Acton, Harold, *More Memoirs of an Aesthete*, Methuen, 1970 [**Acton, *More Memoirs***].

Bowra, C.M., *Memories 1898–1939*, Weidenfeld and Nicolson, 1966 [**Bowra**].

Connolly, Cyril, *Enemies of Promise*, Penguin Books, 1961 (first published by Routledge & Kegan Paul, 1938; revised edition, 1948) [**Connolly, *EP***].

Connolly, Cyril, *The Condemned Playground: Essays: 1927–1944*, Hogarth Press, 1985 (reprint of original edition published by Routledge in 1945) [**Connolly, *CP***].

Driberg, Tom, *Ruling Passions*, Quartet Books, 1978 [**Driberg**].

'Green, Henry' (Henry Yorke), *Pack My Bag: a Self-Portrait*, Hogarth Press, 1979 (first published in 1940) [**Green, *Pack My Bag***].

Hollis, Christopher, *Oxford in the Twenties: Recollections of Five Friends*, Heinemann, 1976 [**Hollis, *OIT***].

James, Edward, *Swans Reflecting Elephants: My Early Years*, edited by George Melly, Weidenfeld and Nicolson, 1982 [**James, *Swans***].

Lancaster, Marie-Jaqueline (ed.), *Brian Howard: Portrait of a Failure*, Anthony Blond, 1968 [**M.-J. Lancaster**].

Lancaster, Osbert, *With an Eye to the Future* (a reissue, in one volume, of that book and *All Done From Memory*, first published respectively in 1967 and 1953), Century, 1986 [**O. Lancaster**].

Pryce-Jones, Alan, *The Bonus of Laughter*, Hamish Hamilton, 1987 [**Pryce-Jones, *Bonus***].

Pryce-Jones, David, *Cyril Connolly: Journal and Memoir*, Collins, 1983 [**P/J, *Connolly***].

Waugh, Arthur, *One Man's Road*, Chapman & Hall, 1921 [***One Man's Road***].

Waugh, Alec, *The Early Years of Alec Waugh*, Cassell, 1962 [***The Early Years of Alec Waugh***].

Waugh, Alec, *My Brother Evelyn and Other Profiles*, Cassell, 1967 [***My Brother Evelyn***].

Williams, Emlyn, *George: an Early Autobiography*, Hamish Hamilton, 1961 [**Williams, *George***].

Appendix C

NOTES ON SOURCES

The quotations used in the text are identified in this list by the number of the page on which they appear, and by the first words quoted. When two or more quotations from the same source follow each other with little intervening narrative, I have generally used only the first few words of the first quotation for identification. Abbreviations refer to the Bibliography (Appendix B), where the full publication details of the work cited are given.

At the head of the notes to each chapter will be found a general note in which principal sources for the chapter are given. Quotations from these sources have not been included in the notes themselves, it being assumed that the reader will have no difficulty in tracing them when consulting these sources.

Part 1 1918–1922: Eton Candle

1 '... THOUGHT THEY MUST BE FOREIGNERS'

Principal sources: Acton; M.-J. Lancaster.

page
3   'Eton . . . has one great', Bernard Crick, *George Orwell*, Secker & Warburg, 1980, 47f.
6   '*Svengali will go*', George du Maurier, *Trilby*, Part Second (with adaptations).
9   '*Les Chansons de Bilitis*', Connolly, *CP*, 138.
10 'Of the ladies', *Eton College Chronicle*, 9 March 1922.

Appendix C

2 COME NEARER, CHILD

Principal sources: Acton; M.-J. Lancaster; Powell, *Infants*; Green, *Pack My Bag*; James, *Swans*; Connolly, *EP*.

18 'How should I', Philip Purser, *Where Is He Now? The Extraordinary Worlds of Edward James*, Quartet Books, 1978, 10.
21 'a sense of desolate', George Orwell, *Collected Essays, Journalism and Letters*, vol. IV, Secker & Warburg, 1968, 334.
22 'He is extraordinarily', Hugo Vickers, *Cecil Beaton*, Weidenfeld & Nicolson, 1985, 17, 13.
23 'faun-like', P/J, *Connolly*, 31f.
24 'Smack, smack', Hollis, *OIT*, 98.
25 'sensibility . . . was', Pryce-Jones, *Bonus*, 42.

3 SUSPENDED BOYHOOD

Principal sources: Connolly, *EP*; M.-J. Lancaster; Acton; *The Eton Candle* (edited by Brian Howard), Spottiswoode, Ballantyne & Co. (Eton), 1922.

28 'driven underground', O. Lancaster, 85.
29 'Here, under the yawns', Green, *Pack My Bag*, 172.
30 'It was the happiest', P/J, *Connolly*, 49.

Part 2 1922–1924: Et in Arcadia

1 OXFORD BROOM

Principal sources: Acton; M.-J. Lancaster; O. Lancaster; Green, *Pack My Bag*; Hollis, *OIT*.

35 'I used to think', *Isis*, 17 May 1922.
38 'They represent', John Betjeman, *An Oxford University Chest*, John Miles, 1938, 129.
39 'the wish to scandalize', *EAR*, 597.
40 'My father', Pryce-Jones, *Bonus*, 37.
41 'trousers very wide', Driberg, 56. 'A tall plumpish', Williams, *George*, 316.
42 'I had probably', Driberg, 56. 'I've settled *them*', Betjeman, *SBB*, 94.
43 'We should not', *Oxford magazine*, 17 May 1923.
44 'Within, the heat', Harold Acton, *'Aquarium*, Duckworth, 1923, 19.

2 '... LONGED TO REMAIN MYSELF AND YET BE ACCEPTED ...'

Principal sources: *ALL; The Early Years of Alec Waugh; My Brother Evelyn; One Man's Road*; Sykes; Davie; Amory; Hollis, *OIT*.

46 'He can't write', *Spectator*, 21 July 1966.

48 'a bit too good', *Waugh Trilogy*. 'too well brought up', 'The Balance', in *Georgian Stories*, *1926*.

51 'unaggressive, benign', *Spectator*, 12 September 1981.

52 'The two brothers', 'Winner Takes All' in *WS*.

53 '*Dilwyn* Thomas', Anthony Powell, *The Strangers All Are Gone*, Heinemann, 1982, 160. 'prim, stuffy', Donaldson, xv, 7.

54 'to the dismay', *EAR*, 366. 'The enthusiasm', ibid.

55 'How often', *EWAHW*, 17. 'complete isolation', *Face to Face*.

56 'indifference to kicks', Dudley Carew, *A Fragment of Friendship*, Everest Books, 1974, 16. 'No. No fault', *Frankly Speaking*.

57 'magnetically brilliant', Driberg, 49.

59 'During the last', *EAR*, 11.

61 'This learned and', *EAR*, 367. 'In the interests', ibid., 10.

62 'Michael ... lay back', Compton Mackenzie, *Sinister Street*, Book 3, Chapter 5. 'an important bad', Connolly, *EP*, 44.

64 'Privacy after years', Betjeman, *SBB*, 93.

65 'We haven't exactly', Nancy Mitford, *Highland Fling*, Chapter 11.

3 HYPOCRITES

Principal sources: *ALL*; Acton; Sykes; Powell, *Infants*; Acton; Powell, *Infants*; Driberg; M.-J. Lancaster; Williams, *George*; Hollis, *OIT*; Green, *Pack My Bag*.

71 'a romantic, yet', *EWAHW*, 36. 'Le faune', Amory, 277. 'When Mr Acton', *Isis*, 20 February 1924.

72 'the most incredible', ibid.

78 'The Hypocrites are', *Isis*, 14 May 1924.

79 'they're supposed', Williams, *George*, 316.

80 'a white wisp', ibid., 393. 'several of the ladies', Humphrey Carpenter, *OUDS: a Centenary History of the Oxford University Dramatic Society*, Oxford University Press, 1985, 86. 'My dear', Williams, *George*, 384.

81 'My father', Hillier, *YB*, Chapter 7. 'never heard an', James, *Swans*, 64. 'it was chic', Pryce-Jones, *Bonus*, 49.

82 'was neither courted', *EWAHW*, 19f.

83 'A small, good-looking', *EAR*, 9. 'Was it chance', Betjeman, *CP*, 152.

84 'a small man', Stannard, 90.

85 'a pre-Raphaelite', conversation with the author, 8 August 1988.

87 'I cut tutorials', Betjeman, *SBB*, 87.

4 DEAR PRIVATE GIGGLES OF A PRIVATE WORLD

Principal sources: P/J, *Connolly*; Cyril Bailey, *Frances Fortescue Urquhart: a Memoir*, Macmillan, 1936; Peter Quennell, *The Marble Foot: an Autobiography*,

1905-1938, Collins, 1976; Hollis, *OIT*; Hugh Lloyd-Jones (ed.), *Maurice Bowra: a Celebration*, Duckworth, 1974; Betjeman, *SBB*; O. Lancaster; Hillier, *LP*; Hillier, *YB*.

89 'Strangers' eyes', Walter Pater, *Miscellaneous Studies* (Vol. 8 of *Collected Works*), Macmillan, 1910, 220f.
90 'Because I'm poor', Sykes, 49.
91 'This is the earthly', Noel Blakiston (ed.), *A Romantic Friendship: the Letters of Cyril Connolly to Noel Blakiston*, Constable, 1975, 12.
93 'I don't think', Kenneth Clark, *Another Part of the Wood: A Self-Portrait*, John Murray, 1974, 100. 'a world authority', C.M.Bowra, *Memories, 1898-1939*, Weidenfeld & Nicolson, 1966, 158.
97 'He said all the', Kenneth Clark, op. cit., 100.
100 'a lachrymose', Pryce-Jones, *Bonus*, 231f.
101 'a convincing impersonation', Carpenter, *OUDS* (see note to p. 80), 102. 'a zany wiseacre', Williams, *George*, 378.
102 'When nine', John Betjeman, *Uncollected Poems*, John Murray, 1982, 26f.
104 'with his gate lodge', John Betjeman, *Ghastly Good Taste*, Chapman & Hall, 1933, xix. 'purely imitative', ibid., xvii.
105 'I have seen Americans', *'Architectural Review*, May 1931.
106 'Sezincote is quite', Davie, 316.

5 HE EMBODIED AUTHORITY

Principal sources: *ASOL*; Allain. (The first volume of Norman Sherry's life of Greene was published as this book was going to press, so that I have only been able to use it as a last-minute source, to add and correct a few details.)

107 'a man of powerful', Claud Cockburn, *In Time of Trouble: an Autobiography*, Rupert Hart-Davis, 1956, 44-6.
110 The poems: Graham Greene, *Babbling April*, Blackwell, 1925.

6 A DREAM TOO AGREEABLE

Principal sources: M.-J. Lancaster; *ALL*; John Fothergill, *An Innkeeper's Diary*, Chatto & Windus, 1927; John Fothergill, *My Three Inns*, Chatto & Windus, 1949; Acton; Sykes; Amory; Powell, *Infants*; O. Lancaster.

113 'I asked her', Williams, *George*, 381.
114 'in hired cars', Lloyd-Jones, op. cit. (see 'principal sources' note to Part 2, Chapter 4), 89.
118 'Less £6', Stannard, 120.
121 'The Great Western', *Cherwell*, 8 December 1923.
122 'Reviewing the prospects', ibid., 1 March 1924.

123 'he emphasized', ibid., 21 June 1924. 'Mr Barrymore', *Isis*, 27 January, 30 January, 6 February 1924.

124 'a badger–like', ibid., 5 March 1924. 'His tutor', ibid., 13 june 1925. 'a boisterous', Peter Quennell, op. cit. (see 'principal sources', note to Part 2, Chapter 4), 117.

126 'at the next', Davie, 161. 'wasted . . .', Pryce–Jones, *Bonus*, 47. 'literature is not', Green, *Pack My Bag*, 213. 'You'd have only', Betjeman, *SBB*, 109.

127 'It was my ambition', Hillier, *YB*, Chapter 9.

Part 3 1924–1929 : Bright Young People

1 STRUGGLE FOR DETACHMENT

Principal sources: *ASOL*; *WOE*; Allain; Betjeman, *SBB*; Betjeman, *CP*; Sykes; *ALL; P/J, Connolly*; Acton; Green, *Pack My Bag*; Davie; Evelyn Waugh, *Rossetti: his Life and Works*, Duckworth, 1928. A print of *The Scarlet Woman* is in the National Film Archive.

133 'the slender banjo–tunes', Cherwell, 9 May 1925.

135 'I never remember', Alan Ross, *Coastwise Lights*, Collins, 1988, 111.

137 'is in the momentary', *EAR*, 15.

138 'a great artist', *EAR*, 337.

140 'a Byronic exercise', *EWAHW*, 41.

143 'fine', Amory, 24.

145 Waugh's *PRB: an Essay on the Pre–Raphaelite Brotherhood, 1847–1854*, was reprinted by the Dalrymple Press in 1982.

146 'They could not settle', Connolly, *EP*, 56.

147 'Such specious', Arthur Waugh, *Alfred, Lord Tennyson*, Heinemann, 1893, 7.

2 A COMIC NOVEL

Principal sources: Davie; Amory.

150 'One night', Powell, *Messengers*, 22. 'ornamental', *EAR*, 57.

151 'a wildly outrageous', quoted on cover of 1968 Penguin edition of 'Saki', *The Chronicles of Clovis*. 'The wit is', *EAR*, 324. 'too often have', ibid., 232. 'grown up in', ibid., 564. 'He inhabits', ibid., 567. 'exquisite felicity', ibid., 565. 'I remember', P.G.Wodehouse, *Jeeves in the Offing*, Penguin, 1963, 48.

152 'At my private', *EAR*, 305. '*Crome Yellow*', Betjeman, *SBB*, 93. 'In quite diverse', *EAR*, 56. 'the chain', *EAR*, 57. 'When something', Connolly, *EP*, 45. 'coy naughtiness', *EAR*, 56.

153 'As no doubt', Amory, 298. 'the idea of futility', Connolly, *EP*, 53. 'This is a satirical', ibid., 112.

154 'startlingly brilliant', *EAR*, 391f. 'frivolous and', ibid., 392. 'I was prostrated', Powell, *Infants*, 145. 'detached observer', Acton, 160.

155 'Max Beerbohm was', EAR, *516*. 'Master', Rupert Hart–Davis 'ed.), *Letters of Max Beerbohm*, John Murray, 1988, 211. 'When I draw', ibid., 35. 'Some people', *PR*. 'The truth is', *EAR*, 195f.

156 'I've burnt it', Powell, *Messengers*, 22. 'groaning loudly', *EWAHW*, 50. 'there was nothing', *Ninety–Two Days*, 7. 'I have the', *Work Suspended*, Chapman & Hall, 1942, 5. 'rightful place', Connolly, *EP*, 126.

158 'It seems to me', *EAR*, 262.

159 '*not* sure', Morton N. Cohen (ed.), *The Letters of Lewis Carroll*, Macmillan, 1979, 781.

160 'Silly to trouble', Henry Green, *Blindness*, Part 2, Chapter 3.

161 'Mr Toad on top', *My Brother Evelyn*, 183.

162 'No, it must', Acton, 203.

163 'half-cynical', Arthur Waugh, *A Hundred Years of Publishing*, Chapman & Hall, 1930, 305f. 'not a satire', *New Statesman*, 3 November 1928. 'At a bungalow', Acton 203.

3 A SORT OF CUMULATIVE FUTILITY

Principal sources: Davie; Amory; Sykes; Stannard; Powell, *Messengers*; M.-J. Lancaster; Anthony Masters, *Rosa Lewis: an Exceptional Edwardian*, Weidenfeld & Nicolson, 1977; P/J, *Connolly*; Acton.

164 'was suddenly transfigured', O. Lancaster, 58.

166 'which we had found', Pryce–Jones, *Bonus*, 34.

168 'Bright Young Henry Yorke', Diana Mosley, *A Life of Contrasts*, Hamish Hamilton, 1977, 79. 'They were just', Harold Acton, *Humdrum*, Chatto & Windus, 1928, 222f.

169 'an unassuming', Pryce–Jones, *Bonus*, 34.

177 'un ravissant', *Evelyn Waugh Newsletter*, No. 1, Spring 1967. 'It was not a nose', *WS*.

178 'an impecunious', Jeffrey Heath, *The Picturesque Prison: Evelyn Waugh and his Writing*, Weidenfeld & Nicolson, 1982, 26. 'the ardour', ibid., 27.

181 'Isn't abroad', Hillier, *YB*, Chapter 14.

183 'Technically, *Living*', *EAR*, 81. 'evidently a burden', Alan Ross, op. cit. (see note to p. 135), 109.

192 'We all used to', *Waugh Trilogy*.

194 'responsible people', *EAR*, 94–6.

195 'They looked like', Harold Acton, *Nancy Mitford*, Hamish Hamilton, 1975, 27. 'as I've been', *My Brother Evelyn*, 191. 'a lonely little', *EAR*, 443.

196 'the marriage', *The Early Years of Alec Waugh*, 155. 'Sex instinct', *EAR*, 95f.

197 'It's terrible', *My Brother Evelyn*, 191.

199 'utterly suicidal', conversation with the author, 8 August 1988. 'showed few signs', Diana Mosley, op. cit. (see note to p. 168), 76. 'I went through', *PR*. 'I asked him', Hollis, *OIT*, 84.

200 'I was in the', *PR*.

Part 4 1930–1934: In Search of a City

1 A NEW ORDER AND ANOTHER CHRISTENDOM

Principal sources: ASOL; *JWM*; Allain; Davie; Hillier, *YB*.

206 'A Visit to Morin' is in Greene's *Collected Short Stories*, Penguin, 1986.

208 'A second novel', *EAR*, 101.

209 'laughed until I', *CH*, 97. 'a further stage', ibid., 107. 'I popularized', *PR*. 'The last time', Amory, 589.

210 'I thought that these', Bowra, op. cit. (see note to p. 93), 174.

217 'one of the great triumphs', Osbert Lancaster, *Here, of All Places*, John Murray, 1959, 66.

218 'crazy and sterile', *EAR*, 63.

220 'was unintelligible', *EAR*, 367. 'in love with religion', *EWAHW*, 40. 'England was Catholic', *EAR*, 367. 'He needed to cling', *Waugh Trilogy*.

221 'the uniquely unattractive', Pryce-Jones, *Bonus*, 157. 'Are you rich', ibid., 156. 'for a long time', Martin D'Arcy, *Catholicism*, Ernest Benn, 1927, 9f. 'a kind of', ibid., 7.

222 'it only remained', *EAR*, 368. 'come to learn', *EWAHW*, 64. 'Evelyn, on the', ibid. 'perhaps inclined', Sykes, 108. 'It is better', Stannard, 297. 'very unsentimentally', Sykes, 107.

223 'I look back', *EAR*, 368. 'a body which', ibid., 404.

225 'to prevent the', Stannard, 228. 'What showed his', Sykes, 108.

226 'Converted To Rome', *EAR*, 103f.

2 REMOTE PEOPLE

Principal sources: *WOE*; P/J, *Connolly*; Acton; Davie; Amory; *Remote People*.

228 'laden by', *ASOL*, 151. 'dreaming of that', 'Palinurus' (Cyril Connolly), *The Unquiet Grave*, Hamish Hamilton, revised edition, 1945, 111.

229 'Innsbruck . . .', Robert Byron, *Europe Through the Looking-Glass*, Routledge, 1926, 36. 'Uncle Matthew's', Nancy Mitford, *The Pursuit of Love*, Chapter 15.

230 'insularity run', *EAR*, 198. 'None of our', Bowra, op. cit. (see note to p. 93), 174. 'fallen from grace', Acton, *More Memoirs*, 19. 'cancer of the', M.-J. Lancaster, 352, 356. 'The more I', ibid., 319.

231 'an American woman', *EAR*, 115.
232 'One morning', Alec Waugh, *A Year to Remember*, W.H.Allen, 1975, 111f.
233 'A Bostonian', Sykes, 110. 'a pious fraud', Stannard, 240. 'an elderly man', Graham Greene, *In Search of Character*, Bodley Head, 1961, 102f.
234 'His articulation', Acton, *More Memoirs*, 175. 'became an enthusiastic', Sykes, 112.
235 'He struck me', Wilfred Thesiger, *The Life of my Choice*, Collins, 1987, 91f. 'the best company', Bowra, op. cit. (see note to p. 93), 173, 175.
239 'When we have', Hollis, *OIT*, 89. 'satanic', *ALL*, 204. 'almost consistently', Basil Murray, 'Autobiographical Sketch', MS in possession of Mrs Ann Paludan. 'did not greatly', *ALL*, 204. 'We've had as', Hollis, *OIT*, 88. 'utterly fascinated', Sykes, 41. 'a man of', *EAR*, 403. 'the sulky', *ALL*, 204.
240 'a man of', Pryce-Jones, *Bonus*, 233. 'In the lining', ibid., 234.
241 'Paul in *Decline*', *My Brother Evelyn*, 166. 'a disgrace to', *CH*, 133.
242 'the bounds of', ibid., 132. Waugh's *Open Letter* is reprinted in Amory.

3 VERY GRIM

Principal sources: Amory; Powell, *Messengers*; Amory; Davie; *Ninety-Two Days*.

246 'It is the point-to-point', Robert Byron, *The Station*, Duckworth, 1928, 13f. 'To my mind', *CH*, 127.
247 'statements of incest', *EWAHW*, 50. 'chocolate-box', Stannard, 283. 'if you weren't', ibid., 298f.
248 'to help me', Diana Cooper, *The Light of Common Day*, Rupert Hart-Davis, 1959, 114f. 'I am ... sceptical', *EAR*, 127. 'He is possessed', Sykes, 126. 'That is an explanation', *EAR*, 132ff.
250 'I had not refused', Stannard, 352f.
252 'wanted to discover', *EAR*, 303. 'not apposite', Sykes, 138.

Part 5 1934–1939: The Gentleman's House

1 BERNERS BETJEMAN COUNTRY

Principal sources: Hillier, *LP*; Hillier, *YB*; James, *Swans*; Amory; Davie; Sykes.

259 'full of private', *EAR*, 403. 'to take on', Jessica Mitford, *Hons and Rebels*, Quartet Books, 1978, 36.
260 'Betjeman is', Selina Hastings, *Nancy Mitford: a Biography*, Hamish Hamilton, 1985, 71. 'of becoming', Jessica Mitford, op. cit. (see note to p. 259), 36. 'Pam, I adore', Betjeman, *CP*, 57f.

261 'a strangely', Bowra, op. cit. (see note to p. 93), 169. 'John's appearance', Pryce–Jones, *Bonus*, 231.

263 'its crystal organ', *Evening Standard*, 21 March 1934. 'On no account', ibid., 4 April 1934. 'the possibilities', ibid., 16 April 1934. 'Be a good', Stannard, 398.

264 'the six most', Wilfrid Blunt, *Married to the Single Life*, Michael Russell, 1983, 182. 'He resembled', Vickers, op. cit. (see note to p. 22), 172.

265 'Lord Berners has', Diana Mosley, op. cit. (see note to p. 168), 112. 'a mecca', ibid., 120. 'Though they were', Nancy Mitford, *The Pursuit of Love*, Chapter 5. 'Oh fair be', text kindly supplied by Bevis Hillier.

266 'combined a missionary', O. Lancaster, 124. 'My dear Penelope', Bowra, op. cit. (see note to p. 93), 171f.

269 'neurotically shy', Donaldson, ix.

271 'pious book', Stannard, 389.

272 'The first time', Frank Pakenham, *Born to Believe*, Jonathan Cape, 1953, 122. 'Augustan Latin', Connolly, *EP*, 15. 'the language in', Evelyn Waugh, *Rossetti: his Life and Works*, Duckworth, 1928, 54.

2 A FASCIST TRACT

Principal sources: *JWM*; Barbara Greene, *Too Late to Turn Back* (a reissue of her 1938 book, *Land Benighted*), Settle Bendall, 1981; *WIA*; Amory; Davie.

274 'Get there if', *The English Auden*, Faber and Faber, 1977, 48.

275 'Prod looked very', Hastings, op. cit. (see note to p. 260), 97n.

276 'very poor', Allain, 68. 'panicked', *WOE*, 38.

277 'The reader has', *EAR*, 362.

279 'a new quarrelsomeness', Pryce–Jones, *Bonus*, 106. Waugh's *Evening Standard* article is reprinted in *EAR*.

281 'They are like children', *EAR*, 177.

284 'a very gloomy', Sykes, 158.

285 'If this book', Stannard, 418.

287 'allowed themselves to', *EAR*, 189.

288 'could after all', *CH*, 188. 'He does not', ibid., 190. 'cynic turned', ibid., 192. 'a Fascist', ibid., 193.

3 SETTING MYSELF UP AS A SQUIRE

Principal sources: Connolly, *CP*; Connolly, *EP*; P/J, *Connolly*; Powell, *Faces*; Amory; Davie; Stannard; Betjeman, *CP*.

290 'public indifference', *WOE*, 54.

291 'mortified', M.-J. Lancaster, 199f.

296 'overcome by', Sykes, 5. 'Lord Cockburn', ibid., 'The larger one's, *EAR*, 137.

297 'the transition', Waugh, *Rossetti* (see note to p. 272), 22.

300 'the style of', *EAR*, 216.

302 'the symbol of', Acton, 155.

303 'art with dandyism', quoted in the *Independent*, 3 October 1988, 27. 'The Victorians', Hillier, *YB*, Chapter 9. 'the younger poets', Arthur Waugh, *Tradition and Change*, Chapman & Hall, 1919, 41, 226, 285, 278.

304 'the new, complicated', *EAR*, 273. 'ganged up', ibid., 394.

305 'how entirely', *New Statesman*, 16 January 1937. 'Aristocracy saved', *EAR*, 276.

306 'It is the most', *EAR*, 301.

307 'not achieved neutrality', *EAR*, 306. 'His belief', Sykes, 245. 'marble halls', Evelyn Waugh, *A Tourist in Africa*, Chapman & Hall, 1960, 19.

308 'the gentleman's house', *EAR*, 214.

309 'a fine eleven o'clock', *EAR*, 212.

4 OURSELVES AGAINST THE WORLD

Principal sources: Davie; Amory; Connolly, *CP*; Connolly, *EP*; *Night and Day* (an anthology, ed by Christopher Hawtree, was published by Chatto & Windus in 1985).

310 'She was in bed', *Observer*, 17 January 1988.

312 'has never existed', *EAR*, 255. 'entirely good-tempered', *CH*, 202.

313 'I know Spain', *EAR*, 187. 'a partisan', Evelyn Waugh, *Robbery Under Law*, Chapman & Hall, 1939, 144.

314 'We motored', P/J, *Connolly*, 282. 'to dislodge *Punch*', Powell, *Faces*, 75.

318 'the only man', *EAR*, 238ff.

319 'A better word', ibid.

320 'Mr Connolly', ibid. 'the preposterous', ibid., 246. 'inextricably involved', *WOE*, 59.

321 'I was discovered', ibid., 58.

323 'a formidable rival', *EAR*, 249.

325 'the only novel', *WOE*, 66.

326 'I was handing', ibid., 65. 'Most of all', A. L. Rowse, *A Cornishman at Oxford*, Jonathan Cape, 1965, 206f. 'His contemplation', Quennell, op. cit. (see note on 'principal sources' to Part 2, Chapter 4), 98.

327 'I belonged', Allain, 25.

Part 6 1939–1945: Arcadia Revisited

1 BUGGERED ABOUT

Principal sources: Davie; Amory; Powell, *Faces*; *WOE*; M.-J. Lancaster.

333 'If we're all', P/J, *Connolly*, 287.
334 'he looking', Pryce–Jones, *Bonus*, 119ff.
343 'Aren't the great', Sykes, 209.

2 A TOTAL MISFIT

Principal sources: Davie; Amory; Sykes.

344 'The war is', *Horizon*, January 1940.
345 'a Left–wing', Cyril Connolly (ed.), *The Golden Horizon*, Weidenfeld & Nicolson, 1953, ix. 'a land richer', *Horizon*, February 1940. 'We must be', ibid., September 1941.
349 'My own normal', Powell, *Faces*, 147.
350 'My eldest', *ALL*, 3.
351 'a total misfit', *Waugh Trilogy*.

3 MAG OP

Principal sources: Davie; Amory.

355 'spam, blackouts', *WOE*, 89. 'the warning example', *My Brother Evelyn*, 166.
362 'I hope you', Sykes, 254.
369 'a little over–written', *Waugh Trilogy*. 'was not intended', quoted in *English Studies*, June 1975.
372 'remains dead', Sykes, 256.

4 UP IN THE BEST–SELLER LIST

Principal sources: Davie; Sykes; Amory. The reviews of *Brideshead Revisited* are quoted from *CH*.

373 'someone to', Kay Halle (ed.), *Randolph Churchill*, Heinemann, 1971, 47.
374 Waugh's comments on *The Unquiet Grave* are taken from Alan Bell, 'Waugh Drops the Pilot', *Spectator*, 7 March 1987, and from *EAR*, 282.
376 'There are two', MS at Humanities Research Center, Austin, Texas; transcription kindly lent by Alan Bell, and quoted with the kind permission of Mrs Deirdre Levi.
377 'best book', *EAR*, 304. '*Cyril*: Brilliant', Hastings, op. cit. (see note to p. 260), 158.

Appendix C

Part 7 1945–1966: Contra Mundum

1 DOWN WITH THE HORRIBLE COUNTER-HONNISH LABOUR PARTY

Principal sources: Amory; Davie; Sykes; Donaldson.

383 'a Tudor house', Janet Morgan (ed.), *The Backbench Diaries of Richard Crossman*, Jonathan Cape and Hamish Hamilton, 1981, 169. 'propaganda', Connolly, *CP*, 285. 'a levelling up', *Horizon*, June 1945.

384 'I have never', Amory, 357; *EAR*, 406; Hollis, *OIT*, 91. 'one of the few', *Horizon*, September 1945. 'the new cocktail', ibid., June 1946.

385 'a sweaty', *WS*, 199. 'through foreign', *EAR*, 313f. 'our nursery', Sykes, 451.

386 'I lunched', *ALL*, 43. 'When they get', *Frankly Speaking*. 'Mr Connolly', *Waugh Trilogy*.

387 'tremendous festivities', ibid., 'He gave glamour', ibid. 'vulgarity', *Spectator*, 4 September 1976. 'a figure', *Waugh Trilogy*.

388 'Did I begin', Hastings, op. cit. (see note to p. 260), 158f.

389 'as though they', *EAR*, 480

391 'There is nothing', *CH*, 296.

393 'It's not really', *Face to Face*.

394 'I . . . find it', *Frankly Speaking*. 'and when the cinema', *Waugh Trilogy*. 'attempted to listen', *EAR*, 429.

395 'dull with death', Betjeman, *CP*, 131.

397 'The ideas', *Horizon*, February 1948. 'unstable, immoral', *CH*, 311. 'Mr Waugh has', *Horizon*, February 1948.

399 'You can do', *WOE*, 51. 'The writer has', *EAR*, 362. 'Evelyn Waugh once', *WOE*, 89. 'vastly more subtle', *EAR*, 361.

400 'It is a', ibid. 'The scales', *WOE*, 89f. 'more responsible', ibid., 69.

401 'The booby', ibid., 92f. 'The reader', *EAR*, 363. 'I did not', Amory, 280n. 'wearied . . . by', *WOE*, 94. 'I believe', *EAR*, 363n.

402 'Under its spell', Cyril Connolly, *Ideas and Places*, Weidenfeld & Nicolson, 1953, 225. 'We are very', *EAR*, 336f.

404 'Those angry', *Strand Magazine*, March 1947.

2 BACK TO PREP SCHOOL AGAIN

Principal sources: Amory; Davie; *WOE*; Barbara Skelton, *Tears Before Bedtime*, Hamish Hamilton, 1987; Powell, *Faces*.

407 'It's just much', *Face to Face*. 'The fact remains', M.-J. Lancaster, 525.

408 'shuffling across', Ross, op. cit. (see note to p. 135), 109f.

409 'shows that', *EAR*, 406.

415 'They can be', *EAR*, 548.

416 'I have few reasons', ibid. 'allow . . . that', Sykes, 431.

Appendix C

3 ACUTE P.M.

Principal sources: Amory; Sykes; Davie; *Frankly Speaking*; Donaldson.

421 'a chronicle', *CH*, 337. 'Waugh dressed', Skelton, op. cit. (see note on 'principal sources' in Book 6, chapter 2), 136.
422 'a sort of sponge–bag', *Waugh Trilogy*. 'If he didn't, Hillier, *YB*, Chapter 9. 'which he must have', Acton, *More Memoirs*, 373.
423 'even going so far', *Waugh Trilogy*.
426 'I never heard', *Spectator*, 20 November 1953.
429 'the fidgeting doubts', *EAR*, 431f.
432 'He looked awful', *Waugh Trilogy*.
434 'talking to the', ibid.
437 'was fairly sure', ibid.
441 'as mad as', ibid. 'was just like', ibid.
442 'parlour pinks', *CH*, 387.

4 THE DEATH WISH

Principal sources: Amory; Sykes; Davie.

444 'I've been absolutely', Hollis, *OIT*, 82. 'originally I had', *PR*.
445 'I am disappointed', *CH*, 369. 'I'm not on', *EAR*, 468ff.
446 'the total first', ibid., 507n. 'mellow and', *Spectator*, 6 May 1966.
447 'I think he', *Waugh Trilogy*. 'The fifties were', *WOE*, 169.
448 'Surrey villas', *EAR*, 461. 'drove me to', *Waugh Trilogy*.
449 'Discussion groups', *EAR*, 390.
450 'I was struck', ibid., 519. 'He is ignoring', *CH*, 389ff.
451 'Not living', *EAR*, 527ff.
454 'Mr Waugh', *CH*, 407f. 'grimly functional', *EAR*, 354.
455 'that charming', *CH*, 473.
457 'few and', *CH*, 272. Reviews of *Officers and Gentlemen*: *CH*, 422ff.
459 'If I had', in Connolly (ed.), *Ideas and Places* (see note to p. 402), 82.
460 'A Visit to Morin' is in Greene's *Collected Short Stories*, Penguin, 1986. 'With the approach', *ASOL*, 120f. 'No, I've broken', Allain, 172f.
461 'quite easy', *Monitor*. 'reticent', *CH*, 457.
463 *Basil Seal Rides Again* is reprinted in *WS*.
467 'longed for death', *Waugh Trilogy*.
468 'a flabby old', quoted *Spectator*, 6 May 1966. 'The main point', ibid. 'Evelyn Waugh', *CH*, 164.
469 'incomparably the best', *Waugh Trilogy*. 'a portrait', *CH*, 90. 'curt, cheap', ibid., 504.
470 'of what made', ibid., 508. 'a triumph of', *Times*, 13 October 1981. 'the vacancy', *TLS*, 20 November 1981. 'in many respects', *New Statesman*, 9 October 1981. 'oafish pooftah', *Spectator*, 19 December 1981.

471 '[Evelyn] Waugh, Betjeman', 'Forward into the', Peter York, *Modern Times*, Futura, 1984, 55, 22.
472 'Back in 1962', *Spectator*, 2 October 1982. 'there will be no', *EAR*, 539f.
473 'An artist', *PR*.

Appendix D

ACKNOWLEDGEMENTS

Some years ago, Hilary Rubenstein suggested to me that a book on this subject ought to be written. I feel embarrassed that he has not profited professionally from it, and I hope that he approves of it. I also need to thank Peter Ackroyd, who declined a publisher's invitation to write a life of Waugh, because I told him that I had ambitions in that direction. It was very generous, and I hope (though I doubt) that I can return the favour one day.

I stand in a not dissimilar relationship to Alan Bell, who himself began work on something very like this book, and who, when he decided not to continue with his own project, greatly helped to launch my own, and continued to offer invaluable advice and answer queries from his own extensive knowledge of the Waugh set.

Pat Kavanagh, one of the successors to Waugh's agent, A.D. Peters, skilfully joined the wires to make the project happen. John Curtis commissioned the book while he was still at Weidenfeld & Nicolson, and saw me off in style; by the time I had completed my journey, Candida Brazil was waiting to edit my manuscript with considerable but charmingly-exercised skill, in collaboration with her copy-editor, Peter James, and, at the Houghton Mifflin Company, my American editor Peter Davison. The book has been fortunate in having Douglas Matthews to provide the index.

Among my friends, John Manger (a Waugh enthusiast) and Andrew Rosenheim (a considerable expert on Waugh) allowed me to try out opinions, and in Andrew's case kindly corrected errors in the first draft. Another Andrew, A.N. Wilson, put up with my speculations about Waugh and his circle during innumerable lunches, and gave me constant encouragement.

Of those who gave me information about Waugh and his contemporaries, I must thank, in alphabetical order, Julia Briggs, Ulick O'Connor, Valentine Cunningham, John Gurney, Bevis Hillier, Father Gerard Irvine, John Kelly, Andrew Lee, Alexander Murray, John Julius Norwich, Ann Paludan, Myfanwy Piper, Martin Stannard, and Auberon Waugh. Sara Forman and Anthony Storr provided medical and psychiatric information.

Mrs Deirdre Levi kindly allowed me to quote from Cyril Connolly's 'profile' of Waugh. Other permissions were given by: the Peters, Fraser & Dunlop Group Ltd, Weidenfeld & Nicolson, Little, Brown & Co, and Ticknor & Fields (a Houghton Mifflin Company), for quotation from the works of Evelyn Waugh; David Higham Associates Ltd and William Heinemann Ltd, for quotation from the works of Anthony Powell; the Estate of Sir Osbert Lancaster, the Estate of Sir John Betjeman, and John Murray (Publishers) Ltd, for the reproduction of poems by Betjeman and drawings by Lancaster; and the Hulton Picture Library and the National Portrait Gallery for photographs.

Lastly, I have a special debt to Sir Harold Acton. I began my work on this book by reading accounts of him at Eton and Oxford, and I concluded my research by visiting him at La Pietra, just outside Florence, on a boiling August day. It was as if one had stepped into Brideshead itself – the nicest aspects of it. At an unforgettable lunch, Sir Harold patiently endured my questions, and quickly made me see how in the Twenties he had charmed a circle of brilliant young men to dance to his tune. Afterwards he was kind enough not merely to read my bulky manuscript, but – with what I imagine to be a typically generous gesture – to send me an international telegram signifying his approval. To him, if it is not an impertinence, I wish to dedicate the book, with the words used by Waugh in the dedication of *Decline and Fall*:

> To Harold Acton
> In homage and affection

Index

Ranks and titles are generally as given in the text.

Index

Arnold, Matthew, 297
Asquith, Katharine *see* Horner, Katharine
Aston Clinton School, 143–4, 146
Astor, John Jacob ('Jakie'), 347
Attlee, Clement, 380
Auden, W. H.: friendship with Betjeman, 101, 214; at Oxford, 128; on Gabbitas and Thring, 131; on Depression, 274; anti-Fascism, 279; and B. Howard, 291; identifies with common people, 303–4; and homosexuality, 304; poems in *Horizon*, 345; *Letters from Iceland* (with MacNeice), 315
Authors Take Sides on the Spanish Civil War, 312

Bailey, Cyril, 89
Bakewell, Jean (The first Mrs C. Connolly), 176, 228, 375
Bakst, Lev S. 127
Baldwin, Ruth, 219
Balfour, Patrick (*later* 3rd Baron Kinross), 92, 200, 238, 281–2, 335, 430–1
Ballets Russes, 3
Balston, Thomas, 28, 134, 187, 192
Banks (headmaster of Arnold House), 140–2
Baring, Maurice, 175
Bates, H. E., 345
Bath, Henry Thynne, 6th Marquess of, 173
Beaton, Cecil: EW bullies at prep school, 21–2, 46, 53; at London party, 166; EW visits, 210; and Victor Watson, 344; contributes to *Horizon*, 345; admires *Brideshead*, 362
Beauchamp, William Lygon, 7th Earl, 247
Beaverbrook press, 424–5, 445
Beaverbrook, William Maxwell Aitken, 1st Baron, 446
Beefsteak Club, 423
Beerbohm, Max: *Zuleika Dobson*, 155
Bell (journal), 378–9
Belloc, Hilaire, 53, 248, 297, 313, 393
Bennett, Arnold, 162, 209, 297, 307
Benson, R. H., 303
Berenson, Bernard, 175
Berlin, Isaiah, 95–6

Berners, Gerald Tyrwhitt-Wilson, 14th Baron, 264–7; death, 414
Betjemann, Bess (*née* Dawson; John B's mother), 100
Betjeman, Candida (John B's daughter), 394
Betjemann, Ernest (John B's father), 100, 102–3; 262, 303, 364, 422
Betjeman, John: on Meadow Building, Christ Church, 38; at Oxford, 64, 73, 87, 101–2; corresponds with Lord Alfred Douglas, 81; romantic experiences, 83; on Bowra, 94–9, 114; background, 100; and C. S. Lewis, 101; appearance and manner, 101–3, 261; teddy bear, 102, 356; poetry, 103–4; interest in Victorian architecture, 104–6; visits Spreadeagle, 114, 118; sent down from Oxford, 126; learning, 127; on Gabbitas and Thring, 131; prep school teaching, 132; reading, 152; on abroad, 181; at Pakenham Hall, 210, 230; works on *Architectural Review*, 210–11, 213, 246, 311; architectural taste, 211–12, 215–18; poems published, 213–15; religious beliefs and faith, 217–18; at London party, 219; in Nancy Mitford's *Christmas Pudding*, 260; courts Pamela Mitford, 260; meets Penelope Chetwode, 261–2; teases Chetwodes, 261–2; marriage to Penelope, 262–3, 296; as film critic, 263; life at Uffington, 263–7; on Berners's folly, 265; and social status, 296; on popular culture and taste, 297–302; contributes to *Night and Day*, 314, 316; and EW's *Work Suspended*, 329; turned down for RAF, 334; in Dublin during war, 338; poems in *Horizon*, 345; at Ministry of Information, 349; and EW's view of Piper, 361; and non-U vocabulary, 388n; EW mocks for money shortage, 393; EW and religious views of, 394–5; broadcasts, 394, 396; separation from Penelope, 396; describes EW, 404; gives washstand to EW, 430–1; writes for *Spectator*, 448; knighthood and laureateship, 469; and Victorian revival, 471; *Antiquarian Prejudice*, 212;

508

Index

Index

Index

Greene, Graham (*contd.*)
126; and career prospects, 131-2;
tutoring, 132-3; novel-writing, 133;
works for *Nottingham Journal*, 135;
works for *The Times*, 205, 209;
engagement and marriage, 205; takes
Catholic instruction, 206-7, 221-2; on
Waugh's Catholicism, 220; on
Whittemore, 233; and political
situation, 275-6; poverty, 276; travels
in Liberia, 276-8, 285-6; narrative
stance, 277; writing output, 290;
attacks suburbia, 300-2; co-founds
Night and Day, 314, 316-17; libel suit
against, 317n; and Spanish Civil War,
320; as Catholic writer, 320-2; in
Mexico, 322-3, 325-6; war service,
333-4, 338-9; with MI6 in West
Africa, 339; and EW's *Brideshead*, 355;
on style of *Brideshead*, 369; EW
encounters, 392; on EW's church
collection money, 394; films, 398-9;
married life and children, 400-1;
pleases EW as writer, 409; and
Catherine Walston, 409-11; troubled
Catholicism, 411, 459-61; and EW's
Men at Arms, 417; travelling, 447; and
Connolly's marriage, 448; EW on
writings of, 448-9, 459; obituary of
EW, 468-9; *Babbling April* (verse), 133;
Brighton Rock, 301, 321, 399-400; *A
Burnt-Out Case*, 459-61; *The Comedians*,
469; *The Confidential Agent*, 339n; *The
End of the Affair*, 409, 411; *England Made
Me*, 276, 316; *A Gun for Sale*, 300, 320;
The Heart of the Matter, 399-402; *The
Human Factor*, 109, 469; *It's a Battlefield*,
275-6, 321; *Journey Without Maps*, 276-
8, 285, 317n; *The Lawless Roads*, 301-2,
322-3, 326-7; *The Living Room* (play),
448; *The Man Within*, 109, 207-9; *The
Ministry of Fear*, 339; *The Name of Action*,
208-9; *Our Man in Havana*, 447; *The
Power and the Glory*, 325-7, 334; *The
Quiet American*, 448; *Rumour at Nightfall*,
208; *A Sense of Reality*, 459; *A Sort of
Life*, 460; *Stamboul Train*, 227-8, 290,
317n; *Travels With My Aunt*, 447n; 'A
Visit to Morin' (short story), 206, 459-
61; *Ways of Escape*, 401
Greene, Hugh, 276

Greene, Raymond, 109
Greene, Vivien (*née* Dayrell-Browning),
205
Greenidge, Terence: friendship with EW
at Oxford, 67-9, 74, 76, 92; at
Spreadeagle, 116; and Railway Club,
121, 123; degree, 126; and films, 137-
8; and EW's conversion, 225
Grey, Sir Edward, 17
Gridiron Club, Oxford ('Grid'), 74
Grigson, Geoffrey, 345
Grisewood, Harman, 70
Gruening, Ernest, 323
Guinness, Beatrice, 223
Guinness, Bryan, 169, 175, 189, 199, 229
Guinness, Diana *see* Mosley, Diana
Guinness, Jonathan, 337
Guinness, Patrick, 175

Haile Selassie I, Emperor of Ethiopia,
230-1, 280, 282-5
Hall Brothers (Oxford tailors), 41
Harcourt, Lewis, 1st Viscount, 18-19
Harland, Henry, 47
Harlow, Jean, 316
Harman, Elizabeth *see* Longford,
Elizabeth, Countess of
Harmsworth, Desmond, 162
Harper, Allanah, 169
Harper's Bazaar, 254, 309, 327
Hartley, L.P., 74
Hartnell, Norman, 167-8
Harton, Father F.P., 266, 270n
Hastings, Hubert de Cronin, 211, 214
'Hatte, Bruno' (invented artist), 169
Hawthornden Prize: EW wins, 293
Haydon, Benjamin Robert, 161
Haydon, Brigadier Charles, 351
Heard, Gerald, 219
Heath Mount School, Hampstead, 22,
46, 52-4
Heath, Edward, 472
Heber-Percy, Robert, 264-5, 414
Heenan, Cardinal John Carmel, 411
Heinemann (publishers), 205, 207-8
Helena, Empress of Rome, 405-7
Hemingway, Ernest: influence, 152-4,
236-7, 244, 273, 303n; and *Spanish
Earth* (film), 314; *The Sun Also Rises* (in
England as *Fiesta*), 154, 244

Index

Index

Scott Moncrieff, C. K., 142
Seafeld, Nina, 175
Selznick, David O., 399
Sezincote (Gloucestershire), 105–6
Shell Guides, 213
Shelton Abbey, Wicklow (Ireland), 104–5
Sherborne school, 53–4
Sitwell family, 303
Sitwell, Edith, 13, 27–8, 44–5, 48, 210, 226; *Façade*, 73
Sitwell, Osbert, 12, 115, 152–3; *Before the Bombardment*, 153
Sitwell, Sacheverell, 12, 115
Skelton, Barbara, 412–13, 421, 448
Smith, Logan Pearsall, 134, 403
Smith, R. D., 397
Spain, 389–91
Spain, Nancy, 445–6
Spanish Civil War, 312–14, 320
Spark, Muriel: *The Comforters*, 450
Sparkes, Gwendoline, 432, 434
Spectator (weekly), 445–6, 448, 450, 470–2
Spence, Roger, 16
Spender, Stephen, 128, 304, 345, 404
Spitzbergen, 270
Spooner, William Archibald, 63
Spreadeagle Hotel, Thame (Oxfordshire), 113–19, 356
Squire, J. C., 213, 303
Stannard, Martin, 84, 194–5, 197–8
Stein, Gertrude, 127–8, 154, 427
Stewart, Lois, 172
Strachey, Lytton, 36, 145–7; *Eminent Victorians*, 92, 144–5
Strand Magazine, 271
Strauss, Dr Eric, 441–2, 444
suburbia, 298–302
Summers, Romney, 78–9
Sutro, John, 119–23, 137, 424
Sykes, Christopher: on EW's family background, 49–50; and EW's homosexual phase, 124–5; on EW's film, 139; on She-Evelyn, 178, 181; on EW's marriage breakdown, 197, 198n; on R. Byron's anti-intellectualism, 229–30; on Whittemore in Abyssinia, 233–4; on Peter Rodd, 239; on *A Handful of Dust*, 252; on Laura Herbert, 269; on EW's view of Pope Pius v, 272; social status, 296; on EW's snobbery, 307; on EW in war,

347–8, 373; and *Brideshead*, 362, 372; on EW's religious fundamentalism, 402; offers book to EW for review, 403; and Eliot, 404; on EW and A. Powell, 416; on EW's dress, 421–2; visits Middle East with EW, 423; on EW's rudeness, 423–4; and EW's radio interview, 425–8; on 'The Box', 431–2; on EW's hallucinations, 434; and EW's offered CBE, 447; and G. Greene, 449; on Combe Florey, 450; and EW's view of Knox, 454; and EW's autobiography, 467; and EW's decline, 468; biography of EW, 469
Symons, A. J. A., 29, 314

Tablet (journal), 241–2, 270, 305, 318, 375, 378–9, 384, 397
Taesas, Lorenzo, 283
Temple, Shirley, 317
Tennyson, Alfred, 1st Baron, 47, 147, 297
Thame (Oxfordshire), 113–19, 199
Thatcher, Margaret, 471
Thesiger, Ernest, 169
Thesiger, Wilfred, 235
Third Man, The (film), 399
Thomson, George Malcolm, 425
Time magazine, 376
Times (newspaper), 231
Times Literary Supplement, 148, 208
Tito, Marshal Josip Broz, 373, 380, 391
Tolkien, J. R. R., 101, 127
Toynbee, Philip, 442, 457
Tree, Sir Herbert Beerbohm, 6
Trefusis, Violet, 265
Trevor-Roper, Hugh, 432
Trollope, Father, 206–7, 221
Truman & Knightley (agents), 140
Twysden, Duff, 245n

U and non-U vocabulary, 388n
Uffington (Berkshire), 263–7, 270
Underhill, Father, 218
United States of America: EW in, 396–8, 423
Urquhart, Francis Fortescue ('Sligger'), 84, 89–90, 92, 97, 131, 134, 137–8

Van Vechten, Carl, 152–3
Vittoria, Francisco de, 389

519

Index

Index